Mastering MATLAB® 6

A Comprehensive Tutorial and Reference

Mastering MATLAB® 6

A Comprehensive Tutorial and Reference

Duane Hanselman
Bruce Littlefield
Department of Electrical and Computer Engineering
University of Maine

Prentice Hall

Prentice Hall
Upper Saddle River, New Jersey 07458

Library of Congress Cataloging-in-Publication Data

Hanselman, Duane C.
Mastering MATLAB 6: a comprehensive tutorial and reference / Duane Hanselman, Bruce Littlefield.
p. cm.
Includes index.
ISBN 0-13-019468-9

1. Numerical analysis—Data processing. 2. MATLAB. I. Littlefield, Bruce. II. Title.
QA297 .H293 2001
519.4'0285'53042—dc21 00-051643

Vice President and Editorial Director, ECS: *Marcia J. Horton*
Publisher: *Tom Robbins*
Editorial Assistant: *Jessica Power*
Vice President of Production and Manufacturing, ESM: *David W. Riccardi*
Executive Managing Editor: *Vince O'Brien*
Managing Editor: *David A. George*
Production Editor: *Carlisle Communications*
Art Director: *Jayne Conte*
Cover Design: *Bruce Kenselaar*
Art Editor: *Adam Velthaus*
Manufacturing Manager: *Trudy Pisciotti*
Manufacturing Buyer: *Dawn Murrin*
Marketing Manager: *Holly Stark*
Marketing Assistant: *Karen Moon*

Printed in the United States of America

10 9 8 7 6 5 4 3

ISBN: 0-13-019468-9

Prentice-Hall International (UK) Limited, *London*
Prentice-Hall of Australia Pty. Limited, *Sydney*
Prentice-Hall Canada Inc., *Toronto*
Prentice-Hall Hispanoamericana, S. A., *Mexico*
Prentice-Hall of India Private Limited, *New Delhi*
Prentice-Hall of Japan, Inc., *Tokyo*
Pearson Education Asia, Pte. Ltd., *Singapore*
Editora Prentice-Hall do Brasil, Ltda., *Rio de Janeiro*

Contents

Preface

This text is about MATLAB. If you use MATLAB or are considering using it, this book is for you. This text represents an alternative to learning MATLAB on your own with or without the help of the documentation that comes with the software. The informal style of this book makes it easy to read and, as the title suggests, it provides the tools you need to master MATLAB. As a programming language and data visualization tool, MATLAB offers a rich set of capabilities for solving problems in engineering, scientific, computing, and mathematical disciplines. The fundamental goal of this text is to help you increase your productivity by showing you how to use these capabilities efficiently. Because of the interactive nature of MATLAB, the material is generally presented in the form of examples that you can duplicate by running MATLAB as you read this book.

This text covers only topics that are of use to a general audience. The material presented applies equally to all computer platforms. None of the *Toolboxes*, *Blocksets*, and other *Libraries* that are available at additional cost are discussed, although some are referred to in appropriate places. There are simply too many additional product items (more than 50 at this time) to consider in one book. However, based on user feedback, this book does discuss linking MATLAB to programs written in C, FORTRAN, and Java. Furthermore, it demonstrates how MATLAB can be dynamically linked to other applications on the PC platform.

Since MATLAB continues to evolve as a software tool, this text focuses on MATLAB version 6. For the most part, the material applies to 5.x versions of MATLAB as well. When appropriate, distinctions between versions are made.

We the authors encourage you to give us feedback on this book. What are the best features of the text? What areas need more work? What topics should be left out? What topics should be added? We can be reached at the e-mail address `mm@eece.maine.edu`. In addition, errata, all examples in the text, and other related material can be found at `http://www.eece.maine.edu/mm`.

1

Getting Started

1.1 INTRODUCTION

This text assumes that you have some familiarity with matrices and computer programming. Matrices and arrays in general are at the heart of MATLAB since all data in MATLAB are stored as arrays. Besides common matrix algebra operations, MATLAB offers array operations that allow one to quickly manipulate sets of data in a wide variety of ways. In addition to its matrix orientation, MATLAB offers programming features similar to those of other computer programming languages. And finally, MATLAB offers graphical user interface (GUI) tools that allow one to use MATLAB as an application development tool. This combination of array data structures, programming features, and GUI tools makes MATLAB an extremely powerful tool for solving problems in many fields. In this text, each of these aspects of MATLAB is discussed in detail. To facilitate learning, detailed examples are presented.

1.2 TYPOGRAPHICAL CONVENTIONS

The following conventions are used throughout this text:

Bold italics	New terms or important facts
Boxed text	Important terms and facts
Bold with initial caps	Keyboard key names, menu names, menu items, and toolbar button names
`Constant-width`	User input, function and file names, commands, and screen displays
`Boxed constant width`	Contents of a script, function, or data file
`Constant-width italics`	User input that is to be replaced and not taken literally, such as » `help` *`functionname`*
Italics	Window names, object names, book titles, toolbox names, company names, example text, and mathematical notation.

1.3 WHAT'S NEW IN MATLAB 6

MATLAB 6 is an evolutionary change from MATLAB 5. That is, there are few revolutionary changes in MATLAB in going from version 5 to version 6. The *Command* window remains the primary user interface, *Figure* windows are used to display graphical information and to create graphical user interfaces (GUIs), and a text editor is provided for writing and editing MATLAB code.

In addition to these standard windows, MATLAB 6 introduces the ***MATLAB desktop,*** which is a window for managing the *Command* window as well as a number of new windows, including the *Help, Command History, Current Directory,* and *Workspace* windows. These new windows facilitate greater productivity when using MATLAB by providing more interactive visual information at the user's fingertips.

While the PC version included a text editor in version 5, UNIX versions did not. This disparity has been eliminated in version 6. All platforms have an identical text editor with an integrated debugger. In addition, the editor includes numerous productivity improvements nonexistent in the PC editor in version 5.

Under the surface, the numerical algorithms used to perform matrix algebra and compute common matrix factorizations have been replaced by faster, more modern, algorithms. As a result, MATLAB execution speed has increased significantly, especially for problems of medium size ($n = 100$) and above. A consequence of this improvement is that floating-point operation counts (*flops*) are no longer calculated.

To facilitate plot customization, interactive *Figure* window tools have been revamped and extended significantly, making it much less cumbersome to create publication-quality artwork. In addition, these same tools promote greater productivity when creating GUIs.

In summary, MATLAB 6 represents an evolutionary change in MATLAB. The basic operation of MATLAB and its capabilities haven't changed in any dramatic way. For the most part, the new and changed features of MATLAB 6 increase one's productivity in solving problems with MATLAB.

1.4 WHAT'S IN *MASTERING MATLAB 6*

MATLAB ships with some printed documentation plus a CD containing only documentation. This CD contains approximately 50 MB of PDF files which form the more than 4500-page documentation set for the base product of MATLAB. In addition the CD contains the complete documentation set for all MATLAB-related products—more than 250 MB of PDF files! If that is not overwhelming enough, the CD also contains more than 150 MB of HTML help files for on-line viewing in the MATLAB *Help* window.

Given this exhaustive documentation set, *Mastering MATLAB 6* does not attempt to be a complete tutorial or reference. Doing so just isn't possible within the confines of a single book. *Mastering MATLAB 6* does not even attempt to document all functions within the base product of MATLAB. This too is not possible, as there are more than 300 built-in functions in MATLAB and approximately 1000 more M-file functions that are part of the base product of MATLAB.

In light of this documentation set, the goals of *Mastering MATLAB 6* include (1) introduce MATLAB to the novice user, (2) illustrate all key features and capabilities of MATLAB, and (3) demonstrate by example how to write efficient MATLAB code. This text is intended to be a valuable resource when the MATLAB documentation set is unavailable. It follows the rule of providing 80% of the information needed in 20% of the space required to cover everything. The book is also intended to be a valuable resource when the MATLAB documentation set is available. In this case, it supplies numerous examples of efficient MATLAB coding, which demonstrate how the many features of MATLAB come together to solve real problems.

This text was written using information about MATLAB version 6.0. As MATLAB evolves between versions 6.0 and 7.0, some things are bound to change. As a result, there may be isolated areas in this book where information about new features is missing and, worse yet, isolated areas where information is incorrect. The authors have no control over MATLAB. We also cannot rewrite the text to reflect minor MATLAB releases. Thankfully the makers of MATLAB are very careful when introducing new features and when changing old features. Historically, old features are grandfathered for one major release, and sometimes more. As a result, even though this text reflects MATLAB version 6.0, it will undoubtedly be useful for all 6.x versions as well.

To support this text the authors maintain a Mastering MATLAB web site at `http://www.eece.maine.edu/mm`. At this site you can find errata for the text as well as MATLAB script M-files for creating all the figures in the book. The authors also encourage constructive feedback about the text at the e-mail address `mm@eece.maine.edu`.

2

Basic Features

Running MATLAB creates one or more windows on your computer monitor. One of these windows, entitled *MATLAB* is called the MATLAB desktop. This window is the primary graphical user interface for MATLAB. Within the *MATLAB* window, there is a window called the ***Command*** window. This is the primary place where you interact with MATLAB. The prompt >> is displayed in the *Command* window, and when the *Command* window is active, a blinking cursor appears to the right of the prompt. This cursor and the MATLAB prompt signify that MATLAB is waiting to perform a mathematical operation.

2.1 SIMPLE MATH

Just like a calculator, MATLAB can do basic math. Consider the following simple example: Mary goes to the office supply store and buys 4 erasers at 25 cents each, 6 memo pads at 52 cents each, and 2 rolls of tape at 99 cents each. How many items did Mary buy and how much did they cost? To solve this problem using a calculator, you enter

```
4 + 6 + 2 = 12 items
4 x 25 + 6 x 52 + 2 x 99 = 610 cents
```

In MATLAB, this problem can be solved in a number of different ways. First, the above-mentioned calculator approach can be taken:

```
>> 4+6+2
ans =
    12
>> 4*25 + 6*52 + 2*99
ans =
   610
```

Note that MATLAB doesn't care about spaces for the most part, and that multiplication takes precedence over addition. Note also that MATLAB calls the result `ans`, which is short for *answer* for both computations.

As an alternative, the above problem can be solved by storing information in ***MATLAB variables:***

```
>> erasers = 4
erasers =
     4
>> pads = 6
pads =
     6
>> tape = 2;
>> items = erasers + pads + tape
items =
    12
>> cost = erasers*25 + pads*52 + tape*99
cost =
   610
```

Here we created three MATLAB variables, `erasers`, `pads`, and `tape`, to store the number of each item. After entering each statement, MATLAB displayed the results, except in the case of `tape`. The semicolon at the end of the line tells MATLAB to evaluate the line but not to display the answer. Finally, rather than calling the results `ans`, we told MATLAB to call the number of items purchased `items` and the total price paid `cost`. At each step, MATLAB remembered past information. Because MATLAB remembers things, let's ask what the average cost per item was:

```
>> average_cost = cost/items
average_cost =
    50.833
```

Because *average cost* is two words and MATLAB variable names must be one word, an underscore was used to create the single MATLAB variable `average_cost`.

In addition to addition and multiplication, MATLAB offers the following basic arithmetic operations:

Operation	Symbol	Example
Addition	+	`3 + 22`
Subtraction	-	`54.4 - 16.5`
Multiplication	*	`3.14 * 6`
Division	/ or \	`19.54/7` or `7\19.54`
Exponentiation	^	`2^8`

The order in which these operations are evaluated in a given expression is given by the usual rules of precedence which can be summarized as follows:

> Expressions are evaluated from left to right with the exponentiation operation having the highest precedence, followed by multiplication and division having equal precedence, followed by addition and subtraction having equal precedence.
>
> Parentheses can be used to alter this ordering, in which case these rules of precedence are applied within each set of parentheses starting with the innermost set and proceeding outward.

2.2 THE MATLAB WORKSPACE

As you work in the *Command* window, MATLAB remembers the commands you enter as well as the values of any variables you create. These commands and variables are said to reside in the ***MATLAB workspace*** or ***Base workspace*** and can be recalled whenever you wish. For example, to check the value of `tape` all you have to do is ask MATLAB for it by entering its name at the prompt:

```
>> tape
tape =
     2
```

If you can't remember the name of a variable, you can ask MATLAB for a list of the variables it knows by using the MATLAB command `who`:

```
>> who
Your variables are:
ans           cost     items    tape
average_cost  erasers  pads
```

Note that MATLAB doesn't tell you the value of all the variables; it merely gives you their names. To find their values, you must enter their names at the MATLAB prompt.

To recall previous commands, MATLAB uses the **Cursor** keys on your keyboard. For example, pressing the ↑ key once recalls the most recent command to the MATLAB prompt. Repeated pressing scrolls back through prior commands one at a time. In a similar manner, pressing the ↓ key scrolls forward through commands. Pressing the → or ← key moves one within a given command at the MATLAB prompt, thereby allowing it to be edited in much the same way that you edit text in a word processing program. Other standard editing keys such as **Delete** or **Backspace, Home,** and **End** perform their commonly assigned tasks. The **Tab** key is useful for variable name completion. Once a scrolled command is acceptable, pressing the **Return** key with the cursor *anywhere* in the command tells MATLAB to process it. Finally, and perhaps most useful, the **Escape** key erases the current command at the prompt. For those of you familiar with the EMACS editor, MATLAB also accepts common EMACS editing control character sequences such as **Control-U** to erase the current command.

2.3 ABOUT VARIABLES

Like any other computer language, MATLAB has rules about variable names. Earlier it was noted that variable names must be a single word containing no spaces. More specifically, MATLAB variable-naming rules are as follows:

Variable-Naming Rules	Comments and Examples
Variable names are case-sensitive.	`Cost`, `cost`, `CoSt`, and `COST` are all different MATLAB variables.
Variable names can contain up to 31 characters. Any characters beyond the 31st are ignored.	`Howaboutthisvariablename`

Variable names must start with a letter, followed by any number of letters, digits, or underscores. Punctuation characters are not allowed since many of them have a special meaning in MATLAB.	`how_about_this_variable_name`
	`X51483`
	`a_b_c_d_e`

There are some specific exceptions to these naming rules. MATLAB has several names that cannot be used for variables. These names form a ***keyword*** or ***reserved word list*** for MATLAB:

Reserved Word List
`for` `end` `if` `while` `function` `return` `elseif` `case` `otherwise` `switch` `continue` `else` `try` `catch` `global` `persistent` `break`

MATLAB will report an error if you try to use a reserved word as a variable. However, you can use words similar to those above by capitalizing one or more letters.

In addition, just as your calculator stores constants such as π, MATLAB has a number of special variables as well:

Special Variables	Description
`ans`	Default variable name used for results.
`beep`	Make computer sound a beep.
`pi`	Ratio of the circumference of a circle to its diameter.
`eps`	Smallest number such that, when added to 1, creates a number greater than 1 on the computer.
`inf`	Stands for infinity, e.g., `1/0`.
`NaN` (or) `nan`	Stands for Not-a-Number, e.g., `0/0`.
`i` (or) `j`	Stands for $\sqrt{-1}$.
`nargin`	Number of function input arguments.
`nargout`	Number of function output arguments.
`realmin`	Smallest usable positive real number.
`realmax`	Largest usable positive real number.
`bitmax`	Largest usable positive integer.
`varargin`	Variable number of function input arguments.
`vararout`	Variable number of function output arguments.

If you reuse a variable such as `tape` in the above example, or assign a value to one of the special variables above, its prior value is overwritten and lost. However, any other expressions computed using the prior values do not change. Consider the following example,

```
>> erasers = 4;
>> pads = 6;
>> tape = 2;
>> items = erasers + pads + tape
items =
    12
>> erasers = 6
erasers =
     6
>> items
items =
    12
```

Here, using the first example again, we found the number of items Mary purchased. Afterward, we changed the number of erasers to 6, overwriting its prior value of 4. In doing so, the value of items has not changed. Unlike a common spreadsheet program, MATLAB does not recalculate the number of items based on the new value of erasers. ***When MATLAB performs a calculation, it does so using the values it knows at the time the requested command is evaluated.*** In the above example, if you wish to recalculate the number of items, the total cost, and the average cost, it will be necessary to recall the appropriate MATLAB commands and ask MATLAB to evaluate them again.

The special variables given above follow this guideline also, with the exception that the special values can be restored. When you start MATLAB, they have the values given above; when you change their values, the original special values are lost. To restore a special value all you have to do is ***clear*** the overwritten value. For example,

```
>> pi
ans =
        3.1416
>> pi = 1.23e-4
pi =
      0.000123
>> clear pi
>> pi
ans =
        3.1416
```

shows that `pi` has the special value 3.1416 to five significant digits, is overwritten with the value 1.23e-4, and then, after being cleared using the `clear` function, has its special value once again.

2.4 COMMENTS, PUNCTUATION, AND ABORTING EXECUTION

As we saw earlier, placing a semicolon at the end of a command suppresses printing of the computed results. This feature is especially useful for suppressing the results of intermediate calculations. For example,

```
>> erasers
erasers =
     6
>> items = erasers + pads + tape;
>> cost = erasers*25 + pads*52 + tape*99;
>> average_cost = cost/items
average_cost =
       47.143
```

displays the average cost of the items Mary bought when she purchased 6 erasers rather than the original 4. The intermediate results `items` and `cost` were not printed because semicolons appear at the end of the commands defining them.

In addition to semicolons, MATLAB uses other punctuation symbols. All text after a percent sign (%) is taken as a comment statement, for example,

```
>> tape = 2  % number of rolls of tape purchased
```

The variable `tape` is given the value 2, and MATLAB simply ignores the percent sign and all text following it.

Multiple commands can be placed on one line if they are separated by commas or semicolons, for example,

```
>> erasers = 6, pads = 6; tape = 2
erasers =
     6
tape =
     2
```

Commas tell MATLAB to display results; semicolons suppress printing.

Sometimes expressions or commands are so long that is convenient to continue them onto additional lines. In MATLAB, statement continuation is denoted by three periods in succession, such as,

```
>> average_cost = cost/items  % command as done earlier
average_cost =
       47.143
>> average_cost = cost/... % command with valid continuation
items
average_cost =
       47.143
>> average_cost = cost... % command with valid continuation
/items
average_cost =
       47.143
```

```
>> average_cost = cost/it... % command with INvalid continuation
ems
??? age_cost=cost/items
                        |
Missing operator, comma, or semi-colon.
```

As shown above, statement continuation works if the three periods appear between variable names and mathematical operators, but not in the middle of a variable name. That is, variable names cannot be split between two lines. In addition, since comment lines are ignored, they cannot be continued either, for example,

```
>> % Comments cannot be continued...
>> either
??? Undefined function or variable 'either'.
```

In this case the ... in the comment line is part of the comment and is not processed by MATLAB.

Finally, MATLAB processing can be interrupted at any time by pressing **Control-C** (pressing the **Ctrl** and **C** keys simultaneously).

2.5 COMPLEX NUMBERS

One of the most powerful features of MATLAB is that it does not require any special handling for complex numbers. Complex numbers are formed in MATLAB in several ways. Examples of complex numbers include:

```
>> c1 = 1-2i  % the appended i signifies the imaginary part
c1 =
   1.0000 - 2.0000i
>> c1 = 1-2j  % j also works
c1 =
   1.0000 - 2.0000i
>> c2 = 3*(2-sqrt(-1)*3)
c2 =
   6.0000 - 9.0000i
>> c3 = sqrt(-2)
c3 =
        0 + 1.4142i
>> c4 = 6+sin(.5)*i
c4 =
   6.0000 + 0.4794i
>> c5 = 6+sin(.5)*j
c5 =
   6.0000 + 0.4794i
```

In the last two examples, the MATLAB default values of `i=j=`$\sqrt{-1}$ are used to form the imaginary part. Multiplication by `i` or `j` is required in these cases since `sin(.5)i` and `sin(.5)j` have no meaning in MATLAB. Termination with the characters `i` and `j`, as shown in the first two examples above, works only with numbers, not with expressions.

Some programming languages require special handling for complex numbers wherever they appear. In MATLAB no special handling is required. Mathematical operations on complex numbers are written the same as those for real numbers:

```
>> c6 = (c1+c2)/c3  % from the above data
c6 =
  -7.7782 - 4.9497i
>> c6r = real(c6)
c6r =
      -7.7782
>> c6i = imag(c6)
c6i =
      -4.9497
>> check_it_out = i^2  % sqrt(-1) squared must be -1!
check_it_out =
    -1
```

In general, operations on complex numbers lead to complex numbers. However, in the last case above, MATLAB is smart enough to drop the zero imaginary part of the result. In addition, the above shows that the functions `real` and `imag` extract the real and imaginary parts of a complex number, respectively.

As a final example of complex arithmetic, consider the Euler (sounds like *oiler*) identity that relates the polar form of a complex number to its rectangular form $M \angle \theta = Me^{j\theta} = a + bj$, where the polar form is given by a magnitude M and an angle θ, and the rectangular form is given by $a + bj$. The relationships among these forms are $M = \sqrt{a^2 + b^2}$, $\theta = \tan^{-1}(b/a)$, $a = M\cos(\theta)$, $b = M\sin(\theta)$.

In MATLAB, the conversion between polar and rectangular forms makes use of the functions `real`, `imag`, `abs`, and `angle`:

```
>> c1
c1 =
   1.0000 - 2.0000i
>> mag_c1 = abs(c1) % magnitude
mag_c1 =
     2.2361
>> angle_c1 = angle(c1) % angle in radians
angle_c1 =
  -1.1071
>> deg_c1 = angle_c1*180/pi % angle in degrees
deg_c1 =
 -63.4349
>> real_c1 = real(c1) % real part
real_c1 =
     1
```

```
>> imag_c1 = imag(c1) % imaginary part
imag_c1 =
   -2
```

The MATLAB function abs computes the magnitude of complex numbers or the absolute value of real numbers, depending on which one you give it. Likewise, the MATLAB function angle computes the angle of a complex number in radians. ***MATLAB does not perform trigonometric operations using units of degrees.***

2.6 FLOATING-POINT ARITHMETIC

In almost all cases numerical values in MATLAB are represented in double-precision arithmetic using a binary (base 2) representation internally. This representation is the most common representation used by computers and is a native format for numerical co-processors. Because of this representation, not all numbers can be represented exactly, there are limiting values that can be represented, and there is a recognizable lower limit for addition.

The largest positive real number that can be represented is:

```
>> format long  % tell MATLAB to display more precision
>> realmax
ans =
   1.797693134862316e+308
```

The smallest positive number that can be represented is:

```
>> realmin
ans =
   2.225073858507201e-308
```

The smallest number that can be added to 1 and produce a number larger than 1 in double precision is:

```
>> eps
ans =
   2.220446049250313e-016
```

The consequences of the limitations of finite precision arithmetic are sometimes strange. For example, addition is not *exactly* commutative.

```
>> 0.42 - 0.5 + 0.08
ans =
  -1.387778780781446e-017
```

```
>> 0.08 - 0.5 + 0.42
ans =
     0
>> 0.08 + 0.42 - 0.5
ans =
     0
```

All three of the above results should be zero, but they are not. In each case the arithmetic was performed from left to right. The issue here is that not all the numbers above can be represented exactly using double-precision arithmetic. In fact, only `0.5` has an exact representation. When numbers cannot be represented exactly, they are approximated with as much precision as possible—leading to inevitable errors in computed results. For the most part, these errors are minor or double-precision arithmetic wouldn't be used in modern computers. In practice, the problems with double-precision arithmetic occur most often when asking MATLAB to compare two numbers for equality or inequality. Clearly, $0.42 - 0.5 + 0.08$ does not equal $0.08 - 0.5 + 0.42$ within MATLAB even though our brains can do the exact arithmetic to show that it does.

A second consequence of finite precision arithmetic appears in function evaluation. In addition to not always being able to represent function arguments exactly, most functions themselves cannot be represented exactly, for example,

```
>> sin(0)
ans =
     0
>> sin(pi)
ans =
    1.224646799147353e-016
```

Here both results should be zero, but $\sin(\pi)$ is not. It is interesting to note that the error here and the error in the previous example are both less than `eps`.

Finally, MATLAB uses double-precision floating-point arithmetic to represent integers as well. With this representation, all integers up to a limit can be represented *exactly.* The limiting value is:

```
>> bitmax
ans =
    9.007199254740991e+015
```

which is $2^{53} - 1$.

2.7 MATHEMATICAL FUNCTIONS

Lists of the common functions that MATLAB supports are shown in the tables below. Most of these functions are used the same way you would write them mathematically:

```
>> x = sqrt(2)/2
x =
    0.7071
>> y = asin(x)
y =
    0.7854
>> y_deg = y*180/pi
y_deg =
   45.0000
```

These commands find the angle where the sine function has a value of $\sqrt{2}/2$. Note again that MATLAB uses radians. Other examples include the following:

```
>> y = sqrt(3^2 + 4^2)  % show 3-4-5 right triangle relationship
y =
     5
>> y = rem(23,4)  % remainder function, 23/4 has a remainder of 3
y =
     3
>> x = 2.6, y1 = fix(x), y2 = floor(x), y3 = ceil(x), y4 = round(x)
x =
    2.6000
y1 =
     2
y2 =
     2
y3 =
     3
y4 =
     3
```

Trigonometric Function	Description
`acos`	Inverse cosine.
`acosh`	Inverse hyperbolic cosine.
`acot`	Inverse cotangent.
`acoth`	Inverse hyperbolic cotangent.
`acsc`	Inverse cosecant.
`acsch`	Inverse hyperbolic cosecant.
`asec`	Inverse secant.

Trigonometric Function	Description
asech	Inverse hyperbolic secant.
asin	Inverse sine.
asinh	Inverse hyperbolic sine.
atan	Inverse tangent.
atan2	Four quadrant inverse tangent.
atanh	Inverse hyperbolic tangent.
cos	Cosine.
cosh	Hyperbolic cosine.
cot	Cotangent.
coth	Hyperbolic cotangent.
csc	Cosecant.
csch	Hyperbolic cosecant.
sec	Secant.
sech	Hyperbolic secant.
sin	Sine.
sinh	Hyperbolic sine.
tan	Tangent.
tanh	Hyperbolic tangent.

Exponential Function	Description
^	Power.
exp	Exponential.
log	Natural logarithm.
log10	Base 10 logarithm.
log2	Base 2 logarithm and floating-point number dissection.

Exponential Function	Description
pow2	Base 2 power and floating-point number scaling.
sqrt	Square root.
nextpow2	Next higher power of 2.

Complex Function	Description
abs	Absolute value or magnitude.
angle	Phase angle in radians.
conj	Complex conjugate.
imag	Imaginary part.
real	Real part.
unwrap	Unwrap phase angle.
isreal	True for real values.
cplxpair	Sort vector into complex conjugate pairs.
complex	Form complex number from real and imaginary parts.

Rounding and Remainder Function	Description
fix	Round toward zero.
floor	Round toward negative infinity.
ceil	Round toward positive infinity.
round	Round toward nearest integer.
mod	Modulus or signed remainder.
rem	Remainder after division.
sign	Signum function.

Coordinate Transformation Function	Description
`cart2sph`	Cartesian to spherical.
`cartpol`	Cartesian to cylindrical or polar.
`pol2cart`	Cylindrical or polar to Cartesian.
`sph2cart`	Spherical to Cartesian.

Number Theoretic Function	Description
`factor`	Prime factors.
`isprime`	True for prime numbers.
`primes`	Generate list of prime numbers.
`gcd`	Greatest common divisor.
`lcm`	Least common multiple.
`rat`	Rational approximation.
`rats`	Rational output.
`perms`	All possible combinations.
`nchoosek`	All combinations of *N* elements taken *K* at a time.

Specialized Function	Description
`airy`	Airy function.
`besselj`	Bessel function of the first kind.
`bessely`	Bessel function of the second kind.
`besselh`	Bessel function of the third kind.
`besseli`	Modified Bessel function of the first kind.

Specialized Function	Description
besselk	Modified Bessel function of the second kind.
beta	Beta function.
betainc	Incomplete beta function.
betaln	Logarithm of beta function.
ellipj	Jacobi elliptic function.
ellipke	Complete elliptic integral.
erf	Error function.
erfc	Complementary error function.
erfcx	Scaled complementary error function.
erfinv	Inverse error function.
expint	Exponential error function.
gamma	Gamma function.
gammainc	Incomplete gamma function.
gammaln	Logarithm of gamma function.
legendre	Associated Legendre function.
cross	Vector cross product.
dot	Vector dot product.

3

The MATLAB Desktop

As stated in the last chapter, running MATLAB creates one or more windows on your computer monitor. One of these windows, entitled *MATLAB,* is called the *MATLAB* desktop. This window contains or manages all other windows that are part of MATLAB. Depending on how you set up MATLAB, some windows associated with the desktop may or may not be visible and some may or may not reside within (i.e., be ***docked***) the *MATLAB* window. Management of the *MATLAB* desktop window and its associated windows is not discussed in this text. If you are familiar with other window-based programs, manipulation of windows in MATLAB will be readily apparent. The *MATLAB* desktop window menu items change depending on which window is active. In addition, there are many helpful contextual menus (which are accessed by pressing the right mouse button over an item). If you are not familiar with window-based programs, it may be beneficial to seek general assistance from other sources. In any case, to find out which windows are associated with the desktop, investigate the items on the **View** menu within the *MATLAB* desktop window.

3.1 MATLAB WINDOWS

The windows utilized in MATLAB include the (1) *Command* (2) *Command History,* (3) *Launch Pad,* (4) *Current Directory* (browser), (5) *Help* (browser), (6) *Workspace* (browser), (7) *Array Editor,* and (8) *Editor/Debugger.* The table shown below gives an overview of the purpose of each of these windows.

Matlab Desktop Windows

Window	Description
Command	Issue commands to MATLAB for processing.
Command History	Running history of prior commands issued in the *Command* window.
Launch Pad	Tree layout for access to tools, demos, and documentation.
Current Directory	GUI for directory and file manipulation in MATLAB.
Help	GUI for finding and viewing on-line documentation.
Workspace	GUI for viewing, loading, and saving MATLAB variables.
Array Editor	GUI for modifying the content of MATLAB variables.
Editor/Debugger	Text editor and debugger for MATLAB text files.

3.2 MANAGING THE MATLAB WORKSPACE

Within the *MATLAB* desktop, actions taken in all windows support computations performed in the *Command* window. As a result, the rest of this chapter provides more detailed information about the *Command* window.

The data and variables created in the *Command* window reside in what is called the ***MATLAB workspace*** or ***Base workspace.*** In addition to viewing variables in the *Workspace* window, to see what variable names exist in the MATLAB workspace, issue the command `who`:

```
>> who
Your variables are:
```

```
angle_c1        c4              cost            pads
ans             c5              deg_c1          real_c1
average_cost    c6              erasers         tape
c1              c6i             imag_c1
c2              c6r             items
c3              check_it_out    mag_c1
```

The variables you see may differ from those above depending on what you've asked MATLAB to do since starting the program. For more detailed information, use the command `whos`:

```
>> whos
  Name              Size            Bytes  Class
  angle_c1          1x1                 8  double array
  ans               1x1                 8  double array
  average_cost      1x1                 8  double array
  c1                1x1                16  double array (complex)
  c2                1x1                16  double array (complex)
  c3                1x1                16  double array (complex)
  c4                1x1                16  double array (complex)
  c5                1x1                16  double array (complex)
  c6                1x1                16  double array (complex)
  c6i               1x1                 8  double array
  c6r               1x1                 8  double array
  check_it_out      1x1                 8  double array
  cost              1x1                 8  double array
  deg_c1            1x1                 8  double array
  erasers           1x1                 8  double array
  imag_c1           1x1                 8  double array
  items             1x1                 8  double array
  mag_c1            1x1                 8  double array
  pads              1x1                 8  double array
  real_c1           1x1                 8  double array
  tape              1x1                 8  double array

Grand total is 21 elements using 216 bytes
```

Here each variable is listed along with its size, the number of bytes used, and its class. Since MATLAB is array-oriented, all the variables belong to the class of double-precision arrays, even though all the above variables are scalars. Later, as other data types or classes are introduced, this last column will provide more useful information. The above list is also displayed in the *Workspace* window, which can be viewed by typing `workspace` at the MATLAB prompt or by choosing the **Workspace** menu item on the **View** menu of the *MATLAB* desktop.

The command `clear` deletes variables from the MATLAB workspace. For example,

```
>> clear real_c1 imag_c1 c*
>> who
Your variables are:
angle_c1       deg_c1         mag_c1
ans            erasers        pads
average_cost   items          tape
```

deletes the variables `real_c1`, `imag_c1`, and all variables starting with the letter `c`. Other options for the `clear` function can be found by asking for information using the command `help` or `helpwin`, for example,

```
>> help clear
 CLEAR  Clear variables and functions from memory.
  CLEAR removes all variables from the workspace.
  CLEAR VARIABLES does the same thing.
  CLEAR GLOBAL removes all global variables.
  CLEAR FUNCTIONS removes all compiled M- and MEX-functions.
  CLEAR ALL removes all variables, globals, functions, and MEX links.
  CLEAR ALL at the command prompt also removes the Java packages
  import list.
  CLEAR IMPORT removes the Java packages import list at the command
  prompt. It cannot be used in a function.
  CLEAR CLASSES is the same as CLEAR ALL except that class definitions
  are also cleared. If any objects exist outside the workspace (say in
  userdata or persistent in a locked m-file) a warning will be issued
  and the class definition will not be cleared. CLEAR CLASSES must be
  used if the number or names of fields in a class are changed.

  CLEAR VAR1 VAR2 ... clears the variables specified. The wild card
  character '*' can be used to clear variables that match a pattern.
  For instance, CLEAR X* clears all the variables in the current
  workspace that start with X.

  If X is global, CLEAR X removes X from the current workspace
  but leaves it accessible to any functions declaring it global.
  CLEAR GLOBAL X completely removes the global variable X.
  CLEAR FUN clears the function specified. If FUN has been locked
  by MLOCK it will remain in memory. Use a partial path (see
  PARTIALPATH) to distiguish between different overloaded versions of
  FUN. For instance, 'clear inline/display' clears only the INLINE
  method for DISPLAY, leaving any other implementations in memory.
  CLEAR ALL, CLEAR FUN, or CLEAR FUNCTIONS also have the side effect of
  removing debugging breakpoints and reinitializing persistent variables
  since the breakpoints for a function and persistent variables are
  cleared whenever the m-file changes or is cleared.

  Use the functional form of CLEAR, such as CLEAR('name'),
  when the variable name or function name is stored in a string.
  See also WHO, WHOS, MLOCK, MUNLOCK, PERSISTENT.
```

Clearly, the `clear` command deletes more than just variables. Its other uses will become apparent as you become more familiar with MATLAB's other features.

3.3 MEMORY MANAGEMENT

MATLAB allocates memory for variables as they are created and for M-file functions as they are used. Depending on the computer you are using, it is possible for MATLAB to run out of memory—making it impossible to do any further work. When you eliminate variables using the `clear` command, MATLAB frees up the memory used by the variables cleared. However, over time it is possible for memory to become fragmented, where MATLAB's memory space is populated by variables surrounded by numerous small fragments of free memory. Since MATLAB always stores variables in contiguous chunks of memory, these fragments of free memory may not be reusable. To alleviate this problem, the `pack` command performs memory garbage collection. This command saves all MATLAB workspace variables to disk, clears all variables from the workspace, and then reloads the variables back into the workspace. On completion, all fragments of free memory are consolidated into one large, usable block. Depending on how much memory is allocated to MATLAB on your computer, how long you've been running a particular MATLAB session, and how many variables you've created, you may or may not ever need to use the `pack` command.

3.4 NUMBER DISPLAY FORMATS

When MATLAB displays numerical results, it follows several rules. By default, if a result is an integer, MATLAB displays it as an integer. Likewise, when a result is a real number, MATLAB displays it with approximately four digits to the right of the decimal point. If the significant digits in the result are outside this range, MATLAB displays the result in scientific notation similar to scientific calculators. You can override this default behavior by specifying a different numerical format within *Command* window preferences on the **Preferences** menu item in the **File** menu or by typing the appropriate MATLAB `format` command at the prompt. With the special variable `pi`, the numerical display formats produced by different `format` selections are as follows:

MATLAB Command	`pi`	Comments
`format short`	`3.1416`	5 digits
`format long`	`3.14159265358979`	16 digits
`format short e`	`3.1416e+000`	5 digits plus exponent
`format long e`	`3.14159265358979e+000`	16 digits plus exponent

MATLAB Command	`pi`	Comments
`format short g`	`3.1416`	Best of `format short` or `format short e`
`format long g`	`3.14159265358979`	Best of `format long` or `format long e`
`format hex`	`400921fb54442d18`	Hexadecimal, floating point
`format bank`	`3.14`	2 decimal digits
`format +`	`+`	Positive (+), negative (−), or zero (0)
`format rat`	`355/113`	Rational approximation

`format debug`	`Structure address = fba34a8`
	`m = 1`
	`n = 1`
	`pr = 8bc8148`
	`pi = 0`
	`3.1416`
		Internal storage information in addition to `short g`

Note: MATLAB does not change the internal representation of a number when different display formats are chosen; only the display changes. All calculations are performed in double-precision arithmetic.

3.5 KEEPING A SESSION LOG

Sometimes it is useful to keep a log of all work performed during a MATLAB session. The *Command History* window keeps a chronological log of the functions and commands executed during current and past MATLAB work sessions but does not show the results. MATLAB provides a command `diary`, which saves all *Command* window activity to a text file in the current directory. The help text for `diary` describes its use:

```
>> help diary
 DIARY Save text of MATLAB session.
    DIARY filename causes a copy of all subsequent command window input
    and most of the resulting command window output to be appended to the
    named file. If no file is specified, the file 'diary' is used.
    DIARY OFF suspends it.
 DIARY ON turns it back on.
 DIARY, by itself, toggles the diary state.
```

3.6 SYSTEM INFORMATION

MATLAB provides a number of commands that provide information about the computer in use as well as the MATLAB version in use. The command `computer` returns a character string identifying the computer in use, for example,

```
>> computer
ans =
PCWIN
```

In this case, the computer is a PC running *Windows 98*. The command `version` returns a character string identifying the MATLAB version, for example,

```
>> version
ans =
6.0.0.51483 (R12)
```

and the command `ver` returns information about MATLAB as well as installed toolboxes, for example,

```
>> ver
-----------------------------------------------
MATLAB Version 5.3.0.10183 (R11) on PCWIN
MATLAB License Number: 51483
-----------------------------------------------
MATLAB Toolbox                  Version 5.3   (R11)     15-Jan-1999
Mastering MATLAB Toolbox        Version 5.0             04-Jun-1999
Symbolic Math Toolbox           Version 2.1   (R11)     11-Sep-1998
Signal Processing Toolbox       Version 4.2   (R11)     10-Jul-1998
Optimization Toolbox            Version 2.0   (R11)     09-Oct-1998
Control System Toolbox          Version 4.2   (R11)     15-Jul-1998
Simulink                        Version 3.0   (R11)     01-Sep-1998
```

MATLAB licensing information can be found by using the commands `license` and `hostid`, for example,

```
>> hostid
    '51483'
>> license
ans =
51483
```

Of course, your results from entering these commands will be different from those shown above since your computer and MATLAB version differ from those used to produce the above.

3.7 THE MATLAB SEARCH PATH

MATLAB uses a ***search path*** to find information stored in files on disk. MATLAB's files are organized into numerous directories and subdirectories.

> The list of all directories where MATLAB's files are found is called the MATLAB search path or simply ***MATLABPATH.***

Use of the MATLAB search path is described as follows. When you enter `cow` at the MATLAB prompt, that is, `>> cow`, MATLAB does the following:

1. It checks to see if `cow` is a ***variable*** in the MATLAB workspace; if not,
2. It checks to see if `cow` is a ***built-in function;*** if not,
3. It checks to see if a file named `cow.m` exists in the ***current directory;*** if not,
4. It checks to see if `cow.m` exists anywhere on the ***MATLAB search path*** by searching in the order in which it is specified.
5. If `cow` isn't found at this point, MATLAB reports an error.

Based on the above search strategy, MATLAB acts accordingly. If `cow` is a variable, MATLAB uses the variable. If it is a built-in function, MATLAB calls the function. If `cow.m` is a file in the current directory or anywhere on the MATLAB search path, the file `cow.m` is opened and MATLAB acts on what is found in the file. As is documented in Chapters 4 and 11, MATLAB has two basic file types that are of common use; both are simple text files containing MATLAB commands. See Chapters 4 and 11 for further information for regarding these ***M-files.***

In reality, the MATLAB search procedure is more complicated than described above because of advanced features in MATLAB. However, for the most part, the above search procedure is sufficient for most MATLAB work. More detailed information regarding the MATLAB search path can be found in Chapter 11.

When MATLAB starts up, it defines a default MATLAB search path that points to all the directories where MATLAB stores its files. This search path can be displayed and modified in several ways. The easiest way to do so is with the ***Path Browser,*** which is a graphical user interface for viewing and modifying the MATLAB search path. The Path Browser is made available by choosing **Set Path. . .** from the **File** menu on the *MATLAB* desktop window. Since the MATLAB search path already points to all directories where MATLAB stores its files, the primary purpose for accessing the Path Browser is to add one's own directories containing MATLAB files to the search path.

To display the MATLAB search path in the *Command* window, MATLAB provides the function `matlabpath`. In addition, the features of the Path Browser can be duplicated in the *Command* window by using the functions `path`, `addpath`, and `rmpath`. For more information regarding these functions, see the on-line documentation.

4

Script M-files

For simple problems, entering your requests at the MATLAB prompt in the *Command* window is fast and efficient. However, as the number of commands increases or when you wish to change the value of one or more variables and reevaluate a number of commands, typing at the MATLAB prompt quickly becomes tedious. MATLAB provides a logical solution to this problem. It allows you to place MATLAB commands in a simple text file and then tell MATLAB to open the file and evaluate the commands exactly as it would if you had typed them at the MATLAB prompt. These files are called ***script files*** or simply ***M-files.*** The term *script* symbolizes the fact that MATLAB simply reads from the script found in the file. The term *M-file* recognizes the fact that script filenames must end with the extension `'.m'`, for example, `example1.m`.

4.1 SCRIPT M-FILE USE

To create a script M-file, click on the blank page icon on the MATLAB desktop toolbar or choose **New** from the **File** menu and select **M-file.** This procedure brings up a text editor window where you can enter MATLAB commands. The script M-file below shows the commands from an example considered earlier.

```
% script M-file example1.m

erasers = 4; % number of each item
pads = 6;
tape = 2;
items = erasers + pads + tape
cost = erasers*25 + pads*52 + tape*99
average_cost = cost/items
```

This file can be saved to disk and executed immediately by selecting the **Run** icon on the **Editor** window toolbar or by pressing the **F5** function key. Alternately, this file can be saved as the M-file `example1.m` on your disk by choosing **Save** from the **File** menu; then it's just a matter of typing the name of the script file without the `.m` extension at the MATLAB prompt:

```
>> example1
items =
    12
cost =
   610
average_cost =
       50.833
```

When MATLAB interprets the `example1` statement above, it follows the hierarchy described in the previous chapter. In brief, MATLAB prioritizes current MATLAB variables and built-in MATLAB commands ahead of M-file names. Thus, if `example1` is not a current MATLAB variable or a built-in MATLAB command (it isn't), MATLAB opens the file `example1.m` (if it can find it) and evaluates the commands found there just as if they had been entered directly at the *Command* window prompt. As a result, commands within the M-file have access to all variables in the MATLAB workspace, and all variables created by the M-file become part of the workspace. Normally, the commands read in from the M-file are not displayed as they are evaluated. The `echo on` command tells MATLAB to display or echo commands to the *Command* window as they are read and evaluated. You can probably guess what the `echo off` command does. Similarly, the command `echo` by itself toggles the echo state.

This ability to create script M-files makes it simple to answer "what if?" questions. For example, one can repeatedly open the `example1.m` M-file, change the number of `erasers`, `pads`, or `tape`, and then save and execute the file using the **F5** key sequence. The power of this capability cannot be overstated. Moreover, by creating M-files, your commands are saved on disk for future MATLAB sessions.

The utility of MATLAB comments is readily apparent when using script files, as shown in `example1.m`. Comments allow you to document the commands found in a script file so that they are not forgotten when viewed in the future. In addition, the use of semicolons at the end of lines to suppress the display of results allows you to control script file output so that only important results are shown. Because of the utility of script files, MATLAB provides several functions that are particularly useful when used in M-files:

Function	Description
`beep`	Make computer beep.
`disp(`*`variablename`*`)`	Display results without identifying variable names.
`echo`	Control *Command* window echoing of script file contents as they are executed.
`input`	Prompt user for input.
`keyboard`	Give control to keyboard temporarily. Type `return` to return control to the executing script M-file.
`pause` or `pause(`*`n`*`)`	Pause until user presses any keyboard key, or pause for *n* seconds and then continue.
`waitforbuttonpress`	Pause until user presses mouse button or keyboard key.

When a MATLAB command is not terminated in a semicolon, the results of the command are displayed in the *Command* window with the variable name identified. For a prettier display it is sometimes convenient to suppress the variable name. In MATLAB this is accomplished with the command `disp`, for example,

```
>> items
items =
    12
>> disp(items)
    12
```

Rather than repeatedly edit a script file when computations for a variety of cases are desired, the `input` command allows one to prompt for input as a script file is executed. For example, reconsider the `example1.m` script file with modifications:

```
% script M-file example1.m

erasers = 4;  % Number of each item
pads = 6;
tape = input('Enter the number of rolls of tape purchased > ');
items = erasers + pads + tape
cost = erasers*25 + pads*52 + tape*99
average_cost = cost/items
```

Running this script M-file produces

```
>> example1
Enter the number of rolls of tape purchased > 3
items =
    13
cost =
   709
average_cost =
        54.538
```

In response to the prompt, the number `3` was entered and the **Return** or **Enter** key was pressed. The remaining commands were evaluated as before. The function `input` accepts any valid MATLAB expression for input. For example, running the script file again and providing different input gives

```
>> example1
Enter the number of rolls of tape purchased > round(sqrt(13))-1
items =
    13
cost =
   709
average_cost =
        54.538
```

In this case, the number of rolls of tape was set equal to the result of evaluating the expression `round(sqrt(13))-1`.

To see the effect of the echo command, add it to the script file and execute it:

```
% script M-file example1.m
echo on
erasers = 4;  % Number of each item
pads = 6;
tape = input('Enter the number of rolls of tape purchased > ');
items = erasers + pads + tape
cost = erasers*25 + pads*52 + tape*99
average_cost = cost/items
echo off
```

```
>> example1
erasers = 4;  % Number of each item
pads = 6;
input('Enter the number of rolls of tape purchased > ');
Enter the number of rolls of tape purchased > 2
items = erasers + pads + tape
items =
    12
cost = erasers*25 + pads*52 + tape*99
cost =
   610
average_cost = cost/items
average_cost =
       50.833
echo off
```

As you can see in this case, the echo command made the result much harder to read. On the other hand, the echo command can be very helpful when debugging more complicated script files.

4.2 STARTUP AND FINISH

When MATLAB starts up, it executes two script M-files, matlabrc.m and startup.m. Of these, matlabrc.m comes with MATLAB and generally should not be modified. The commands in this M-file set the default *Figure* window size and placement as well as a number of other default features. The default MATLAB search path is set by calling the script file pathdef.m from matlabrc.m. The *Path Browser* and *Command* window functions for editing the MATLAB search path maintain the file pathdef.m, and so there is no need to edit it using a text editor.

Commands in matlabrc.m check for the existence of the script M-file startup.m on the MATLAB search path. If it exists, the commands in it are executed. This optional M-file startup.m typically contains commands that add personal default features to MATLAB. For example, it is common to put one or more addpath or path commands in startup.m to append additional directories to the MATLAB search path. Similarly, the default number display format can be changed, for example, format compact. If you have a grayscale monitor, the command graymon is useful for setting default grayscale graphics features. Further still, if you want plots to have different default characteristics, a call to colordef could appear in startup.m. Since startup.m is a standard script M-file, there are no restrictions as to what commands can be placed in it. However, it's probably not wise to include the command quit in startup.m! On single-user installations, startup.m is commonly stored in the toolbox/local subdirectory on the MATLAB path. On network installations, a convenient location for your startup.m file is the default directory where you start MATLAB sessions.

When you terminate MATLAB via the **Exit MATLAB** item on the **File** menu in the *MATLAB* desktop window or by typing exit or quit at the MATLAB prompt, MATLAB searches the MATLAB path for a script M-file named finish.m. If one is found, the commands in it are executed before MATLAB terminates. For example, the following finish.m prompts the user for confimation using a dialog box before quitting. The command quit cancel provides a way to cancel quitting.

```
%FINISH Confirm Desire for Quitting MATLAB
question = 'Are You Sure You Want To Quit?';
button = questdlg(question,'Exit Request','Yes','No','No');

switch button
case 'No'
   quit cancel;  % how to cancel quitting!
end
% 'Yes' lets script and MATLAB end.
```

5

Arrays and Array Operations

All the computations considered to this point have involved single numbers called scalars. Operations involving scalars are the basis of mathematics. At the same time, when one wishes to perform the same operation on more than one number at a time, repeated scalar operations are time-consuming and cumbersome. To solve this problem, MATLAB defines operations on data arrays.

5.1 SIMPLE ARRAYS

Consider the problem of computing values of the sine function over one half of its period, namely, $y = \sin(x)$ over $0 \leq x \leq \pi$. Since it is impossible to compute $\sin(x)$ at all points over this range (there are an infinite number of them), we must choose a finite number of points. In doing so we sample the function. To pick a number, let's evaluate $\sin(x)$ every 0.1π in this range; that is, let $x = 0, 0.1\pi, 0.2\pi, ..., 1.0\pi$. If you were using a scientific calculator to compute these values, you would start by making a list or array of the values of x. Then you would enter each value of x into your calculator, find its sine, and write down the result as the second array *y*. Perhaps you would write them in an organized fashion as follows.

x	0	0.1π	0.2π	0.3π	0.4π	0.5π	0.6π	0.7π	0.8π	0.9π	π
y	0	0.31	0.59	0.81	0.95	1	0.95	0.81	0.59	0.31	0

As shown, x and y are ordered lists of numbers; that is, the first value or element in y is associated with the first value or element in x, the second element in y is associated with the second element in x, and so on. Because of this ordering, it is common to refer to individual values or elements in x and y with subscripts; for example, x_1 is the first element in x, y_5 is the fifth element in y, and x_n is the nth element in x.

MATLAB handles arrays in a straightforward, intuitive way. Creating arrays is easy—just follow the visual organization given above:

```
>> x = [0 .1*pi .2*pi .3*pi .4*pi .5*pi .6*pi .7*pi .8*pi .9*pi pi]
x =
  Columns 1 through 7
         0    0.3142    0.6283    0.9425    1.2566    1.5708    1.8850
  Columns 8 through 11
    2.1991    2.5133    2.8274    3.1416
>> y = sin(x)
y =
  Columns 1 through 7
         0    0.3090    0.5878    0.8090    0.9511    1.0000    0.9511
  Columns 8 through 11
    0.8090    0.5878    0.3090    0.0000
```

To create an array in MATLAB all you have to do is start with a left bracket, enter the desired values separated by spaces (or commas), and then close the array with a right bracket. Notice that finding the sine of the values in `x` follows naturally. MATLAB understands that you want to find the sine of each element in `x` and place the results in an associated array called `y`. This fundamental capability makes MATLAB different than other computer languages.

Since spaces separate array values, complex numbers entered as array values cannot have embedded spaces unless expressions are enclosed in parentheses. For example, `[1 -2i 3 4 5+6i]` contains five elements, whereas the identical arrays `[(1 - 2i) 3 4 5+6i]` and `[1-2i 3 4 5+6i]` contain four.

5.2 ARRAY ADDRESSING OR INDEXING

Now since `x` in the above example has more than one element, (it has 11 values separated into columns), MATLAB gives you the result back with the columns identified. As shown above, x is an array having one row and 11 columns, or in mathematical jargon it is a row vector, a 1-by-11 array or simply an array of length 11.

In MATLAB, individual array elements are accessed using subscripts; for example, x(1) is the first element in x, x(2) is the second element in x, and so on. For example,

```
>> x(3)   % The third element of x
ans =
    0.6283
>> y(5)   % The fifth element of y
ans =
    0.9511
```

To access a block of elements at one time MATLAB provides ***colon notation:***

```
>> x(1:5)
ans =
          0    0.3142    0.6283    0.9425    1.2566
```

These are the first through fifth elements in x. The notation 1:5 says start with 1 and count up to 5.

```
>> x(7:end)
ans =
        1.885         2.1991         2.5133         2.8274         3.1416
```

starts with the seventh element and continues to the last element. Here the word end signifies the last element in the array x.

```
>> y(3:-1:1)
ans =
    0.5878    0.3090         0
```

These are the third, second, and first elements in reverse order. The notation 3:-1:1 says start with 3, count down by 1, and stop at 1.

```
>> x(2:2:7)
ans =
    0.3142    0.9425    1.5708
```

These are the second, fourth, and sixth elements in x. The notation 2:2:7 says start with 2, count up by 2, and stop when you get to 7. In this case adding 2 to 6 gives 8, which is greater than 7, and so the eighth element is not included.

```
>> y([8 2 9 1])
ans =
    0.8090    0.3090    0.5878         0
```

Here we used another array, `[8 2 9 1]`, to extract the elements of the array `y` in the order we wanted them! The first element taken is the eighth, the second is the second, the third is the ninth, and the fourth is the first. In reality `[8 2 9 1]` itself is an array that addresses the desired elements of `y`.

```
>> y([1 1 3 4 2 2])
ans =
         0         0    0.5878    0.8090    0.3090    0.3090
```

As shown above, there is no requirement that the array used as an index contain unique elements. This allows one to rearrange and duplicate array elements arbitrarily. Using this feature leads to efficient MATLAB coding.

Addressing one array with another works as long as the addressing array contains integers between 1 and the length of the array. For example,

```
>> y(3.2)
Warning: Subscript indices must be integer values.
ans =
      0.5878
>> y(3.7)
Warning: Subscript indices must be integer values.
ans =
      0.8090
>> y(11.6)
Warning: Subscript indices must be integer values.
???  Index exceeds matrix dimensions.
```

In the above examples, MATLAB accepted the noninteger indices but gave a warning message. In addition, MATLAB attempted to return the value of `y` with the indices rounded to the nearest integer. For the last example above, 11.6 rounds to 12, and since there is no 12th element in `y`, an error message is returned in lieu of a numerical result.

5.3 ARRAY CONSTRUCTION

Earlier we entered the values of `x` by typing each individual element in `x`. While this is fine when there are only 11 values in `x`, what if there are 111 values? Using the colon notation, two other ways of entering `x` are

```
>> x = (0:0.1:1)*pi
x =
  Columns 1 through 7
         0    0.3142    0.6283    0.9425    1.2566    1.5708    1.8850
  Columns 8 through 11
    2.1991    2.5133    2.8274    3.1416
```

```
>> x = linspace(0,pi,11)
x =
  Columns 1 through 7
         0    0.3142    0.6283    0.9425    1.2566    1.5708    1.8850
  Columns 8 through 11
    2.1991    2.5133    2.8274    3.1416
```

In the first case above, the colon notation (0:0.1:1) creates an array that starts at 0, increments or counts by 0.1, and ends at 1. Each element in this array is then multiplied by π to create the desired values in x. In the second case, the MATLAB function linspace is used to create x. This function's arguments are described by

```
linspace(first_value,last_value,number_of_values)
```

Both of these array creation forms are common in MATLAB. The colon notation form allows you to directly specify the increment between data points but not the number of data points. linspace, on the other hand, allows you to directly specify the number of data points but not the increment between the data points.

Both of the above array creation forms result in arrays in which the individual elements are linearly spaced with respect to each other. For the special case where a logarithmically spaced array is desired, MATLAB provides the logspace function:

```
>> logspace(0,2,11)
ans =
  Columns 1 through 7
    1.0000    1.5849    2.5119    3.9811    6.3096   10.0000   15.8489
  Columns 8 through 11

   25.1189   39.8107   63.0957  100.0000
```

Here, we created an array starting at 10^0, ending at 10^2, and containing 11 values. The function arguments are described by

```
logspace(first_exponent,last_exponent,number_of_values)
```

Though it is common to begin and end at integer powers of 10, logspace works equally well with nonintegers.

When using colon notation or the functions linspace and logspace, there is often a temptation to enclose expressions in brackets, for example,

```
>> a = [1:7]
a =
     1     2     3     4     5     6     7
>> b = [linspace(1,7,5)]
b =
          1          2.5            4          5.5            7
```

While using brackets does not change results and may add clarity to the statements, the added brackets force MATLAB to do more work and take more time because brackets signify concatenation. In the above examples no concatenation is performed, and so there's no need to ask MATLAB to take the time to consider that posibility.

Parentheses do not signify concatenation and therefore do not slow MATLAB down. As a result, parentheses can be used as needed, for example,

```
>> a = (1:7)' % change row to column
a =
     1
     2
     3
     4
     5
     6
     7
```

Sometimes an array is required that is not conveniently described by a linearly or logarithmically spaced element relationship. There is no uniform way to create these arrays. However, array addressing and the ability to combine expressions can help eliminate the need to enter individual elements one at a time. For example,

```
>> a = 1:5, b = 1:2:9
a =
     1     2     3     4     5
b =
     1     3     5     7     9
```

creates two arrays. Remember that multiple statements can appear on a single line if they are separated by commas or semicolons.

```
>> c = [b a]
c =
     1     3     5     7     9     1     2     3     4     5
```

creates an array c composed of the elements of b followed by those of a.

```
>> d = [a(1:2:5) 1 0 1]
d =
     1     3     5     1     0     1
```

creates an array d composed of the first, third, and fifth elements of a followed by three additional elements.

The simple array construction features of MATLAB are summarized in the following table.

Array Construction Technique	Description
`x=[2 2*pi sqrt(2) 2-3j]`	Create row vector x containing arbitrary elements.
`x=first:last`	Create row vector x starting with first, counting by 1, and ending at or before last. Note that x=[first:last] produces the same result but takes longer since MATLAB considers both bracket and colon array creation forms.
`x=first:increment:last`	Create row vector x starting with first, counting by increment, and ending at or before last.
`x=linspace(first,last,n)`	Create linearly spaced row vector x starting with first, ending at last, and having n elements.
`x=logspace(first,last,n)`	Create logarithmically spaced row vector x starting with 10^{first}, ending at 10^{last}, and having n elements.

5.4 ARRAY ORIENTATION

In the above examples, arrays contained one row and multiple columns. As a result of this row orientation they are commonly called row vectors. It is also possible for an array to be a column vector having one column and multiple rows. In this case, all of the above array manipulation and mathematics apply without change. The only difference is that results are displayed as columns rather than rows. Since the array creation functions illustrated above all create row vectors, there must be some way to create column vectors. The most straightforward way to create a column vector is to specify it element by element and use ***semicolons*** to separate values:

```
>> c = [1;2;3;4;5]
c =
     1
     2
     3
     4
     5
```

> Based on this example, separating elements by spaces or commas specifies elements in different columns, whereas separating elements by semicolons specifies elements in different rows.

To create a column vector using the colon notation `start:increment:end` or the functions `linspace` and `logspace`, one must ***transpose*** the resulting row into a column using the MATLAB transpose operator ('). For example,

```
>> a = 1:5
a =
      1     2     3     4     5
```

creates a row vector using the colon notation format.

```
>> b = a'
b =
      1
      2
      3
      4
      5
```

uses the transpose operator to change the row vector `a` into the column vector `b`.

```
>> w = b'
w =
      1     2    3     4     5
```

applies the transpose again and changes the column back to a row.

In addition to the simple transpose above, MATLAB also offers a transpose operator with a preceding dot. In this case the ***dot-transpose operator*** is interpreted as the noncomplex conjugate transpose. When an array is complex, the transpose (') gives the complex-conjugate transpose, that is, the sign on the imaginary part is changed as part of the transpose operation. On the other hand, the dot-transpose (.') transposes the array but does not conjugate it.

```
>> c = a.'
c =
      1
      2
      3
      4
      5
```

shows that `.'` and `'` are identical for real data.

```
>> d = a + i*a
d =
  Columns 1 through 4
   1.0000 + 1.0000i   2.0000 + 2.0000i   3.0000 + 3.0000i   4.0000 + 4.0000i
  Column 5
   5.0000 + 5.0000i
```

creates a simple complex row vector from the array `a` using the default value `i`$=\sqrt{-1}$.

```
>> e = d'
e =
   1.0000 - 1.0000i
   2.0000 - 2.0000i
   3.0000 - 3.0000i
   4.0000 - 4.0000i
   5.0000 - 5.0000i
```

creates a column vector `e` that is the complex conjugate transpose of `d`.

```
>> f = d.'
f =
   1.0000 + 1.0000i
   2.0000 + 2.0000i
   3.0000 + 3.0000i
   4.0000 + 4.0000i
   5.0000 + 5.0000i
```

creates a column vector `f` that is the transpose of `d`.

If an array can be a row vector or a column vector, it makes intuitive sense that arrays can just as well have both multiple rows and multiple columns. That is, arrays can also be in the form of matrices. The creation of matrices follows that of row and column vectors. ***Commas or spaces are used to separate elements in a specific row, and semicolons are used to separate individual rows:***

```
>> g = [1 2 3 4;5 6 7 8]
g =
     1     2     3     4
     5     6     7     8
```

Here `g` is an array or matrix having 2 rows and 4 columns; that is, it is a 2-by-4 matrix or it is a matrix of dimension 2 by 4. The semicolon tells MATLAB to start a new row between the 4 and 5.

```
>> g = [1 2 3 4
5 6 7 8
9 10 11 12]
g =
     1     2     3     4
     5     6     7     8
     9    10    11    12
```

In addition to semicolons, pressing the ***Return*** or ***Enter*** key while entering an array also tells MATLAB to start a new row.

```
>> h = [1 2 3;4 5 6 7]
???  All rows in the bracketed expression must have the same
number of columns.
```

MATLAB strictly enforces the fact that all rows must contain the same number of columns.

5.5 SCALAR-ARRAY MATHEMATICS

In the first array example above, the array x is multiplied by the scalar π. Other simple mathematical operations between scalars and arrays follow the same natural interpretation. Addition, subtraction, multiplication, and division by a scalar simply applies the operation to all elements of the array.

```
>> g-2
ans =
    -1     0     1     2
     3     4     5     6
     7     8     9    10
```

subtracts 2 from each element in g.

```
>> 2*g - 1
ans =
     1     3     5     7
     9    11    13    15
    17    19    21    23
```

multiplies each element in g by 2 and subtracts 1 from each element of the result.

```
>> 2*g/5 + 1
ans =
          1.4          1.8          2.2          2.6
            3          3.4          3.8          4.2
          4.6            5          5.4          5.8
```

multiplies each element of g by 2, then divides each element of the result by 5, and finally adds 1 to each element.

Note that scalar-array mathematics uses the same order of precedence used in scalar expressions to determine the order of evaluation.

5.6 ARRAY-ARRAY MATHEMATICS

Mathematical operations between arrays are not quite as simple as those between scalars and arrays. Clearly, array operations between arrays of different sizes or dimensions are difficult to define and of even more dubious value. However, when two arrays have the same dimensions, addition, subtraction, multiplication, and division apply on an element-by-element basis in MATLAB, for example,

```
>> g  % recall previous array
g =
     1     2     3     4
     5     6     7     8
     9    10    11    12
>> h = [1 1 1 1;2 2 2 2;3 3 3 3]  % create new array
h =
     1     1     1     1
     2     2     2     2
     3     3     3     3
>> g + h  % add h to g on an element-by-element basis
ans =
     2     3     4     5
     7     8     9    10
    12    13    14    15
>> ans - h  % subtract h from the previous answer to get g back
ans =
     1     2     3     4
     5     6     7     8
     9    10    11    12
>> 2*g - h  % multiplies g by 2 and subtracts h from the result
ans =
     1     3     5     7
     8    10    12    14
    15    17    19    21
>> 2*(g-h)  % use parentheses to change order of operation
ans =
     0     2     4     6
     6     8    10    12
    12    14    16    18
```

Note that array-array mathematics also uses the same order of precedence used in scalar expressions to determine the order of evaluation, and that parentheses can be used as desired to change the order of operation.

Element-by-element multiplication and division work similarly but use slightly unconventional notation:

```
>> g.*h
ans =
     1     2     3     4
    10    12    14    16
    27    30    33    36
```

Here we multiplied the arrays g and h element by element using the dot multiplication symbol .*.

> The dot preceding the standard asterisk multiplication symbol tells MATLAB to perform element-by-element array multiplication. Multiplication without the dot signifies matrix multiplication, which is discussed later.

For this particular example matrix multiplication is not defined:

```
>> g*h
??? Error using ==> *
Inner matrix dimensions must agree.
```

Element-by-element division, or dot division, also requires use of the dot symbol, for example,

```
>> g./h
ans =
    1.0000    2.0000    3.0000    4.0000
    2.5000    3.0000    3.5000    4.0000
    3.0000    3.3333    3.6667    4.0000
>> h.\g
ans =
    1.0000    2.0000    3.0000    4.0000
    2.5000    3.0000    3.5000    4.0000
    3.0000    3.3333    3.6667    4.0000
```

As with scalars, division is defined using both forward and backward slashes. In both cases, the array below the slash is divided into the array above the slash.

> The dot preceding the forward or backward slash symbol tells MATLAB to perform element-by-element array division. Division without the dot signifies matrix inversion, which is discussed later.

Array or dot division also applies if the numerator is a scalar, for example,

```
>> 1./g
ans =
           1          0.5      0.33333         0.25
         0.2      0.16667      0.14286        0.125
     0.11111          0.1     0.090909     0.083333
```

In this case, the scalar 1 in the numerator is expanded to an array the same size as the denominator, and then element-by-element division is performed. That is, the above represents a shorthand way of computing

```
>> f=[1 1 1 1; 1 1 1 1; 1 1 1 1] % create numerator by scalar expansion
f =
     1     1     1     1
     1     1     1     1
     1     1     1     1
>> f./g
ans =
           1          0.5      0.33333         0.25
         0.2      0.16667      0.14286        0.125
     0.11111          0.1     0.090909     0.083333
>> f./h
ans =
           1            1            1            1
         0.5          0.5          0.5          0.5
     0.33333      0.33333      0.33333      0.33333
```

This process of automatically expanding scalar values so that element-by-element arithmetic applies is called ***scalar expansion.*** Scalar expansion is used extensively in MATLAB.

Division without the dot is the matrix division operation, which is an entirely different operation, for example,

```
>> g/h
Warning: Rank deficient, rank = 1  tol =   5.3291e-015.
ans =
           0            0      0.83333
           0            0       2.1667
           0            0          3.5
```

```
>> h/g
Warning: Rank deficient, rank = 2  tol =   1.8757e-014.
Ans =
        -0.125             0          0.125
         -0.25             0           0.25
        -0.375             0          0.375
```

Matrix division gives results that are not necessarily the same size as `g` and `h`. Matrix operations are discussed in the chapter on matrix algebra.

Array exponentiation is defined in several ways. As with multiplication and division, ^ is reserved for matrix exponentiation and .^ is used to denote element-by-element exponentiation. When the exponent is a scalar, the scalar is applied to each element of the array. For example,

```
>> g, h  % recalls the arrays used earlier
g =
     1     2     3     4
     5     6     7     8
     9    10    11    12
h =
     1     1     1     1
     2     2     2     2
     3     3     3     3

>> g.^2
ans =
     1     4     9    16
    25    36    49    64
    81   100   121   144
```

squares the individual elements of `g`, whereas

```
>> g^2
??? Error using ==> ^
Matrix must be square.
```

is matrix exponentiation, which is defined only for square matrices, that is, matrices with equal row and column counts.

```
>> g.^-1
ans =
             1           0.5       0.33333          0.25
           0.2       0.16667       0.14286         0.125
       0.11111           0.1      0.090909      0.083333
```

finds the reciprocal of each element in g,

```
>> 1./g
ans =
           1         0.5     0.33333        0.25
         0.2     0.16667     0.14286       0.125
     0.11111         0.1    0.090909    0.083333
```

which produces the same result as the scalar expansion approach seen earlier.

When the exponent is an array operating on a scalar, each element of the array is applied to the scalar. For example,

```
>> 2.^g
ans =
           2           4           8          16
          32          64         128         256
         512        1024        2048        4096
```

raises 2 to the power of each element in the array g.

If both components are arrays of the same size, exponentiation is applied element by element. For example,

```
>> g.^h
ans =
           1           2           3           4
          25          36          49          64
         729        1000        1331        1728
```

raises the elements of g to the corresponding elements in h. In this case, the first row is unchanged since the first row of h contains ones; the second row is squared, and the third row is cubed.

```
>> g.^(h-1)
ans =
     1     1     1     1
     5     6     7     8
    81   100   121   144
```

shows that scalar and array operations can be combined.

The two forms of exponentiation that have scalar parts are yet further examples of scalar expansion. The results make intuitive sense if the scalars involved are first expanded to the size of the array and element-by-element exponentiation is then applied.

The following table summarizes basic array operations.

Element-by-Element Operation	Representative Data A = [a_1 a_2 ... a_n], B = [b_1 b_2 ... b_n], c = <a *scalar*>
Scalar addition	A+c = [a_1+c a_2+c ... a_n+c]
Scalar subtraction	A-c = [a_1-c a_2-c ... a_n-c]
Scalar multiplication	A*c = [a_1*c a_2*c ... a_n*c]
Scalar division	A/c = c\A = [a_1/c a_2/c ... a_n/c]
Array addition	A+B = [a_1+b_1 a_2+b_2 ... a_n+b_n]
Array multiplication	A.*B = [a_1*b_1 a_2*b_2 ... a_n*b_n]
Array right division	A./B = [a_1/b_1 a_2/b_2 ... a_n/b_n]
Array left division	B.\A = [a_1/b_1 a_2/b_2 ... a_n/b_n]
Array exponentiation	A.^c = [a_1^c a_2^c ... a_n^c] c.^A = [c^a_1 c^a_2 ... c^a_n] A.^B = [a_1^b_1 a_2^b_2 ... a_n^b_n]

5.7 STANDARD ARRAYS

Because of their general utility, MATLAB provides functions for creating a number of standard arrays. These include arrays containing all ones or all zeros, identity matrices, arrays of random numbers, diagonal arrays, and arrays whose elements are a given constant.

```
>> ones(3)
ans =
     1     1     1
     1     1     1
     1     1     1
>> zeros(2,5)
ans =
     0     0     0     0     0
     0     0     0     0     0
>> size(g)
ans =
     3     4
>> ones(size(g))
ans =
     1     1     1     1
     1     1     1     1
     1     1     1     1
```

When called with a single input argument, `ones(n)` or `zeros(n)`, MATLAB creates an `n`-by-`n` array containing ones or zeros, respectively. When called with two input arguments, `ones(r,c)` or `zeros(r,c)`, MATLAB creates an array having `r` rows and `c` columns. To create an array of ones or zeros the same size as another array, use the `size` function (discussed later in this chapter) in the argument to `ones` or `zeros`.

```
>> eye(4)
ans =
     1     0     0     0
     0     1     0     0
     0     0     1     0
     0     0     0     1
>> eye(2,4)
ans =
     1     0     0     0
     0     1     0     0
>> eye(4,2)
ans =
     1     0
     0     1
     0     0
     0     0
```

As shown above, the function `eye` produces identity matrices using the same syntax style as that used to produce arrays of zeros and ones. An identity matrix or array is all zeros except for the elements `A(i,i)`, where `i = 1:min(r,c)` in which `min(r,c)` is the minimum of the number of rows and columns in `A`.

```
>> rand(3)
ans =
      0.9501      0.4860      0.4565
      0.2311      0.8913      0.0185
      0.6068      0.7621      0.8214
>> rand(1,5)
ans =
       0.4447      0.6154      0.7919      0.9218      0.7382
>> b = eye(3)
  b =
     1     0     0
     0     1     0
     0     0     1
>> rand(size(b))
ans =
      0.1763      0.9169      0.0579
      0.4057      0.4103      0.3529
      0.9355      0.8937      0.8132
```

The function `rand` produces uniformly distributed random arrays whose elements lie between 0 and 1.

```
>> randn(2)
ans =
     -0.4326        0.1253
     -1.6656        0.2877
>> randn(2,5)
ans =
      -1.1465        1.1892        0.3273       -0.1867       -0.5883
       1.1909       -0.0376        0.1746        0.7258        2.183
```

On the other hand, the function `randn` produces arrays whose elements are samples from a ***zero-mean, unit-variance*** normal distribution.

```
>> a = 1:4  % start with a simple vector
a =
     1     2     3     4
>> diag(a)  % place elements on the main diagonal
ans =
     1     0     0     0
     0     2     0     0
     0     0     3     0
     0     0     0     4
>> diag(a,1)  % place elements 1 place up from diagonal
ans =
     0     1     0     0     0
     0     0     2     0     0
     0     0     0     3     0
     0     0     0     0     4
     0     0     0     0     0
>> diag(a,-2)  % place elements 2 places down from diagonal
ans =
     0     0     0     0     0     0
     0     0     0     0     0     0
     1     0     0     0     0     0
     0     2     0     0     0     0
     0     0     3     0     0     0
     0     0     0     4     0     0
```

As shown above, the function `diag` creates diagonal arrays in which a vector can be placed at any location parallel to the main diagonal of an array.

With the above standard arrays there are several ways to create an array whose elements all have the same value. Some of them include

```
>> d = pi;  % choose pi for this example
>> d*ones(3,4)  % slowest method (scalar-array multiplication)
ans =
      3.1416      3.1416      3.1416      3.1416
      3.1416      3.1416      3.1416      3.1416
      3.1416      3.1416      3.1416      3.1416
>> d+zeros(3,4) % slower method (scalar-array addition)
ans =
      3.1416      3.1416      3.1416      3.1416
      3.1416      3.1416      3.1416      3.1416
      3.1416      3.1416      3.1416      3.1416
>> d(ones(3,4))  % fast method (array addressing)
ans =
      3.1416      3.1416      3.1416      3.1416
      3.1416      3.1416      3.1416      3.1416
      3.1416      3.1416      3.1416      3.1416
>> repmat(d,3,4)  % fastest method (optimum array addressing)
ans =
      3.1416      3.1416      3.1416      3.1416
      3.1416      3.1416      3.1416      3.1416
      3.1416      3.1416      3.1416      3.1416
```

For small arrays all of the above methods are fine. However, as the array grows in size, the multiplications required in the scalar multiplication approach slow the procedure down. Since addition is often faster than multiplication, the next best approach is to add the desired scalar to an array of zeros. Although they are not intuitive, the last two methods are the fastest for large arrays. They both involve array indexing as described earlier.

The solution `d(ones(r,c))` creates an `r`-by-`c` array of ones and then uses this array to index and duplicate the scalar `d`. Creating the temporary array of ones takes time and uses memory, thereby slowing this approach down despite the fact that no floating-point mathematics is used. The solution `repmat(d,r,c)` calls the function `repmat`, which stands for replicate matrix. For scalar `d`, this function performs the following steps.

```
D(r*c) = d;          % a row vector whose (r*c)-th element is d
D(:) = d;            % scalar expansion to fill all elements of D with d
D = reshape(D,r,c); % reshape the vector into the desired r-by-c shape
```

The above MATLAB code uses scalar expansion to create a vector having `r*c` elements all equal to `d`. This vector is then reshaped using the function `reshape` into an `r`-by-`c` array. The functions `repmat` and `reshape` are discussed further later.

5.8 ARRAY MANIPULATION

Since arrays are fundamental to MATLAB, there are many ways to manipulate them in MATLAB. Once arrays are formed, MATLAB provides powerful ways to insert, extract, and rearrange subsets of them by identifying subscripts of interest. Knowledge of these features is a key to using MATLAB efficiently. To illustrate the array manipulation features of MATLAB, consider the following examples.

```
>> A = [1 2 3;4 5 6;7 8 9]
A =
      1     2     3
      4     5     6
      7     8     9
>> A(3,3) = 0  % set element in 3rd row, 3rd column to zero
A =
      1     2     3
      4     5     6
      7     8     0
```

changes the element in the third row and third column to zero.

```
>> A(2,6) = 1  % set element in 2nd row, 6th column to one
A =
      1     2     3     0     0     0
      4     5     6     0     0     1
      7     8     0     0     0     0
```

places one in the second row, sixth column. Since A does not have six columns, the size of A is increased as necessary and filled with zeros so that the array remains rectangular.

```
>> A(:,4) = 4
A =
      1     2     3     4     0     0
      4     5     6     4     0     1
      7     8     0     4     0     0
```

sets the fourth column of A equal to 4. Since 4 is a scalar, it is expanded to fill all the elements specified. This is another example of scalar expansion. MATLAB performs scalar expansion to simplify statements that can be interpreted unambiguously. For example, the above statement is equivalent to the more cumbersome statement

```
>> A(:,4) = [4;4;4]
A =
      1     2     3     4     0     0
      4     5     6     4     0     1
      7     8     0     4     0     0
```

```
>> A(:,4) = [4 4 4]  % but a row can't be squeezed into a column!

??? In an assignment  A(:,matrix) = B, the number of elements in
the subscript of A and the number of columns in B must be the same.
```

Let's start over and look at other array manipulations.

```
>> A = [1 2 3;4 5 6;7 8 9];  % restore original data

>> B = A(3:-1:1,1:3)
B =
     7     8     9
     4     5     6
     1     2     3

>> B = A(end:-1:1,1:3)  % same as above
B =
     7     8     9
     4     5     6
     1     2     3
```

creates an array B by taking the rows of A in reverse order. The word end automatically denotes the final or largest index for a given dimension. In this example, end signifies the largest row index 3.

```
>> B = A(3:-1:1,:)
B =
     7     8     9
     4     5     6
     1     2     3
```

does the same as the above example. Here the final single colon means take all columns. That is, : is equivalent to 1:3 in this example because A has three columns.

```
>> C = [A B(:,[1 3])]
C =
     1     2     3     7     9
     4     5     6     4     6
     7     8     9     1     3
```

creates C by appending or concatenating all rows in the first and third columns of B to the right of A.

```
>> B = A(1:2,2:3)
B =
     2     3
     5     6
```

```
>> B = A(1:2,2:end)  % same as above
B =
     2     3
     5     6
```

creates B by extracting the first two rows and last two columns of A. Once again, colon notation is used to create index vectors identifying the array elements to extract. In the second instance above, `end` is used to denote the final or largest column index.

```
>> C = [1 3]
C =
     1     3
>> B = A(C,C)
B =
     1     3
     7     9
```

uses the array C to index the array A rather than specifying them directly using the colon notation *start:increment:end* or *start:end*. In this example, B is formed from the first and third rows and first and third columns of A.

```
>> B = A(:)
B =
     1
     4
     7
     2
     5
     8
     3
     6
     9
```

builds B by stretching A into a column vector, taking its columns one at a time in order. This is the simplest form of reshaping an array into an array having different dimensions but the same number of total elements.

```
>> B = B.'
B =
     1     4     7     2     5     8     3     6     9

>> B = reshape(A,1,9)  % reshape A into 1-by-9
B =
     1     4     7     2     5     8     3     6     9

>> B = reshape(A,[1 9])
B =
     1     4     7     2     5     8     3     6     9
```

illustrates the dot-transpose operation introduced earlier as well as the function `reshape`. In this case `reshape` works with the indices supplied as separate function arguments or supplied as a single vector argument.

```
>> B = A  % copy A into B
B =
     1     2     3
     4     5     6
     7     8     9
>> B(:,2) = []
B =
     1     3
     4     6
     7     9
```

redefines `B` by throwing away all rows in the second column of the original `B`. When you set something equal to the empty matrix or empty array `[]`, it is deleted, causing the array to collapse to what remains. Note that you must delete whole rows or columns so that the result remains rectangular.

```
>> C = B.'
C =
     1     4     7
     3     6     9
>> reshape(B,2,3)  % reshape is not equivalent to transpose
ans =
     1     7     6
     4     3     9
```

illustrates the transpose of an array and demonstrates that `reshape` is not the same. The transpose converts the *i*th row to the *i*th column of the result, and so the original 3-by-2 array becomes a 2-by-3 array.

```
>> C(2,:) = []
C =
     1     4     7
```

throws out the second row of `C`, leaving a row vector.

```
>> A(2,:) = C
A =
     1     2     3
     1     4     7
     7     8     9
```

replaces the second row of `A` with `C`.

```
>> B = A(:,[2 2 2 2])  % create new B array
B =
     2     2     2     2
     4     4     4     4
     8     8     8     8
>> B = A(:,2+zeros(1,4))  % [2 2 2 2]=2+zeros(1,4)
B =
     2     2     2     2
     4     4     4     4
     8     8     8     8
>> B = repmat(A(:,2),1,4)  % replicate 2nd column into 4 columns
B =
     2     2     2     2
     4     4     4     4
     8     8     8     8
```

creates B three ways by duplicating all rows in the second column of A four times. The last approach is fastest for large arrays.

```
>> A, C  % show A and C again
A =
     1     2     3
     1     4     7
     7     8     9
C =
     1     4     7
>> A(2,2) = []
???  Indexed empty matrix assignment is not allowed.
```

shows that you can throw out only entire rows or columns. MATLAB simply does not know how to collapse an array when partial rows or columns are thrown out.

```
>> C = A(4,:)
???  Index exceeds matrix dimensions.
```

Since A does not have a fourth row, MATLAB doesn't know what to do and says so. Based on this result, indices must follow the guideline below.

> If A(r,c) appears on the left-hand side of an equal sign and one or more elements specified by (r,c) do not exist, zeros are added to A as needed so that A(r,c) addresses known elements. However, on the right-hand side of an equal sign all elements addressed by A(r,c) must exist or an error is returned.

Continuing on, consider the following.

```
>> C(1:2,:) = A
??? In an assignment A(matrix,:) = B, the number of columns in
A and B must be the same.
```

shows that you can't squeeze one array into another one having a different size.

```
>> C(3:4,:) = A(2:3,:)
C =
     1     4     7
     0     0     0
     1     4     7
     7     8     9
```

But you can place the second and third columns of A into the same-size area of C. Since the second through fourth rows of C did not exist, they are created as necessary. Moreover, the second row of C is unspecified, and so it is filled with zeros.

```
>> A = [1 2 3;4 5 6;7 8 9]  % fresh data
A =
     1     2     3
     4     5     6
     7     8     9
>> A(:,2:3)             % a peek at what's addressed next
ans =
     2     3
     5     6
     8     9
>> G(1:6) = A(:,2:3)
G =
     2     5     8     3     6     9
```

creates a row vector G by extracting all rows in the second and third columns of A. Note that the shapes of the matrices are different on both sides of the equal sign. The elements of A are inserted into the elements of G by going down the rows of the first column and then down the rows of the second column.

```
>> H = ones(6,1);    % create a column array

>> H(:) = A(:,2:3)   % fill H without changing its shape
H =
     2
     5
     8
     3
     6
     9
```

When `(:)` appears on the left-hand side of the equal sign, it means to take elements from the right-hand side and stick them into the array on the left-hand side without changing its shape. In the above example, this process extracts the second and third columns of A and inserts them into the column vector H. Obviously, for the above to work, both sides must address the same number of elements.

When the right-hand side of an assignment is a scalar and the left-hand side is an array, ***scalar expansion*** is used. For example,

```
>> A(2,:) = 0
A =
     1     2     3
     0     0     0
     7     8     9
```

replaces the second row of A with zeros. The single zero on the right-hand side is expanded to fill all the indices specified on the left. This example is equivalent to

```
>> A(2,:) = [0 0 0]
A =
     1     2     3
     0     0     0
     7     8     9
```

Scalar expansion occurs whenever a scalar is used in a location calling for an array. MATLAB automatically expands the scalar to fill all requested locations and then performs the operation dictated.

```
>> A(1,[1 3]) = pi
A =
    3.1416    2.0000    3.1416
         0         0         0
    7.0000    8.0000    9.0000
```

This is yet another example in which the scalar π is expanded to fill two locations. Consider again what the function `reshape` does with scalar input. Let's create a 2-by-4 array containing the number 2:

```
>> D(2*4) = 2  % create array with 8 elements
D =
     0     0     0     0     0     0     0     2
>> D(:) = 2  % scalar expansion
D =
     2     2     2     2     2     2     2     2
>> D = reshape(D,2,4)  % reshape
D =
     2     2     2     2
     2     2     2     2
```

The first line `D(2*4) = 2` causes a row vector of length `8` to be created and places `2` in the last column. Next `D(:) = 2` uses scalar expansion to fill all elements of `D` with `2`. Finally the result is reshaped into the desired dimensions.

Sometimes it is desirable to perform some mathematical operation between a vector and a two-dimensional (2-D) array. For example, consider the arrays:

```
>> A = reshape (1:12,3,4)'
A =
        1     2     3
        4     5     6
        7     8     9
       10    11    12
>> r = [3 2 1]
r =
        3     2     1
```

Suppose we wish to subtract `r(i)` from the *i*th column of `A`. One way of accomplishing this is

```
>> Ar = [A(:,1)-r(1) A(:,2)-r(2) A(:,3)-r(3)]
Ar =
       -2     0     2
        1     3     5
        4     6     8
        7     9    11
```

Alternatively one can use indexing:

```
>> R = r([1 1 1 1],:) % duplicate r to have 4 rows
R =
        3     2     1
        3     2     1
        3     2     1
        3     2     1
>> Ar = A - R % now use element by element subtraction
Ar =
       -2     0     2
        1     3     5
        4     6     8
        7     9    11
```

The array `R` can also be computed faster and more generally using the functions `ones` and `size` or using the function `repmat`, all of which are discussed later. Consider the following example.

```
>> R = r(ones(size(A,1),1),:) % historically this is Tony's trick
R =
     3     2     1
     3     2     1
     3     2     1
     3     2     1
>> R = repmat(r,size(A,1),1)  % often faster than Tony's trick
R =
     3     2     1
     3     2     1
     3     2     1
     3     2     1
```

In the above, `size(A,1)` returns the number of rows in `A`.

Sometimes it is more convenient to address array elements with a single index. ***When a single index is used in MATLAB, the index counts elements down the columns starting with the first.*** For example,

```
>> D = reshape(1:12,3,4)  % new data
D =
     1     4     7    10
     2     5     8    11
     3     6     9    12
>> D(2)
ans =
     2
>> D(5)
ans =
     5

>> D(end)
ans =
    12
>> D(4:7)
ans =
     4     5     6     7
```

The MATLAB functions `sub2ind` and `ind2sub` perform the arithmetic to convert to and from a single index to row and column subscripts, for example,

```
>> sub2ind(size(D),2,4)  % find single index from row and column
ans =
    11
>> [r,c] = ind2sub(size(D),11)  % find row and column from single index
r =
     2
c =
     4
```

The element in the second row, fourth column is the 11th element. Note that these two functions want to know the size of the array to search, that is, `size(D)`, rather than the array `D` itself.

In addition to addressing arrays based on their subscripts, ***logical arrays*** that result from logical operations (to be discussed more thoroughly later) can also be used if the size of the array is equal to that of the array it is addressing. In this case, True (1) elements are retained and False (0) elements are discarded. For example,

```
>> x = -3:3  % Create data
x =
    -3    -2    -1     0     1     2     3
>> abs(x)>1
ans =
     1     1     0     0     0     1     1
```

returns a logical array with ones (True) where the absolute value of `x` is greater than one, and zeros (False) elsewhere. The chapter on logical expressions contains more detailed information on logical expressions.

```
>> y = x(abs(x)>1)
y =
    -3    -2     2     3
```

creates `y` by taking those values of `x` where its absolute value is greater than 1.

Note, however, that even though `abs(x)>1` produces the array `[1 1 0 0 0 1 1]`, it is not equivalent to a numerical array containing those values; that is,

```
>> y = x([1 1 0 0 0 1 1])
??? Index into matrix is negative or zero. See release notes on
changes to logical indices.
```

gives an error even though the `abs(x)>1` and `[1 1 0 0 0 1 1]` appear to be the same vector. In the second case, `[1 1 0 0 0 1 1]` is a ***numeric array*** as opposed to a ***logical array.*** As a result, MATLAB tries to address the element numbers specified in `[1 1 0 0 0 1 1]` and generates an error because there is no element `0`. Naturally MATLAB provides the function `logical` for converting numerical arrays to logical arrays:

```
>> y = x(logical([1 1 0 0 0 1 1]))
y =
    -3    -2     2     3
```

Once again we have the desired result. Logical arrays are another ***data type*** in MATLAB. Up to now we've considered only numerical arrays. To summarize:

> Specifying array subscripts with numerical arrays extracts the elements having the given numerical indices. On the other hand, specifying array subscripts with logical arrays, which are returned by logical expressions and the function `logical`, extracts elements which are logical True (1).

Logical arrays work on two-dimensional arrays as well as vectors, for example,

```
>> B = [5 -3;2 -4]  % new data
B =
     5    -3
     2    -4
>> x = abs(B)>2  % logical result
x =
     1     1
     0     1
>> y = B(x)  % grab True values
y =
     5
    -3
     4
```

However, the final result above is returned as a column vector since there is no way to define a two-dimensional array having only three elements. No matter how many elements are extracted, MATLAB extracts all the true elements using single-index order and then forms or reshapes the result into a column vector.

The above array addressing techniques are summarized in the following table.

Array Addressing	Description
`A(r,c)`	Addresses a subarray within `A` defined by the index vector of desired rows in `r` and an index vector of desired columns in `c`.
`A(r,:)`	Addresses a subarray within `A` defined by the index vector of desired rows in `r` and all columns.
`A(:,c)`	Addresses a subarray within `A` defined by all rows and the index vector of desired columns in `c`.
`A(:)`	Addresses all elements of `A` as a column vector taken column by column. If `A(:)` appears on the left-hand side of the equal sign, it means to fill `A` with elements from the right-hand side of the equal sign without changing its shape.

Array Addressing	Description
`A(k)`	Addresses a subarray within `A` defined by the single index vector `k`, as if `A` were the column vector `A(:)`.
`A(x)`	Addresses a subarray within `A` defined by the logical array `x`. `x` must be the same size as `A`.

5.9 ARRAY SORTING

Given a data vector, a common task required in numerous applications is sorting. In MATLAB, the function `sort` performs this task, for example,

```
>> x = randperm(8)  % new data
x =
     7     5     2     1     3     6     4     8
>> xs = sort(x)  % sort ascending
xs =
     1     2     3     4     5     6     7     8
>> [xs,idx] = sort(x)  % return sort index as well
xs =
     1     2     3     4     5     6     7     8
idx =
     4     3     5     7     2     6     1     8
```

As shown above, the `sort` function returns one or two outputs. The first is an ascending sort of the input argument, and the second is the sort index, for example, `xs(k) = x(idx(k))`.

> Note that when a MATLAB function returns two or more variables, they are enclosed by square brackets on the left-hand side of the equal sign. This is different than the array manipulation syntax discussed above in which `[a,b]` on the right-hand side of the equal sign builds a new array with `b` appended to the right of `a`.

If a descending sort is desired, the output must be turned around using indexing techniques illustrated earlier, for example,

```
>> xsd = xs(end:-1:1)
xsd =
     8     7     6     5     4     3     2     1
```

```
>> idxd = idx(end:-1:1)
idxd =
  8     1     6     2     7     5     3     4
```

When presented with a two-dimensional array, `sort` acts differently, for example,

```
>> A = [randperm(6);randperm(6);randperm(6);randperm(6)] % new data
A =
     1     2     5     6     4     3
     4     2     6     5     3     1
     2     3     6     1     4     5
     3     5     1     2     4     6
>> [As,idx] = sort(A)
As =
     1     2     1     1     3     1
     2     2     5     2     4     3
     3     3     6     5     4     5
     4     5     6     6     4     6
idx =
     1     1     4     3     2     2
     3     2     1     4     1     1
     4     3     2     2     3     3
     2     4     3     1     4     4
```

Here the `sort` function sorts in ascending order each column independently of the others, and the indices returned are those for each column. In many cases one is more interested in sorting an array based on the sort of a specific column. In MATLAB this task is easy, for example,

```
>> [tmp,idx] =  sort(A(:,4)); % sort 4-th column only

>> As = A(idx,:) % rearrange rows in all columns using idx
As =
     2     3     6     1     4     5
     3     5     1     2     4     6
     4     2     6     5     3     1
     1     2     5     6     4     3
```

Now the rows of `As` are just the rearranged rows of `A`, in which the fourth column of `As` is sorted ascending.

It is also possible to sort each row rather than each column as shown above, for example,

```
>> As = sort(A,2) % sort across 2-nd dimension
As =
     1     2     3     4     5     6
     1     2     3     4     5     6
     1     2     3     4     5     6
     1     2     3     4     5     6
```

```
>> As = sort(A,1)  % same as sort(A)
As =
     1     2     1     1     3     1
     2     2     5     2     4     3
     3     3     6     5     4     5
     4     5     6     6     4     6
```

By using a second argument to `sort`, one can specify in which direction to sort. Since in `A(r,c)` the row dimension appears first, `sort(A,1)` means sort down the rows. Since the column dimension appears second, `sort(A,2)` means sort across the columns.

The chapter on data analysis contains much more information about the `sort` function.

5.10 SUBARRAY SEARCHING

Many times it is desirable to know the indices or subscripts of the elements of an array that satisfy some relational expression. In MATLAB this task is performed by the function `find`, which returns the subscripts when a relational expression is True, for example,

```
>> x = -3:3
x =
    -3    -2    -1     0     1     2     3
>> k = find(abs(x)>1)  % finds those subscripts where abs(x)>1
k =
     1     2     6     7
>> y = x(k)  % creates y using the indices in k.
y =
    -3    -2     2     3
>> y = x(abs(x)>1) % creates the same y vector by logical addressing
y =
    -3    -2     2     3
```

The `find` function also works for two-dimensional arrays, for example,

```
>> A = [1 2 3;4 5 6;7 8 9] % new data
A =
     1     2     3
     4     5     6
     7     8     9
>> [i,j] = find(A>5) % i and j are not equal to sqrt(-1) anymore
i =
     3
     3
     2
     3
```

```
j =
     1
     2
     3
     3
```

Here the indices stored in `i` and `j` are the associated row and column indices, respectively, where the relational expression is True. That is, `A(i(1),j(1))` is the first element of `A`, where `A>5`, and so on.

Alternatively, `find` returns single indices for two-dimensional arrays, for example,

```
>> k = find(A>5)
k =
     3
     6
     8
     9
```

Of the two index sets returned for two-dimensional arrays, this latter single-index form is often more useful, for example,

```
>> A(k)  % look at elements greater than 5
ans =
     7
     8
     6
     9

>> A(k) = 0  % set elements addressed by k to zero
A =
     1     2     3
     4     5     0
     0     0     0
>> A = [1 2 3;4 5 6;7 8 9]  % restore data
A =
     1     2     3
     4     5     6
     7     8     9

>> A(i,j)  % this is A([3 3 2 3],[1 2 3 3])
ans =
     7     8     9     9
     7     8     9     9
     4     5     6     6
     7     8     9     9
```

```
>> A(i,j) = 0  % this is A([3 3 2 3],[1 2 3 3]) also
A =
     1     2     3
     0     0     0
     0     0     0
```

The `A(i,j)` cases above are not as clearly understood as the preceding single-index cases. Assuming that `A(k)` is equivalent to `A(i,j)` is a common MATLAB indexing mistake. `A(i,j)` above is equivalent to

```
>> [A(3,1) A(3,2) A(3,3) A(3,3)
    A(3,1) A(3,2) A(3,3) A(3,3)
    A(2,1) A(2,2) A(2,3) A(2,3)
    A(3,1) A(3,2) A(3,3) A(3,3)]
ans =
     7     8     9     9
     7     8     9     9
     4     5     6     6
     7     8     9     9
```

Here the first row index in `i` is coupled with all the column indices in `j` to form the first row in the result. Then the second row index in `i` is coupled with the column indices in `j` to form the second row in the result, and so on. Given the above form, the diagonal elements of `A(i,j)` are equal to those of `A(k)`. Therefore, the two approaches are equal if the diagonal elements of `A(i,j)` are retained,

```
>> diag(A(i,j))
ans =
     7
     8
     6
     9
```

While `diag(A(i,j)) = A(k)`, `A(k)` is preferred since it does not create an intermediate square array.

Similarly, `A(i,j) = 0` is equivalent to

```
>> A(3,1)=0; A(3,2)=0; A(3,3)=0; A(3,3)=0; % i(1) with all j
>> A(3,1)=0; A(3,2)=0; A(3,3)=0; A(3,3)=0; % i(2) with all j
>> A(2,1)=0; A(2,2)=0; A(2,3)=0; A(2,3)=0; % i(3) with all j
>> A(3,1)=0; A(3,2)=0; A(3,3)=0; A(3,3)=0  % i(4) with all j
A =
     1     2     3
     0     0     0
     0     0     0
```

Based on the above equivalents, it is clear that `A(i,j)` is not generally as useful as `A(k)` for subarray searching using `find`.

The above concepts are summarized in the following table.

Array Searching	Description
`i=find(X)`	Return single indices of the array `X` where its elements are nonzero.
`[r,c]=find(X)`	Return row and column indices of the array `X` where its elements are nonzero.

In addition to using the function `find` to identify specific values within an array, the maximum and minimum values and their locations within an array are often useful. MATLAB provides the functions `max` and `min` to accomplish these tasks. Consider the following example.

```
>> v = rand(1,6)  % new data
v =
    0.3046    0.1897    0.1934    0.6822    0.3028    0.5417

>> max(v)  % return maximum value
ans =
    0.6822

>> [mx,i] = max(v)  % maximum value and its index
mx =
    0.6822
i =
     4

>> min(v)  % return minimum value
ans =
    0.1897

>> [mn,i] = min(v)  % minimum value and its index
mn =
    0.1897
i =
     2
```

For two-dimensional arrays `min` and `max` behave a little differently, for example,

```
>> A = rand(4,6)  % new data
A =
    0.1509    0.8537    0.8216    0.3420    0.7271    0.3704
    0.6979    0.5936    0.6449    0.2897    0.3093    0.7027
    0.3784    0.4966    0.8180    0.3412    0.8385    0.5466
    0.8600    0.8998    0.6602    0.5341    0.5681    0.4449
```

```
>> [mx,r] = max(A)
mx =
    0.8600    0.8998    0.8216    0.5341    0.8385    0.7027
r =
     4     4     1     4     3     2
>> [mn,r] = min(A)
mn =
    0.1509    0.4966    0.6449    0.2897    0.3093    0.3704
r =
     1     3     2     2     2     1
```

In the above mx is a vector containing the maximum of each column of A, and r is the row index where the maximum appears. The same principle applies to mn and r relative to the function min. To find the overall minimum or maximum of a 2-D array, one can take two approaches:

```
>> mmx = max(mx)  % apply max again to prior result
mmx =
    0.8998
>> [mmx,i] = max(A(:)) % reshape A as a column vector first
mmx =
    0.8998
i =
     8
```

The first of these is essentially max(max(A)), which requires two function calls. The second is preferred in many situations because it also returns the single index where the maximum occurs, that is, mmx = A(i). This latter approach also works for multidimensional arrays, which are discussed in the next chapter.

When an array has duplicate minima or maxima, the indices returned by min and max are the first ones encountered. To find all minima and maxima requires use of the find function, for example,

```
>> x = [1 4 6 3 2 1 6]
x =
     1     4     6     3     2     1     6
>> mx = max(x)
mx =
     6
>> i = find(x==mx) % indices of values equal to mx
i =
     3     7
```

The chapter on data analysis contains more information about the functions min and max.

5.11 ARRAY MANIPULATION FUNCTIONS

In addition to the arbitrary array addressing and manipulation capabilities described in the preceding sections, MATLAB provides several functions that implement common array manipulations. Many of these manipulations are easy to follow, such as the following.

```
>> A = [1 2 3;4 5 6;7 8 9]  % fresh data
A =
     1     2     3
     4     5     6
     7     8     9
>> flipud(A)  % flip array in up-down direction
ans =
     7     8     9
     4     5     6
     1     2     3
>> fliplr(A)  % flip array in the left-right direction
ans =
     3     2     1
     6     5     4
     9     8     7
>> rot90(A)  % rotate array 90 degrees counterclockwise
ans =
     3     6     9
     2     5     8
     1     4     7
>> rot90(A,2)  % rotate array 2*90 degrees counterclockwise
ans =
     9     8     7
     6     5     4
     3     2     1
>> B = 1:12  % more data
B =
     1     2     3     4     5     6     7     8     9    10    11    12
>> reshape(B,2,6)  % reshape to 2 rows, 6 columns, fill by columns
ans =
     1     3     5     7     9    11
     2     4     6     8    10    12

>> reshape(B,[2 6]) % equivalent to above
ans =
     1     3     5     7     9    11
     2     4     6     8    10    12
>> reshape(B,3,4)  % reshape to 3 rows, 4 columns, fill by columns
ans =
     1     4     7    10
     2     5     8    11
     3     6     9    12
```

```
>> reshape(A,3,2)  % A has more than 3*2 elements, OOPS!
??? To RESHAPE the number of elements must not change.
>> reshape(A,1,9)  % stretch A into a row vector
ans =
     1     4     7     2     5     8     3     6     9
```

The following functions extract parts of an array to create another array.

```
>> A  % remember what A is
A =
     1     2     3
     4     5     6
     7     8     9
>> diag(A)  % extract diagonal using diag
ans =
     1
     5
     9
>> diag(ans)  % remember this? same function, different action
ans =
     1     0     0
     0     5     0
     0     0     9
>> triu(A)  % extract upper triangular part
ans =
     1     2     3
     0     5     6
     0     0     9
>> tril(A)  % extract lower triangular part
ans =
     1     0     0
     4     5     0
     7     8     9
>> tril(A) - diag(diag(A)) % lower triangular part with no diagonal
ans =
     0     0     0
     4     0     0
     7     8     0
```

The following functions create arrays from other arrays.

```
>> a = [1 2;3 4]  % a smaller data array
a =
     1     2
     3     4
>> b = [0 1;-1 0]  % another smaller data array
b =
     0     1
    -1     0
```

```
>> kron(a,b)  % the Kronecker tensor product of a and b
ans =
     0     1     0     2
    -1     0    -2     0
     0     3     0     4
    -3     0    -4     0
```

The above `kron(a,b)` is equivalent to

```
>> [1*b 2*b
    3*b 4*b]
ans =
     0     1     0     2
    -1     0    -2     0
     0     3     0     4
    -3     0    -4     0
>> kron(b,a)  % the Kronecker tensor product of b and a
ans =
     0     0     1     2
     0     0     3     4
    -1    -2     0     0
    -3    -4     0     0
```

The above `kron(b,a)` is equivalent to

```
>> [0*a 1*a
   -1*a 0*a]
ans =
     0     0     1     2
     0     0     3     4
    -1    -2     0     0
    -3    -4     0     0
```

So `kron(a,b)` takes each element of its first argument and multiplies it by the second argument and creates a block array.

One of the most useful array manipulation functions is `repmat`, which was introduced earlier.

```
>> a  % recall data
a =
     1     2
     3     4
>> repmat(a,1,3) % replicate a once down, 3 across
ans =
     1     2     1     2     1     2
     3     4     3     4     3     4
```

```
>> repmat(a,[1 3]) % equivalent to above
ans =
     1     2     1     2     1     2
     3     4     3     4     3     4

>> [a a a] % equivalent to above
ans =
     1     2     1     2     1     2
     3     4     3     4     3     4

>> repmat(a,2,2) % replicate a twice down, twice across
ans =
     1     2     1     2
     3     4     3     4
     1     2     1     2
     3     4     3     4
>> repmat(a,2) % same as repmat(a,2,2) and repmat(a,[2 2])
ans =
     1     2     1     2
     3     4     3     4
     1     2     1     2
     3     4     3     4
>> [a a; a a] % equivalent to above
ans =
     1     2     1     2
     3     4     3     4
     1     2     1     2
     3     4     3     4
```

As illustrated above and earlier, the functions `repmat` and `reshape` accept indexing arguments in two ways. The indexing arguments can be passed as separate input arguments or they can be passed as individual elements in a single-vector argument. In addition, for `repmat` a single second-input argument `repmat(A,n)` is interpreted as `repmat(A,[n n])`.

Finally, to replicate a scalar to create an array the same size as another array, one can simply use `repmat(d,size(A))`, where the function `size` is discussed in the next section. For example,

```
>> A=reshape(1:12,[3 4]) % new data
A =
     1     4     7    10
     2     5     8    11
     3     6     9    12
>> repmat(pi,size(A)) % pi replicated to be the size of A
ans =
        3.1416        3.1416        3.1416        3.1416
        3.1416        3.1416        3.1416        3.1416
        3.1416        3.1416        3.1416        3.1416
```

5.12 ARRAY SIZE

In cases where the size of an array or vector is unknown and is needed for some mathematical manipulation, MATLAB provides the utility functions `size`, `length`, and `numel`, for example,

```
>> A = [1 2 3 4;5 6 7 8]
A =
     1     2     3     4
     5     6     7     8
>> s = size(A)
s =
     2     4
```

With one output argument, the `size` function returns a row vector whose first element is the number of rows and whose second element is the number of columns.

```
>> [r,c] = size(A)
r =
     2
c =
     4
```

With two output arguments, `size` returns the number of rows in the first variable and the number of columns in the second variable.

```
>> r = size(A,1)   % number of rows
r =
     2
>> c = size(A,2)   % number of columns
c =
     4
```

Called with two arguments, `size` returns either the number or rows or columns. The correspondence between the second argument to `size` and the number returned follows the order in which array elements are indexed. `A(r,c)` has its row index `r` specified first, and so `size(A,1)` returns the number of rows. `A(r,c)` has its column index `c` specified second, and so `size(A,2)` returns the number of columns.

The function `numel` returns the total number of elements in an array. For example,

```
>> numel(A)
ans =
     8
```

and `length` returns the number of elements along the largest dimension. For example,

```
>> length(A)
ans =
     4
```

returns the number of rows or the number of columns, whichever is larger. For vectors `length` returns the vector length, for example,

```
>> B = -3:3
B =
    -3    -2    -1     0     1     2     3
>> length(B) % length of a row vector
ans =
     7
>> length(B') % length of a column vector
ans =
     7
```

The functions `size` and `length` also work for an array of zero dimension, for example,

```
>> c = [] % you can create an empty variable!
c =
     []
>> size(c)
ans =
     0     0
>> d = zeros(3,0) % an array with one dimension nonzero!
d =
   Empty matrix: 3-by-0
>> size(d)
ans =
     3     0
>> length(d)
ans =
     0
>> max(size(d)) % maximum of elements of size(d)
Warning: Use length(x) instead of max(size(x)) when x might be empty.
ans =
     3
```

As shown above, MATLAB allows arrays to have one zero and one nonzero dimension. For these arrays length and maximum dimension are not the same and causes MATLAB to issue a warning.

The above array size concepts are summarized in the table below.

Array Size	Description
`s=size(A)`	Returns a row vector `s` whose first element is the number of rows in `A` and whose second element is the number of columns in `A`.
`[r,c]=size(A)`	Returns two scalars, `r` and `c`, containing the number of rows and columns, respectively.
`r=size(A,1)`	Returns the number of rows in `A`.
`c=size(A,2)`	Returns the number of columns in `A`.
`n=length(A)`	Returns `max(size(A))` for nonempty `A`, `0` when `A` has either zero rows or zero columns, and the length of `A` if `A` is a vector.
`n=max(size(A))`	Returns `length(A)` for nonempty `A`, and for empty `A` returns the length of the largest nonzero dimension of `A`.
`n=numel(A)`	Returns the total number of elements in `A`.

5.13 ARRAYS AND MEMORY UTILIZATION

In most modern computers transferring data to and from memory is often more time-consuming than floating-point arithmetic, which has been fully integrated into most processors. Memory speed just hasn't kept pace with processor speed, forcing computer manufacturers to incorporate multiple levels of memory cache in an attempt to keep processors supplied with data. In addition, computer users work with increasingly larger data sets (variables), which can easily exceed cache capacity. Consequently, efficient memory utilization is critical to effective computing.

MATLAB itself does not perform any explicit memory management. Memory allocation and deallocation within MATLAB utilize calls to standard C functions (`malloc`, `calloc`, `free`). Therefore, MATLAB relies on the compiler's implementation of these library functions to take appropriate, efficient, system-specific steps for memory allocation and deallocation. Given that there is an inherent tradeoff between memory use and execution speed, MATLAB purposely chooses to use more memory if doing so increases execution speed. Since MATLAB uses memory to gain performance, it is beneficial to consider how memory is allocated in MATLAB and what can be done to minimize memory overuse and fragmentation.

When a variable is created with an assignment statement, such as,

```
>> P = zeros(100);
```

MATLAB requests a contiguous chunk of memory to store the variable, letting the compiler and the operating system determine where that chunk is allocated. If a variable is reassigned, such as,

```
>> P = rand(5,6);
```

the original memory is deallocated and a new allocation request is made for the new variable in its new size. Once again, it is up to the compiler and the operating system to figure out how to implement these tasks. Clearly, when the reassigned variable is larger than the original, a different chunk of contiguous memory is required to store the new data.

In a case where the variable reassignment just so happens to use exactly the same amount of memory, for example,

```
>> P = zeros(5,6); % same size as earlier
>> P = ones(6,5);  % same number of elements as earlier
```

MATLAB still goes through the memory allocation/deallocation process. As a result, reusing variable names does not eliminate memory allocation/deallocation overhead. However, it does clear the memory used by prior data that is no longer needed. The exception to this reallocation is with scalars. For example, `a = 1` followed by `a = 2` simply copies the new value into the old memory location.

On the other hand, if an assignment statement addresses indices that already exist in a variable, the associated memory locations are updated and no allocation/deallocation overhead is incurred. For example,

```
>> P(3,3) = 1;
```

does not force any memory allocation calls because `P(3,3)` already exists. The variable size remains the same, and so there's no need to find a different contiguous chunk of memory to store it. However, if an assignment statement increases the size of a variable, for example,

```
>> P(8,1) = 1;
>> size(P)
ans =
     8     5
```

which makes `P` grow from 6-by-5 or 30 elements to 8-by-5 or 40 elements, MATLAB requests memory for the revised variable, copies the old variable into the new memory, and then deallocates the old memory chunk, thereby incurring allocation/deallocation overhead.

When all the indices of a variable are addressed in an assignment statement, such as,

```
>> P(:) = ones(1,40);
```

the number of elements on the left- and right-hand sides must be equal. When this is true, MATLAB simply copies the data on the right-hand side into the memory that already exists on the left-hand side. No allocation/deallocation overhead is incurred. Furthermore, the dimensions of `P` remain unchanged:

```
>> size(P)
ans =
     8     5
```

In MATLAB, variables can be declared global in scope using the `global` command, which is discussed elsewhere in this text. From a memory management point of view, global variables do not behave any differently than ordinary variables. So there is neither benefit nor penalty for using them.

One interesting thing that MATLAB does to improve performance is a feature called ***delayed copy.*** Consider the following example.

```
>> A = zeros(10);
>> B = zeros(10);
>> C = B;
```

Here the variables `A` and `B` each have memory for 100 elements allocated to them. However, the variable `C` does not have any memory allocated to it. It shares the memory allocated to `B`. Copying of the data in `B` to a chunk of memory allocated to `C` does not take place until either `B` or `C` is modified. That is, a simple assignment such as the above does *not* immediately create a copy of the right-hand-side array in the left-hand-side variable. When an array is large, it is advantageous to delay the copy. That is, future references to `C` simply access the associated contents of `B`, and so to the user it appears that `C` is equal to `B`. Time is taken to copy the array `B` into the variable `C` only if the contents of `B` are about to change or if the contents of `C` are about to be assigned new values by some MATLAB statement. While the time saved by this *delayed copy* feature is insignificant for smaller arrays, it can lead to significant performance improvements for very large arrays.

This delayed copy scheme applies to functions as well. When a function is called, for example, `myfunc(a,b,c)`, the arrays `a`, `b`, and `c` are not copied into the workspace of the function unless the function modifies them in some way. By implementing a delayed copy, memory allocation overhead is avoided unless the function modifies the variable. As a result, there is no performance penalty for passing a large array to a function if that function only reads data from the array. This feature is covered in the chapter on M-file functions as well.

When one calls a function, it is not uncommon to pass the result of a computation or a function output as part of the function call itself, for example,

```
>> prod(size(A))
ans =
   100
```

Here the results from the function `size(A)` are passed directly to the function `prod` without explicitly storing the result in a named variable. The memory used to execute the above statement is identical to

```
>> tmp=size(A);
```

```
>> prod(tmp)
ans =
   100
```

In other words, even though the first statement did not explicitly create a variable to store the results from `size(A)`, MATLAB created an implicit variable and then passed it to the function `prod`. The only benefit gained by the first approach is that the implicit variable is automatically cleared after the function call.

In many applications it is convenient to increase the size of an array as part of a computational procedure. Usually this procedure is part of some looping structure, but for now let's consider a simpler example:

```
>> A=1:5
A =
     1     2     3     4     5
>> B=6:10;

>> A=[A;B]
A =
     1     2     3     4     5
     6     7     8     9    10
>> C=11:15;

>> A=[A;C]
A =
     1     2     3     4     5
     6     7     8     9    10
    11    12    13    14    15
```

Every time the variable `A` is reassigned above, new memory is allocated, old data is copied, and old memory is deallocated. If the arrays involved are large or the reassignment occurs numerous times, memory overhead can significantly reduce algorithm speed. To alleviate this problem, one should ***preallocate*** all the memory required and then fill it as required. Doing so for the above example gives

```
>> A=zeros(3,5)  % grab all required memory up front
A =
     0     0     0     0     0
     0     0     0     0     0
     0     0     0     0     0
>> A(1,:)=1:5;   % no memory allocation here

>> B=6:10;
>> A(2,:)=B;     % no memory allocation here
>> C=11:15;
```

```
>> A(3,:)=C        % no memory allocation here
A =
     1     2     3     4     5
     6     7     8     9    10
    11    12    13    14    15
```

While the above example is somewhat silly, it serves to illustrate that the memory allocation process for the variable A is performed only once, rather than once at every reassignment of A.

The table below summarizes the facts discussed in this section.

Syntax	Description
`P=zeros(100);` `P=rand(5,6);`	Reassignment of a variable incurs memory allocation/deallocation overhead.
`P(3,3)=1;`	If the indices on the left exist, no memory allocation/deallocation is performed.
`P(8,1)=1;`	If the indices on the left do not exist, memory allocation/deallocation occurs.
`P=zeros(5,6);` `P=ones(5,6);`	Reassignment of a variable incurs memory allocation/deallocation overhead even if the reassignment does not change the number of elements involved.
`P(:)=rand(1,30)`	If P exists, contents from the right-hand side are copied into the memory allocated on the left. No memory allocation/deallocation is performed.
`B=zeros(10);` `C=B;`	Delayed copy. C and B share the memory allocated to B until either B or C is modified.

`prod(size(A))`
`tmp=size(A);`
`prod(tmp)`
	Implicit and explicit variables require the same memory allocation. However, the implicit variable is automatically cleared.

`myfunc(a,b,c)`	Delayed copy. The variables a, b, and c are not copied into the function workspace unless the function modifies them. No memory allocation/deallocation overhead is incurred if the variables are not modified.

`A=zeros(3,5);`
`A(1,:)=1:5;`
`A(2,:)=6:10;`
`A(3,:)=11:15;`
	Preallocate all memory for a variable that grows as an algorithm progresses. Memory allocation/deallocation overhead is incurred only once, rather than once per iteration or reassignment.

6

Multidimensional Arrays

In the previous chapter, 1- and 2-D arrays and their manipulation were illustrated. Since MATLAB version 5 appeared several years ago, MATLAB has added support for arrays of arbitrary dimensions. For the most part, MATLAB supports multidimensional arrays (i.e., *n*-D arrays) using the same functions and addressing techniques that apply to 1- and 2-D arrays. In general, the third dimension is numbered by ***pages,*** while higher dimensions have no generic name. Thus, a 3-D array has rows, columns, and pages. Each page contains a 2-D array of rows and columns. In addition, just as all the columns of a 2-D array must have the same number of rows, and vice versa, all the pages of a 3-D array must have the same number of rows and columns. One way to visualize 3-D arrays is to think of the residential listings (white pages) in a phone book. Each page has the same number of columns and the same number of names (rows) in each column. The stack of all pages forms a 3-D array of names and phone numbers.

Even though there is no limit to the number of dimensions, 3-D arrays are used predominately in this chapter because they are more easily visualized and displayed.

6.1 ARRAY CONSTRUCTION

Multidimensional arrays can be created in several ways, for example,

```
>> A = zeros(4,3,2)
A(:,:,1) =
 0     0     0
 0     0     0
 0     0     0
 0     0     0
A(:,:,2) =
 0     0     0
 0     0     0
 0     0     0
 0     0     0
```

This is an array of zeros having four rows, three columns, and two pages. The first page is displayed first, followed by the second page. The other common array generation functions `ones`, `rand`, and `randn` work the same way by simply adding dimensions to the input arguments.

Direct indexing also works, for example,

```
>> A = zeros(2,3)  % start with a 2-D array
A =
     0     0     0
     0     0     0
>> A(:,:,2) = ones(2,3)  % add a second page to go 3-D!
A(:,:,1) =
     0     0     0
     0     0     0
A(:,:,2) =
     1     1     1
     1     1     1
>> A(:,:,3) = 4  % add a third page by scalar expansion
A(:,:,1) =
     0     0     0
     0     0     0
A(:,:,2) =
     1     1     1
     1     1     1
A(:,:,3) =
     4     4     4
     4     4     4
```

The above approach starts with a 2-D array which is the first page of a 3-D array. Then, additional pages are added by straightforward array addressing.

The functions `reshape` and `repmat` can also be used to create *n*-D arrays, for example,

```
>> B = reshape(A,2,9) % 2-D data, stack pages side-by-side
B =
     0     0     0     1     1     1     4     4     4
     0     0     0     1     1     1     4     4     4

>> B = [A(:,:,1) A(:,:,2) A(:,:,3)] % equivalent to above
B =
     0     0     0     1     1     1     4     4     4
     0     0     0     1     1     1     4     4     4

>> reshape(B,2,3,3) % recreate A!
ans(:,:,1) =
     0     0     0
     0     0     0
ans(:,:,2) =
     1     1     1
     1     1     1
ans(:,:,3) =
     4     4     4
     4     4     4

>> reshape(B,[2 3 3]) % alternative to reshape(B,2,3,3)
ans(:,:,1) =
     0     0     0
     0     0     0
ans(:,:,2) =
     1     1     1
     1     1     1
ans(:,:,3) =
     4     4     4
     4     4     4
```

Based on the above, `reshape` can change any dimensional array into any other dimensional array.

```
>> C = ones(2,3) % new data
C =
     1     1     1
     1     1     1

>> repmat(C,1,1,3) % this form not allowed above 2-D!
??? Error using ==> repmat
Too many input arguments.
```

```
>> repmat(C,[1 1 3])
ans(:,:,1) =
     1     1     1
     1     1     1
ans(:,:,2) =
     1     1     1
     1     1     1
ans(:,:,3) =
     1     1     1
     1     1     1
```

The above replicates C once in the *row* dimension, once in the *column* dimension, and three times in the *page* dimension.

The cat function creates *n*-D arrays from lower-dimensional arrays:

```
>> a = zeros(2); % new data
>> b = ones(2);
>> c = repmat(2,2,2);
>> D = cat(3,a,b,c)  % conCATenate a,b,c along the 3rd dimension
D(:,:,1) =
     0     0
     0     0
D(:,:,2) =
     1     1
     1     1
D(:,:,3) =
     2     2
     2     2
>> D = cat(4,a,b,c)  % try the 4th dimension!
D(:,:,1,1) =
     0     0
     0     0
D(:,:,1,2) =
     1     1
     1     1
D(:,:,1,3) =
     2     2
     2     2

>> D(:,1,:,:)  % look at elements in column 1
ans(:,:,1,1) =
     0
     0
ans(:,:,1,2) =
     1
     1
ans(:,:,1,3) =
     2
     2
```

```
>> size(D)
ans =
     2     2     1     3
```

D has 2 rows, 2 columns, 1 page, and 3 fourth-dimension parts.

6.2 ARRAY MATHEMATICS AND MANIPULATION

As additional dimensions are created, array mathematics and manipulation become more cumbersome. Scalar-array arithmetic remains straightforward, but array-array arithmetic requires that the two arrays have the same size in all dimensions. Since scalar-array and array-array arithmetic remains unchanged from the 2-D case presented in the last chapter, further illustrations are not presented here.

MATLAB provides several functions for the manipulation of *n*-D arrays. The function squeeze eliminates ***singleton dimensions;*** that is, it eliminates dimensions of size 1. For example,

```
>> E = squeeze(D)  % squeeze dimension 4 down to dimension 3
E(:,:,1) =
     0     0
     0     0
E(:,:,2) =
     1     1
     1     1
E(:,:,3) =
     2     2
     2     2
>> size(E)
ans =
     2     2     3
```

E contains the same data as D but has 2 rows, 2 columns, and 3 pages. How about a 3-D vector?

```
>> v(1,1,:) = 1:6  % a vector along the page dimension
v(:,:,1) =
     1
v(:,:,2) =
     2
v(:,:,3) =
     3
v(:,:,4) =
     4
v(:,:,5) =
     5
v(:,:,6) =
     6
```

```
>> squeeze(v) % squeeze it into a column vector
ans =
     1
     2
     3
     4
     5
     6

>> v(:) % this always creates a column vector
ans =
     1
     2
     3
     4
     5
     6
```

The function `reshape` allows you to change the row, column, page, and higher-order dimensions without changing the total number of elements, for example,

```
>> F = cat(3,2+zeros(2,4),ones(2,4),zeros(2,4)) % new 3-D array
F(:,:,1) =
     2     2     2     2
     2     2     2     2
F(:,:,2) =
     1     1     1     1
     1     1     1     1
F(:,:,3) =
     0     0     0     0
     0     0     0     0

>> G = reshape(F,[3 2 4]) % change it to 3 rows, 2 columns, 4 pages
G(:,:,1) =
     2     2
     2     2
     2     2
G(:,:,2) =
     2     1
     2     1
     1     1
G(:,:,3) =
     1     1
     1     0
     1     0
G(:,:,4) =
     0     0
     0     0
     0     0
```

```
>> H = reshape(F,[4 3 2]) % or 4 rows, 3 columns, 2 pages
H(:,:,1) =
     2     2     1
     2     2     1
     2     2     1
     2     2     1
H(:,:,2) =
     1     0     0
     1     0     0
     1     0     0
     1     0     0

>> K = reshape(F,2,12) % 2 rows, 12 columns, 1 page
K =
     2     2     2     2     1     1     1     1     0     0     0     0
     2     2     2     2     1     1     1     1     0     0     0     0
```

The above reshaping is confusing until you become comfortable visualizing arrays in *n*-D space. In addition, some reshaping requests make more practical sense than others. For example, `G` above has little practical value, whereas `K` is much more practical since it stacks the pages of `F` side by side as additional columns.

The reshaping process follows the same pattern as that for 2-D arrays. Data is gathered first by rows, then by columns, then by pages, and so on into higher dimensions. That is, all the rows in the first column are gathered, then all the rows in the second column, and so on. Then when the first page has been gathered, one moves on to the second page and starts over with all the rows in the first column.

The order in which array elements are gathered is the order in which the functions `sub2ind` and `ind2sub` consider single index addressing:

```
>> sub2ind(size(F),1,1,1) % 1st row, 1st column, 1st page is element 1
ans =
     1
>> sub2ind(size(F),1,2,1) % 1st row, 2nd column, 1st page is element 3
ans =
     3
>> sub2ind(size(F),1,2,3) % 1st element, 2nd column, 3rd page is element 19
ans =
    19

>> [r,c,p]=ind2sub(size(F),19) % inverse of above
r =
     1
c =
     2
p =
     3
```

The *n*-D equivalent to `flipud` and `fliplr` is `flipdim`, for example,

```
>> M = reshape(1:18,2,3,3) % new data
M(:,:,1) =
     1     3     5
     2     4     6
M(:,:,2) =
     7     9    11
     8    10    12
M(:,:,3) =
    13    15    17
    14    16    18
>> flipdim(M,1) % flip row order
ans(:,:,1)
     2     4     6
     1     3     5
ans(:,:,2) =
     8    10    12
     7     9    11
ans(:,:,3) =
    14    16    18
    13    15    17
>> flipdim(M,2) % flip column order
ans(:,:,1) =
     5     3     1
     6     4     2
ans(:,:,2) =
    11     9     7
    12    10     8
ans(:,:,3) =
    17    15    13
    18    16    14

>> flipdim(M,3) % flip page order
ans(:,:,1) =
    13    15    17
    14    16    18
ans(:,:,2) =
     7     9    11
     8    10    12
ans(:,:,3) =
     1     3     5
     2     4     6
```

The function `shiftdim` shifts the dimensions of an array. That is, if an array has `r` rows, `c` columns, and `p` pages, a shift by one dimension creates an array with `c` rows, `p` columns, and `r` pages, for example,

```
>> M  % recall data
M(:,:,1) =
     1     3     5
     2     4     6
M(:,:,2) =
     7     9    11
     8    10    12
M(:,:,3) =
    13    15    17
    14    16    18

>> shiftdim(M,1) % shift one dimension
ans(:,:,1) =
     1     7    13
     3     9    15
     5    11    17
ans(:,:,2) =
     2     8    14
     4    10    16
     6    12    18
```

Shifting dimensions by 1 causes the first row on page 1 to become the first column on page 1, the second row on page 1 to become the first column on page 2, and so on.

```
>> shiftdim(M,2) % shift two dimensions
ans(:,:,1) =
     1     2
     7     8
    13    14
ans(:,:,2) =
     3     4
     9    10
    15    16
ans(:,:,3) =
     5     6
    11    12
    17    18
```

Here the first column on page 1 of `M` becomes the first row on page 1, the first column on page 2 becomes the second row on page 1, and so on. If you are like the authors of this text, shifting dimensions is not immediately intuitive. For the 3-D case, it helps if you visualize `M` forming a rectangular box with page 1 on the front, followed by page 2 behind page 1, and then page 3 forming the back of the box. Then shifting dimensions is equivalent to rotating the box so that a different side faces you.

The function shiftdim also accepts negative shifts. In this case, the array is pushed into higher dimensions, leaving singleton dimensions behind, for example,

```
>> M % recall data
M(:,:,1) =
     1     3     5
     2     4     6
M(:,:,2) =
     7     9    11
     8    10    12
M(:,:,3) =
    13    15    17
    14    16    18

>> size(M) % M has 2 rows, 3 columns, and 3 pages
ans =
     2     3     3

>> shiftdim(M,-1) % shift dimensions out by 1
ans(:,:,1,1) =
     1     2
ans(:,:,2,1) =
     3     4
ans(:,:,3,1) =
     5     6
ans(:,:,1,2) =
     7     8
ans(:,:,2,2) =
     9    10
ans(:,:,3,2) =
    11    12
ans(:,:,1,3) =
    13    14
ans(:,:,2,3) =
    15    16
ans(:,:,3,3) =
    17    18
>> size(ans)
ans =
     1     2     3     3
```

The result now has four dimensions. The reader is left to figure out the correspondence between the original data and the shifted result.

When dealing with 2-D arrays, the transpose operator swapped rows and columns, converting an r-by-c array into a c-by-r array. The functions permute and ipermute are the *n*-D equivalents of the transpose operator. By itself, permute is a generalization of the function shiftdim. Consider the following example.

```
>> M  % recall data
M(:,:,1) =
     1     3     5
     2     4     6
M(:,:,2) =
     7     9    11
     8    10    12
M(:,:,3) =
    13    15    17
    14    16    18

>> permute(M,[2 3 1]) % same as shiftdim(M,1)
ans(:,:,1) =
     1     7    13
     3     9    15
     5    11    17
ans(:,:,2) =
     2     8    14
     4    10    16
     6    12    18
>> shiftdim(M,1)
ans(:,:,1) =
     1     7    13
     3     9    15
     5    11    17
ans(:,:,2) =
     2     8    14
     4    10    16
     6    12    18
```

In the above, `[2 3 1]` instructs the function to make the second dimension the first, the third dimension the second, and the first dimension the third. Consider a simpler example:

```
>> permute(M,[2 1 3])
ans(:,:,1) =
     1     2
     3     4
     5     6
ans(:,:,2) =
     7     8
     9    10
    11    12
ans(:,:,3) =
    13    14
    15    16
    17    18
```

Here [2 1 3] instructs permute to transpose the rows and columns but leave the third dimension alone. As a result, each page in the result is a conventional transpose of the original data.

The second argument to permute, called ORDER, must be a permutation of the dimensions of the array passed as the first argument; otherwise the requested permutation doesn't make sense. Consider the example

```
>> permute(M,[2 1 1])
??? Error using ==> permute
ORDER cannot contain repeated permutation indices.

>> permute(M,[2 1 4])
??? Error using ==> permute
ORDER contains an invalid permutation index.
```

The function permute can also be used to push an array into higher dimensions. For example, shiftdim(M,-1) shown earlier is equivalent to

```
>> permute(M,[4 1 2 3])
ans(:,:,1,1) =
     1     2
ans(:,:,2,1) =
     3     4
ans(:,:,3,1) =
     5     6
ans(:,:,1,2) =
     7     8
ans(:,:,2,2) =
     9    10
ans(:,:,3,2) =
    11    12
ans(:,:,1,3) =
    13    14
ans(:,:,2,3) =
    15    16
ans(:,:,3,3) =
    17    18
```

An array always has a unit dimension past its size; for example, a 2-D array has one page. That is, all dimensions past the nonunity size of an array are singletons. As a result, the singleton fourth dimension in M above is made the first dimension of the result shown.

For 2-D arrays, issuing the transpose operator a second time returns the array to its original form. Because of the added generality of n-D arrays, the function ipermute is used to undo the actions performed by permute. For example,

```
>> M  % recall data
M(:,:,1) =
     1     3     5
     2     4     6
M(:,:,2) =
     7     9    11
     8    10    12
M(:,:,3) =
    13    15    17
    14    16    18
>> permute(M,[3 2 1]) % sample permutation
ans(:,:,1) =
     1     3     5
     7     9    11
    13    15    17
ans(:,:,2) =
     2     4     6
     8    10    12
    14    16    18
>> ipermute(M,[3 2 1]) % back to original data
ans(:,:,1) =
     1     3     5
     7     9    11
    13    15    17
ans(:,:,2) =
     2     4     6
     8    10    12
    14    16    18
```

6.3 ARRAY SIZE

As demonstrated in the prior chapter and earlier in this chapter, the function `size` returns the size of an array along each of its dimensions. The functionality of `size` is unchanged from the features demonstrated in the last chapter. In addition, the function `numel` remains unchanged as well. Consider the following example.

```
>> size(M)  % return array of dimensions
ans =
     2     3     3

>> numel(M) % number of elements
ans =
    18
```

```
>> [r,c,p] = size(M) % return individual variables
r =
     2
c =
     3
p =
     3
>> r = size(M,1) % return just rows
ans =
     2
>> c = size(M,2) % return just columns
c =
     3
>> p = size(M,3) % return just pages
p =
     3

>> v = size(M,4) % default for all higher dimensions
v =
     1
```

When the number of dimensions is unknown or variable, the function `ndims` is useful:

```
>> ndims(M)
ans =
     3
>> ndims(M(:,:,1)) % just the 2-D first page of M
ans =
     2
```

In this last example, `M(:,:,1)` is a 2-D array because it has only one page. That is, it has a singleton third dimension. The function `ndims` is equivalent to the following simple code fragment.

```
>>> length(size(M))
ans =
     3
```

The following table summarizes the functions illustrated in this chapter.

n-D Function	Description

`ones(r,c,...)`
`zeros(r,c,...)`
`rand(r,c,...)`
`randn(r,c,...)`
	Basic *n*-D array creation.

n-D Function	Description
`reshape(B,2,3,3)` `reshape(B,[2 3 3])`	Reshape array into arbitrary dimensions.
`repmat(C,[1 1 3])`	Replicate array into arbitrary dimensions.
`cat(3,a,b,c)`	Concatenate array along a specified dimension.
`squeeze(D)`	Eliminate dimensions of size equal to 1, i.e., singleton dimensions.
`sub2ind(size(F),1,1,1)` `[r,c,p]=ind2sub(size(F),19)`	Subscript to single index conversion and single index to subscript conversion.
`flipdim(M,1)`	Flip order along a given dimension. *n*-D equivalent to `flipud` and `fliplr`.
`shiftdim(M,2)`	Shift dimensions. Circular shift for positive second argument. Push out for negative second argument.
`permute(M,[2 1 3])` `ipermute(M,[2 1 3])`	Arbitrary permutation and inverse of dimensions. Generalization of transpose operator to *n*-D arrays.
`size(M)` `[r,c,p]=size(M)`	Size of *n*-D array along its dimensions.
`r=size(M,1)`	Number of rows in array.
`c=size(M,2)`	Number of columns in array.
`p=size(M,3)`	Number of pages in array.
`ndims(M)`	Number of dimensions in an array.
`numel(M)`	Number of elements in an array.

7

Cell Arrays and Structures

MATLAB 5 introduced two data types called ***cell arrays*** and ***structures.*** These data types allow one to group dissimilar but related arrays into a single variable. Data management then becomes easier since groups of related data can be organized and accessed through a cell array or structure. Since cell arrays and structures are *containers* for other data types, mathematical operations on them are not defined. One must address the *contents* of a cell or structure to perform mathematical operations.

One way to visualize cell arrays is to consider a collection of post office boxes covering a wall at the post office. The collection of boxes is the cell array, with each box being one cell in the cell array. The contents of each post office box are different, just as the contents of each cell in a cell array are different types or sizes of MATLAB data such as character strings or numerical arrays of varying dimensions. Just as each post office box is identified by a number, each cell in a cell array is indexed by a number. When you send mail to a post office box, you identify the box number you want it put in. When you put data in a particular cell, you identify the cell number you want it put in. The number is also used to identify which box or cell to take data out of.

Structures are almost identical to cell arrays except that the individual post office boxes or data storage locations are not identified by number. Instead they are identified by name. Based on the post office box analogy, the collection of post office boxes is the structure and each box is identified by its owner's name rather than by a number. To send mail to a post office box, you identify the name of the box you want it put in. To place data in a particular structure element, you identify the name (i.e., field) of the structure element to put the data in.

7.1 CELL ARRAY CREATION

Cell arrays are MATLAB arrays whose elements are cells. Each cell in a cell array can hold any MATLAB data type including numerical arrays, character strings, symbolic objects, other cell arrays, and structures. For example, one cell of a cell array might contain a numerical array, another an array of character strings, and another a vector of complex values. Cell arrays can be created with any number of dimensions, just as numerical arrays can. However, in most cases cell arrays are created as a simple vector of cells.

Cell arrays can be created using assignment statements or by preallocating the array using the `cell` function and then assigning data to the cells. If you have trouble with these examples, it is very likely that you have another variable in the workspace of the same name. If any of the following examples give unexpected results, clear the array from the workspace and try again.

> If you assign a cell to an existing variable that is not a cell, MATLAB will stop and report an error.

Like other kinds of arrays, cell arrays can be built by assigning data to individual cells, one at a time. There are two different ways to access cells. If you use standard array syntax to index the array, you must enclose the cell contents in curly braces, `{ }`. It is these curly braces that MATLAB uses to define cell arrays. For example,

```
>> clear A  % make sure A is not being used
>> A(1,1) = { [1 2 3; 4 5 6; 7 8 9] };
>> A(1,2) = { 2+3i }; % semicolons suppress display
>> A(2,1) = { 'A character string' };
>> A(2,2) = { 12:-2:0 } % no semicolon, so display requested
A =
              [3x3 double]    [2.0000+ 3.0000i]
      'A character string'          [1x7 double]
```

Note that MATLAB shows that `A` is a 2-by-2 cell array, but that it does not show the contents of all cells. Basically, MATLAB shows the cell contents if they do not take up much space and describes the cell contents if they do take up significant space. The curly braces on the right side of the equal sign indicate that the expression represents a cell rather than numerical values. This is called ***cell indexing.*** Alternatively, the following statements create the same cell array:

```
>> A{1,1} = [1 2 3; 4 5 6; 7 8 9];
>> A{1,2} = 2+3i;
>> A{2,1} = 'A character string';
>> A{2,2} = 12:-2:0;
A =
            [3x3 double]    [2.0000+ 3.0000i]
    'A character string'         [1x7 double]
```

Here, the curly braces appear on the left side of the equal sign. `A{1,1}` indicates that `A` is a cell array and that the contents of the first row and first column of the cell array are on the right-hand side of the equal sign. This is called ***content addressing.*** Both methods can be used interchangeably.

Based on the above example, curly braces `{ }` are used to access the contents of cells, whereas parentheses `( )` are used to identify cells, but not their contents. To use the post office box analogy, curly braces are used to look at the contents of post office boxes, whereas parentheses are used to identify post office boxes without looking inside at their contents.

> `A(i,j) = {x};` and `A{i,j} = x;` both tell MATLAB to store the content of variable `x` in the `(i,j)` element of the cell array `A`. `A(i,j)` is called **cell indexing.** `A{i,j}` is called **content addressing.** That is, curly braces `{ }` access the contents of cells, whereas parentheses `( )` identify cells without looking at their content.

The `celldisp` function forces MATLAB to display the contents of cells in the usual manner, for example,

```
>> celldisp(A)
A{1,1} =
     1     2     3
     4     5     6
     7     8     9
A{2,1} =
     A character string
A{1,2} =
     2.0000+  3.0000i
A{2,2} =
     12    10     8     6     4     2     0
```

If a cell array has many elements, `celldisp` can produce a lot of output to the *Command* window. As an alternative, the contents of a single cell are displayed by requesting the contents of the cell using content addressing. This is different from cell indexing, which identifies the cell but not its content, for example,

```
>> A{2,2} % content addressing
ans =
    12    10     8     6     4     2     0
>> A(2,2) % cell indexing
ans =
     [1x7 double]

>> A{1,:} % address contents of the first row
ans =
     1     2     3
     4     5     6
     7     8     9
ans =
   2.0000 + 3.0000i

>> A(1,:)
ans =
     [3x3 double]    [2.0000+ 3.0000i]
```

Note that the contents of all the cells above are generically named `ans` because the cells store data that does not have associated names.

Square brackets were used in previous chapters to create numerical arrays. Curly braces work the same way for cells. Commas separate columns. Semicolons separate rows. Consider the following example.

```
>> B = { [1 2], 'John Smith'; 2+3i, 5 }
B =
           [1x2 double]     'John Smith'
     [2.0000+ 3.0000i]     [           5]
```

When dealing with numerical arrays it is common to preallocate an array with zeros and then fill the array as needed. The same can be done with cell arrays. The `cell` function creates a cell array and fills it with empty numerical matrices, `[]`. For example,

```
>> C = cell(2,3)
C =
     []      []      []
     []      []      []
```

Once the cell array has been defined, both cell indexing and content addressing can be used to populate the cells, as in the following example.

```
>> C(1,1) = 'This doesn''t work'
??? Conversion to cell from char is not possible.
```

The left-hand side here uses cell indexing, and so the right-hand side must be a cell, which it is not because it lacks curly braces surrounding the contents. As a result, MATLAB reports an error.

```
>> C(1,1) = { 'This does work' }
C =
    'This does work'      []       []
                  []      []       []
>> C{2,3} = 'This works too'
C =
    'This does work'      []                    []
                  []      []      'This works too'
```

Because curly braces appear on the left-hand side of the last statement, MATLAB makes the character string the contents of the addressed cell. Once again this is content addressing, whereas the prior statement is an example of cell indexing.

7.2 CELL ARRAY MANIPULATION

The numerical array manipulation techniques presented in preceding chapters apply to cell arrays as well. In a sense, cell array manipulation is just a natural extension of these techniques to a different type of array. If you assign data to a cell outside the dimensions of the current cell array, MATLAB automatically expands the array and fills the intervening cells with the empty numerical array `[]`.

Square brackets are used to combine cell arrays into larger cell arrays, just as they are used to construct larger numerical arrays, for example,

```
>> A  % recall prior cell arrays
A =
              [3x3 double]    [2.0000+ 3.0000i]
    'A character string'           [1x7 double]
>> B
B =
          [1x2 double]    'John Smith'
    [2.0000+ 3.0000i]    [          5]
>> C = [A;B]
C =
              [3x3 double]    [2.0000+ 3.0000i]
    'A character string'           [1x7 double]
              [1x2 double]    'John Smith'
    [   2.0000+ 3.0000i]    [                5]
```

A subset of cells can be extracted to create a new cell array by conventional array addressing techniques, for example,

```
>> D = C([1 3],:) % first and third rows
D =
    [3x3 double]     [2.0000+ 3.0000i]
    [1x2 double]     'John Smith'
```

An entire row or column of a cell array can be deleted using the empty array:

```
>> C(3,:) = []
C =
              [3x3 double]     [2.0000+ 3.0000i]
    'A character string'            [1x7 double]
    [    2.0000+ 3.0000i]     [                5]
```

Note that curly braces do not appear in either of the above expressions because we are working with the cell array itself, not the contents of the cells. Once again, curly braces are used to address the contents of cells, whereas parentheses are used to identify the cells without regard for their content.

The `reshape` function can be used to change the configuration of a cell array but cannot be used to add or remove cells, for example,

```
>> X = cells(3,4);
>> size(X) % size of the cell array, not the contents
ans =
     3     4

>> Y = reshape(X,6,2);
>> size(Y)
ans =
     6     2
```

So the function `reshape` naturally reshapes any array without regard to its type. Similarly, the `size` function returns the size of any array type.

The function `repmat` also works even though its name implies that it replicates matrices. The function `repmat` was created when MATLAB's only data type was matrices. If it had been written after the introduction of cell arrays and other array types, perhaps it would have been called `reparray`. Consider the following `repmat` example.

```
>> Y  % recall data
Y =
      []     []
      []     []
      []     []
      []     []
      []     []
      []     []
```

```
>> Z = repmat(Y,1,3)
Z =
     []     []     []     []     []     []
     []     []     []     []     []     []
     []     []     []     []     []     []
     []     []     []     []     []     []
     []     []     []     []     []     []
     []     []     []     []     []     []
```

7.3 RETRIEVING CELL ARRAY CONTENTS

To retrieve the contents of a cell in a cell array one must use content addressing, which involves curly braces, for example,

```
>> B  % recall cell array
B =
          [1x2 double]     'John Smith'
    [2.0000+ 3.0000i]     [          5]
>> x = B{2,2} % content addressing uses { }
x =
     5
```

The variable x now contains the numerical value 5, making x a numerical array (a scalar in this case). The class function can be used to confirm that this is true, as in the following example,

```
>> class(x) % return argument's data type
ans =
        double
```

Numerical arrays are double precision, thus class returns a character string identifying x as being double. If cell indexing had been used mistakenly, the result would be different:

```
>> y = B(2,2)    % cell indexing uses ( )
y =
    [5]

>> y = B(4)      % same as above using single index
y =
    [5]

>> class(y)      % y is not a double, but a cell!
ans =
cell
>> class(y{1})  % but the contents of y is a double!
ans =
double
```

By now you are either bored with this distinction between cell indexing and content addressing, or your head is spinning from the confusion.

There are other functions for testing variable types as well. The following examples return logical results, where True = 1 and False = 0.

```
>> iscell(y)        % yes, y is a cell
ans =
     1
>> iscell(y{1})     % contents of y is NOT a cell
ans =
     0
>> isa(y,'cell')    % yes, y is a cell
ans =
     1
>> isdouble(y{1})  % this function doesn't exist (yet?)
??? Undefined function or variable 'isdouble'
>> isnumeric(y{1}) % contents of y is numerical
ans =
     1
>> isa(y{1},'double')  % contents of y is a double
ans =
     1
>> isa(y{1},'numeric') % contents of y is also numeric
ans =
     1
>> isa(y{1},'cell')    % contents of y is NOT a cell
ans =
     0
```

While you can display the contents of more than one cell array at a time, it is not possible to assign more than one at a time to a variable using a standard assignment statement. Consider the following example.

```
>> B{:,2}
ans =
John Smith
ans =
     5
>> d = B{:,2}
??? Illegal right-hand side in assignment. Too many elements.
```

If you think about it, the above error makes sense. How can one assign two pieces of data to a single variable? If the above method did work, would `d` be a 2-by-1 array with a character string in its first location and a scalar in its second? Extracting data from multiple cells at a time simply cannot be done so casually.

When one addresses the contents of a single cell, it is possible to further address a subset of the contents by simply appending the desired subscript range, for example,

```
>> A  % recall prior data
A =
              [3x3 double]     [2.0000+ 3.0000i]
    'A character string'           [1x7 double]
>> celldisp(A) % display contents
A{1,1} =
     1     2     3
     4     5     6
     7     8     9
A{2,1} =
A character string
A{1,2} =
   2.0000 + 3.0000i
A{2,2} =
    12    10     8     6     4     2     0
>> A{1,1}(3,:)  % third row of 3-by-3 array
ans =
     7     8     9
>> A{4}(2:5)    % second through fifth elements of A{2,2}
ans =
    10     8     6     4
>> A{1,2}(2)    % second element doesn't exist
??? Index exceeds matrix dimensions.
>> A{2,1}(3:11) % extract part of the character string
ans =
character
```

7.4 COMMA-SEPARATED LISTS

To extract the contents of more than one cell at a time, MATLAB provides comma-separated list syntax. This syntax applies in any place where variables appear in a list separated by commas. For example, it appears in array construction:

```
>> a = ones(2,3);
>> b = zeros(2,1);
>> c = (3:4)';
>> d = [a,b,c] % same as [a b c]
d =
  1     1     1     0     3
  1     1     1     0     4
```

It also appears in function input and output argument lists, for example,

```
>> d = cat(2,a,b,c)
d =
      1     1     1     0     3
      1     1     1     0     4
>> [m,n] = size(d)
m =
  2
n =
  5
```

Based on the above idea, comma-separated list syntax is implemented as follows. Placing a content-addressed cell array in locations where comma-separated lists appear causes MATLAB to extract the contents of the addressed cell arrays and place them sequentially separated by commas, as in the following example.

```
>> F = {a b c}  % create a cell array
F =
    [2x3 double]    [2x1 double]    [2x1 double]
>> d = cat(2,F{:}) % same as cat(2,a,b,c)
d =
      1     1     1     0     3
      1     1     1     0     4
>> d = cat(2,F(:)) % not content addressing
d =
    [2x3 double]
    [2x1 double]
    [2x1 double]
```

In the above example, `cat(2,F{:})` is interpreted by MATLAB as `cat(2,F{1},F{2},F{3})`, which is equal to `cat(2,a,b,c)`. That is, comma-separated list syntax dictates that `F{:}` is interpreted as a listing of all addressed parts of `F{:}` separated by commas. Note that content addressing must be used. Cell indexing as shown in the second case above acts on the cells, not on their contents. As a result, there is no comma-separated list in the second case, `cat(2,F(:))`. Consider another example:

```
>> d = [F{:}]
d =
      1     1     1     0     3
      1     1     1     0     4
>> d = [F{1},F{2},F{3}] % what is implied by the above
d =
      1     1     1     0     3
      1     1     1     0     4
```

```
>> e = [F{2:3}] % can also content address any subset
e =
        0     3
        0     4

>> e = [F{2},F{3}] % what is implied by the above
e =
        0     3
        0     4
```

At first comma-separated list syntax may seem strange. However, with familiarity one recognizes its power. For more information, see the on-line help for `lists` or search for the phrase `comma-separated list`.

Given comma-separated list syntax, the function `deal` provides a way to extract the contents of numerous cells into separate variables. If you have ever used playing cards, you know that to deal means to pass out the cards in some organized way. The function `deal` does just that; it passes out the cell array contents to individual variables. Consider the following example.

```
>> celldisp(F) % recall data
F{1} =
        1     1     1
        1     1     1
F{2} =
        0
        0
F{3} =
        3
        4
>> [r,s,t] = deal(F{:}) % deal out contents of F
r =
        1     1     1
        1     1     1
s =
        0
        0
t =
        3
        4
```

The variables `r`, `s`, and `t` are numerical variables, with `r = F{1}`, `s = F{2}`, `t = F{3}`. If you think about it, the above example is equal to

```
>> [r,s,t] = deal(F{1},F{2},F{3})
r =
        1     1     1
        1     1     1
```

```
s =
     0
     0
t =
     3
     4
```

So the function deal is in reality pretty simple. It just assigns the contents of the first input argument to the first output argument, the second to the second, and so on. Despite its simplicity, deal is a very powerful tool for extracting data from multiple cells with one statement.

Because the output of deal is also a comma-separated list, deal can be used to assign the contents of multiple cells in one statement, for example,

```
>> [G{:}] = deal(a,b,c)
??? Error using ==> deal
The number of outputs should match the number of inputs.

>> [G{1:3}] = deal(a,b,c)
G =
    [2x3 double]    [2x1 double]    [2x1 double]
>> F = {a b c}
F =
    [2x3 double]    [2x1 double]    [2x1 double]
>> isequal(F,G) % True since F = G
ans =
     1
```

The first statement produced an error since G{:} doesn't identify how many cell array elements to separate by commas, whereas the second statement identifies the three needed. Since the syntax {a b c} produces an identical cell array, using deal to populate multiple cells with one statement isn't necessary (and it's slower).

7.5 CELL FUNCTIONS

Besides the functions celldisp, cell, iscell, isa, and deal, there are several other functions that are useful when dealing with cell arrays. The function cellfun provides a way to apply certain functions to all cells in a cell array, thereby eliminating the need to apply them to each cell individually. Consider the following example.

```
>> A  % recall data
A =
               [3x3 double]    [2.0000+ 3.0000i]
    'A character string'            [1x7 double]
```

```
>> cellfun('isreal',A) % True=1 where not complex
ans =
     1     0
     1     1
>> cellfun('length',A) % length of contents
ans =
     3     1
    18     7
>> cellfun('prodofsize',A) % number of elements in each cell
ans =
     9     1
    18     7
>> cellfun('isclass',A,'char') % True for character strings
ans =
     0     0
     1     0
```

The function `cellfun` offers other functions as well. For further information, see on-line help.

Another function that is sometimes useful is `num2cell`. This function takes an array of any type (not just numbers as the function name suggests) and fills a cell array with its components, for example,

```
>> a = rand(3,6) % new numerical data
a =
    0.7266    0.2679    0.6833    0.6288    0.6072    0.5751
    0.4120    0.4399    0.2126    0.1338    0.6299    0.4514
    0.7446    0.9334    0.8392    0.2071    0.3705    0.0439
>> c = num2cell(a)   % c{i,j}=a(i,j)
c =
    [0.7266]    [0.2679]    [0.6833]    [0.6288]    [0.6072]    [0.5751]
    [0.4120]    [0.4399]    [0.2126]    [0.1338]    [0.6299]    [0.4514]
    [0.7446]    [0.9334]    [0.8392]    [0.2071]    [0.3705]    [0.0439]
>> d = num2cell(a,1) % d{i}=a(:,i)
d =
  Columns 1 through 4
    [3x1 double]    [3x1 double]    [3x1 double]    [3x1 double]
  Columns 5 through 6
    [3x1 double]    [3x1 double]
>> e = num2cell(a,2)  % e{i}=a(i,:)
e =
    [1x6 double]
    [1x6 double]
    [1x6 double]
```

With numerical data as input, `num2cell(a)` isn't useful in many applications, but packing larger pieces of an array into cells is often more useful as illustrated in the last two cases above.

7.6 CELL ARRAYS OF STRINGS

Although a rigorous discussion of character strings doesn't occur until the next chapter, the use of character strings and their storage in cell arrays are described here. If the concept of a character string is foreign to you, read the next chapter and then come back to this material.

In MATLAB character strings are formed by enclosing characters within quotes, for example,

```
>> s = 'Is that your final answer?'
s =
Is that your final answer?
```

The variable s contains a string of characters. In many applications, groups of character strings are associated with each other. When this occurs, it is convenient to group them into a cell array rather than store them in individual variables, for example,

```
>> cs = {'Regis, I''d like to use a lifeline.'
s
'Yes, that''s my final answer.'}
cs =
     'Regis, I'd like to use a lifeline.'
     'Is that your final answer?'
     'Yes, that's my final answer.'

>> size(cs)  % a column cell array
ans =
      3     1
>> iscell(cs) % yes, it is a cell array
ans =
      1
```

The cell array cs has three cells, each containing a character string. In MATLAB, this is simply called a ***cell array of strings.*** Because cell arrays are commonly used to store sets of character strings, MATLAB provides several functions to support them, as in the following example.

```
>> iscellstr(cs)
ans =
 1
```

The function iscellstr returns True = 1 if all the cells in its cell array argument contain character strings, otherwise it returns False = 0.

Before cell arrays were introduced in MATLAB, groups of character strings were stored in character string arrays, that is, 2-D arrays just like the numerical arrays discussed earlier, with each string occupying a separate row in the array. Each character in the ***string array*** occupies its own location and is indexed just like a numerical array.

MATLAB provides functions to convert a cell array of strings to a string array, and vice versa, as in the following example.

```
>> cs  % recall cell array of strings
cs =
    'Regis, I'd like to use a lifeline.'
    'Is that your final answer?'
    'Yes, that's my final answer.'
>> sa = char(cs) % convert to a string array
sa =
Regis, I'd like to use a lifeline.
Is that your final answer?
Yes, that's my final answer.
>> ischar(sa) % True for string array
ans =
     1
>> iscell(sa) % True for cell array
ans =
     0
>> size(sa)   % size of string array
ans =
     3    34
>> size(cs)   % size of cell array
ans =
     3     1
>> cst = cellstr(sa) % convert back to cell array
cst =
    'Regis, I'd like to use a lifeline.'
    'Is that your final answer?'
    'Yes, that's my final answer.'
>> iscell(cst)       % True for cell array
ans =
     1
>> isequal(cs,cst)   % True for equal variables
ans =
     1
>> isequal(cs,sa)    % cell array not equal to string array
ans =
     0
```

So the MATLAB functions `char` and `cellstr` are inverses of each other. In addition, since a string array must have the same number of columns in each row, blank spaces are added to rows as necessary to make the string array rectangular.

7.7 STRUCTURE CREATION

Structures are like cell arrays in that they allow one to group collections of dissimilar data into a single variable. However, instead of addressing elements by number, structure elements are addressed by names called ***fields.*** Like cell arrays, structures can have any number of dimensions, but a simple scalar or vector array is most common.

Whereas cell arrays used curly braces to access data, structures use dot notation to access data in fields. Creating a structure can be as simple as assigning data to individual fields, for example,

```
>> circle.radius = 2.5;       % semicolon, no display
>> circle.center = [0 1];
>> circle.linestyle = '--';
>> circle.color = 'red'       % no semicolon, so display
circle =
       radius: 2.5
       center: [0 1]
    linestyle: '--'
        color: 'red'
```

The above data is stored in a structure variable called `circle`. It has case-sensitive fields entitled `radius`, `center`, `linestyle`, and `color`. Structure field names have the same restrictions as variable names in that they can contain up to 31 characters and must begin with a letter.

```
>> size(circle)
ans =
     1     1
>> whos
  Name          Size            Bytes  Class

  ans           1x2                16  double array
  circle        1x1               530  struct array

Grand total is 14 elements using 546 bytes
```

`circle` is a scalar structure since `size` says that it is 1-by-1. The `whos` command also shows its size, says that it is a structure array, and says that it uses 530 bytes of memory. If one has more than one circle, it can be stored as a second element in the `circle` variable, for example,

```
>> circle(2).radius = 3.4;
>> circle(2).color = 'green';
>> circle(2).linestyle = ':';
>> circle(2).center = [2.3 -1.2]
circle =
1x2 struct array with fields:
    radius
    center
    linestyle
    color
```

Now `circle` is a structure array having two elements. The `(2)` appears immediately after the variable name because it is the variable that is having an element added to it. The `.fieldname` suffix identifies the field where data is to be placed. Note that the structure fields are filled in a different order this time and that the size of the data differs between the two elements. That is, the `color` fields are `'red'` and `'green'`. There are no restrictions on what can be placed in fields from one array element to the next, for example,

```
>> circle(2).radius = 'sqrt(2)'
circle =
1x2 struct array with fields:
    radius
    center
    linestyle
    color
>> circle.radius  % display radius contents
ans =
         2.5
ans =
sqrt(2)
```

Now `circle(1).radius` holds numerical data and `circle(2).radius` holds a character string.

If the value of structures is not apparent, consider how this data would be stored without structures, for example,

```
>> Cradius = [2.5 3.4]; % ignore sqrt(2) change above
>> Ccenter = [0 1 ; 2.3 -1.2];
>> Clinestyle = {'--' ':'};  % cell array of strings
>> Ccolor = {'red' 'green'};
```

Now, rather than having a single variable storing the information for two circles, there are four variables that must be indexed properly to extract data for each circle. Its easy to add another circle to the structure but more cumbersome to add them to the above variables. Consider the following example.

```
>> circle(3).radius = 25.4;
>> circle(3).center = [-1 0];
>> circle(3).linestyle = '-.';
>> circle(3).color = 'blue'    % third circle added
circle =
1x3 struct array with fields:
    radius
    center
    linestyle
    color
```

```
>> Cradius(3) = 25.4
Cradius =
         2.5          3.4          25.4
>> Ccenter(3,:) = [-1 0]
Ccenter =
           0            1
         2.3         -1.2
          -1            0
>> Cradius(3) = 25.4
Cradius =
         2.5          3.4          25.4

>> Clinestyle{3} = '-.'
Clinestyle =
    '--'    ':'    '-.'
>> Ccolor(3) = {'blue'}
Ccolor =
  'red'    'green'    'blue'
```

Based on the above, the clarity provided by structures should be readily apparent. In addition, consider passing the circle data to a function. For example, as a structure the data is passed simply as `myfunc(circle)`, whereas the other approach requires `myfunc(Cradius,Ccenter,Clinestyle,Ccolor)`.

Suppose that at some later date one wanted to add another field to `circle`, for example,

```
>> circle(1).filled = 'yes'
circle =
1x3 struct array with fields:
    radius
    center
    linestyle
    color
    filled
>> circle.filled  % display all .filled fields
ans =
yes
ans =
     []
ans =
     []
```

Now all the elements of `circle` have the field `filled`. Those not assigned by default contain the empty array `[]`. The other `filled` fields are easily assigned, for example,

```
>> circle(2).filled = 'no';
>> circle(3).filled = 'yes';
```

```
>> circle.filled
ans =
yes
ans =
no
ans =
yes
```

When structure creation by direct assignment isn't possible, MATLAB provides the function `struct`. For example, to recreate the above structure,

```
>> values1 = {2.5 'sqrt(2)' 25.4}; % cell arrays with field data
>> values2 = {[0 1] [2.3 -1.2] [-1 0]};
>> values3 = {'--' ':' '-.'};
>> values4 = {'red' 'green' 'blue'};
>> values5 = {'yes' 'no' 'yes'};

>> CIRCLE = struct('radius',values1,'center',values2,...
           'linestyle',values3,'color',values4,'filled',values5)
CIRCLE =
1x3 struct array with fields:
    radius
    center
    linestyle
    color
    filled
>> isequal(circle,CIRCLE) % True since structures are equal
ans =
     1
```

7.8 STRUCTURE MANIPULATION

Structures are arrays and therefore can be combined and indexed like numerical arrays and cell arrays. When combining structure arrays, the only restriction is that the arrays combined share the same fields, for example,

```
>> square.width = 5;  % a new structure
>> square.height = 14;
>> square.center = zeros(1,2);
>> square.rotation = pi/4
square =
       width: 5
      height: 14
      center: [0 0]
    rotation: 0.7854
```

```
>> A = [circle CIRCLE]
A =
1x6 struct array with fields:
    radius
    center
    linestyle
    color
    filled
>> B = [circle square]
??? Number of fields does not match in [] concatenation.
```

The structures `circle` and `CIRCLE` are both 1-by-3 and share the same fields, and so concatenating them produces a 1-by-6 structure array. However, the structure `square` does not have the same fields and therefore cannot be concatenated.

It is also possible to address a subarray of a structure, for example,

```
>> C = [circle(1:2) CIRCLE(3)]
C =
1x3 struct array with fields:
    radius
    center
    linestyle
    color
    filled
>> isequal(C,circle) % True since equal
ans =
     1
```

Here `C` and `circle` are equal because `CIRCLE(3) = circle(3)`. Once again, basic array addressing and concatenation apply to structure arrays as well. For concatenation, field names must match exactly.

Although they are not as useful in this case, structures can also be manipulated with the functions `reshape` and `repmat`, for example,

```
>> Aa = reshape(A,3,2)
Aa =
3x2 struct array with fields:
    radius
    center
    linestyle
    color
    filled
>> Aaa = reshape(A,1,2,3)
Aaa =
1x2x3 struct array with fields:
    radius
    center
```

```
    linestyle
    color
    filled
```

Since there is seldom a practical reason to have anything other than a structure array with vector orientation, `reshape` is seldom needed or used with structures. However, it is often convenient to create a structure array with default data in all the fields of all array elements. The function `repmat` performs this task with ease, for example,

```
>> S = repmat(square,3,1)
S =
3x1 struct array with fields:
    width
    height
    center
    rotation

>> S.width  % look at all width fields
ans =
     5
ans =
     5
ans =
     5
```

All three elements of the structure `S` contain the data originally assigned to the structure `square`. At this point the structure fields can be modified as needed to describe different squares.

7.9 RETRIEVING STRUCTURE CONTENT

When one knows the names of the fields associated with a structure array, retrieving the data in a particular structure element and field simply requires identifying it, for example,

```
>> rad2 = circle(2).radius
rad2 =
sqrt(2)
>> circle(1).radius
ans =
          2.5

>> area1 = pi*circle(1).radius^2
area1 =
       19.635
```

Here `circle(1).radius` identifies the value 2.5, which is used to compute the area of the first circle.

When the contents of a field are an array, it is also possible to retrieve a subset of that field by appending an array index to the structure request, for example,

```
>> circle(1).filled          % the entire field
ans =
yes
>> circle(1).filled(1)       % first element of field
ans =
y
>> circle(1).filled(2:end) % rest of field
ans =
es
```

As is true for cell arrays, retrieving the contents of more than one structure array element and field cannot be accomplished by direct addressing, for example,

```
>> col = circle.color
??? Illegal right hand side in assignment. Too many elements.
```

The above attempts to extract three pieces of data and store it in one variable. MATLAB solves this problem the same way it does for cell arrays.

7.10 COMMA-SEPARATED LISTS (AGAIN)

To extract the contents of more than one structure array element at a time, MATLAB provides comma-separated list syntax. This syntax applies in any place where variables appear in a list separated by commas. For example, it appears in array construction:

```
>> a = ones(2,3);
>> b = zeros(2,1);
>> c = (3:4)';
>> d = [a,b,c] % same as [a b c]
d =
  1     1     1     0     3
  1     1     1     0     4
```

It also appears in function input and output argument lists, for example,

```
>> d = cat(2,a,b,c)
d =
     1     1     1     0     3
     1     1     1     0     4
```

```
>> [m,n] = size(d)
m =
 2
n =
 5
```

Based on this idea, comma-separated list syntax is implemented as follows. Placing a structure array with appended field name in locations where comma-separated lists appear causes MATLAB to extract the contents of the addressed fields and place them sequentially separated by commas, for example,

```
>> cent = cat(1,circle.center) % comma separated list syntax
cent =
            0            1
          2.3         -1.2
           -1            0
>> cent =
cat(1,circle(1).center,circle(2).center,circle(3).center)
cent =
            0            1
          2.3         -1.2
           -1            0
>> some = cat(1,circle(2:end).center)
some =
          2.3         -1.2
           -1            0
```

Here the `cat` function concatenates the circle centers into rows of the numerical array `cent`. By comma-separated list syntax, the first two statements above are identical. The third statement shows that one can index and extract a subarray as well.

Since the `color` fields of the structure `circle` are character strings of different lengths, they cannot be extracted into a string array, but they can be extracted into a cell array. Consider the following example.

```
>> circle.color
ans =
red
ans =
green
ans =
blue

>> col = cat(1,circle.color) % elements have different lengths
??? Error using ==> cat
CAT arguments dimensions are not consistent.
>> col = [circle.color] % no error but not much use!
col =
redgreenblue
```

```
>> col = {circle.color} % cell array of strings
col =
    'red'    'green'    'blue'

>> col = char(col) % if needed, convert to string array
col =
red
green
blue
```

MATLAB does not provide tools for extracting all the fields of a single structure array element. For example, there is no way to retrieve the `radius`, `center`, `linestyle`, `color`, and `filled` fields of the first circle in one statement. In a sense, there is no need to have such a function since each of these can be directly addressed and used in computations, for example, `area1 = pi*circle(1).radius^2`.

Given comma-separated list syntax, the function `deal` provides a way to extract the contents of numerous structure elements into separate variables. If you have ever used playing cards, you know that to deal means to pass out the cards in some organized way. The function `deal` does just that; it passes out the structure array contents associated with a single field to individual variables, for example,

```
>> [c1,c2,c3] = deal(circle.color) % get all colors
c1 =
red
c2 =
green
c3 =
blue
>> [rad1,rad3]=deal(circle([1 3]).radius) % 1st and 3rd radius
rad1 =
         2.5
rad3 =
        25.4
```

Because the output of `deal` is also a comma-separated list, `deal` can be used to assign the contents of multiple structure array elements with a single field in one statement, for example,

```
>> [circle.radius] = deal(5,14,83)
circle =
1x3 struct array with fields:
    radius
    center
    linestyle
    color
    filled
```

```
>> circle.radius  % confirm assignments
ans =
     5
ans =
    14
ans =
    83
>> [triangle(:).type] = deal('right','isosceles','unknown')
??? Error using ==> deal
The number of outputs should match the number of inputs.
>> [triangle(1:3).type] = deal('right','isosceles','unknown')
triangle =
1x3 struct array with fields:
    type
>> triangle.type
ans =
right
ans =
isosceles
ans =
unknown
```

In the first statement above the structure `circle` already existed and has three elements. Therefore, the output argument was expanded into three elements. In the second statement containing `deal` the structure `triangle` didn't exist. An error was returned because it wasn't possible to determine how many elements to create in a comma-separated list. However, in the last statement containing `deal` the number of elements was given explicitly and the `type` field of the newly created structure `triangle` was populated with the given data.

7.11 STRUCTURE FUNCTIONS

In the *Command* window it is easy to identify the field names of a given structure by simply entering the structure name at the MATLAB prompt, for example,

```
>> circle
circle =
1x3 struct array with fields:
    radius
    center
    linestyle
    color
    filled
>> square
square =
       width: 5
      height: 14
      center: [0 0]
    rotation: 0.7854
```

When a structure is passed to a function, for example, `myfunc(circle)`, the function internally must have some way to obtain the field names or one cannot extract data from the structure. (Writing functions in MATLAB is covered in Chapter 11.) In MATLAB the function `fieldnames` provides this information, for example,

```
>> fieldnames(circle)
ans =
    'radius'
    'center'
    'linestyle'
    'color'
    'filled'
```

The output of `fieldnames` is a cell array of strings identifying the fields associated with the input structure.

It is also possible to guess the field names and ask if they exist using the logical function `isfield`, for example,

```
>> isfield(circle,'color') % True
ans =
     1
>> isfield(circle,'width') % False
ans =
     0
```

If one doesn't know whether a variable is a structure or not, the functions `class` and `isstruct` are helpful, for example,

```
>> class(square)    % ask for class of variable square
ans =
struct
>> isstruct(circle) % True for structures
ans =
     1
>> d = pi;
>> isstruct(d)      % False for doubles
ans =
     0
```

When the field names are known, the functions `rmfield`, `setfield`, and `getfield` allow one to remove fields, set field contents, and get field contents, respectively. Consider the following examples.

```
>> fnames = fieldnames(circle);
```

Store the field names in a cell array.

```
>> circle2 = rmfield(circle,fnames{5})
circle2 =
1x3 struct array with fields:
    radius
    center
    linestyle
    color
```

The above code removes the field `filled` from `circle` and assigns the result to a new structure `circle2`.

```
>> rad1 = getfield(circle,{1},fnames{1})
rad1 =
     5

>> rad3 = getfield(circle,{3},fnames{1})
rad3 =
    83
```

The first statement retrieves the field `radius` from the first element of `circle`. The second statement retrieves the field `radius` from the third element.

```
>> circle3 = setfield(circle,{3},fnames{1},rad3)
circle3 =
1x3 struct array with fields:
    radius
    center
    linestyle
    color
    filled
>> circle3(3).radius
ans =
    83
```

Finally, `setfield` is used to set the `radius` field of the third `circle` element to `rad3`. The features of these functions are more thoroughly covered in the on-line documentation.

Given the similarity between cell arrays and structures based on the post office box analogy, it's not hard to believe that MATLAB provides the functions `cell2struct` and `struct2cell` to convert cell arrays to structures and back. Documentation of these functions can be found in the on-line documentation.

MATLAB supports arrays with an unlimited number of dimensions. Cell arrays and structures can store any array type including cell arrays and structures. So it is possible to have a cell in a cell array contain a structure with a field that contains another structure that has a field containing a cell array of which one cell contains another cell array. Needless to say, there comes a point where the power of cell arrays and structures becomes indecipherable and not of much practical use. So to end this chapter, try to decipher the following legal MATLAB statements.

```
>> one(2).three(4).five = {circle}
one =
1x2 struct array with fields:
    three
>> test = {{{circle}}}
test =
    {1x1 cell}
```

How many structures are involved in the first statement? What is the total number of structure elements, including empty arrays, created by the statement? Can the structure `circle` be extracted from the second statement with a single MATLAB statement?

8

Character Strings

MATLAB's true power is in its ability to crunch numbers. However, there are times when it is desirable to manipulate text, such as when placing labels and titles on plots. In MATLAB, text is referred to as character strings, or simply strings. Character strings represent another variable ***class*** or data type in MATLAB.

8.1 STRING CONSTRUCTION

Character strings in MATLAB are special numerical arrays of ASCII values that are displayed as their character string representation, for example,

```
>> t = 'How about this character string?'
t =
How about this character string?
>> size(t)
ans =
     1    32
```

```
>> whos
  Name        Size            Bytes  Class

  ans         1x2                16  double array
  t           1x32               64  char array

Grand total is 34 elements using 80 bytes
```

A character string is simply text surrounded by single quotes. Each character in a string is one element in an array that requires 2 bytes per character for storage. This is different than the 8 bytes per element required for numerical or double arrays as shown above.

To see the underlying ASCII representation of a character string, one need only perform some arithmetic operation on the string or use the dedicated function `double`. Consider the following example.

```
>> u = double(t)
u =
  Columns 1 through 12
    72   111   119    32    97    98   111   117   116    32   116   104
  Columns 13 through 24
   105   115    32    99   104    97   114    97    99   116   101   114
  Columns 25 through 32
    32   115   116   114   105   110   103    63
>> abs(t)
ans =
  Columns 1 through 12
    72   111   119    32    97    98   111   117   116    32   116   104
  Columns 13 through 24
   105   115    32    99   104    97   114    97    99   116   101   114
  Columns 25 through 32
    32   115   116   114   105   110   103    63
```

The function `char` performs the inverse transformation:

```
>> char(u)
ans =
How about this character string?
```

Numerical values less than 0 produce a warning message when converted to character; values greater than 255 are converted after finding their remainder, that is, `rem(n,256)` is computed, for example,

```
>> a = double('a')
a =
    97
```

```
>> char(a)
ans =
a

>> char(a+256) % adding 256 does not change result
ans =
a

>> char(a-256) % negative value produces a blank character
Warning: Out-of-range or noninteger values truncated during
conversion from double to character.
ans =
```

Since strings are arrays, they can be manipulated with all the array manipulation tools available in MATLAB, for example,

```
>> u = t(16:24)
u =
character
```

Strings are addressed just like arrays. Here elements 16 through 24 contain the word `character`.

```
>> u = t(24:-1:16)
u =
retcarahc
```

This is the word `character` spelled backward.

```
>> u = t(16:24)'
u =
c
h
a
r
a
c
t
e
r
```

Using the transpose operator changes the word `character` to a column.

```
>> v = 'I can''t find the manual!'
v =
I can't find the manual!
```

Single quotes within a character string are symbolized by two consecutive quotes. String concatenation follows directly from array concatenation:

```
>> u = 'If a woodchuck could chuck wood,';
>> v = ' how much wood could a woodchuck chuck?';

>> w = [u v]
w =
If a woodchuck could chuck wood, how much wood could a woodchuck chuck?
```

The function disp allows you to display a string without printing its variable name, for example,

```
>> disp(u)
If a woodchuck could chuck wood,
```

Note that the u = statement is suppressed. This feature is useful for displaying help text within a script file.

Like other arrays, character strings can have multiple rows, but each row must have an equal number of columns. Therefore, blanks are explicitly required to make all rows the same length, for example,

```
>> v = ['Character strings having more than'
        'one row must have the same number '
        'of columns just like arrays!      ']
v =
Character strings having more than
one row must have the same number
of columns just like arrays!
```

The functions char and strvcat create multiple-row string arrays from individual strings of varying lengths, for example,

```
>> legends = char('Wilt','Russel','Kareem','Bird','Magic','Jordan')
legends =
Wilt
Russel
Kareem
Bird
Magic
Jordan
```

```
>> legends = strvcat('Wilt','Russel','Kareem','Bird','Magic','Jordan')
legends =
Wilt
Russel
Kareem
Bird
Magic
Jordan
>> size(legends)
ans =
     6     6
```

The only difference between char and strvcat is that strvcat ignores empty string inputs, whereas char inserts blank rows for empty strings, as in the following example.

```
>> char('one','','two','three')
ans =
one

two
three

>> strvcat('one','','two','three')
ans =
one
two
three
```

Horizontal concatenation of string arrays having the same number of rows is accomplished by the function strcat. Padded blanks are ignored. Consider the following example.

```
>> a = char('apples','bananas')
a =
apples
bananas
>> b = char('oranges','grapefruit')
b =
oranges
grapefruit
>> strcat(a,b)
ans =
applesoranges
bananasgrapefruit
```

Once a string array is created with padded blanks, the function deblank is useful for eliminating the extra blanks from individual rows extracted from the array, for example,

```
>> c = legends(4,:)
c =
Bird

>> size(c)
ans =
     1     6

>> c = deblank(legends(4,:))
c =
Bird

>> size(c)
ans =
     1     4
```

8.2 NUMBERS TO STRINGS TO NUMBERS

There are numerous contexts in which it is desirable to convert numerical results to character strings and to extract numerical data from character strings. MATLAB provides the functions `int2str`, `num2str`, `mat2str`, `sprintf`, and `fprintf` for converting numerical results to character strings. Examples of these functions include

```
>> int2str(eye(3)) % convert integer arrays
ans =
1  0  0
0  1  0
0  0  1

>> size(ans) % it's a character array, not a numerical matrix
ans =
     3     7

>> num2str(rand(2,4)) % convert noninteger arrays
ans =
0.95013     0.60684      0.8913     0.45647
0.23114     0.48598      0.7621     0.01850

>> size(ans) % again it is a character array
ans =
     2    40

>> mat2str(pi*eye(2)) % convert to MATLAB input syntax form!
ans =
[3.14159265358979 0; 0 3.14159265358979]
```

```
>> size(ans)
ans =
     1    40

>> fprintf('%.4g\n',sqrt(2)) % display in Command window
1.414

>> sprintf('%.4g',sqrt(2)) % create character string
ans =
1.414

>> size(ans)
ans =
     1     5
```

The last two functions above are general-purpose conversion functions that closely resemble their ANSI C language counterparts. As a result, they offer the most flexibility. Normally `fprintf` is used to convert numerical results to ASCII format and append it to a data file. However, if no file identifier is provided as the first argument to `fprintf` or if a file identifier of 1 is used, the resulting output is displayed in the *Command* window. `sprintf` is identical to `fprintf` except that it simply creates a character array that can be displayed, passed to a function, or modified like any other character array. Because `sprintf` and `fprintf` are nearly identical, consider the usage of `sprintf` in the following example.

```
>> radius = sqrt(2);
>> area = pi * radius ^ 2;

>> s=sprintf('A circle of radius %.5g has an area of %.5g.',radius,area)
s =
A circle of radius 1.4142 has an area of 6.2832.
```

Here `%.5g`, the format specification for the variable `radius` indicates that five significant digits in general conversion format are desired. The most common usage of `sprintf` is to create a character string for annotating a graph, for displaying numerical values in a graphical user interface, or for creating a sequence of data file names. A rudimentary example of this last usage is as follows.

```
>> i = 3;
>> fname = sprintf('mydata%.0f.dat',i)
fname =
mydata3.dat
```

In the past, the functions `int2str` and `num2str` were nothing more than a simple call to `sprintf` with `%.0f` and `%.4g` format specifiers, respectively. In MATLAB 5 `int2str` and `num2str` were enhanced to work with numerical arrays as illustrated above. As a result of their former simplicity, it was common in prior versions of MATLAB to create the above example as

```
s = ['A circle of radius ' num2str(radius) ' has an area of ' ...
num2str(area) '.']
s =
A circle of radius 1.4142 has an area of 6.2832.
```

While the result is the same as that shown above, this latter form requires more computational effort, is more prone to typographical errors such as missing spaces or single quotes, and requires more effort to read. As a result, it is suggested that usage of `int2str` and `num2str` be limited to the conversion of arrays as illustrated earlier in this section. In almost all other cases, it is more productive to use `sprintf` directly.

The help text for `sprintf` concisely describes its use:

```
>> help sprintf
 SPRINTF Write formatted data to string.
    [S,ERRMSG] = SPRINTF(FORMAT,A,...) formats the data in the real
    part of matrix A (and in any additional matrix arguments), under
    control of the specified FORMAT string, and returns it in the
    MATLAB string variable S. ERRMSG is an optional output argument
    that returns an error message string if an error occurred or an
    empty matrix if an error did not occur. SPRINTF is the same as
    FPRINTF except that it returns the data in a MATLAB string
    variable rather than writing it to a file.

    FORMAT is a string containing C language conversion specifications.
    Conversion specifications involve the character %, optional flags,
    optional width and precision fields, optional subtype specifier, and
    conversion characters d, i, o, u, x, X, f, e, E, g, G, c, and s.
    See the Language Reference Guide or a C manual for complete details.

    The special formats \n,\r,\t,\b,\f can be used to produce linefeed,
    carriage return, tab, backspace, and formfeed characters respectively.
    Use \\ to produce a backslash character and %% to produce the percent
    character.

    SPRINTF behaves like ANSI C with certain exceptions and extensions.
    These include:
    1. The following non-standard subtype specifiers are supported for
       conversion characters o, u, x, and X.
       t    - The underlying C datatype is a float rather than an
              unsigned integer.
       b    - The underlying C datatype is a double rather than an
              unsigned integer.
       For example, to print out in hex a double value use a format like
       '%bx'.
```

```
  2. SPRINTF is "vectorized" for the case when A is nonscalar. The
     format string is recycled through the elements of A (columnwise)
     until all the elements are used up. It is then recycled in a similar
     manner through any additional matrix arguments.

  Examples
     sprintf('%0.5g',(1+sqrt(5))/2)       1.618
     sprintf('%0.5g',1/eps)               4.5036e+15
     sprintf('%15.5f',1/eps)              4503599627370496.00000
     sprintf('%d',round(pi))              3
     sprintf('%s','hello')                hello
     sprintf('The array is %dx%d.',2,3)   The array is 2x3.
     sprintf('\n') is the line termination character on all platforms.

  See also FPRINTF, SSCANF, NUM2STR, INT2STR.
```

The table below shows how `pi` is displayed under a variety of conversion specifications.

Command	Result
`sprintf('%.0e',pi)`	`3e+000`
`sprintf('%.1e',pi)`	`3.1e+000`
`sprintf('%.3e',pi)`	`3.142e+000`
`sprintf('%.5e',pi)`	`3.14159e+000`
`sprintf('%.10e',pi)`	`3.1415926536e+000`
`sprintf('%.0f',pi)`	`3`
`sprintf('%.1f',pi)`	`3.1`
`sprintf('%.3f',pi)`	`3.142`
`sprintf('%.5f',pi)`	`3.14159`
`sprintf('%.10f',pi)`	`3.1415926536`
`sprintf('%.0g',pi)`	`3`
`sprintf('%.1g',pi)`	`3`
`sprintf('%.3g',pi)`	`3.14`
`sprintf('%.5g',pi)`	`3.1416`
`sprintf('%.10g',pi)`	`3.141592654`
`sprintf('%8.0g',pi)`	`       3`

Command	Result
`sprintf('%8.1g',pi)`	3
`sprintf('%8.3g',pi)`	3.14
`sprintf('%8.5g',pi)`	3.1416
`sprintf('%8.10g',pi)`	3.141592654

In the above table, the format specifier `e` signifies exponential notation, `f` signifies fixed-point notation, and `g` signifies the use of `e` or `f`, whichever is shorter. Note that for the `e` and `f` formats, the number to the right of the decimal point indicates how many digits to the right of the decimal point to be displayed. On the other hand, in the `g` format, the number to the right of the decimal specifies the total number of digits to be displayed. In addition, note that in the last five entries, a width of 8 characters is specified for the result and the result is right-justified. In the very last case, the 8 is ignored because more than 8 digits were specified.

Though it is not as common, sometimes it is necessary to convert or extract a numerical value from a character string. The MATLAB functions `str2num`, `sscanf`, and `str2double` provide this capability, for example,

```
>> s = num2str(pi*eye(2)) % create string data
s =
3.1416          0
     0     3.1416
>> ischar(s) % True for string
ans =
     1
>> m = str2num(s) % convert string to number
m =
        3.1416             0
             0        3.1416

>> isdouble(m)  % Oops, this function doesn't exist
??? Undefined function or variable 'isdouble'.

>> isnumeric(m) % True for numbers
ans =
     1

>> pi*eye(2) - m % accuracy is lost
ans =
 -7.3464e-006              0
             0 -7.3464e-006
```

The function str2num can contain expressions but not variables in the workspace, for example,

```
>> x = pi; % create a variable

>> ss = '[sqrt(2) j; exp(1) 2*pi-x]' % string with variable x
ss =
[sqrt(2) j; exp(1) 2*pi-x]
>> str2num(ss) % conversion fails because of x
ans =
     []

>> ss = '[sqrt(2) j; exp(1) 2*pi-6]' % replace x with 6
ss =
[sqrt(2) j; exp(1) 2*pi-6]
>> str2num(ss) % now it works
ans =
 1.4142                          0 +          1i
 2.7183                    0.28319

>> class(ans)  % yes, its a double
ans =
double
```

The function sscanf is the counterpart to sprintf. sscanf reads data from a string under format control, for example,

```
>> v = version     % get MATLAB version as a string
v =
6.0.0.51483 (R12)

>> sscanf(v,'%f')  % get floating-point numbers
ans =
           6
           0
     0.51483
>> sscanf(v,'%f',1) % get just one floating-point number
ans =
     6
>> sscanf(v,'%d')   % get an integer
ans =
     6
>> sscanf(v,'%s')   % get a string
ans =
6.0.0.51483(R12)
```

Because one can specify the format under which sscanf operates, it is very powerful and flexible. See its on-line help text for more thorough information about its capabilities.

When the conversion to a single double-precision value is required, the function `str2double` is useful. While the function `str2num` performs this task as well, `str2double` is generally quicker because of its more limited scope. Consider the example

```
>> str2double('Inf') % It does convert infinity
ans =
   Inf
>> class(ans)
ans =
double
>> str2double('34.6 - 23.2j') % complex numbers work
ans =
        34.6 -        23.2i
>> str2double('pi') % variables and expressions don't work
ans =
   NaN
```

8.3 STRING EVALUATION

There are many applications in which it is convenient to evaluate a character string as if it were a MATLAB expression. This is a generalization of what `str2num` and `str2double` do. They are limited to extracting numerical values from strings. The MATLAB function `eval` brings in the entire MATLAB interpreter to evaluate any string that conforms to MATLAB syntax. For example, in the last chapter we used the function `getfield` to retrieve the contents of a structure field whose field name was a string in the workspace. This action can be performed by `eval`, as in the following example.

```
>> % structure creation first
>> [triangle(1:3).type] = deal('right','isosceles','unknown');
>> [triangle.center] = deal(zeros(1,2),ones(1,2),rand(1,2))
triangle =
1x3 struct array with fields:
    type
    center

>> fnames = fieldnames(triangle) % get field names
fnames =
    'type'
    'center'

>> % create string to evaluate with sprintf
>> estr = sprintf('t=triangle(%d).%s',1,fnames(1))
??? Error using ==> sprintf
Function 'sprintf' not defined for variables of class 'cell'.
```

```
>> estr = sprintf('t=triangle(%d).%s',1,fnames{1})
estr =
t=triangle(1).type

>> eval(estr) % evaluate above string
t =
right

>> % put it all together without an intermediate variable
>> eval(sprintf('t=triangle(%d).%s',3,fnames{1}))
t =
unknown

>> t = eval(sprintf('triangle(%d).%s',3,fnames{1}))
t =
unknown
```

In the above example, `sprintf` is used to create the evaluation string because of its flexibility and readability. The first attempt to create the evaluation string failed because `sprintf` requires a string array `fnames{1}` as opposed to a cell `fnames(1)`. Once the string was created, using it as the argument to `eval` created the variable `t` in the workspace containing the desired field value. The last statement shows that `eval` provides the result of the evaluation as an output argument when it is not part of the evaluation string itself.

Just as in all work in MATLAB, errors are likely to appear from time to time, for example,

```
>> t = eval(sprintf('Triangle(%d).%s',3,fnames{1}))
??? Undefined variable 'Triangle'.
```

Here `triangle` became `Triangle`, which is a nonexistent variable, causing MATLAB to report an error and not assigning anything to the variable `t`. To give the user the ability to control what happens when the MATLAB interpreter finds an error, `eval` can be called as `eval(try,catch)`, where `try` is the string to be evaluated first. If an error in `try` is found, the string `catch` is evaluated and no error is reported unless one appears in `catch`. Consider the example

```
>> t=eval(sprintf('Triangle(%d).%s',3,fnames{1}),'NaN')
t =
   NaN
```

Here `t` is assigned the value of `NaN` because of the error in the `try` string. There is no limit to the number of statements that can be executed in `try` or `catch` strings, for example,

```
>> eval(sprintf('t=triangle(%d).%s',3,fnames{1})) % recall statement
t =
unknown
```

```
>> eval(sprintf('t=Triangle(%d).%s',3,fnames{1}),'t=NaN;Flag=1;')
>> lasterr
ans =
Undefined variable 'Triangle'.

>> t,Flag
t =
   NaN
Flag =
     1
```

In this example, the second statement contains a `catch` string having two statements both terminated by semicolons. As a result, when the `catch` string is evaluated, because of the error in the `try` string, `t` and `Flag` are created but not displayed until requested. In addition, the function `lasterr` contains the error string generated by the error encountered in the `try` string. This string is available for the `catch` string to parse, so that the `catch` string can take different actions depending on the error generated.

On some occasions the results of the `eval` function are displayed as text in a window other than the *Command* window, perhaps in a GUI. To support this capability, MATLAB provides the function `evalc`. This function acts just like `eval` except that it returns the character string representation of the results, not the results themselves:

```
>> evalc(sprintf('t=triangle(%d).%s',3,fnames{1}))
ans =
t =
unknown

>> class(ans) % the above is a string, not a number
ans =
char
>> evalc(sprintf('t=Triangle(%d).%s',3,fnames{1}),'t=NaN;Flag=1')
ans =
Flag =
     1

>> class(ans) % above is a string, not a number
ans =
char
```

Because `eval` and `evalc` bring in the entire MATLAB interpreter to evaluate a string expression, they incur significant overhead. As a result, they generally should not be used unless there is no other alternative. However, this is not to say that they shouldn't be used at all.

To minimize usage of `eval`, MATLAB provides the function `feval` for the common, specific case of evaluating functions defined by character strings. Because of its limited scope, `feval` does not bring in the entire MATLAB interpreter to evaluate a string. It automatically assumes the string is a valid function name. As a result, `feval` is significantly faster than `eval`. Consider the example

```
>> fname = 'cos' % choose a function
fname =
cos
>> x = linspace(0,pi,5) % data for function
x =
        0      0.7854      1.5708      2.3562      3.1416
>> y = feval(fname,x)
y =
        1     0.70711  6.1232e-017   -0.70711          -1
>> y = cos(x) % direct call
y =
        1     0.70711  6.1232e-017   -0.70711          -1
```

While the above example is purely academic, it illustrates the basic features of `feval`. The function `feval` is not limited to functions having a single input and output argument. Any number of input and output arguments can be handled. `[x,y,z,...]= feval('func',a,b,c,...)` is evaluated as `[x,y,z,...] = func(a,b,c,...)`. More information about `feval` can be found in Chapter 11.

8.4 STRING FUNCTIONS

MATLAB provides a variety of string-related functions, some of which have been discussed already. The table below briefly describes many of the string functions in MATLAB.

Function	Description
`char(S1,S2,...)`	Create character array from strings or cell arrays.
`double(S)`	Convert string to ASCII representation.
`cellstr(S)`	Create cell array of strings from character array.
`blanks(n)`	Create string of `n` blanks.
`deblank(S)`	Remove trailing blanks.
`eval(S), evalc(S)`	Evaluate string expression.
`ischar(S)`	True for string array.
`iscellstr(C)`	True for cell array of strings.
`isletter(S)`	True for letters of the alphabet.
`isspace(S)`	True for whitespace characters.
`strcat(S1,S2,...)`	Concatenate strings horizontally.
`strvcat(S1,S2,...)`	Concatenate strings vertically, ignoring blanks.

Function	Description
`strcmp(S1,S2)`	True if strings are equal.
`strncmp(S1,S2,n)`	True if `n` characters of strings are equal.
`strcmpi(S1,S2)`	True if strings are equal ignoring case.
`strncmpi(S1,S2,n)`	True if `n` characters of strings are equal ignoring case.
`findstr(S1,S2)`	Find one string within another.
`strjust(S1,type)`	Justify string array left, right, or center.
`strmatch(S1,S2)`	Find indices of matching strings.
`strrep(S1,S2,S3)`	Replace occurrences of `S2` in `S1` with `S3`.
`strtok(S1,D)`	Find tokens in string given delimiters.
`upper(S)`	Convert to uppercase.
`lower(S)`	Convert to lowercase.
`num2str(x)`	Convert number to string.
`int2str(k)`	Convert integer to string.
`mat2str(X)`	Convert matrix to string for `eval`.
`str2double(S)`	Convert string to double-precision value.
`str2num(S)`	Convert string array to numerical array.
`sprintf(S)`	Create string under format control.
`sscanf(S)`	Read string under format control.

Consider the following examples of the usage of the above functions. The function `findstr` returns the starting indices of one string within another.

```
>> b = 'Peter Piper picked a peck of pickled peppers';

>> findstr(b,' ')     % find indices of spaces
ans =
     6    12    19    21    26    29    37
>> findstr(b,'p')     % find the letter p
ans =
     9    13    22    30    38    40    41
```

```
>> find(b=='p')       % for single-character searches find works too
ans =
     9    13    22    30    38    40    41
>> findstr(b,'cow')  % cow does not exist
ans =
     []
>> findstr(b,'pick') % find the string pick
ans =
    13    30
```

Note that this function is case-sensitive and returns the empty matrix when no match is found. `findstr` does not work on string arrays with multiple rows.

Tests on character strings include

```
>> c = 'a2 : b_c'
c =
a2 : b_c
>> ischar(c)   % it is a character string
ans =
     1
>> isletter(c) % where are the letters?
ans =
     1     0     0     0     0     1     0     1
>> isspace(c)  % where are the spaces?
ans =
     0     0     1     0     1     0     0     0
```

To illustrate string comparison consider the situation where a user types a string (perhaps into an editable text *uicontrol*) that must match at least in part one of a list of strings. The function `strmatch` provides this capability:

```
>> S = char('apple','banana','peach','mango','pineapple')
S =
apple
banana
peach
mango
pineapple
>> strmatch('pe',S)   % pe is in 3rd row
ans =
     3
>> strmatch('p',S)      % p is in 3rd and 5th rows
ans =
     3
     5
>> strmatch('banana',S) % banana is in 2nd row
ans =
     2
```

```
>> strmatch('Banana',S) % but Banana is nowhere
ans =
     []
>> strmatch(lower('Banana'),S) % changing B to b finds banana
ans =
     2
```

8.5 CELL ARRAYS OF STRINGS

The fact that all rows in string arrays must have the same number of columns is sometimes cumbersome, especially when the nonblank portions vary significantly from row to row. This cumbersome issue is eliminated by using cell arrays. All data forms can be placed in cell arrays, but their most frequent use is with character strings. A cell array is a data type that simply allows one to name a group of data of various sizes and types, as in the following example.

```
>> C = {'How';'about';'this for a';'cell array of strings?'}
C =
    'How'
    'about'
    'this for a'
    'cell array of strings?'
>> size(C)
ans =
     4     1
```

Note that curly brackets {} are used to create cell arrays and that the quotes around each string are displayed. In this example, the cell array C has 4 rows and 1 column. However, each element of the cell array contains a character string of different length.

Cell arrays are addressed just like other arrays, for example,

```
>> C(2:3)
ans =
    'about'
    'this for a'
>> C([4 3 2 1])
ans =
    'cell array of strings?'
    'this for a'
    'about'
    'How'
>> C(1)
ans =
    'How'
```

Here the results are still cell arrays. That is, C(indices) addresses given cells but not the contents of these cells. To retrieve the contents of a particular cell use curly brackets, as in the example

```
>> s = C{4}
s =
cell array of strings?
>> size(s)
ans =
     1    22
```

To extract more than one cell the function `deal` is useful:

```
>> [a,b,c,d] = deal(C{:})
a =
How
b =
about
c =
this for a
d =
cell array of strings?
```

Here `C{:}` denotes all the cells as a list. That is, it's the same as

```
>> [a,b,c,d] = deal(C{1},C{2},C{3},C{4})
a =
How
b =
about
c =
this for a
d =
cell array of strings?
```

Partial cell array contents can also be dealt, for example,

```
>> [a,b] = deal(C{2:2:4}) % get 2nd and 4th cell contents
a =
about
b =
cell array of strings?
```

A subset of the contents of a particular cell array can also be addressed:

```
>> C{4}(1:10) % 4th cell, elements 1 through 10
ans =
cell array
```

The multipurpose function `char` converts the contents of a cell array to a conventional string array, as in the following example.

```
>> s = char(C)
s =
How
about
this for a
cell array of strings?
>> size(s)  % result is a standard string array with blanks
ans =
     4    22
>> ss = char(C(1:2))  % naturally you can convert subsets
ss =
How
about
>> size(ss)  % result is a standard string array with blanks
ans =
     2     5
```

The inverse conversion is performed by the function `cellstr`, which deblanks the strings as well, for example,

```
>> cellstr(s)
ans =
    'How'
    'about'
    'this for a'
    'cell array of strings?'
```

One can test if a particular variable is a cell array of strings by using the function `iscellstr`, for example,

```
>> iscellstr(C)    % True for cell arrays of strings
ans =
     1
>> ischar(C)       % True for string arrays
ans =
     0
>> ischar(C{3})    % Contents of 3rd cell is a string array
ans =
     1
>> iscellstr(C(3)) % but 3rd cell itself is a cell
ans =
     1
>> ischar(C(3))    % and not a string array
ans =
     0
```

```
>> class(C)         % get data type or class string
ans =
cell
>> class(s)         % get data type or class string
ans =
char
```

Most of the string functions in MATLAB work with either string arrays or cell arrays of strings. In particular, the functions `deblank`, `strcat`, `strcmp`, `strncmp`, `strcmpi`, `strncmpi`, `strmatch`, and `strrep` all work with either string arrays or cell arrays of strings. Further information regarding cell arrays in general can be found in Chapter 7.

9

Relational and Logical Operations

In addition to traditional mathematical operations, MATLAB supports relational and logical operations. You may be familiar with these if you've had some experience with other programming languages. The purpose of these operators and functions is to provide answers to True/False questions. One important use of this capability is to control the flow or order of execution of a series of MATLAB commands (usually in a M-file) based on the results of True/False questions.

> As inputs to all relational and logical expressions, MATLAB considers any nonzero number to be True and zero to be False. The output of all relational and logical expressions produces logical arrays with one for True and zero for False.

Logical arrays are a special type of numerical array that can be used for logical array addressing as shown in the chapter on arrays as well as in any numerical expression.

9.1 RELATIONAL OPERATORS

MATLAB relational operators include all common comparisons as shown in the table below.

Relational Operator	Description
<	Less than
<=	Less than or equal to
>	Greater than
>=	Greater than or equal to
==	Equal to (not to be confused with =)
~=	Not equal to

MATLAB relational operators can be used to compare two arrays of the same size or to compare an array to a scalar. In the latter case, scalar expansion is used to compare the scalar to each array element and the result has the same size as the array. For example,

```
>> A = 1:9, B = 9-A
A =
     1     2     3     4     5     6     7     8     9
B =
     8     7     6     5     4     3     2     1     0
>> tf = A>4
tf =
     0     0     0     0     1     1     1     1     1
```

finds elements of A that are greater than 4. Zeros appear in the result where A≤4, and ones appear where A>4.

```
>> tf = (A==B)
tf =
     0     0     0     0     0     0     0     0     0
```

finds elements of A that are equal to those in B.

> Note that = and == mean two different things: == compares two variables and returns ones where they are equal and zeros where they are not; =, on the other hand, is used to assign the output of an operation to a variable.

Also note that testing for equality sometimes produces confusing results for floating-point numbers, for example,

```
>> tf = (-0.08 + 0.5 -0.42)==(0.5 - 0.42 - 0.08) % equal ?
tf =
     0

>> tf = (-0.08 + 0.5 -0.42)~=(0.5 - 0.42 - 0.08) % not equal ?
tf =
     1
>> (-0.08 + 0.5 -0.42)-(0.5 - 0.42 - 0.08) % not exactly equal!
ans =
  -1.3878e-017
```

This is the example we used in Chapter 2 to illustrate that arithmetic is not *exactly* commutative using finite precision. Visually we would expect the result to be `True = 1`, but it is not because the two expressions differ by a number less than `eps`. This fundamental fact of finite precision arithmetic is posed as a ***bug*** in MATLAB on the MATLAB newsgroup on regular basis.

It is possible to combine relational expressions with mathematical expressions. For example,

```
>> tf = B - (A>2)
tf =
     8     7     5     4     3     2     1     0    -1
```

finds where `A>2` and subtracts the resulting vector from `B`.

```
>> B = B + (B==0)*eps
B =
  Columns 1 through 7
    8.0000    7.0000    6.0000    5.0000    4.0000    3.0000    2.0000
  Columns 8 through 9
    1.0000    0.0000
```

is a demonstration of how to replace zero elements in an array with the special MATLAB number eps, which is approximately 2.2e-16. This particular expression is sometimes useful to avoid dividing by zero, as in the example,

```
>> x = (-3:3)/3
x =
   -1.0000   -0.6667   -0.3333         0    0.3333    0.6667    1.0000
>> sin(x)./x
Warning: Divide by zero.
ans =
    0.8415    0.9276    0.9816       NaN    0.9816    0.9276    0.8415
```

Computing the function sin(x)/x gives a warning because the fifth data point is zero. Since sin(0)/0 is undefined, MATLAB returns NaN (meaning Not-a-Number) at that location in the result. This can be avoided by replacing the zero with eps, for example,

```
>> x = x + (x==0)*eps;
>> sin(x)./x
ans =
    0.8415    0.9276    0.9816    1.0000    0.9816    0.9276    0.8415
```

Now sin(x)/x for x=0 gives the correct limiting answer. Alternatively, one can avoid the computation at x=0, for example,

```
>> x = (-3:3)/3 % recreate x
x =
  Columns 1 through 6
           -1     -0.66667     -0.33333            0      0.33333      0.66667
  Column 7
            1
>> y = ones(size(x)) % create default output
y =
     1     1     1     1     1     1     1
>> tf = x~=0  % find nonzero locations
tf =
     1     1     1     0     1     1     1
>> y(tf) = sin(x(tf))./x(tf) % operate only on nonzeros
y =
  Columns 1 through 6
      0.84147      0.92755      0.98158            1      0.98158      0.92755
  Column 7
      0.84147
```

While the above may seem cumbersome compared to adding eps to x, the concept of avoiding computations with selected components of an array is used often in efficient MATLAB programming.

9.2 LOGICAL OPERATORS

Logical operators provide a way to combine or negate relational expressions. MATLAB logical operators include those shown in the table below.

Logical Operator	Description
&	AND
|	OR
~	NOT

Some examples of the use of logical operators are the following.

```
>> A = 1:9; B = 9-A; % recall data
>> tf = A>4
tf =
     0     0     0     0     1     1     1     1     1
```

finds where A is greater than 4.

```
>> tf = ~(A>4)
tf =
     1     1     1     1     0     0     0     0     0
```

negates the above result, that is, swaps the positions of the ones and zeros.

```
>> tf = (A>2) & (A<6)
tf =
     0     0     1     1     1     0     0     0     0
```

returns ones where A is greater than 2 AND less than 6.

Finally, the above capabilities make it easy to generate arrays representing signals with discontinuities or signals composed of segments of other signals. The basic idea is to multiply the values in an array that you wish to keep by ones, and multiply all other values by zeros. For example,

```
>> x = linspace(0,10,100);    % create data
>> y = sin(x);                % compute sine
>> z = (y>=0).*y;             % set negative values of sin(x) to zero
>> z = z + 0.5*(y<0);         % where sin(x) is negative add 1/2
>> z = (x<=8).*z;             % set values past x=8 to zero
>> plot(x,z)
>> xlabel('x'), ylabel('z=f(x)'),
>> title('Figure 9.1: A Discontinuous Signal')
```

Figure 9.1: A Discontinuous Signal

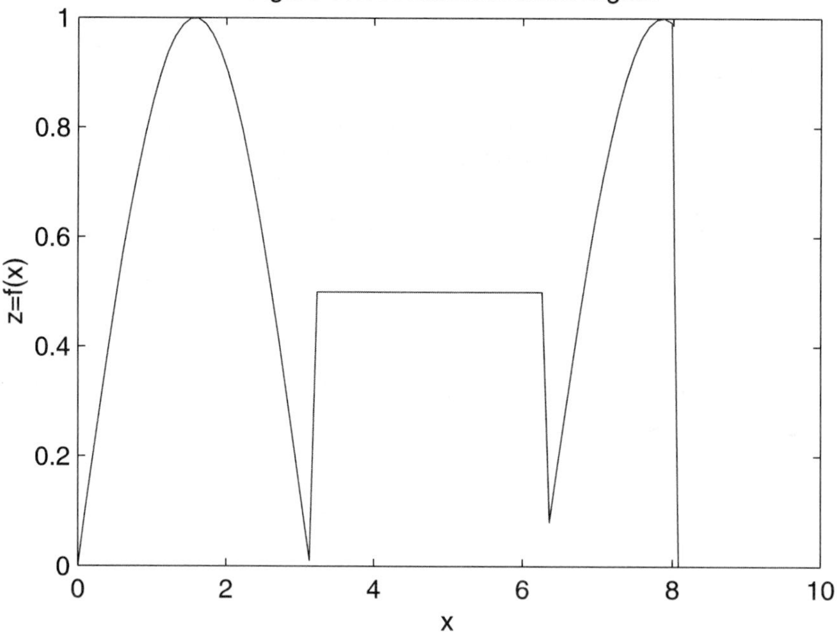

9.3 OPERATOR PRECEDENCE

When evaluating an expression, MATLAB follows a set of rules governing operator precedence. Operators having higher precedence are evaluated before operators of lower precedence. Operators of equal precedence are evaluated left to right. The table below illustrates the operator precedence rules used by MATLAB.

Operator	Precedence Level
Parentheses ( )	Highest
Transpose (.'), conjugate transpose ('), power (.^), matrix power (^)	
Unary plus (+), unary minus (-), negation (~)	
Multiplication (.*), matrix multiplication (*), right division (./), left division (.\), matrix right division (/), matrix left division (\)	
Addition (+), subtraction (-)	

Operator	Precedence Level
Colon operator (:)	
Less than (<), less than or equal to (<=), greater than (>), greater than or equal to (>=), equal to (==), not equal to (~=)	
Logical AND (&)	
Logical OR (|)	Lowest

The above order of precedence is similar or exactly equal to the order used by most computer programming languages. As a result, you are probably already comfortable writing expressions that conform to the above rules. As in other programming languages, parentheses can and should be used to control the order in which an expression is evaluated. Within each level of parentheses, the above rules hold, for example,

```
>> 3|2&0
Warning: The logical expression(s) involving OR and AND operators
may have returned a different result in previous versions of
MATLAB due to a change in logical operator precedence.
Use parentheses to make your code insensitive to this change.
Please type "help precedence" for more information.
ans =
     1

>> 3|(2&0)
ans =
     1

>> (3|2)&0
ans =
     0
```

The above discussion points out the fact that the preceding order of precedence table is different than it was in prior versions of MATLAB. Before MATLAB version 6, logical AND and logical OR shared the same order of precedence, whereas logical AND now has higher precedence than logical OR.

9.4 RELATIONAL AND LOGICAL FUNCTIONS

In addition to basic relational and logical operators, MATLAB provides a number of additional relational and logical functions including the following.

Function	Description
`xor(x,y)`	Exclusive OR operation. Return True for each element where either `x` or `y` is nonzero. Return False where both `x` and `y` are zero or both are nonzero.
`any(x)`	Return True if any element in a vector `x` is nonzero. Return True for each column in an array `x` that has any nonzero elements.
`all(x)`	Return True if all elements in a vector `x` are nonzero. Return True for each column in an array `x` that has all nonzero elements.

In addition to these functions MATLAB provides numerous functions that test for the existence of specific values or conditions and return logical results.

Function	Description
`ispc`	True for the PC (Windows) version of MATLAB.
`isstudent`	True for MATLAB Student Edition.
`isunix`	True for the UNIX version of MATLAB.
`ismember`	True for set member.
`isglobal`	True for global variables.
`mislocked`	True if M-file cannot be cleared.
`isempty`	True for empty matrix.
`isequal`	True if arrays of any data type are equal.
`isfinite`	True for finite elements.
`isinf`	True for infinite elements.
`islogical`	True for logical array.
`isnan`	True for Not-a-Number.
`isnumeric`	True for numeric arrays.
`isreal`	True for real array.
`isprime`	True for prime numbers.
`automesh`	True if the inputs should be automatically meshgridded.
`inpolygon`	True for points inside polygonal region.

Function	Description
`isvarname`	True for valid variable name.
`iskeyword`	True for keywords or reserved words.
`issparse`	True for sparse matrix.
`isappdata`	True if application-defined data exists.
`ishandle`	True for graphics handles.
`figflag`	True if figure is currently displayed on screen.
`iscellstr`	True for cell array of strings.
`ischar`	True for character string array.
`isletter`	True for letters of the alphabet.
`isspace`	True for white space characters.
`isa`	True if object is a given class.
`iscell`	True for cell array.
`isfield`	True if field is in structure array.
`isjava`	True for Java object arrays.
`isobject`	True for objects.
`isstruct`	True for structures.
`isvalid`	True for serial port objects that can be connected to hardware.

9.5 NaNS AND EMPTY ARRAYS

`NaN`s (Not-a-Numbers) and empty arrays (`[]`) require special treatment in MATLAB, especially when used in logical or relational expressions. According to IEEE mathematical standards, almost all operations on `NaN`s result in `NaN`s. Consider the example

```
>> a = [1 2 nan inf nan]  % Note: NaN and nan are equivalent
a =
     1     2   NaN    Inf    NaN

>> b = 2*a
b =
     2     4   NaN    Inf    NaN
```

```
>> c = sqrt(a)
c =
    1.0000    1.4142       NaN          Inf          NaN
>> d = (a==nan)
d =
     0     0     0     0     0
>> f = (a~=nan)
f =
     1     1     1     1     1
```

The first two computations above give NaN results for NaN inputs. However, the final two relational computations produce somewhat surprising results. (a==nan) produces all zeros or False results even when NaN is compared to NaN. At the same time (a~=nan) produces all ones or True results. Thus, individual NaNs are not equal to each other. As a result of this property of NaNs, MATLAB has a built-in logical function for finding NaNs, called isnan. For example,

```
>> g = isnan(a)
g =
     0     0     1     0     1
```

This function makes it possible to find the indices of NaNs using the find command, for example,

```
>> i = find(isnan(a))  % find indices of NaNs
i =
     3     5
>> a(i) = zeros(size(i))  % changes NaNs in a to zeros
a =
     1     2     0   Inf     0
```

Whereas NaNs are well-defined mathematically by IEEE standards, empty arrays are defined by the creators of MATLAB and have their own interesting properties. Empty arrays are simply that. They are MATLAB variables having zero length in one or more dimensions, for example,

```
>> size([])  % simplest empty array
ans =
     0     0
>> c = zeros(0,5)  % an empty array with multiple columns!
c =
   Empty matrix: 0-by-5

>> size(c)
ans =
     0     5
```

```
>> d = ones(4,0)  % an empty array with multiple rows!
d =
   Empty matrix: 4-by-0
>> size(d)
ans =
     4     0
>> length(d)  % it's length is zero even though it has 4 rows
ans =
     0
```

The above may seem strange, but allowing an empty array to have zero length in any dimension is sometimes useful. `[]` is just the simplest empty array.

In MATLAB, many functions return empty arrays when no other result is appropriate. Perhaps the most common example is the `find` function, for example,

```
>> x = -2:2  % new data
x =
    -2    -1     0     1     2
>> y = find(x>2)
y =
     []
```

In this example, `x` contains no values greater than 2, and so there are no indices to return. To test for empty results, MATLAB provides the logical function `isempty`:

```
>> isempty(y)
ans =
     1
```

When performing relational tests for the empty array, it is important to use `isempty` because of ambiguities, such as,

```
>> c==[] % compare 0-by-5 to 0-by-0 empty arrays
Warning: X == [] is technically incorrect. Use isempty(X) instead.
ans =
     0
>> a = [] % create an empty variable
a =
     []
>> a==[] % equal, but still not good
Warning: X == [] is technically incorrect. Use isempty(X) instead.
ans =
     1
```

In MATLAB, the empty array is not equal to any nonzero array or scalar. This fact leads to the following example,

```
>> y = []; % new data

>> a = (y==0)
Warning: Future versions will return [] for [] == scalar comparisons.
a =
     0
>> a = (y==1)
Warning: Future versions will return [] for [] == scalar comparisons.
a =
     0
>> b = (y~=0)
Warning: Future versions will return [] for [] ~= scalar comparisons.
b =
     1
```

which shows that an empty array is not equal to a scalar and that at some point a version of MATLAB will define `empty == scalar` as being empty. This warning existed in MATLAB version 5 as well, and so it may be a while before this change is implemented. Until then one must be careful in situations like the following.

```
>> find(y==0)
Warning: Future versions will return [] for [] == scalar comparisons.
ans =
     []
```

says there are no indices to return. Likewise,

```
>> b = (y~=0)
Warning: Future versions will return [] for [] ~= scalar comparisons.
b =
     1
```

says an empty matrix is not equal to a scalar yet again. But

```
>> j = find(y~=0)
Warning: Future versions will return [] for [] ~= scalar comparisons.
j =
     1
```

and now there is an index even though `y` has zero size! Therefore, until the promised changes in empty array treatment are made, one must check variables with `isempty` before conducting relational tests. The current interpretation usually leads to problems since `y(find(y~=0))` does not exist. But the new treatment leads to

```
>> find([])
ans =
     []
```

which is generally what is desired.

10

Control Flow

Computer programming languages and programmable calculators offer features that allow you to control the flow of command execution based on decision-making structures. If you have used these features before, this section will be very familiar to you. On the other hand, if control flow is new to you, this material may seem complicated the first time through.

Control flow is extremely powerful since it lets past computations influence future operations. MATLAB offers five decision-making or control flow structures. They are For Loops, While Loops, If-Else-End constructions, Switch-Case constructions, and Try-Catch blocks. Because these constructions often encompass numerous MATLAB commands, they often appear in M-files rather than being typed directly at the MATLAB prompt.

10.1 FOR LOOPS

For Loops allow a group of commands to be repeated a fixed, predetermined number of times. The general form of a For Loop is

```
for x = array
   (commands)
end
```

The *(commands)* between the for and end statements are executed once for every **column** in array. At each iteration, x is assigned to the next column of array; that is, during the nth time through the loop, x = array(:,n). For example,

```
>> for n = 1:10
      x(n) = sin(n*pi/10);
   end
>> x
x =
  Columns 1 through 7
    0.3090    0.5878    0.8090    0.9511    1.0000    0.9511    0.8090
  Columns 8 through 10
    0.5878    0.3090    0.0000
```

In words, the first statement says: for n equals 1 to 10 evaluate all statements until the next end statement. The first time through the For Loop, n=1, the second time, n=2, and so on through the n=10 case. After the n=10 case, the For Loop ends and any commands after the end statement are evaluated, which in this case is to display the computed elements of x.

Since the loop variable is assigned to successive columns of the array on the right-hand side of the equal sign, arbitrary indexing or inadvertent errors can occur. Consider the following example.

```
>> for n = 10:-1:1  % decrementing loop
      x(n) = sin(n*pi/10);
   end
>> x
x =
  Columns 1 through 7
    0.3090    0.5878    0.8090    0.9511    1.0000    0.9511    0.8090
  Columns 8 through 10
    0.5878    0.3090    0.0000
```

In this example, the loop variable n counts down from 10 to 1. The expression 10:-1:1 is a standard array creation statement that creates a row vector with multiple columns. Any numerical array can be used.

```
>> i = 0; % count loop iterations
>> for n = (1:10)' % right hand side is a column
      i = i+1;
      x(n) = sin(n*pi/10);
   end
```

```
>> i  % Only one time through the loop!
i =
     1
>> x
x =
  Columns 1 through 7
    0.3090    0.5878    0.8090    0.9511    1.0000    0.9511    0.8090
  Columns 8 through 10
    0.5878    0.3090    0.0000
```

In this example, the For Loop executes only one pass! The expression `(1:10)'` is a column vector, and so `n` is set equal to the entire array `(1:10)'` on its first pass. Since there are no additional columns in the right-hand side array, the loop terminates.

```
>> array = randperm(10)
array =
     8     2    10     7     4     3     6     9     5     1
>> for n = array
      x(n) = sin(n*pi/10);
   end
>> x
x =
  Columns 1 through 7
    0.3090    0.5878    0.8090    0.9511    1.0000    0.9511    0.8090
  Columns 8 through 10
    0.5878    0.3090    0.0000
```

In this example the loop variable `n` takes on the numbers 1 to 10 in the random order given by `array`.

A For Loop cannot be terminated by reassigning the loop variable `n` within the For Loop, for example,

```
>> for n = 1:10
      x(n) = sin(n*pi/10);
      n = 10;
  end
>> x
x =
  Columns 1 through 7
    0.3090    0.5878    0.8090    0.9511    1.0000    0.9511    0.8090
  Columns 8 through 10
    0.5878    0.3090    0.0000
```

To repeat, the right-hand-side array in the For Loop statement can be any valid array creation statement, for example,

```
>> i = 1;
>> for x = rand(4,5)
      y(i) = sum(x);
      i = i+1;
   end
>> y
y =
  1.7325      2.3954      1.6326      1.7201      2.0872
```

Here the loop variable x is assigned to the successive 4-by-1 columns of a random array. Since the For Loop has no natural loop index, i was added.

Naturally, For Loops can be nested as desired, for example,

```
>> for n = 1:5
      for m = 5:-1:1
          A(n,m) = n^2 + m^2;
      end
      disp(n)
   end
     1
     2
     3
     4
     5
>> A
A =
     2     5    10    17    26
     5     8    13    20    29
    10    13    18    25    34
    17    20    25    32    41
    26    29    34    41    50
```

Just because the above examples were used to illustrate For Loop usage doesn't mean that they are examples of efficient MATLAB programming. For Loops should be avoided whenever there is an equivalent array approach to solving a given problem. The equivalent array approach, called a ***vectorized*** solution, is often orders of magnitude faster. Consider the example

```
>> n = 1:10;
>> x = sin(n*pi/10)
x =
  Columns 1 through 7
    0.3090    0.5878    0.8090    0.9511    1.0000    0.9511    0.8090
  Columns 8 through 10
    0.5878    0.3090    0.0000
```

These two statements duplicate the repeated example of computing the sine function at 10 angles. In addition to being orders of magnitude faster, the above vectorized solution is more intuitive, is easier to read, and requires less typing.

The above nested For Loop is equivalent to the vectorized code below.

```
>> n = 1:5;
>> m = 1:5;
>> [nn,mm] = meshgrid(n,m);

>> A = nn.^2 + mm.^2
A =
     2     5    10    17    26
     5     8    13    20    29
    10    13    18    25    34
    17    20    25    32    41
    26    29    34    41    50
```

As discussed in Chapter 5, arrays should be preallocated before a For Loop (or While Loop) is executed. Doing so minimizes the amount of memory allocation required. For example, in the first case considered above, every time the commands within the For Loop are executed, the size of the variable `x` is increased by 1. This forces MATLAB to take the time to allocate more memory for `x` every time through the loop. To eliminate this step, the For Loop example should be rewritten as

```
>> x = zeros(1,10); % preallocated memory for x
>> for n = 1:10
      x(n) = sin(n*pi/10);
   end
```

Now, only the values of `x(n)` need to be changed each time through the loop.

10.2 WHILE LOOPS

As opposed to a For Loop that evaluates a group of commands a fixed number of times, a While Loop evaluates a group of statements an indefinite number of times.

The general form of a While Loop is

```
while expression
    (commands)
end
```

The *`(commands)`* between the `while` and `end` statements are executed as long as ***all*** elements in *`expression`* are True. Usually evaluation of *`expression`* gives a scalar result, but array results are also valid. In the array case, *all* elements of the resulting array must be True. Consider the following example.

```
>> num = 0; EPS = 1;
>> while (1+EPS)>1
      EPS = EPS/2;
      num = num+1;
   end
>> num
num =
    53

>> EPS=2*EPS
EPS =
   2.2204e-16
```

This example shows one way of computing the special MATLAB value `eps`, which is the smallest number that can be added to 1 such that the result is greater than 1 using finite precision. Here we used uppercase `EPS` so that the MATLAB value `eps` is not overwritten. In this example `EPS` starts at 1. As long as `(1+EPS)>1` is True (nonzero), the commands inside the While Loop are evaluated. Since `EPS` is continually divided in two, `EPS` eventually gets so small that adding `EPS` to 1 is no longer greater than 1. (Recall that this happens because a computer uses a fixed number of digits to represent numbers. Double precision specifies approximately 16 digits, and so one would expect `eps` to be near 10^{-16}.) At this point, `(1+EPS)>1` is False (zero) and the While Loop terminates. Finally, `EPS` is multiplied by 2 because the last division by 2 made it too small by a factor of 2.

For array expressions, the While Loop continues only when *all* elements in *`expression`* are True. If you want the While Loop to continue when *any* element is True, simply use the function `any`, for example, `while any(`*`expression`*`)`, which returns a scalar logical True whenever any of its contents are True.

10.3 IF-ELSE-END CONSTRUCTIONS

Many times, sequences of commands must be conditionally evaluated based on a relational test. In programming languages this logic is provided by some variation of an If-Else-End construction. The simplest If-Else-End construction is

```
if expression
    (commands)
end
```

The *`(commands)`* between the `if` and `end` statements are evaluated if ***all*** elements in *`expression`* are True (nonzero).

In cases where *expression* involves several logical subexpressions, only the minimum number required to determine the final logical state are evaluated. For example, if *expression* is *(expression1 | expression2)*, then *expression2* is evaluated only if *expression1* is False. Similarly, if *expression* is *(expression1 & expression2)*, then *expression2* is not evaluated if *expression1* is False.

Consider the following example.

```
>> apples = 10;            % number of apples
>> cost = apples*25        % cost of apples
cost =
   250

>> if apples>5             % give 20% discount for larger purchases
      cost = (1-20/100)*cost;
   end
>> cost
cost =
   200
```

In cases where there are two alternatives, the If-Else-End construction is

```
if expression
     (commands evaluated if True)
else
     (commands evaluated if False)
end
```

Here the first set of commands are evaluated if *expression* is True; the second set are evaluated if *expression* is False.

When there are three or more alternatives, the If-Else-End construction takes the form

```
if expression1
     (commands evaluated if expression1 is True)
elseif expression2
     (commands evaluated if expression2 is True)
elseif expression3
     (commands evaluated if expression3 is True)
elseif expression4
     (commands evaluated if expression4 is True)
```

```
elseif expression5
      .
      .
      .
else
   (commands evaluated if no other expression is True)
end
```

In this last form only the commands associated with the first True expression encountered are evaluated; ensuing relational expressions are not tested, and the rest of the If-Else-End construction is skipped. Furthermore, the final `else` command may or may not appear.

Now that we know how to make decisions with If-Else-End constructions, it is possible to show a legal way to break out of For Loops and While Loops:

```
>> EPS = 1;
>> for num = 1:1000
      EPS = EPS/2;
      if (1+EPS)<=1
         EPS = EPS*2
         break
      end
   end
EPS =
   2.2204e-16

>> num
num =
    53
```

This example demonstrates another way of estimating `eps`. In this case, the For Loop is instructed to run some sufficiently large number of times. The If-Else-End structure tests to see if `EPS` has gotten small enough. If it has, `EPS` is multiplied by 2 and the `break` command forces the For Loop to end prematurely, that is, at `num=53` in this case.

In this example, when the `break` statement is executed, MATLAB jumps to the next statement outside the loop in which it appears. In this case, it returns to the MATLAB prompt and displays `EPS`. If a `break` statement appears in a nested For Loop or While Loop structure, MATLAB only jumps out of the immediate loop in which it appears. It does not jump all the way out of the entire nested structure.

MATLAB version 6 introduces the command `continue` for use in For Loops and While Loops. When MATLAB encounters a `continue` statement inside a For Loop or While Loop, it immediately jumps to the `end` statement of the loop, bypassing all the commands between the `continue` command and the `end` statement. In doing so, the `continue` command moves immediately to the expression test for the next pass through the loop. Consider the example

```
>> EPS = 1;
>> for num = 1:1000
      EPS = EPS/2;
      if (1+EPS)>1
         continue
      end
      EPS = EPS*2
      break
   end
EPS =
   2.2204e-016
```

Here the prior example is rewritten to use the `continue` command. Note that the `continue` command has no affect on the If-End construction.

10.4 SWITCH-CASE CONSTRUCTIONS

When sequences of commands must be conditionally evaluated based on repeated use of an equality test with one common argument, a Switch-Case construction is often easier. Switch-Case constructions have the form

```
switch expression
   case test_expression1
      (commands1)
   case {test_expression2,test_expression3,test_expression4}
      (commands2)
   otherwise
      (commands3)
end
```

Here *expression* must be either a scalar or a character string. If *expression* is a scalar, *expression==test_expressionN* is tested by each `case` statement. If *expression* is a character string, `strcmp(`*expression,test_expression*`)` is tested. In the above example, *expression* is compared with *test_expression1* at the first `case` statement. If they are equal, *(commands1)* are evaluated and the rest of the statements before the `end` statement are skipped. If the first comparison is not true, the second is considered. In the above example, *expression* is compared with *test_expression2, test_expression3,* and *test_expression4,* which are contained in a cell array. If ***any*** of these are equal to *expression, (commands2)* are evaluated and the rest of the statements before `end` are skipped. If all `case` comparisons are false, *(commands3)* following the optional `otherwise` statement are executed.

Note that this implementation of the Switch-Case construction allows at most one of the command groups to be executed.

A simple example demonstrating the Switch-Case construction is

```
x = 2.7;
units = 'm';
switch units
   case {'inch','in'}
      y = x*2.54;
   case {'feet','ft'}
      y = x*2.54/12;
   case {'meter','m'}
      y = x/100;
   case {'millimeter','mm'}
     y = x*10;
   case {'centimeter','cm'}
      y = x;
   otherwise
      disp(['Unknown Units: ' units])
      y = nan;
end
```

Executing the above example gives a final value of `y=0.027`.

10.5 TRY-CATCH BLOCKS

A Try-Catch block provides user-controlled error-trapping capabilities. That is, with a Try-Catch block, errors found by MATLAB are captured, giving the user the ability to control how MATLAB responds to errors. Try-Catch blocks have the form

```
try
  (commands1)
catch
  (commands2)
end
```

Here all MATLAB expressions in *(commands1)* are executed. If no MATLAB errors are generated, control is passed to the `end` statement. However, if a MATLAB error appears while executing *(commands1)*, control is immediately passed to the `catch` statement and subsequent expressions *(commands2)*. Within the `catch` block the function `lasterr` contains the string generated by the error encountered in the `try` block. As a result, the `catch` block expressions *(commands2)* can retrieve the error string and act accordingly.

Consider the following example implemented in a script M-file for convenience.

```
x = ones(4,2);
y = 4*eye(2);
try
   z = x*y;
catch
   z = nan;
   disp('X and Y are not conformable.')
end
z
```

With the above data for x and y, this code segment produces the output

```
z =
      4     4
      4     4
      4     4
      4     4
```

In this case only the code in the `try` block executed. Changing the variable y creates an error,

```
x = ones(4,2);
y = 4*eye(3);   % now wrong size
try
   z = x*y;
catch
   z = nan;
   disp('X and Y are not conformable.')
end
z
```

Executing the code this time generates the following output in the *Command* window.

```
X and Y are not conformable.
z =
   NaN
```

In addition, the function `lasterr` describes the error found:

```
>> lasterr
ans =
Error using ==> *
Inner matrix dimensions must agree.
```

11

Function M-files

When you use MATLAB functions such as `inv`, `abs`, `angle`, and `sqrt`, MATLAB takes the variables you pass it, computes the required results using your input, and then passes these results back to you. The commands evaluated by the function, as well as any intermediate variables created by these commands, are hidden. All you see is what goes in and what comes out; that is, a function is a black box.

These properties make functions very powerful tools for evaluating commands that encapsulate useful mathematical functions or sequences of commands that appear often when solving some larger problem. Because of this power, MATLAB provides a structure for creating functions of your own in the form of text M-files. The function `mmempty` shown on the next page is a good example of an M-file function.

A function M-file is similar to a script M-file in that it is a text file having a `.m` extension. Like script M-files, function M-files are not entered in the *Command* window but rather are external text files created with a text editor, probably the Editor/Debugger that comes with MATLAB. A function M-file is different than a script file in that a function communicates with the MATLAB workspace only through the variables passed to it and through

```
function d=mmempty(a,b)
%MMEMPTY Substitute Value if Empty.
% MMEMPTY(A,B) returns A if A is not empty,
% otherwise B is returned.
%
% Example: The empty array problem in logical statements
% let a=[]; then use MMEMPTY to set default logical state
% (a==1) is false, but MMEMPTY(a,1)==1 is true
% (a==0) is false, but MMEMPTY(a,0)==0 is true
% Also:
% sum(a) is 0,  but sum(MMEMPTY(a,b))=sum(b)
% prod(a) is 1, but prod(MMEMPTY(a,b))=prod(b)
% find(a~=0) is 1, but find(MMEMPTY(a,0)~=0) is []
%
% See also ISEMPTY, SUM, PROD, FIND
if isempty(a)
    d=b;
else
    d=a;
end
```

the output variables it creates. Intermediate variables within the function do not appear in or interact with the MATLAB workspace. As can be seen in the above example, the first line of a function M-file defines the M-file as a function and specifies its name, which is the same as its filename without the `.m` extension. It also defines its input and output variables. The next continuous sequence of comment lines are the text displayed in response to the help command `help mmempty` or `helpwin mmempty`. The first help line, called the H1 line, is the line searched by the `lookfor` command. Finally, the remainder of the M-file contains MATLAB commands that create the output variables. Note that there is no `return` command in `mmempty`; the function simply terminates after it executes the last command.

11.1 M-FILE CONSTRUCTION RULES

Function M-files must satisfy a number of criteria. In addition, there are a number of desirable features they should have. These criteria and desirable features are itemized below.

1. The function M-file name and the function name, for example, `mmempty`, that appear in the first line of the file should be identical. In reality, MATLAB ignores the function name in the first line and executes functions based on the file name stored on disk.
2. Function M-file names can have up to 31 characters. This maximum may be limited by the operating system, in which case the lower limit applies. MATLAB ignores char-

acters beyond the 31st or the operating system limit, and so longer names can be used, provided the legal characters point to a unique file name.

3. Function M-file names are case-sensitive on UNIX platforms but are not case-sensitive on Windows platforms. To avoid platform dependencies, it has always been customary to use only lowercase letters in M-file names.
4. Function names must begin with a letter. Any combination of letters, numbers, and underscores can appear after the first character. This naming rule is identical to that for variables.
5. The first line of a function M-file is called the ***function-declaration line*** and must contain the word `function` followed by the calling syntax for the function in its most general form. The input and output variables identified in the first line are variables local to the function. The input variables contain data passed to the function, and the output variables contain data passed back from the function. It is not possible to pass data back through the input variables.
6. The first set of contiguous comment lines after the function-declaration line are the help text for the function. The first comment line is called the H1 line and is the line searched by the `lookfor` command. The H1 line typically contains the function name in uppercase characters and a concise description of the function's purpose. Comment lines after the first describe possible calling syntaxes, algorithms used, and simple examples if appropriate.
7. Function names appearing in the help text of a function are normally capitalized only to give them visual distinction. Functions are called using lowercase letters.
8. All statements after the first set of contiguous comment lines compose the body of the function. The body of a function contains MATLAB statements that operate on the input arguments and produce results in the output arguments.
9. A function M-file terminates after the last line in the file is executed or whenever a `return` statement is encountered.
10. A function can abort operation and return control to the *Command* window by calling the function `error`. This function is useful for flagging improper function usage as shown in the following file fragment.

```
if length(val) > 1
   error('VAL must be a scalar.')
end
```

When the function `error` is executed as shown above, the string `'VAL must be a scalar.'` is displayed in the *Command* window after a line identifying the file the error message originated from. Passing an empty string to `error`, for example, `error('')`, causes no action to be taken. After being issued, the error character string is passed to the function `lasterr` for later recall.

11. A function can report a warning and then continue operation by calling the function `warning`. This function is useful for reporting exceptions and other anomalous behavior. `warning('`*`some message`*`')` simply displays a character string in the *Command* window. The difference between the function `warning` and the function `disp` is that warning messages can be turned on or off globally by issuing the command

`warning on` or `warning off`, respectively. Passing an empty string to `warning`, for example, `warning('')`, causes no action to be taken.

12. Function M-files can contain calls to script files. When a script file is encountered, it is evaluated in the function's workspace, not in the MATLAB workspace.
13. Multiple functions can appear in a single function M-file. Additional functions, called subfunctions or local functions, are simply appended to the end of the primary function. Subfunctions begin with a standard function statement line and follow all function construction rules.
14. Subfunctions can be called by the primary function in the M-file as well as by other subfunctions in the same M-file. Like all functions, subfunctions have their own individual workspaces.
15. Subfunctions can appear in any order after the primary function in an M-file. Help text for subfunctions can be displayed by entering `>> helpwin` *`func/subfunc`*, where *`func`* is the main function name and *`subfunc`* is the subfunction name.
16. It is suggested that subfunction names begin with the word `local`, for example, `local_myfun`. This practice improves the readability of the primary function because calls to local functions are clearly identifiable. All local function names can have up to 31 characters.
17. In addition to subfunctions, M-files can call private M-files, which are standard function M-files that reside in a subdirectory of the calling function entitled `private`. Only functions in the immediate parent directory of private M-files have access to private M-files. Private subdirectories are meant to contain utility functions useful to several functions in the parent directory. Private function M-file names need not be unique because of their higher precedence and limited scope.
18. It is suggested that private M-file names begin with the word `private`, for example, `private_myfun`. This practice improves the readability of the primary function because calls to private functions are clearly identifiable. Like other function names, the names of all private M-files can have up to 31 characters.

11.2 INPUT AND OUTPUT ARGUMENTS

MATLAB functions can have any number of input and output arguments. The features of and criteria for these arguments are listed below.

1. Function M-files can have zero input and zero output arguments.
2. Functions can be called with fewer input and output arguments than the function-definition line in the M-file specifies. Functions cannot be called with more input or output arguments than the M-file specifies.
3. The number of input and output arguments used in a function call can be determined by calls to the functions `nargin` and `nargout`, respectively. Since `nargin` and `nargout` are functions, not variables, one cannot reassign them with statements such as `nargin = nargin - 1`. The function `mmdigit` illustrates the use of `nargin`:

```
function y=mmdigit(x,n,b,t)
%MMDIGIT Round Values to Given Significant Digits.
% MMDIGIT(X,N,B) rounds array X to N significant places in base B.
% If B is not given, B=10 is assumed.
% If X is complex the real and imaginary parts are rounded separately.
% MMDIGIT(X,N,B,'fix') uses FIX instead of ROUND.
% MMDIGIT(X,N,B,'ceil') uses CEIL instead of ROUND.
% MMDIGIT(X,N,B,'floor') uses FLOOR instead of ROUND.
if nargin<2
   error('Not enough input arguments.')
elseif nargin==2
   b=10;
   t='round';
elseif nargin==3
   t='round';
end
n=round(abs(n(1)));
if isempty(b), b=10;
else           b=round(abs(b(1)));
end
if isreal(x)
   y=abs(x)+(x==0);
   e=floor(log(y)./log(b)+1);
   p=repmat(b,size(x)).^(n-e);
   if strncmpi(t,'round',1)
      y=round(p.*x)./p;
   elseif strncmpi(t,'fix',2)
      y=fix(p.*x)./p;
   elseif strncmpi(t,'ceil',1)
      y=ceil(p.*x)./p;
   elseif strncmpi(t,'floor',2)
      y=floor(p.*x)./p;
   else
      error('Unknown rounding requested')
   end
else % complex input
   y=complex(mmdigit(real(x),n,b,t),mmdigit(imag(x),n,b,t));
end
```

In `mmdigit`, `nargin` is used to assign default values to input arguments not supplied by the user.

4. When a function is called, the input variables are not copied into the function's workspace, but their values are made ***readable*** within the function. However, if any

values in the input variables are changed, the array is then copied into the function's workspace. Thus, to conserve memory and increase speed, it is best to extract elements from large arrays and then modify them, rather than forcing the entire array to be copied into the function's workspace. Note that using the same variable name for both an input and an output argument causes an immediate copying of the contents of the variable into the function's workspace. For example, `function y=myfunction(x,y,z)` causes the variable `y` to be immediately copied into the workspace of `myfunction`.

5. If a function declares one or more output arguments but no output is desired, simply do not assign the output variable or variables any values. Or use the function `clear` to delete them before terminating the function.

6. Functions can accept a variable, unlimited number of input arguments by specifying `varargin` as the last input argument in the function-declaration line. `varargin` is a predefined cell array whose *i*th cell is the *i*th argument starting from where `varargin` appears. For example, consider a function having the function-declaration line

```
function a=myfunction(varargin)
```

If this function is called as `a=myfunction(x,y,z)`, then inside the function `varargin{1}` contains the array `x`, `varargin{2}` contains the array `y`, and `varargin{3}` contains the array `z`. Likewise, if the function is called as `a=myfunction(x)`, `varargin` has length 1 and `varargin{1}=x`. Every time `myfunction` is called, it can be called with a different number of arguments. In any case, the function `nargin` returns the actual number of input arguments used.

In cases where one or more input arguments are fixed, `varargin` must appear as the last argument, such as,

```
function a=myfunction(x,y,varargin)
```

If this function is called as `a=myfunction(x,y,z)`, then inside the function `x` and `y` are available and `varargin{1}` contains `z`. For further information on cell arrays, see Chapter 7.

7. Functions can accept a variable, unlimited number of output arguments by specifying `varargout` as the last output argument in the function-declaration line. `varargout` is a predefined cell array whose *i*th cell is the *i*th argument starting from where `varargout` appears. For example, consider a function having the function-declaration line

```
function varargout=myfunction(x)
```

If this function is called as `[a,b]=myfunction(x)`, then inside the function the contents of `varargout{1}` must be assigned to the data that becomes the variable `a`, and `varargout{2}` must be assigned to the data that becomes the variable `b`. As with `varargin`, discussed above, the length of `varargout` is equal to the number of output arguments used and `nargout` returns this length. In cases where one or more output arguments are fixed, `varargout` must appear as the last argument in the function-declaration line, for example, `function [a,b,varargout]=myfunction(x)`. For further information on cell arrays, see Chapter 7.

8. The functions `nargchk` and `nargoutchk` provide simple error checking for the number of valid input and output arguments, respectively. Since functions automatically return an error if called with more input or output arguments than appear in their function definitions, these functions have limited value but may be useful when a function definition declares an arbitrary number of input or output arguments.

11.3 FUNCTION WORKSPACES

As stated earlier, functions are black boxes. They accept inputs, act on these inputs, and create outputs. Any and all variables created within the function are hidden from the MATLAB or base workspace. Each function has its own temporary workspace that is created with each function call and deleted when the function completes execution. MATLAB functions can be called recursively, and each call has a separate workspace. In addition to input and output arguments, MATLAB provides several techniques for communicating among function workspaces and the MATLAB or base workspace. These techniques are itemized below.

1. Functions can share variables with other functions, the MATLAB workspace, and recursive calls to themselves if the variables are declared `global`. To gain access to a global variable within a function or the MATLAB workspace, the variable must be declared `global` within each desired workspace, for example, `global myvariable`. The MATLAB functions `tic` and `toc` illustrate the use of global variables:

```
function tic
%TIC Start a stopwatch timer.
%   The sequence of commands
%       TIC, operation, TOC
%   prints the number of seconds required for the operation.
%
%   See also TOC, CLOCK, ETIME, CPUTIME.

%   Copyright (c) 1984-1999 The MathWorks, Inc. All Rights Reserved.
%   $Revision: 5.7 $  $Date: 1999/01/12 16:43:03 $
% TIC simply stores CLOCK in a global variable.
global TICTOC
TICTOC = clock;
```

(Reprinted with permission of The MathWorks, Inc., Natick, MA.)

```
function t = toc
%TOC Read the stopwatch timer.
%   TOC prints the elapsed time (in seconds) since TIC was used.
%   t = TOC; saves the elapsed time in t, instead of printing it out.
%
%   See also TIC, ETIME, CLOCK, CPUTIME.

%   Copyright (c) 1984-1999 The MathWorks, Inc. All Rights Reserved.
%   $Revision: 5.8 $  $Date: 1999/01/12 16:43:03 $
% TOC uses ETIME and the value of CLOCK saved by TIC.
global TICTOC
if isempty(TICTOC)
  error('You must call TIC before calling TOC.');
end
if nargout < 1
   elapsed_time = etime(clock,TICTOC)
else
   t = etime(clock,TICTOC);
end
```

(Reprinted with permission of The MathWorks, Inc., Natick, MA.)

The functions `tic` and `toc` form a simple stopwatch for timing MATLAB operations. When `tic` is called, it declares the variable `TICTOC` global, assigns the current time to it, and then terminates. Later when `toc` is called, `TICTOC` is declared global in the `toc` workspace, thereby providing access to its contents and the elapsed time is computed. It is important to note that the variable `TICTOC` exists only in the workspaces of the functions `tic` and `toc`; it does not exist in the MATLAB workspace unless `global TICTOC` is issued there.

> As a matter of programming practice, the use of global variables is discouraged whenever possible. However, if they are used, it is suggested that global variable names be long, contain all capital letters, and optionally start with the name of the M-file where they appear, for example, `MYFUN_ALPHA`. If followed, these suggestions will minimize unintended conflicts among global variables.

2. In addition to sharing data through global variables, function M-files can have restricted access to variables for repeated or recursive calls to themselves by declaring a variable `persistent`, for example, `persistent myvariable`. Persistent variables act like global variables whose scope is limited to the function where they are declared. Persistent variables exist as long as an M-file remains in memory in MATLAB. The function `mmclass` illustrates the use of persistent variables:

```
function c=mmclass(arg)
%MMCLASS MATLAB Object Class Existence.
% MMCLASS returns a cell array of strings containing the
% names of MATLAB object classes available with this license.
%
% MMCLASS('ClassName') returns logical True (1) if the class
% having the name 'ClassName' exists with this license.
% Otherwise logical False (0) is returned.
%
% MMCLASS searches the MATLABPATH for class directories.
% Classes not on the MATLABPATH are ignored.
%
% See also CLASS, ISA, METHODS, ISOBJECT
persistent clist  % save data for future calls

if isempty(clist)
   clist=cell(0);
   cstar=[filesep '@*'];
   dlist=[pathsep matlabpath];
   sidx=findstr(pathsep,dlist)+1;      % path segment starting indices
   eidx=[sidx(2:end)-2 length(dlist)]; % path segment ending indices
   for i=1:length(sidx)-1     % look at each path segment
      cdir=dir([dlist(sidx(i):eidx(i)) cstar]); % dir @* on segment
      clist=[clist {cdir.name}];                % add results to list
   end
   clist=char(clist);         % convert to string array
   clist(:,1)=[];             % eliminate initial '@'
   clist=unique(clist,'rows');% alphabetize and make unique
   clist=cellstr(clist);      % back to a cell array
end
if nargin==0
   c=clist;
elseif ischar(arg)
   c=~isempty(strmatch(arg,clist));
else
   error('Character String Argument Expected.')
end
```

In `mmclass`, the variable `clist` is declared persistent. The first time `mmclass` is called during a MATLAB session, `clist` is empty. When the function finds it empty, it creates it with the first If-End construction in the function. For future calls to `mmclass`, `clist` exists because of its persistence, and the effort undertaken to create it is avoided.

3. MATLAB provides the function `evalin` that allows one to reach into another workspace, evaluate an expression, and return the result to the current workspace. The function `evalin` is similar to `eval`, except that the string is evaluated in either the ***caller*** or the ***base*** workspace. The caller workspace is the workspace where the current function was called from. The base workspace is the MATLAB workspace in the *Command* window. For example, `A=evalin('caller','expression')` evaluates `'expression'` in the caller workspace and returns the results to the variable `A` in the current workspace. Alternatively, `A=evalin('base','expression')` evaluates `'expression'` in the MATLAB workspace and returns the results to the variable `A` in the current workspace. `evalin` also provides error trapping with the syntax `evalin('workspace','try','catch')`, where `'workspace'` is either `'caller'` or `'base'`, `'try'` is the first expression evaluated, and `'catch'` is an expression that is evaluated in the ***current*** workspace if the evaluation of `'try'` produces an error.

4. Since one can evaluate an expression in another workspace, it makes sense that one can also assign the results of some expression in the current workspace to a variable in another workspace. The function `assignin` provides this capability. `assignin('workspace','vname',X)`, where `'workspace'` is either `'caller'` or `'base'`, assigns the contents of the variable `X` in the current workspace to a variable in the `'caller'` or `'base'` workspace named `'vname'`.

5. The function `inputname` provides a way to determine the variable names used when a function is called. For example, suppose a function is called as

```
>> y = myfunction(xdot,time,sqrt(2))
```

Issuing `inputname(1)` inside `myfunction` returns the character string `'xdot'`, `inputname(2)` returns `'time'`, and `inputname(3)` returns an empty array because `sqrt(2)` is not a variable but rather an expression that produces an unnamed temporary result.

The function `mmswap` illustrates the use of `evalin`, `assignin`, and `inputname`:

```
function mmswap(x,y)
%MMSWAP Swap Two Variables.
% MMSWAP(X,Y) or MMSWAP X Y  swaps the contents of the
% variable X and Y in the workspace where it is called.
% X and Y must be variables not literals or expressions.
%
% For example: Rat=ones(3); Tar=pi; MMSWAP(Rat,Tar) or MMSWAP Rat Tar
% swaps the contents of the variables named Rat and Tar in the
% workspace where MMSWAP is called giving Rat=pi and Tar=ones(3).
if nargin~=2
   error('Two Input Arguments Required.')
end
if ischar(x) & ischar(y)   % MMSWAP X Y 'string arguments'
   xx=['exist(''' x ''',''var'')']; % check existence of arguments
   yy=['exist(''' y ''',''var'')']; % in caller, e.g., exist('x','var')

   t=[evalin('caller',xx) evalin('caller',yy)];
   if all(t)                     % both x and y are valid
      xx=evalin('caller',x);  % get contents of x
      yy=evalin('caller',y);  % get contents of y
      assignin('caller',y,xx) % assign contents of x to y
      assignin('caller',x,yy) % assign contents of y to x
   elseif isequal(t,[0 1])       % x is not valid
      error(['Undefined Variable: ''' x ''''])
   elseif isequal(t,[1 0])       % y is not valid
      error(['Undefined Variable: ''' y ''''])
   else                          % neither is valid
      error(['Undefined Variables: ''' x ''' and ''' y ''''])
   end
else                          % MMSWAP(X,Y) 'numerical arguments'
  xname=inputname(1);         % get x argument name if it exists
  yname=inputname(2);         % get x argument name if it exists
   if ~isempty(xname) & ~isempty(yname)   % both x and y are valid
      assignin('caller',xname,y)          % assign contents of y to x
      assignin('caller',yname,x)          % assign contents of x yo y
   else
      error('Arguments Must be Valid Variables.')
   end
end
```

6. The name of the M-file being executed is available within a function in the variable `mfilename`. For example, when the M-file `myfunction.m` is being executed, the workspace of the function contains the variable `mfilename`, which contains the character

string `'myfunction'`. This variable also exists within script files, in which case it contains the name of the script file being executed.

11.4 FUNCTIONS AND THE MATLAB SEARCH PATH

Function M-files are one of the fundamental strengths of MATLAB. They allow one to encapsulate sequences of useful commands and apply them over and over. Since M-files exist as text files on disk, it is important that MATLAB maximize the speed at which the files are found, opened, and executed. The techniques that MATLAB uses to maximize speed are itemized below.

1. The first time MATLAB executes a function M-file, it opens the corresponding text file and ***compiles*** the commands into an internal pseudocode representation in memory that speeds execution for all later calls to the function. If the function contains references to other M-file functions and script M-files, they too are compiled into memory.
2. The function `inmem` returns a cell array of strings containing a list of functions and script files currently compiled into memory.
3. Issuing the command `mlock` within an M-file locks the compiled function so that it cannot be cleared from memory; for example, `clear functions` does not clear a locked function from memory. By locking an M-file, persistent variables declared in a function are guaranteed to exist from one call to the next. The function call `munlock('FUN')` unlocks the function `FUN` so that it can be cleared from memory. The function `mislocked('FUN')` returns True if the function `FUN` is currently locked in memory. By default function M-files are unlocked.
4. It is possible to store the compiled or P-code version of a function M-file to disk using the `pcode` command. When this is done, MATLAB loads the compiled function into memory rather than the M-file. For most functions this step does not significantly shorten the amount of time required to execute a function the first time. However, it can speed up large M-files associated with complex graphical user interface functions. P-code files are created by issuing

   ```
   >> pcode myfunction
   ```

   where *`myfunction`* is the M-file name to be compiled. P-code files are encrypted platform-independent binary files that have the same name as the original M-file but end in `.p` rather than `.m`. P-code files provide a level of security since they are visually indecipherable and can be run without the corresponding M-file.
5. As discussed in Chapter 3, when MATLAB encounters a name it doesn't recognize, it follows a set of rules to determine what to do. Given the information presented here, the set of rules can be stated as follows.

When you enter `cow` at the MATLAB prompt or if MATLAB encounters a reference to `cow` in a script or function M-file,

a. it checks to see if `cow` is a ***variable*** in the current workspace; if not,

b. it checks to see if `cow` is a ***built-in function;*** if not,

c. it checks to see if `cow` is a ***subfunction*** in the file in which `cow` appears; if not,

d. it checks to see if `cow` is a ***private*** function to the file in which `cow` appears; if not,

e. it checks to see if `cow` exists in the ***current directory;*** if not,

f. it checks to see if `cow` exists in each directory specified on the ***MATLAB search path*** by searching in the order in which the search path is specified.

MATLAB uses the first match it finds. In addition, it prioritizes file types in steps d, e, and f above by considering MEX-files first, followed by P-code files, followed last by M-files. So if `cow.`*`mex`*, `cow.p`, and `cow.m` exist, MATLAB uses `cow.`*`mex`*, where *`mex`* is replaced by the platform-dependent MEX-file extension. If `cow.p` and `cow.m` exist, MATLAB uses `cow.p`.

6. When MATLAB is started, it ***caches*** the name and location of all M-files stored within the `toolbox` subdirectory and in all subdirectories of the `toolbox` directory. This allows MATLAB to find and execute function M-files much faster.

M-file functions that are cached are considered read-only. If they are executed and then later altered, MATLAB simply executes the function that was previously compiled into memory, ignoring the changed M-files. Moreover, if new M-files are added within the `toolbox` directory after MATLAB is already running, their presence will not be noted in the cache, and thus they will be unavailable for use.

As a result, in the development of M-file functions, it is best to store them outside the `toolbox` directory, perhaps in the MATLAB directory, until they are considered complete. When they are complete, move them to a subdirectory inside the read-only `toolbox` directory. Finally, make sure the MATLAB search path is changed to recognize their existence.

7. When new M-files are added to a ***cached*** location, MATLAB finds them only if the cache is refreshed by issuing the command `rehash toolbox`. On the other hand, when cached M-files are modified, MATLAB recognizes the changes only if a previously compiled version is dumped from memory by issuing the `clear` command; for example, `>> clear` *`myfun`* clears the M-file function *`myfun`* from memory, or `>> clear functions` clears all unlocked compiled functions from memory.

8. MATLAB keeps track of the modification date of M-files outside the `toolbox` directory. As a result, when an M-file function is encountered that was previously compiled into memory, MATLAB compares the modification dates of the compiled M-file with that of the M-file on disk. If the dates are the same, MATLAB executes the compiled M-file. On the other hand, if the M-file on disk is newer, MATLAB dumps the previously compiled M-file and compiles the newer, revised M-file for execution.

9. It is possible to check all the file dependencies for a function M-file by using the function `depfun`. This function rigorously parses an M-file for all calls to other M-file functions, built-in functions, and function calls in `eval` strings and callbacks, and identifies variable and Java classes used. This function is helpful for identifying function dependencies in M-files being shared with others who may not have the same ***Toolboxes*** installed. The function `depdir` uses `depfun` to return a listing of the dependent directories of an M-file.

11.5 CREATING YOUR OWN TOOLBOX

It is common to organize a group of M-files into a subdirectory on the MATLAB search path. If the M-files are considered complete, the subdirectory should be placed in the `toolbox` directory so that the M-file names are cached as described earlier. When a `toolbox` subdirectory is created, it is beneficial to include two additional script M-files containing only MATLAB comments, that is, lines that begin with a percent sign `%`. These M-files named `Readme.m` and `Contents.m` are described below.

1. The script file `Readme.m` typically contains comment lines that describe late-breaking changes or descriptions of undocumented features. Issuing the command `>> whatsnew` *`MyToolbox`*, where *`MyToolbox`* is the name of the directory containing the group of M-files, displays the file in the *Help* window. If the Toolbox is posted to the Mathworks FTP site, the `Readme.m` file should include a disclaimer such as the following to avoid legal problems.

```
% These M-files are User-Contributed Routines that are being redistributed
% by The Mathworks, upon request, on an "as is" basis. A User-Contributed
% Routine is not a product of The Mathworks, Inc. and The Mathworks assumes
% no responsibility for any errors that may exist in these routines.
```

2. The script file `Contents.m` contains comment lines that list all M-files in the Toolbox. Issuing the command `>> helpwin` *`MyToolbox`*, where *`MyToolbox`* is the name of the directory containing the group of M-files, displays the file listing in the *Help* window. The first line in the `Contents.m` file should specify the name of the Toolbox, and the second line should state the Toolbox version and date as shown below.

```
% Toolbox Description
% Version xxx dd-mmm-yyyy
```

When this is done, the `ver` command in MATLAB decodes the first two lines and includes this information in its list of version information, for example,

```
>> ver
-------------------------------------
MATLAB Version 6.0.0.51483 on PCWIN
MATLAB License Number: 51483
-------------------------------------
MATLAB Toolbox                    Version 6.0   (R12)     30-Dec-2000
Optimization Toolbox              Version 3.0   (R12)     09-Oct-2000
Spline Toolbox                    Version 3.0   (R12)     13-Mar-2000
Mastering MATLAB Toolbox          Version 6.0             01-Jan-2001
```

3. When writing a collection of M-files to form a Toolbox, it sometimes convenient to allow the user to maintain a set of preferences for Toolbox use, or to set preferences for one or more functions in the Toolbox. While it is always possible to store this information in a MAT-file and retrieve it in later MATLAB sessions, doing so requires choosing a directory location for the preferences file and guaranteeing that the file isn't moved or deleted between sessions. To eliminate the weaknesses of the data file approach, MATLAB provides the functions `getpref`, `setpref`, `addpref`, and `rmpref`. These functions allow one to get, set, add, and remove preferences, respectively. Preferences are organized in groups so that preferences for multiple activities are supported. Within each group, individual preferences are named with character strings, and the values stored can be any MATLAB variable. This is similar to the way structures work. For example, `group.prefname=values` is a way to store values for `prefname` in a structure named `group`. By using these functions, the handling of preference files is hidden from the user. Where they are stored is system-dependent, and they are persistent across MATLAB sessions.

11.6 COMMAND-FUNCTION DUALITY

In addition to creating function M-files, it is also possible to create MATLAB ***commands.*** Examples of MATLAB commands include `clear`, `who`, `dir`, `ver`, `help`, and `whatsnew`. MATLAB commands are very similar to functions. In fact, there are only two differences between commands and functions:

1. Commands do not have output arguments, and
2. Input arguments to commands are not enclosed in parentheses.

For example, `clear functions` is a command that accepts the input argument `functions` without parentheses, performs the action of clearing all compiled functions from memory, and produces no output. A function, on the other hand, usually places data in one or more output arguments and must have its input arguments separated by commas and enclosed in parentheses, for example, `a=atan2(x,y)`.

In reality, MATLAB commands are function calls that obey the two differences mentioned above. For example, the command `whatsnew` is a function M-file. When called from the MATLAB prompt as

```
>> whatsnew MyToolbox
```

MATLAB interprets the command as a call to the function `whatsnew` with the syntax

```
>> whatsnew('MyToolbox')
```

In other words, as long as there are no output arguments requested, MATLAB interprets command arguments as character strings, places them in parentheses, and then calls the requested function. This interpretation applies to all MATLAB commands.

Both command and function forms can be entered at the MATLAB prompt, although the command form generally requires less typing. A function M-file can also be interpreted as a function if it obeys the rules for calling functions. For example, the command

```
>> which fname
```

displays the directory path string to the M-file *fname*, and the function call

```
>> s = which('fname')
```

returns the directory path string in the variable `s`. At the same time,

```
>> s = which fname
??? s = which fname
                |
Missing operator, comma, or semi-colon.
```

causes an error because it mixes function and command syntaxes. ***Whenever MATLAB encounters an equal sign, it interprets the rest of the statement as a function, which requires comma-separated arguments enclosed in parentheses.***

To summarize, commands and functions both call functions. Commands are translated into function calls by interpreting command arguments as character strings, placing them in parentheses, and then calling the requested function. Any function call can be made in the form of a command if it produces no output arguments and if it requires only character string input.

11.7 FUNCTION EVALUATION USING FEVAL

There are a number of occasions when the character string name of a function is passed to a function for evaluation. For example, many of the numerical analysis functions in MATLAB require the name of a function to be evaluated. MATLAB provides the function `feval` to facilitate this evaluation. For example,

```
>> a = feval('myfunction',x)
```

is equivalent to

```
>> a = myfunction(x)
```

Now you might be thinking that `feval` isn't necessary because the function `eval` can also be used to evaluate a character string, that is,

```
>> a = eval('myfunction(x)')
```

The difference between these two functions is that `eval` calls in the entire MATLAB interpreter to evaluate the string, whereas `feval` does only what it says it does. As a result, `feval` is much more efficient, especially if the function must be evaluated many times as part of some iterative procedure.

The function `feval` also supports multiple input and output arguments, as in

```
>> [a,b] = feval('myfunction',x,y,z,t)
```

which is equivalent to

```
>> [a,b] = myfunction(x,y,z,t)
```

MATLAB supports two alternatives to the above approach of using `feval`. The first uses ***function handles,*** which are new in MATLAB version 6. To speed up `feval` it is necessary to have more information about a function to be evaluated than just its character string name. In creating a function handle object, MATLAB extracts all needed information and hides it within the function handle data type. Once created, a function handle simply replaces the character string name in `feval`. Consider the example

```
>> fhan = @humps     % direct creation of humps(x)
fhan =
    @humps
>> fhan(2) = @cos    % direct creation of cos(x)
fhan =
    @humps    @cos
>> func2str(fhan)    % get the strings back
ans =
    'humps'    'cos'

>> feval(fhan(1),3) % evaluate humps(3)
ans =
      -5.6383
>> feval(fhan(2),pi/2) % evaluate cos(pi/2)
ans =
  6.1232e-017
```

Direct creation of a function handle uses the @ symbol followed immediately by the character string name of the function to be converted. Furthermore, just as is true with other MATLAB data types or classes, function handles are arrays. So the above function handle array contains two function handles, one named `@humps` and the other `@cos`. The utility function `func2str` extracts the strings associated with the handles into a cell array.

When the character string name of a function is known, the function `str2func` can be used to create function handles, for example,

```
>> func = str2func('humps'); % create humps(x)
>> func(2) = str2func('cos') % create cos(x)
func =
    @humps    @cos
>> fstr = {'humps' 'cos'}    % create cell array
fstr =
 'humps'    'cos'

>> func = str2func(fstr)    % create both from cells
func =
    @humps    @cos
```

Here the function handle array `func` is created two ways. First the individual elements are created, and then the simultaneous creation of both is demonstrated using a cell array input.

Once a function handle has been created, the function `functions` provides feedback about its content, for example,

```
>> functions(func(1))
ans =
    function: 'humps'
     default: 'C:\MATLABR12\toolbox\matlab\demos\humps.m'
>> functions(func(2))
ans =
    function: 'cos'
     methods: [1x1 struct]
```

More information about function handles can be found in the on-line documentation.

The second alternative to using `feval` with a character string function argument pertains to the case where the string expresses the function itself, for example,

```
>> myfun = '100*(y -x^2)^2 + (1-x)^2';
```

The function `feval` cannot evaluate `myfun` because `myfun` is not an M-file function and because there is no way for `feval` to know what the function arguments are. While `feval` cannot be used, `eval` still works. That is,

```
>> a = eval(myfun);
```

evaluates the function provided `x` and `y` have been assigned the desired values in the workspace.

To make both these function definitions work with `feval`, MATLAB created an object called an ***in-line function*** that overloads `feval` with the capability to handle cases such as `myfun` above. In-line functions are created and manipulated by the functions `inline`, `fcnchk`, `argnames`, and `formula`. Consider the following example.

```
>> x = 1.2; % pick some values for x and y
>> y = 2;
>> myfun    % show function
myfun =
100*(y -x^2)^2 + (1-x)^2

>> a = eval(myfun) % traditional evaluation
a =
         31.4
>> myfuni = inline(myfun,'x','y') % convert to in-line function
myfuni =
     Inline function:
     myfuni(x,y) = 100*(y -x^2)^2 + (1-x)^2
>> a = feval(myfuni,x,y) % now feval works
a =
         31.4
>> b = feval(myfuni,-1.2,0) % and works for any arguments
b =
        212.2
>> argnames(myfuni) % what are the function arguments?
ans =
    'x'
    'y'
>> formula(myfuni) % what is the formula for this function?
ans =
100*(y -x^2)^2 + (1-x)^2
```

As shown above, the `inline` object type overloads the function `feval` with the function `@inline/feval.m`, which takes the `inline` function, evaluates it, and returns results just as the standard or built-in function `feval` does. For further information on this topic see Chapter 33.

When the M-file name, function handle, or string function definition is passed to a function for evaluation, the function must determine what function representation is being used. Because most of the numerical analysis functions in MATLAB support all three function forms, the utility function `fcnchk` accepts an input and does the right thing. That is, if the input is just an M-file name, it returns it for use with the built-in `feval`. If the input is a function handle, it returns it for use with the built-in `feval`. And finally, if the input is an entire string function definition, it creates and returns an in-line function that calls the overloaded `feval` for evaluation. Consider the following example.

```
>> fcnchk(fhan(1))  % function handle
ans =
    @humps
```

```
>> FUN = 'humps';      % M-file function name
>> fcnchk(FUN)         % check M-file name
ans =
humps
>> FUN = '100*(y -x^2)^2 + (1-x)^2' % function definition
FUN =
100*(y -x^2)^2 + (1-x)^2
>> fcnchk(FUN) % inline function needed? Yes
ans =
     Inline function:
     ans(x) = 100*(y -x^2)^2 + (1-x)^2
>> argnames(ans)
ans =
    'x'
```

The function argnames makes a number of assumptions regarding what the variable or argument of a character string function is. In general, it looks for only one argument, although this argument can be a vector. So in the above example, rather than have x and y as the variables, let the variables be x(1) and x(2), respectively, for example,

```
>> FUN % recall FUN
FUN =
100*(y -x^2)^2 + (1-x)^2
>> FUN = strrep(FUN,'x','x(1)') % change x to x(1)
FUN =
100*(y -x(1)^2)^2 + (1-x(1))^2
>> FUN = strrep(FUN,'y','x(2)') % change y to x(2)
FUN =
100*(x(2) -x(1)^2)^2 + (1-x(1))^2
>> fcnchk(FUN) % create inline function with vector argument x
ans =
     Inline function:
     ans(x) = 100*(x(2) -x(1)^2)^2 + (1-x(1))^2

>> argnames(ans)
ans =
    'x'
```

The utility of in-line functions is that feval works for functions defined by M-file names as well as for in-line functions. The utility function fcnchk deciphers whether its input contains just an M-file name, a function handle, or the string function description. The output of fcnchk in all three cases can be passed to feval for evaluation. For further assistance see the on-line documentation.

12

M-file Debugging and Profiling

In the process of developing function M-files, it is inevitable that errors, that is, ***bugs,*** appear. MATLAB provides a number of approaches and functions to assist in ***debugging*** M-files. MATLAB also provides a tool to help you improve the execution speed of M-files. In ***profiling*** the execution of an M-file, MATLAB identifies which lines of code take the most time to complete.

12.1 DEBUGGING TOOLS

Two types of errors can appear in MATLAB expressions: syntax errors and run-time errors. Syntax errors (such as misspelled variables or function names or missing quotes or parentheses) are found when MATLAB evaluates an expression or when a function is compiled into memory. MATLAB flags these errors immediately and provides feedback about the type of error encountered and the line number in the M-file where it occurs. Given this feedback, these errors are usually easy to spot. A exception to this situation occurs in syntax errors within GUI callback strings. These errors are not detected until the strings themselves are evaluated during the operation of the GUI.

Run-time errors, on the other hand, are generally more difficult to find, even though MATLAB flags them also. When a run-time error is found, MATLAB returns control to the *Command* window and the MATLAB workspace. Access to the function workspace where the error occurred is lost, and so one cannot interrogate the contents of the function workspace in an effort to isolate the problem.

Based on the authors' experience, the most common run-time errors occur when the result of some operation leads to empty arrays or `NaN`s. All operations on `NaN`s return `NaN`s, so if `NaN`s are a possible result, it is good to use the logical function `isnan` to perform some default action when `NaN`s occur. Addressing arrays that are empty always leads to an error since empty arrays have a zero dimension. The `find` function represents a common situation where an empty array may result. If the empty array output of the `find` function is used to index some other array, the result returned will also be empty. That is, empty matrices tend to propagate empty matrices, for example,

```
>> x = pi*(1:4)  % example data
x =
     3.1416     6.2832     9.4248    12.5664
>> i = find(x>20)  % use find function
i =
     []
>> y = 2*x(i)  % propagate the empty matrix
y =
     []
```

Clearly when `y` is expected to have a finite dimension and values, a run-time error is likely to occur. When performing operations or using functions that can return empty results, the logical function `isempty` is useful to define a default result for the empty matrix case, thereby avoiding a run-time error.

There are several approaches to debugging function M-files. For simple problems, it is straightforward to use a combination of the following.

1. Remove semicolons from selected lines within the function so that intermediate results are displayed in the *Command* window.
2. Add statements that display variables of interest within the function.
3. Place the `keyboard` command at selected places in the M-file to give temporary control to the keyboard. By doing so, the function workspace can be interrogated and values changed as necessary. Resume function execution by issuing a `return` command at the keyboard prompt, that is, `K>> return`.
4. Change the function M-file into a script M-file by placing a `%` before the function definition statement at the beginning of the M-file. When executed as a script file, the workspace is the MATLAB workspace, and thus it can be interrogated after the error occurs.

When the M-file is large, the M-file is recursive, or the M-file is highly nested, that is, it calls other M-file functions that call still other functions, and so on, it is more convenient to use the MATLAB graphical debugging functions found on the **Debug** and **Break-**

points menus of the Editor/Debugger. *Command* window equivalents of these functions exist but are more cumbersome to use. If you insist on using these functions rather than the graphical debugger, see the on-line help text for `debug`, that is, `>> helpwin debug`.

The graphical debugging tools in MATLAB allow one to stop at user-set breakpoints and at MATLAB warnings and errors, as well as at expressions that create `NaNs` and `Infs`. When a breakpoint is reached, MATLAB stops execution before the affected line completes execution and returns results. While stopped, the *Command* window keyboard prompt `K>>` appears, allowing one to interrogate the function workspace, change the values of variables in the workspace, and so on, as required to track down the bug. In addition the *Editor/Debugger* window shows the line where execution stopped and provides the means for stepping into the workspace of other functions called by the M-file being debugged. When one is ready to move beyond a breakpoint, the Editor/Debugger provides menu items for single-stepping, continuing until the next breakpoint, continuing until the cursor position is reached, or terminating the debugging activity.

Describing the use of the graphical debugging tools is difficult because of their graphical nature and because the process of debugging is unique to each debugging session. However, the authors have found the debugging tools to be intuitive and easy to use. Once the basic steps are mastered, the graphical debugging features of MATLAB are extremely powerful and productive in the process of creating good MATLAB code.

12.2 FILE DEPENDENCIES

Given the ease with which M-files can be transferred electronically, it is not uncommon to run an M-file only to find out that it fails to run because it calls one or more M-file functions not found on your MATLAB path. MATLAB provides the function `depfun`, which parses an M-file for file dependencies. This function recursively searches for all function dependencies including the dependencies within functions called by the function in question as well as any dependencies found in the callbacks of Handle Graphics objects. For example, consider the function `mmlog10`, which is shown below.

```
function [m,e]=mmlog10(x)
%MMLOG10 Dissect Decimal Floating-Point Numbers. (MM)
% [M,E]=MMLOG10(X) returns the mantissa M and exponent E of X,
% such that X=M.*(10.^(E)). M is in the range 1<= M <10.
% E contains integers.
%
% See also LOG2, LOG10
% create output arrays
m=zeros(size(x));
e=m;
```

```
% capture exceptions
tmpa=isnan(x);  % NaN's
m(tmpa)=nan;
e(tmpa)=nan;

tmpb=isinf(x);  % +/- infs
m(tmpb)=1;
e(tmpb)=x(tmpb);

tmpc=(x==0);    % 0's
%m(tmpc)=0; e(tmpc)=0; %these values are already zero!

% now for "good" numbers
tmp=~(tmpa|tmpb|tmpc);
e(tmp)=floor(log10(abs(x(tmp))));
e(tmp)=e(tmp)+(abs(x(tmp))>=10.^(e(tmp)+1));
m(tmp)=x(tmp)./10.^e(tmp);
```

The file dependencies in `mmlog10` are found by executing the following.

```
>> [trace_list,builtins] = depfun('mmlog10','-toponly')
Examining file C:\MATLABR12\toolbox\mm6\mmlog10.m
trace_list =
    'C:\MATLABR12\toolbox\mm6\mmlog10.m'
    'C:\MATLABR12\toolbox\matlab\elfun\log10.m'
builtins =
    'size'
    'zeros'
    'isnan'
    'isinf'
    '=='
    '|'
    '~'
    'abs'
    'floor'
    '+'
    '.^'
    '>='
    './'
```

By default `depfun` creates Handle Graphics objects to see if the function in question stores any function calls in the callbacks associated with the Handle Graphics objects. Clearly `mmlog10` does not since it performs array arithmetic. The cell array variable `trace_list` contains the complete path and function name listing of M-file functions called by `mmlog10`, inclusive of itself. The cell array variable `builtins` contains a listing of all built-in MATLAB commands called by `mmlog10`.

In the calling syntax, the second input argument was `'-toponly'`. This argument instructs `depfun` to avoid recursive searching. In other words, in this example, `depfun` does not open `log10` to find its dependencies and then open these dependencies until it has exhausted all the functions called as a result of a call to `mmlog10`. Without the `'-toponly'` second argument, `depfun` can require significant time and can return an overwhelming amount of information. If you need confirmation of this fact, ask `depfun` to analyze the 1183 lines it contains, that is, `[trace_list,builtins]=depfun('depfun')`.

The function `depfun` does an exhaustive search. In addition to the two outputs `trace_list` and `builtins` shown above, it can return other information as well. The most general calling syntax for `depfun` is

```
[trace_list, builtins, class_names, prob_files, prob_symbols,...
eval_strings, called_from, java_classes] = depfun(fun);
```

In this syntax, `class_names` is a cell array of all classes used by the function; `prob_files` is a structure array of files that could not be parsed; `prob_symbols` is a structure array of symbols that could not be resolved as functions of variables; `eval_strings` is a structure array indicating where `trace_list` files call `eval`, `evalc`, `evalin`, or `feval`; `called_from` is a cell array that indicates who calls whom; and `java_classes` is a cell array of Java class names used by one or more of the files in `trace_list`.

12.3 PROFILING M-FILES

Even when a function M-file works correctly, there may be ways to fine-tune the code to avoid unnecessary calculations or function calls. Performance improvements can be obtained by simply storing the result of a calculation to avoid a complex recalculation or by using vectorization techniques to avoid an iterative procedure such as a For Loop. When writing a function it is difficult to guess where most execution time is spent. In today's high-speed processors with integrated floating-point units, it may be faster to calculate a result more than once than to store it in a variable and recall it again later. There is an inherent tradeoff between memory usage and the number of computations performed. Depending on the data being manipulated, it may be faster to use more memory to store intermediate results or it may be faster to perform more computations. Furthermore, the tradeoff between memory and computations is almost always dependent on the size of the data set being considered. If a function operates on large data sets, the optimum implementation may be much different than that when the data set is small. Complicating things even further is the fact that the best implementation of a given algorithm is often much different than how one writes the algorithm on paper.

MATLAB provides ***profiling*** tools to optimize the execution of M-file functions. These tools monitor the execution of M-files and identify which lines consume the greatest amount of time relative to the rest of the code. For example, if one line or function call consumes 50% of the time in a given M-file, the attention paid to this line or function call will have the greatest impact on overall execution speed. Sometimes one can rewrite the code to eliminate the offending line or lines. Other times one can minimize the amount of data manipulated in the line, thereby speeding it up. And still other times there may be nothing one can do to increase speed. In any case, a great deal of insight is gained by profiling the operation of M-file functions.

MATLAB uses the `profile` command to determine which lines of code in an M-file take the most time to execute. Using `profile` is straightforward. For example, the execution profile of `mmlog10` (shown earlier) is found by executing the commands

```
>> profile on

>> for i=1:100
      [m,e] = mmlog10(x);
   end

>> profile report
```

First the profiler is turned on, then `mmlog10` is executed some sufficient number of times, and finally a profile report is generated. The profile report is an HTML file displayed in either the *Help* window or in your computer's default browser. Displaying the details for `mmlog10` on the author's computer gives the following execution summary.

Time (s)	Percent of time	Line No.	Line Contents
		13:	`% create output arrays`
0.05	7%	14:	`m=zeros(size(x));`
		15:	`e=m;`
		17:	`tmpa=isnan(x); % NaN's`
0.11	15%	18:	`m(tmpa)=nan;`
0.06	8%	19:	`e(tmpa)=nan;`
0.06	8%	20:	`tmpb=isinf(x); % +/- infs`

Time (s)	Percent of time	Line No.	Line Contents
		21:	`m(tmpb)=1;`
		25:	`% now for "good" numbers`
0.06	8%	26:	`tmp=~(tmpa | tmpb | tmpc);`
0.20	28%	27:	`e(tmp)=floor(log10(abs(x(tmp))));`
0.05	7%	28:	`e(tmp)=e(tmp)+(abs(x(tmp)).=10.^(e(tmp)+1));`
0.06	8%	29:	`m(tmp)=x(tmp)./10.^e(tmp);`

As shown above, line 27 requires the greatest amount of time. It consumes 0.20 second or 28% of the time needed to execute the function. The reason `mmlog10` was executed 100 times in the For Loop is that the profiler does not have infinite time precision. The function `profile` typically deals with time quantized on the order of 0.05 second. As a result, on a fast computer the function in question must be run multiple times to accumulate sufficient data. When the For Loop is eliminated from the above profiling example, no useful information is returned in the profile report.

The `profile` command has a number of features in addition to those illustrated above. Three detail levels can be selected. A log showing the chronological sequence of function calls made can be requested. And statistics can be returned in a structure. For further help on profiling see the on-line help for `profile`.

13

File and Directory Management

MATLAB opens and saves data files in a variety of file formats, some of which are formats custom to MATLAB, others are industry standards, and still others are file formats custom to other applications. The techniques used to open and save data files includes GUIs as well as *Command* window functions.

Like most modern applications, MATLAB uses the current directory as the default location for data files and M-files. Directory management tools and changing the current directory are accomplished through GUIs as well as *Command* window functions.

This chapter covers file and directory management features in MATLAB.

13.1 NATIVE DATA FILES

Variables in the MATLAB workspace can be saved in a format native to MATLAB by using the `save` command. For example,

```
>> save
```

stores all variables in the MATLAB workspace in MATLAB binary format in the file `matlab.mat` in the current directory. These native binary MAT-files maintain full double precision as well as the names of the variables saved. MAT-files are not platform-independent but are completely cross-platform-compatible. Variables saved on one platform can be opened on other MATLAB platforms without any special treatment.

The `save` command can be used to store specific variables as well. For example,

```
>> save var1 var2 var3
```

saves just the variables `var1`, `var2`, and `var3` to `matlab.mat`. The file name can be specified as a first argument to `save`. For example,

```
>> save filename var1 var2 var3
```

saves `var1`, `var2`, and `var3` to the file named `filename.mat`.

Using command-function duality, the above command form can also be written in function form as

```
>> save('filename','var1','var2,','var3')
```

This particular format is useful if the file name is stored in a MATLAB character string, for example,

```
>> fname = 'myfile';
>> save(fname,'var1','var2,','var3')
```

Here, the named variables are stored in a file named `myfile.mat`.

In addition to the above simple forms, the `save` command supports options for saving in ASCII text format and can be used to append data to a file that already exists. For help with these features refer to the on-line help.

The complement to `save` is the `load` command. This command opens data files that were created by the `save` command or that are compatible with the `save` command. For example,

```
>> load
```

loads all variables found in `matlab.mat` wherever it is first found in the current directory or on the MATLAB search path. The variable names originally stored in `matlab.mat` are restored in the workspace, and they overwrite any like-named variables that may exist there.

To load specific variables from a MAT-file one must include the file name and a variable list, for example,

```
>> load filename var1 var2 var3
>> load('filename','var1','var2','var3')
```

Here filename.mat is opened and variables var1, var2, and var3 are loaded into the workspace. The second statement demonstrates the functional form of the load command, which allows the data file to be specified as a character string. Though not shown, the filename string can include a complete or a partial path, thereby restricting load to looking in a specific directory for the data file.

The latter example above provides a way to open a sequence of enumerated data files, such as mydata1.mat, mydata2.mat, and so on, as in the example

```
for i=1:N
   fname=sprintf('mydata%d',i);
   load(fname)
end
```

This code segment uses sprintf to create file name strings inside a For Loop so that a sequence of data files are loaded into the workspace.

When one does not wish to overwrite workspace variables, the load command can be written in function form and given an output argument. For example,

```
>> vnew = load('filename','var1','var2');
```

opens the file filename.mat and loads the variables var1 and var2 into a ***structure*** variable named vnew having fields var1 and var2. That is, vnew.var1 = var1 and vnew.var2 = var2.

The load command can also open ASCII text files as well. In particular, if the data file consists of MATLAB comment lines and rows of space-separated values, the syntax

```
>> load filename.ext
```

opens the file filename.ext and loads the data into a single double-precision data array named filename. For further information regarding the load command, see the on-line help.

To find out whether a data file exists and what variables it holds, the MATLAB commands exist and whos are valuable. For example,

```
>> exist('matlab.mat','file')
```

returns 0 if the file doesn't exist, and 2 if it does.

```
>> whos -file matlab.mat
```

returns the standard whos *Command* window display for the variables contained in the file matlab.mat. Alternatively,

```
>> w = whos('-file','matlab.mat')
w =
3x1 struct array with fields:
    name
    size
    bytes
    class
```

returns a structure array with fields named for the columns of the `whos` display. Used in this way the variable names, sizes, memory, and class are stored in variables.

Last, but not least, data files can be deleted by using the *Command* window command `delete`. For example,

```
>> delete filename.ext
```

deletes the file named `filename.ext`.

In MATLAB version 6 data file management functions can be accessed from the *Workspace* browser as well as from the *Import* wizard. The *Workspace* browser can be viewed by choosing **Workspace** from the **View** menu on the *MATLAB* desktop. The *Import* wizard, which appears by selecting **Import Data...** from the **File** menu or by typing `uiimport` in the *Command* window, is a general-purpose GUI that facilitates loading data in a variety of formats, not just MATLAB's native MAT-file format.

13.2 DATA IMPORT AND EXPORT

In addition to MATLAB's native MAT-file format and conventional ASCII text format, MATLAB supports a variety of industry standard formats and other custom file formats. Some formats are restricted to reading, others to writing. Some formats are restricted to images, others to multimedia or spreadsheets. These data import and export functions and capabilities make it possible for MATLAB to exchange data with other programs.

Figure window images can be saved in a native MATLAB FIG-file format using the **Save** item on the *Figure* window **File** menu. In addition, *Figure* window images can be exported to a variety of formats by selecting **Export...** on the **File** menu of a *Figure* window. The *Command* window function `saveas` provides an alternative to this GUI-based approach. For assistance in using `saveas`, see the on-line documentation.

Data-specific import and export functions available in MATLAB include those listed in the table below.

Function	Description
`dlmread`	Read delimited text file.
`dlmwrite`	Write delimited text file.
`textread`	Read formatted text from file.
`wk1read`	Read spreadsheet file.
`wk1write`	Write spreadsheet file.
`xlsread`	Read spreadsheet file.
`aviread`	Read movie file.
`imread`	Read image file.
`imwrite`	Write image file.

Function	Description
`auread`	Read Sun sound file.
`auwrite`	Write Sun sound file.
`wavread`	Read Microsoft sound file.
`wavwrite`	Write Microsoft sound file.
`hdf`	Gateway to HDF file capabilities.

The help text for each of these functions provides information on their use. The functions `imread` and `imwrite` in particular support multiple formats. The formats supported include JPEG, TIFF, BMP, PNG, HDF, PCX, and XWD. The help text for `fileformats` provides a more complete listing of the file formats supported by MATLAB, for example,

```
>> help fileformats

  Readable file formats.

   Text formats                          Command    Returns
    MAT  - MATLAB workspace              load       Variables in file.
    CSV  - Comma separated numbers       csvread    Double array.
    DLM  - Delimited text                dlmread    Double array.
    TAB  - Tab separated text            dlmread    Double array.

   Spreadsheet formats
    XLS  - Excel worksheet               xlsread    Double array and cell array.
    WK1  - Lotus 123 worksheet           wk1read    Double array and cell array.

   Movie formats                         Command    Returns
    AVI  - Movie                         aviread    MATLAB movie.

   Image formats
    JPEG - JPEG image                    imread     MxNx3 truecolor image data.
    TIFF - TIFF image                    imread     MxNx3 truecolor image data.
    GIF  - GIF image                     imread     Indexed data and colormap.
    BMP  - BMP image                     imread     Indexed data and colormap.
    PNG  - PNG image                     imread     MxNx3 truecolor image data.
    HDF  - HDF image                     imread     MxNx3 truecolor image data.
    PCX  - PCX image                     imread     Indexed data and colormap.
    XWD  - XWD image                     imread     Indexed data and colormap.

   Audio file formats
    AU   - NeXT/Sun sound                auread     Sound data and sample rate.
    WAV  - Microsoft Wave sound          wavread    Sound data and sample rate.
```

13.3 LOW-LEVEL FILE I/O

Because an infinite variety of file types exists, MATLAB provides low-level file I/O functions for reading or writing any binary or formatted ASCII file imaginable. These functions closely resemble their ANSI C programming language counterparts but do not necessarily match their characteristics exactly. In fact, many of the special-purpose file I/O commands described above use these commands internally. The low-level file I/O functions in MATLAB are shown in the following table.

Category	Function	Description/Syntax Example
File opening and closing	`fopen`	Open file. `fid = fopen('filenename','permission')`
	`fclose`	Close file. `status = fclose(fid)`
Binary I/O	`fread`	Read part or all of a binary file. `A = fread(fid,num,precision)`
	`fwrite`	Write array to a binary file. `count = fwrite(fid,array,precision)`
Formatted I/O	`fscanf`	Read formatted data from file. `A = fscanf(fid,format,num)`
	`fprintf`	Write formatted data to file. `count = fprintf(fid,format,A)`
	`fgetl`	Read line from file; discard newline character. `line = fgetl(fid)`
	`fgets`	Read line from file; keep newline character. `line = fgets(fid)`
String conversion	`sprintf`	Write formatted data to string. `S = sprintf(format,A)`
	`sscanf`	Read string under format control. `A = sscanf(string,format,num)`
File positioning	`ferror`	Inquire about file I/O status. `message = ferror(fid)`
	`feof`	Test for end of file. `TF = feof(fid)`
	`fseek`	Set file position indicator. `status = fseek(fid,offset,origin)`

Category	Function	Description/Syntax Example
	`ftell`	Get file position indicator. `position = ftell(fid)`
	`frewind`	Rewind file. `frewind(fid)`

In the above table, *fid* is a file identifier number and *permission* is a character string identifying the permissions requested. Possible strings include `'r'` for reading only, `'w'` for writing only, `'a'` for appending only, and `'r+'` for both reading and writing. Since the PC distinguishes between text and binary files, a `'b'` must often be appended when working with binary files, for example, `'rb'`. In the above table *format* is a character string defining the desired formatting. *format* follows ANSI standard C very closely. More information regarding the use of these functions can be found in the on-line documentation for each function.

13.4 DIRECTORY MANAGEMENT

With all the new windows in MATLAB version 6, it makes sense to have management of the current directory and its files available in a GUI. The *Current Directory* window displayed by choosing **Current Directory** from the **View** menu in the *MATLAB* desktop window performs these tasks. In addition to traversing the directory tree, this GUI allows one to preview the files in the current directory, see their modification dates, search for text in M-files, create new directories and new M-files, and so on. Because of the fundamental utility of knowing the current directory, it is also displayed in a pop-up menu in the *MATLAB* desktop window. Therefore, the current directory can always be known simply by looking at the toolbar on the desktop.

Prior to MATLAB version 6, directory management was conducted through the use of *Command* window functions. Though these functions are not as important in version 6, they still serve a valuable purpose. In particular, most functions have the capability of returning directory and file information in MATLAB variables, thereby allowing complex manipulation of files and directories to be done within function M-files. The *Command* window directory management functions available in MATLAB are summarized in the table below.

Function	Description
`cd` `pwd`	Show present working directory.
`S = cd;`	Return present working directory as a string in `S`.
`cd dirname`	Change present working directory to *dirname*.

Function	Description
`copyfile(oldname,dirname)` `copyfile(oldname,newname)`	Copy file *oldname* to directory *dirname*. Copy file *oldname* to *newname*.
`delete filename.ext`	Delete file *filename.ext*.

`dir`
`ls`
`S = dir;`
	Display files in current directory.
	
	Return directory information in structure `S`.

`mkdir dirname`	Make directory *dirname* in current directory.

`what`
 	
`S = what;`
	Display an organized listing of all MATLAB files in the current directory.
	Return listing information in structure `S`.

`which filename` `S = which('filename');`	Display directory path to *filename*. Return directory path to *filename* as a string in `S`.

`who`
`who -file filename`
`S = who('-file','filename');`
	Display variables in workspace.
	Display variables in MAT-file *filename*`.mat`.
	Return variables names in *filename*`.mat` in a cell array `S`.

`whos`
 	
`whos -file filename`
 	
`S = whos('-file','filename');`
	Display variables, size, and class in workspace.
	Display variables, size, and class in MAT-file *filename*`.mat`.
	Return variables, size, and class in *filename*`.mat` in structure `S`.

`help filename`
 	
`S = help('filename');`
	Display help text for *filename* in *Command* window.
	Return help text for *filename* in a character string `S`.

`type filename`	Display M-file *filename* in *Command* window.

Most of the above functions require only partial path information to locate a particular file. That is, *filename* may or may not include part of its directory path. If no directory path is included in *filename*, the current directory then the MATLAB search path is used to find the requested file. If some part of the directory path is provided, MATLAB traverses the MATLAB search path to find the subdirectory and file specified. For example, if `filename ='mystuff/myfile'`, MATLAB restricts its search to a subdirectory named `mystuff` on the MATLAB path.

To illustrate the usefulness of the above functions consider the function `mmbytes` shown below.

```
function y=mmbytes(arg)
%MMBYTES Variable Memory Usage.
% MMBYTES and MMBYTES('base') returns the total memory in bytes
% currently used in the base workspace.
% MMBYTES('caller') returns the total memory in bytes currently
% used in the workspace where MMBYTES is called from.
% MMBYTES('global') returns the total memory in bytes currently
% used in the global workspace.
if nargin==0
    arg='base';
end
if strcmp(arg,'global')
    x=evalin('base','whos(''global'')');
else
    x=evalin(arg,'whos');
end
y=sum(cat(1,x.bytes));
```

This function uses the `whos` function to gather information about the variables that exist within MATLAB. The output of the `whos` function generates a structure array `x`. The `bytes` field of this structure contains the memory allocated to all variables. The final statement in the function concatentates all the memory-allocated numbers into a vector, which is summed using the `sum` function.

Because of its varied uses, the function `exist` was not listed in the above table. This function tests for the existence of variables, files, directories, and so on. The help text for this function shown below describes its many uses.

```
>> help exist
 EXIST  Check if variables or functions are defined.
    EXIST('A') returns:
      0 if A does not exist
      1 if A is a variable in the workspace
      2 if A is an M-file on MATLAB's search path. It also returns 2 when
           A is the full pathname to a file or when A is the name of an
           ordinary file on MATLAB's search path
```

```
  3 if A is a MEX-file on MATLAB's search path
  4 if A is a MDL-file on MATLAB's search path
  5 if A is a built-in MATLAB function
  6 if A is a P-file on MATLAB's search path
  7 if A is a directory
  8 if A is a Java class
EXIST('A') or EXIST('A.EXT') returns 2 if a file named 'A' or 'A.EXT'
exists and the extension isn't a P or MEX function extension.
EXIST('A','var') checks only for variables.
EXIST('A','builtin') checks only for built-in functions.
EXIST('A','file') checks for files or directories.
EXIST('A','dir') checks only for directories.
EXIST('A','class') checks only for Java classes.
EXIST returns 0 if the specified instance isn't found.
```

To facilitate manipulation of character strings containing directory paths and filenames, MATLAB provides several useful functions. These functions are summarized in the table below.

Function	Description
`addpath('`*`dirname`*`')`	Prepend directory *`dirname`* to the MATLAB search path.
`[path,name,ext] =...` `fileparts(`*`filename`*`)`	Return path, name, and extension for file *`filename`*.
`filesep`	Return file separator character for this computer platform. The file separator is the character used to separate directories and the file name. For example, on the PC the file separator is `'\'`.
`fullfile(`*`d1,d2,...,filename`*`)`	Return full path and file specification for *`filename`* using directory tree strings, *`d1,d2, ...`*.
`matlabroot`	Return a string containing the path to the root directory of MATLAB.
`mexext`	Return MEX-file extension for this computer platform.
`pathsep`	Return path separator for this platform. The path separator is the character used to separate entries on the MATLAB search path string.

Function	Description
`prefdir`	Return MATLAB preferences directory for this platform.
`rmpath('dirname')`	Remove directory *dirname* from the MATLAB search path.
`tempdir`	Return name of a temporary directory for this platform.
`tempname`	Return name of a temporary file for this platform.

These functions, along with those in the preceding table, facilitate creation of file and directory management functions as M-files. More assistance for each function can be found by consulting the on-line help.

14

Set, Bit, and Base Functions

14.1 SET FUNCTIONS

Since arrays are ordered collections of values, they can be thought of as sets. With that understanding, MATLAB provides several functions for testing and comparing sets. The simplest test is for equality, for example,

```
>> a = rand(2,5);  % random array
>> b = randn(2,5); % a different random array
>> isequal(a,b)    % a and b are not equal
ans =
     0
>> isequal(a,a)    % but a is certainly equal to a
ans =
     1

>> isequal(a,a(:)) % a with a as a column
ans =
     0
```

For two arrays to be equal they must have the same dimensions and the same contents. This function applies to all MATLAB data types, not just numerical arrays, for example,

```
>> a = 'a string';
>> b = 'a String';
>> isequal(a,b)  % character string equality
ans =
     0
>> a = {'one' 'two' 'three'};
>> b = {'one' 'two' 'four'};
>> isequal(a,b)  % cell array equality
ans =
     0
>> isequal(a,a)
ans =
     1
>> a.one = 'one';
>> a.two = 2;
>> a.three = pi;
>> b.two = 2;
>> b.one = 'one';
>> b.three = pi;
>> isequal(a,b) % structure equality
ans =
     0
>> isequal(a,a)
ans =
     1
```

MATLAB variables are equal if they have the same size and exactly the same content. Two structures are identical if they have the same size, if they have the same contents, ***and if the fields are created in the same order.***

The function `unique` removes duplicate items from a given set:

```
>> a = [2:2:8;4:2:10] % new data
a =
     2     4     6     8
     4     6     8    10
>> unique(a) % unique elements sorted into a column
ans =
     2
     4
     6
     8
    10
```

`unique` returns a sorted column vector because removal of duplicate values makes it impossible to maintain the array dimensions. `unique` also applies to cell arrays of strings, for example,

```
>> c = {'Shania' 'Britney' 'Dixie' 'Shania' 'Faith'};
>> unique(c)
ans =
    'Britney'    'Dixie'    'Faith'    'Shania'
```

Set membership is determined with the function `ismember`, for example,

```
>> a = 1:9
a =
     1     2     3     4     5     6     7     8     9
>> b = 2:2:9
b =
     2     4     6     8
>> ismember(a,b) % which elements in a are in b
ans =
     0     1     0     1     0     1     0     1     0
>> ismember(b,a) % which elements in b are in a
ans =
     1     1     1     1
```

For vector arguments, `ismember` returns a logical array the same size as its first argument with ones appearing at the indices where the two vectors share common values.

```
>> A = eye(3);  % new data
>> B = ones(3);
>> ismember(A,B) % those elements in A that are also in B
ans =
     1
     0
     0
     0
     1
     0
     0
     0
     1
>> ismember(B,A)
ans =
     1
     1
     1
     1
     1
     1
     1
     1
     1
```

For 2-D arrays `ismember` returns a column vector with ones appearing at the *single* indices of the first argument where the two arguments share common values. The function `ismember` also applies to cell arrays of strings, for example,

```
>> ismember(c,'Dixie')
ans =
     0     0     1     0     0
```

Set arithmetic is accomplished with the functions `union`, `intersect`, `setdiff`, and `setxor`. Examples of the use of these functions include the following.

```
>> a,b             % recall prior data
a =
     1     2     3     4     5     6     7     8     9
b =
     2     4     6     8
>> union(a,b) % union of a and b
ans =
     1     2     3     4     5     6     7     8     9
>> intersect(a,b) % intersection of a and b
ans =
     2     4     6     8
>> setxor(a,b)     % set exclusive or of a and b
ans =
     1     3     5     7     9
>> setdiff(a,b)    % values in a that are not in b
ans =
     1     3     5     7     9
>> setdiff(b,a)    % values in b that are not in a
ans =
     []
>> union(A,B, 'rows') % matrix inputs produce combined rows with
no repetitions
ans =
     0     0     1
     0     1     0
     1     0     0
     1     1     1
```

Like prior functions discussed in this chapter, these set functions also apply to cell arrays of strings.

14.2 BIT FUNCTIONS

In addition to the logical operators discussed in the last chapter, MATLAB provides functions that allow logical operations on individual bits of floating-point integers. Because MATLAB represents all numerical values as double-precision floating-point numbers (IEEE arithmetic), integers are represented as floating-point integers called ***flints***. As a result, IEEE arithmetic–compliant computers can uniquely represent integers in the range from 0 to $2^{53} - 1$. The MATLAB bitwise functions `bitand`, `bitcmp`, `bitor`, `bitxor`, `bitset`, `bitget`, and `bitshift` work on integers in this range.

The maximum integer representable using bit operations is `bitmax`, which is $2^{53} - 1$ on computers that perform IEEE arithmetic.

```
>> format hex % change format to hexadecimal
>> bitmax
ans =
   433fffffffffffff
```

Examples of bit operations include the following.

```
>> a = (2^24)-1 % data
a =
   416fffffe0000000
>> b = 123456789 % data
b =
   419d6f3454000000
>> bitand(a,b) % (a & b)
ans =
   4156f34540000000
>> bitor(a,b) % (a | b)
ans =
   419ffffffc000000
>> bitxor(a,b) % xor(a,b)
ans =
   419e90cba8000000
>> bitcmp(0,10) % complement 0 as a 10 bit number
ans =
   408ff80000000000
>> bitget(a,1) % get first bit of a
ans =
   3ff0000000000000
>> bitset(a,30) % set 30th bit of a to 1
ans =
   41c07ffff800000
>> format short g % reset display format
```

14.3 BASE CONVERSIONS

MATLAB provides a number of utility functions for converting decimal numbers to other bases ***in the form of character strings.*** Conversions between decimals and binary numbers are performed by the functions `dec2bin` and `bin2dec`, for example,

```
>> a = dec2bin(17) % find binary representation of 17
a =
10001
>> class(a) % result is a character string
ans =
char
>> bin2dec(a) % convert a back to decimal
ans =
    17
>> class(ans) % result is a double-precision decimal
ans =
double
```

Conversions between decimals and hexadecimals are performed by `dec2hex` and `hex2dec`, as in the example

```
>> a = dec2hex(2047) % hex representation of 2047
a =
7FF
>> class(a) % result is a character string
ans =
char
>> hex2dec(a) % convert a back to decimal
ans =
        2047
>> class(ans) % result is a double-precision decimal
ans =
double
```

Conversions between decimals and any base between 2 and 36 are performed by `dec2base` and `base2dec`, for example,

```
>> a = dec2base(26,3)
a =
222
>> class(a)
ans =
char
>> base2dec(a,3)
ans =
    26
```

Base 36 is the maximum usable base because it uses the numbers `0` through `9` and the letters `A` through `Z` to represent the 36 distinct digits of a base 36 number.

15

Time Computations

MATLAB offers a number of functions to manipulate time. You can do arithmetic with dates and times, print calendars, and find specific days. MATLAB does this by storing the date and time as a double-precision number representing the number of days since the beginning of year zero. For example, January 1, 2000, at midnight is represented as 730486, and the same day at noon is 730486.5. This format may make calculations easier for a computer, but it is difficult to interpret visually. That's why MATLAB supplies a number of functions to convert between date numbers and character strings and to manipulate dates and times.

15.1 CURRENT DATE AND TIME

The function `clock` returns the current date and time in an array, for example,

```
>> T = clock
T =
        2000          6         27         15         37      47.04
```

This is the time when this part of the text was written. The above data is organized as `T = [year month day hour minute seconds]`. So the above time is the year 2000, the 6th month, 27th day, 15th hour, 37th minute, 47.04 seconds.

The function `now` returns the current date and time as a double-precision date number or simply a date number.

```
>> format long
>> t = now
t =
     7.306646527226851e+005
>> format short g
```

Both `T` and `t` represent essentially the same information.

The function `date` returns the current date as a character string in the dd-mmm-yyyy format.

```
>> date
ans =
27-Jun-2000
```

15.2 DATE FORMAT CONVERSIONS

In general, mathematics with time involves converting times to date number format, performing standard mathematical operations on the times, and then converting the result back to a format that makes human sense. As a result, converting time among different formats is very important. MATLAB supports three formats for dates: (1) double-precision date number, (2) date (character) strings in a variety of styles, and (3) numerical date vector where each element contains a different date component, that is, `[year,month,day,hour,minute,seconds]`.

The function `datestr` converts the date number to a date string. The syntax for using `datestr` is `datestr(date,dateform)`, where `dateform` is described by the help text for `datestr`:

```
>> help datestr
 DATESTR String representation of date.
    DATESTR(D,DATEFORM) converts a serial data number D (as returned by
    DATENUM) or a free-format date string into a date string with a
    format specified by format number or string DATEFORM (see table below).
    By default, DATEFORM is 1, 16, or 0 depending on whether D contains
    dates, times or both. Date strings with 2 character years are interpreted
```

```
to be within the 100 years centered around the current year.
DATESTR(D,DATEFORM,PIVOTYEAR) uses the specified pivot year as the
starting year of the 100-year range in which a two-character year
resides. The default pivot year is the current year minus 50 years.
DATEFORM = -1 uses the default format.

DATEFORM number   DATEFORM string           Example
   0             'dd-mmm-yyyy HH:MM:SS'   01-Mar-2000 15:45:17
   1             'dd-mmm-yyyy'            01-Mar-2000
   2             'mm/dd/yy'               03/01/00
   3             'mmm'                    Mar
   4             'm'                      M
   5             'mm'                     03
   6             'mm/dd'                  03/01
   7             'dd'                     01
   8             'ddd'                    Wed
   9             'd'                      W
  10             'yyyy'                   2000
  11             'yy'                     00
  12             'mmmyy'                  Mar00
  13             'HH:MM:SS'               15:45:17
  14             'HH:MM:SS PM'             3:45:17 PM
  15             'HH:MM'                  15:45
  16             'HH:MM PM'                3:45 PM
  17             'QQ-YY'                  Q1-96
  18             'QQ'                     Q1
  19             'dd/mm'                  01/03
  20             'dd/mm/yy'               01/03/00
  21             'mmm.dd,yyyy HH:MM:SS'   Mar.01,2000 15:45:17
  22             'mmm.dd,yyyy'            Mar.01,2000
  23             'mm/dd/yyyy'             03/01/2000
  24             'dd/mm/yyyy'             01/03/2000
  25             'yy/mm/dd'               00/03/01
  26             'yyyy/mm/dd'             2000/03/01
  27             'QQ-YYYY'                Q1-1996
  28             'mmmyyyy'                Mar2000

See also DATE, DATENUM, DATEVEC, DATETICK.
```

Some examples of datestr usage include

```
>> t = now
t =
  7.3066e+005
>> datestr(t)
ans =
27-Jun-2000 16:22:56
```

```
>> class(ans)
ans =
char

>> datestr(t,12)
ans =
Jun00
>> datestr(t,23)
ans =
06/27/2000
>> datestr(t,24)
ans =
27/06/2000
>> datestr(t,25)
ans =
00/06/27
>> datestr(t,13)
ans =
16:22:56
```

The function `datenum` is the inverse of `datestr`. That is, `datenum` converts a date string to a date number using the form `datenum(str)`. Alternatively, it converts individual date specifications using the form `datenum(year,month,day)` or `datenum(year,month,day,hour,minute,second)`. Consider the example

```
>> t = now
t =
    7.306647000825232e+005
>> ts = datestr(t)
ts =
27-Jun-2000 16:48:07
>> datenum(ts)
ans =
    7.306647000810185e+005
>> datenum(2000,6,27,16,48,07)
ans =
    7.306647000810185e+005
>> datenum(2000,6,27)
ans =
      730664
```

The `datevec` function converts a date string using `datestr` formats 0, 1, 2, 6, 13, 14, 15, or 16 to a numerical vector containing the date components. Alternatively, it converts a date number to a numerical vector of date components, for example,

```
>> c = datevec('12/24/1984')
c =
   1984    12    24     0     0     0
>> [yr,mo,day,hr,min,sec] = datevec('24-Dec-1984 08:22')
yr =
   1984
mo =
   12
day =
   24
hr =
   8
min =
   22
sec =
   0
```

15.3 DATE FUNCTIONS

The numerical day of the week can be found from a date string or a date number using the function `weekday`. ***MATLAB uses the convention where Sunday is day 1 and Saturday is day 7.*** For example,

```
>> [d,w] = weekday(728647)
d =
   2
w =
   Mon
>> [d,w] = weekday('21-Dec-1994')
d =
   4
w =
   Wed
```

The last day of any month can be found using the function `eomday`. Because of leap year, both the year and month are required, for example,

```
>> eomday(1996,2) % divisible by 4 is a leap year
ans =
   29
>> eomday(1900,2) % divisible by 100 not a leap year
ans =
   28
>> eomday(2000,2) % divisible by 400 is a leap year
ans =
   29
```

MATLAB can generate a calendar for any month you request and display it in the *Command* window or place it in a 6-by-7 matrix using the function `calendar`, for example,

```
>> calendar(date)
                    Jun 2000
     S      M     Tu      W     Th      F      S
     0      0      0      0      1      2      3
     4      5      6      7      8      9     10
    11     12     13     14     15     16     17
    18     19     20     21     22     23     24
    25     26     27     28     29     30      0
     0      0      0      0      0      0      0
>> calendar(2000,6)
                    Jun 2000
     S      M     Tu      W     Th      F      S
     0      0      0      0      1      2      3
     4      5      6      7      8      9     10
    11     12     13     14     15     16     17
    18     19     20     21     22     23     24
    25     26     27     28     29     30      0
     0      0      0      0      0      0      0
>> x = calendar(2000,6)
x =
     0      0      0      0      1      2      3
     4      5      6      7      8      9     10
    11     12     13     14     15     16     17
    18     19     20     21     22     23     24
    25     26     27     28     29     30      0
     0      0      0      0      0      0      0
>> class(x)
ans =
double
```

15.4 TIMING FUNCTIONS

The functions `tic` and `toc` are used to time a sequence of MATLAB operations. `tic` starts a stopwatch; `toc` stops the stopwatch and displays the elapsed time:

```
>> tic; plot(rand(50,5)); toc
elapsed_time =
   0.33
>> tic; plot(rand(50,5)); toc
elapsed_time =
   0.11
```

Note the difference in elapsed times for identical `plot` commands. The second `plot` was significantly faster because MATLAB had already created the *Figure* window and compiled the functions it needed into memory.

The function `cputime` returns the amount of central processing unit (CPU) time in seconds that MATLAB has used since the current session was started. The function `etime` calculates the elapsed time between two time vectors in six-element row vector form such as that returned by the functions `clock` and `datevec`. Both `cputime` and `etime` can be used to compute the time it takes for an operation to be completed. In fact, the functions `tic` and `toc` just automate the use of `clock` and `etime` to compute elapsed time. Usage of `cputime` and `etime` are demonstrated by the following examples in which `myoperation` is a script file containing a number of MATLAB commands:

```
>> t0 = cputime; myoperation; cputime-t0
ans =
    0.149999999999991
>> t1 = clock; myoperation; etime(clock,t1)
ans =
    11.284853
```

15.5 PLOT LABELS

Sometimes it is useful to plot data and use dates or time strings for one or more of the axis labels. The `datetick` function automates this task. ***Use of this function requires that the axis to be marked be plotted with a vector of date numbers, for example, the output of the*** `datenum` ***function.*** Consider the following examples.

```
>> t = (1900:10:1990)';
>> p = [ 75.995;  91.972; 105.711; 123.203; 131.669;
        150.697; 179.323; 203.212; 226.505; 249.633];
>> plot(datenum(t,1,1),p)
>> datetick('x','yyyy')    % use 4-digit year on the x-axis
>> title('Figure 15.1: Population by Year')
```

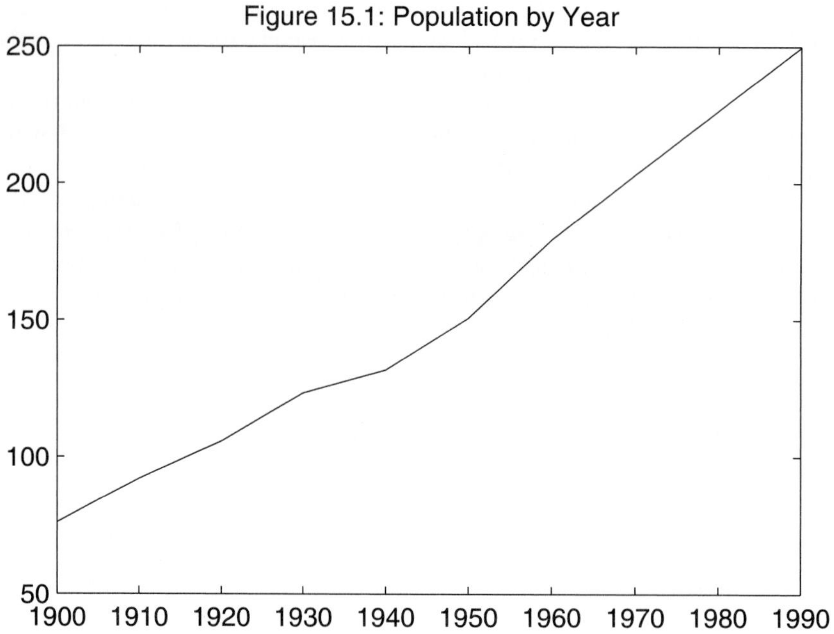

Here we create a bar chart of company sales from November 1998 to December 1999:

```
>> y = [1998 1998 1999*ones(1,12)]';
>> m = [11 12 (1:12)]';
>> s = [1.1 1.3 1.2 1.4 1.6 1.5 1.7 1.6 1.8 1.3 1.9 1.7 1.6 1.95]';
>> bar(datenum(y,m,1),s)
>> datetick('x','mmmyy')
>> ylabel('$ Million')
>> title('Figure 15.2: Monthly Sales')
```

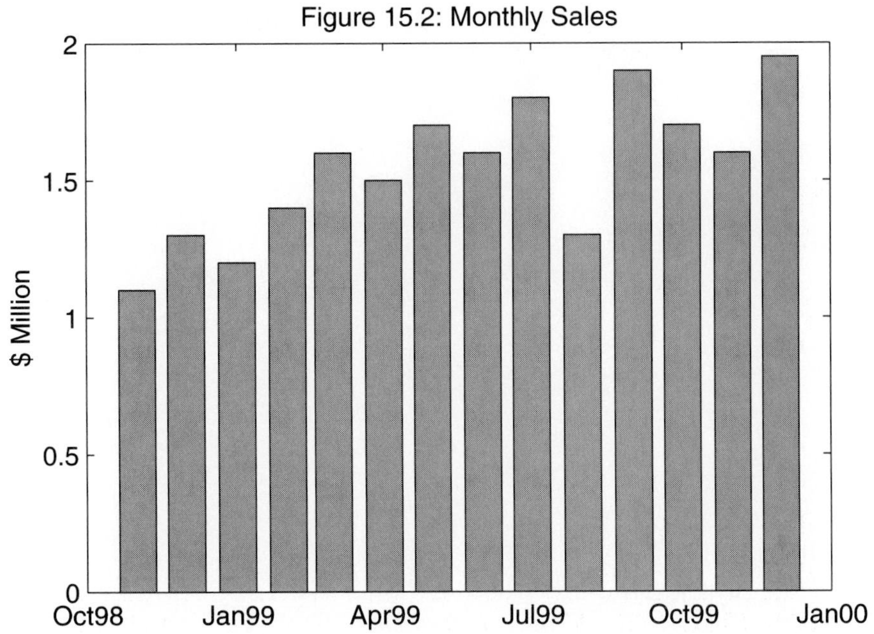
Figure 15.2: Monthly Sales
$ Million
2
1.5
1
0.5
0
Oct98
Jan99
Apr99
Jul99
Oct99
Jan00

16

Matrix Algebra

MATLAB was originally written to provide an easy-to-use interface to professionally developed numerical linear algebra subroutines. As it has evolved over the years, other features such as graphics and graphical user interfaces have made the numerical linear algebra routines less prominent. Nevertheless, MATLAB offers a wide range of valuable matrix algebra functions.

> It is important to note that while MATLAB supports *n*-dimensional arrays, matrix algebra is defined only for 2-D arrays, that is, vectors and matrices.

16.1 SETS OF LINEAR EQUATIONS

One of the most common linear algebra problems is the solution of a linear set of equations. For example, consider the set of equations

$$\begin{bmatrix} 1 & 2 & 3 \\ 4 & 5 & 6 \\ 7 & 8 & 0 \end{bmatrix} \cdot \begin{bmatrix} x_1 \\ x_2 \\ x_3 \end{bmatrix} = \begin{bmatrix} 366 \\ 804 \\ 351 \end{bmatrix}$$

$$\boldsymbol{A} \cdot \boldsymbol{x} = \boldsymbol{y}$$

where the mathematical multiplication symbol $(\cdot)$ is now defined in the matrix sense as opposed to the array sense discussed earlier. In MATLAB, this matrix multiplication is denoted with the asterisk notation *. The above equations define the product of the matrix $\boldsymbol{A}$ and the vector $\boldsymbol{x}$ as being equal to the vector $\boldsymbol{y}$. The existence of solutions to the above equation is a fundamental problem in linear algebra. Moreover, when a solution does exist, there are numerous approaches to finding the solution, such as Gaussian elimination, LU factorization, or direct use of $\boldsymbol{A}^{-1}$. It is clearly beyond the scope of this text to discuss the many analytical and numerical issues of matrix algebra. We only wish to demonstrate how MATLAB can be used to solve problems like the one above.

To solve the above problem it is necessary to enter $\boldsymbol{A}$ and $\boldsymbol{y}$:

```
>> A = [1 2 3;4 5 6
7 8 0]
A =
     1     2     3
     4     5     6
     7     8     0
>> y = [366;804;351]
y =
   366
   804
   351
```

As discussed earlier, the entry of the matrix `A` shows the two ways that MATLAB distinguishes between rows. The semicolon between the 3 and 4 signifies the start of a new row, as does the new line between the 6 and 7. The vector `y` is a column because each semicolon signifies the start of a new row.

With a background in linear algebra it is easy to show that this problem has a unique solution if the rank of `A` and the rank of the augmented matrix `[A y]` are both equal to 3. Alternatively, one can check the condition number of `A`. If the condition number is not excessively large, then `A` has an inverse with good numerical properties. Testing this problem produces

```
>> rank(A)
ans =
     3
```

```
>> rank([A y])
ans =
     3

>> cond(A) % close to one is best
ans =
        35.106
```

Since the rank and condition number tests hold, MATLAB can find the solution of $\boldsymbol{A} \cdot \boldsymbol{x} = \boldsymbol{y}$ in two ways, one of which is preferred. The less favorable but more straightforward method is to take $\boldsymbol{x} = \boldsymbol{A}^{-1} \cdot \boldsymbol{y}$ literally. For example,

```
>> x = inv(A)*y
x =
           25
           22
           99
```

Here `inv(A)` is a MATLAB function that computes A^{-1} and the multiplication operator `*` is matrix multiplication. The preferable solution is found using the matrix left division operator or backward slash, for example,

```
>> x = A\y
x =
           25
           22
           99
```

This equation utilizes an LU factorization approach and expresses the answer as the left division of `A` into `y`. The left division operator \ has no preceding dot, as this is a matrix operation, not an element-by-element array operation. There are many reasons why this second solution is preferable. Of these, the simplest is that the latter method requires fewer floating-point operations and as a result is significantly faster. In addition, this solution is generally more accurate, especially for larger problems. In either case, if MATLAB cannot find a solution or cannot find it accurately, it displays a warning message.

If the transpose of the above set of linear equations is taken, that is, $(\boldsymbol{A} \cdot \boldsymbol{x})' = \boldsymbol{y}'$, then the above set of linear equations can be written as $\boldsymbol{x}' \cdot \boldsymbol{A}' = \boldsymbol{y}'$, where $\boldsymbol{x}'$ and $\boldsymbol{y}'$ are now row vectors. As a result, it is equally valid to express a set of linear equations in terms of the product of a row vector and a matrix being equal to another row vector, for example, $\boldsymbol{u} \cdot \boldsymbol{B} = \boldsymbol{v}$. In MATLAB, this case is solved by the same internal algorithms using the matrix right division operator or forward slash as `u = v/B`.

It is important to note that when MATLAB encounters a forward (/) or backward (\) slash, it checks the structure of the coefficient matrix to determine what internal algorithm to use to find the solution. In particular, if the matrix is upper or lower triangular or a permutation of an upper or lower triangular matrix, MATLAB does not refactor the matrix but rather just performs the forward or backward substitution steps required to find the solution.

As a result, MATLAB makes use of the properties of the coefficient matrix to compute the solution as fast as possible.

If you've studied linear algebra rigorously, you know that when the number of equations and number of unknowns differ, a single unique solution usually does not exist. However, with further constraints a solution of practical use can usually be found. In MATLAB, when rank($\boldsymbol{A}$) = min(r,c) where r and c are the number of rows and columns in $\boldsymbol{A}$, respectively, and there are more equations than unknowns ($r > c$), that is, the ***overdetermined*** case, use of a division operator / or \ automatically finds the solution that minimizes the norm of the squared residual or error $\boldsymbol{e} = \boldsymbol{A} \cdot \boldsymbol{x} - \boldsymbol{y}$. This solution is of great practical value and is called the ***least squares solution.*** Consider the example shown below.

```
>> A = [1 2 3;4 5 6;7 8 0;2 5 8]  % 4 equations in 3 unknowns
A =
     1     2     3
     4     5     6
     7     8     0
     2     5     8
>> y = [366 804 351 514]'  % a new r.h.s. vector
y =
   366
   804
   351
   514
>> x = A\y      % least squares solution
x =
      247.98
     -173.11
      114.93
>> e = A*x-y   % this residual has the smallest norm.
e =
  -119.4545
    11.9455
     0.0000
    35.8364

>> norm(e)
ans =
  125.2850
```

In addition to the least squares solution computed with the left and right division operators, MATLAB also offers the functions `lscov` and `lsqnonneg`. The function `lscov` solves the weighted least squares problem when the covariance matrix of the data is known, and `lsqnonneg` finds the nonnegative least squares solution where all solution components are constrained to be positive.

When there are fewer equations than unknowns ($r < c$), that is, the ***underdetermined*** case, an infinite number of solutions exist. Of these solutions, MATLAB computes two in a straightforward way. Use of the division operator gives a solution that has a maximum number of zeros in the elements of $\boldsymbol{x}$. Alternatively, computing `x=pinv(A)*y` gives a solution where the length or norm of x is smaller than all other possible solutions. This solution, based on the pseudoinverse, also has great practical value and is called the ***minimum norm solution.*** For example,

```
>> A = A'  % create 3 equations in 4 unknowns
A =
     1     4     7     2
     2     5     8     5
     3     6     0     8
>> y = y(1:3) % new r.h.s. vector
y =
   366
   804
   351
>> x = A\b  % solution with maximum zero elements
x =
         0
 -165.9000
   99.0000
  168.3000
>> xn = pinv(A)*b % minimum norm solution
xn =
   30.8182
 -168.9818
   99.0000
  159.0545
>> norm(x)  % norm of solution with zero elements
ans =
  256.2200
>> norm(xn) % minimum norm solution has smaller norm!
ans =
  254.1731
```

16.2 MATRIX FUNCTIONS

In addition to the solution of linear sets of equations, MATLAB offers numerous matrix functions that are useful for solving numerical linear algebra problems. A thorough discussion of these functions is beyond the scope of this text. In general, MATLAB provides functions for all common and some uncommon numerical linear algebra problems. A brief description of many of the matrix functions is given in the table below.

Function	Description
`A^n`	Exponentiation, e.g., `A^3 = A*A*A`.
`balance(A)`	Scale to improve eigenvalue accuracy.
`[V,D]=cdf2rdf(V,D)`	Complex diagonal form to real block diagonal form.

Function	Description
chol(A)	Cholesky factorization.
cond(A)	Matrix condition number.
condest(A)	1-norm condition number estimate.
[V,D,s]=condeig(A)	Condition number with respect to repeated eigenvalues.
det(A)	Determinant.
eig(A)	Vector of eignenvalues.
[V,D]=eig(A)	Matrix of eignenvectors, and diagonal matrix containing eigenvalues.
expm(A)	Matrix exponential.
funm(A)	General matrix function.
gsvd(A)	Generalized singular values.
[U,V,X,C,S]=gsvd(A)	Generalized singular value decomposition.
hess(A)	Hessenburg form of a matrix.
inv(A)	Matrix inverse.
logm(A)	Matrix logarithm.
lscov(A,y,V)	Least squares with covariance matrix.
lsqnonneg(A,y)	Nonnegative least squares solution.
[L,U]=lu(A)	LU decomposition.
minres(A,y)	Minimum residual method.
norm(A,type)	Matrix and vector norms.
null(A)	Null space.
orth(A)	Orthogonal range space.
pinv(A)	Pseudoinverse.
poly(A)	Characteristic polynomial.
polyeig(A0,A1,...)	Polynomial eigenvalue solution.
polyvalm(A)	Evaluate matrix polynomial.

Function	Description
`qr(A)`	Orthogonal-triangular decomposition.
`qz(A,B)`	Generalized eigenvalues.
`rank(A)`	Matrix rank.
`rcond(A)`	LAPACK reciprocal condition estimator.
`rref(A)`	Reduced row echelon form.
`rsf2csf(A)`	Real Schur form to complex Schur form.
`schur(A)`	Schur decomposition.
`sqrtm(A)`	Matrix square root.
`subspace(A,B)`	Angle between two subspaces.
`svd(A)`	Singular values.
`[U,S,V]=svd(A)`	Singular value decomposition.
`symmlq(A,y)`	Symmetric LQ solution method.
`trace(A)`	Sum of matrix diagonal elements.

16.3 SPECIAL MATRICES

MATLAB offers a number of special matrices; some of them are general utilities, while others are matrices of interest to specialized disciplines. These and other special matrices include those given in the table below. Use the on-line help to learn more about these matrices.

Matrix	Description
`[]`	Empty matrix.
`blkdiag(a0,a1,...)`	Block diagonal concatenation of input arguments.
`compan(P)`	Companion matrix to polynomial.
`eye(r,c)`	Identity matrix.
`gallery`	More than 50 test matrices.
`hadamard(n)`	Hadamard matrix of order `n`.

Matrix	Description
`hankel(C)`	Hankel matrix.
`hilb(n)`	Hilbert matrix of order `n`.
`invhilb(n)`	Inverse Hilbert matrix of order `n`.
`magic(n)`	Magic matrix of order `n`.
`ones(r,c)`	Matrix containing all ones.
`pascal(n)`	Pascal matrix of order `n`.
`rand(r,c)`	Uniformly distributed random matrix with elements between 0 and 1.
`randn(r,c)`	Normally distributed random matrix with elements having zero mean and unit variance.
`rosser`	Classic symmetric eigenvalue test problem.
`toeplitz(C,R)`	Toeplitz matrix.
`vander(C)`	Vandermonde matrix.
`wilkinson(n)`	Wilkinson's eigenvalue test matrix of order `n`.
`zeros(r,c)`	Matrix containing all zeros.

16.4 SPARSE MATRICES

In many practical applications, matrices are generated that contain only a few nonzero elements. As a result, these matrices are said to be ***sparse.*** For example, circuit simulation and finite element analysis programs routinely deal with matrices containing fewer than 1% nonzero elements. If a matrix is large, for example, `max(size(A)) > 100`, and has a high percentage of zero elements, it is both wasteful of computer storage to store the zero elements and wasteful of computational power to perform arithmetic operations using the zero elements. To eliminate the storage of zero elements, it is common to store only the nonzero elements of a sparse matrix and two sets of indices identifying the row and column positions of these elements. Similarly, to eliminate arithmetic operations on the zero elements, special algorithms have been developed to solve typical matrix problems such as solving a set of linear equations in which operations involving zeros are minimized and intermediate matrices have minimum nonzero elements.

The techniques used to optimize sparse matrix computations are complex in implementation as well as in theory. Fortunately, MATLAB hides this complexity. In MATLAB, sparse matrices are stored in variables just as regular full matrices are. Moreover, most computations with sparse matrices use the same syntax as that used for full matrices. In particular, all the array manipulation capabilities of MATLAB work equally well on sparse matrices. For example, `s(i,j) = value` adds a nonzero element to the `i`th row and `j`th column of the sparse matrix `s`.

In this text, only the creation of sparse matrices and the conversion to and from sparse matrices is illustrated. In general, operations on full matrices produce full matrices and operations on sparse matrices produce sparse matrices. In addition, operations on a mixture of full and sparse matrices generally produce sparse matrices unless the operation makes the result too densely populated with nonzeros to make sparse storage efficient.

Sparse matrices are created using the MATLAB function `sparse`. For example,

```
>> As = sparse(1:10,1:10,ones(1,10))
As =
   (1,1)         1
   (2,2)         1
   (3,3)         1
   (4,4)         1
   (5,5)         1
   (6,6)         1
   (7,7)         1
   (8,8)         1
   (9,9)         1
  (10,10)        1
```

creates a 10-by-10 identity matrix. In this usage `sparse(i,j,s)` creates a sparse matrix whose *k*th nonzero element is `s(k)`, and `s(k)` appears in the row `i(k)` and column `j(k)`. Note the difference in how sparse matrices are displayed. Nonzero elements and their row and column positions are displayed. The above sparse matrix can also be created by conversion. For example,

```
>> As = sparse(eye(10))
As =
   (1,1)         1
   (2,2)         1
   (3,3)         1
   (4,4)         1
   (5,5)         1
   (6,6)         1
   (7,7)         1
   (8,8)         1
   (9,9)         1
  (10,10)        1
```

creates the 10-by-10 identity matrix again, this time by converting the full matrix `eye(10)` to sparse format. While this method of creating a sparse matrix works, it is seldom used in practice because the initial full matrix wastes a great deal of memory.

Given a sparse matrix, the function `full` generates the conventional full matrix equivalent. For example,

```
>> A = full(As)
A =
     1     0     0     0     0     0     0     0     0     0
     0     1     0     0     0     0     0     0     0     0
     0     0     1     0     0     0     0     0     0     0
     0     0     0     1     0     0     0     0     0     0
     0     0     0     0     1     0     0     0     0     0
     0     0     0     0     0     1     0     0     0     0
     0     0     0     0     0     0     1     0     0     0
     0     0     0     0     0     0     0     1     0     0
     0     0     0     0     0     0     0     0     1     0
     0     0     0     0     0     0     0     0     0     1
```

converts the sparse matrix `As` back to its full form.

To compare sparse matrix storage to full matrix storage consider the following example.

```
>> B = eye(200);
>> Bs = sparse(B);
>> whos
  Name       Size          Bytes  Class

  B        200x200        320000  double array
  Bs       200x200          3204  sparse array

Grand total is 40200 elements using 323204 bytes
```

Here the sparse matrix `Bs` contains only 0.5% nonzero elements and requires 3204 bytes of storage. On the other hand, `B`, the same matrix in full matrix form requires two orders of magnitude more storage!

16.5 SPARSE MATRIX FUNCTIONS

MATLAB provides numerous sparse matrix functions. Many involve different aspects of and techniques for the solution of sparse simultaneous equations. A discussion of these functions is beyond the scope of this text. The functions available are listed in the table below.

Sparse Matrix Function	Description
`bic`	Biconjugate gradient iterative linear equation solution.
`bicstab`	Biconjugate gradient stabilized iterative linear equation solution.
`cgs`	Conjugate gradients squared iterative linear equation solution.

Sparse Matrix Function	Description
`cholinc`	Incomplete Cholesky factorization.
`colamd`	Column approximate minimum degree reordering method.
`colamdtree`	`colamd` followed by column elimination tree postordering.
`colmmd`	Column minimum degree reordering method.
`colperm`	Column permutation.
`condest`	1-norm condition number estimate.
`dmperm`	Dulmage-Mendelsohn reordering method.
`eigs`	A few eigenvalues using ARPACK.
`etree`	Elimination tree.
`etreeplot`	Plot elimination tree.
`find`	Find indices of nonzero elements.
`full`	Convert sparse matrix to full matrix.
`gmres`	Generalized minimum residual iterative linear equation solution.
`gplot`	Construct graph theory plot.
`issparse`	True for sparse matrix.
`lsqr`	LSQR implementation of conjugate gradients on normal equations.
`luinc`	Incomplete LU factorization.
`minres`	Minimum residual iterative linear equation solution.
`nnz`	Number of nonzero matrix elements.
`nonzeros`	Nonzero matrix elements.
`normest`	Estimate of matrix 2-norm.
`nzmax`	Storage allocated for nonzero elements.
`pcg`	Preconditioned conjugate gradients iterative linear equation solution.
`qmr`	Quasi-minimal residual iterative linear equation solution.

Sparse Matrix Function	Description
`randperm`	Random permutation.
`spalloc`	Allocate space for sparse matrix.
`sparse`	Create sparse matrix.
`spaugment`	Form least squares augmented system.
`spconvert`	Import from sparse matrix external format.
`spdiags`	Sparse matrix formed from diagonals.
`speye`	Sparse identity matrix.
`spfun`	Apply function to nonzero elements.
`spones`	Replace nonzeros with ones.
`spparms`	Set parameters for sparse matrix routines.
`sprand`	Sparse uniformly distributed matrix.
`sprandn`	Sparse normally distributed matrix.
`sprandsym`	Sparse random symmetric matrix.
`sprank`	Structural rank.
`spy`	Visualize sparsity pattern.
`svds`	A few singular values.
`symbfact`	Symbolic factorization analysis.
`symamd`	Symmetric approximate minimum degree reordering method.
`symamdtree`	`symamd` followed by symmetric elimination tree postordering.
`symmd`	Symmetric minimum degree reordering method.
`symmlq`	Symmetric LQ iterative linear equation solution.
`symrcm`	Symmetric reverse Cuthill-Mckee reordering method.
`treelayout`	Lay out tree or forest.
`treeplot`	Plot tree.

17

Data Analysis

Because of its array orientation, MATLAB readily performs statistical analyses on data sets. While MATLAB by default considers data sets stored in column-oriented arrays, data analysis can be conducted along any specified dimension.

> That is, unless specified otherwise, each column of an array represents a different measured variable and each row represents individual samples or observations.

17.1 BASIC STATISTICAL ANALYSIS

For example, let's assume that the daily high temperature (in Celsius) of three cities over a 31-day month was recorded and assigned to the variable `temps` in a script M-file. Running the M-file puts the variable `temps` in the MATLAB workspace. Doing this work, the variable `temps` contains the data

```
>> temps
temps =
    12     8    18
    15     9    22
    12     5    19
    14     8    23
    12     6    22
    11     9    19
    15     9    15
     8    10    20
    19     7    18
    12     7    18
    14    10    19
    11     8    17
     9     7    23
     8     8    19
    15     8    18
     8     9    20
    10     7    17
    12     7    22
     9     8    19
    12     8    21
    12     8    20
    10     9    17
    13    12    18
     9    10    20
    10     6    22
    14     7    21
    12     5    22
    13     7    18
    15    10    23
    13    11    24
    12    12    22
```

Each row contains the high temperatures for a given day. Each column contains the high temperatures for a different city. To visualize the data, plot it:

```
>> d = 1:31;    % number the days of the month
>> plot(d,temps)
```

```
>> xlabel('Day of Month'), ylabel('Celsius')
>> title('Figure 17.1: Daily High Temperatures in Three Cities')
```

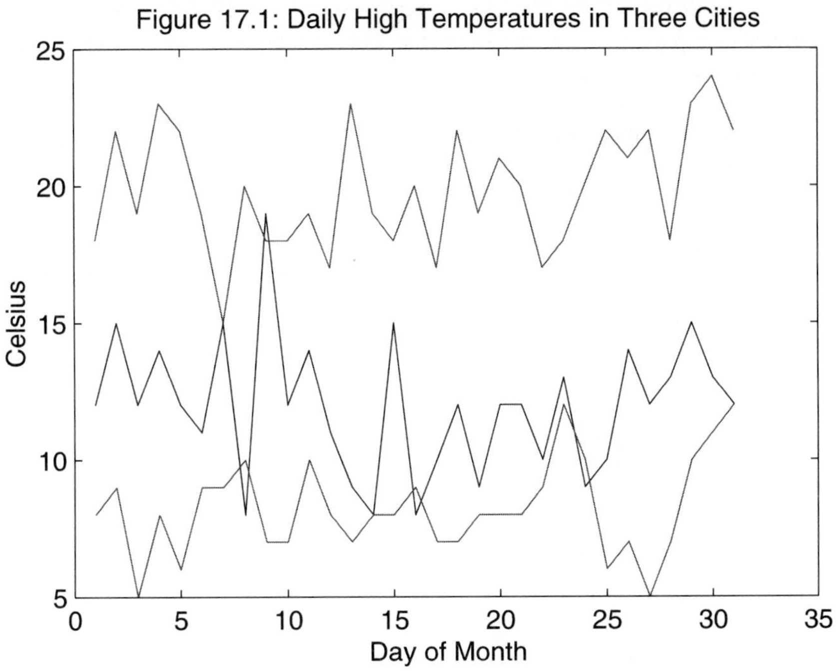

The plot command above illustrates yet another form of plot command usage. The variable d is a vector of length 31, whereas temps is a 31-by-3 matrix. Given this data, the plot command plots each column of temps versus d.

To illustrate some of the data analysis capabilities of MATLAB, consider the following commands based on the above temperature data.

```
>> avg_temp = mean(temps)
avg_temp =
   11.968    8.2258   19.871
```

shows that the third city has the highest average temperature. Here MATLAB found the average of each column individually. Taking the average again gives

```
>> avg_avg = mean(avg_temp)
avg_avg =
   13.3548
```

which returns the overall average temperature of the three cities.

> When the input to a data analysis function is a row or column vector, MATLAB simply performs the operation on the vector, returning a scalar result.

Alternately, you can specify the dimension to work on:

```
>> avg_temp = mean(temps,1)  % same as above, work down the rows
avg_temp =
       11.968        8.2258        19.871
>> avg_tempr = mean(temps,2)  % compute means across columns
avg_tempr =
       12.667
       15.333
           12
           15
       13.333
           13
           13
       12.667
       14.667
       12.333
       14.333
           12
           13
       11.667
       13.667
       12.333
       11.333
       13.667
           12
       13.667
       13.333
           12
       14.333
           13
       12.667
           14
           13
       12.667
           16
           16
       15.333
```

This is the three-city average temperature on each day. The scalar second argument to `mean` dictates the dimension to be analyzed; for example, 1 is the row dimension number, so perform the analysis accumulating information down the rows; 2 is the column dimension number, so perform the analysis accumulating information across the columns.

If `temps` were n-dimensional, the mean and other statistical functions could be used along any dimension. Consider the following example.

```
>> temps2 = temps+round(2*rand(size(temps))-1);
>> temps3 = cat(3,temps,temps2);
>> size(temps3)
ans =
    31     3     2
>> mean(temps3)  % same as mean(temps3,1)
ans(:,:,1) =
        11.968         8.2258         19.871
ans(:,:,2) =
        11.677         8.0968         19.903

>> squeeze(mean(temps3))' % squeeze to two dimensions
ans =
        11.968         8.2258         19.871
        11.677         8.0968         19.903

>> reshape(mean(temps3),3,2)' % alternate squeeze
ans =
        11.968         8.2258         19.871
        11.677         8.0968         19.903
>> mean(temps3,3)
ans =
            12              8             18
          14.5              9           22.5
            12            5.5             19
            14            7.5           23.5
          11.5            6.5           21.5
          10.5            9.5           18.5
            15            8.5           15.5
             8            9.5             20
          18.5            6.5           18.5
          11.5            6.5             18
          13.5             10             19
            11            7.5             17
           8.5            7.5           22.5
             8            7.5           18.5
            15            7.5           17.5
             8            9.5             20
            10              7           17.5
          11.5              7             22
             9              8           19.5
            12              8             21
            12              8             20
```

```
        9.5           9          17
         13        11.5          18
          9         9.5        20.5
         10           6        21.5
         14         7.5          21
         12         5.5        21.5
       12.5           7          18
         15         9.5          23
         13        11.5        24.5
       12.5        11.5          22
```

Here temps2 contains randomly generated data for the temperatures in the three cities for a second month. The variable temps3 contains the first month's temperatures on page 1 and the second month's temperatures on page 2. The function call mean(temps3) computes the means down each column on each page, giving a result that has 1 row, 3 columns, and 2 pages. This data can be squeezed to two rows and three columns using squeeze or reshape. The function call mean(temps3,3) computes the mean along the page dimension, which is the month-to-month mean of the temperatures on a given day, in a given city. The result is an array having 31 rows, 3 columns, and 1 page, that is, a 2-D array.

Going back to the 2-D case, consider the problem of finding the daily deviation from the mean of each city. That is, avg_temp(i) must be subtracted from column i of temps. One cannot simply issue the statement

```
>> temps - avg_temp
??? Error using ==> -
Matrix dimensions must agree.
```

because the operation is not a defined array operation (temps is 31 by 3, and avg_temp is 1 by 3). Perhaps the most straightforward approach is to use a For Loop, for example,

```
>> for c=1:3
      tdev(:,c) = temps(:,c) - avg_temp(c);
   end
```

While the above approach works, it is slower than using the array manipulation features of MATLAB. It is much faster to duplicate avg_temp to make it the size of temps and then do the subtraction:

```
>> tdev = temps - avg_temp(ones(31,1),:)
tdev =
    0.0323   -0.2258   -1.8710
    3.0323    0.7742    2.1290
    0.0323   -3.2258   -0.8710
    2.0323   -0.2258    3.1290
    0.0323   -2.2258    2.1290
   -0.9677    0.7742   -0.8710
    3.0323    0.7742   -4.8710
```

```
  -3.9677    1.7742    0.1290
   7.0323   -1.2258   -1.8710
   0.0323   -1.2258   -1.8710
   2.0323    1.7742   -0.8710
  -0.9677   -0.2258   -2.8710
  -2.9677   -1.2258    3.1290
  -3.9677   -0.2258   -0.8710
   3.0323   -0.2258   -1.8710
  -3.9677    0.7742    0.1290
  -1.9677   -1.2258   -2.8710
   0.0323   -1.2258    2.1290
  -2.9677   -0.2258   -0.8710
   0.0323   -0.2258    1.1290
   0.0323   -0.2258    0.1290
  -1.9677    0.7742   -2.8710
   1.0323    3.7742   -1.8710
  -2.9677    1.7742    0.1290
   0.0323   -3.2258    2.1290
   1.0323   -1.2258   -1.8710
   3.0323    1.7742    3.1290
   1.0323    2.7742    4.1290
   0.0323    3.7742    2.1290
```

Here `avg_temp(ones(31,1),:)` duplicates the first (and only) row of `avg_temp` 31 times, creating a 31-by-3 matrix whose *i*th column is `avg_temp(i)`. Alternatively, `avg_temp(ones(31,1),:)` can be replaced by `repmat(avg_temp,31,1)`, which replicates the row vector `avg_temp` 31 times in the row dimension and once in the column dimension.

MATLAB can also find minima and maxima. For example,

```
>> max_temp = max(temps)
max_temp =
    19    12    24
```

finds the maximum high temperature of each city over the month.

```
>> [max_temp,maxday] = max(temps)
max_temp =
    19    12    24
maxday =
     9    23    30
```

finds the maximum high temperature of each city and the row index `maxday` where the maximum appears. For this example, `maxday` identifies the day of the month when the highest temperature occurred.

```
>> min_temp = min(temps)
min_temp =
     8     5    15
```

finds the minimum high temperature of each city.

```
>> [min_temp,minday] = min(temps)
min_temp =
     8     5    15
minday =
     8     3     7
```

finds the minimum high temperature of each city and the row index `minday` where the minimum appears. For this example, `minday` identifies the day of the month when the lowest high temperature occurred.

Other standard statistical measures are also provided in MATLAB, for example,

```
>> s_dev = std(temps) % standard deviation in each city
s_dev =
    2.5098    1.7646    2.2322
>> median(temps) % median temperature in each city
ans =
    12     8    20
>> cov(temps) % covariance
ans =
        6.2989        0.04086       -0.13763
       0.04086          3.114       0.063441
      -0.13763       0.063441         4.9828
>> corrcoef(temps) % correlation coefficients
ans =
             1      0.0092259      -0.024567
     0.0092259              1       0.016106
     -0.024567       0.016106              1
```

You can also compute differences from day to day by using the function `diff`:

```
>> daily_change = diff(temps)
daily_change =
     3     1     4
    -3    -4    -3
     2     3     4
    -2    -2    -1
    -1     3    -3
     4     0    -4
    -7     1     5
    11    -3    -2
    -7     0     0
     2     3     1
    -3    -2    -2
    -2    -1     6
    -1     1    -4
     7     0    -1
    -7     1     2
```

```
     2    -2    -3
     2     0     5
    -3     1    -3
     3     0     2
     0     0    -1
    -2     1    -3
     3     3     1
    -4    -2     2
     1    -4     2
     4     1    -1
    -2    -2     1
     1     2    -4
     2     3     5
    -2     1     1
    -1     1    -2
```

computes the difference between daily high temperatures, which describes how much the daily high temperature varied from day to day. For example, between the first and second days of the month, the first row of `daily_change` is the amount the daily high changed. As with other functions, the difference can be computed along other dimensions as well, for example,

```
>> city_change = diff(temps,1,2)
city_change =
    -4    10
    -6    13
    -7    14
    -6    15
    -6    16
    -2    10
    -6     6
     2    10
   -12    11
    -5    11
    -4     9
    -3     9
    -2    16
     0    11
    -7    10
     1    11
    -3    10
    -5    15
    -1    11
    -4    13
    -4    12
    -1     8
    -1     6
     1    10
    -4    16
    -7    14
```

```
    -7    17
    -6    11
    -5    13
    -2    13
     0    10
```

Here `diff(temps,1,2)` says to compute a first-order difference along dimension 2. Therefore, the above result is the city difference. The first column is the difference between city 2 and city 1; the second column is the difference between city 3 and city 2.

It is common to use the value `NaN` to signify missing data. When this is done, most statistical functions require special treatment because operations on `NaN`s generally produce `NaN`s. For example,

```
>> temps4 = temps;     % copy data
>> temps4(5,1) = nan; % insert some NaNs
>> temps4(29,2) = nan;
>> temps4(13:14,3) = nan
temps4 =
    12     8    18
    15     9    22
    12     5    19
    14     8    23
   NaN     6    22
    11     9    19
    15     9    15
     8    10    20
    19     7    18
    12     7    18
    14    10    19
    11     8    17
     9     7   NaN
     8     8   NaN
    15     8    18
     8     9    20
    10     7    17
    12     7    22
     9     8    19
    12     8    21
    12     8    20
    10     9    17
    13    12    18
     9    10    20
    10     6    22
    14     7    21
    12     5    22
    13     7    18
    15   NaN    23
    13    11    24
    12    12    22
```

```
>> max(temps4) % max and min work with NaNs
ans =
    19    12    24
>> mean(temps4) % other statistical functions do not
ans =
   NaN   NaN   NaN
>> std(temps4)
ans =
   NaN   NaN   NaN
```

One solution to this NaN problem is to write your own functions that exclude NaN elements, for example,

```
>> m = zeros(1,3); % preallocate memory for results
>> for i=1:3
       idx = ~isnan(temps4(:,i));
       m(i)=mean(temps4(idx,i));
   end
>> m
m =
           13       7.3333       19.667
```

Here the function isnan is used to locate elements containing NaN. Then the mean down each column is found by indexing only non-NaN elements. It is not possible to exclude NaN elements over all columns simultaneously because not all columns have the same number of NaN elements.

17.2 BASIC DATA ANALYSIS

In addition to statistical data analysis, MATLAB offers a variety of general-purpose data analysis functions. For example, the temperature data above can be filtered using the function filter(b,a,data):

```
>> filter(ones(1,4),4,temps)
ans =
            3            2          4.5
         6.75         4.25           10
         9.75          5.5        14.75
        13.25          7.5         20.5
        13.25            7         21.5
        12.25            7        20.75
           13            8        19.75
         11.5          8.5           19
        13.25         8.75           18
         13.5         8.25        17.75
        13.25          8.5        18.75
```

```
     14          8         18
   11.5          8      19.25
   10.5       8.25       19.5
  10.75       7.75      19.25
     10          8         20
  10.25          8       18.5
  11.25       7.75      19.25
   9.75       7.75       19.5
  10.75        7.5      19.75
  11.25       7.75       20.5
  10.75       8.25      19.25
  11.75       9.25         19
     11       9.75      18.75
   10.5       9.25      19.25
   11.5       8.75      20.25
  11.25          7      21.25
  12.25       6.25      20.75
   13.5       7.25         21
  13.25       8.25      21.75
  13.25         10      21.75
```

Here the filter implemented is $4y_n = x_n + x_{n-1} + x_{n-2} + x_{n-3}$ or, equivalently, $y_n = (x_n + x_{n-1} + x_{n-2} + x_{n-3})/4$. That is, each column of `temps` is passed through a moving average filter of length 4. Any realizable filter structure can be applied by specifying different coefficients for the input and output coefficient vectors.

The function `y=filter(b,a,x)` implements the following general tapped delay-line algorithm:

$$\sum_{k=0}^{N} a_{k+1} y_{n-k} = \sum_{k=0}^{M} b_{k+1} x_{n-k}$$

where the vector `a` is the tap weight vector a_{k+1} on the output, and the vector `b` is the tap weight vector b_{k+1} on the input. For $N = 2$ and $M = 3$, the above equation is equivalent to

$$a_1 y_n + a_2 y_{n-1} + a_3 y_{n-2} = b_1 x_n + b_2 x_{n-1} + b_3 x_{n-2} + b_4 x_{n-3}$$

Data can also be sorted, for example,

```
>> data = rand(10,1) % create some data
data =
        0.61543
        0.79194
        0.92181
        0.73821
        0.17627
        0.40571
        0.93547
        0.9169
        0.41027
        0.89365
```

```
>> [sdata,sidx] = sort(data) % sort in ascending order
sdata =
      0.17627
      0.40571
      0.41027
      0.61543
      0.73821
      0.79194
      0.89365
       0.9169
      0.92181
      0.93547
sidx =
     5
     6
     9
     1
     4
     2
    10
     8
     3
     7
```

The second output of the `sort` function is the sorted index order. That is, the fifth element in `data` has the lowest value, and the seventh element in `data` has the largest value.

Sometimes it is important to know the ***rank*** of the data. For example, what is the rank or position of the *i*th data point in the unsorted array with respect to the sorted array? With MATLAB array indexing, the rank is found by the single statement

```
>> ridx(sidx) = 1:10 % ridx is rank
ridx =
     4     6     9     5     1     2    10     8     3     7
```

That is, the first element of the unsorted data appears fourth in the sorted data, and the last element is seventh.

The function `sort` always sorts in ascending order. If descending order is desired, the results from `sort` must be flipped, for example,

```
>> sdata = sdata(end:-1:1); % turn sort around

>> sidx=sidx(end:-1:1)      % turn sort index around
sidx =
     7
     3
     8
    10
```

```
    2
    4
    1
    9
    6
    5
```

When the array to be sorted is a matrix like `temps` above, each column is sorted and each column produces a column in the optional index matrix. As with the other data analysis functions, the dimension to perform analysis on can be specified as a final input argument.

Very often it is desirable to use the results of sorting one column of an array and apply that sort order to all remaining columns. For example,

```
>> newdata = randn(10,4) % new data for sorting
newdata =
    -0.43256    -0.18671     0.29441    -0.39989
     -1.6656     0.72579     -1.3362        0.69
     0.12533    -0.58832     0.71432     0.81562
     0.28768      2.1832      1.6236     0.71191
     -1.1465     -0.1364    -0.69178      1.2902
      1.1909     0.11393       0.858      0.6686
      1.1892      1.0668       1.254      1.1908
   -0.037633    0.059281     -1.5937     -1.2025
     0.32729   -0.095648      -1.441    -0.01979
     0.17464    -0.83235     0.57115    -0.15672
>> [tmp,idx] = sort(newdata(:,2)); % sort second column
>> newdatas = newdata(idx,:) % shuffle rows using idx from 2nd column
newdatas =
     0.17464    -0.83235     0.57115    -0.15672
     0.12533    -0.58832     0.71432     0.81562
    -0.43256    -0.18671     0.29441    -0.39989
     -1.1465     -0.1364    -0.69178      1.2902
     0.32729   -0.095648      -1.441    -0.01979
   -0.037633    0.059281     -1.5937     -1.2025
      1.1909     0.11393       0.858      0.6686
     -1.6656     0.72579     -1.3362        0.69
      1.1892      1.0668       1.254      1.1908
     0.28768      2.1832      1.6236     0.71191
```

Here, the second column of the random array is sorted in increasing order. Then the sort index is used to shuffle rows in all columns. For example, the last row of `newdata` is now the first row in `newdatas` because the last element in the second column is the smallest element in the second column.

A vector is strictly monotonic if its elements either always increase or always decrease as one proceeds down the array. The function `diff` is useful for determining monotonicity, for example,

```
>> A = diff(data) % check random data
A =
        0.1765
       0.12988
      -0.18361
      -0.56194
       0.22944
       0.52976
     -0.018565
      -0.50663
       0.48338
>> mono = all(A>0) | all(A<0) % as expected, not monotonic
mono =
     0
>> B = diff(sdata) % check random data after sorting
B =
       0.22944
      0.004564
       0.20516
       0.12277
       0.05373
       0.10171
      0.023255
     0.0049085
      0.013657
>> mono = all(B>0) | all(B<0) % as expected, monotonic
mono =
     1
```

Furthermore, a monotonic vector is equally spaced if

```
>> all(diff(diff(sdata))==0) % random data is not equally spaced
ans =
     0
>> all(diff(diff(1:25))==0) % but numbers 1 to 25 are equally spaced
ans =
     1
```

17.3 DATA ANALYSIS AND STATISTICAL FUNCTIONS

By default, data analysis in MATLAB is performed on column-oriented matrices. Different variables are stored in individual columns, and each row represents a different observation of each variable. Many data analysis functions work along any dimension, provided it is specified as the last input argument. The data analysis and statistical functions in MATLAB are shown in the following table.

Function	Description
`corrcoef(A)`	Correlation coefficients.
`cov(A)`	Covariance matrix.
`cplxpair(v)`	Sort vector into complex conjugate pairs.
`cumprod(A)`	Cumulative product of elements.
`cumsum(A)`	Cumulative sum of elements.
`cumtrapz(A)`	Cumulative trapezoidal integration.
`del2(A)`	Discrete Laplacian (surface curvature).
`diff(A)`	Differences between elements.
`gradient(Z,dx,dy)`	Approximate surface gradient.
`histc(X,edges)`	Histogram count and bin locations using bins marked by `edges`.
`max(A)`	Maximum values.
`median(A)`	Median values.
`min(A)`	Minimum values.
`prod(A)`	Product of elements.
`sort(A)`	Ascending sort.
`sortrows(A)`	Sort rows in ascending order, i.e., dictionary sort.
`std(A)`	Standard deviation.
`sum(A)`	Sum of elements.
`trapz(A)`	Trapezoidal integration.
`var(A)`	Variance, i.e., square of standard deviation.

18

Data Interpolation

Interpolation is a way of estimating values of a function between those given by some set of data points. In particular, interpolation is a valuable tool when one cannot quickly evaluate the function at the desired intermediate points. For example, this is true when the data points are the result of some experimental measurements or lengthy computational procedure. MATLAB provides tools for interpolating in any number of dimensions by using multidimensional arrays. To illustrate interpolation, only 1- and 2-D interpolation are considered in depth here. However, the functions used for higher dimensions are briefly discussed.

18.1 ONE-DIMENSIONAL INTERPOLATION

Perhaps the simplest example of interpolation is MATLAB plots. By default, MATLAB draws straight lines connecting the data points used to make a plot. This linear interpolation guesses that intermediate values fall on a straight line between the entered points. Certainly as the number of data points increases and the distance between them decreases, linear interpolation becomes more accurate, for example,

```
>> x1 = linspace(0,2*pi,60);
>> x2 = linspace(0,2*pi,6);
>> plot(x1,sin(x1),x2,sin(x2),'--')
>> xlabel('x'),ylabel('sin(x)')
>> title('Figure 18.1: Linear Interpolation')
```

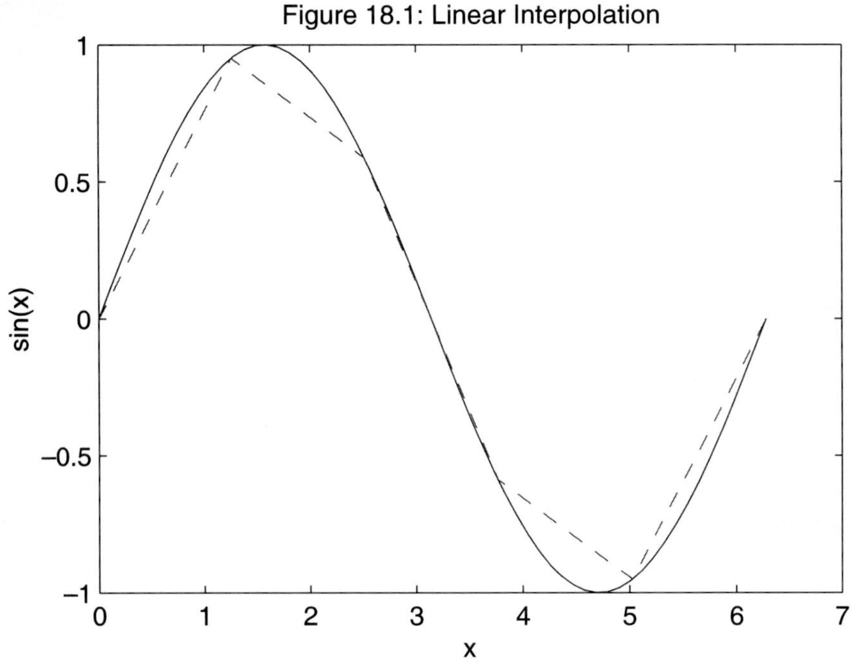

Of the two plots of the sine function shown, the one using 60 points is much more accurate between the data points than the one using only 6 points.

To illustrate 1-D interpolation consider the following example. The threshold of audibility, that is, the lowest perceptible sound level, of the human ear varies with frequency. Typical data are given below.

```
>> Hz=[20:10:100 200:100:1000 1500 2000:1000:10000];  % frequencies in Hertz
>> spl =[76 66 59  54  49  46  43 40 38 22 ... % sound pressure level in dB
        14  9  6 3.5 2.5 1.4 0.7  0 -1 -3 ...
        -8 -7 -2   2   7   9  11 12];
```

The sound pressure levels are normalized so that 0 dB appears at 1000 Hz. Since the frequencies span such a large range, plot the data using a logarithmic x-axis:

```
>> semilogx(Hz,spl,'-o')
>> xlabel('Frequency, Hz')
```

```
>> ylabel('Relative Sound Pressure Level, dB')
>> title('Figure 18.2: Threshold of Human Hearing')
>> grid on
```

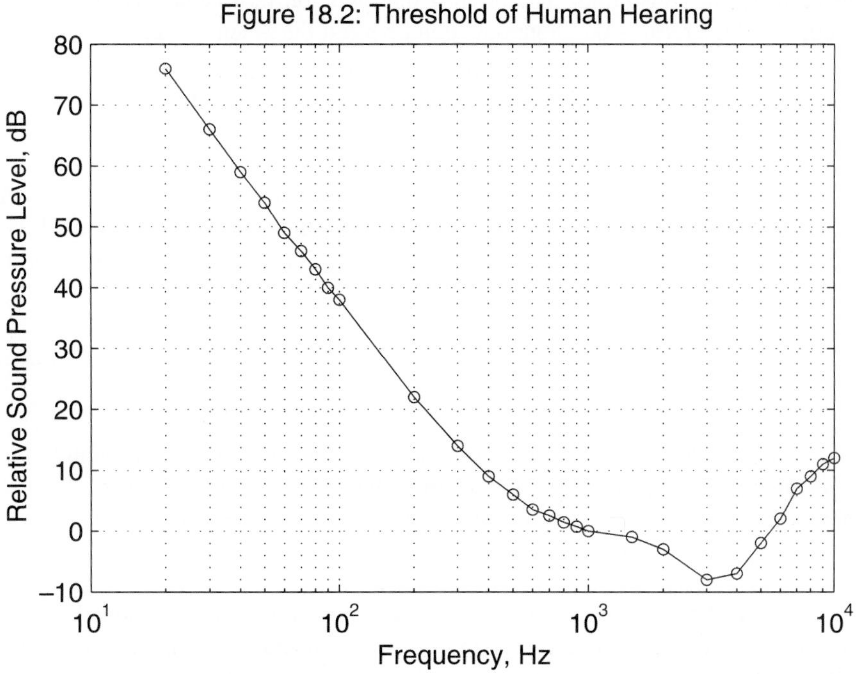

Based on this plot, the human ear is most sensitive to tones around 3 kHz. Given this data, let's use the function `interp1` to estimate the sound pressure level in several different ways at a frequency of 2.5 kHz.

```
>> s = interp1(Hz,spl,2.5e3)            % linear interpolation
s =
        -5.5
>> s = interp1(Hz,spl,2.5e3,'linear')  % linear interpolation again
s =
        -5.5
>> s = interp1(Hz,spl,2.5e3,'cubic')   % cubic interpolation
s =
     -6.0488
>> s = interp1(Hz,spl,2.5e3,'spline')  % cubic spline interpolation
s =
      -5.869
>> s = interp1(Hz,spl,2.5e3,'nearest') % nearest-neighbor interpolation
s =
    -8
```

Note the differences in these results. The first two results return exactly what is shown in the figure at 2.5 kHz since MATLAB linearly interpolates between data points on plots. Cubic and spline interpolation fit cubic, that is, third-order, polynomials to each data interval using different constraints. The poorest interpolation in this case is the nearest-neighbor method, which returns the input data point nearest the given value.

> The function `interp1` has changed in MATLAB version 6. The `'cubic'` method is now based on a piecewise cubic Hermite interpolating polynomial, which preserves monotonicity and data extrema. The MATLAB version 5 `'cubic'` method is specified by using `'v5cubic'` for the method string.

So how do you choose an interpolation method for a given problem? In many cases linear interpolation is sufficient. In fact, that's why it is the default method. While the nearest-neighbor method produced poor results here, it is often used when speed is important or the data set is large. The most time-consuming method is spline, but it often produces the most desirable results.

While the above case considered only a single interpolation point, `interp1` can handle any arbitrary number of points. In fact, one of the most common uses of cubic or spline interpolation is to smooth data. That is, given a set of data, use interpolation to evaluate the data at a finer interval, for example,

```
>> Hzi = linspace(2e3,5e3);  % look closely near minimum
>> spli = interp1(Hz,spl,Hzi,'spline');  % interpolate near minimum
>> i = find(Hz>=2e3 & Hz<=5e3);  % find original data indices near minimum

>> semilogx(Hz(i),spl(i),'--o',Hzi,spli)  % plot old and new data
>> xlabel('Frequency, Hz')
>> ylabel('Relative Sound Pressure Level, dB')
>> title('Figure 18.3: Threshold of Human Hearing')
>> grid on
```

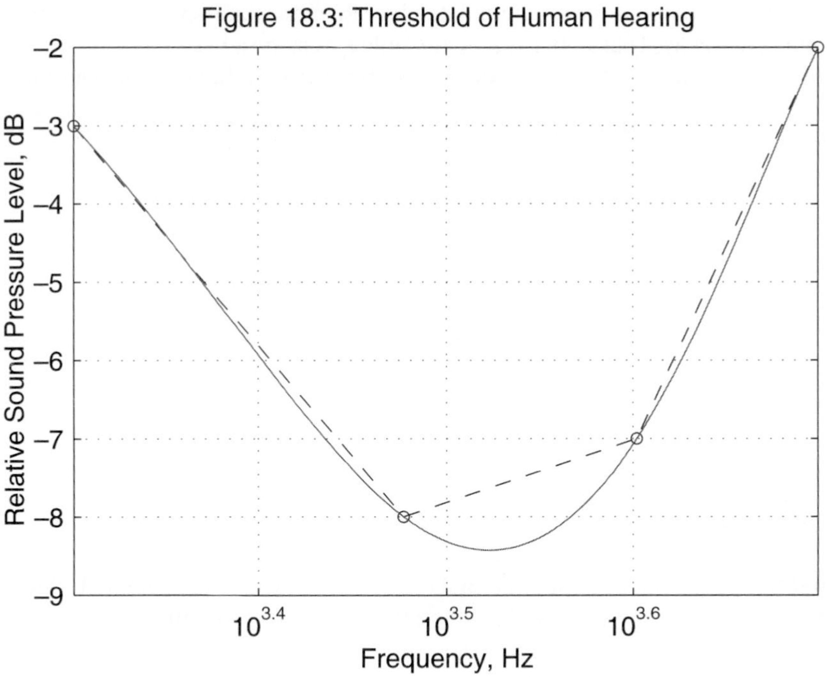

In the plot, the dashed line is the linear interpolation, the solid line is the cubic interpolation, and the original data is marked with `'o'`. By asking for a finer resolution on the frequency axis and using spline interpolation, we have a smoother estimate of the sound pressure level. In particular, note how the slope of the spline solution does not change abruptly at the data points.

With this data we can make a better estimate of the frequency of greatest sensitivity, for example,

```
>> [spl_min,i] = min(spli) % minimum and index of minimum
spl_min =
      -8.4245
i =
    45
>> Hz_min = Hzi(i)  % frequency at minimum
Hz_min =
       3333.3
```

According to this analysis, the human ear is most sensitive to tones near 3.33 kHz.

It is important to recognize the major restriction enforced by `interp1`, namely, the independent variable must be monotonic. That is, the first variable must always increase or must always decrease. In our example, `Hz` is monotonic.

Finally, it is possible to interpolate more than one data set at a time if y is a column-oriented data array. That is, if x is a vector, either y can be a vector as shown above or it can be an array having length(x) rows and any number of columns. Consider the example

```
>> x = linspace(0,2*pi,11)'; % example data
>> y = [sin(x) cos(x) tan(x)];
>> size(y) % three columns
ans =
    11     3
>> xi = linspace(0,2*pi); % interpolate on a finer scale
>> yi = interp1(x,y,xi,'cubic');
>> size(yi) % result is all three columns interpolated
ans =
   100     3
```

Here, sin(x), cos(x), and tan(x) are all interpolated at the points in xi.

18.2 TWO-DIMENSIONAL INTERPOLATION

Two-dimensional interpolation is based on the same underlying ideas as 1-D interpolation. However as the name implies, 2-D interpolation interpolates functions of two variables, $z = f(x,y)$. To illustrate this added dimension consider the following example. An exploration company is using sonar to map the ocean floor. At points every 0.5 km on a rectangular grid, the ocean depth in meters is recorded for later analysis. A portion of the data collected is entered into MATLAB in the script M-file ocean.m, as shown below.

```
% ocean.m, example test data
% ocean depth data
x = 0:.5:4;  % x-axis (varies across the rows of z)
y = 0:.5:6;  % y-axis (varies down the columns of z)
z=[100    99   100    99   100    99    99    99   100
   100    99    99    99   100    99   100    99    99
    99    99    98    98   100    99   100   100   100
   100    98    97    97    99   100   100   100    99
   101   100    98    98   100   102   103   100   100
   102   103   101   100   102   106   104   101   100
    99   102   100   100   103   108   106   101    99
    97    99   100   100   102   105   103   101   100
   100   102   103   101   102   103   102   100    99
   100   102   103   102   101   101   100    99    99
   100   100   101   101   100   100   100    99    99
   100   100   100   100   100    99    99    99    99
   100   100   100    99    99   100    99   100    99];
```

A plot of this data can be displayed by entering

```
>> mesh(x,y,z)
>> xlabel('X-axis, km')
>> ylabel('Y-axis, km')
>> zlabel('Ocean Depth, m')
>> title('Figure 18.4: Ocean Depth Measurements')
```

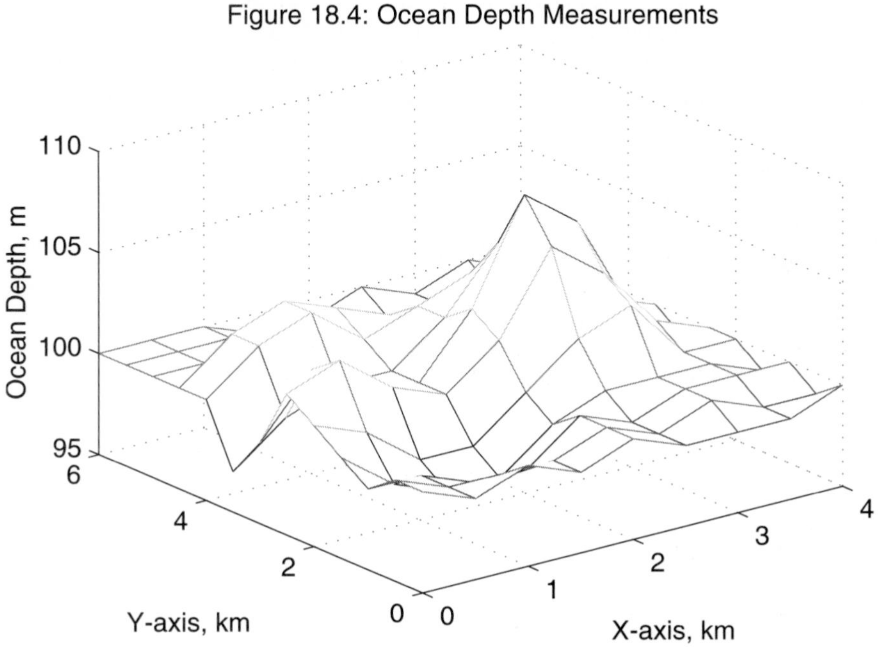

With this data, the depth at arbitrary points within the rectangle can be found by using the function `interp2`, for example,

```
>> zi = interp2(x,y,z,2.2,3.3)
zi =
       103.92
>> zi = interp2(x,y,z,2.2,3.3,'linear')
zi =
       103.92
>> zi = interp2(x,y,z,2.2,3.3,'cubic')
zi =
       104.19
>> zi = interp2(x,y,z,2.2,3.3,'nearest')
zi =
   102
```

As was the case with 1-D interpolation, several interpolation methods are available, with the default method being linear.

Once again, we can interpolate on a finer scale or mesh to smooth the plot, for example,

```
>> xi = linspace(0,4,30);  % finer x-axis
>> yi = linspace(0,6,40);  % finer y-axis
```

For each value in `xi`, we wish to interpolate at all values in `yi`. That is, we wish to create a grid of all combinations of the values of `xi` and `yi` and then interpolate at all these points. The function `meshgrid` accepts two vectors and produces two arrays containing duplicates of its inputs so that all combinations of the inputs are considered, for example,

```
>> xtest = 1:5
xtest =
     1     2     3     4     5
>> ytest = 6:9
ytest =
     6     7     8     9
>> [xx,yy] = meshgrid(xtest,ytest)
xx =
     1     2     3     4     5
     1     2     3     4     5
     1     2     3     4     5
     1     2     3     4     5
yy =
     6     6     6     6     6
     7     7     7     7     7
     8     8     8     8     8
     9     9     9     9     9
```

As shown above, `xx` has `length(ytest)` rows, each containing `xtest`, and `yy` has `length(xtest)` columns, each containing `ytest`. With this structure, `xx(i,j)` and `yy(i,j)` for all `i` and `j` cover all combinations of the original vectors `xtest` and `ytest`.

Applying `meshgrid` to our ocean depth example produces

```
>> [xxi,yyi] = meshgrid(xi,yi);  % grid of all combinations
>> size(xxi) % xxi has 40 rows each containing xi
ans =
    40    30
>> size(yyi) % yyi has 30 columns each containing yi
ans =
    40    30
```

Given `xxi` and `yyi`, the ocean depth can now be interpolated on the finer scale by entering

```
>> zzi = interp2(x,y,z,xxi,yyi,'cubic');  % interpolate
>> size(zzi) % zzi is the same size as xxi and yyi
ans =
    40    30
>> mesh(xxi,yyi,zzi)  % plot smoothed data
>> hold on
>> [xx,yy] = meshgrid(x,y); % grid original data
>> plot3(xx,yy,z+0.1,'ok')  % plot original data up a bit to show nodes
>> hold off
>> xlabel('X-axis, km')
>> ylabel('Y-axis, km')
>> zlabel('Ocean Depth, m')
>> title('Figure 18.5: 2-D Smoothing')
```

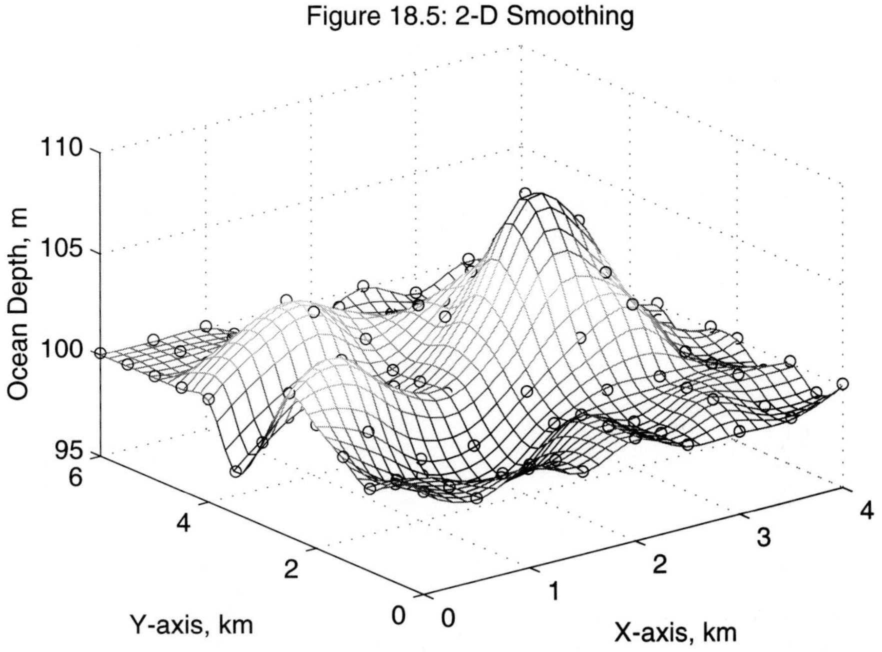

Using this data, we can now estimate the peak and its location:

```
>> zmax = max(max(zzi))
zmax =
       108.05
>> [i,j] = find(zmax==zzi);
>> xmax = xi(j)
xmax =
       2.6207
>> ymax = yi(i)
ymax =
       2.9231
```

The concepts discussed in these first two sections extend naturally to higher dimensions where `ndgrid`, `interp3`, and `interpn` apply. `ndgrid` is the multidimensional equivalent of `meshgrid`. Multidimensional interpolation uses multidimensional arrays in a straightforward way to organize the data and perform the interpolation. `interp3` performs interpolation in 3-D space, and `interpn` performs interpolation in higher-order dimensions. Both `interp3` and `interpn` offer method choices of `'linear'`, `'cubic'` and `'nearest'`. For more information regarding these functions see the MATLAB documentation and the on-line help.

18.3 TRIANGULATION AND SCATTERED DATA

In a number of applications such as those involving geometric analysis, data points are often scattered rather than appearing on a rectangular grid like the ocean data in the example discussed in the last section. For example, consider the 2-D random data

```
>> x = randn(1,12);
>> y = randn(1,12);
>> z = zeros(1,12); % no z component for now
>> plot(x,y,'o')
>> title('Figure 18.6: Random Data')
```

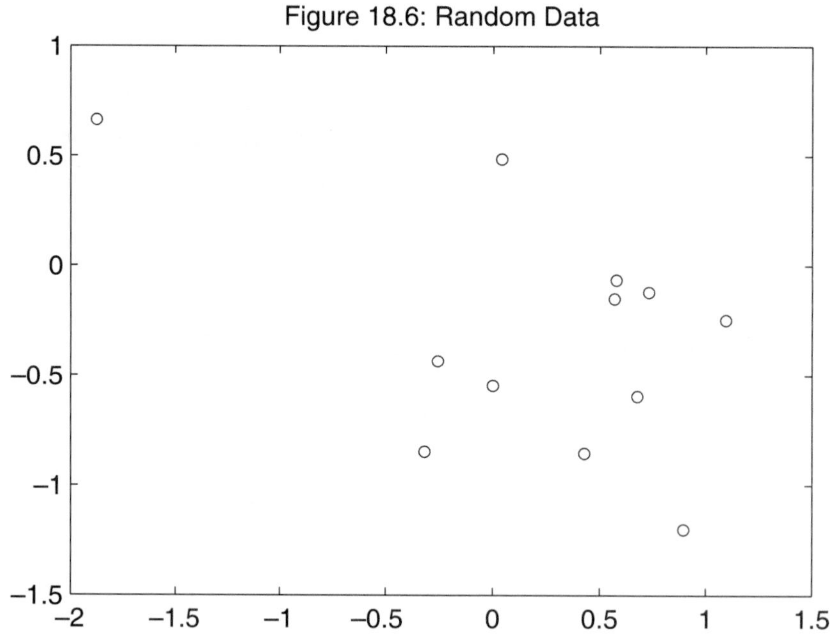

Given scattered data such as that shown, it is common to apply Delaunay triangulation, which returns a set of triangles connecting the data points such that no data points are contained within any triangle. The MATLAB function `delaunay` accepts data points and returns a list of indices into the data that identify the triangle vertices. For the above data `delaunay` returns

```
>> tri = delaunay(x,y)
tri =
     2     5     6
    10     6     5
     1     5     2
    12     1     2
     3     6    10
     1    10     5
    11     7    10
     7     3    10
     1    11    10
     8     7    11
     1     8    11
    12     8     1
     9     8    12
     4    12     2
     4     9    12
     9     7     8
     9     3     7
```

Each row contains indices into `x` and `y` that identify triangle vertices. For example, the first triangle is described by the data points in `x([2 5 6])` and `y([2 5 6])`. The triangles can be plotted using the function `trimesh`:

```
>> hold on, trimesh(tri,x,y,z), hold off
>> hidden off
>> title('Figure 18.7: Delaunay Triangulation')
```

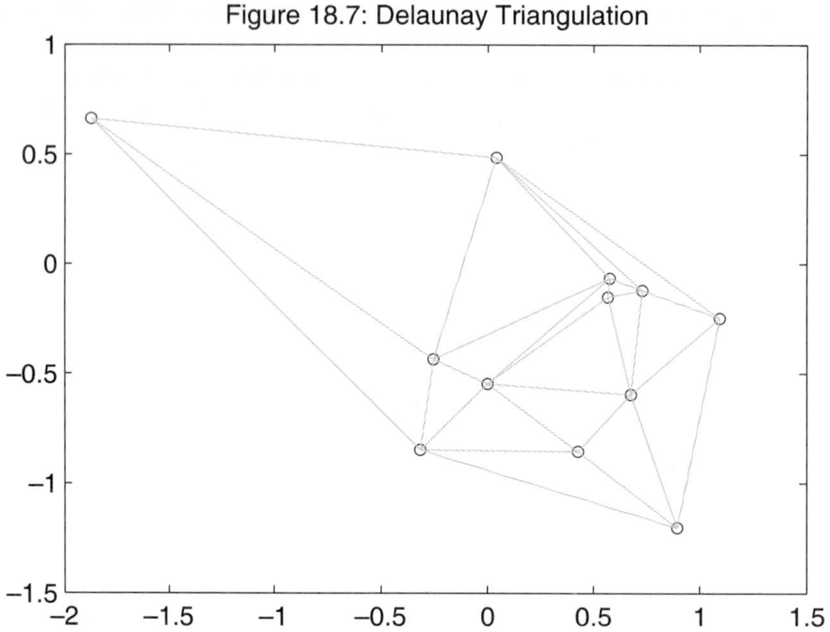

Once the Delaunay triangulation is known, the functions tsearch and dsearch can be used to interpolate it. For example, the triangle enclosing the origin is

```
>> tsearch(x,y,tri,0,0) % find row of tri closest to (0,0)
ans =
    13
>> tri(ans,:) % vertices of triangle closest to (0,0)
ans =
     9     8    12
```

Naturally tsearch accepts multiple values, for example,

```
>> tsearch(x,y,tri,[-.5 1],[.1 .5])
ans =
    15   NaN
```

Here, the 15th triangle encloses the point $(-0.5, 0.1)$, and no triangle encloses the point $(1, 0.5)$.

Rather than returning the triangle enclosing one or more data points, the function dsearch returns the indices into x and y that are closest to the desired points, for example,

```
>> dsearch(x,y,tri,[-.5 .1],[.1 .5])
ans =
    12     7
```

Here, the point `(x(12),y(12))` is closest to the point $(-0.5, 1)$, and the point `(x(7), y(7))` is closest to (0.1, 0.5).

In addition to interpolating the data, it is often useful to know which points form the outer boundary or ***convex hull*** for the set. The function `convhull` returns indices into `x` and `y` that describe the convex hull, as in the following example.

```
>> k = convhull(x,y)'
k =
     2     6     3     9     4     2
```

Note that `convhull` returns the indices of a closed curve since the first and last index values are the same. Based on the data returned by `convhull`, the boundary can be drawn, for example,

```
>> plot(x,y,'o',x(k),y(k))
>> title('Figure 18.8: Convex Hull')
```

Figure 18.8: Convex Hull

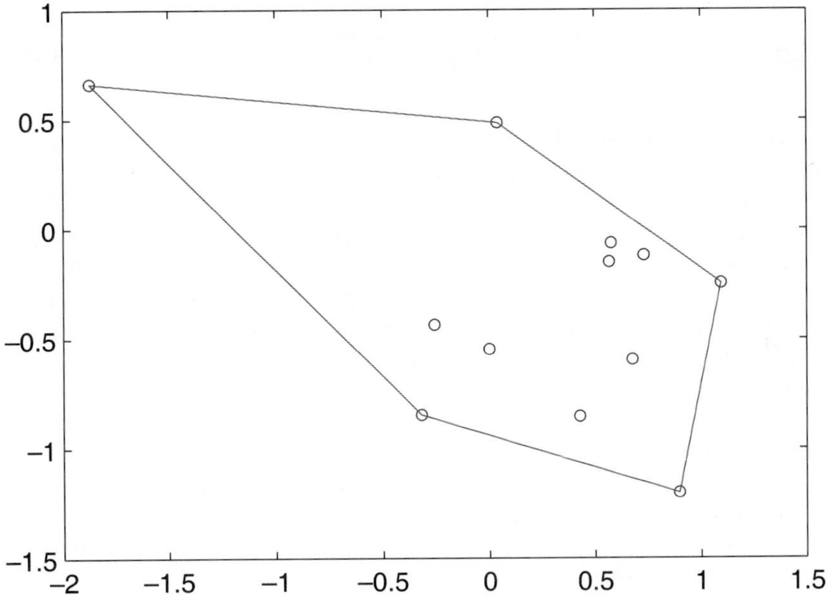

It is also possible to define and draw the lines that separate regions in the plane that are closest to a particular data point. These lines form what is called a ***Voronoi polygon.*** In MATLAB these lines are drawn by the function `voronoi`, for example,

```
>> voronoi(x,y,tri)
>> title('Figure 18.9: Voronoi Diagram')
```

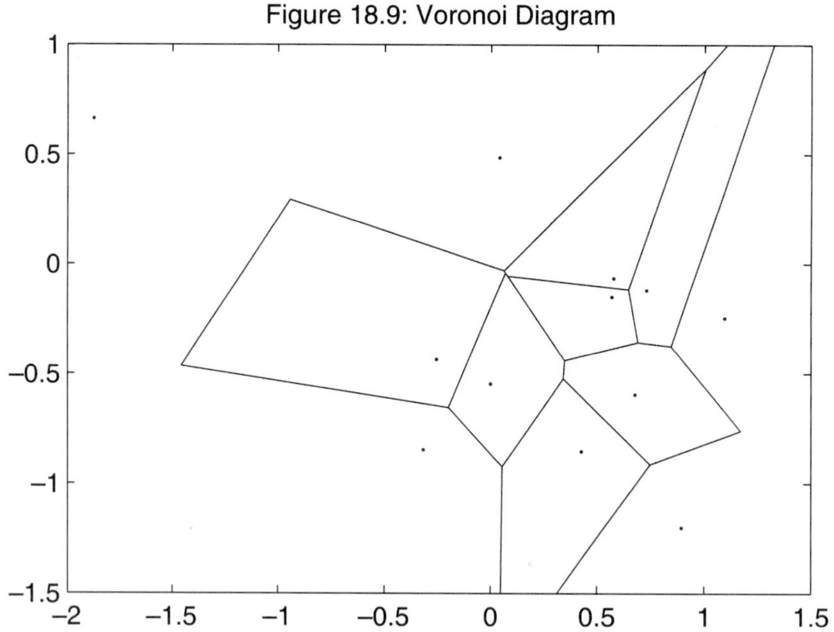

Finally, it is possible to interpolate a Delaunay triangulation to produce interpolated points on a rectangular grid using the function `griddata`. In particular, this step is required to use functions such as `surf` and other standard plotting routines. These plotting routines require data that contains information at a complete sequence of points along two coordinate axes rather than the scattered data that `trimesh` utilizes. Think about a map analogy. Delaunay triangulation allows you to identify specific scattered points on a map. The function `griddata` uses this information to construct an approximation to the rest of the map, filling in data in a user-specified rectangular region in two coordinate directions. Consider the following.

```
>> z = rand(1,12); % now use some random z axis data
>> xi = linspace(min(x),max(x),30);  % x interpolation points
>> yi = linspace(min(y),max(y),30);  % y interpolation points
>> [Xi,Yi] = meshgrid(xi,yi);        % create grid of x and y
>> Zi = griddata(x,y,z,Xi,Yi);       % grid the data at Xi,Yi points
>> mesh(Xi,Yi,Zi)
>> hold on
>> plot3(x,y,z,'ko')  % show original data as well
>> hold off
>> title('Figure 18.10: Griddata Example')
```

Figure 18.10: Griddata Example

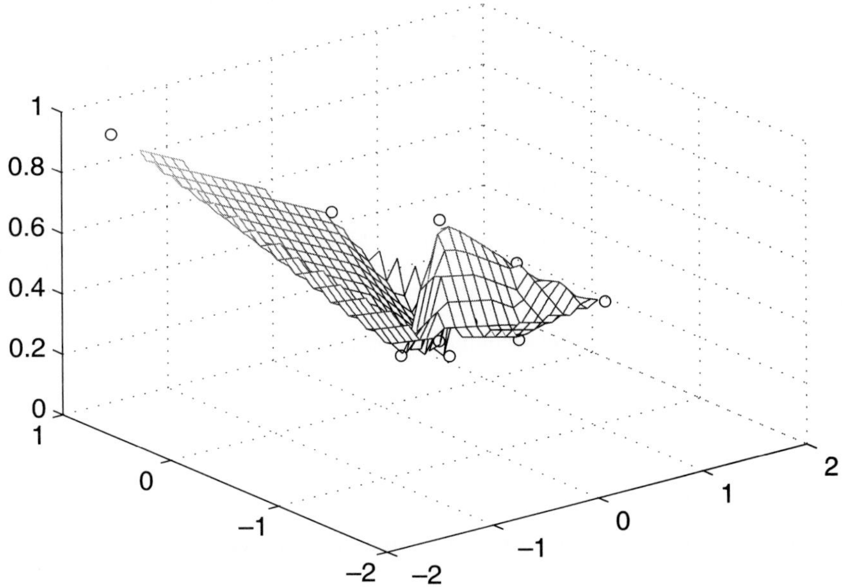

In the above example, the information at the 12 scattered data points was interpolated to produce an array of data on a 30-by-30 grid in the *x*-*y* plane. The variable `Zi` contains a 30-by-30 array of points linearly interpolated from the triangulation of the data in `x`, `y` and `z`. Just as `interp1` and `interp2` support other interpolations, `griddata` also supports others. For example,

```
>> Zi = griddata(x,y,z,Xi,Yi,'linear')  % same as above (default)
>> Zi = griddata(x,y,z,Xi,Yi,'cubic')   % triangle based cubic interpolation
>> Zi = griddata(x,y,z,Xi,Yi,'nearest') % triangle based nearest neighbor
>> Zi = griddata(x,y,z,Xi,Yi,'invdist') % inverse distance method
```

18.4 SUMMARY

In MATLAB version 6, the triangulation functions discussed in this chapter have *n*-dimensional forms as well. The data interpolation functions in MATLAB are summarized in the table below.

Function	Description
`interp1`	1-D interpolation.
`interp1q`	1-D quick interpolation (no error checking).

Function	Description
interp2	2-D interpolation.
interp3	3-D interpolation.
interpft	1-D interpolation using FFT method.
interpn	*n*-D interpolation.
griddata	2-D rectangular gridding.
griddata3	3-D rectangular gridding.
griddatan	*n*-D rectangular gridding.
delaunay	Delaunay triangulation.
delaunay3	3-D Delaunay tesselation.
delaunayn	*n*-D Delaunay tesselation.
dsearch	Nearest point search in Delaunay triangulation.
tsearch	Closest triangle search.
tsearchn	*n*-D closest triangle search.
convhull	Convex hull.
convhulln	*n*-D convex hull.
voronoi	Voronoi diagram.
voronoin	*n*-D Voronoi diagram.

19

Polynomials

MATLAB provides a number of functions for manipulating polynomials. Polynomials are easily differentiated, and integrated, and it is straightforward to find polynomial roots. However, higher-order polynomials pose numerical difficulties in a number of situations and therefore should be used with caution.

19.1 ROOTS

Finding the roots of a polynomial, that is, the values for which the polynomial is zero, is a problem common to many disciplines. MATLAB solves this problem and provides other polynomial manipulation tools as well. In MATLAB a polynomial is represented by a row vector of its coefficients in descending order. For example, the polynomial $x^4 - 12x^3 + 0x^2 + 25x + 116$ is entered as

```
>> p = [1 -12 0 25 116]
p =
     1   -12     0    25   116
```

Note that terms with zero coefficients must be included. MATLAB has no way of knowing which terms are zero unless you specifically identify them. Given this form, the roots of a polynomial are found by using the function `roots`, for example,

```
>> r = roots(p)
r =
  11.7473
   2.7028
  -1.2251 + 1.4672i
  -1.2251 - 1.4672i
```

Since in MATLAB both a polynomial and its roots are vectors, ***MATLAB adopts the convention that polynomials are row vectors and roots are column vectors.***

Given the roots of a polynomial it is also possible to construct the associated polynomial. In MATLAB, the command `poly` performs this task. Consider the example

```
>> pp = poly(r)
pp =
            1           -12 -2.3093e-014            25           116
>> pp(abs(pp)<1e-12) = 0  % change small element to zero!
pp =
            1           -12            0            25           116
```

Because of truncation errors it is not uncommon for the results of `poly` to have near-zero components or to have components with small imaginary parts. As shown above, near-zero components can be corrected by array manipulation. Similarly, eliminating spurious imaginary parts is simply a matter of using the function `real` to extract the real part of the result.

19.2 MULTIPLICATION

Polynomial multiplication is supported by the function `conv`, which performs the convolution of two arrays. Consider the product of the two polynomials $a(x) = x^3 + 2x^2 + 3x + 4$ and $b(x) = x^3 + 4x^2 + 9x + 16$:

```
>> a = [1 2 3 4];  b = [1 4 9 16];
>> c = conv(a,b)
c =
     1     6    20    50    75    84    64
```

This result is $c(x) = x^6 + 6x^5 + 20x^4 + 50x^3 + 75x^2 + 84x + 64$. Multiplication of more than two polynomials requires repeated use of `conv`.

19.3 ADDITION

MATLAB does not provide a direct function for adding polynomials. Standard array addition works if both polynomial vectors are the same size, for example,

```
>> d = a + b
d =
        2       6      12      20
```

which is $d(x) = 2x^3 + 6x^2 + 12x + 20$. When two polynomials are of different orders, the polynomial of lower order must be padded with leading zeros so that it has the same effective order as the higher-order polynomial. Consider the addition of polynomials `c` and `d` above:

```
>> e = c + [0 0 0 d]
e =
        1       6      20      52      81      96      84
```

which is $e(x) = x^6 + 6x^5 + 20x^4 + 52x^3 + 81x^2 + 96x + 84$. Leading zeros are required rather than trailing zeros because coefficients associated with like powers of x must line up. The M-file function shown below automates polynomial addition.

```
function p=mmpadd(a,b)
%MMPADD Polynomial Addition.
% MMPADD(A,B) adds the polynomials A and B.

if nargin<2
   error('Not Enough Input Arguments.')
end
a=a(:).';          % make sure inputs are polynomial row vectors
b=b(:).';
na=length(a);   % find lengths of a and b
nb=length(b);
p=[zeros(1,nb-na) a]+[zeros(1,na-nb) b];  % pad with zeros as necessary
```

To illustrate the use of `mmpadd` reconsider the above example,

```
>> f = mmpadd(c,d)
f =
        1       6      20      52      81      96      84
```

which is the same as `e` above. Of course, `mmpadd` can also be used for subtraction, for example,

```
>> g = mmpadd(c,-d)
g =
        1       6      20      48      69      72      44
```

which is $g(x) = x^6 + 6x^5 + 20x^4 + 48x^3 + 69x^2 + 72x + 44$.

19.4 DIVISION

In some special cases it is necessary to divide one polynomial into another. In MATLAB, this is accomplished with the function `deconv`, for example,

```
>> [q,r] = deconv(c,b)
q =
     1     2     3     4
r =
     0     0     0     0     0     0     0
```

This result says that `b` divided into `c` gives the quotient polynomial `q` and the remainder `r`, which is zero in this case since the product of `b` and `q` is exactly `c`. Another example gives a remainder:

```
>> [q,r] = deconv(f,b)
q =
     1     2     3     6
r =
     0     0     0     0    -2    -6   -12
```

Here `b` divided into `f` gives the quotient polynomial `q` and the remainder `r`. The leading zeros in `r` simply make `r` the same length as `f`. In this case the quotient is $q(x) = x^3 + 2x^2 + 3x + 6$ and the remainder term is $r(x) = -2x^2 - 6x - 12$.

19.5 DERIVATIVES AND INTEGRALS

Because differentiation of a polynomial is simple to express, MATLAB offers the function `polyder` for polynomial differentiation, for example,

```
>> g  % recall polynomial
g =
     1     6    20    48    69    72    44
>> h = polyder(g)
h =
     6    30    80   144   138    72
```

Similarly, the integral of a polynomial is easy to express. Given an integration constant, the function `polyint` returns the integral, for example,

```
>> polyint(h,44) % get g back from h=polyder(g)
ans =
     1     6    20    48    69    72    44
```

19.6 EVALUATION

Given that you can add, subtract, multiply, divide, and differentiate polynomials based on row vectors of their coefficients, one should be able to evaluate them also. In MATLAB this is accomplished with the function `polyval`, as in the example

```
>> p = [1 4 -7 -10];     % the polynomial
>> x = linspace(-1,3); % evaluation points
>> v = polyval(p,x);    % evaluate p at points in x
>> plot(x,v)            % plot results
>> title('Figure 19.1: x{^3} + 4x{^2} - 7x -10')
>> xlabel('x')
```

Figure 19.1: $x^3 + 4x^2 - 7x - 10$

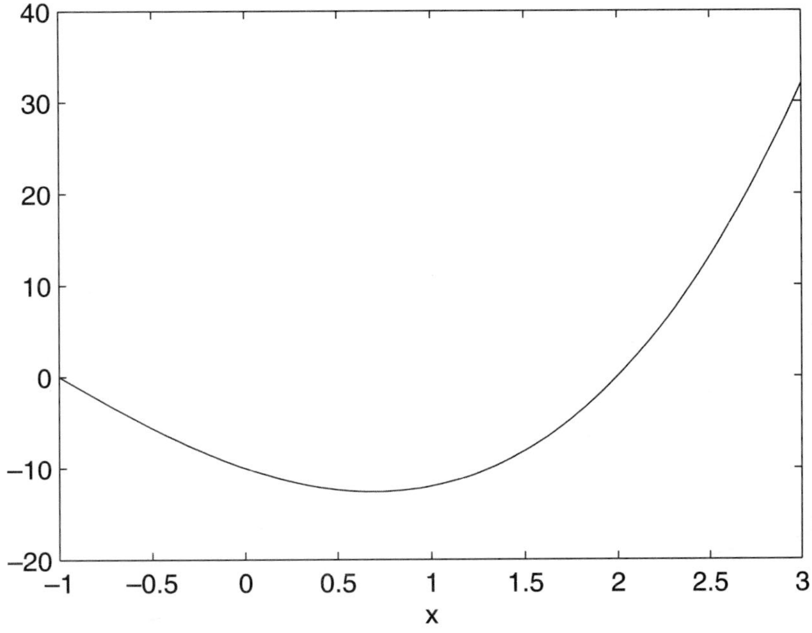

19.7 RATIONAL POLYNOMIALS

Sometimes one encounters ratios of polynomials, for example, transfer functions and Pade approximations to functions. In MATLAB, these are manipulated by considering the numerator and denominator polynomials separately, for example,

```
>> n = [1 -10 100]  % a numerator
n =
     1   -10   100
```

```
>> d = [1 10 100 0]  % a denominator
d =
       1     10    100      0
>> z = roots(n)  % the zeros of n(x)/d(x)
z =
             5 +       8.6603i
             5 -       8.6603i
>> p = roots(d)  % the poles of n(x)/d(x)
p =
             0
            -5 +       8.6603i
            -5 -       8.6603i
```

The derivative of this rational polynomial with respect to x is found using `polyder`:

```
>> [nd,dd] = polyder(n,d)
nd =
          -1            20          -100         -2000        -10000
dd =
  Columns 1 through 6
           1            20           300          2000         10000            0
  Column 7
           0
```

Here `nd` and `dd` are the respective numerator and denominator polynomials of the derivative.

Another common operation is to find the partial fraction expansion of a rational polynomial, for example,

```
>> [r,p,k] = residue(n,d)
r =
  9.7954e-17 +       1.1547i
  9.7954e-17 -       1.1547i
            1
p =
           -5 +       8.6603i
           -5 -       8.6603i
            0
k =
      []
```

In this case, the `residue` function returns the residues or partial fraction expansion coefficients `r`, their associated poles `p`, and the direct term polynomial `k`. Since the order of the numerator is less than that of the denominator, there are no direct terms. For this example, the partial fraction expansion of the rational polynomial is

$$\frac{n(x)}{d(x)} = \frac{1.1547i}{x + 5 - 8.6603i} + \frac{-\,1.1547i}{x + 5 + 8.6603i} + \frac{1}{x}$$

Given this information the original rational polynomial is found by using `residue` yet again:

```
>> [nn,dd] = residue(r,p,k)
nn =
            1          -10          100
dd =
            1           10          100            0
```

So, in this case, the function `residue` performs two operations that are inverses of one another based on how many input and output arguments are used.

19.8 CURVE FITTING

In numerous application areas, one is faced with the task of fitting a curve to measured data. Sometimes the chosen curve passes through the data points, but at other times the curve comes close to, but does not necessarily pass through, the data points. In the most common situation, the curve is chosen so that the sum of the squared errors at the data points is minimized. This choice results in a ***least squares*** curve fit. While least squares curve fitting can be done using any set of basis functions, it is straightforward and common to use a truncated power series, that is, a polynomial.

In MATLAB, the function `polyfit` solves the least squares polynomial curve-fitting problem. To illustrate the use of this function let's start with the data

```
>> x = [0 .1 .2 .3 .4 .5 .6 .7 .8 .9 1];
>> y = [-.447 1.978 3.28 6.16 7.08 7.34 7.66 9.56 9.48 9.30 11.2];
```

To use `polyfit`, we must give it the above data and the order or degree of the polynomial we wish to best fit to the data. If we choose $n = 1$ as the order, the best straight-line approximation will be found. This is often called ***linear regression.*** On the other hand, if we choose $n = 2$ as the order, a quadratic polynomial will be found. For now, let's choose a quadratic polynomial:

```
>> n = 2;
>> p = polyfit(x,y,n)
p =
   -9.8108   20.1293   -0.0317
```

The output of `polyfit` is a row vector of the polynomial coefficients. Here the solution is $y(x) = -9.8108x^2 + 20.1293x - 0.0317$. To compare the curve-fit solution to the data points, let's plot both:

```
>> xi = linspace(0,1,100);
>> yi = polyval(p,xi);
>> plot(x,y,'-o',xi,yi,'--')
>> xlabel('x'), ylabel('y=f(x)')
>> title('Figure 19.2: Second Order Curve Fitting')
```

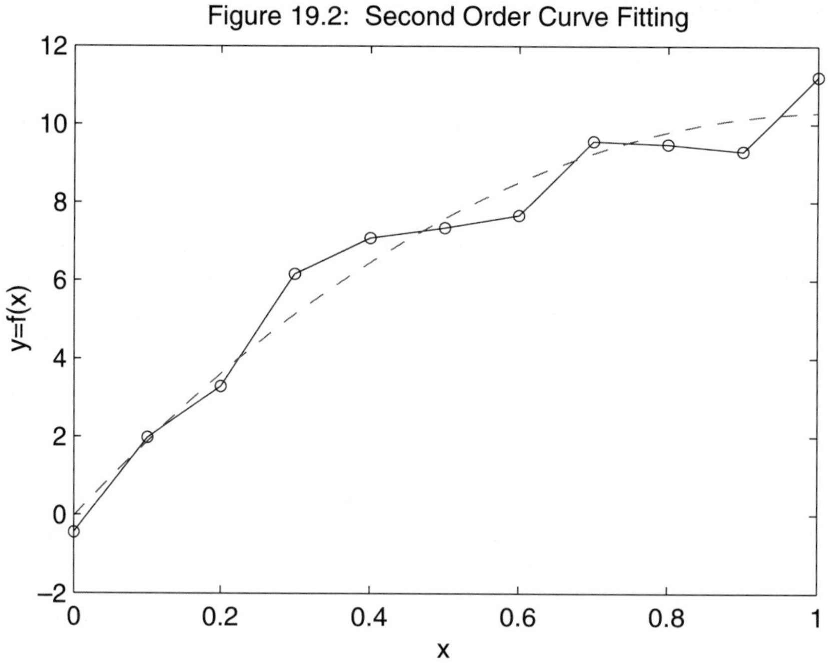

This plot contains the original data `x` and `y`, marking the data points with `'o'` and connecting them with straight lines. In addition it plots the evaluated polynomial data `xi` and `yi` using a dashed line `'--'`.

The choice of polynomial order is somewhat arbitrary. It takes two points to define a straight line or first-order polynomial. (If this isn't clear to you, mark two points and draw a straight line between them.) It takes three points to define a quadratic or second-order polynomial. Following this progression, it takes $n + 1$ data points to uniquely specify an nth-order polynomial. Thus, in the above case where there are 11 data points, we could choose up to a 10th-order polynomial. However, given the poor numerical properties of higher-order polynomials, one should not choose a polynomial order any higher than necessary. In addition, as the polynomial order increases, the approximation becomes less smooth since higher-order polynomials can be differentiated more times before they become zero. For example, consider choosing a 10th-order polynomial.

```
>> pp = polyfit(x,y,10);
>> pp.'  % display polynomial coefficients as a column
ans =
  -4.6436e+005
   2.2965e+006
  -4.8773e+006
   5.8233e+006
```

```
  -4.2948e+006
   2.0211e+006
  -6.0322e+005
   1.0896e+005
        -10626
        435.99
        -0.447
```

Note the size of the polynomial coefficients in this case compared to those of the earlier quadratic fit. Note also the seven orders of magnitude difference between the last (`-0.447`) and first (`-4.6436e+005`) coefficients and the alternating signs on the coefficients. To see how this polynomial differs from the quadratic fit earlier, consider a plot of both.

```
>> y10 = polyval(pp,xi);  % evaluate 10th-order polynomial
>> plot(x,y,'o',xi,yi,'--',xi,y10) % plot data
>> xlabel('x'), ylabel('y=f(x)')
>> title('Figure 19.3: 2nd and 10th Order Curve Fitting')
```

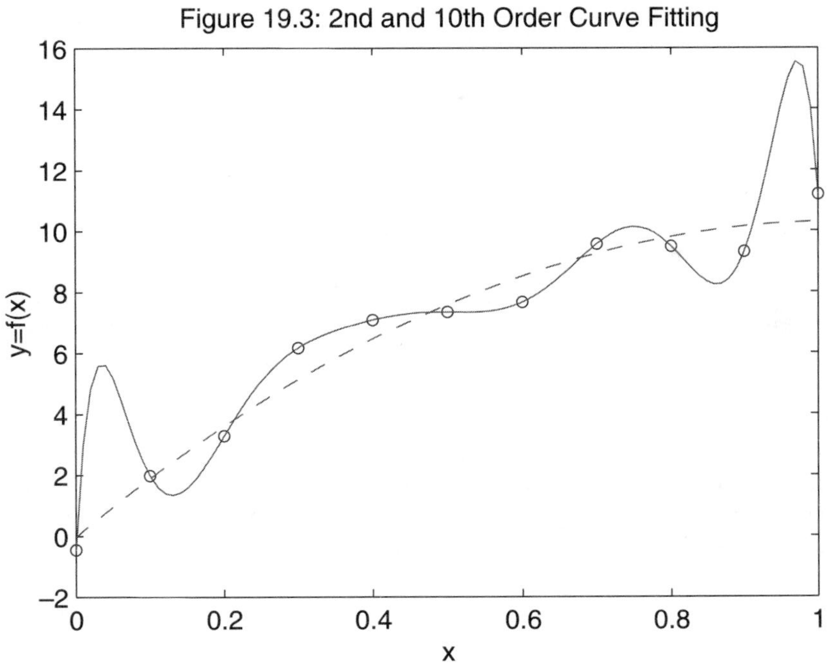

In the plot, the original data is marked with `'o'`, the quadratic curve fit is dashed, and the 10th order fit is solid. Note the wavelike ripples that appear between the data points at the left and right extremes in the 10th order fit. This example clearly demonstrates the difficulties with higher-order polynomials.

20

Cubic Splines

It is well known that interpolation using high-order polynomials often produces ill-behaved results. There are numerous approaches to eliminating this poor behavior. Of these approaches, cubic splines are very popular. In MATLAB, basic cubic splines interpolation is accomplished by the functions `spline`, `ppval`, `mkpp`, and `unmkpp`. Of these, only `spline` appears in the MATLAB documentation. However, help text is available for all these functions. In the following sections, the basic features of cubic splines as implemented in these M-file functions is demonstrated. In addition, an alternative to cubic splines, called a piecewise cubic Hermite interpolating polynomial, is considered. This piecewise polynomial is computed by the function `pchip` and returns a piecewise polynomial just as `spline` does.

20.1 BASIC FEATURES

In cubic splines, cubic polynomials are found to approximate the curve between each pair of data points. In the language of splines, these data points are called breakpoints. Since a straight line is uniquely defined by two points, an infinite number of cubic polynomials can be used to approximate a curve between two points. Therefore, in cubic splines, additional constraints are placed on the cubic polynomials to make the result unique. By constraining the first and second derivatives of each cubic polynomial to match at the breakpoints, all internal cubic polynomials are well defined. Moreover, both the slope and curvature of the approximating polynomials are continuous across the breakpoints. However, the first and last cubic polynomials do not have adjoining cubic polynomials beyond the first and last breakpoints. As a result, the remaining constraints must be determined by some other means. The most common approach, which is the default for the function `spline`, is to adopt a ***not-a-knot*** condition. This condition forces the third derivative of the first and second cubic polynomials to be identical, and likewise for the last and second-to-last cubic polynomials.

Based on the above description, one could guess that finding cubic spline polynomials requires solving a large set of linear equations. In fact, given n breakpoints, there are $n - 1$ cubic polynomials to be found, each having 4 unknown coefficients. Thus, the set of equations to be solved involves $4(n - 1)$ unknowns. By writing each cubic polynomial in a special form and by applying the constraints, the cubic polynomials can be found by solving a reduced set of n equations in n unknowns. Thus, if there are 50 breakpoints, there are 50 equations in 50 unknowns. Luckily, these equations can be concisely written and solved using sparse matrices, which is what the function `spline` uses to compute the unknown coefficients.

20.2 PIECEWISE POLYNOMIALS

In its most simple use, `spline` takes data `x` and `y` and desired values `xi`, finds the cubic spline interpolation polynomials that fit `x` and `y`, and then evaluates the polynomials to find the corresponding `yi` values for each `xi` value. This matches the use of `yi = interp1(x,y,xi,'spline')`. Consider the example

```
>> x = 0:12;
>> y = tan(pi*x/25);
>> xi = linspace(0,12);

>> yi = spline(x,y,xi);

>> plot(x,y,'o',xi,yi)
>> title('Figure 20.1: Spline Fit')
```

Figure 20.1: Spline Fit

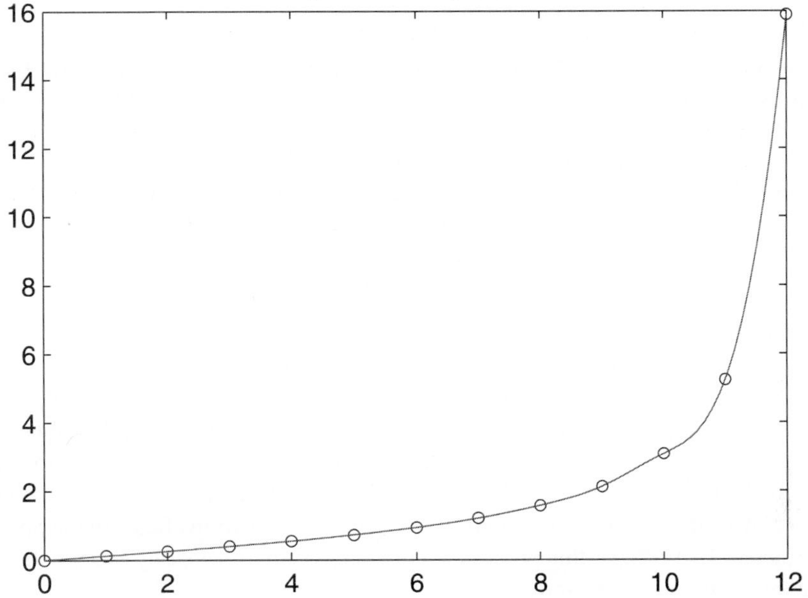

This approach is appropriate if only one set of interpolated values is required. However, if another set is needed from the same set of data, it doesn't make sense to recompute the same set of cubic spline coefficients a second time. In this situation, one can call `spline` with only the first two arguments, for example,

```
>> pp = spline(x,y)
pp =
       form: 'pp'
     breaks: [0 1 2 3 4 5 6 7 8 9 10 11 12]
      coefs: [12x4 double]
     pieces: 12
      order: 4
        dim: 1
```

When called in this way, `spline` returns a structure containing the ***pp-form,*** or piecewise polynomial form, of the cubic splines. This structure contains all the information necessary to evaluate the cubic splines for any set of desired interpolation values. The pp-form structure is also compatible with the optional *Spline Toolbox* available with MATLAB. Given the pp-form, the function `ppval` evaluates the cubic splines. For example,

```
>> yi = ppval(pp,xi);
```

computes the same `yi` values computed earlier. Similarly,

```
>> xi2 = linspace(10,12);
>> yi2 = ppval(pp,xi2);
```

uses the pp-form again to evaluate the cubic splines over a finer spacing restricted to the region between 10 and 12.

```
>> xi3 = 10:15;
>> yi3 = ppval(pp,xi3)
yi3 =
    3.0777    5.2422   15.8945   44.0038   98.5389  188.4689
```

shows that cubic splines can be evaluated outside the region over which the cubic polynomials were computed. When data appears beyond the last or before the first breakpoint, the last and first cubic polynomials are used respectively to find interpolated values.

The cubic splines pp-form given above stores the breakpoints and polynomial coefficients, as well as other information regarding the cubic splines representation. This form is a convenient data structure in MATLAB since all information is stored in a single structure. When a cubic spline representation is evaluated, the various fields in the pp-form must be extracted. In MATLAB this process is conveniently performed by the function `unmkpp`. Using this function on the above pp-form gives

```
>> [breaks,coefs,npolys,ncoefs,dim] = unmkpp(pp)
breaks =
  Columns 1 through 12
     0     1     2     3     4     5     6     7     8     9    10    11
  Column 13
    12
coefs =
    0.0007   -0.0001    0.1257         0
    0.0007    0.0020    0.1276    0.1263
    0.0010    0.0042    0.1339    0.2568
    0.0012    0.0072    0.1454    0.3959
    0.0024    0.0109    0.1635    0.5498
    0.0019    0.0181    0.1925    0.7265
    0.0116    0.0237    0.2344    0.9391
   -0.0083    0.0586    0.3167    1.2088
    0.1068    0.0336    0.4089    1.5757
   -0.1982    0.3542    0.7967    2.1251
    1.4948   -0.2406    0.9102    3.0777
    1.4948    4.2439    4.9136    5.2422
npolys =
    12
ncoefs =
     4
dim =
     1
```

Here `breaks` contains the breakpoints, `coefs` is a matrix whose *i*th row is the *i*th cubic polynomial, `npolys` is the number of polynomials, `ncoefs` is the number of coefficients per polynomial, and `dim` is the spline dimension. Note that this pp-form is sufficiently general that the spline polynomials need not be cubic. This fact is useful when the spline is integrated or differentiated.

In prior versions of MATLAB, the pp-form was stored in a single numerical array rather than a structure. As a result, `unmkpp` was valuable in separating the parts of the pp-form from the numerical array. Given the simplicity of the structure form, one can easily address the fields directly and avoid using `unmkpp` entirely. However, `unmkpp` continues to support the prior numerical array pp-form, thereby making the process of extracting the parts of a pp-form transparent to the user.

Given the broken-apart form above, the function `mkpp` restores the pp-form, for example,

```
>> pp = mkpp(breaks,coefs)
pp =
      form: 'pp'
    breaks: [0 1 2 3 4 5 6 7 8 9 10 11 12]
     coefs: [12x4 double]
    pieces: 12
     order: 4
       dim: 1
```

Since the size of the matrix `coefs` determines `npolys` and `ncoefs`, they are not needed by `mkpp` to reconstruct the pp-form.

20.3 CUBIC HERMITE POLYNOMIALS

When the underlying data to be interpolated represents a smooth function, cubic splines return appropriate values. However, when the underlying data is not so smooth, cubic splines can predict minima and maxima that do not exist and can destroy monotonicity. Therefore, for nonsmooth data a different piecewise polynomial interpolation is called for. In MATLAB 6, the function `pchip` returns a piecewise cubic polynomial that has the properties described in the help text shown below.

```
>> help pchip

  PCHIP  Piecewise Cubic Hermite Interpolating Polynomial.
  X is a row or column vector. Y is a row or column vector of the same
  length as X, or a matrix with length(X) columns.
  YI = PCHIP(X,Y,XI) evaluates an interpolant at the elements of XI.
  PP = PCHIP(X,Y) returns a piecewise polynomial structure for use by PPVAL.
```

```
The PCHIP interpolating function, P(x), satisfies:
  P(x) is a different cubic on each subinterval, x(k) <= x <= x(k+1).
  P(x) interpolates y, i.e. P(x(k)) = y(k).
  The first derivative, P'(x), is continuous.
  The second derivative, P''(x), is piecewise linear.
  P''(x) is probably not continuous; there may be jumps at x(k).
  P(x) is "shape preserving" and "respects monotonicity".
  On intervals where the data is monotonic, so is P(x).
  At points where the data has a local extremum, so does P(x).
Comparing PCHIP with SPLINE:
  Spline is smoother, i.e. S''(x) is continuous.
  Spline is more accurate if the data are values of a smooth function.
  Pchip has no overshoots and less oscillation if the data are not smooth.
  Pchip is less expensive to set up.
  The two are equally expensive to evaluate.
```

The following example demonstrates the similarities and differences between `spline` and `pchip`.

```
>> x = [0 2 4 5 7.5 10];% sample data
>> y = exp(-x/6).*cos(x);

>> cs = spline(x,y);    % cubic spline
>> ch = pchip(x,y);     % cubic Hermite

>> xi = linspace(0,10);
>> ysi = ppval(cs,xi);  % interpolate spline
>> yhi = ppval(ch,xi);  % interpolate Hermite

>> plot(x,y,'o',xi,ysi,':',xi,yhi)
>> legend('data','spline','hermite')
>> title('Figure 20.2: Spline and Hermite Interpolation')
```

Figure 20.2: Spline and Hermite Interpolation

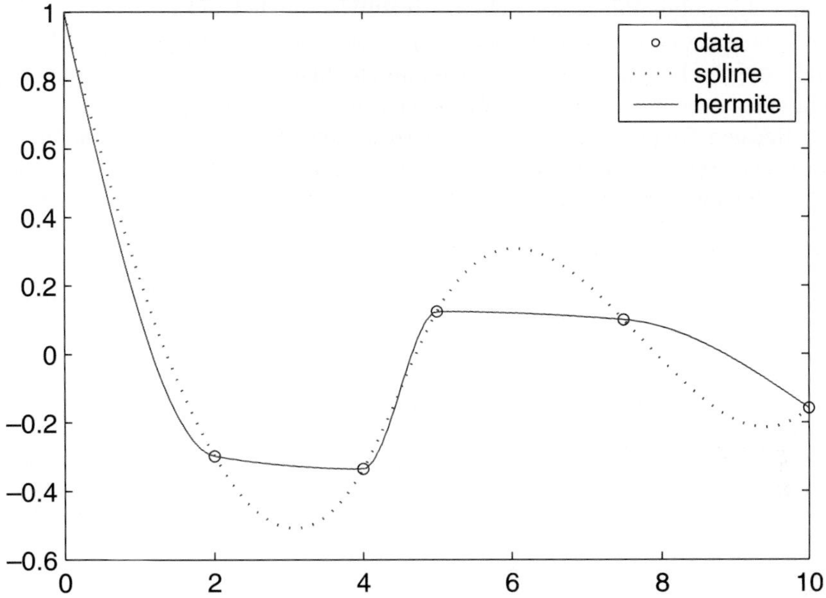

20.4 INTEGRATION

In many situations it is desirable to know the area under a function described by piecewise polynomials as a function of the independent variable x. That is, if the piecewise polynomials are denoted $y = s(x)$, we are interested in computing

$$S(x) = \int_{x_1}^{x} s(x)dx + C$$

where x_1 is the first breakpoint and C is the integration constant. Since $s(x)$ is composed of connected cubic polynomials, with the kth cubic polynomial being

$$s_k(x) = a_k(x - x_k)^3 + b_k(x - x_k)^2 + c_k(x - x_k) + d_k \qquad x_k \le x \le x_{k+1}$$

and whose area over the region $[x_k, x]$ where $x_k <= x <= x_{k+1}$ is

$$S_k(x) = \int_{x_k}^{x} s_k(x)\,dx = \frac{a_k}{4}(x - x_k)^4 + \frac{b_k}{3}(x - x_k)^3 + \frac{c_k}{2}(x - x_k)^2 + d_k(x - x_k)$$

The area under a piecewise polynomial is easily computed as

$$S(x) = \sum_{i=1}^{k-1} S_i(x_{i+1}) + S_k(x)$$

where $x_k \le x \le x_{k+1}$. The summation term is the cumulative sum of the areas under all preceding cubic polynomials. As such, it is readily computed and forms the constant term in the polynomial describing $S(x)$ since $S_k(x)$ is a polynomial. With this understanding, the integral itself can be written as a piecewise polynomial. In this case, it is a quartic piecewise polynomial since the individual polynomials are of order four.

Because the pp-form used in MATLAB can support piecewise polynomials of any order, the above piecewise polynomial integration is embodied in the function `mmppint`. The body of this function is as follows.

```
function ppi=mmppint(pp,c)
%MMPPINT Cubic Spline Integral Interpolation.
% PPI=MMPPINT(PP,C) returns the piecewise polynomial vector PPI
% describing the integral of the cubic spline described by
% the piecewise polynomial in PP and having integration constant C.

if prod(size(c))~=1
   error('C Must be a Scalar.')
end
[br,co,npy,nco]=unmkpp(pp);              % take apart pp
sf=nco:-1:1;                             % scale factors for integration
ico=[co./sf(ones(npy,1),:) zeros(npy,1)];      % integral coefficients
nco=nco+1;                               % integral spline has higher order
ico(1,nco)=c;                            % integration constant
for k=2:npy                              % find constant terms in polynomials
      ico(k,nco)=polyval(ico(k-1,:),br(k)-br(k-1));
end
ppi=mkpp(br,ico);                        % build pp form for integral
```

Consider the following example using `mmppint`.

```
>> x = (0:.1:1)*2*pi;
>> y = sin(x); % create rough data
>> pp = spline(x,y);       % pp-form fitting rough data
>> ppi = mmppint(pp,0);    % pp-form of integral
>> xi = linspace(0,2*pi); % finer points for interpolation
>> yi = ppval(pp,xi);      % evaluate curve
>> yyi = ppval(ppi,xi);    % evaluate integral
```

```
>> plot(x,y,'o',xi,yi,xi,yyi,'--') % plot results
>> title('Figure 20.3: Spline Integration')
```

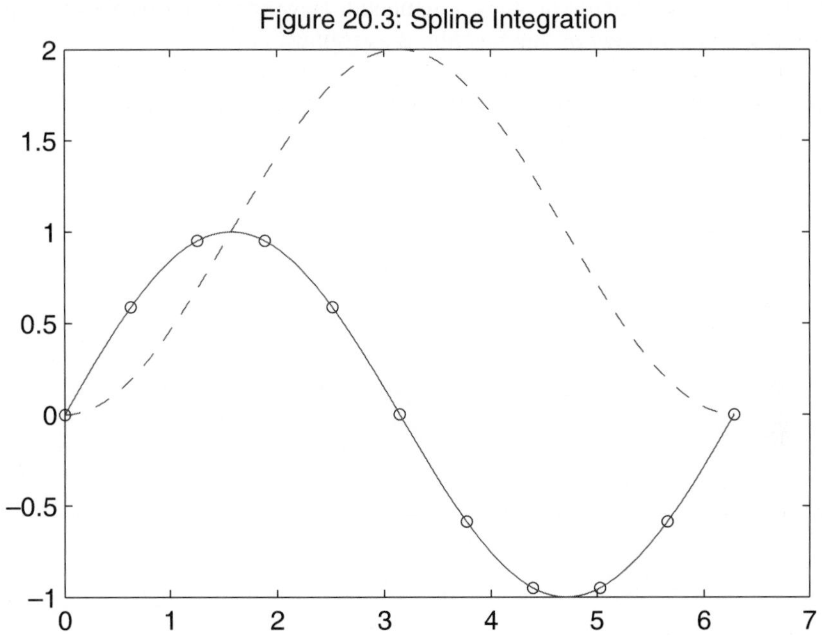

Note that this plot qualitatively shows the identity

$$\int_0^x \sin(x)dx = 1 - \cos(x)$$

20.5 DIFFERENTIATION

Just as one may be interested in piecewise polynomial integration, the derivative or slope of a function described by piecewise polynomials is also useful. Given that the kth cubic polynomial is

$$s_k(x) = a_k(x - x_k)^3 + b_k(x - x_k)^2 + c_k(x - x_k) + d_k \qquad x_k \le x \le x_{k+1}$$

the derivative of $s_k(x)$ is easily written as

$$\frac{ds_k(x)}{dx} = 3a_k(x - x_k)^2 + 2b_k(x - x_k) + c_k$$

where $x_k \leq x \leq x_{k+1}$. As with integration, the derivative is also a piecewise polynomial. However, in this case it is a quadratic piecewise polynomial since the order of the polynomial is two.

Based on the above expression, the function mmppder performs piecewise polynomial differentiation. The body of this function is as follows.

```
function ppd=mmppder(pp)
%MMPPDER Cubic Spline Derivative Interpolation.
% PPD=MMPPDER(PP) returns the piecewise polynomial vector PPD
% describing the cubic spline derivative of the curve described
% by the piecewise polynomial in PP.

[br,co,npy,nco]=unmkpp(pp);           % take apart pp
sf=nco-1:-1:1;                        % scale factors for differentiation
dco=sf(ones(npy,1),:).*co(:,1:nco-1); % derivative coefficients
ppd=mkpp(br,dco);                     % build pp form for derivative
```

To demonstrate the use of mmppder, consider the following example.

```
>> x = (0:.1:1)*2*pi; % same data as earlier
>> y = sin(x);
>> pp = spline(x,y);       % pp-form fitting rough data
>> ppd = mmppder(pp);      % pp-form of derivative
>> xi = linspace(0,2*pi); % finer points for interpolation
>> yi = ppval(pp,xi);      % evaluate curve
>> yyd = ppval(ppd,xi);    % evaluate derivative
>> plot(x,y,'o',xi,yi,xi,yyd,'--') % plot results
>> title('Figure 20.4: Spline Differentiation')
```

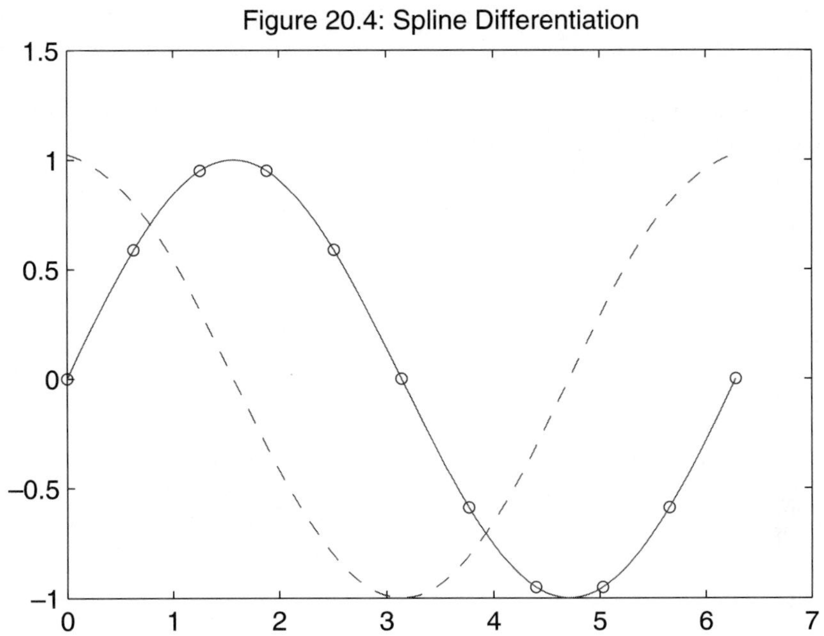

Note that this qualitatively shows the identity

$$\frac{d}{dx}\sin(x) = \cos(x)$$

20.6 SPLINE INTERPOLATION ON A PLANE

Spline interpolation as implemented by the function `spline` assumes that the independent variable is monotonic. That is, the spline $y = s(x)$ describes a continuous function. When it is not continuous, there is no one-to-one relationship between x and y and the function `ppval` has no way of knowing what y value to return for a given x. A common situation where this occurs is when a curve is defined on a plane, for example,

```
>> t = linspace(0,3*pi,15);
>> x = sqrt(t).*cos(t);
>> y = sqrt(t).*sin(t);

>> plot(x,y)
>> xlabel('X')
>> ylabel('Y')
>> title('Figure 20.5: Spiral Y=f(X)')
```

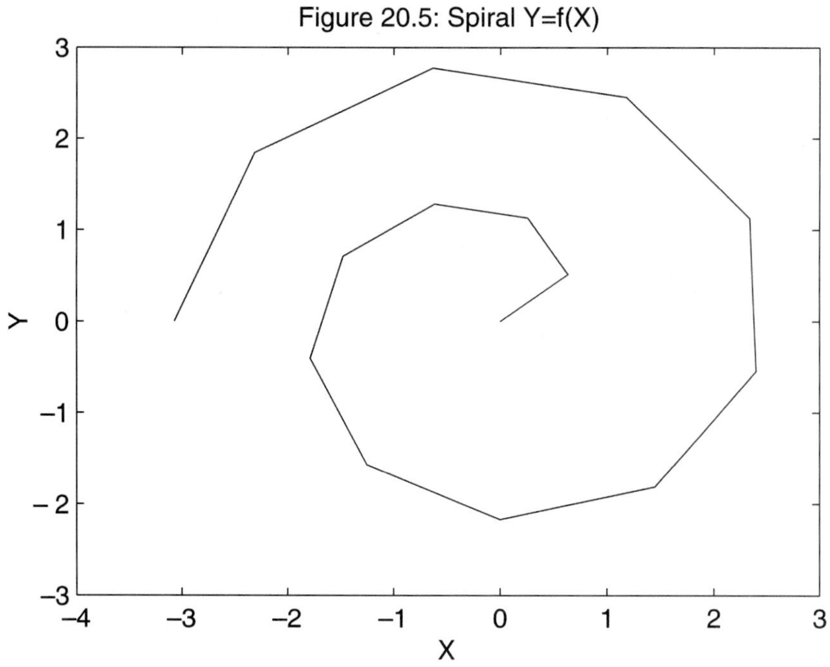

It is not possible to compute a cubic spline for the spiral as a function of x since there are multiple y values for each x near the origin. However, it is possible to compute a spline for each axis with respect to the variable or parameter `t`. This can be accomplished in two ways in MATLAB. First, one could make two calls to `spline` to fit a spline to $x(t)$ and then make another call to fit a spline to $y(t)$. Alternatively, the `spline` function can fit both splines simultaneously and return a single pp-form structure containing both fits. Consider the second approach:

```
>> ppxy = spline(t,[x;y])
ppxy =
      form: 'pp'
    breaks: [1x15 double]
     coefs: [28x4 double]
    pieces: 14
     order: 4
       dim: 2
```

Here the second argument to `spline` is an array containing two ***rows,*** each of which is fit with a spline using the independent variable `t`, which is monotonic. Elsewhere in MATLAB, data arrays are column-oriented, with different columns representing different variables. However, the function `spline` adopts a row-oriented approach in which different rows represent different variables. Not recognizing this subtle fact can lead to errors, for example,

```
>> ppz = spline(t,[x;y]') % try "normal" column-oriented data
??? Error using ==> spline
Abscissa and ordinate vector should be of the same length.
```

In addition, the new pp-form structure returned above now identifies `ppxy.dim = 2`, meaning that `ppxy` describes a 2-D spline.

Given the above spline fit, the original data can be interpolated as desired, for example,

```
>> ti = linspace(0,3*pi); % total range, 100 points
>> xy = ppval(ppxy,ti);   % evaluate both splines
>> size(xy)               % results are row-oriented too!
ans =
     2   100
>> plot(x,y,'d',xy(1,:),xy(2,:))
>> xlabel('X')
>> ylabel('Y')
>> title('Figure 20.6: Interpolated Spiral Y=f(X)')
```

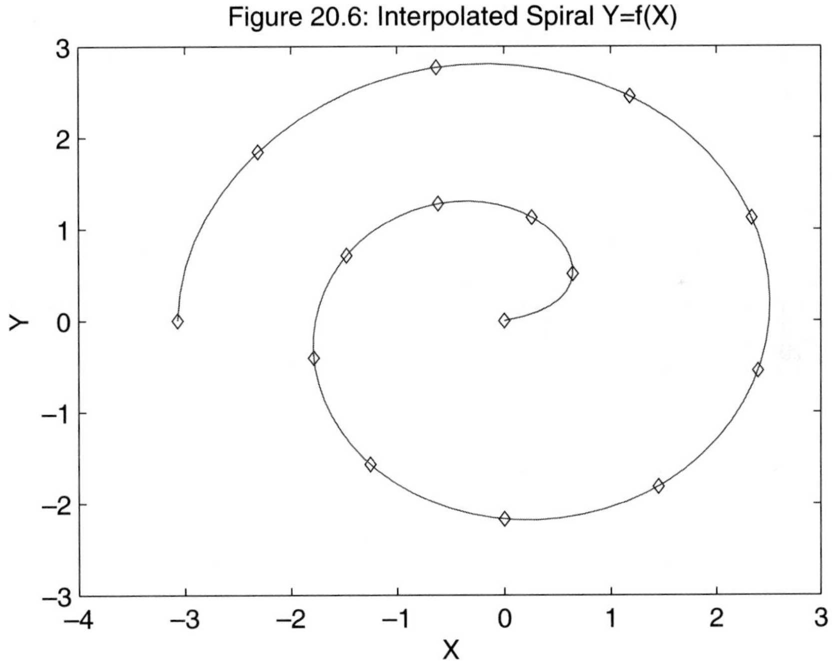

In the example, the results of `ppval` are also row-oriented, the first row being associated with the first spline, and so on. Therefore, to plot y versus x, the second row `xy(2,:)` is plotted versus the first row `xy(1,:)`.

Finally, the above approach is not limited to two dimensions. The pp-form structure and MATLAB piecewise polynomial functions all handle n-dimensional splines.

21

Fourier Analysis

Frequency domain tools such as Fourier series, Fourier transforms, and their discrete time counterparts form a cornerstone in signal processing. These transforms decompose a signal into a sequence or continuum of sinusoidal components that identify the frequency domain content of the signal. MATLAB provides the functions `fft`, `ifft`, `fft2`, `ifft2`, `fftn`, `ifftn`, `fftshift`, and `ifftshift` for Fourier analysis. This collection of functions performs the discrete Fourier transform and its inverse in one or more dimensions. More extensive signal-processing tools are available in the optional *Signal Processing Toolbox.*

Because signal processing encompasses such a diverse area, it is beyond the scope of this text to illustrate even a small sample of the type of problems that can be solved using the discrete Fourier transform functions in MATLAB. Therefore, only one example using the function `fft` to approximate the Fourier transform of a continuous time signal is illustrated. In addition, use of the function `fft` to approximate the Fourier series of a periodic continuous time signal is demonstrated.

21.1 DISCRETE FOURIER TRANSFORM

In MATLAB, the function `fft` computes the discrete Fourier transform of a signal. In cases where the length of the data is a power of 2, or a product of prime factors, fast Fourier transform (FFT) algorithms are utilized to compute the discrete Fourier transform.

> Because of the substantial increase in computational speed that occurs when data length is a power of 2, whenever possible it is important to choose data lengths equal to a power of 2, or to pad data with zeros to give it a length equal to a power of 2.

The fast Fourier transform implemented in MATLAB follows that commonly used in engineering texts:

$$F(k) = \text{FFT}\{f(n)\} = \sum_{n=0}^{N-1} f(n)e^{-j2\pi nk/N} \qquad k = 0,1,\ldots, N-1$$

Since MATLAB does not support zero indices, the values are shifted by one index value to

$$F(k) = \text{FFT}\{f(n)\} = \sum_{n=1}^{N} f(n)e^{-j2\pi(n-1)(k-1)/N} \qquad k = 1,2,\ldots, N$$

The inverse transform follows accordingly as

$$f(n) = \text{FFT}^{-1}\{F(k)\} = \frac{1}{N}\sum_{k=1}^{N} F(k)e^{j2\pi(n-1)(k-1)/N} \qquad n = 1,2,\ldots, N$$

Specific details on the use of the `fft` function are described in its help text:

```
>> help fft
 FFT Discrete Fourier transform.
    FFT(X) is the discrete Fourier transform (DFT) of vector X. If the
    length of X is a power of two, a fast radix-2 fast-Fourier
    transform algorithm is used. If the length of X is not a
    power of two, a slower non-power-of-two algorithm is employed.
    For matrices, the FFT operation is applied to each column.
    For N-D arrays, the FFT operation operates on the first
    non-singleton dimension.

    FFT(X,N) is the N-point FFT, padded with zeros if X has less
    than N points and truncated if it has more.

    FFT(X,[],DIM) or FFT(X,N,DIM) applies the FFT operation across the
    dimension DIM.
```

```
For length N input vector x, the DFT is a length N vector X,
with elements
                  N
   X(k) =       sum  x(n)*exp(-j*2*pi*(k-1)*(n-1)/N), 1 <= k <= N.
                 n=1
The inverse DFT (computed by IFFT) is given by
                  N
   x(n) = (1/N) sum  X(k)*exp( j*2*pi*(k-1)*(n-1)/N), 1 <= n <= N.
                 k=1

The relationship between the DFT and the Fourier coefficients a and b in
             N/2
x(n) = a0 + sum a(k)*cos(2*pi*k*t(n)/(N*dt))+b(k)*sin(2*pi*k*t(n)/(N*dt))
             k=1
is
   a0 = X(1)/N, a(k) = 2*real(X(k+1))/N, b(k) = -2*imag(X(k+1))/N,
where x is a length N discrete signal sampled at times t with spacing dt.

See also IFFT, FFT2, IFFT2, FFTSHIFT.
```

To illustrate use of the FFT, consider the problem of estimating the continuous Fourier transform of the signal

$$f(t) = 2e^{-3t} \qquad t \geq 0$$

Analytically, the Fourier transform of $f(t)$ is given by

$$F(\omega) = \frac{2}{3 + j\omega}$$

Although using the FFT has little real value in this case since the analytical solution is known, this example illustrates an approach to estimating the Fourier transform of less common signals, especially than whose Fourier transform is not readily found analytically. The following MATLAB statements estimate $|F(\omega)|$ using the FFT and graphically compare it to the analytical expression above.

```
N = 128;                 % choose a power of 2 for speed
t = linspace(0,3,N);     % time points for function evaluation
f = 2*exp(-3*t);         % evaluate function, minimize aliasing: f(3) ~ 0
Ts = t(2) - t(1);        % the sampling period
Ws = 2*pi/Ts;            % the sampling frequency in rad/sec
F = fft(f);              % compute the fft
Fc = fftshift(F)*Ts;     % shift and scale
```

```
W = Ws*(-N/2:(N/2)-1)/N; % frequency axis
Fa = 2./(3+j*W);         % analytical Fourier transform
plot(W,abs(Fa),W,abs(Fc),'o') % generate plot, 'o' marks fft
xlabel('Frequency, Rad/s')
ylabel('|F(\omega)|')
title('Figure 21.1: Fourier Transform Approximation')
```

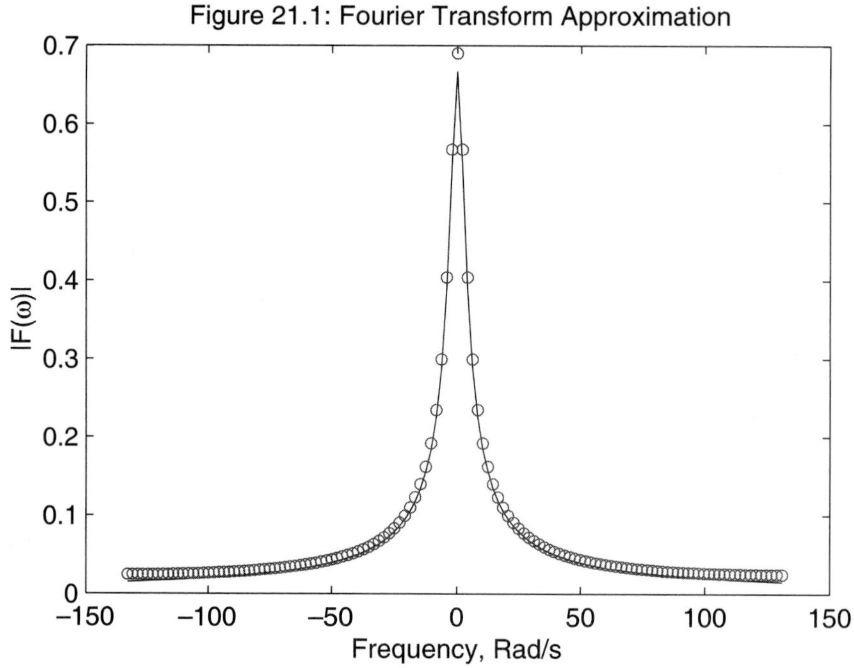

The function `fftshift` flips the halves of `F` so that the $(N/2) + 1$ element of `Fc` is the DC component of the result. Elements less than this are negative frequency components, while those greater are positive frequency components. Using this fact, `W` creates the appropriate analog frequency axis with `W(N/2 + 1) = 0`. Graphically, the FFT approximation is good at low frequencies but demonstrates some aliasing at higher frequencies near the Nyquist frequency.

The FFT-related functions in MATLAB include those in the table below.

Function	Description
`conv`	Convolution.
`conv2`	2-D convolution.
`convn`	n-D convolution.
`deconv`	Deconvolution.

Function	Description
`filter`	Discrete time filter.
`filter2`	2-D discrete time filter.
`fft`	Discrete Fourier transform.
`fft2`	2-D discrete Fourier transform.
`fftn`	*n*-D discrete Fourier transform.
`ifft`	Inverse discrete Fourier transform.
`ifft2`	2-D inverse discrete Fourier transform.
`ifftn`	*n*-D inverse discrete Fourier transform.
`fftshift`	Shift FFT results so that negative frequencies appear first.
`ifftshift`	Undo actions performed by `fftshift`.
`abs`	Magnitude of complex array.
`angle`	Radian angle of complex array.
`unwrap`	Remove phase angle jumps.
`cplxpair`	Sort vector into complex conjugate pairs.
`nextpow2`	Next higher power of 2.

21.2 FOURIER SERIES

MATLAB itself offers no functions specifically tailored to Fourier series analysis and manipulation. However, they are easily added when one understands the relationship between the discrete Fourier transform of samples of a periodic signal and its Fourier series.

The Fourier series representation of a real-valued periodic signal $f(t)$ can be written in complex exponential form as

$$f(t) = \sum_{n=-\infty}^{\infty} F_n e^{jn\omega_o t}$$

where the Fourier series coefficients are given by

$$F_n = \frac{1}{T_o}\int_t^{t+T_o} f(t)e^{-jn\omega_o t}\,dt$$

and the fundamental frequency is $\omega_0 = 2\pi/T_o$, where T_o is the period. The complex exponential form of the Fourier series can be rewritten in trigonometric form as

$$f(t) = A_o + \sum_{n=1}^{\infty}\{A_n \cos(n\omega_o t) + B_n \sin(n\omega_o t)\}$$

where the coefficients are given by

$$A_o = \frac{1}{T_o}\int_t^{t+T_o} f(t)\, dt$$

$$A_n = \frac{2}{T_o}\int_t^{t+T_o} f(t)\cos(n\omega_o t)\, dt$$

$$B_n = \frac{2}{T_o}\int_t^{t+T_o} f(t)\sin(n\omega_o t)\, dt$$

Of these two forms, the complex exponential Fourier series is generally easier to manipulate analytically, whereas the trigonometric form provides a more intuitive understanding because it is easier to visualize sine and cosine waveforms. The relationships between the coefficients of the two forms are

$$A_o = F_o \qquad A_n = 2\ \mathrm{Re}\{F_n\} \qquad B_n = -2\ \mathrm{Im}\{F_n\}$$

$$F_n = F^*_{-n} = (A_n - jB_n)/2$$

Using these relationships, one can use the complex exponential form analytically and then convert results to the trigonometric form for display.

The discrete Fourier transform can be used to compute the Fourier series coefficients provided the time samples are appropriately chosen and the transform output is scaled. For example, consider computing the Fourier series coefficients of the sawtooth waveform shown next.

Figure 21.2: Sawtooth Waveform

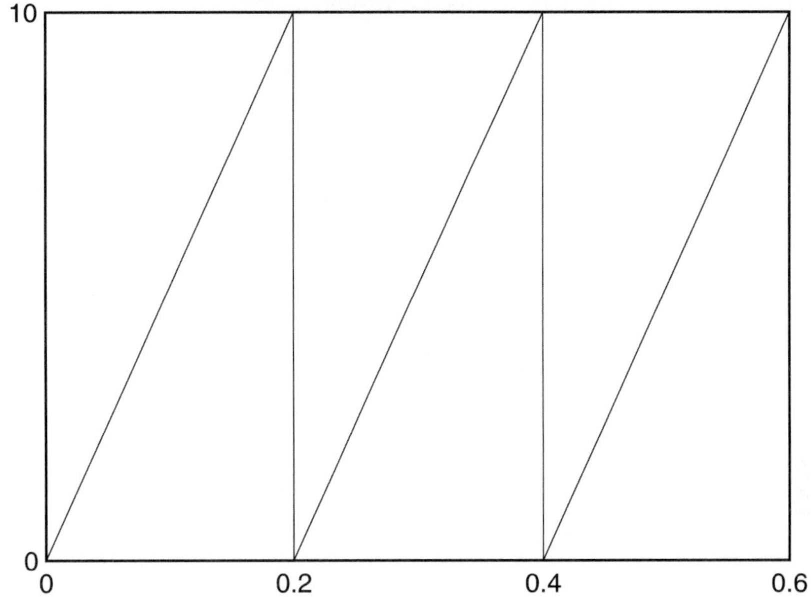

First, one must create a function to evaluate the sawtooth at arbitrary points, for example,

```
function f=sawtooth(t,To)
%SAWTOOTH Sawtooth Waveform Generation.
% SAWTOOTH(t,To) computes values of a sawtooth having
% a period To at the points defined in the vector t.
f = 10*rem(t,To)/To;
f(f==0 | f==10) = 5; % must average value at discontinuity!
```

To minimize aliasing it is necessary to compute enough harmonics so that the highest harmonic amplitude is negligible. In this case choose

```
>> N = 25;   % number of harmonics
>> To = 0.2; % choose period
```

The number of terms to consider in the discrete Fourier transform is twice the number of harmonics since the discrete Fourier transform computes both positive and negative harmonics:

```
>> n = 2*N;
```

The function must be evaluated at n points over one period in such a manner that the $(n + 1)$th point is one period away from the first point, that is,

```
>> t = linspace(0,To,n+1); % (n+1)th point is one period away
>> t(end) = [];            % throw away undesired last point
>> f = sawtooth(t,To);     % compute sawtooth
```

We are now ready to compute the transform, rearrange the components, and scale the results:

```
>> Fn = fft(f);                                 % compute FFT
>> Fn = [conj(Fn(N+1)) Fn(N+2:end) Fn(1:N+1)]; % rearrange values
>> Fn = Fn/n;                                   % scale results
```

The vector `Fn` now contains the complex exponential Fourier series coefficients in ascending order. That is, `Fn(1)` is F_{-25}, `Fn(26)` is F_0, the DC component, and `Fn(51)` is F_{25}, the 25th harmonic component.

From these data the trigonometric Fourier series coefficients are as follows.

```
>> A0 = Fn(N+1) % DC component
A0 =
     5

>> An = 2*real(Fn(N+2:end)) % Cosine terms
An =
  1.0e-015 *
  Columns 1 through 7
   -0.1176   -0.0439   -0.2555    0.3814    0.0507   -0.2006    0.1592
  Columns 8 through 14
   -0.1817    0.0034         0    0.0034   -0.1141   -0.1430   -0.0894
  Columns 15 through 21
   -0.0685   -0.0216    0.0537   -0.0496   -0.0165         0   -0.0165
  Columns 22 through 25
   -0.0079    0.2405    0.3274    0.2132

>> Bn = -2*imag(Fn(N+2:end)) % Sine terms
Bn =
  Columns 1 through 7
   -3.1789   -1.5832   -1.0484   -0.7789   -0.6155   -0.5051   -0.4250
  Columns 8 through 14
   -0.3638   -0.3151   -0.2753   -0.2418   -0.2130   -0.1878   -0.1655
  Columns 15 through 21
   -0.1453   -0.1269   -0.1100   -0.0941   -0.0792   -0.0650   -0.0514
  Columns 22 through 25
   -0.0382   -0.0253   -0.0126         0
```

Since the sawtooth waveform has odd symmetry except for its DC component, it makes sense that the cosine coefficients `An` are negligible (note that they are scaled by 10^{-15}).

Comparing the actual Fourier series coefficients for this sawtooth waveform to the `Bn` terms above gives a relative error of

```
>> idx = -N:N;          % harmonic indices
>> Fna = 5j./(idx*pi); % complex exponential terms
>> Fna(N+1) = 5;
>> Bna = -2*imag(Fna(N+2:end)); % sine terms

>> Bn_error = (Bn-Bna)./Bna     % relative error
Bn_error =
  Columns 1 through 7
   -0.0013   -0.0053   -0.0119   -0.0211   -0.0331   -0.0478   -0.0653
  Columns 8 through 14
   -0.0857   -0.1089   -0.1352   -0.1645   -0.1971   -0.2330   -0.2723
  Columns 15 through 21
   -0.3152   -0.3620   -0.4128   -0.4678   -0.5273   -0.5917   -0.6612
  Columns 22 through 25
   -0.7363   -0.8174   -0.9051   -1.0000
```

As with the earlier Fourier transform example, aliasing causes errors that increase with increasing frequency. Since all practical signals are not band-limited, aliasing is inevitable and a decision must be made about the degree of aliasing that can be tolerated in a given application. As the number of requested harmonics increases, the degree of aliasing decreases. Therefore, to minimize aliasing one can request a larger number of harmonics and then chose a subset of them for viewing and further manipulation.

Finally, the line spectra of the complex exponential Fourier series can be plotted using the `stem` function.

```
>> stem(idx,abs(Fn))
>> xlabel('Harmonic Index')
>> title('Figure 21.3: Sawtooth Harmonic Content')
>> axis tight
```

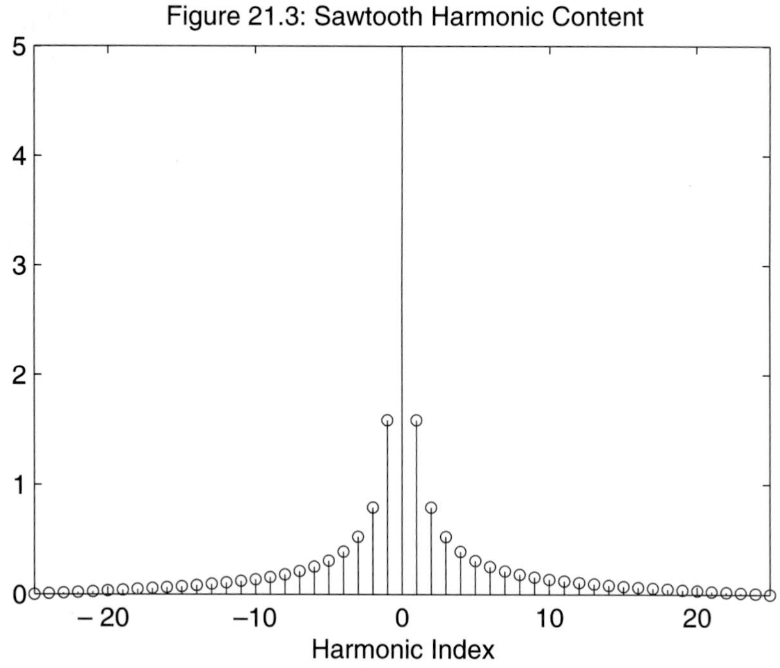
Figure 21.3: Sawtooth Harmonic Content
5
4
3
2
1
0
– 20
–10
0
10
20
Harmonic Index

22

Optimization

Optimization in the context of this chapter refers to the process of determining where a function $y = g(x)$ takes on either specific or extreme values. When a function is defined simply, the corresponding inverse function $x = g^{-1}(y)$ can often be found, in which case one can determine what x values produce a given y by evaluating the inverse function. On the other hand, many functions including many simple ones have no inverse. When this is the case, one must estimate the x that produces a known y by some iterative procedure. In practice, this iterative procedure is called ***zero finding*** because finding x such that $y = g(x)$ for some y is equivalent to finding x such that $f(x) = 0$, where $f(x) = y - g(x)$.

In addition to knowing where a function takes on specific values, it is also common to know its extreme values, that is, where it achieves maximum or minimum values. As before, there are numerous times when these extreme values must be estimated by some iterative procedure. Since a function maximum is the minimum of its negative, that is, $\max f(x) = \min \{-f(x)\}$, iterative procedures for finding extreme values typically find only minimum values and the procedures are called ***minimization*** algorithms.

In this chapter, the optimization functions available in basic MATLAB are covered. Many more functions are available in the optional *Optimization Toolbox.*

22.1 ZERO FINDING

Finding a zero of a function can be interpreted in a number of ways depending on the function. When the function is 1-D, the MATLAB function fzero can be used to find a zero. The algorithm used by this function is a combination of bisection and inverse quadratic interpolation. When the function is multidimensional, that is, the function definition consists of multiple scalar functions of a vector variable, one must look beyond basic MATLAB for a solution. The *Optimization Toolbox* or other third-party toolboxes are required to solve the multidimensional case.

To illustrate the use of the function fzero, consider the function humps:

```
>> x = linspace(-.5,1.5);
>> y = humps(x);
>> plot(x,y)
>> grid on
>> title('Figure 22.1: Humps Function')
```

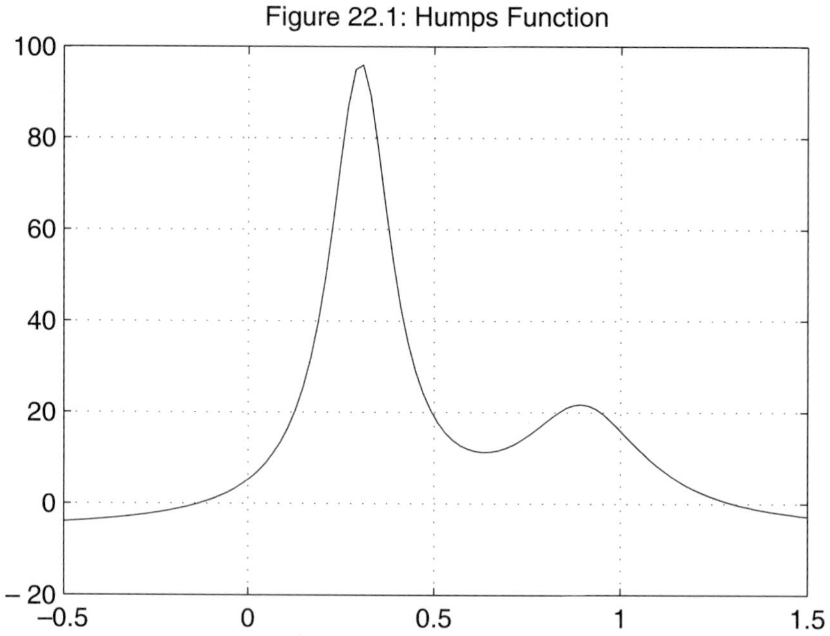

The humps M-file evaluates the function

$$\text{humps}(x) = \frac{1}{(x-0.3)^2+0.01} + \frac{1}{(x-0.9)^2+0.04} - 6$$

This function crosses zero near $x = -0.2$ and $x = 1.3$. The function fzero provides a way to find a better approximation to these zero crossings:

```
>> format long  % display more precision
>> x = fzero('humps',1.3)
x =
   1.29954968258482
>> humps(x) % how close is it to 0?
ans =
     0
>> [x,value] = fzero('humps',-0.2)
x =
  -0.13161801809961
value =
    8.881784197001252e-016
```

Here the two zeros of the function were found. The first zero is very close to 1.3, and evaluation of the function at the zero produced zero. The second zero was found to be close to -0.13. In this call to `fzero` a second output argument was supplied, which returned the function evaluated at the zero. Therefore, it wasn't necessary to call `humps(x)` to check the accuracy of the solution found by `fzero`. It is important to note that `fzero` returns just one zero—the zero found closest to the initial guess. So if a function has more than one zero, it is up to the user to call `fzero` multiple times with different initial guesses.

When initially called, the function `fzero` searches on either side of the initial guess for a sign change in the function. When a sign change is found, the two endpoints that produced the sign change form a ***bracket*** on the number line. If a function is continuous, it must cross through zero somewhere in the bracket. Knowing this, the function `fzero` then searches for the zero crossing and returns the value of x that comes closest to making this happen.

Rather than supplying an initial guess or estimate of the zero, in many cases a bracket is already known based on the properties of the problem to be solved. When this occurs, one can simply supply `fzero` with the bracket rather than an initial guess of the zero location, for example,

```
>> [x,value] = fzero('humps',[-2 0])
x =
  -0.13161801809961
value =
     0
>> [x,value] = fzero('humps',[0 1.2])
??? Error using ==> fzero
The function values at the interval endpoints must differ in sign.
```

In the first example, `[-2 0]` is a bracket around the zero near -0.13. As a result, `fzero` finds the zero. In the second example, `[0 1.2]` is not a bracket around a zero, forcing `fzero` to report an error and abort its search. So if a two-element array is supplied to `fzero`, it must bracket a zero or the function terminates without doing a zero search.

In the above examples, the function to be searched was provided to `fzero` as a character string identifying the appropriate function M-file. As discussed in Chapter 11, the function to be searched can also be supplied as a ***function handle,*** an ***in-line function*** object, or a ***string expression,*** depending on how the function is known. Since `humps` is an M-file, it can be used as shown earlier or as a function handle, for example,

```
>> [x,value] = fzero(@humps,[-2 0]) % function handle approach
x =
   -0.13161801809961
value =
       0
```

If the M-file `humps` did not exist, but one wrote the humps(x) expression, the in-line function object and string expression approaches would apply. Consider the following example.

```
>> humpstr = '1 ./ ((x-.3).^2 + .01) + 1 ./ ((x-.9).^2 + .04) - 6'
humpstr =
1 ./ ((x-.3).^2 + .01) + 1 ./ ((x-.9).^2 + .04) - 6
>> [x,value] = fzero(humpstr,[-2 0]) % string expression
x =
  -0.13161801809961
value =
     0
>> hinline = inline(humpstr)
hinline =
     In-line function:
     hinline(x) = 1 ./ ((x-.3).^2 + .01) + 1 ./ ((x-.9).^2 + .04) - 6
>> [x,value] = fzero(hinline,[-2 0]) % in-line function object
x =
  -0.13161801809961
value =
     0
```

Here `humpstr` is the character string expression evaluating humps(x). Passing this string to the function `inline` produces the in-line function object `hinline`. Using either of these as the first argument to `fzero` provides the desired result.

In reality in the first example above, `fzero` determines that its first argument is a string expression and then calls `inline` to convert it to an in-line function object. So both of the above examples are equivalent; its just a matter of where the in-line function conversion occurs. In the first case, `fzero` performed the conversion; in the second the user did it.

It is important to note that all four forms of function definition apply to all the optimization functions discussed in this chapter. Furthermore, while all forms are equivalent in terms of results, they are not equivalent in terms of execution speed. Writing an M-file function and creating a function handle pointing to it is the fastest approach, followed by using the function M-file directly, followed by either the in-line function object or string expression approach.

All functions in this chapter have various settable parameters. These functions as well as those in the *Optimization Toolbox* share the same format for managing parameters. The functions `optimset` and `optimget` are used to set and get parameters for all functions. For `fzero` there are two settable parameters, `'Display'`, and `'TolX'`. The first parameter controls the amount of detail returned while the function is working; the second sets a tolerance range for accepting the final answer. Consider the following example.

```
>> options = optimset('Display','iter'); % show iteration history
>> [x,value] = fzero(@humps,[-2 0],options)
  Func-count        x              f(x)           Procedure
     1             -2          -5.69298           initial
     2              0           5.17647           initial
     3       -0.952481         -5.07853           interpolation
     4       -0.480789         -3.87242           interpolation
     5       -0.240394         -1.94304           bisection
     6       -0.120197          0.28528           bisection
     7       -0.135585       -0.0944316           interpolation
     8       -0.131759      -0.00338409           interpolation
     9       -0.131618     1.63632e-006           interpolation
    10       -0.131618    -7.14819e-010           interpolation
    11       -0.131618                0           interpolation
Zero found in the interval: [-2, 0].
x =
  -0.13161801809961
value =
     0
>> options = optimset('Display','none'); % show nothing
>> [x,value] = fzero(@humps,[-2 0],options)
x =
  -0.13161801809961
value =
     0
```

```
>> options = optimset('Display','final','TolX',0.1);
>> [x,value] = fzero(@humps,[-2 0],options)
Zero found in the interval: [-2, 0].
x =
  -0.24039447250762
value =
  -1.94303825972565

>> options = optimset('Display','iter','TolX',0.1); % set both
>> [x,value] = fzero(@humps,[-2 0],options)
  Func-count      x             f(x)             Procedure
    1              -2        -5.69298           initial
    2               0         5.17647           initial
    3       -0.952481        -5.07853           interpolation
    4       -0.480789        -3.87242           interpolation
    5       -0.240394        -1.94304           bisection
Zero found in the interval: [-2, 0].
x =
  -0.24039447250762
value =

  -1.94303825972565
```

In these examples an options structure was created with the desired parameters, and then passed as a third argument to `fzero`. The `'Display'` option has four settings, `'final'`, `'iter'`, `'none'`, and `'notify'` with `'notify'` being the default. The `'TolX'` option sets the tolerance for the final answer, which is equal to `eps` by default. See the on-line help for `optimset` and `optimget` for more information regarding parameters for MATLAB optimization functions.

22.2 MINIMIZATION IN ONE DIMENSION

In addition to the visual information provided by plotting, it is often necessary to determine other more specific attributes of a function. Of particular interest in many applications are function extremes, that is, its maxima (peaks) and its minima (valleys). Mathematically, these extremes are found analytically by determining where the derivative (slope) of a function is zero. This idea can be readily understood by inspecting the slope of the `humps` plot at its peaks and valleys. Clearly, when a function is simply defined, this process often works. However, even for many simple functions that can be differentiated readily, it is often not possible to find where the derivative is zero. In these cases and in cases where it is difficult or impossible to find the derivative analytically, it is necessary to search for function extremes numerically. MATLAB provides two functions that perform this task, `fminbnd` and `fminsearch`. These two functions find minima of 1-D and n-D functions, respectively. `fminbnd` utilizes a combination of golden section search and parabolic interpolation. Since a maximum of $f(x)$ is equal to a minimum of $-f(x)$, `fminbnd` and `fminsearch` can be used to find both minima and maxima. If this notion is not clear, visualize the preceding humps(x) plot flipped upside down. In the upside-down state, peaks become valleys and valleys become peaks.

To illustrate 1-D minimization and maximization, consider the preceding humps(x) example once again. From the figure, there is a maximum near $x = 0.3$ and a minimum near $x = 0.6$. With `fminbnd`, these extremes can be found with more accuracy, for example,

```
>> [xmin,value] = fminbnd('humps',0.5,0.8)
xmin =
   0.63700821196362
value =
  11.25275412587769
>> options=optimset('Display','iter');
>> [xmin,value] = fminbnd('humps',0.5,0.8,options)
 Func-count       x              f(x)          Procedure
    1          0.61459         11.4103          initial
    2          0.68541         11.9288          golden
    3          0.57082         12.7389          golden
    4         0.638866         11.2538          parabolic
    5         0.637626         11.2529          parabolic
    6         0.637046         11.2528          parabolic
    7         0.637008         11.2528          parabolic
    8         0.636975         11.2528          parabolic
Optimization terminated successfully:
the current x satisfies the termination criteria using
OPTIONS.TolX of 1.000000e-004
xmin =
   0.63700821196362
value =
  11.25275412587769
```

In the above two calls to `fminbnd`, 0.5 and 0.8 denote the range over which to search for minimum. In the second case options were set to display the iterations performed by `fminbnd`.

To find the maximum near $x = 0.3$, we can either modify the `humps.m` file to negate the expression, or we can just use the string expression input approach, for example,

```
>> [xmax,value] = fminbnd('-humps(x)',0.2,0.4,options)
 Func-count       x              f(x)          Procedure
    1         0.276393         -91.053          initial
    2         0.323607        -91.4079          golden
    3         0.352786        -75.1541          golden
    4         0.300509        -96.5012          parabolic
    5         0.300397        -96.5014          parabolic
    6         0.300364        -96.5014          parabolic
    7         0.300331        -96.5014          parabolic
```

```
Optimization terminated successfully:
the current x satisfies the termination criteria using
OPTIONS.TolX of 1.000000e-004
xmax =
   0.30036413790024
value =
 -96.50140724387050
```

In the above example, `'-humps(x)'` is a string expression identifying what is to be minimized. On termination, the maximum is found to be very close to 0.3, and the peak has an amplitude of +96.5. The value returned by `fminbnd` is the negative of the actual value because `fminbnd` computes the minimum of $-\text{humps}(x)$.

22.3 MINIMIZATION IN HIGHER DIMENSIONS

As described above, the function `fminsearch` provides a simple algorithm for minimizing a function of several variables. That is, `fminsearch` attempts to find the minimum of $f(\boldsymbol{x})$, where $f(\boldsymbol{x})$ is a scalar function of a vector argument $\boldsymbol{x}$. `fminsearch` implements the Nelder-Mead simplex search algorithm, which modifies the components of $\boldsymbol{x}$ to find the minimum of $f(\boldsymbol{x})$. This algorithm is not as efficient on smooth functions as some other algorithms are, but on the other hand, it does not require gradient information that is often expensive to compute. It also tends to be more robust on functions that are not smooth where gradient information is less valuable. If the function to be minimized is inexpensive to compute, the Nelder-Mead algorithm usually works very well.

To illustrate usage of `fminsearch`, consider the banana function, also called Rosenbrock's function:

$$f(\boldsymbol{x}) = 100(x_2 - x_1{}^2)^2 + (1 - x_1)^2$$

This function can be visualized by creating a 3-D mesh plot with x_1 as the x-dimension and x_2 as the y-dimension:

```
x = [-1.5:0.125:1.5];  % range for x1 variable
y = [-.6:0.125:2.8];   % range for x2 variable
[X,Y] = meshgrid(x,y); % grid of all x and y
Z = 100.*(Y-X.*X).^2 + (1-X).^2; % evaluate banana
mesh(X,Y,Z)
hidden off
xlabel('x(1)')
ylabel('x(2)')
title('Figure 22.2: Banana Function')
hold on
plot3(1,1,1,'k.','markersize',30)
hold off
```

Figure 22.2: Banana Function

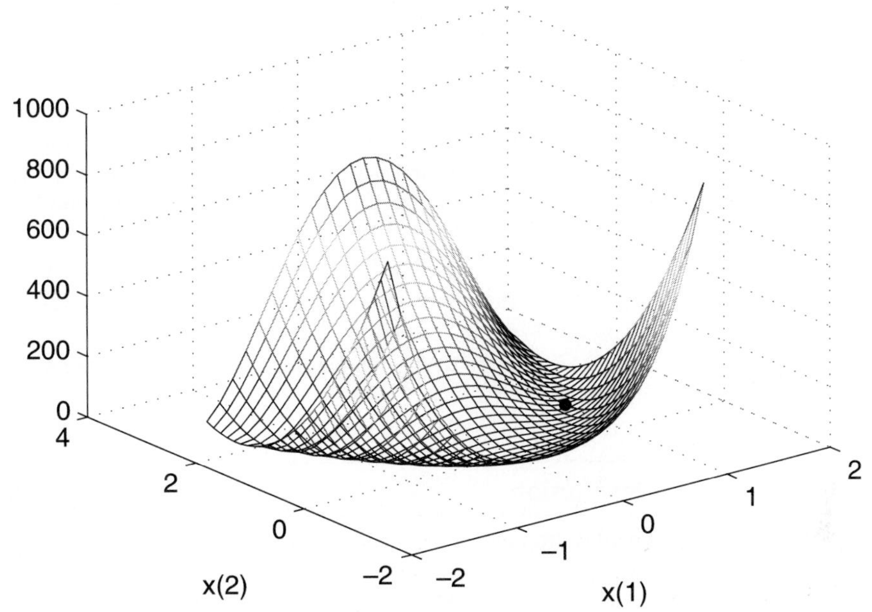

As shown in the plot, the banana function has a unique minimum of zero at $\boldsymbol{x} = [1; 1]$. To find the minimum of this function it must be rewritten in terms of $x_1 =$ `x(1)` and $x_2 =$ `x(2)`, as shown mathematically above. It can be entered as the M-file

```
function f=banana(x)
% Rosenbrock's banana function
f=100*(x(2)-x(1)^2)^2 + (1-x(1))^2;
```

Using this function M-file, `fminsearch` produces

```
>> [xmin,value,flag,output] = fminsearch('banana',[-1.9,2])
xmin =
   1.00001666889480   1.00003447386277
value =
    4.068551535063419e-010
flag =
     1
```

```
output =
     iterations: 114
      funcCount: 210
      algorithm: 'Nelder-Mead simplex direct search'
```

Here four output parameters are shown: the minimum found, the function evaluated at the minimum, a flag signifying success, and finally an algorithm statistics structure. Finding the minimum with a tolerance of 1e-4 required 114 iterations and 210 banana function evaluations. If less output is desired, it is simply a matter of providing fewer output variables.

As with `fminbnd`, `fminsearch` accepts an `options` structure. The options that can be set for `fminsearch` are listed in the table below. As shown earlier, preferences are set by calling `optimset` as `options = optimset('Name',value,'Name',value,...)`. Setting `'Display'` to `'iter'` in `fminsearch` can lead to a tremendous amount of output to the *Command* window.

Option Name	Description	Default Value
'Display'	Display frequency, 'iter', 'final', 'none', or 'notify'.	'notify'
'MaxFunEvals'	Maximum function evaluations.	200*length(x)
'MaxIter'	Maximum algorithm iterations.	200*length(x)
'TolFun'	Function solution tolerance.	1.00E-004
'TolX'	Variable solution tolerance.	1.00E-004

To demonstrate how to use the options shown in the table, consider finding the solution to the above problem with tighter function and variable tolerances:

```
>> options = optimset('Display','none','TolFun',1e-8,'TolX',1e-8);
>> [xmin,value,flag,output] = fminsearch('banana',[-1.9,2],options)
xmin =
   1.00000000126077   1.00000000230790
value =
    6.153858843361103e-018
flag =
     1
output =
    iterations: 144
     funcCount: 266
     algorithm: 'Nelder-Mead simplex direct search'
```

With the tighter tolerances, `xmin` is now within 1e-8 of the actual minimum, the function evaluates to well within `eps` of the minimum of zero, and the number of algorithm iterations and function evaluations increases by approximately 26%. From this information it is clear that `fminsearch` requires a lot of function evaluations and therefore can be slow for functions that are computationally expensive.

22.4 PRACTICAL ISSUES

Iterative solutions such as those found by `fzero`, `fminbnd`, and `fminsearch` all make some assumptions about the function to be iterated. Since there are essentially no limits to the function provided, it makes sense that these ***function functions*** may not converge or may take many iterations to converge. At worst, these functions can produce a MATLAB error that terminates the iteration without producing a result. And even if they do terminate promptly, there is no guarantee that they have stopped at the desired result. To make the most efficient use of these function functions, consider the following points.

1. Start with a good initial guess. This is the most important consideration. A good guess keeps the problem in the neighborhood of the solution where its numerical properties are hopefully stable.
2. If components of the solution (e.g., in `fminsearch`) are separated by several orders of magnitude or more, consider scaling them to improve iteration efficiency and accuracy. For example, if `x(1)` is known to be near `1`, and `x(2)` is known to be near `1e6`, scale `x(2)` by `1e-6` in the function definition and then scale the returned result by `1e6`.
3. If the problem is complicated, look for ways to simplify it into a sequence of simpler problems that have fewer variables.
4. Make sure your function cannot return complex numbers, `Inf`, or `NaN`, which usually results in convergence failure. The functions `isreal`, `isfinite`, and `isnan` can be used to test results before returning them.
5. Avoid functions that are discontinuous. Functions such as `abs`, `min`, and `max` all produce discontinuities that can lead to divergence.
6. Constraints on the allowable range of x can be included by adding a penalty term to the function to be iterated such that the algorithm is persuaded to avoid out-of-range values.

23

Integration and Differentiation

Integration and differentiation are fundamental tools in calculus. Integration computes the area under a function, and differentiation describes the slope or gradient of a function. MATLAB provides functions for numerically approximating the integral and slope of a function. Functions are provided for making approximations when functions exist as M-files or in-line functions, as well as when functions are tabulated at uniformly spaced points over the region of interest.

23.1 INTEGRATION

MATLAB provides three functions for computing integrals of functions described by M-files or in-line functions: `quad`, `quadl`, and `dblquad`.

Note that quad8, which appeared in prior versions of MATLAB, is now obsolete and has been replaced by quadl. The algorithm used in quad has also been changed. In addition, both quad and quadl now support function handles, inline functions, and string arguments.

To illustrate integration, consider the function humps(x) as shown in Figure 23.1 below. As is apparent in the figure, the sum of the trapezoidal areas approximates the integral of the function. Clearly, as the number of trapezoids increases, the fit between the function and the trapezoids gets better, leading to a better integral or area approximation.

Figure 23.1: Integral Approximation with Trapezoids

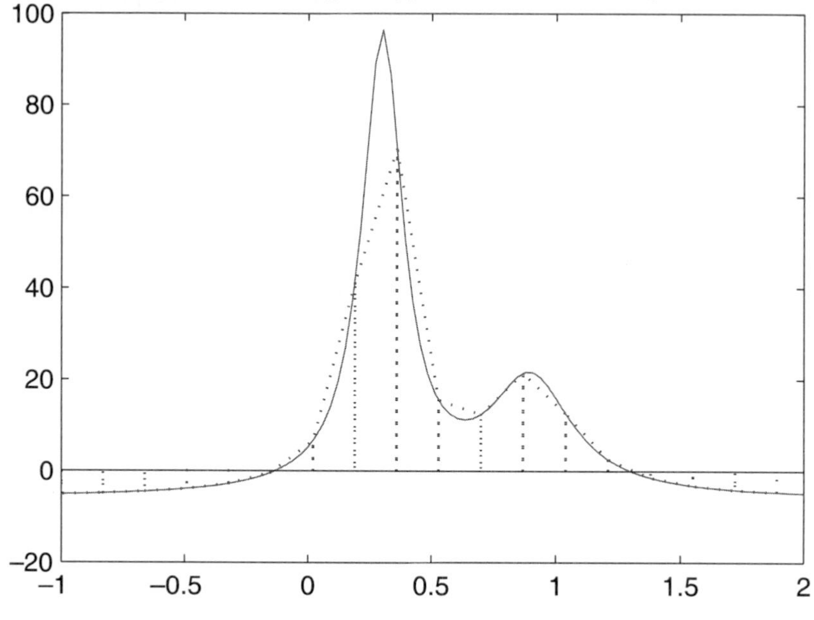

Using tabulated values from the humps function, the MATLAB function trapz approximates the area using the trapezoidal approximation. Duplicating the trapezoids shown in the preceding figure produces

```
>> x = -1:.17:2;
>> y = humps(x);
>> area = trapz(x,y)
area =
        25.917
```

Based on the figure, this is probably not a very accurate estimate of the area. However, when a finer discretization is used, more accuracy is achieved, for example,

```
>> x = linspace(-1,2,100); % linear spacing required!
>> y = humps(x);
>> format long
>> area = trapz(x,y)
area =
      26.34473119524596
```

This area agrees with the analytical integral through five significant digits.

Sometimes one is interested in the integral as a function of x, that is,

$$\int_{x_1}^{x} f(x)dx$$

where x_1 is a known lower limit of integration. The definite integral from x_1 to any point x is then found by evaluating the function at x. Based on the trapezoidal rule, tabulated values of the cumulative integral are computed using the function `cumtrapz`, for example,

```
>> x = linspace(-1,2,100);
>> y = humps(x);
>> z = cumtrapz(x,y);
>> size(z)
ans =
     1   100
>> plotyy(x,y,x,z)
>> grid on
>> xlabel('x')
>> ylabel('humps(x) and integral of humps(x)')
>> title('Figure 23.2: Cumulative Integral of humps(x)')
```

Figure 23.2: Cumulative Integral of humps(x)

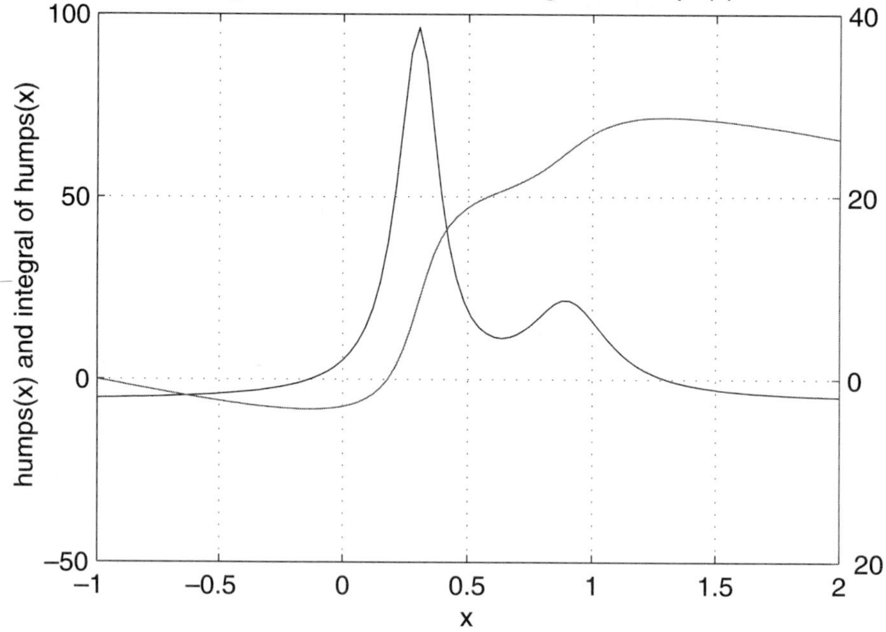

Depending on the properties of the function at hand, it may be difficult to determine an optimum trapezoidal width. Clearly, if one could somehow vary the individual trapezoid widths to match the characteristics of the function, much greater accuracy could be achieved.

The MATLAB functions `quad` and `quadl`, which are based on a mathematical concept called ***quadrature,*** take this approach. These integration functions operate in the same way. Both evaluate the function to be integrated at whatever intervals are necessary to achieve accurate results. Moreover, both functions make higher-order approximations than a simple trapezoid, with `quadl` being more rigorous than `quad`. As an example, consider computing the integral of the `humps` function again:

```
>> z(end)              % cumtrapz result
ans =
   26.34473119524596

>> quad(@humps,-1,2)
ans =
   26.34496047137833
```

```
>> quadl(@humps,-1,2)
ans =
  26.34496047137833
```

For this example, quad and quadl both return the same result, which demonstrates eight significant digit accuracy. The use of cumtrapz achieves five significant digit accuracy.

The function to be integrated, that is, the integrand, must support a vector input argument. That is, the integrand must return a vector of outputs for a vector of inputs. Doing so means using dot-arithmetic operators, .*, ./, .\, and .^. For example, the function in humps.m is given by the statement

```
y = 1 ./ ((x-.3).^2 + .01) + 1 ./ ((x-.9).^2 + .04) - 6;
```

The functions quad and quadl also allow one to specify an absolute error tolerance as a fourth input argument. The default absolute tolerance is 15*eps*(an estimate of the integral).

In addition to 1-D integration, MATLAB supports 2-D integration with the function dblquad. That is, dblquad approximates the integral

$$\int_{y_{min}}^{y_{max}} \int_{x_{min}}^{x_{max}} f(x,y)\,dx\,dy$$

To use dblquad, one must first create a function that evaluates $f(x,y)$. For example, consider the function myfun.m shown below.

```
function z=myfun(x,y)
%MYFUN(X,Y) an example function of two variables

z = sin(x).*cos(y) + 1; % must handle vector x input
```

This function can be plotted by issuing the commands

```
>> x = linspace(0,pi,20);    % xmin to xmax
>> y = linspace(-pi,pi,20); % ymin to ymax
>> [xx,yy] = meshgrid(x,y);
>> zz = myfun(xx,yy);
>> mesh(xx,yy,zz)
>> xlabel('x'), ylabel('y')
>> title('Figure 23.3: myfun.m plot')
```

Figure 23.3: myfun.m plot

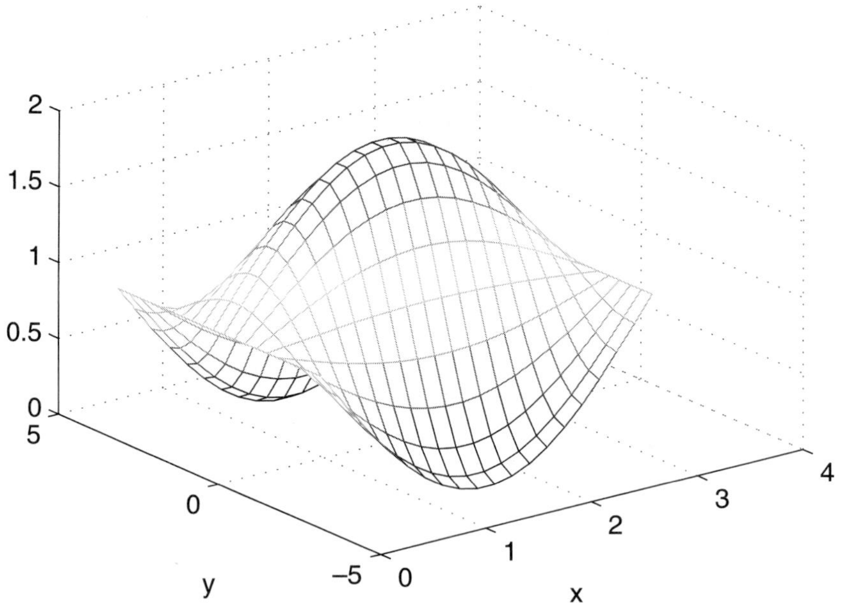

The volume under this function is computed by calling `dblquad` as

```
>> area = dblquad('myfun',0,pi,-pi,pi)
area =
  19.73921476256606
>> relerr = (area-2*pi^2)/(2*pi^2)
relerr =
  3.0196e-007
```

Here `dblquad` is called as `dblquad(Fname,xmin,xmax,ymin,ymax)`. Based on the relative error computed above, the results produced by `dblquad` are fairly accurate even though the function `quad` is called by `dblquad` to do the actual integration.

23.2 DIFFERENTIATION

As opposed to integration, numerical differentiation is much more difficult. Integration describes an overall or macroscopic property of a function, whereas differentiation describes the slope of a function at a point, which is a microscopic property of a function. As a result, integration is not sensitive to minor changes in the shape of a function, whereas differentiation is. Any small change in a function can easily create large changes in its slope in the neighborhood of the change.

Because of this inherent sensitivity in differentiation, numerical differentiation is avoided whenever possible, especially if the data to be differentiated is obtained experimentally. In this case, it is best to perform a least squares curve fit to the data and then differentiate the resulting polynomial. Or alternatively, one could fit cubic splines to the data and then find the spline representation of the derivative as discussed in Chapter 20. For example, reconsider the example from Chapter 19:

```
>> x = [0 .1 .2 .3 .4 .5 .6 .7 .8 .9 1];
>> y = [-.447 1.978 3.28 6.16 7.08 7.34 7.66 9.56 9.48 9.30 11.2];
>> n = 2; % order of fit
>> p = polyfit(x,y,n)  % find polynomial coefficients
p =
   -9.8108    20.1293    -0.0317
>> xi = linspace(0,1,100);
>> yi = polyval(p,xi); % evaluate polynomial
>> plot(x,y,'-o',xi,yi,'--')
>> xlabel('x'), ylabel('y=f(x)')
>> title('Figure 23.4: Second Order Curve Fitting')
```

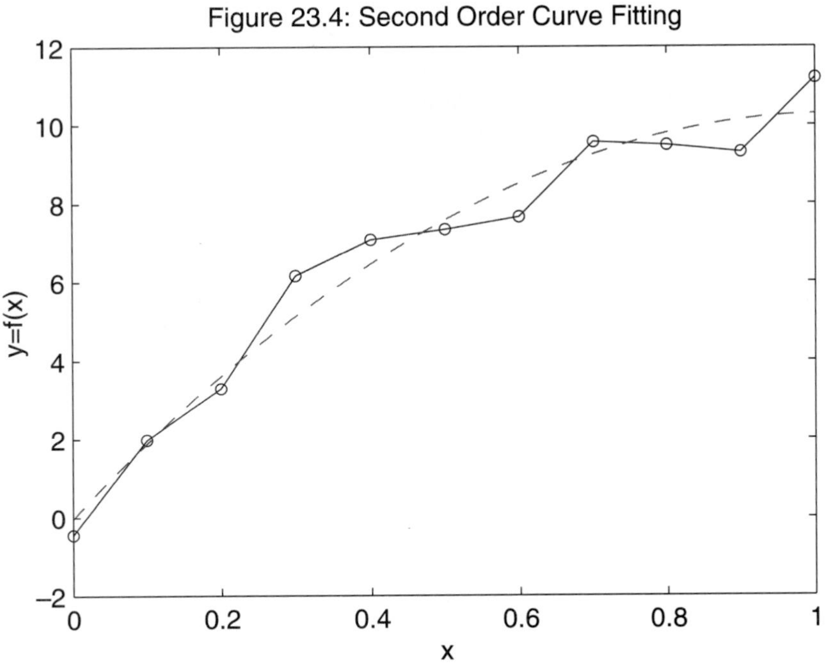

The derivative in this case is found by using the polynomial derivative function `polyder`:

```
>> pd = polyder(p)
pd =
  -19.6217   20.1293
```

The derivative of $y(x) = -9.8108x^2 + 20.1293x - 0.0317$ is $dy/dx = -19.6217x + 20.1293$. Since the derivative of a polynomial is yet another polynomial of the next lowest order, the derivative can also be evaluated at any point. In this case, the polynomial fit is second order, making the resulting derivative first order. As a result, the derivative is a straight line, meaning that it changes linearly with x.

MATLAB provides a function for computing an approximate derivative given tabulated data describing some function. This function, named `diff`, computes the difference between elements in an array. Since differentiation is defined as

$$\frac{dy}{dx} = \lim_{\Delta x \to 0} \frac{f(x + \Delta x) - f(x)}{\Delta x}$$

the derivative of $y = f(x)$ can be approximated by

$$\frac{dy}{dx} \approx \frac{\Delta y}{\Delta x} = \frac{f(x + \Delta x) - f(x)}{\Delta x}$$

which is the forward finite difference in y divided by the finite difference in x. Since `diff` computes differences between array elements, differentiation can be approximated in MATLAB. Continuing with the prior example:

```
>> dyp = polyval(dp,x);     % poly derivative for comparison
>> dy = diff(y)./diff(x);   % compute differences and use array division
>> xd = x(1:end-1);         % new x axis array since dy is shorter than y
>> plot(xd,dy,x,dyp,':')
>> ylabel('dy/dx'), xlabel('x')
>> title('Figure 23.5: Forward Difference Derivative Approximation')
```

Figure 23.5: Forward Difference Derivative Approximation

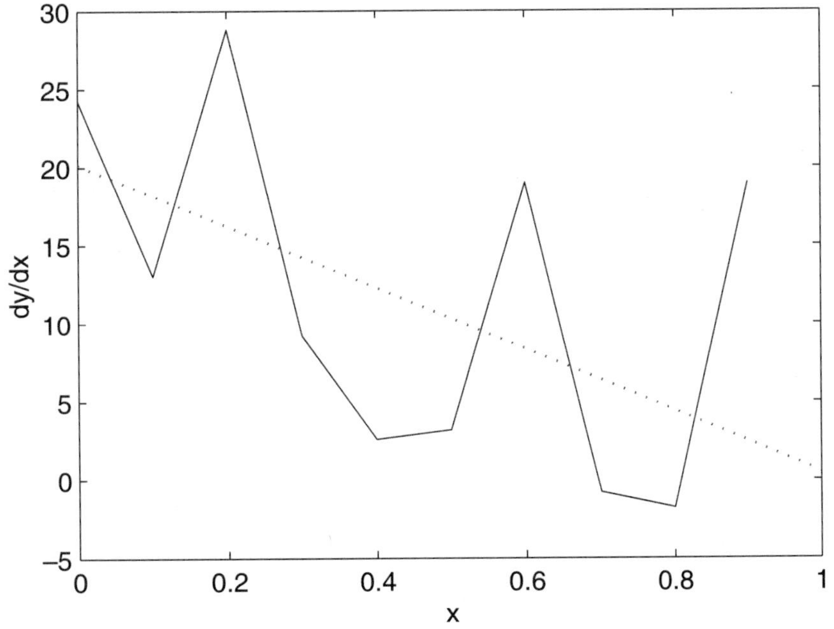

Since `diff` computes the difference between elements of an array, the resulting output contains one less element than the original array. Thus, to plot the derivative, one element of the `x` array must be thrown out. When the first element of `x` is thrown out, the above procedure gives a backward difference approximation, which uses information at `x(n-1)` and `x(n)` to approximate the derivative at `x(n)`. On the other hand, throwing out the last element gives a forward difference approximation, which uses `x(n+1)` and `x(n)` to compute results at `x(n)`. Comparing the derivative found using `diff` to that found from polynomial approximation, it is overwhelmingly apparent that approximating the derivative by finite differences can lead to poor results, especially if the data originates from experimental or noisy measurements. When the data used does not have uncertainty, the results of using `diff` can be acceptable, especially for visualization purposes, for example,

```
>> x = linspace(0,2*pi);
>> y = sin(x);
>> dy = diff(y)/(x(2)-x(1));
>> xd = x(2:end);
>> plot(x,y,xd,dy)
>> xlabel('x'), ylabel('sin(x) and cos(x)')
>> title('Figure 23.6: Backward Difference Derivative Approximation')
```

Figure 23.6: Backward Difference Derivative Approximation

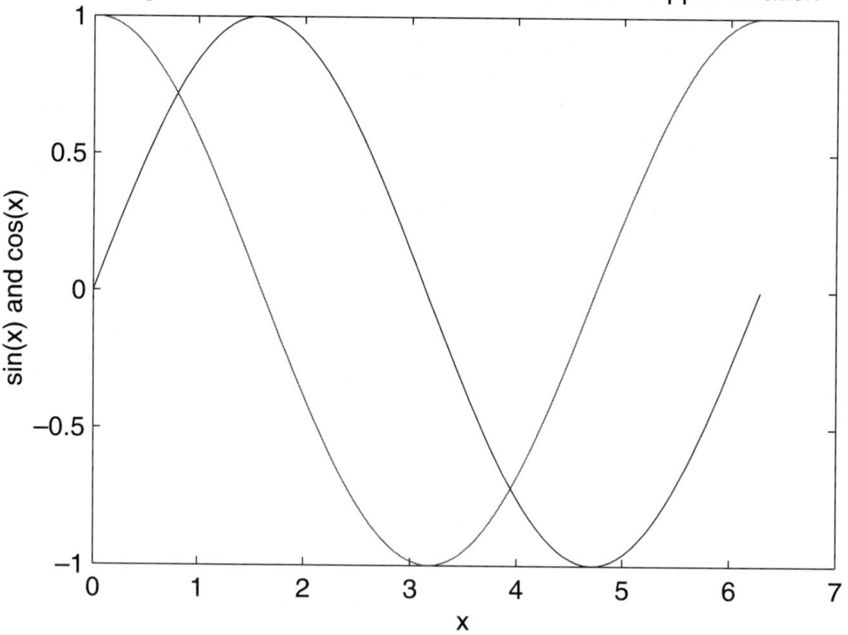

In this example, `x` was linearly spaced, and so dividing by `x(2)-x(1)` gives the same answer as `diff(x)`, which is required if `x` is not linearly spaced. In addition, the first element in `x` is thrown out, making the result a backward difference derivative approximation. Visually, the above derivative is quite accurate. In fact, the maximum error is

```
>> max(abs(cos(xd)-dy))
ans =
    0.0317
```

When forward or backward difference approximations are not sufficient, central differences can be computed by performing the required array operations directly. The first central difference for linearly spaced data is given by

$$\frac{dy(x_n)}{dx} \approx \frac{f(x_{n+1}) - f(x_{n-1})}{x_{n+1} - x_{n-1}}$$

Therefore, the slope at x_n is a function of its neighboring data points. Repeating the previous example gives

```
>> dy = (y(3:end)-y(1:end-2)) / (x(3)-x(1));
>> xd = x(2:end-1);
>> max(abs(cos(xd)-dy))
ans =
  0.00067086
```

In this case, the first and last data points do not have a central difference approximation because there is no data at `n = 0` and `n = 101`, respectively. However, at all intermediate points, the central difference approximation is nearly two orders of magnitude more accurate than the forward or backward difference approximations.

When dealing with 2-D data, the function `gradient` uses central differences to compute the slope in each direction at each tabulated point. Forward differences are used at the initial points, and backward differences are used at the final points so that the output has the same number of data points as the input. The function `gradient` is used primarily for graphical data visualization, for example,

```
>> [x,y,z] = peaks(20);     % simple 2-D function
>> dx = x(1,2) - x(1,1);    % spacing in x direction
>> dy = y(2,1) - y(1,1);    % spacing in y direction
>> [dzdx,dzdy] = gradient(z,dx,dy);
>> contour(x,y,z)
>> hold on
>> quiver(x,y,dzdx,dzdy)
>> hold off
>> title('Figure 23.7: Gradient Arrow Plot')
```

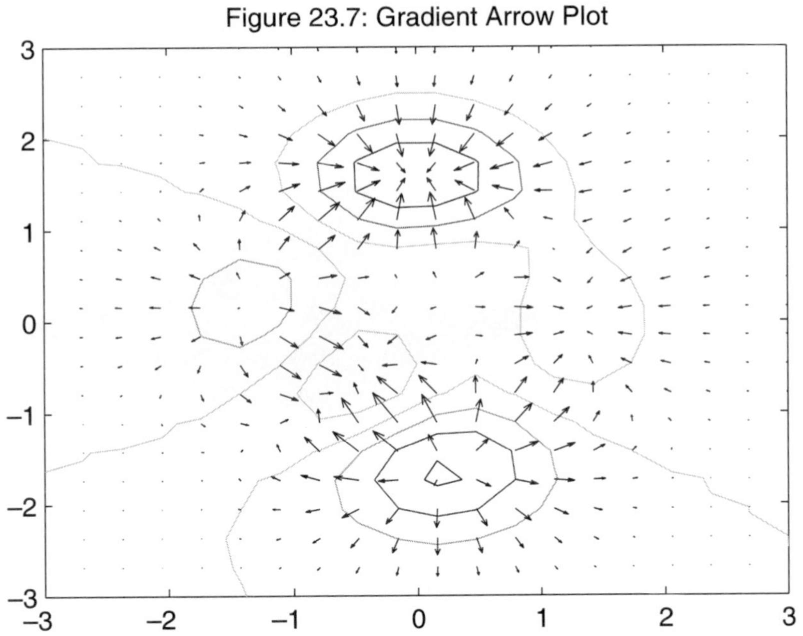

In the above example, `gradient` computes *dz/dx* and *dz/dy* from the tabulated data output of `peaks`. This data is supplied to the function `quiver`, which draws arrows normal to the underlying surface with lengths scaled by the slope at each point.

In addition to the gradient, it is sometimes useful to know the curvature of a surface. The curvature or change in slope at each point is calculated by the function `del2`, which computes the discrete approximation to the Laplacian:

$$\nabla^2 z(x,y) = \frac{d^2 z}{dx^2} + \frac{d^2 z}{dy^2}$$

In its simplest form, this value is computed by taking each surface element and subtracting from it the average of its four neighbors. If the surface is flat in each direction at a given point, the element does not change. Since MATLAB version 5, central second differences have been used at interior points to produce more accurate results. Consider the following example in which the absolute surface curvature influences the color of the surface.

```
>> [x,y,z] = peaks; % default output of peaks
>> dx = x(1,2) - x(1,1); % spacing in x direction
>> dy = y(2,1) - y(1,1); % spacing in y direction
>> L = del2(z,dx,dy);
>> surf(x,y,z,abs(L))
>> shading interp
>> title('Figure 23.8: Discrete Laplacian Color')
```

Figure 23.8: Discrete Laplacian Color

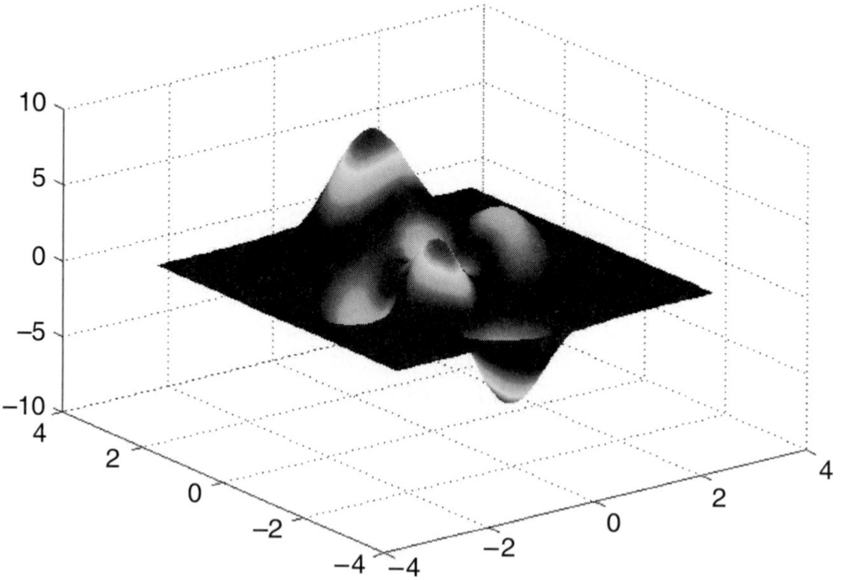

24

Differential Equations

In 1995 MATLAB introduced a collection of M-files, called the MATLAB ODE suite, for solving ordinary differential equations (ODEs). With the introduction of MATLAB 5, the MATLAB ODE suite became a standard part of MATLAB. Now, in MATLAB 6, the ODE suite has added two initial value problem (IVP) solvers. In addition, functions have been added in MATLAB 6 to solve boundary value problems (BVPs) and partial differential equations (PDEs).

Taken as a whole, MATLAB now has the capability to solve a wide variety of problems involving differential equations, however, discussing each of these is beyond the scope of this text. Because initial value problems involving ODEs appear most often in applications, the MATLAB ODE suite is discussed here. Information on all three problem types can be found in the on-line documentation and on *The Mathworks Inc.* web site. In particular, the files `ode_suite.pdf` and `bvptutorial.pdf` offer extensive insight into algorithm development as well as function usage through the use of examples.

24.1 IVP FORMAT

The MATLAB ODE suite computes the time history of a set of coupled first-order differential equations with known initial conditions. In mathematical terms, these problems are called initial value problems and have the form

$$\dot{\mathbf{y}} = \mathbf{f}(t, \mathbf{y}) \qquad \mathbf{y}(t_o) = \mathbf{y}_o$$

which is vector notation for the set of differential equations

$$\begin{aligned} \dot{y}_1 &= f_1(t, y_1, y_2, \ldots, y_n) & y_1(t_o) &= y_{1o} \\ \dot{y}_2 &= f_2(t, y_1, y_2, \ldots, y_n) & y_2(t_o) &= y_{2o} \\ &\vdots & &\vdots \\ \dot{y}_n &= f_n(t, y_1, y_2, \ldots, y_n) & y_n(t_o) &= y_{no} \end{aligned}$$

where $\dot{y}_i = dy_i/dt$, n is the number of first-order differential equations, and y_{io} is the initial condition associated with the ith equation. When an initial value problem is not specified as a set of first-order differential equations, it must be rewritten as one. For example, consider the classic van der Pol equation

$$\ddot{x} - \mu(1 - x^2)\dot{x} + x = 0$$

where μ is a parameter greater than zero. If we choose $y_1 = x$ and $y_2 = dx/dt$, the van der Pol equation becomes

$$\begin{aligned} \dot{y}_1 &= y_2 \\ \dot{y}_2 &= \mu(1 - y_1^2) - y_1 \end{aligned}$$

This initial value problem is used throughout this chapter to demonstrate aspects of the MATLAB ODE suite.

24.2 ODE SUITE SOLVERS

The MATLAB ODE suite offers seven initial value problem solvers. Each has characteristics appropriate for different initial value problems. The calling syntax for each solver is identical, making it relatively easy to change solvers for a given problem. A description of each solver is given in the following table.

Solver	Description
`ode23`	An explicit one-step Runge-Kutta low-order (2nd- to 3rd-order) solver. Suitable for problems that exhibit mild stiffness, problems where lower accuracy is acceptable, or problems where ***f(t,y)*** is not smooth, e.g., discontinuous.
`ode23s`	An implicit one-step modified Rosenbrock solver of order two. Suitable for stiff problems where lower accuracy is acceptable or where ***f(t,y)*** is discontinuous. ***Stiff problems are generally described as problems in which the underlying time constants vary by several orders of magnitude or more.***
`ode23t`	An implicit one-step trapezoidal rule using a *free* interpolant. Suitable for moderately stiff problems. Can be used to solve differential-algebraic equations (DAEs).
`ode23tb`	An implicit trapezoidal rule followed by a backward differentiation rule of order two. Similar to `ode23s`. Can be more efficient than `ode15s` for crude tolerances.
`ode45`	An explicit one-step Runge Kutta medium-order (4th- to 5th-order) solver. Suitable for nonstiff problems that require moderate accuracy. ***This is typically the first solver to try on a new problem.***
`ode113`	A multistep Adams-Bashforth-Moulton PECE solver of varying order (1st- to 13th-order). Suitable for nonstiff problems that require moderate to high accuracy involving problems where ***f(t,y)*** is expensive to compute. Not suitable for problems where ***f(t,y)*** is not smooth.
`ode15s`	An implicit, multistep numerical differentiation solver of varying order (1st- to 5th-order). Suitable for stiff problems that require moderate accuracy. ***This is typically the solver to try if*** `ode45` ***fails or is too inefficient.***

The above table uses terminology, for example, explicit, implicit, and stiff, that requires a substantial theoretical background to understand. If you understand the terminology, the above table describes the basic properties of each solver. If you don't understand the terminology, just follow the guidelines presented in the table where `ode45` and `ode15s` are the first and second respective solvers to be tried for a given problem.

It is important to note that the MATLAB ODE suite is provided as a set of M-files that can be viewed. In addition, these same solvers are included internally in SIMULINK for the simulation of dynamic systems.

24.3 BASIC USE

Before a set of differential equations can be solved, they must be coded in a function M-file as `ydot=odefile(t,y)`. That is, the file must accept a time `t` and a solution `y` and return values for the derivatives. For the van der Pol equation, this ODE file can be written as follows.

```
function ydot=vdpol(t,y)
%VDPOL van der Pol equation.
% Ydot=VDPOL(t,Y)
% Ydot(1) = Y(2)
% Ydot(2) = mu*(1-Y(1)^2)*Y(2)-Y(1)
% mu = 2

mu = 2;
ydot = [y(2); mu*(1-y(1)^2)*y(2)-y(1)];
```

Note that the input arguments are `t` and `y` but that the function does not use `t`. Note also that the output `ydot` must be a column vector.

Given the above ODE file, this set of ODEs is solved using the following commands.

```
>> tspan = [0 20];  % time span to integrate over
>> yo = [2; 0];     % initial conditions (must be a column)
>> [t,y] = ode45(@vdpol,tspan,yo);
>> size(t)          % number of time points
ans =
   333     1
>> size(y)          % (i)th column is y(i) at t(i)
ans =
   333     2
>> plot(t,y(:,1),t,y(:,2),'--')
>> xlabel('time')
>> title('Figure 24.1: van der Pol Solution')
```

Figure 24.1: van der Pol Solution

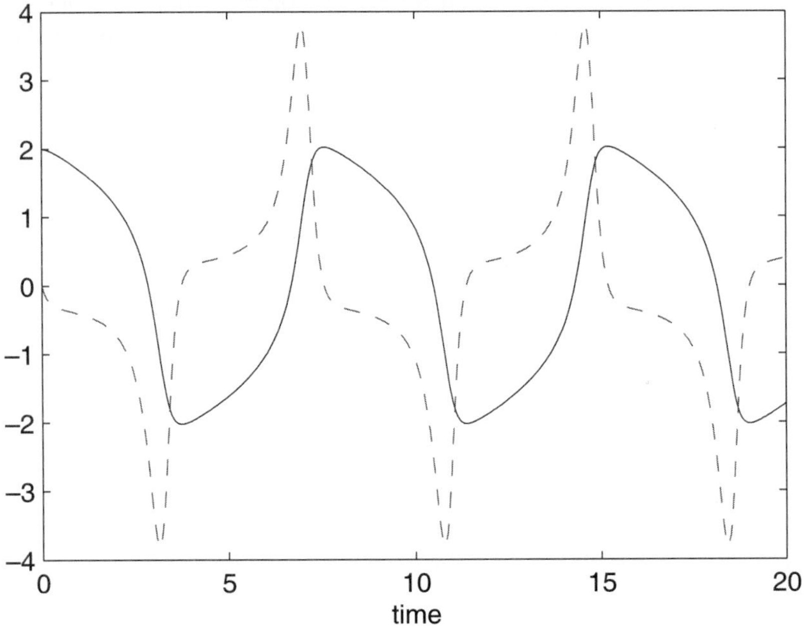

As shown above, the use of function handles is appropriate in this case since differential equations are always written as M-files, and they are evaluated many times in the process of generating a solution over a reasonable time span. By default, if a solver is called with no output arguments, for example, `ode45(@vdpol,tspan,yo)`, the solver generates no output variables but generates a time plot similar to that shown in the above figure.

In addition to specifying the initial and final time points in `tspan`, one can identify the specific solution time points desired by simply adding them to `tspan`, for example,

```
>> yo = [2; 0];
>> tspan = linspace(0,20,100);
>> [t,y] = ode45(@vdpol,tspan,yo);
>> size(t)
ans =
   100     1
>> size(y)
ans =
   100     2
```

Here 100 points are gathered over the same time interval as in the earlier example. When called in this way, the solver still uses automatic step size control to maintain accuracy. ***It does not use fixed step integration.*** To gather the solution at the desired points, the solver interpolates its own solution in an efficient way that does not deteriorate the solution's accuracy.

Sometimes the set of differential equations to be solved contains a set of parameters that the user wishes to vary. Rather than open the ODE file and change the parameters before each call to a solver, the parameters can be added to the solver and ODE file input arguments, for example,

```
function ydot=vdpol(t,y,mu)
%VDPOL van der Pol equation.
% Ydot=VDPOL(t,Y,mu)
% Ydot(1) = Y(2)
% Ydot(2) = mu*(1-Y(1)^2)*Y(2)-Y(1)

% mu = ?; now passed as an input argument

if nargin<3 % supply default if not given
   mu=2;
end
ydot = [y(2); mu*(1-y(1)^2)*y(2)-y(1)];
```

```
>> mu = 10 % set mu in Command window
mu =
    10
>> ode45(@vdpol,tspan,yo,[],mu)
>> title('Figure 24.2: van der Pol Solution, \mu=10')
```

Figure 24.2: van der Pol Solution, μ=10

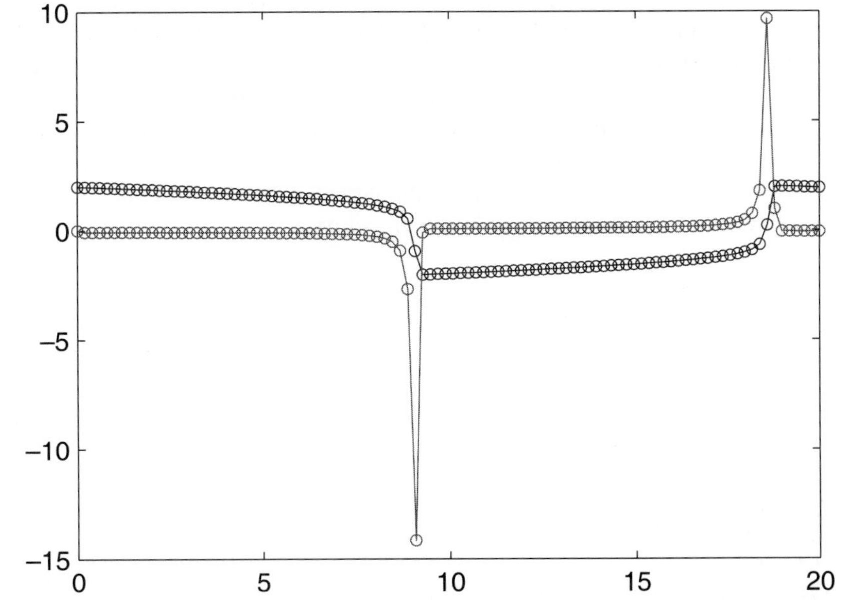

The preceding solves the van der Pol equation with $\mu = 10$. Here `mu` is added as a third input argument to `vdpol.m`. Then the differential equations are solved by adding two input arguments to the `ode45` function call. The first added argument is an empty array, which tells the function to use default solver options. The second added argument contains the value of the parameter. Since no output arguments were specified, the plotted solution is automatically created. While the above example describes the use of one parameter, any number of parameters can be added after the first one shown above. In addition, each parameter can be an array of any data type.

> Prior to MATLAB 6 the ODE file could contain initial conditions, settable options, Jacobian evaluation, and all other features required to solve a general set of ODEs. While these features are grandfathered in MATLAB 6, this general use of the ODE file has been eliminated in favor of techniques that lead to more efficient ODE solution.

24.4 SETTING OPTIONS

Up to this point we have just accepted all default tolerances and options. When these are not sufficient, an options structure can be passed to a solver as a fourth input argument. The MATLAB ODE suite contains the functions `odeset` and `odeget` to manage this options structure. `odeset` works similarly to the Handle Graphics `set` function in that parameters are specified in name/value pairs, for example, `options = odeset('Name1',Value1, 'Name2',Value2,...);`. The available parameter names and values are described in the on-line help for `odeset`, which is shown below.

```
>> help odeset
 ODESET Create/alter ODE OPTIONS structure.
    OPTIONS = ODESET('NAME1',VALUE1,'NAME2',VALUE2,...) creates an integrator
    options structure OPTIONS in which the named properties have the
    specified values. Any unspecified properties have default values. It is
    sufficient to type only the leading characters that uniquely identify the
    property. Case is ignored for property names.
    OPTIONS = ODESET(OLDOPTS,'NAME1',VALUE1,...) alters an existing options
    structure OLDOPTS.
    OPTIONS = ODESET(OLDOPTS,NEWOPTS) combines an existing options structure
    OLDOPTS with a new options structure NEWOPTS. Any new properties
    overwrite corresponding old properties.
    ODESET with no input arguments displays all property names and their
    possible values.

 ODESET PROPERTIES
 RelTol - Relative error tolerance  [ positive scalar {1e-3} ]
    This scalar applies to all components of the solution vector, and
    defaults to 1e-3 (0.1% accuracy) in all solvers. The estimated error in
    each integration step satisfies e(i) <= max(RelTol*abs(y(i)),AbsTol(i)).
 AbsTol - Absolute error tolerance  [ positive scalar or vector {1e-6} ]
    A scalar tolerance applies to all components of the solution vector.
    Elements of a vector of tolerances apply to corresponding components of
    the solution vector. AbsTol defaults to 1e-6 in all solvers. See RelTol.
 NormControl -  Control error relative to norm of solution  [ on | {off} ]
    Set this property 'on' to request that the solvers control the error in
    each integration step with norm(e) <= max(RelTol*norm(y),AbsTol). By
    default the solvers use a more stringent component-wise error control.
 Refine - Output refinement factor  [ positive integer ]
    This property increases the number of output points by the specified
    factor producing smoother output. Refine defaults to 1 in all solvers
    except ODE45, where it is 4. Refine doesn't apply if length(TSPAN) > 2.
 OutputFcn - Installable output function  [ function ]
    This output function is called by the solver after each time step. When
    a solver is called with no output arguments, OutputFcn defaults to the
    function odeplot. Otherwise, OutputFcn defaults to [].
```

```
OutputSel - Output selection indices  [ vector of integers ]
   This vector of indices specifies which components of the solution vector
   are passed to the OutputFcn. OutputSel defaults to all components.
Stats - Display computational cost statistics  [ on | {off} ]
Jacobian - Jacobian function [ function | constant matrix ]
   Set this property to a function FJac (if FJac(t,y) returns dF/dy) or to
   the constant value of dF/dy.
JPattern - Jacobian sparsity pattern [ sparse matrix ]
   Set this property to a sparse matrix S with S(i,j) = 1 if component i of
   F(t,y) depends on component j of y, and 0 otherwise.
Vectorized - Vectorized ODE function  [ on | {off} ]
   Set this property 'on' if the ODE function F is coded so that
   F(t,[y1 y2 ...]) returns [F(t,y1) F(t,y2) ...].
Events - Locate events  [ function ]
   To detect events, set this property to the event function.
Mass - Mass matrix [ constant matrix | function ]
   For problems M*y' = f(t,y) set this property to the value of the constant
   mass matrix. For problems with time- or state-dependent mass matrices,
   set this property to a function that evaluates the mass matrix.
MStateDependence - Dependence of the mass matrix on y [ none | {weak} | strong ]
   Set this property to 'none' for problems M(t)*y' = F(t,y). Both 'weak' and
   'strong' indicate M(t,y), but 'weak' will result in implicit solvers
   using approximations when solving algebraic equations.
MassSingular - Mass matrix is singular  [ yes | no | {maybe} ]
   Set this property to 'no' if the mass matrix is not singular.
MvPattern - dMv/dy sparsity pattern [ sparse matrix ]
   Set this property to a sparse matrix S with S(i,j) = 1 if for any k, the
   (i,k) component of M(t,y) depends on component j of y, and 0 otherwise.
InitialSlope - Consistent initial slope yp0 [ vector ]
   yp0 satisfies M(t0,y0)*yp0 = F(t0,y0).
InitialStep - Suggested initial step size  [ positive scalar ]
   The solver will try this first. By default the solvers determine an
   initial step size automatically.
MaxStep - Upper bound on step size  [ positive scalar ]
   MaxStep defaults to one-tenth of the tspan interval in all solvers.
BDF - Use Backward Differentiation Formulas in ODE15S  [ on | {off} ]
   This property specifies whether the Backward Differentiation Formulas
   (Gear's methods) are to be used in ODE15S instead of the default
   Numerical Differentiation Formulas.
MaxOrder - Maximum order of ODE15S  [ 1 | 2 | 3 | 4 | {5} ]
```

Consider the following examples of using the above options.

```
>> odeset
          AbsTol: [ positive scalar or vector {1e-6} ]
          RelTol: [ positive scalar {1e-3} ]
     NormControl: [ on | {off} ]
       OutputFcn: [ function ]
       OutputSel: [ vector of integers ]
```

```
           Refine: [ positive integer ]
            Stats: [ on | {off} ]
      InitialStep: [ positive scalar ]
          MaxStep: [ positive scalar ]
              BDF: [ on | {off} ]
         MaxOrder: [ 1 | 2 | 3 | 4 | {5} ]
         Jacobian: [ matrix | function ]
         JPattern: [ sparse matrix ]
       Vectorized: [ on | {off} ]
             Mass: [ matrix | function ]
 MStateDependence: [ none | {weak} | strong ]
        MvPattern: [ sparse matrix ]
     MassSingular: [ yes | no | {maybe} ]
     InitialSlope: [ vector ]
           Events: [ function ]
```

Invoking odeset without input or output arguments returns an option listing, their possible values, and default values in braces.

```
>> tspan = [0 20]; % set time span to solve
>> yo = [2; 0];    % intial conditions
>> mu = 10;        % parameter mu
>> options = odeset('AbsTol',1e-12,'RelTol',1e-6)
options =
              AbsTol: 1e-012
                 BDF: []
              Events: []
         InitialStep: []
            Jacobian: []
           JConstant: []
            JPattern: []
                Mass: []
        MassConstant: []
        MassSingular: []
            MaxOrder: []
             MaxStep: []
         NormControl: []
           OutputFcn: []
           OutputSel: []
              Refine: []
              RelTol: 1e-006
               Stats: []
          Vectorized: []
    MStateDependence: []
           MvPattern: []
        InitialSlope: []
```

```
>> [t,y] = ode45(@vdpol,tspan,yo,[],mu);  % default tolerances
>> length(t)
ans =
   593
>> [t,y] = ode45(@vdpol,tspan,yo,options,mu);  % tight tolerances
>> length(t)
ans =
          1689
>> [t,y] = ode15s(@vdpol,tspan,yo,[],mu);  %  different solver
>> length(t)
ans =
   232
>> [t,y] = ode15s(@vdpol,tspan,yo,options,mu);
>> length(t)
ans =
   651
```

Here the steps needed to integrate the first 20 seconds are shown. Default tolerances, that is, `AbsTol=1e-6` and `RelTol=1e-3`, forces `ode45` to take 593 time steps. Decreasing the tolerances to `AbsTol=1e-12` and `RelTol=1e-6` takes 1689 time steps. However, changing to the stiff solver `ode15s` requires only 651 steps at the tighter tolerances.

The stiff solvers `ode15s`, `ode23s`, `ode23t`, and `ode23tb` allow one to specify an analytical Jacobian rather than a numerically computed approximation, which is the default. The Jacobian is a matrix of partial derivatives, which has the form

$$\begin{bmatrix} \frac{\partial f_1}{\partial y_1} & \frac{\partial f_1}{\partial y_2} & \cdots & \frac{\partial f_1}{\partial y_n} \\ \frac{\partial f_2}{\partial y_1} & \frac{\partial f_2}{\partial y_2} & \cdots & \frac{\partial f_2}{\partial y_n} \\ \vdots & \vdots & \ddots & \vdots \\ \frac{\partial f_n}{\partial y_1} & \frac{\partial f_n}{\partial y_2} & \cdots & \frac{\partial f_n}{\partial f_n} \end{bmatrix}$$

This matrix or a numerical approximation of it is used by the stiff solvers to compute the solution of a set of nonlinear equations at each time step. If at all possible, an analytical Jacobian should be supplied as shown in the following.

```
function jac=vdpoljac(t,y,mu)
%VDPOLJAC van der Pol equation Jacobian.

% mu = ?; passed as an input argument
if nargin<3 % supply default if not given
   mu=2;
end
jac = [      0                     1
      (-2*mu*y(1)*y(2)-1) (mu*(1-y(1)^2))];
```

```
>> options = odeset(options,'Jacobian',@vdpoljac);
>> [t,y] = ode15s(@vdpol,tspan,yo,options,mu);
>> length(t)
ans =
   670
```

In the above, the function handle of the M-file that computes the Jacobian is added to the options structure set earlier. Running the solver now shows that it takes 670 steps. While this is more than the 651 shown earlier, providing the analytical Jacobian significantly increases execution speed.

When it is not possible to supply an analytical Jacobian, it is beneficial to supply a ***vectorized*** ODE file. Vectorizing the ODE file usually means replacing `y(i)` with `y(i,:)` and using array operators. Doing so allows computation of the numerical Jacobian to proceed as fast as possible, for example,

```
function ydot=vdpol(t,y,mu)
%VDPOL van der Pol equation.
% Ydot=VDPOL(t,Y)
% Ydot(1) = Y(2)
% Ydot(2) = mu*(1-Y(1)^2)*Y(2)-Y(1)

% mu = ?; now passed as an input argument
if nargin<3 % supply default if not given
   mu=2;
end
ydot = [y(2,:); mu*(1-y(1,:)^2)*y(2,:)-y(1,:)];
```

The 'Refine' property determines how much output data to generate. It does not affect the step sizes chosen by the solvers or the solution accuracy. It merely dictates how many intermediate points to interpolate the solution at within each integration step, as in the following example.

```
>> options = odeset('Refine',1);
>> [t,y] = ode45(@vdpol,tspan,yo,options,mu);
>> length(t) % # of time points
ans =
   149
>> options = odeset('Refine',4);
>> [t,y] = ode45(@vdpol,tspan,yo,options,mu);
>> length(t) % # of time points
ans =
   593
```

With 'Refine' set to one, 149 time points are returned over the 20-second time span. Setting 'Refine' to 4 increases the number of time points returned to 593.

The 'Events' property allows one to flag one or more events that occur as an ODE solution evolves in time. For example, a simple event could be when some solution component reaches a maximum, a minimum, or crosses through zero. Optionally, the occurrence of an event can force a solver to stop integrating. To make use of this feature one must simply supply a function handle that computes the values of the events to be tracked. At each time step the solver computes the events and marks in time those that cross through zero, for example,

```
function [value,isterminal,direction]=vdpolevents(t,y,mu)
%VDPOLEVENTS  van der Pol equation events.

value(1)=abs(y(2))-2; % find where |y(2)|=2
isterminal(1)=0;      % don't stop integration
direction(1)=0;       % don't care about crossing direction
```

```
>> mu = 2;
>> options = odeset('Events',@vdpolevents);
>> [t,y,te,ye] = ode45(@vdpol,tspan,yo,options,mu);
>> plot(t,y,te,ye(:,2),'o')
>> title('Figure 24.3: van der Pol Solution, |y(2)|=2')
```

Figure 24.3: van der Pol Solution, ly(2)l=2

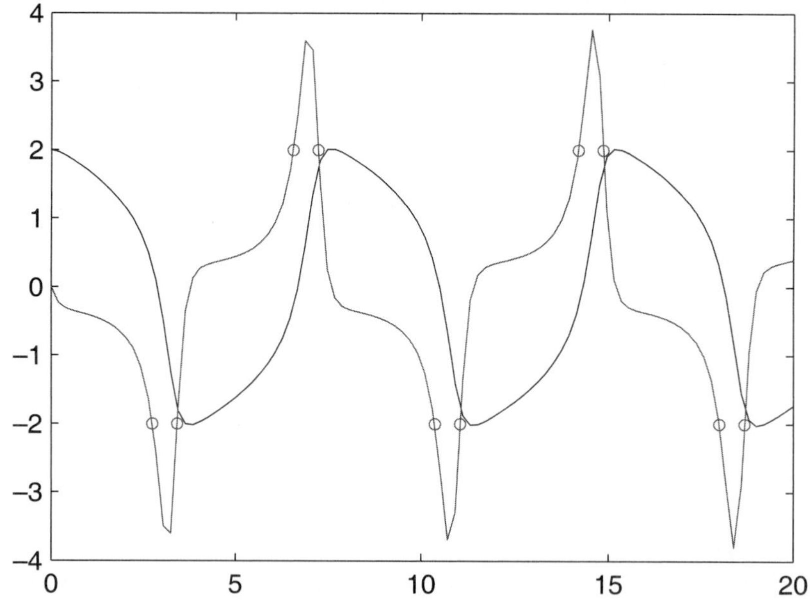

The function `vdpolevents` receives the same three arguments as the other functions. It returns three numerical vectors. The first is the value of the events; the second is a logical array dictating whether the solver should terminate execution on a zero crossing in one or more of the computed events; the third gives the user the ability to specify whether the direction of event crossing should be considered. In the above example, the points where $\text{abs}(y_2(t)) = 2$ is selected as the only event. The solver is told to not halt on sensing events and to not care about the direction of event crossing. The generated plot shows the system solution and the points where the chosen events occur.

24.5 BVPS AND PDES

In addition to the seven MATLAB solvers for solving initial value ordinary differential equations, MATLAB 6 includes functions for the solution of boundary value problems and partial differential equations. The functions used to solve BVPs are shown in the table below.

Function	Description
`bvp4c`	BVP solver.
`bvpget`	Get BVP options structure.
`bvpinit`	Form the initial solution guess, which is refined by `bvp4c`.

Function	Description
`bvpset`	Set the BVP options structure.
`bvpval`	Evaluate/interpolate the solution found using `bvp4c`.

Further information regarding the solution of BVPs can be found in the on-line documentation as well as in the file `bvptutorial.pdf` as mentioned earlier.

The functions used to solve PDEs are shown in the table below.

Function	Description
`pdepe`	Solve IVPs for parabolic-elliptic PDEs in one dimension.
`pdeval`	Evaluate/interpolate the solution found using `pdepe`.

Further information regarding the solution of PDEs can be found in the on-line documentation.

25

Two-Dimensional Graphics

Throughout this text several of MATLAB's graphics features have been introduced. In this and the next several chapters, the graphics features in MATLAB are more rigorously illustrated. Many of the features and capabilities illustrated here are available as menu items from the top of a *Figure* window or are available as buttons on the *Figure* or *Camera* toolbar, which appears by default when plots are generated or can be chosen via the **View** menu in a *Figure* window.

The general rule is to use the toolbar and menu features of *Figure* windows if you want to customize a single *Figure.* Or use *Command* window functions to automate the process of customizing plots. This text concentrates on the *Command* window functions since they perform the actions taken when menu and toolbar items are used.

25.1 THE `plot` FUNCTION

As you have seen in earlier examples, the most common function for plotting 2-D data is the `plot` function. This versatile function plots sets of data arrays on appropriate axes and connects the points with straight lines, for example,

```
>> x = linspace(0,2*pi,30);
>> y = sin(x);
>> plot(x,y), title('Figure 25.1: Sine Wave')
```

This example creates 30 data points over $0 \le x \le 2\pi$ to form the horizontal axis of the plot and creates another vector `y` containing the sine of the data points in `x`. The `plot` function opens a graphics window, called a *Figure* window, scales the axes to fit the data, plots the points, and then connects the points with straight lines. It also adds numerical scales and tick marks to the axes automatically. If a *Figure* window already exists, `plot` generally clears the current *Figure* window and draws a new plot.

It is possible to plot more than one curve or line on a plot, for example,

```
>> z = cos(x);
>> plot(x,y,x,z)
>> title('Figure 25.2: Sine and Cosine')
```

Just by giving plot another pair of arguments instructs it to generate a second line. This time sin(x) versus x and cos(x) versus x were plotted on the same plot. Although the figure doesn't show color, `plot` automatically draws the second curve in a different color. The function `plot` generates as many curves as it receives pairs of input arguments.

If one of the arguments is a matrix and the other a vector, the `plot` function plots each column of the matrix versus the vector, for example,

```
>> W = [y;z]; % create a matrix of the sine and cosine
>> plot(x,W)  % plot the columns of W vs. x
```

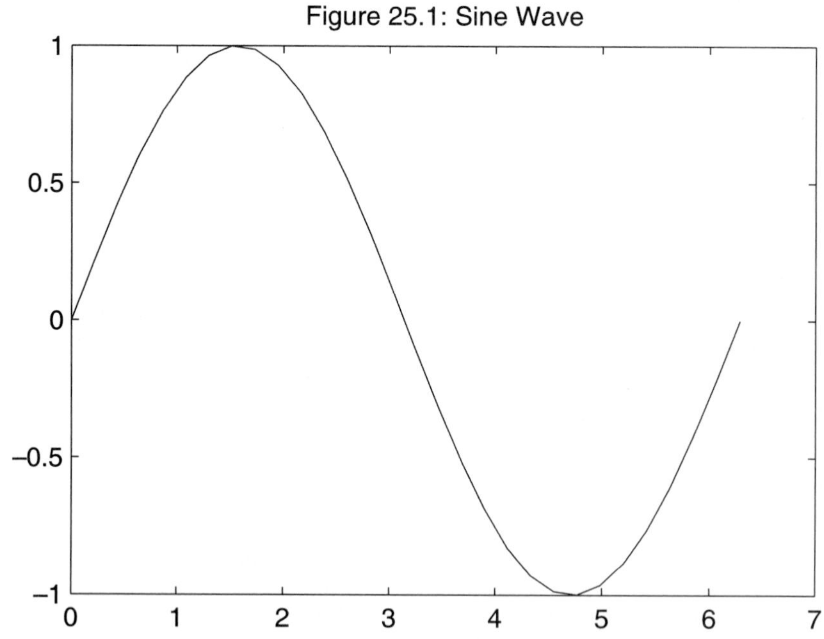

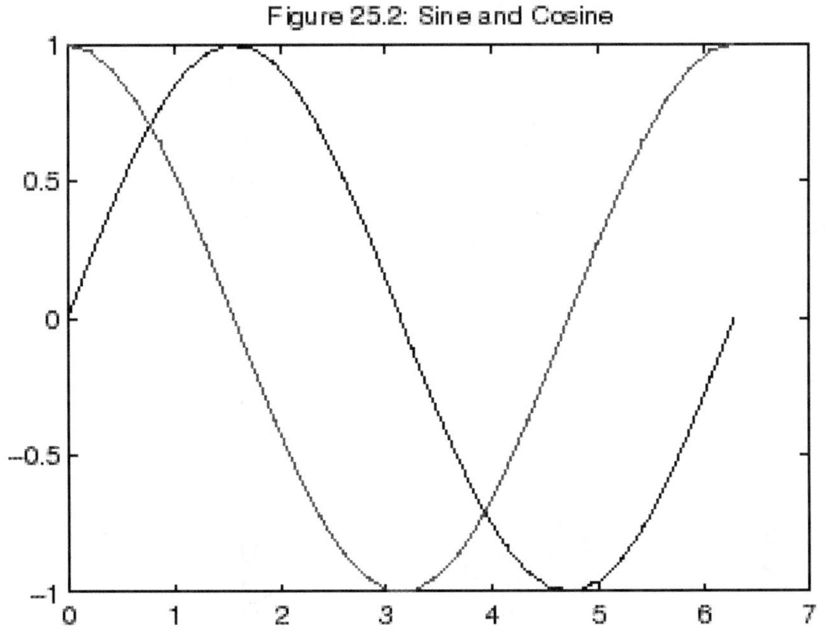

reproduces the preceding plot.

If you change the order of the arguments, the orientation of the plot changes accordingly, for example,

```
>> plot(W,x) % plot x vs. the columns of W
>> title('Figure 25.3: Change Argument Order')
```

When the `plot` function is called with only one argument, for example, `plot(Y)`, the `plot` function acts differently depending on the data contained in `Y`. If `Y` is a ***complex-valued*** vector, `plot(Y)` is interpreted as `plot(real(Y),imag(Y))`. In all other cases, the imaginary components of the input vectors are *ignored.* On the other hand, if `Y` is ***real-valued***, then `plot(Y)` is interpreted as `plot(1:length(Y),Y)`; that is, `Y` is plotted versus an index of its values. When `Y` is a matrix, the above interpretations are applied to each column of `Y`.

25.2 LINESTYLES, MARKERS, AND COLORS

In the previous examples, MATLAB chose the solid linestyle, and the colors blue and green for the plots. You can specify your own colors, markers, and linestyles by giving `plot` a third argument after each pair of data arrays. This optional argument is a character string consisting of one or more characters from the table on page 352.

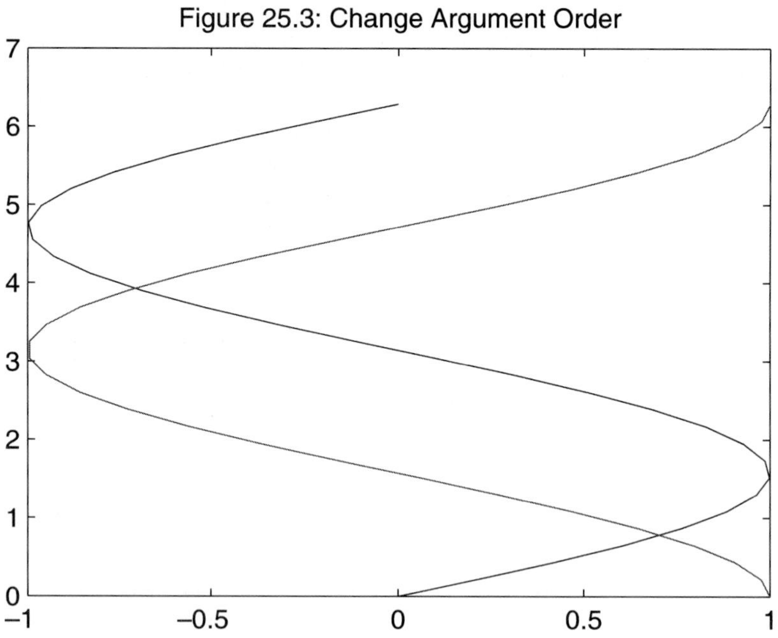

Symbol	Color	Symbol	Marker	Symbol	Linestyle
b	Blue	.	Point	-	Solid line
g	Green	o	Circle	:	Dotted line
r	Red	x	Cross	-.	Dash-dot line
c	Cyan	+	Plus sign	--	Dashed line
m	Magenta	*	Asterisk		
y	Yellow	s	Square		
k	Black	d	Diamond		
w	White	v	Triangle (down)		
		^	Triangle (up)		
		<	Triangle (left)		
		>	Triangle (right)		
		p	Pentagram		
		h	Hexagram		

If you do not specify a color and you are using the default color scheme, MATLAB starts with blue and cycles through the first seven colors in the preceding table for each additional line. The default linestyle is a solid line unless you explicitly specify a different linestyle. There is no default marker. If no marker is selected, no markers are drawn. The use of any marker places the chosen symbol at each data point but does not connect the data points with a straight line unless a linestyle is specified as well.

If a color, a marker, and a linestyle are all included in the string, the color applies to both the marker and the line. To specify a different color for the marker, plot the same data with a different specification string, for example,

```
>> plot(x,y,'b:p',x,z,'c-',x,1.2*z,'m+')
>> title('Figure 25.4: Linestyles and Markers')
```

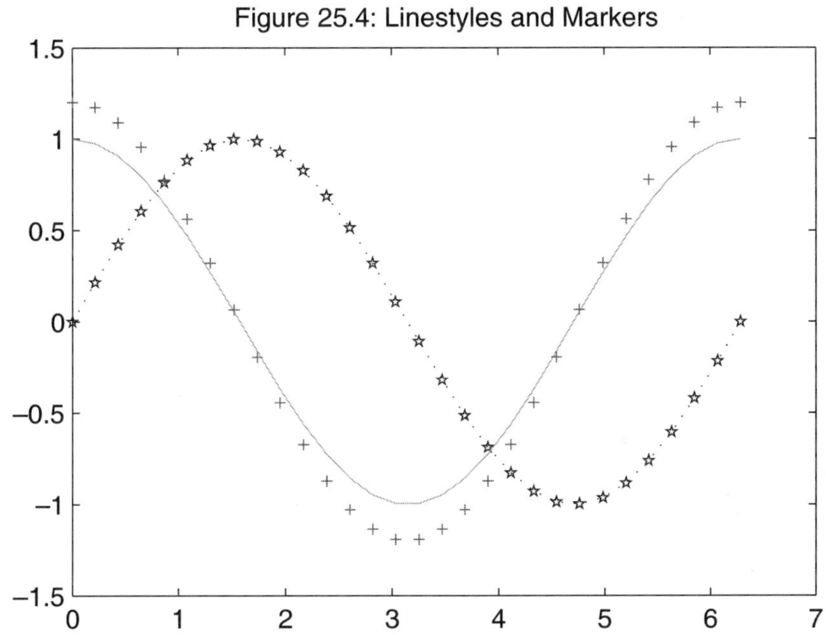

As with many of the plots in this section, your computer displays color but the figures shown here do not. If you are following along in MATLAB, just enter the commands listed in the examples to see the effects of color.

25.3 PLOT GRIDS, AXES BOX, AND LABELS

The `grid on` command adds grid lines to the current plot at the tick marks. The `grid off` command removes the grid. `grid` with no arguments alternately turns the grid lines on and off; that is, it ***toggles*** them. MATLAB starts up with `grid off` for most plots by default. If you like to have grid lines on all your plots by default, add the following lines to your `startup.m` file.

```
set(0,'DefaultAxesXgrid','on')
set(0,'DefaultAxesYgrid','on')
set(0,'DefaultAxesZgrid','on')
```

These lines illustrate the use of Handle Graphics features in MATLAB and the setting of default behavior. More information on these topics can be found in Chapter 30.

Normally, 2-D axes are fully enclosed by solid lines called an ***axes box.*** This box can be turned off with `box off`. `box on` restores the axes box. The `box` command toggles the state of the axes box. Horizontal and vertical axes can be labeled with the `xlabel` and `ylabel` functions, respectively. The `title` function adds a line of text at the top of the plot. Consider the following example.

```
>> x = linspace(0,2*pi,30);
>> y = sin(x);
>> z = cos(x);
>> plot(x,y,x,z)
>> box off                                % turn off the axes box
>> xlabel('Independent Variable X')       % label horizontal axis
>> ylabel('Dependent Variables Y and Z') % label vertical axis
>> title('Figure 25.5: Sine and Cosine Curves, No Box') % title
```

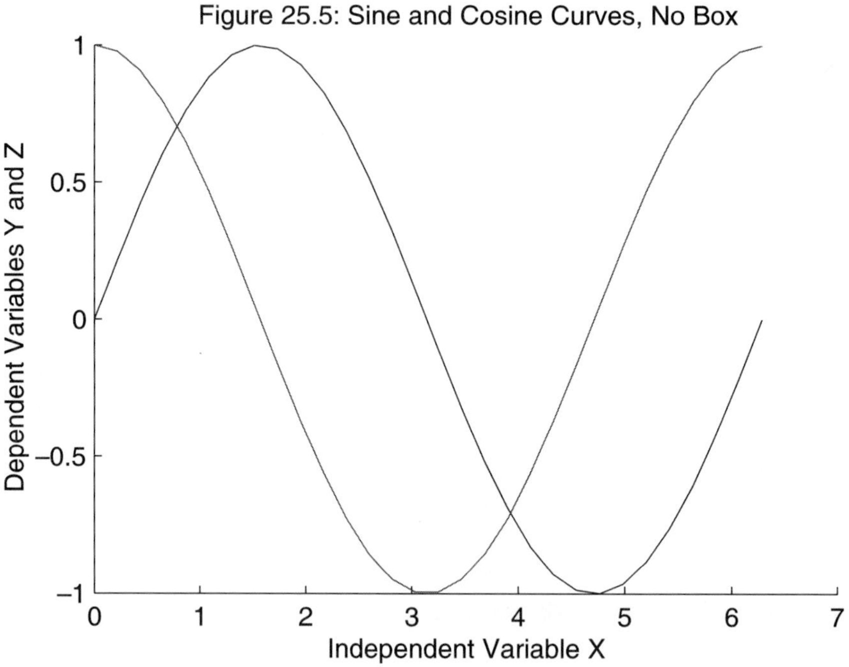

You can add a label or any other text string to any specific location on your plot with the `text` function. The syntax for `text` is `text(x,y,'string')`, where `(x,y)` represents the coordinates of the center left edge of the text string in units taken from the plot axes.

For example, the following code segment places the text `'sin(x)'` at the location $x = 2.5$, $y = 0.7$.

```
>> grid on, box on % turn axes box and grid lines on
>> text(2.5,0.7,'sin(x)')
>> title('Figure 25.6: Sine and Cosine Curves, Added Label')
```

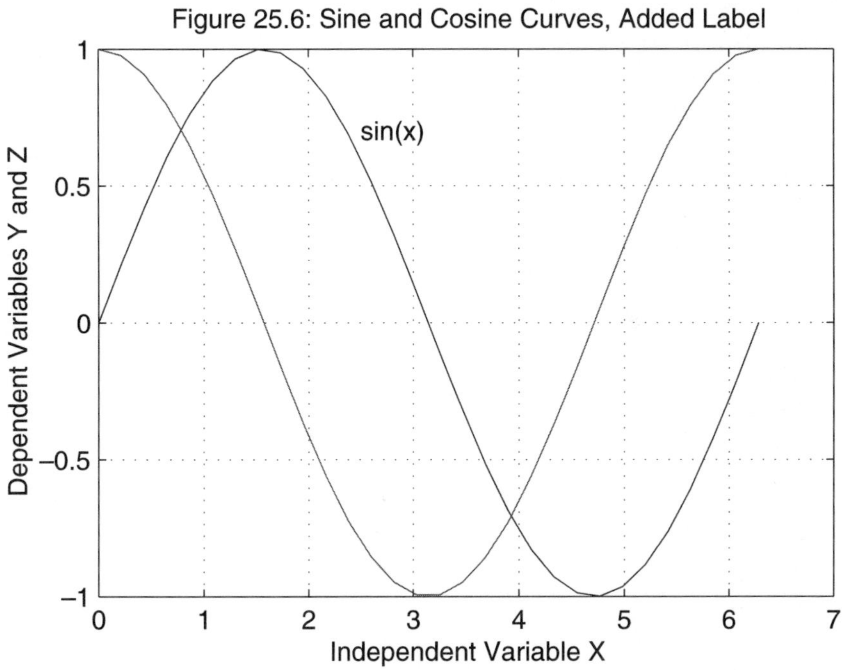

If you want to add a label but don't want to stop to figure out the coordinates to use, you can place a text string with the mouse. The `gtext('text')` function switches to the current *Figure* window, puts up a cross-hair that follows the mouse, and waits for a mouse click or key press. When either one occurs, the string argument to `gtext` is placed with the lower left corner of the first character at that location.

25.4 CUSTOMIZING PLOT AXES

MATLAB gives you complete control over the scaling and appearance of both the horizontal and vertical axes of your plot with the `axis` command. Because this command has so many features, only the most useful are described here. The primary features of the `axis` command are given in the following table.

Command	Description
`axis([xmin xmax ymin ymax])`	Set axis limits on the current plot.
`V = axis`	Return a row vector containing the current axis limits.
`axis auto`	Return axis scaling to automatic defaults.
`axis manual`	Freeze axis scaling so that if `hold` is `on`, subsequent plots use the same axis limits.
`axis tight`	Set axis limits to the range of the plotted data.
`axis fill`	Set the axis limits and aspect ratio so that the axis fills the allotted space. This option has an effect only if `PlotBoxAspectRatio` or `DataAspectRatioMode` is `manual`.
`axis ij`	Put axis in ***matrix*** mode. The horizontal axis increases from left to right. The vertical axis increases from top to bottom.
`axis xy`	Put axis in Cartesian mode. The horizontal axis increases from left to right. The vertical axis increases from bottom to top.
`axis equal`	Set the aspect ratio so that equal tick mark increments on each axis are equal in size.
`axis image`	Set axis limits appropriate for displaying an image.
`axis square`	Make the axis box square in size.
`axis normal`	Restore the current axis box to full size and removes any restrictions on unit scaling.
`axis vis3d`	Freeze the aspect ratio to enable rotation of 3-D objects without axis size changes.
`axis off`	Turn off all axis labeling, tick marks, and background.
`axis on`	Turn on all axis labeling, tick marks, and background.

Multiple commands to `axis` can be given at once. For example, `axis auto on xy` is the default axis scaling. The `axis` command affects only the current plot. Therefore, it is issued after the plot command, just as grid, xlabel, ylabel, title, text, and so on, are issued after the plot is on the screen. Consider the example

```
x = linspace(0,2*pi,30);
y = sin(x);
plot(x,y)
title('Figure 25.7: Fixed Axis Scaling')
axis([0 2*pi -1.5 2])  % change axis limits
```

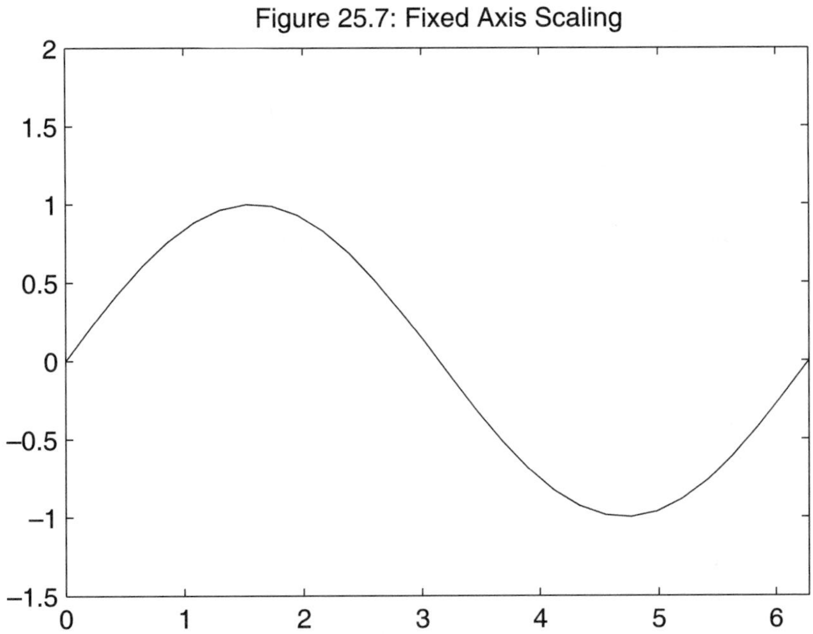

Note that by specifying the maximum x-axis value to be 2*pi, the plot axis ends at exactly 2*pi rather than rounding the axis limit up to 7. The simplest way to see what the various axis command arguments do is to generate a simple plot as shown above and then issue multiple axis commands and view the resulting changes.

When one simply wants to change the axis limits on a single axis, the axis command is cumbersome because it requires one to enter limits for all the axes. To solve this problem, MATLAB provides the functions xlim, ylim, and zlim, which are described by the help text for xlim, with the obvious change for ylim and zlim.

```
>> help xlim
 XLIM X limits.
    XL = XLIM               gets the x limits of the current axes.
    XLIM([XMIN XMAX])       sets the x limits.
    XLMODE = XLIM('mode') gets the x limits mode.
    XLIM(mode)              sets the x limits mode.
                               (mode can be 'auto' or 'manual')
    XLIM(AX,...)            uses axes AX instead of current axes.
    XLIM sets or gets the XLim or XLimMode property of an axes.
    See also PBASPECT, DASPECT, YLIM, ZLIM.
```

25.5 MULTIPLE PLOTS

You can add new plots to an existing plot using the `hold` command. When you enter `hold on`, MATLAB does not remove the existing axes when new `plot` functions are issued. Instead, it adds new curves to the current axes. However, if the new data does not fit within the current axes limits, the axes are rescaled. Entering `hold off` releases the current *Figure* window for new plots. The `hold` command without arguments toggles the `hold` setting, for example,

```
>> x = linspace(0,2*pi,30);
>> y = sin(x);
>> z = cos(x);
>> plot(x,y)
>> hold on
>> ishold  % return 1 (True) if hold is ON
ans =
     1
>> plot(x,z,'m')
>> hold off
>> ishold  % hold is no longer ON
ans =
     0
>> title 'Figure 25.8: Use of hold command'
```

Notice that this example specifies the color of the second curve. Since there is only one set of data arrays in each `plot` function, the line color for each `plot` function would otherwise default to the first color in the color order list, resulting in two lines plotted in the same color on the plot. Note also that the title text is not enclosed in parentheses but that the effect remains unchanged. In the alternative form above `title` is interpreted as a command rather than a function.

Figure 25.8: Use of hold command

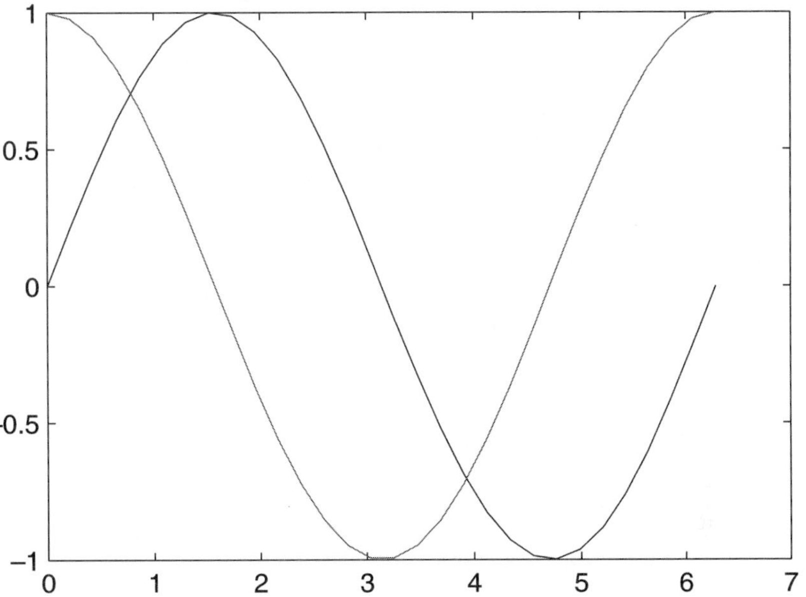

25.6 MULTIPLE FIGURES

It is possible to create multiple *Figure* windows and plot different data sets in different ways in each one. To create new *Figure* windows, use the `figure` command in the *Command* window or the **New Figure** selection from the **File** menu in the *Command* or *Figure* window. You can choose a specific *Figure* window to be the active or current figure by clicking on it with the mouse or by using `figure(n)`, where `n` is the number of the window. The current *Figure* window is the window that is active for subsequent plotting functions.

Every time a new *Figure* window is created, a number identifying it, that is, its ***handle,*** is returned and stored for future use. The figure handle is also displayed in the *Figure* window title bar. When a new *Figure* window is created, it is placed in the default figure position on the screen. As a result, when more than one *Figure* window is created, each new window covers all preceding windows. To see the windows simultaneously, simply drag them around using the mouse on the *Figure* window title bar.

To reuse a *Figure* window for a new plot, it must be made the active, or current figure. Clicking on the figure of choice with the mouse makes it the current figure. From within MATLAB, `figure(h)` where `h` is the figure handle, makes the corresponding figure active or current. Only the current figure is responsive to `axis`, `hold`, `xlabel`, `ylabel`, `title`, and `grid` commands.

Figure windows can be deleted by closing them with the mouse similar to the way you close windows on your computer, if such a feature exists. Alternatively, the command `close` can be issued. For example,

```
>> close
```

closes the current *Figure* window.

```
>> close(h)
```

closes the *Figure* window having handle h.

```
>> close all
```

closes all *Figure* windows.

If you simply want to erase the contents of a *Figure* window without closing it, use the command clf. For example,

```
>> clf
```

clears the current *Figure* window.

```
>> clf reset
```

clears the current *Figure* window and resets all properties such as hold to their default state.

25.7 SUBPLOTS

One *Figure* window can hold more than one set of axes. The subplot(m,n,p) command subdivides the current *Figure* window into an m-by-n array of plotting areas and chooses the pth area to be active. The subplots are numbered left to right along the top row, then along the second row, and so on, for example,

```
x = linspace(0,2*pi,30);
y = sin(x);
z = cos(x);
a = 2*sin(x).*cos(x);
b = sin(x)./(cos(x)+eps);

subplot(2,2,1) % pick the upper left of a 2-by-2 grid of subplots
plot(x,y), axis([0 2*pi -1 1]), title('Figure 25.09a: sin(x)')

subplot(2,2,2) % pick the upper right of the 4 subplots
plot(x,z), axis([0 2*pi -1 1]), title('Figure 25.09b: cos(x)')

subplot(2,2,3) % pick the lower left of the 4 subplots
plot(x,a), axis([0 2*pi -1 1]), title('Figure 25.09c: 2sin(x)cos(x)')

subplot(2,2,4) % pick the lower right of the 4 subplots
plot(x,b), axis([0 2*pi -20 20]), title('Figure 25.09d: sin(x)/cos(x)')
```

Note that when a particular subplot is active, it is the only subplot or axis that is responsive to axis, hold, xlabel, ylabel, title, grid, and box commands. The other subplots are

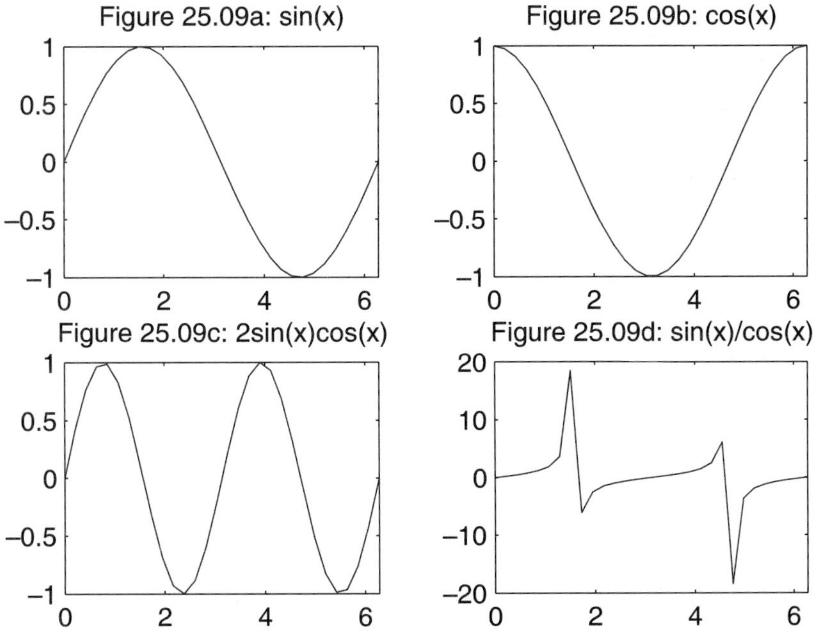

not affected. In addition, the active subplot remains active until another `subplot` or `figure` command is issued. When a new `subplot` command changes the number of subplots in the *Figure* window, previous subplots are erased to make room for the new orientation. To return to the default mode and use the entire *Figure* window for a single set of axes, use the command `subplot(1,1,1)`. When you print a *Figure* window containing multiple plots, all of them are printed on the same page. For example, when the current *Figure* window contains four subplots and the orientation is landscape mode, each of the plots uses one-quarter of the printed page.

25.8 INTERACTIVE PLOTTING TOOLS

Before the *Figure* window menu bar and toolbars existed, MATLAB offered several functions for annotating plots interactively. These functions are described in this section, and most are available from the *Figure* menu bar and toolbars.

Rather than using individual text strings to identify the data sets on your plot, a legend can be used. The `legend` command creates a legend box on the plot, keying any text you supply to each line in the plot. If you wish to move the legend, simply click and hold down the mouse button near the lower left edge of the legend and drag the legend to the desired location. `legend off` deletes the legend. Consider the following example.

```
>> x = linspace(0,2*pi,30);
>> y = sin(x);
>> z = cos(x);
>> plot(x,y,x,z)
```

```
>> legend('sin(x)','cos(x)')
>> title('Figure 25.10: Legend Example')
```

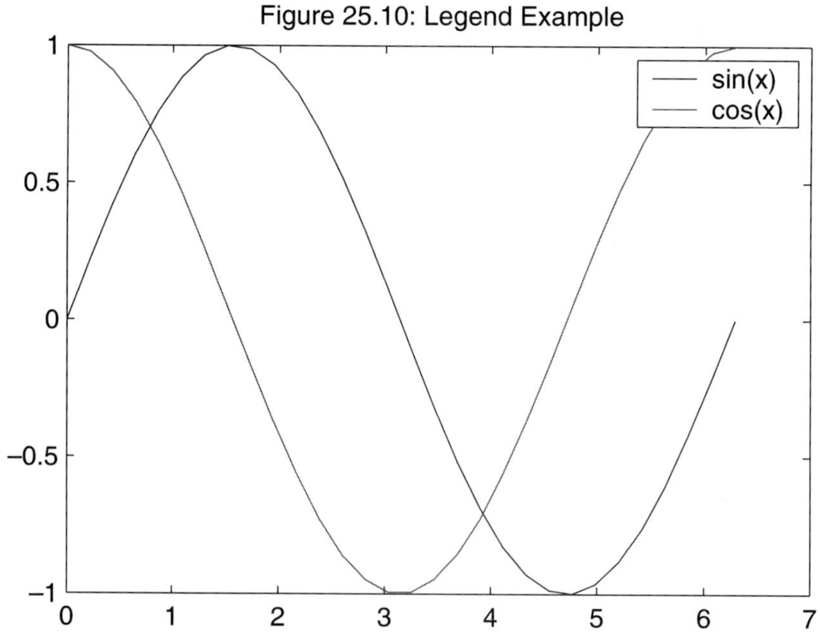

MATLAB provides an interactive tool to expand sections of a 2-D plot to see more detail or to ***zoom in*** on a region of interest. The command `zoom on` turns on the zoom mode. Clicking the left mouse button within the *Figure* window expands the plot by a factor of 2 centered around the point under the mouse pointer. Each time you click, the plot expands. Click the right mouse button to zoom out by a factor of 2. You can also click and drag a rectangular area to zoom in on a specific area. `zoom(n)` zooms in by a factor of `n`. `zoom out` returns the plot to its initial state. `zoom off` turns off the zoom mode. `zoom` with no arguments toggles the zoom state of the active *Figure* window. The *Figure* toolbar and *Figure* window menus offer a GUI approach to implementing this feature as well.

In some situations it is convenient to select coordinate points from a plot in a *Figure* window. In MATLAB this feature is embodied in the `ginput` function. The form `[x,y]=ginput(n)` gets `n` points from the current plot or subplot based on mouse-click positions within the plot or subplot. If you press the **Return** or **Enter** key before all `n` points are selected, `ginput` terminates with fewer points. The points returned in the vectors `x` and `y` are the respective x and y data coordinate points selected. The returned data are not necessarily points from the plotted data but rather the explicit x- and y-coordinate values where the mouse was clicked. If points are selected outside the plot or subplot axes limits, for example, outside the plot box, the points returned are extrapolated values.

This function can be somewhat confusing when used in a *Figure* window containing subplots. The data returned is with respect to the current or active subplot. Thus, if `ginput` is issued after a `subplot(2,2,3)` command, the data returned is with respect to the axes of the data plotted in `subplot(2,2,3)`. If points are selected from other subplots, the data is still with respect to the axes of the data in `subplot(2,2,3)`. When an unspecified number of data points are desired, the form `[x,y]=ginput` without an input argument can be used. Here data points are gathered until the **Return** key is pressed. The `gtext` function described earlier in this chapter utilizes the function `ginput` along with the function `text` for placing text with the mouse.

25.9 SCREEN UPDATES

Because screen rendering is relatively time-consuming, MATLAB does not always update the screen after each graphics command. For example, if the following commands are entered at the MATLAB prompt, MATLAB updates the screen after each graphics command (`plot`, `axis`, and `grid`).

```
>> x = linspace(0,2*pi); y = sin(x);
>> plot(x,y)
>> axis([0 2*pi -1.2 1.2])
>> grid
```

However, if the same graphics commands are entered on a single line, that is,

```
>> plot(x,y), axis([0 2*pi -1.2 1.2]), grid
```

MATLAB renders the figure only once—when the MATLAB prompt reappears. A similar procedure occurs when graphics commands appear as part of a script or function M-file. In this case, even if the commands appear on separate lines in the file, the screen is rendered only once—when all commands are completed and the MATLAB prompt reappears.

In general, five events cause MATLAB to render the screen:

1. A return to the MATLAB prompt
2. Encountering a function that temporarily stops execution, such as `pause`, `keyboard`, `input`, and `waitforbuttonpress`
3. Execution of a `getframe` command
4. Execution of a `drawnow` command
5. Resizing of a *Figure* window.

Of these, the `drawnow` command specifically allows one to force MATLAB to redraw the screen at arbitrary times.

25.10 SPECIALIZED 2-D PLOTS

Up to this point the basic plotting function `plot` has been illustrated. In many situations, plotting lines or points on linearly scaled axes does not convey the desired information. As a result, MATLAB offers other basic 2-D plotting functions, as well as specialized plotting functions that are embodied in function M-files.

In addition to `plot`, MATLAB provides the functions `semilogx` for plotting with a logarithmically scaled *x*-axis, `semilogy` for plotting with a logarithmically scaled *y*-axis, and `loglog` for plotting with both axes logarithmically spaced. All the features discussed above with respect to the function `plot` apply to these functions as well.

The `area` function is useful for building a stacked area plot. `area(x,y)` is the same as `plot(x,y)` for vectors `x` and `y`, except that the area under the plot is filled in with color. The lower limit for the filled area may be specified but defaults to zero. To stack areas, use the form `area(X,Y)`, where `Y` is a matrix and `X` is a matrix or vector whose length equals the number of rows in `Y`. If `X` is omitted, `area` uses the default value `X=1:size(Y,1)`, for example,

```
>> z = -pi:pi/5:pi;
>> area([sin(z); cos(z)])
>> title('Figure 25.11: Stacked Area Plot')
```

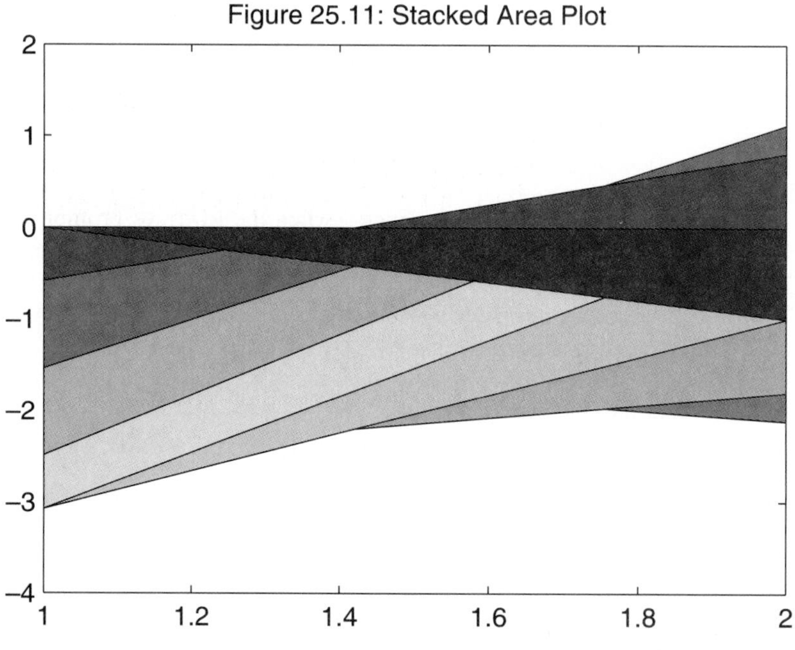

Filled polygons can be drawn using the `fill` function. `fill(x,y,'c')` fills the 2-D polygon defined by the column vectors `x` and `y` with the color specified by `c`. The vertices of the polygon are specified by the pairs `(x(i),y(i))`. If necessary, the polygon is closed by connecting the last vertex to the first. Like the `plot` function, `fill` can have any number of pairs of vertices and associated colors. Moreover, when `x` and `y` are matrices of the same dimension, the columns of `x` and `y` are assumed to describe separate polygons. Consider the example

```
>> t = (1:2:15)'*pi/8;
>> x = sin(t);
>> y = cos(t);
>> fill(x,y,'r') % a filled red circle using only 8 data points
>> axis square off
>> text(0,0,'STOP', ...
   'Color',[1 1 1], ...
   'FontSize',80, ...
   'FontWeight','bold', ...
   'HorizontalAlignment','center')
>> title('Figure 25.12: Stop Sign')
```

Figure 25.12: Stop Sign

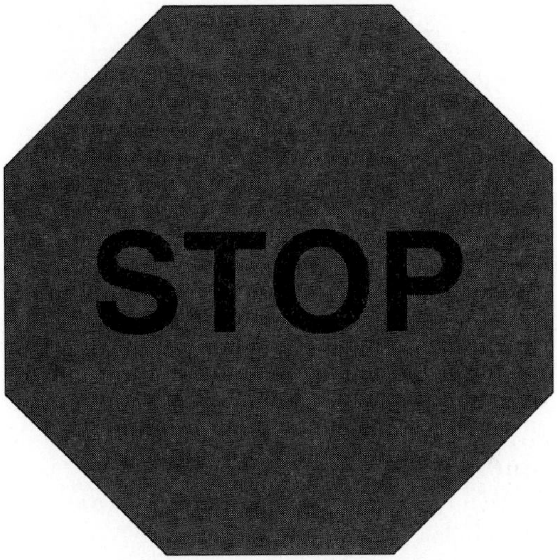

This example uses the `text(x,y,'string')` function with extra arguments. The `Color`, `FontSize`, `FontWeight`, and `HorizontalAlignment` arguments tell MATLAB to use Handle Graphics to modify the text. Handle Graphics is the name of MATLAB's underlying graphics functions. You can access this rich set of powerful, versatile graphics functions yourself. See Chapter 30 for more information on these features.

Standard pie charts can be created using the `pie(a,b)` function, where `a` is a vector of values and `b` is an optional logical vector describing a slice or slices to be pulled out of the pie chart. The `pie3` function renders the pie chart with a 3-D appearance. Consider the example

```
>> a = [.5 1 1.6 1.2 .8 2.1];
>> pie(a,a==max(a));   % chart a and pull out the biggest slice
>> title('Figure 25.13: Example Pie Chart')
```

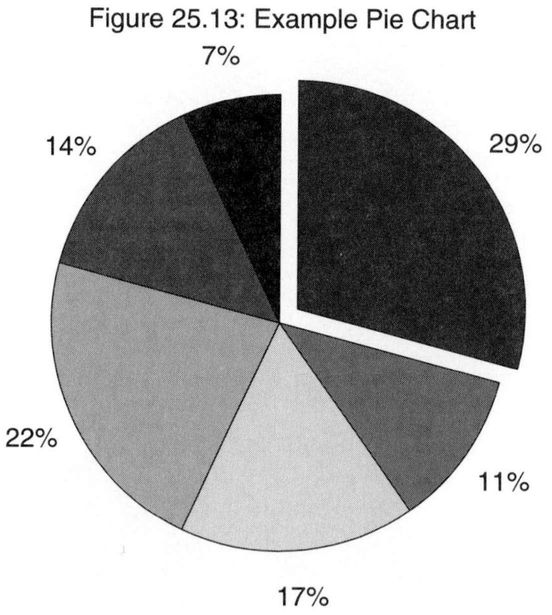

Sometimes it is desirable to plot two different functions on the same axes using different *y*-axis scales. The function `plotyy` does just that, for example,

```
>> x = -2*pi:pi/10:2*pi;
>> y = sin(x);
>> z = 3*cos(x);
>> subplot(2,1,1), plot(x,y,x,z)
>> title('Figure 25.14a: Two plots on the same scale.');
>> subplot(2,1,2), plotyy(x,y,x,z)
>> title('Figure 25.14b: Two plots on different scales.');
```

Bar and stair plots can be generated using the `bar`, `barh`, and `stairs` plotting functions. The `bar3` and `bar3h` functions render the bar charts with a 3-D appearance. Consider the following example.

```
>> x = -2.9:0.2:2.9;
>> y = exp(-x.*x);
>> subplot(2,2,1)
>> bar(x,y)
>> title('Figure 25.15a: 2-D Bar Chart')
>> subplot(2,2,2)
>> bar3(x,y,'r')
>> title('Figure 25.15b: 3-D Bar Chart')
>> subplot(2,2,3)
>> stairs(x,y)
```

Figure 25.14a: Two plots on the same scale.

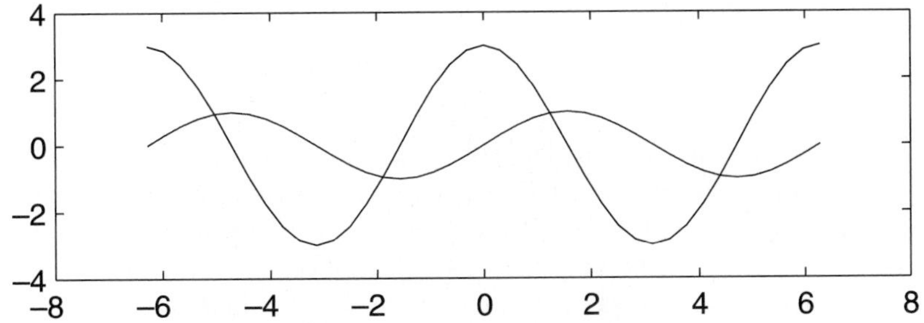

Figure 25.14b: Two plots on different scales.

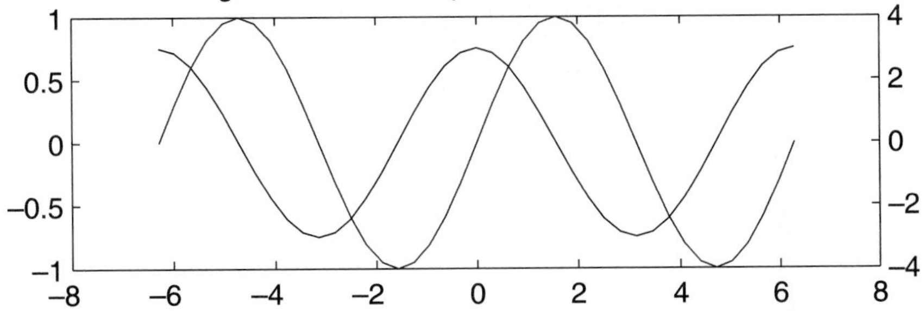

Figure 25.15a: 2-D Bar Chart

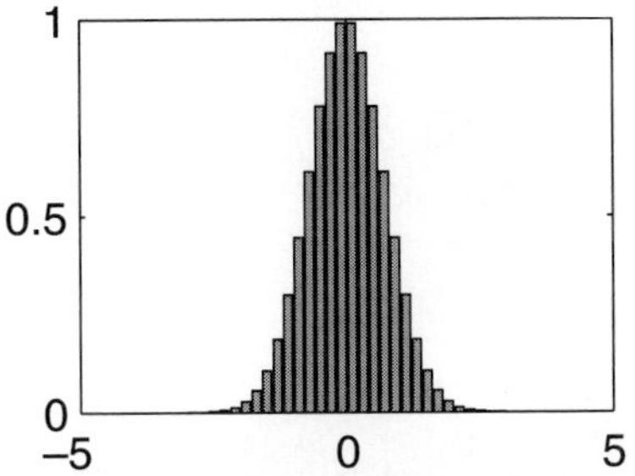

Figure 25.15b: 3-D Bar Chart

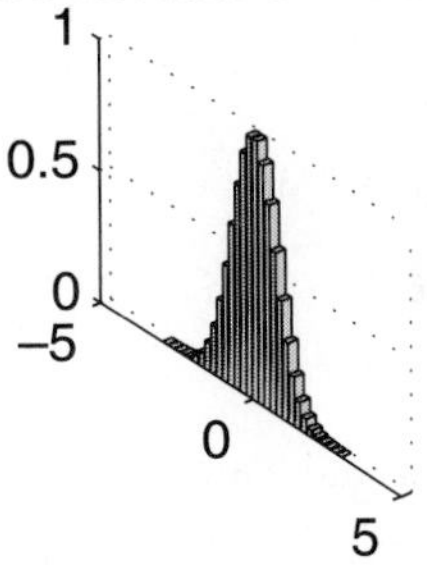

Figure 25.15c: Stair Chart

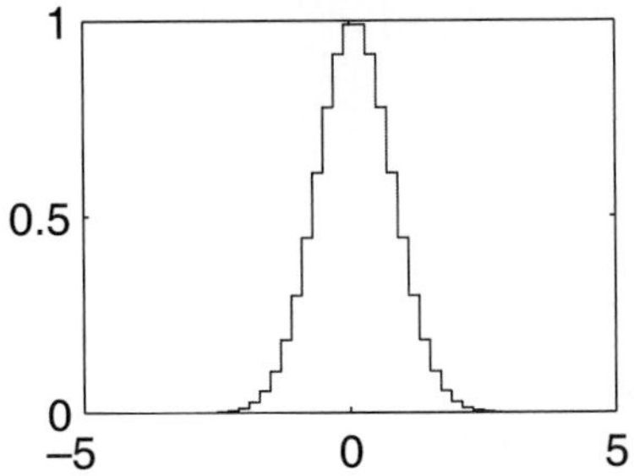

Figure 25.15d: Horizontal Bar Chart

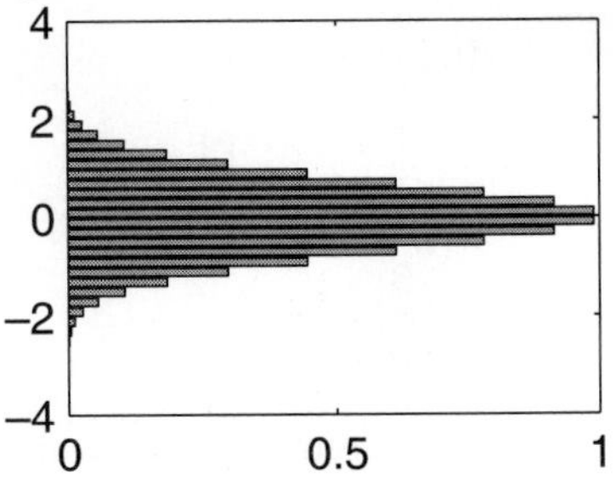

```
>> title('Figure 25.15c: Stair Chart')
>> subplot(2,2,4)
>> barh(x,y)
>> title('Figure 25.15d: Horizontal Bar Chart')
```

The various `bar` functions accept a single color argument for all bars. Bars can be grouped or stacked as well. The form `bar(x,Y)` for vector `x` and matrix `Y` draws groups of bars corresponding to the columns of `Y`. `bar(x,Y,'stacked')` draws the bars stacked vertically. `barh`, `bar3`, and `bar3h` have similar options.

Histograms illustrate the distribution of values in a vector. `hist(y)` draws a 10-bin histogram for the data in vector `y`. `hist(y,n)`, where `n` is a scalar, draws a histogram with `n` bins. `hist(y,x)`, where `x` is a vector, draws a histogram using the bins specified in `x`. Consider the example

```
>> x = -2.9:0.2:2.9;  % specify the bins to use
>> y = randn(5000,1); % generate 5000 random data points
>> hist(y,x)          % draw the histogram
>> title('Figure 25.16: Histogram of Gaussian Data')
```

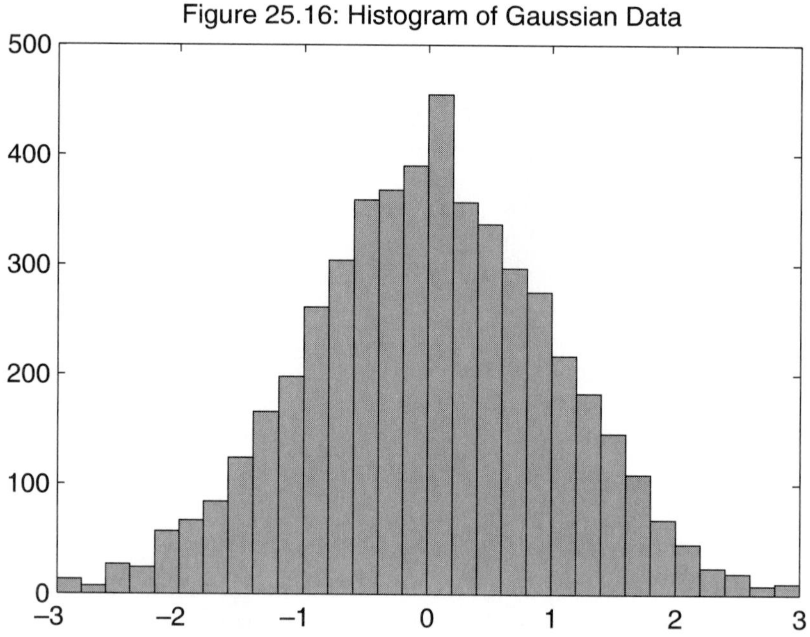

Discrete sequence data can be plotted using the `stem` function. `stem(z)` creates a plot of the data points in vector `z` connected to the horizontal axis by a line. An optional character string argument can be used to specify linestyle. `stem(x,z)` plots the data points in `z` at the values specified in `x`, as in the example

```
>> z = randn(30,1);          % create some random data
>> stem(z,'--')              % draw a stem plot using dashed linestyle
>> set(gca,'YGrid','on') % turn grid on Y-axis only
>> title('Figure 25.17: Stem Plot of Random Data')
```

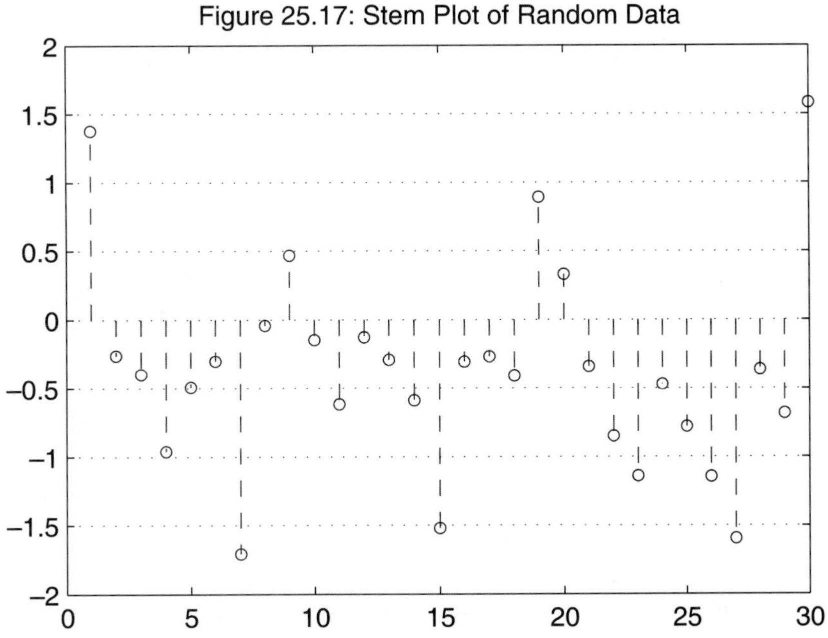

A plot can include error bars at the data points. `errorbar(x,y,e)` plots the graph of vector `x` versus vector `y` with error bars specified by vector `e`. All vectors must be the same length. For each data point `(x(i),y(i))`, an error bar is drawn a distance `e(i)` above and `e(i)` below the data point, for example,

```
>> x = linspace(0,2,21); % create a vector
>> y = erf(x);           % y is the error function of x
>> e = rand(size(x))/10; % e contains random error values
>> errorbar(x,y,e)       % create the plot
>> title('Figure 25.18: Errorbar Plot')
```

Plots in polar coordinates can be created using the `polar(t,r,S)` function, where `t` is the angle vector in radians, `r` is the radius vector, and `S` is an optional character string describing color, marker symbol, and/or linestyle, for example,

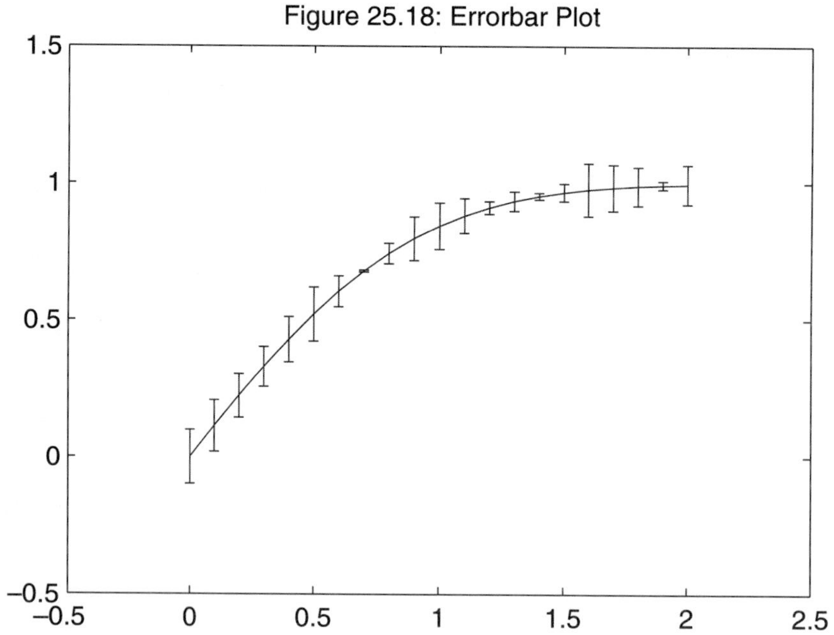


```
>> t = linspace(0,2*pi);
>> r = sin(2*t).*cos(2*t);
>> subplot(2,2,1)
>> polar(t,r), title('Figure 25.19a: Polar Plot')
```

Complex data can be plotted using `compass` and `feather`. `compass(z)` draws a plot that displays the angle and magnitude of the complex elements of `z` as arrows emanating from the origin. `feather(z)` plots the same data using arrows emanating from equally spaced points on a horizontal line. `compass(x,y)` and `feather(x,y)` are equivalent to `compass(x+i*y)` and `feather(x+i*y)`. Consider the example

```
>> z = eig(randn(20));
>> subplot(2,2,2)
>> compass(z)
>> title('Figure 25.19b: Compass Plot')
>> subplot(2,2,3)
>> feather(z)
>> title('Figure 25.19c: Feather Plot')
```

The function `rose(v)` draws a 20-bin polar histogram for the angles in vector `v`. `rose(v,n)`, where `n` is a scalar, draws a histogram with `n` bins. `rose(v,x)`, where `x` is a vector, draws a histogram using the bins specified in `x`. Consider the example

```
>> subplot(2,2,4)
>> v = randn(1000,1)*pi;
>> rose(v)
>> title('Figure 25.19d: Angle Histogram')
```

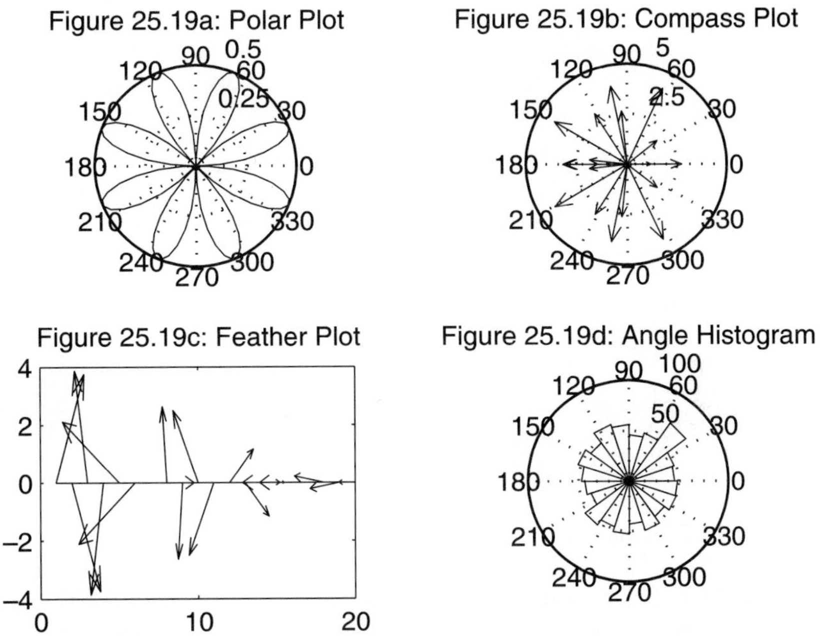

The function `scatter` generates a scatter plot, that is, a plot of circles at data points, where the circle size or color can vary point by point. Consider the example

```
>> x = rand(40,1);
>> y = randn(40,1);
>> area = 20+(1:40);
>> scatter(x,y,area)
>> box on
>> title('Figure 25.20: A scatter plot')
```

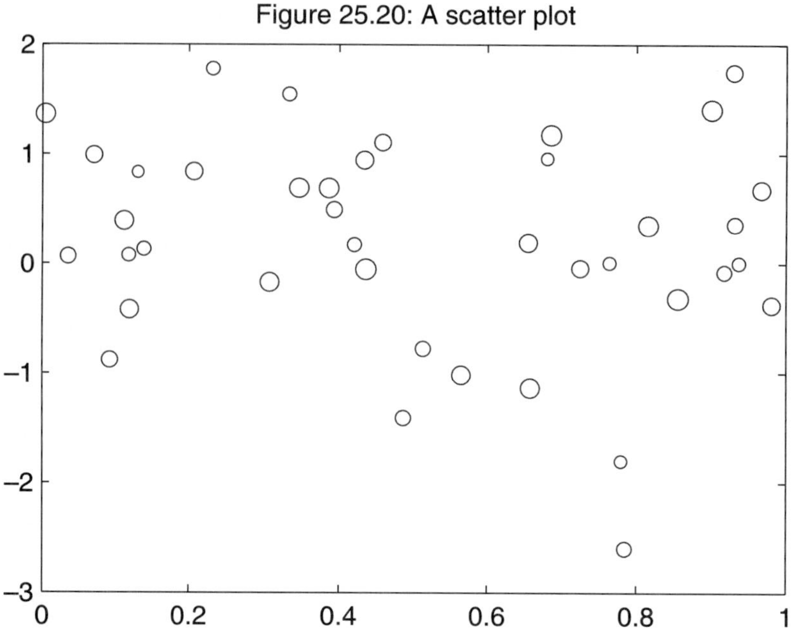

25.11 EASY PLOTTING

When one doesn't want to take the time to specify the data points explicitly for a plot, MATLAB provides the functions `fplot`, `ezplot`, and `ezpolar`. The function `fplot` plots functions defined by M-file names or function handles. The functions `ezplot` and `ezpolar` plot functions defined by string expressions or symbolic math objects, with the obvious difference in plot type. These functions simply spare the user from having to define the data for the independent variable, for example,

```
>> fplot(@humps,[-.5 3])
>> title('Figure 25.21: Fplot of the Humps Function')
>> xlabel('x')
>> ylabel('humps(x)')
>> pause(5)
>> fstr = 'sin(x)/(x)';
>> ezplot(fstr,[-15,15])
>> title(['Figure 25.22: ' fstr])
>> pause(5)
>> istr = '(x-2)^2/(2^2) + (y+1)^2/(3^2) - 1';
>> ezplot(istr,[-2 6 -5 3])
>> axis square
>> grid
>> title(['Figure 25.23: ' istr])
```

Figure 25.21: Fplot of the Humps Function

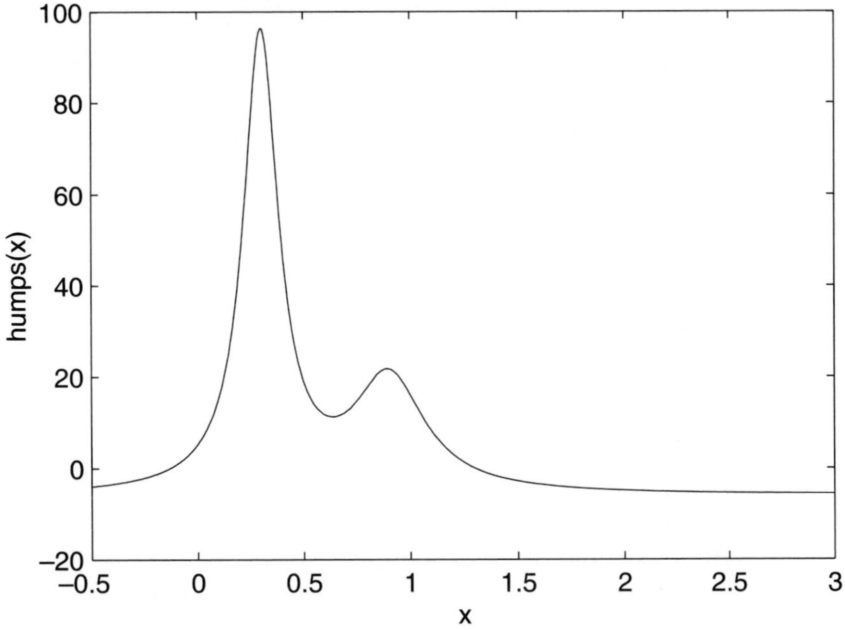

Figure 25.22: sin(x)/(x)

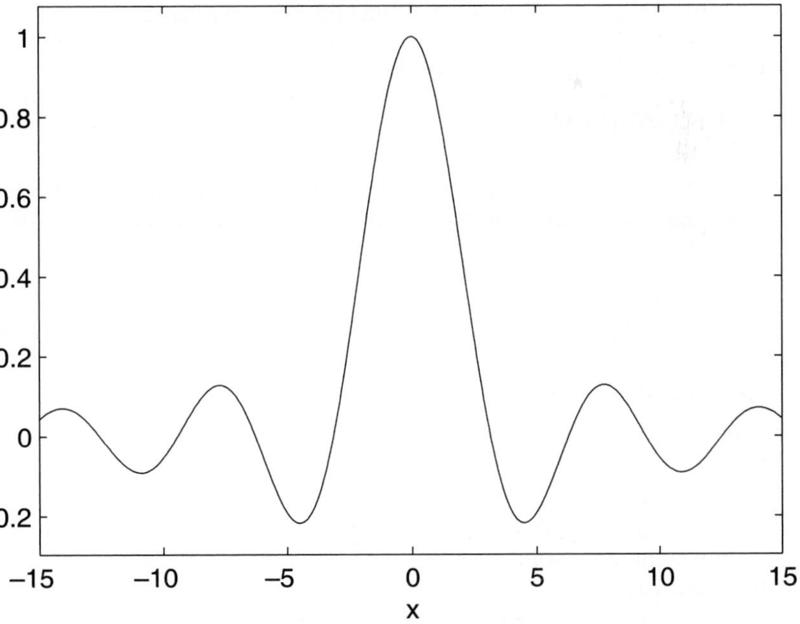

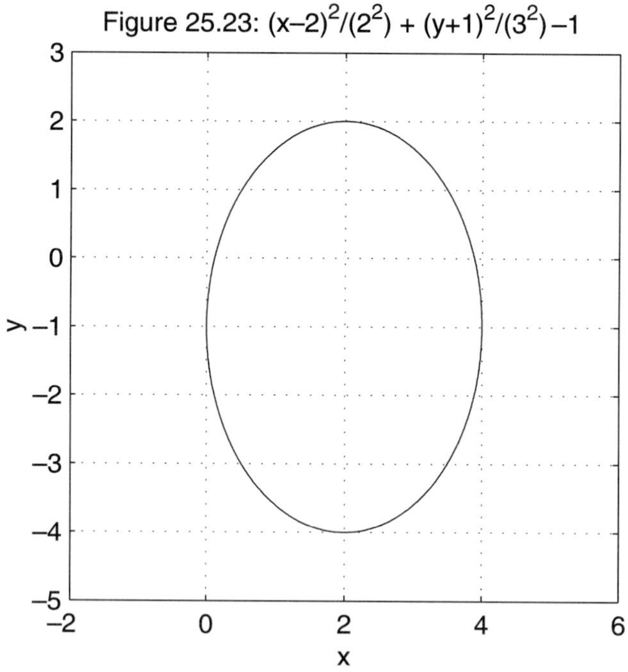

The last example shows that `ezplot` can be used to plot implicit functions. In this case the string expression is that of an elipse centered at $(2,-1)$.

25.12 TEXT FORMATTING

Multiline text can be used in any text string, including titles and axis labels as well as the `text` and `gtext` functions. Simply use string arrays or cell arrays for multiline text. For example,

```
>> xlabel({'This is the first line','and this is the second.'});
```

labels the x-axis with two lines of text. Note that the string separator can be a space, a comma, or a semicolon; each style produces the same result. See Chapter 8 for more details on cell arrays of strings.

A selection of more than 75 symbols, including Greek letters and other special characters, can be included in MATLAB text strings by embedding a subset of TeX commands within the string. The available symbols and the character strings used to define them are listed in the following table. This information can also be found by viewing the `string` property of the *text* Handle Graphics object in the on-line documentation.

Character Sequence	Symbol	Character Sequence	Symbol	Character Sequence	Symbol
\alpha	α	\upsilon	υ	\sim	∼
\beta	β	\phi	ϕ	\leq	≤
\gamma	γ	\chi	χ	\infty	∞
\delta	δ	\psi	ψ	\clubsuit	♣
\epsilon	ϵ	\omega	ω	\diamondsuit	♦
\zeta	ζ	\Gamma	Γ	\heartsuit	♥
\eta	η	\Delta	Δ	\spadesuit	♠
\theta	θ	\Theta	Θ	\leftrightarrow	↔
\vartheta	ϑ	\Lambda	Λ	\leftarrow	←
\iota	ι	\Xi	Ξ	\uparrow	↑
\kappa	κ	\Pi	Π	\rightarrow	→
\lambda	λ	\Sigma	Σ	\downarrow	↓
\mu	μ	\Upsilon	ϒ	\circ	∘
\nu	ν	\Phi	Φ	\pm	±
\xi	ξ	\Psi	Ψ	\geq	≥
\pi	π	\Omega	Ω	\propto	∝
\rho	ρ	\forall	∀	\partial	∂
\sigma	σ	\exists	∃	\bullet	•
\varsigma	ς	\ni	∍	\div	÷
\tau	τ	\cong	≅	\neq	≠
\equiv	≡	\approx	≈	\aleph	ℵ
\Im	ℑ	\Re	ℜ	\wp	℘
\otimes	⊗	\oplus	⊕	\oslash	ø
\cap	∩	\cup	∪	\supseteq	⊇
\supset	⊃	\subseteq	⊆	\subset	⊂
\int	∫	\in	∈	\o	o

Character Sequence	Symbol	Character Sequence	Symbol	Character Sequence	Symbol
\rfloor	⌋	\lceil	⌈	\nabla	∇
\lfloor	⌊	\cdot	·	\ldots	...
\perp	⊥	\neg	¬	\prime	′
\wedge	∧	\times	×	\0	∅
\rceil	⌉	\surd	√	\mid	∣
\vee	∨	\varpi	ϖ	\copyright	©
\langle	⟨	\rangle	⟩		

A limited subset of TeX formatting commands is also available. Superscripts and subscripts are specified by ^ and _, respectively. The text font and size can be selected using the `\fontname` and `\fontsize` commands, and a style can be specified using the `\bf`, `\it`, `\sl`, or `\rm` command to select a boldface, italic, oblique or slant, or normal Roman font, respectively. To print the special characters used to define TeX strings, prefix them with the backslash (\) character. The characters affected are the backslash (\), left and right curly braces { }, underscore (_), and carat (^). The following example illustrates the use of TeX formatting commands.

```
>> axes;  % blank axes
>> axis([0 1 0 0.5])
>> text(0.2,0.1,'\itE = M\cdotC^{\rm2}')
>> text(0.2,0.2,'\fontsize{16} \nabla \times H = J + \partialD/\partialt')
>> text(0.2,0.3,'\fontname{courier} \fontsize{16} \bf x_{\alpha} + y^{2\pi}')
>> fsstr='f(t) = A_o + \fontsize{30}_\Sigma\fontsize{10}';
>> text(0.2,0.4,[fsstr '[A_ncos(n\omega_ot) + B_nsin(n\omega_ot)]'])
>> title('Figure 25.24: TeX Formatting Examples')
```

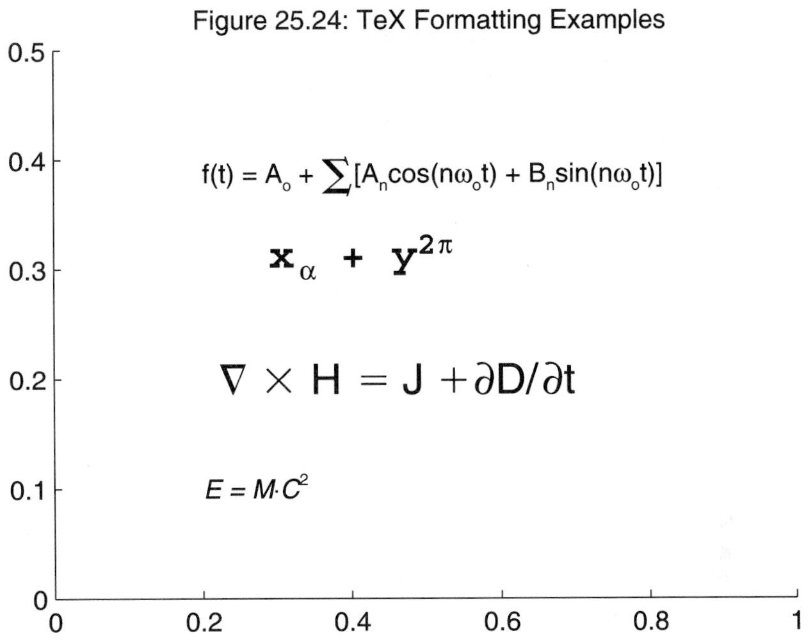

25.13 SUMMARY

The table below lists MATLAB functions for 2-D plotting.

Function	Description
`plot`	Linear plot.
`loglog`	Log-log plot.
`semilogx`	Semilog *x*-axis plot.
`semilogy`	Semilog *y*-axis plot.
`polar`	Polar coordinate plot.
`plotyy`	Linear plot with two *y*-axes.
`axis`	Control axis scaling and appearance.
`xlim`	*x*-axis limits.
`ylim`	*y*-axis limits.
`zlim`	*z*-axis limits.
`daspect`	Set and get data aspect ratio, i.e., `axis equal`.

Function	Description
`pbaspect`	Set and get plot box aspect ratio, i.e., `axis square`.
`zoom`	Zoom in and out.
`grid`	Grid line visibility.
`box`	Axis box visibility.
`hold`	Hold current plot.
`subplot`	Create multiple axes in *Figure* window.
`figure`	Create *Figure* windows.
`legend`	Add legend.
`title`	Title at top of plot.
`xlabel`	*x*-axis label.
`ylabel`	*y*-axis label.
`text`	Place text on plot.
`gtext`	Place text with mouse.
`ginput`	Get coordinates at cursor.
`area`	Filled area plot.
`bar`	Bar graph.
`barh`	Horizontal bar graph.
`bar3`	3-D bar graph.
`bar3h`	3-D horizontal bar graph.
`compass`	Compass graph.
`errorbar`	Linear plot with error bars.
`ezplot`	Easy line plot of string expression.
`ezpolar`	Easy polar plot of string expression.
`feather`	Feather plot.
`fill`	Filled 2-D polygons.
`fplot`	Plot function.
`hist`	Histogram.

Function	Description
pareto	Pareto chart.
pie	Pie chart.
pie3	3-D pie chart.
plotmatrix	Scatter plot matrix.
ribbon	Linear plot with 2-D lines as ribbons.
scatter	Scatter plot.
stem	Discrete sequence or stem plot.
stairs	Stairstep plot.

26

Three-Dimensional Graphics

MATLAB provides a variety of functions to display 3-D data. Some functions plot lines in three dimensions, while others draw surfaces and wire frames. In addition, color can be used to represent a fourth dimension. When color is used in this manner, it is called ***pseudocolor*** since color is not an inherent or natural property of the underlying data in the way that color in a photograph is a natural characteristic of the image. To simplify the discussion of 3-D graphics, the use of color is postponed until the next chapter. In this chapter, the fundamental concepts of producing useful 3-D plots are discussed.

26.1 LINE PLOTS

The `plot` function from the 2-D world is extended into three dimensions with `plot3`. The format is the same as the 2-D `plot`, except that the data is supplied in triples rather than pairs. The general format of the function call is `plot3(x1,y1,z1,S1,x2,y2,z2,S2,...)`, where xn, yn, and zn are vectors or matrices and Sn are optional character strings specifying color, marker symbol, and/or linestyle. plot3 is commonly used to plot a 3-D function of a single variable, for example,

```
>> t = linspace(0,10*pi);
>> plot3(sin(t),cos(t),t)
>> xlabel('sin(t)'), ylabel('cos(t)'), zlabel('t')
>> text(0,0,0,'Origin')
>> grid on
>> title('Figure 26.1: Helix')
>> v = axis
v =
    -1     1    -1     1     0    35
```

From this simple example it is apparent that all the basic features of 2-D graphics exist in 3-D also. The axis command extends to 3-D by returning the *z*-axis limits (0 and 35) as two additional elements in the axis vector. There is a zlabel function for labeling the *z*-axis. The grid command toggles a 3-D grid underneath the plot, and the box command creates a 3-D box around the plot. The defaults for plot3 are grid off and box off. The function text(x,y,z,'string') places a character string at the position identified by the triplet x,y,z. In addition, subplots and multiple *Figure* windows apply directly to 3-D graphics functions.

In the last chapter, multiple lines or curves were plotted on top of one another by specifying multiple arguments to the plot function or by using the hold command. plot3 and the other 3-D graphics functions offer the same capabilities. For example, the added dimension of plot3 allows multiple 2-D plots to be stacked next to one another along one dimension, rather than directly on top of one another. Consider the following example.

```
>> x = linspace(0,3*pi);   % x-axis data
>> z1 = sin(x);            % plot in x-z plane
>> z2 = sin(2*x);
>> z3 = sin(3*x);
>> y1 = zeros(size(x));    % spread out along y-axes by giving
>> y3 = ones(size(x));     % each curve different y-axis values
>> y2 = y3/2;
>> plot3(x,y1,z1,x,y2,z2,x,y3,z3)
>> grid on
>> xlabel('X-axis'), ylabel('Y-axis'), zlabel('Z-axis')
>> title('Figure 26.2: sin(x), sin(2x), sin(3x)')
>> pause(5)
>> plot3(x,z1,y1,x,z2,y2,x,z3,y3)
>> grid on
>> xlabel('X-axis'), ylabel('Y-axis'), zlabel('Z-axis')
>> title('Figure 26.3: sin(x), sin(2x), sin(3x)')
```

Figure 26.1: Helix

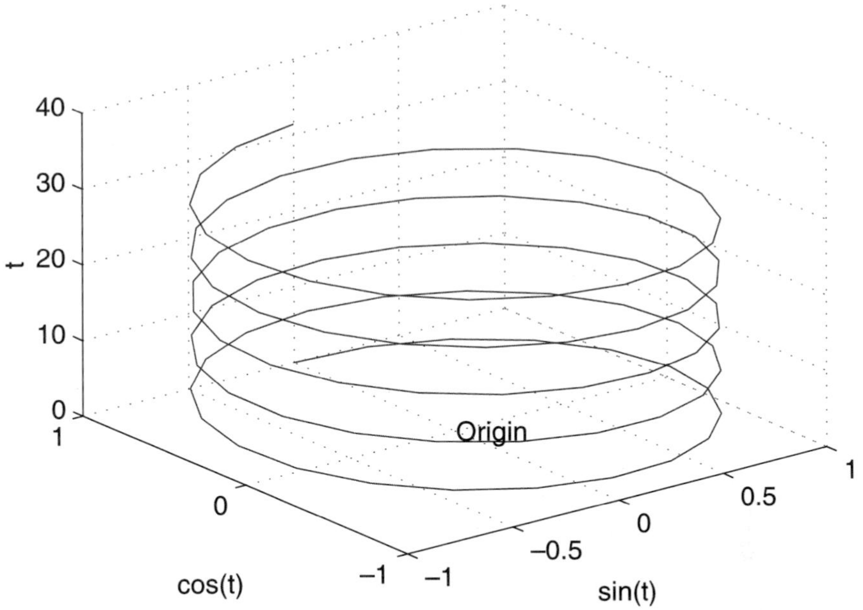

Figure 26.2: sin(x), sin(2x), sin(3x)

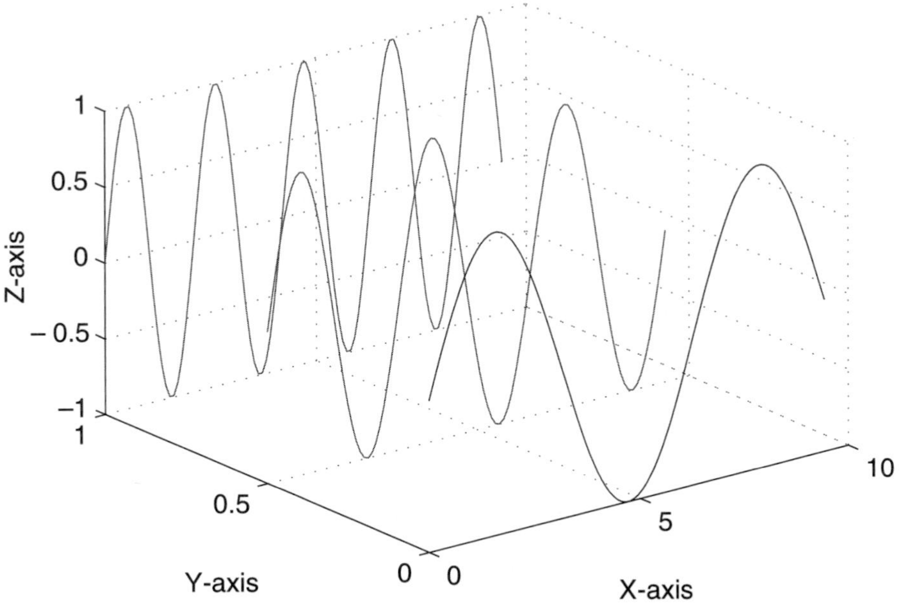

Figure 26.3: sin(x), sin(2x), sin(3x)

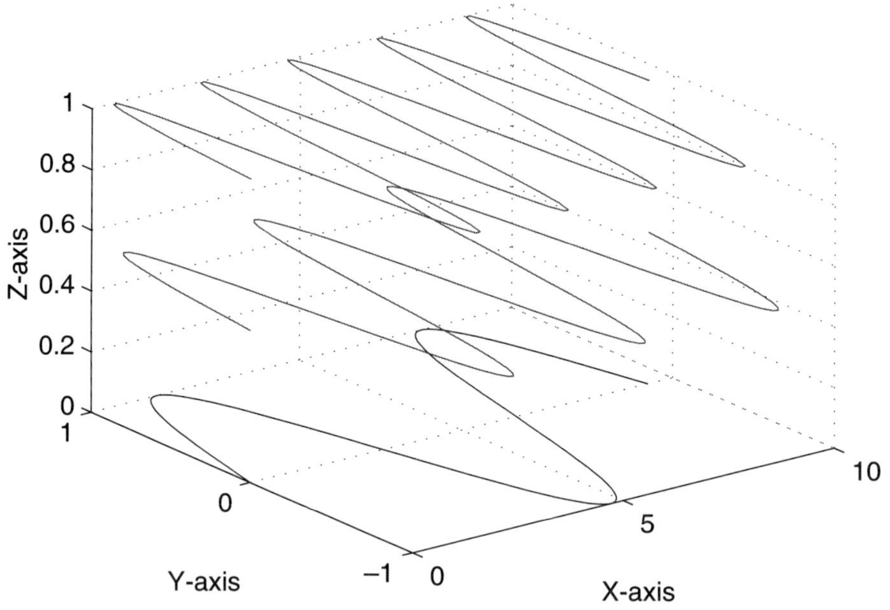

26.2 SCALAR FUNCTIONS OF TWO VARIABLES

As opposed to generating line plots with `plot3`, it is often desirable to visualize a scalar function of two variables, that is,

$$z = f(x,y)$$

Here each pair of values for x and y produces a value for z. A plot of z as a function of x and y is a surface in three dimensions. To plot this surface in MATLAB, the values for z are stored in a matrix. As described in the section on 2-D interpolation, given that `x` and `y` are the independent variables, `z` is a matrix of the dependent variable and the association of `x` and `y` with `z` is

`z(i,:) = f(x,y(i))` and `z(:,j) = f(x(j),y)`

That is, the ith row of `z` is associated with the ith element of `y`, and the jth column of `z` is associated with the jth element of `x`.

When `z=f(x,y)` can be expressed simply, it is convenient to use array operations to compute all the values of `z` in a single statement. To do so requires that we create matrices of all x- and y-values in the proper orientation. This orientation is sometimes called ***plaid*** by *The Mathworks Inc.* MATLAB provides the function `meshgrid` to perform this step, for example,

```
>> x = -3:3;   % choose x-axis values
>> y = 1:5;   % y-axis values
>> [X,Y] = meshgrid(x,y)
X =
    -3    -2    -1     0     1     2     3
    -3    -2    -1     0     1     2     3
    -3    -2    -1     0     1     2     3
    -3    -2    -1     0     1     2     3
    -3    -2    -1     0     1     2     3
Y =
     1     1     1     1     1     1     1
     2     2     2     2     2     2     2
     3     3     3     3     3     3     3
     4     4     4     4     4     4     4
     5     5     5     5     5     5     5
```

As you can see, `meshgrid` duplicated `x` for each of the five rows in `y`. Similarly, it duplicated `y` as a column for each of the seven columns in `x`.

> An easy way to remember which variable is duplicated which way by `meshgrid` is to think about 2-D plots. The x-axis varies from left to right, just as the `X` output of `meshgrid` does. Similarly, the y-axis varies from bottom to top, just as the `Y` output of `meshgrid` does.

Given `X` and `Y`, if $z = f(x,y) = (x + y)^2$, the matrix of data values defining the 3-D surface is given simply as

```
>> Z = (X+Y).^2
Z =
     4     1     0     1     4     9    16
     1     0     1     4     9    16    25
     0     1     4     9    16    25    36
     1     4     9    16    25    36    49
     4     9    16    25    36    49    64
```

When a function cannot be expressed simply as shown above, one must use For Loops or While Loops to compute the elements of `Z`. In many cases it may be possible to compute the elements of `Z` rowwise or columnwise. For example, if it is possible to compute `Z` rowwise, the following script file fragment can be helpful.

```
x= ???  % statement defining vector of x-axis values
y= ???  % statement defining vector of y-axis values

nx = length(x);     % length of x is no. of rows in Z
ny = length(y);     % length of y is no. of columns in Z
Z = zeros(nx,ny);   % initialize Z matrix for speed

for r=1:nx
  (preliminary commands)
  Z(r,:)= {a function of y and x(r) defining r-th row of Z}
end
```

On the other hand, if Z can be computed columnwise, the following script file fragment can be helpful.

```
x= ???  % statement defining vector of x-axis values
y= ???  % statement defining vector of y-axis values

nx = length(x);     % length of x is no. of rows in Z
ny = length(y);     % length of y is no. of columns in Z
Z = zeros(nx,ny);   % initialize Z matrix for speed

for c=1:ny
  (preliminary commands)
  Z(:,c)= {a function of y(c) and x defining c-th column of Z}
end
```

Only when the elements of Z must be computed element by element does the computation usually require a nested For Loop such as the following script file fragment.

```
x= ???  % statement defining vector of x-axis values
y= ???  % statement defining vector of y-axis values
nx = length(x);     % length of x is no. of rows in Z
```

```
ny = length(y);      % length of y is no. of columns in Z
Z = zeros(nx,ny);    % initialize Z matrix for speed
for r=1:nx
  for c=1:ny
    (preliminary commands)
    Z(r,c)= {a function of y(c) and x(r) defining (r,c)-th element}
  end
end
```

26.3 MESH PLOTS

MATLAB defines a ***mesh*** surface by the z-coordinates of points above a rectangular grid in the x-y plane. It forms a mesh plot by joining adjacent points with straight lines. The result looks like a fishing net with knots at the data points. Consider the example

```
>> [X,Y,Z] = peaks(30);
>> mesh(X,Y,Z)
>> xlabel('X-axis'), ylabel('Y-axis'), zlabel('Z-axis')
>> title('Figure 26.4: Mesh Plot of Peaks')
```

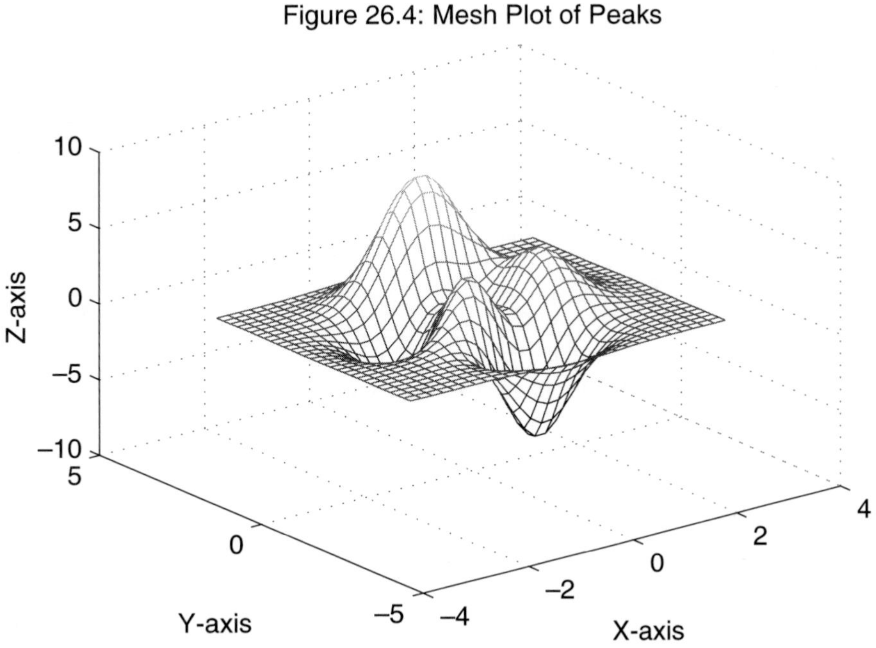

Note on your monitor how the line colors are related to the height of the mesh. In general, `mesh` accepts optional arguments to control color use in the plot. This ability to change how MATLAB uses color is discussed in the next chapter. In any case, the use of color is called pseudocolor since color is used to add a fourth effective dimension to the graph. Note also that the plot was drawn with a grid. ***Most 3-D plots other than*** `plot3` ***and a few other exceptions default to*** `grid on`**.**

In addition to the above input arguments, `mesh` and most 3-D plot functions can also be called with a variety of input arguments. The syntax used here is the most specific in that information is supplied for all three axes. `mesh(Z)` plots the matrix `Z` versus its row and column indices. The most common variation is to use the vectors that were passed to `meshgrid` for the *x*- and *y*- axes, for example, `mesh(x,y,Z)`.

As shown in the above figure, the areas between the mesh lines are opaque rather than transparent. The MATLAB command `hidden` controls this aspect of mesh plots, for example,

```
>> [X,Y,Z]=sphere(12);
>> subplot(1,2,1)
>> mesh(X,Y,Z), title('Figure 26.5a: Opaque')
>> hidden on
>> axis square off
>> subplot(1,2,2)
>> mesh(X,Y,Z), title('Figure 26.5b: Transparent')
>> hidden off
>> axis square off
```

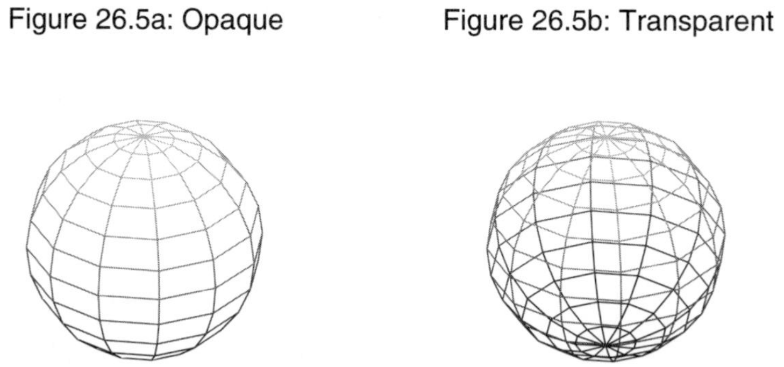

The sphere on the left is opaque (the lines are hidden), whereas the one on the right is transparent (the lines are not hidden).

The MATLAB `mesh` function has two siblings: `meshc`, which is a mesh plot and underlying contour plot, and `meshz`, which is a mesh plot including a zero plane. Consider the example

```
>> [X,Y,Z] = peaks(30);
>> meshc(X,Y,Z)  % mesh plot with underlying contour plot
>> title('Figure 26.6: Mesh Plot with Contours')
```

```
>> pause(5)
>> meshz(X,Y,Z)  % mesh plot with zero plane
>> title('Figure 26.7: Mesh Plot with Zero Plane')
```

Figure 26.6: Mesh Plot with Contours

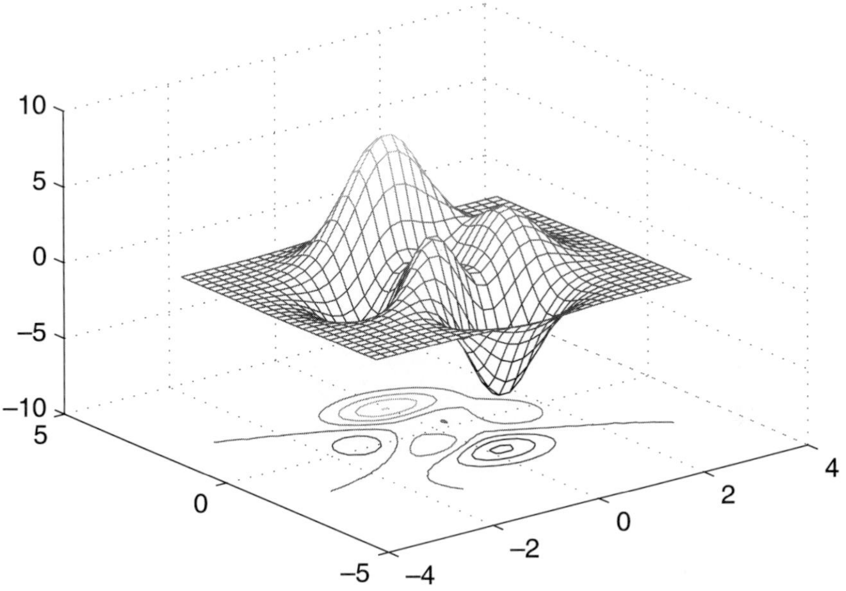

Figure 26.7: Mesh Plot with Zero Plane

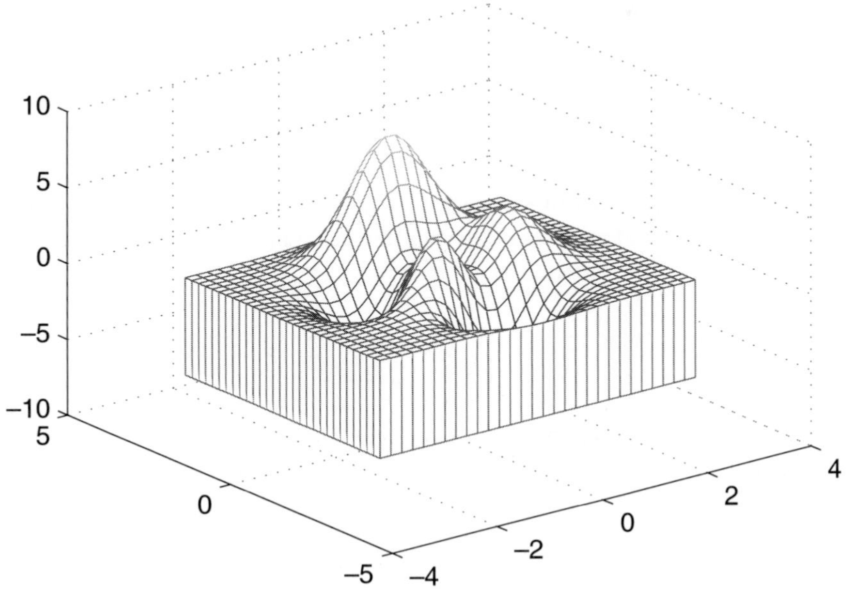

The function `waterfall` is identical to `mesh` except that the mesh lines appear only in the x-direction, for example,

```
>> waterfall(X,Y,Z)
>> xlabel('X-axis'), ylabel('Y-axis'), zlabel('Z-axis')
>> title('Figure 26.8: Waterfall Plot')
```

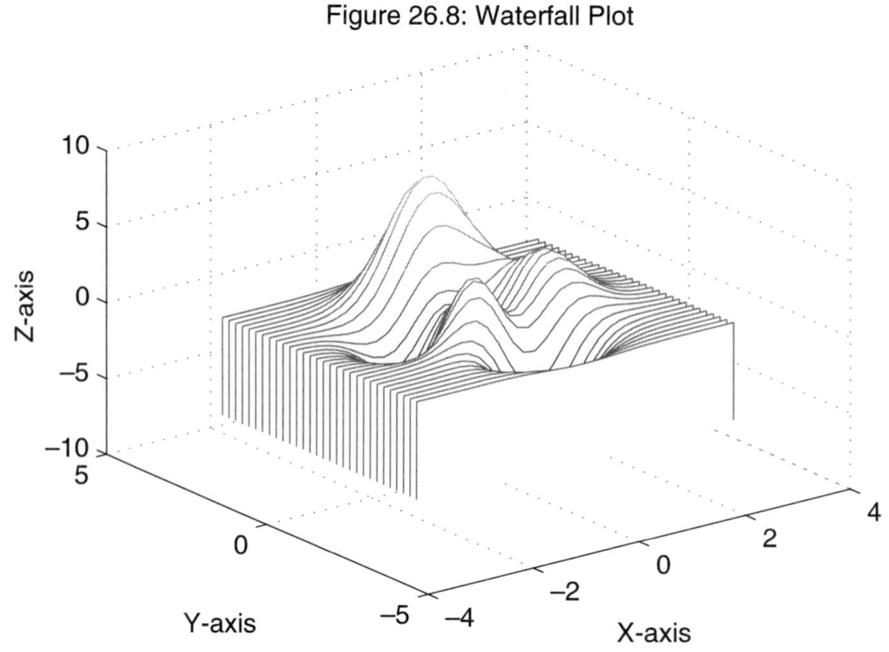

26.4 SURFACE PLOTS

A ***surface*** plot looks like a mesh plot, except that the spaces between the lines, called ***patches,*** are filled in. Plots of this type are generated using the `surf` function, for example,

```
>> [X,Y,Z] = peaks(30);
>> surf(X,Y,Z)
>> xlabel('X-axis'), ylabel('Y-axis'), zlabel('Z-axis')
>> title('Figure 26.09: Surface Plot of Peaks')
```

Note how this plot type is a ***dual*** of sorts to a `mesh` plot. Here the lines are black and the patches have color, whereas in `mesh`, the patches are the color of the axes and the lines have color. As with `mesh`, color varies along the z-axis with each patch or line having constant color. Surface plots default to `grid on` also.

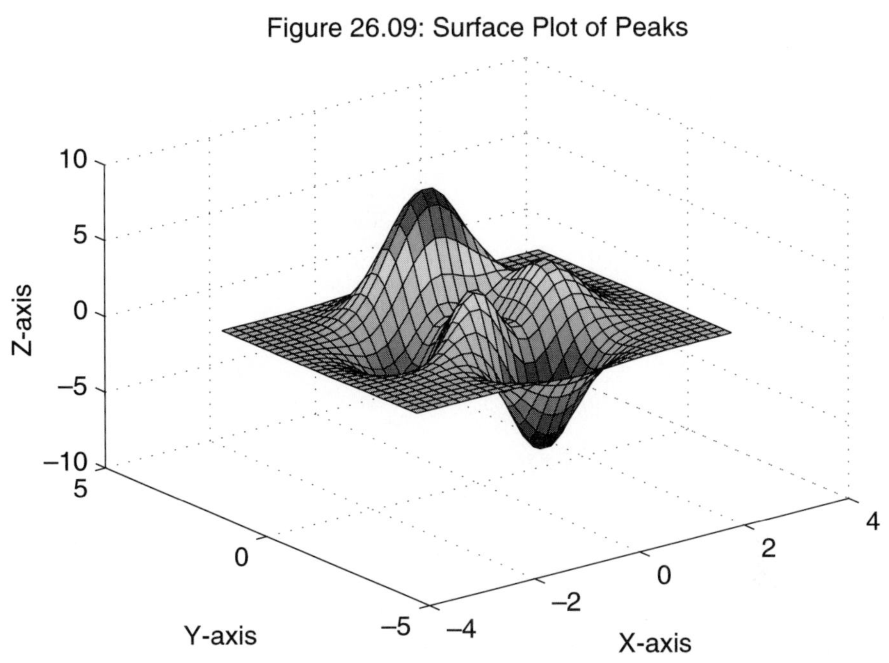

In a surface plot one does not think about hidden line removal as in a `mesh` plot but rather about different ways to shade the surface. In the above `surf` plot, the shading is ***faceted*** like a stained-glass window or object, where the black lines are the joints between the constant-color patches. In addition to faceted, MATLAB provides ***flat*** shading and ***interpolated*** shading. These are applied by using the function `shading`, for example,

```
>> [X,Y,Z] = peaks(30);
>> surf(X,Y,Z)  % same plot as above
>> shading flat
>> xlabel('X-axis'), ylabel('Y-axis'), zlabel('Z-axis')
>> title('Figure 26.10: Surface Plot with Flat Shading')
>> pause(5)
>> shading interp
>> title('Figure 26.11: Surface Plot with Interpolated Shading')
```

In the flat shading shown on the next page, the black lines are removed and each patch retains its single color, whereas in interpolated shading, the lines are also removed but each patch is given interpolated shading. That is, the color of each patch is interpolated over its area based on the color values assigned to each of its vertices. Needless to say, interpolated shading requires much more computation than faceted and flat shading. While shading has a significant visual impact on `surf` plots, it also applies to `mesh` plots, although in this case the visual impact is relatively minor since only the lines have color. Shading also affects `pcolor` and `fill` plots.

Figure 26.10: Surface Plot with Flat Shading

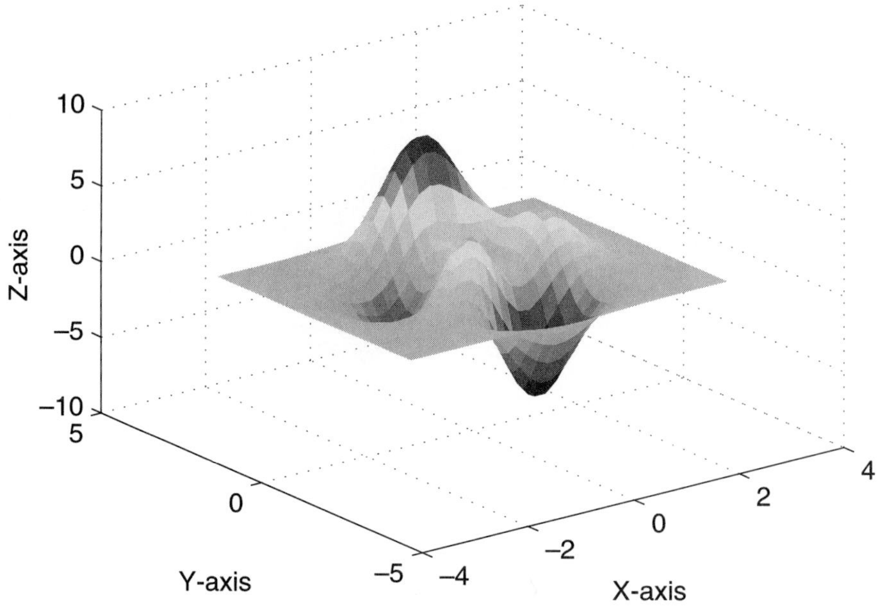

Figure 26.11: Surface Plot with Interpolated Shading

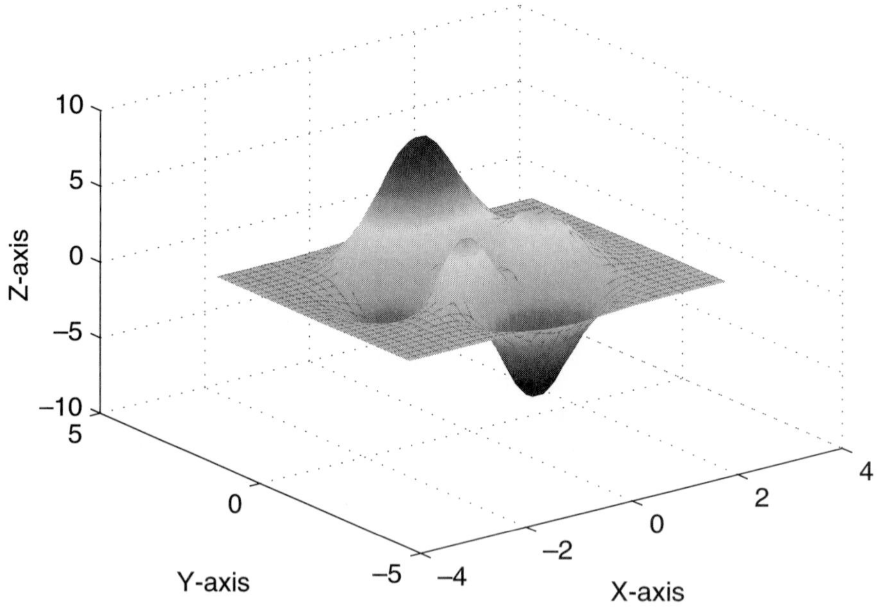

On some computer systems, interpolated shading creates extremely long printing delays or, at worst, printing errors. These problems are not due to the size of the PostScript data file but rather to the enormous amount of computation required in the printer to generate shading that continually changes over the surface of the plot. Often the easiest solution to this problem is to use flat shading for printouts.

In some situations it may be convenient to remove part of a surface so that underlying parts of the surface can be seen. In MATLAB this is accomplished by setting the data values where holes are desired to the special value `NaN`. ***Since `NaN`s have no value, all MATLAB plotting functions simply ignore `NaN` data points, leaving a hole in the plot where they appear.*** Consider the example

```
>> [X,Y,Z] = peaks(30);
>> x = X(1,:);                % vector of x-axis
>> y = Y(:,1);                % vector of y-axis
>> i = find(y>.8 & y<1.2);    % find y-axis indices of hole
>> j = find(x>-.6 & x<.5);    % find x-axis indices of hole
>> Z(i,j) = nan;              % set values at hole indices to NaNs
>> surf(X,Y,Z)
>> xlabel('X-axis'), ylabel('Y-axis'), zlabel('Z-axis')
>> title('Figure 26.12: Surface Plot with a Hole')
```

The MATLAB `surf` function also has two siblings: `surfc` which is a surface plot and underlying contour plot, and `surfl` which is a surface plot with lighting, for example,

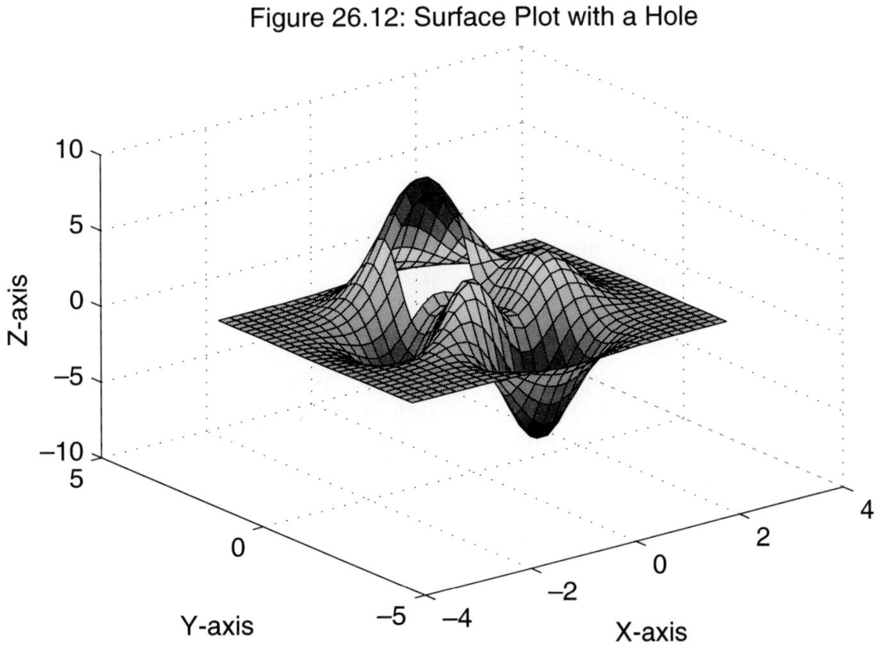

```
>> [X,Y,Z] = peaks(30);
>> surfc(X,Y,Z)  % surf plot with contour plot
>> xlabel('X-axis'), ylabel('Y-axis'), zlabel('Z-axis')
>> title('Figure 26.13: Surface Plot with Contours')
>> pause(5)
>> surfl(X,Y,Z)     % surf plot with lighting
>> shading interp  % surfl plots look best with interp shading
>> colormap pink    % they also look better with shades of a single color
>> xlabel('X-axis'), ylabel('Y-axis'), zlabel('Z-axis')
>> title('Figure 26.14: Surface Plot with Lighting')
```

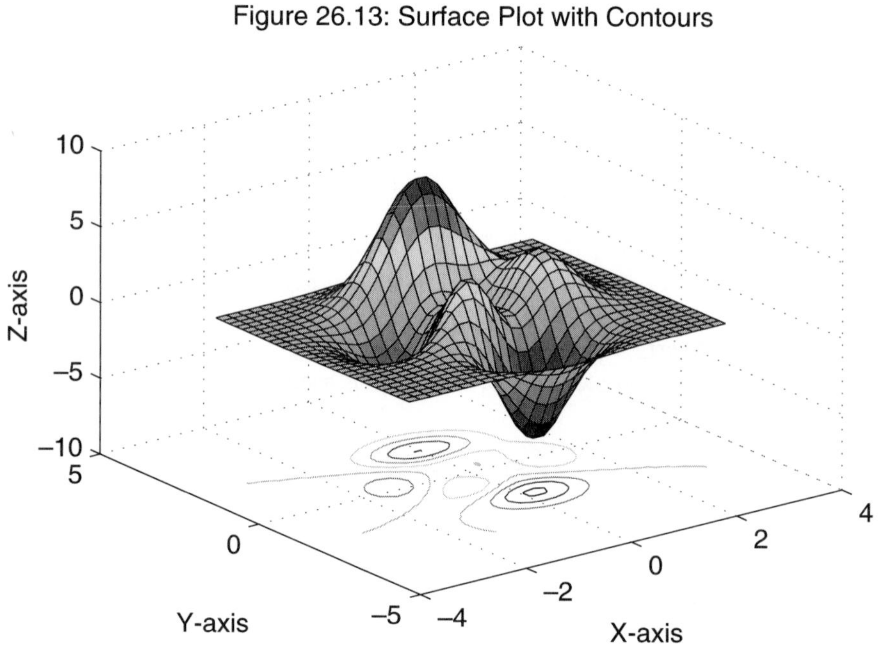

The function surfl makes a number of assumptions regarding the light applied to the surface. It does not use the *light* object discussed in the next chapter. Rather, it simply modifies the color of the surface to give the appearance of lighting. The next chapter provides more rigorous information regarding light properties. Also, in the above executed commands, colormap is a MATLAB function for applying a different set of colors to a figure. This function is discussed in the next chapter as well.

The surfnorm(X,Y,Z) function computes surface normals for the surface defined by X, Y, and Z, plots the surface, and plots vectors normal to the surface at the data points. The surface normals are unnormalized and valid at each vertex. The form [Nx,Ny,Nz]=surfnorm(X,Y,Z) computes the 3-D surface normals and returns their components but does not plot the surface, for example,

```
>> [X,Y,Z] = peaks(15);
>> surfnorm(X,Y,Z)
>> xlabel('X-axis'), ylabel('Y-axis'), zlabel('Z-axis')
>> title('Figure 26.15: Surface Plot with Normals')
```

Figure 26.14: Surface Plot with Lighting

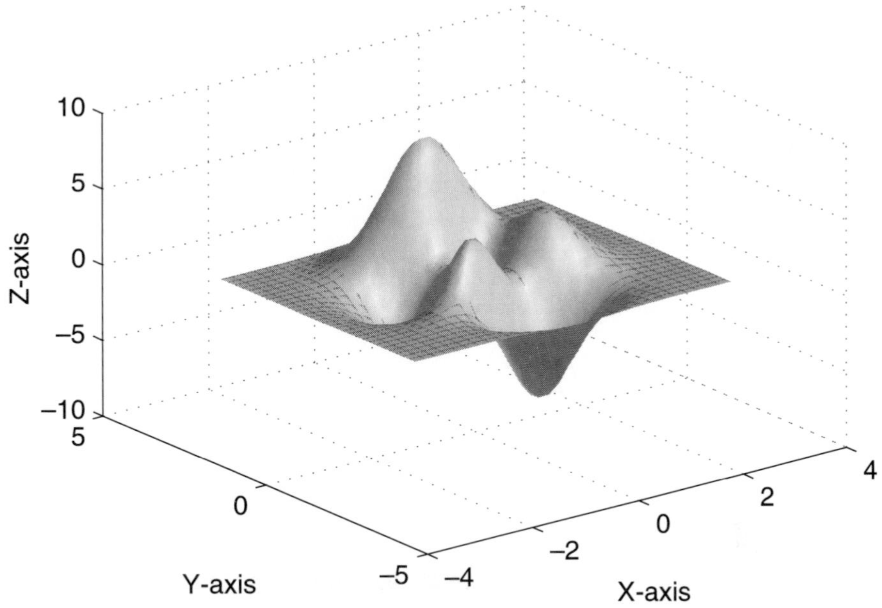

Figure 26.15: Surface Plot with Normals

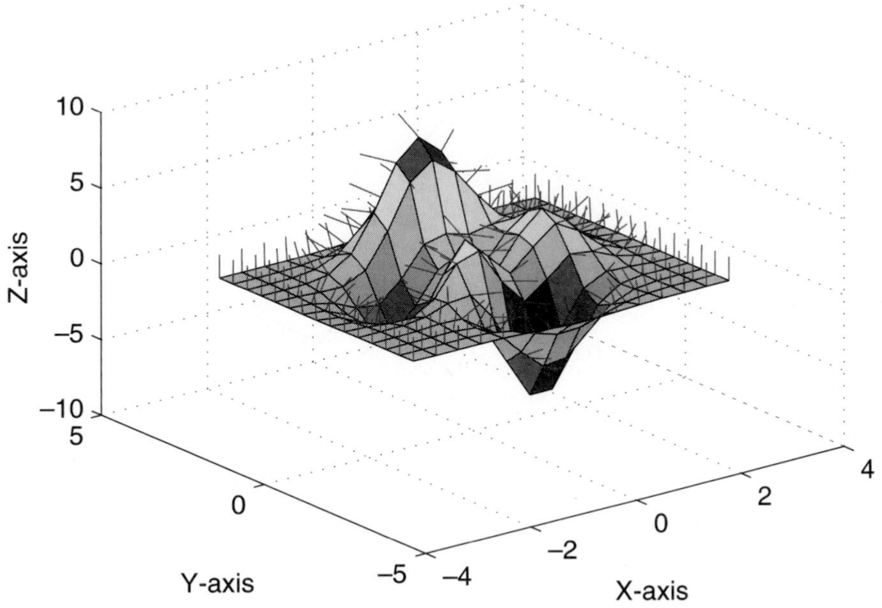

26.5 MESH AND SURFACE PLOTS OF IRREGULAR DATA

Irregular or nonuniformly spaced data can be visualized using the functions `trimesh`, `trisurf`, and `voronoi`, for example,

```
>> x = rand(1,50);
>> y = rand(1,50);
>> z = peaks(x,y*pi);
>> t = delaunay(x,y);
>> trimesh(t,x,y,z)
>> hidden off
>> title('Figure 26.16: Triangular Mesh Plot')
>> pause(5)
>> trisurf(t,x,y,z)
>> title('Figure 26.17: Triangular Surface Plot')
>> pause(5)
>> voronoi(x,y,t)
>> title('Figure 26.18: Voronoi Plot')
```

Figure 26.16: Triangular Mesh Plot

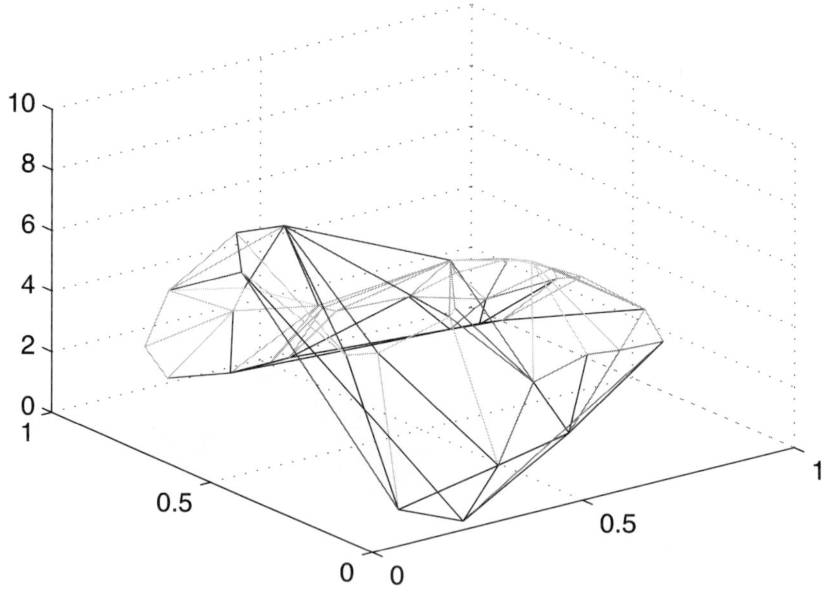

See Chapter 18 for more information on Delaunay triangulation and Voronoi diagrams.

Figure 26.17: Triangular Surface Plot

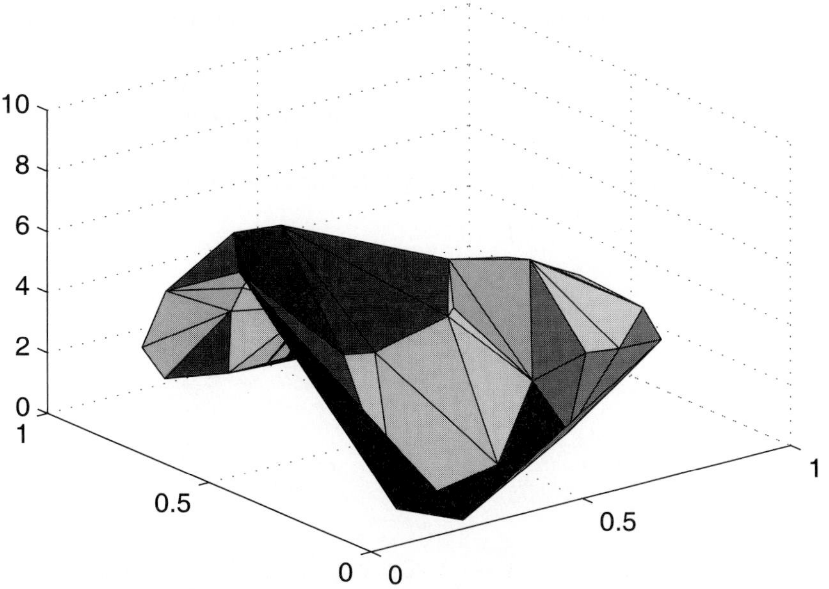

Figure 26.18: Voronoi Plot

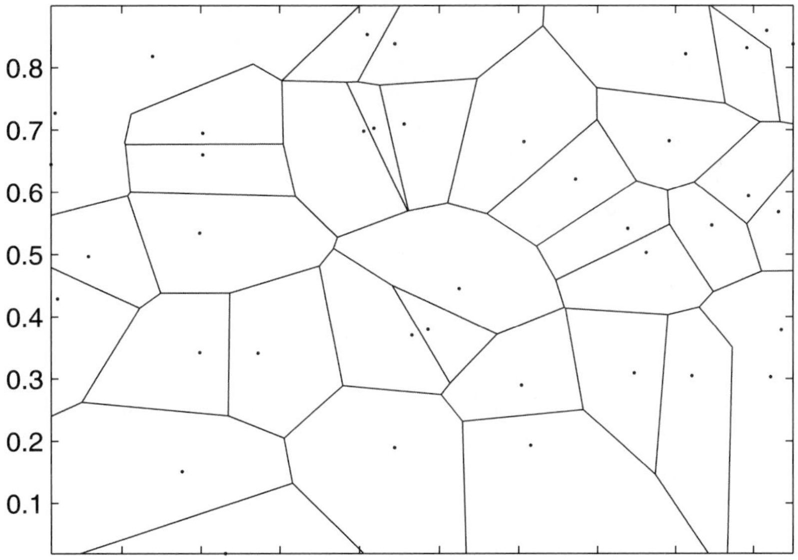

26.6 CHANGING VIEWPOINTS

Note that the default viewpoint of 3-D plots is looking down at the $z = 0$ plane at an angle of 30 degrees and looking up at the $x = 0$ plane at an angle of 37.5 degrees. The angle of orientation with respect to the $z = 0$ plane is called the ***elevation,*** and the angle with respect to the $x = 0$ plane is called the ***azimuth.*** Thus, the default 3-D viewpoint is an elevation of 30 degrees and an azimuth of -37.5 degrees. The default 2-D viewpoint is an elevation of 90 degrees and an azimuth of 0 degrees. The concepts of azimuth and elevation are described visually below.

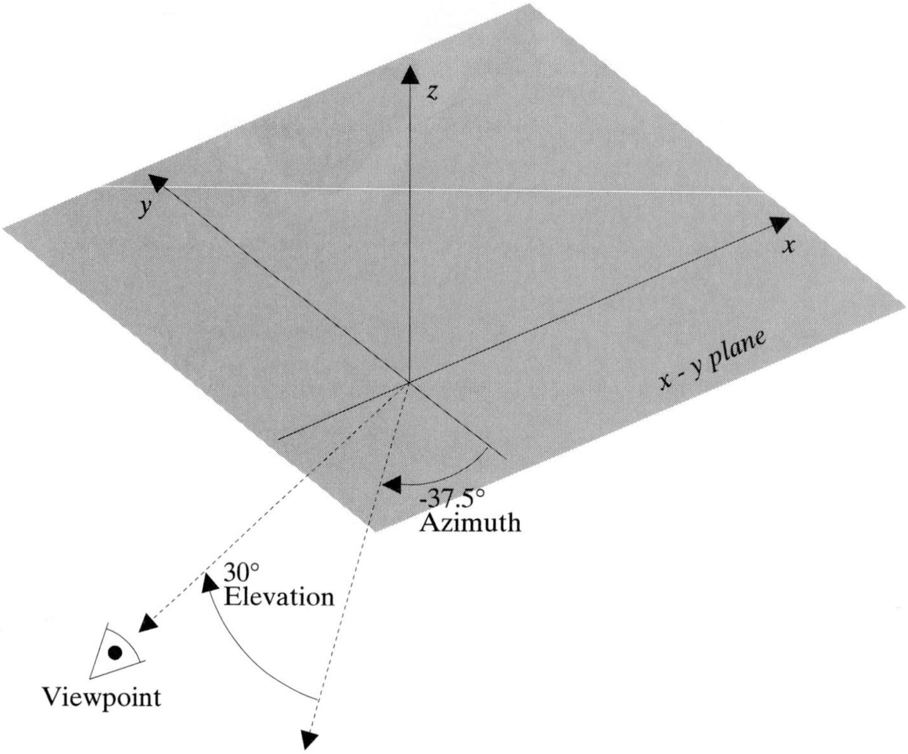

In MATLAB, the function `view` changes the graphical viewpoint for all types of 2-D and 3-D plots. `view(az,el)` and `view([az,el])` change the viewpoint to the specified azimuth `az` and elevation `el`. Consider the following example.

```
>> x = -7.5:.5:7.5; y = x;          % create a data set
>> [X,Y] = meshgrid(x,y);
>> R = sqrt(X.^2+Y.^2)+eps;
```

```
>> Z = sin(R)./R;
>> subplot(2,2,1)
>> surf(X,Y,Z)
>> view(-37.5,30)
>> xlabel('X-axis'), ylabel('Y-axis'), zlabel('Z-axis')
>> title('Figure 26.19a: Az = -37.5, El = 30')

>> subplot(2,2,2)
>> surf(X,Y,Z)
>> view(-37.5+90,30)
>> xlabel('X-axis'), ylabel('Y-axis'), zlabel('Z-axis')
>> title('Figure 26.19b: Az Rotated to 52.5')

>> subplot(2,2,3)
>> surf(X,Y,Z)
>> view(-37.5,60)
>> xlabel('X-axis'), ylabel('Y-axis'), zlabel('Z-axis')
>> title('Figure 26.19c: El Increased to 60')

>> subplot(2,2,4)
>> surf(X,Y,Z)
>> view(0,90)
>> xlabel('X-axis'), ylabel('Y-axis')
>> title('Figure 26.19d: Az = 0, El = 90')
```

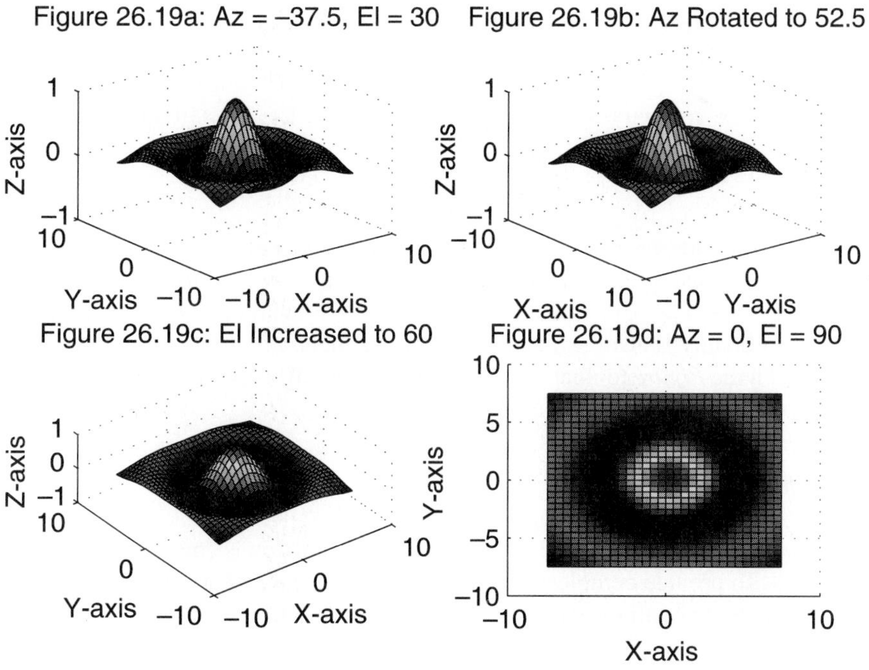

In addition to the above form, `view` also offers additional features summarized in its help text shown below.

```
>> help view
 VIEW   3-D graph viewpoint specification.
   VIEW(AZ,EL) and VIEW([AZ,EL]) set the angle of the view from which an
   observer sees the current 3-D plot. AZ is the azimuth or horizontal
   rotation and EL is the vertical elevation (both in degrees). Azimuth
   revolves about the z-axis, with positive values indicating counter-
   clockwise rotation of the viewpoint. Positive values of elevation
   correspond to moving above the object; negative values move below.
   VIEW([X Y Z]) sets the view angle in cartesian coordinates. The
   magnitude of vector X,Y,Z is ignored.

   Here are some examples:

   AZ = -37.5, EL = 30 is the default 3-D view.
   AZ = 0, EL = 90 is directly overhead and the default 2-D view.
   AZ = EL = 0 looks directly up the first column of the matrix.
   AZ = 180 is behind the matrix.

   VIEW(2) sets the default 2-D view, AZ = 0, EL = 90.
   VIEW(3) sets the default 3-D view, AZ = -37.5, EL = 30.

   [AZ,EL] = VIEW returns the current azimuth and elevation.

   VIEW(T) accepts a 4-by-4 transformation matrix, such as
   the perspective transformations generated by VIEWMTX.

   T = VIEW returns the current general 4-by-4 transformation matrix.

   See also VIEWMTX, the AXES properties View, Xform.
```

In addition to the `view` function, the viewpoint can be set interactively with the mouse by using the function `rotate3d`. `rotate3d on` turns on mouse-based view rotation, `rotate3d off` turns it off, and `rotate3d` with no arguments toggles the state. This functionality is also available on the **Tools** menu in a *Figure* window as well as on a button on the *Figure* toolbar. In reality, the **Rotate 3D** menu item and toolbar button both call `rotate3d` to do the work.

26.7 CAMERA CONTROL

The viewpoint control provided by the `view` function is convenient but limited in capabilities. To provide complete control of a 3-D scene, camera capabilities are needed. That is, one must have all the capabilities available when filming a movie with a camera. Or alternately, one must have all the capabilities available in a 3-D computer or console game environment. In this environment there are two 3-D coordinate systems to manage—one at the camera and one at what the camera is pointed at, that is, the camera target. The camera functions in MATLAB manage and manipulate the relationships between these two coordinate systems and provide control over the camera lens.

Use of the camera functions in MATLAB is generally not easy for a novice. Therefore, to simplify the use of these functions, most are made available interactively from the **Tools** menu or from the *Camera* toolbar in a *Figure* window. To view the *Camera* toolbar, choose it from the **View** menu in the *Figure* window. By using the interactive camera tools, one avoids dealing with the input and output arguments that the *Command* window functions require. Given the ease with which the interactive tools can be used, the complexity involved in using and describing the camera functions, and the relatively small number of potential users, camera functions are not described in this text. The *Using MATLAB Graphics* manual (`graphg.pdf`) that accompanies MATLAB contains a rigorous discussion of these functions and their use. The camera functions available in MATLAB are listed at the end of this chapter.

26.8 CONTOUR PLOTS

Contour plots show lines of constant elevation or height. If you've ever seen a topographical map, you know what a contour plot looks like. In MATLAB, contour plots in 2-D and 3-D are generated using the `contour` and `contour3` functions, respectively, for example,

```
>> [X,Y,Z] = peaks;
>> contour(X,Y,Z,20)          % generate 20 2-D contour lines
>> xlabel('X-axis'), ylabel('Y-axis')
>> title('Figure 26.20: 2-D Contour Plot')
>> pause(5)
>> contour3(X,Y,Z,20)         % the same contour plot in 3-D
>> xlabel('X-axis'), ylabel('Y-axis'), zlabel('Z-axis')
>> title('Figure 26.21: 3-D Contour Plot')
```

The `pcolor` function maps height to a set of colors and presents the same information as the contour plot at the same scale, for example,

```
>> pcolor(X,Y,Z)
>> shading interp  % remove the grid lines
>> title('Figure 26.22: Pseudocolor Plot')
```

Combining the idea of a pseudocolor plot with a 2-D contour produces a filled contour plot. In MATLAB this plot is generated by the function `contourf`, for example,

```
>> contourf(X,Y,Z,12)         % filled contour plot with 12 contours
>> xlabel('X-axis'), ylabel('Y-axis')
>> title('Figure 26.23: Filled Contour Plot')
```

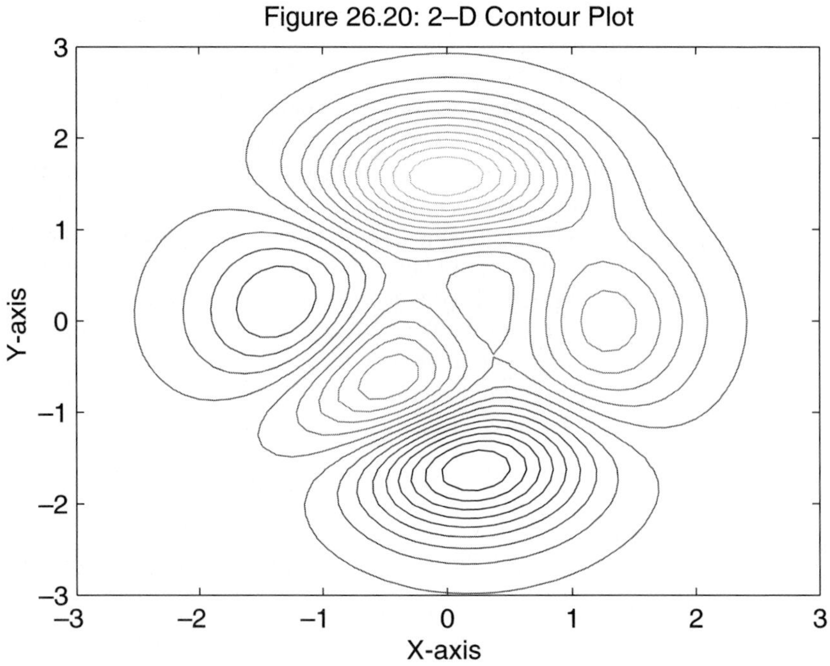
Figure 26.20: 2–D Contour Plot
3
2
1
0
–1
–2
–3
Y-axis
–3
–2
–1
0
1
2
3
X-axis

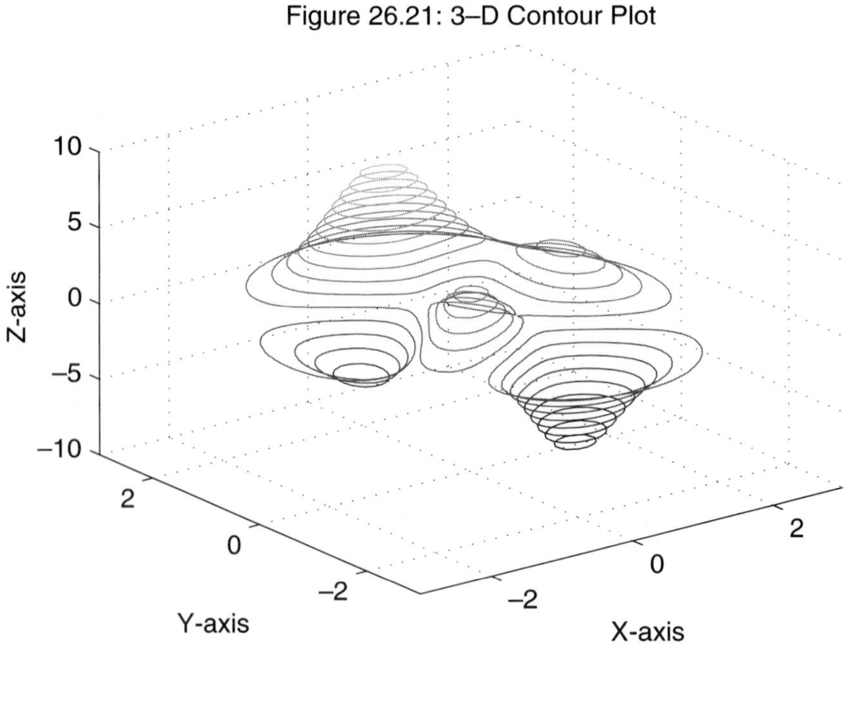
Figure 26.21: 3–D Contour Plot
10
5
0
–5
–10
Z-axis
2
0
–2
Y-axis
2
0
–2
X-axis

Figure 26.22: Pseudocolor Plot

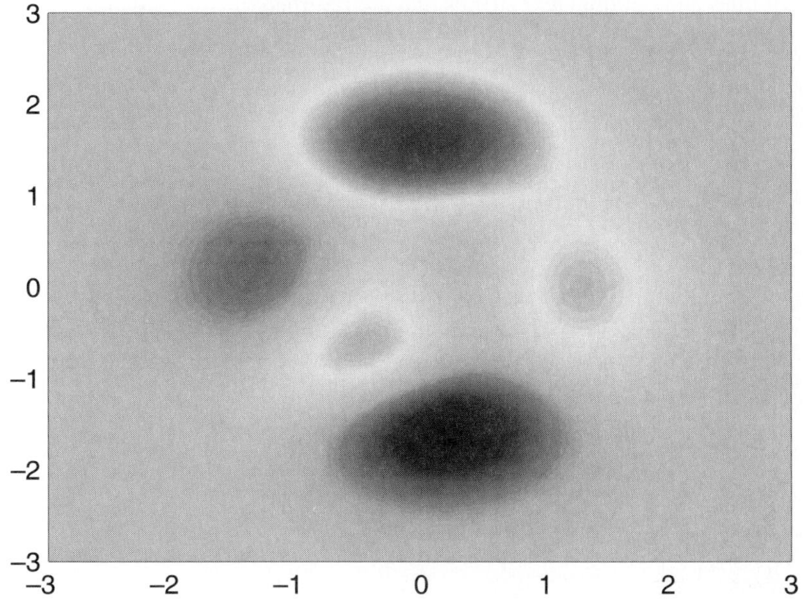

Figure 26.23: Filled Contour Plot

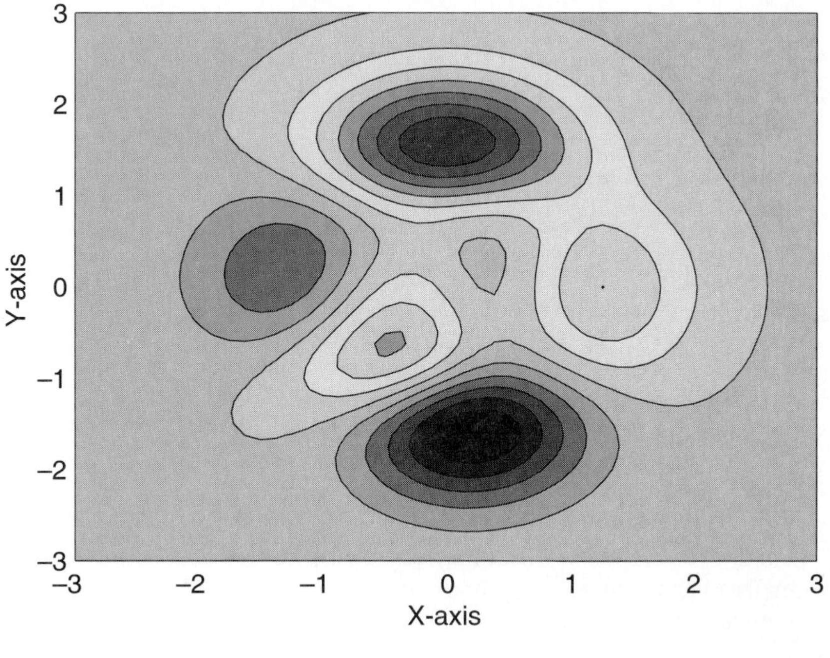

Contour lines can be labeled using the `clabel` function. `clabel` requires a matrix of lines and optional text strings that are returned by `contour`, `contourf`, and `contour3`, for example,

```
>> C = contour(X,Y,Z,12);
>> clabel(C)
>> title('Figure 26.24: Contour Plot With Labels')
```

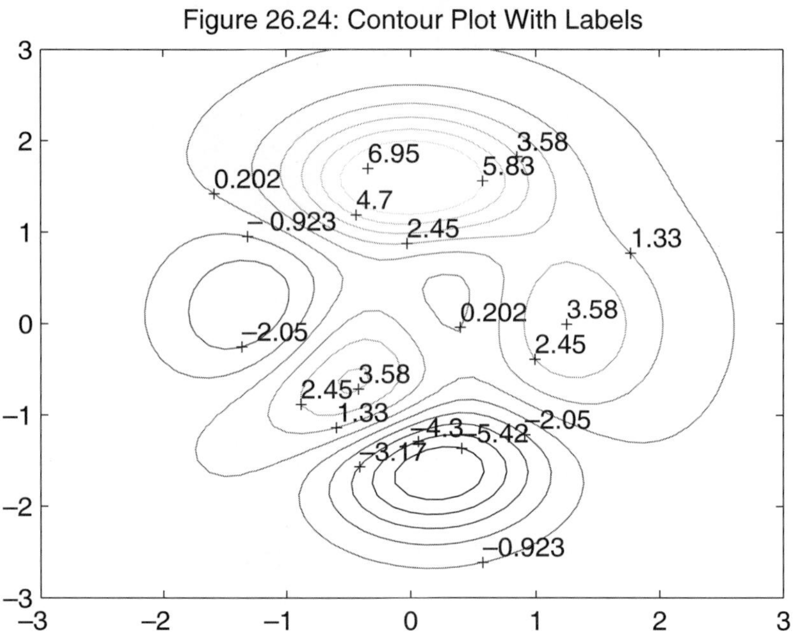

Alternatively, in-line labels are generated using two arguments. These labels appear only where there is sufficient room, for example,

```
>> [C,h] = contour(X,Y,Z,8);
>> clabel(C,h)
>> title('Figure 26.25: Contour Plot With In-line Labels')
```

Finally, you can select which contours to label using the mouse by providing `'manual'` as the last input argument to `clabel`. In-line or horizontal labels are used depending on the presence of the second argument `h` as illustrated above.

Figure 26.25: Contour Plot With In-line Labels

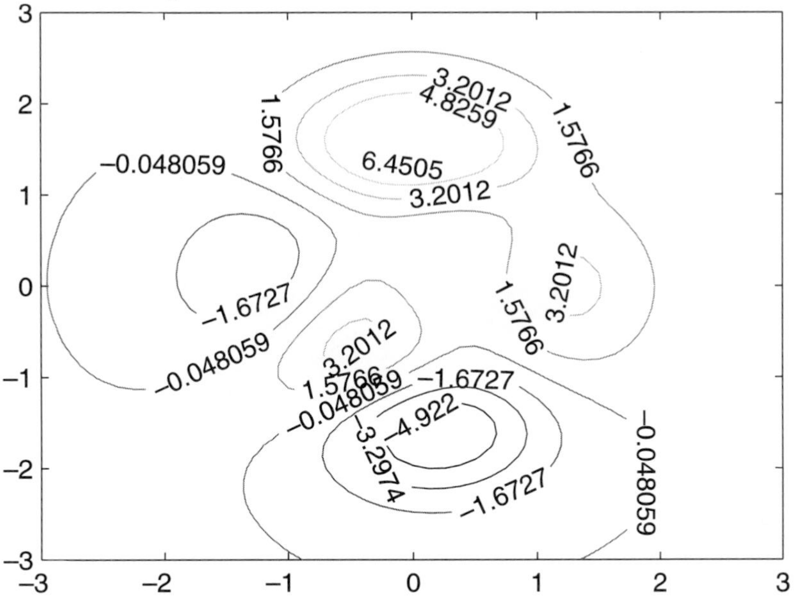

26.9 SPECIALIZED 3-D PLOTS

MATLAB provides a number of specialized plotting functions in addition to those discussed above. The function `ribbon(Y)` plots the columns of `Y` as separate ribbons. `ribbon(x,Y)` plots `x` versus the columns of `Y`. The width of the ribbons can also be specified using the syntax `ribbon(x,Y,width)`, where the default width is 0.75. Consider the example

```
>> Z = peaks;
>> ribbon(Z)
>> title('Figure 26.26: Ribbon Plot of Peaks')
```

The function `quiver(x,y,dx,dy)` draws directional or velocity vectors `(dx,dy)` at the points `(x,y)`, for example,

```
>> [X,Y,Z] = peaks(16);
>> [DX,DY] = gradient(Z,.5,.5);
>> contour(X,Y,Z,10)
>> hold on
>> quiver(X,Y,DX,DY)
>> hold off
>> title('Figure 26.27: 2-D Quiver Plot')
```

Three-dimensional quiver plots of the form `quiver3(x,y,z,Nx,Ny,Nz)` display the vectors `(Nx,Ny,Nz)` at the points `(x,y,z)`, for example,

Figure 26.26: Ribbon Plot of Peaks

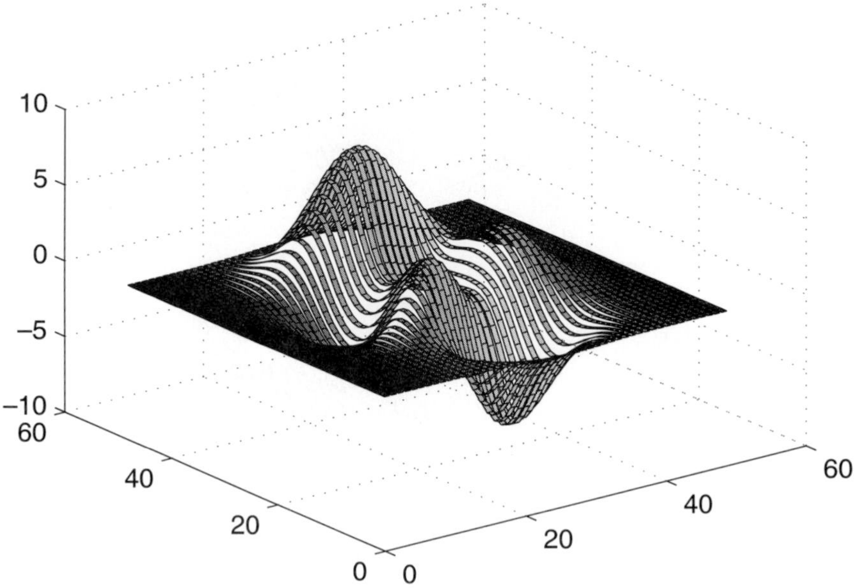

Figure 26.27: 2-D Quiver Plot

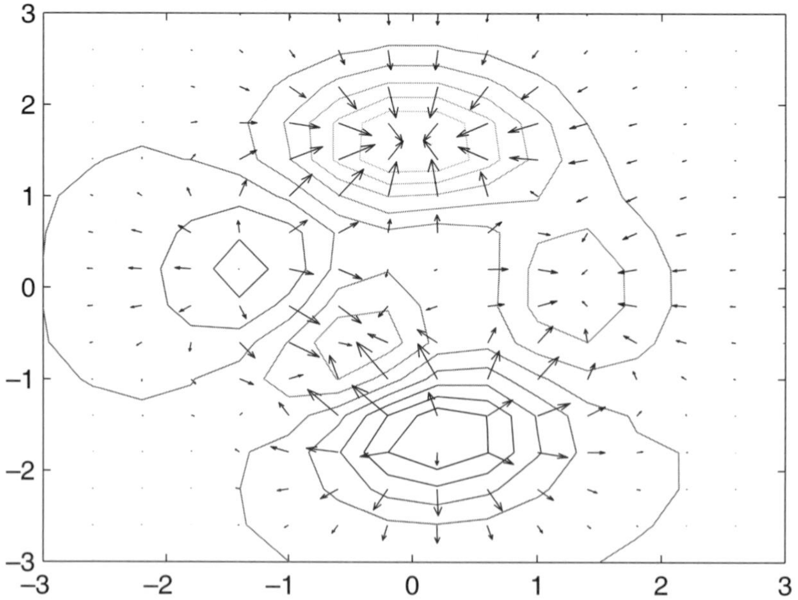

```
>> [X,Y,Z] = peaks(20);
>> [Nx,Ny,Nz] = surfnorm(X,Y,Z);
>> surf(X,Y,Z)
>> hold on
>> quiver3(X,Y,Z,Nx,Ny,Nz)
>> hold off
>> title('Figure 26.28: 3-D Quiver Plot')
```

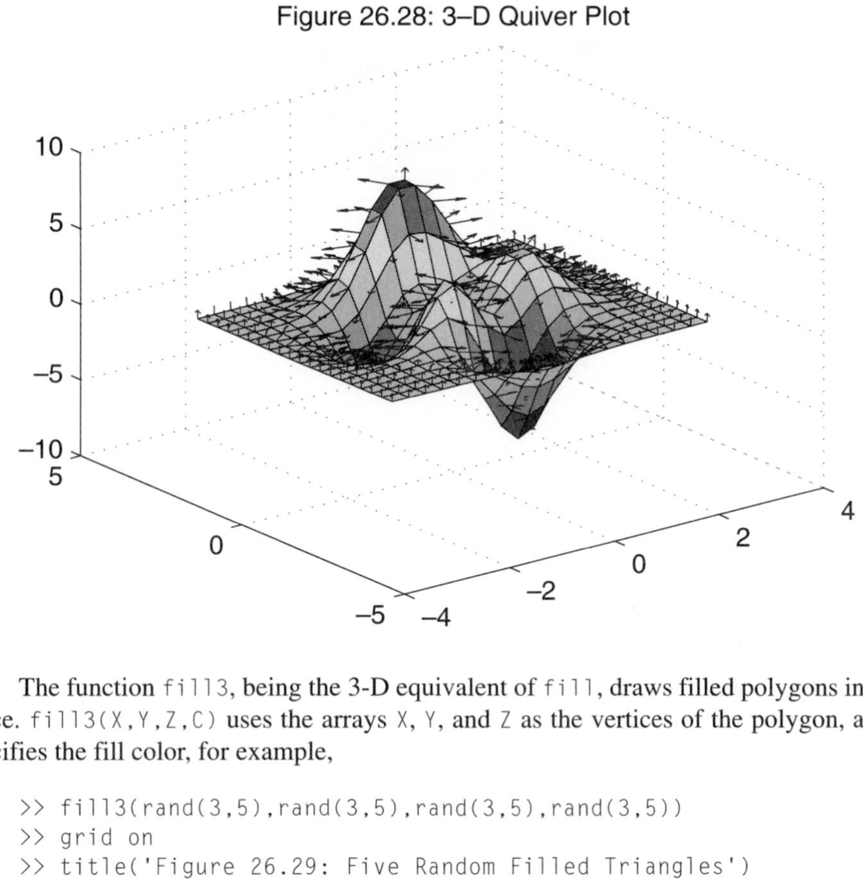

The function fill3, being the 3-D equivalent of fill, draws filled polygons in 3-D space. fill3(X,Y,Z,C) uses the arrays X, Y, and Z as the vertices of the polygon, and C specifies the fill color, for example,

```
>> fill3(rand(3,5),rand(3,5),rand(3,5),rand(3,5))
>> grid on
>> title('Figure 26.29: Five Random Filled Triangles')
```

The 3-D equivalent of stem plots discrete sequence data in 3-D space. stem3(X,Y,Z,C,'filled') plots the data points in (X,Y,Z) with lines extending to the *x*-*y* plane. The optional argument C specifies the marker style and/or color, and the optional 'filled' argument causes the marker to be filled in. stem3(Z) plots the points in Z and automatically generates X and Y values. For example,

```
>> Z = rand(5);
>> stem3(Z,'ro','filled');
>> grid on
>> title('Figure 26.30: Stem Plot of Random Data')
```

Figure 26.29: Five Random Filled Triangles

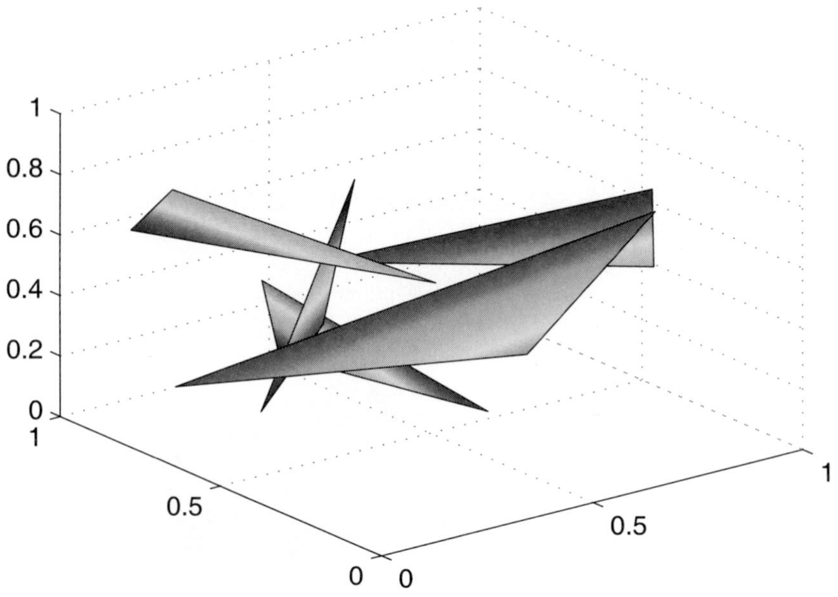

Figure 26.30: Stem Plot of Random Data

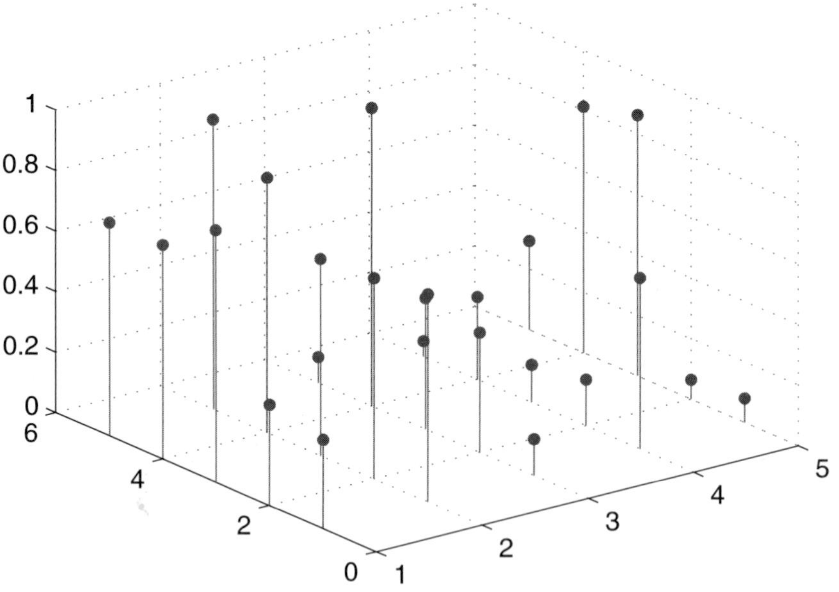

26.10 VOLUME VISUALIZATION

In addition to the common mesh, surface, and contour plots, MATLAB offers a variety of more complex volume and vector visualization functions. These functions construct plots of scalar and vector quantities in 3-D space. Because they generally construct volumes rather than surfaces, their input arguments are 3-D arrays, one for each axis, *x, y,* and *z*. The points in each 3-D array define a grid of coordinates or data at the coordinates. For scalar functions, four 3-D arrays are required, one for each of the three coordinate axes plus one for the scalar data at the coordinate points. These arrays are commonly identified as `X`, `Y`, `Z`, and `V`, respectively. For vector functions, six 3-D arrays are required, one for each of the three coordinate axes plus one for each axis component of the vector at the coordinate points. These arrays are commonly identified as `X`, `Y`, `Z`, `U`, `V`, and `W`, respectively.

Use of the volume and vector visualization functions in MATLAB requires an understanding of volume and vector terminology. For example, ***divergence*** and ***curl*** describe vector processes, and ***isosurfaces*** and ***isocaps*** describe visual aspects of volumes. If you are unfamiliar with these terms, using MATLAB volume and visualization functions can be confusing. It is beyond the scope of this text to cover the terminology required to rigorously use these volume and vector visualization functions. However, the structure of the data arrays and the use of several functions are demonstrated in what follows. For further information, see the *Using MATLAB Graphics* manual (`graphg.pdf`) that accompanies MATLAB. In addition, issuing the command `volvec` provides a GUI for interactive discovery of most volume visualization functions in MATLAB.

Consider the construction of a scalar function defined over a volume. First, the volume coordinate axes must be constructed, for example,

```
>> x = linspace(-3,3,13);       % x-coordinate points
>> y = 1:20;                    % y-coordinate points
>> z = -5:5;                    % z-coordinate points
>> [X,Y,Z] = meshgrid(x,y,z);  % meshgrid works here too!
>> size(X)
ans =
    20    13    11
```

Here, `X`, `Y`, `Z` are 3-D arrays defining the grid. `X` contains `x` duplicated for as many rows as `length(y)` and as many pages as `length(z)`. Similarly, `Y` contains `y` transposed to a column and duplicated for as many columns as `length(x)` and as many pages as `length(z)`. And `Z` contains `z` permuted to a 1-by-1-by-`length(z)` vector and duplicated for as many rows as `length(y)` and as many columns as `length(x)`. As described, this is a direct extension of `meshgrid` to 3-D.

Next, we need to define a function of this data, for example,

```
>> V = sqrt(X.^2 + cos(Y).^2 + Z.^2);
```

Now, the 3-D arrays `X`, `Y`, `Z`, and `V` define a scalar function $v = f(x,y,z)$ defined over a volume. To visualize what this looks like we can look at slices along planes, for example,

```
>> slice(X,Y,Z,V,[0 3],[5 15],[-3 5])
>> xlabel('X-axis')
>> ylabel('Y-axis')
>> zlabel('Z-axis')
>> title('Figure 26.31: Slice Plot Through a Volume')
```

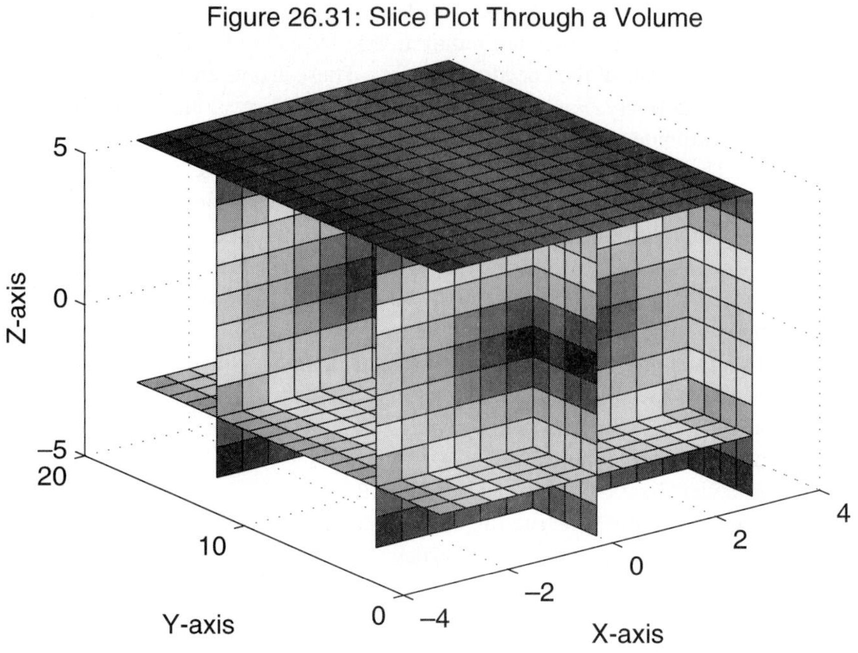

This plot shows slices on planes defined by $x = 0$, $x = 3$, $y = 5$, $y = 15$, $z = -3$, and $z = 5$ as shown by the last three arguments to the function `slice`. The color of the plot is mapped to the values in `V` on the slices.

The slices displayed need not be planes. They can be any surface, for example,

```
>> [xs,ys] = meshgrid(x,y);
>> zs = sin(-xs+ys/2); % a surface to use
>> slice(X,Y,Z,V,xs,ys,zs)
>> xlabel('X-axis')
>> ylabel('Y-axis')
>> zlabel('Z-axis')
>> title('Figure 26.32: Slice Plot Using a Surface')
```

Here `xs`, `ys`, and `zs` defines a surface to slice through the volume.

Going back to the original slice plot, it is possible to add contour lines to selected planes using the `contourslice` function, for example,

Figure 26.32: Slice Plot Using a Surface

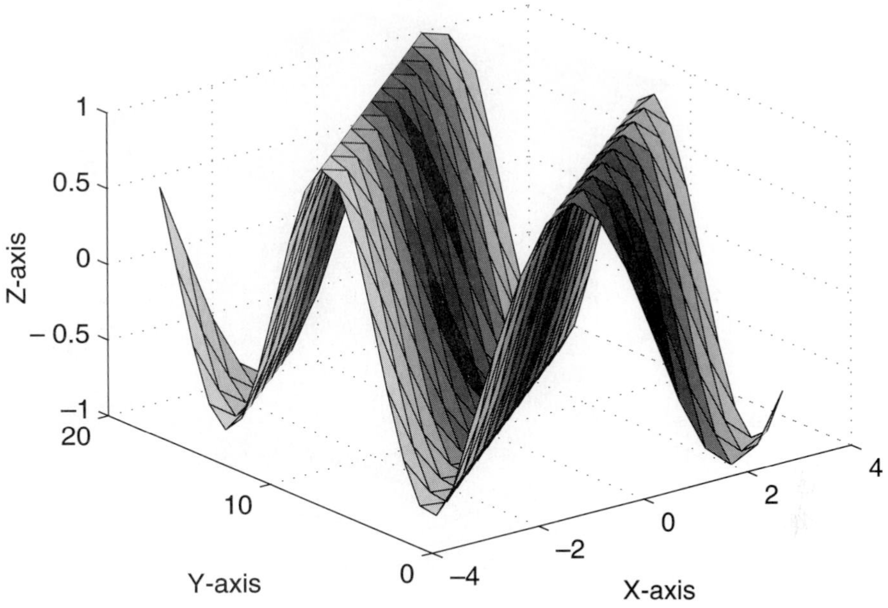


```
>> slice(X,Y,Z,V,[0 3],[5 15],[-3 5])
>> h = contourslice(X,Y,Z,V,3,[5 15],[]);
>> set(h,'EdgeColor','k','Linewidth',1.5)
>> xlabel('X-axis')
>> ylabel('Y-axis')
>> zlabel('Z-axis')
>> title('Figure 26.33: Slice Plot with Selected Contours')
```

Here contour lines are added to the $x = 3$, $y = 5$, and $y = 15$ planes. With the use of Handle Graphics features, the contour lines are set to black and their width is set to 1.5 points.

In addition to looking at slices through a volume, surfaces where the scalar volume data `V` has a specified value can be plotted using the `isosurface` function. This function returns triangle vertices in a manner similar to Delaunay triangulation, the results being in the form required by the `patch` function, which plots the triangles. Consider the following example.

```
>> [X,Y,Z,V] = flow(13);                   % get flow data
>> fv = isosurface(X,Y,Z,V,-2);            % find surface of value -2
>> subplot(1,2,1)
>> p = patch(fv);                          % plot V = -2 surface
>> set(p,'FaceColor',[.5 .5 .5],'EdgeColor','Black'); % modify patches
>> view(3), axis equal tight, grid on % pretty it up
>> title({'Figure 26.34a:' 'Isosurface Plot, V = 2'})
>> subplot(1,2,2)
```

Figure 26.33: Slice Plot with Selected Contours

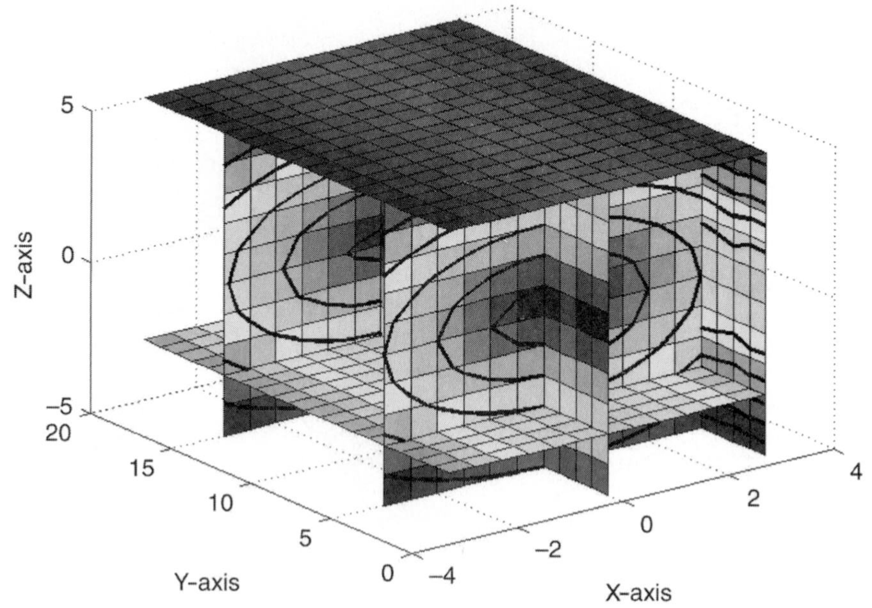


```
>> p = patch(shrinkfaces(fv,.3));      % shrink faces to 30% of original
>> set(p,'Facecolor',[.5 .5 .5],'EdgeColor','Black'); % modify patches
>> view(3), axis equal tight, grid on % pretty it up
>> title({'Figure 26.34b:' 'Shrunken Face Isosurface Plot, V = 2'})
```

Figure 26.34a:
Isosurface Plot, V = 2

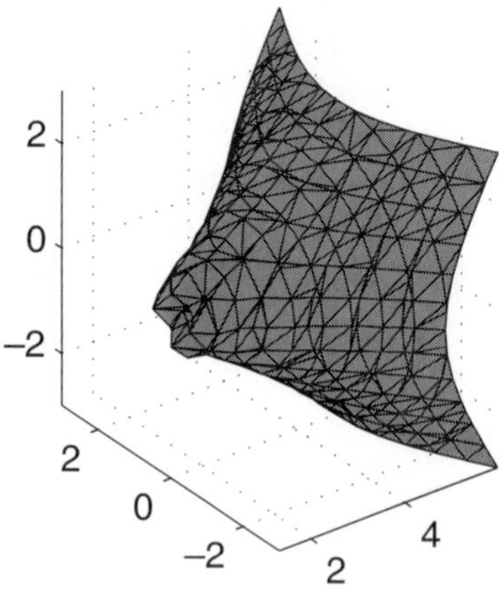

Figure 26.34b:
Shrunken Face Isosurface Plot, V = 2

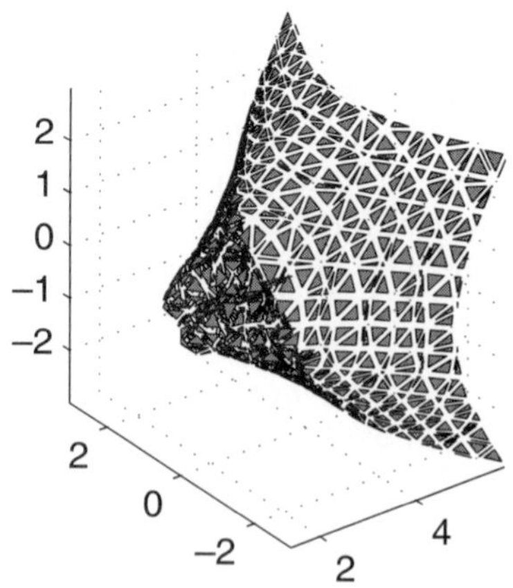

The preceding plots also demonstrate use of the function `shrinkfaces`, which does exactly what its name suggests.

Sometimes volume data contains too many points for efficient display. The functions `reducevolume` and `reducepatch` represent two ways to improve the display of an isosurface. The function `reducevolume` eliminates data before the isosurface is formed, whereas `reducepatch` seeks to eliminate patches while minimizing distortion in the underlying surface. Consider the following example.

```
>> [X,Y,Z,V] = flow;
>> fv = isosurface(X,Y,Z,V,-2);
>> subplot(2,2,1) % Original
>> p = patch(fv);
>> Np = size(get(p,'Faces'),1);
>> set(p,'FaceColor',[.5 .5 .5],'EdgeColor','Black');
>> view(3), axis equal tight, grid on  % pretty it up
>> zlabel(sprintf('%d Patches',Np))
>> title('Figure 26.35a: Original')

>> subplot(2,2,2) % Reduce Volume
>> [Xr,Yr,Zr,Vr] = reducevolume(X,Y,Z,V,[3 2 2]);
>> fvr = isosurface(Xr,Yr,Zr,Vr,-2);
>> p = patch(fvr);
>> Np = size(get(p,'Faces'),1);
>> set(p,'FaceColor',[.5 .5 .5],'EdgeColor','Black');
>> view(3), axis equal tight, grid on  % pretty it up
>> zlabel(sprintf('%d Patches',Np))
>> title('Figure 26.35b: Reduce Volume')

>> subplot(2,2,3) % Reduce Patch
>> p = patch(fv);
>> set(p,'FaceColor',[.5 .5 .5],'EdgeColor','Black');
>> view(3), axis equal tight, grid on  % pretty it up
>> reducepatch(p,.15) % keep 15 percent of the faces
>> Np = size(get(p,'Faces'),1);
>> zlabel(sprintf('%d Patches',Np))
>> title('Figure 26.35c: Reduce Patches')

>> subplot(2,2,4) % Reduce Volume and Patch
>> p = patch(fvr);
>> set(p,'FaceColor',[.5 .5 .5],'EdgeColor','Black');
>> view(3), axis equal tight, grid on  % pretty it up
>> reducepatch(p,.15) % keep 15 percent of the faces
>> Np = size(get(p,'Faces'),1);
>> zlabel(sprintf('%d Patches',Np))
>> title('Figure 26.35d: Reduce Both')
```

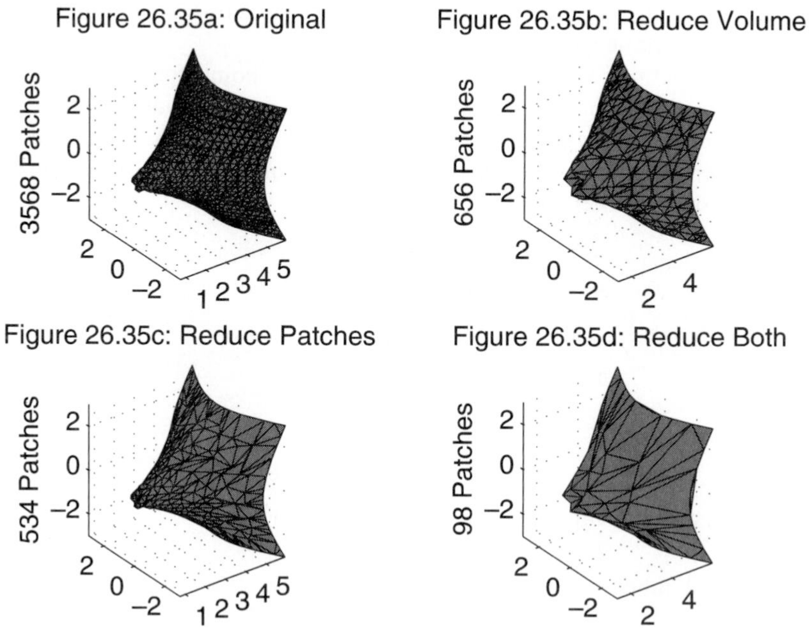

Three-dimensional data can also be smoothed by filtering it using the `smooth3` function, for example,

```
>> data = rand(10,10,10);          % random data
>> datas = smooth3(data,'box',3); % smoothed data

>> subplot(1,2,1) % random data
>> p = patch(isosurface(data,.5), ...
     'FaceColor','Blue','EdgeColor','none');
>> patch(isocaps(data,.5), ...
     'FaceColor', 'interp', 'EdgeColor', 'none');
>> isonormals(data,p)
>> view(3); axis vis3d tight off
>> camlight; lighting phong
>> title({'Figure 26.36a:' 'Random Data'})

>> subplot(1,2,2) % smoothed random data
>> p = patch(isosurface(datas,.5), ...
     'FaceColor','Blue','EdgeColor','none');
>> patch(isocaps(datas,.5), ...
     'FaceColor', 'interp', 'EdgeColor', 'none');
>> isonormals(datas,p)
>> view(3); axis vis3d tight off
>> camlight; lighting phong
>> title({'Figure 26.36b:' 'Smoothed Data'})
```

Figure 26.36a:
Random Data

Figure 26.36b:
Smoothed Data

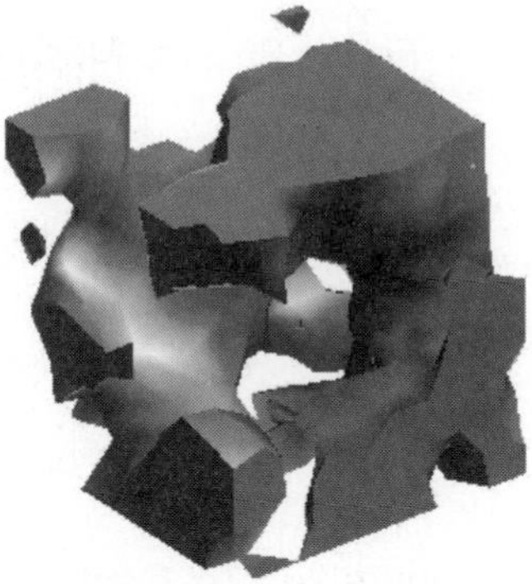

The above example demonstrates the use of the functions `isocaps` and `isonormals`. The function `isocaps` creates the faces on the outer surfaces of the block. The function `isonormals` modifies properties of the drawn patches so that lighting works correctly.

For further information regarding volume and vector visualization features in MATLAB, see the *Using MATLAB Graphics* manual and experiment with the `volvec` function.

26.11 EASY PLOTTING

When one doesn't want to take the time to specify the data points explicitly for a 3-D plot, MATLAB provides the functions `ezcontour`, `ezcontour3`, `ezmesh`, `ezmeshc`, `ezplot3`, `ezsurf`, and `ezsurfc`. These functions construct plots like their equivalents without the `ez` prefix. However, the input arguments are functions defined by string expressions or symbolic math objects and optionally the axis limits over which the plot is to be generated. Internally, the functions compute the data and generate the desired plot, for example,

```
>> fstr = ['3*(1-x).^2.*exp(-(x.^2) - (y+1).^2)' ...
   ' - 10*(x/5 - x.^3 - y.^5).*exp(-x.^2-y.^2)' ...
   ' - 1/3*exp(-(x+1).^2 - y.^2)'];
>> subplot(2,2,1)
>> ezmesh(fstr)
>> title('Figure 26.37a: Mesh of peaks(x,y)')
>> subplot(2,2,2)
>> ezsurf(fstr)
>> title('Figure 26.37b: Surf of peaks(x,y)')
>> subplot(2,2,3)
>> ezcontour(fstr)
>> title('Figure 26.37c: Contour of peaks(x,y)')
```

```
>> subplot(2,2,4)
>> ezcontourf(fstr)
>> title('Figure 26.37d: Contourf of peaks(x,y)')
```

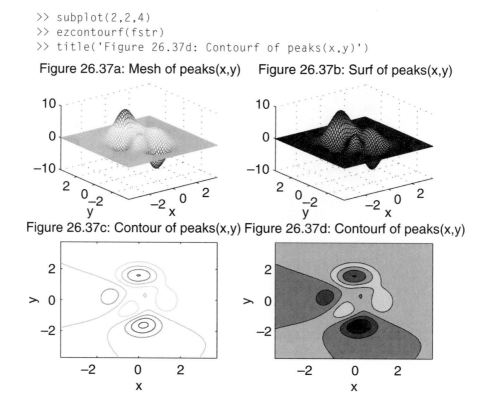

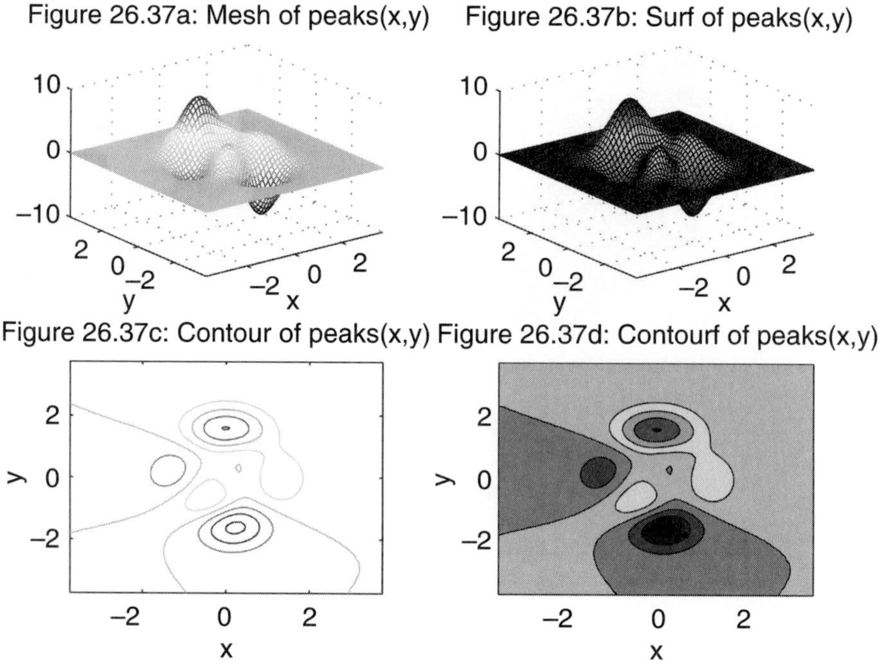

26.12 SUMMARY

The table below documents MATLAB functions for 3-D plotting.

Function	Description
`plot3`	Plot lines and points in 3-D space.
`mesh`	Mesh surface.
`meshc`	Mesh with underlying contour plot.
`meshz`	Mesh with zero plane.
`surf`	Surface plot.
`surfc`	Surface plot with underlying contour plot.
`surfl`	Surface plot with basic lighting.

Function	Description
fill3	Filled 3-D polygons.
shading	Color shading mode.
hidden	Mesh hidden line removal.
surfnorm	Surface normals.
axis	Control axis scaling and appearance.
grid	Grid line visibility.
box	Axis box visibility.
hold	Hold current plot.
subplot	Create multiple axes in *Figure* window.
daspect	Data aspect ratio.
pbaspect	Plot box aspect ratio.
xlim	*x*-axis limits.
ylim	*y*-axis limits.
zlim	*z*-axis limits.
view	3-D viewpoint specification.
viewmtx	View transformation matrix.
rotate3d	Interactive axes rotation.
campos	Camera position.
camtarget	Camera target.
camva	Camera view angle.
camup	Camera up vector.
camproj	Camera projection.
camorbit	Camera orbit.
campan	Pan camera.
camdolly	Dolly camera.
camzoom	Zoom camera.
camroll	Roll camera.

Function	Description
camlookat	Look at specific object.
camlight	Camera lighting creation and placement.
title	Plot title.
xlabel	x-axis label.
ylabel	y-axis label.
zlabel	z-axis label.
text	Place text on plot.
gtext	Place text with mouse.
contour	Contour plot.
contourf	Filled contour plot.
contour3	3-D contour plot.
clabel	Contour labeling.
pcolor	Pseudocolor plot.
voronoi	Voronoi diagram.
trimesh	Triangular mesh plot.
trisurf	Triangular surface plot.
scatter3	3-D scatter plot.
stem3	3-D stem plot.
waterfall	Waterfall plot.
ezmesh	Easy mesh plot of string expression.
ezmeshc	Easy mesh plot with contour plot of string expression.
ezplot3	Easy 3-D linear plot of string expression.
ezsurf	Easy surface plot of string expression.
ezsurfc	Easy surface plot with contour plot of string expression.
ezcontour	Easy contour plot of string expression.

Function	Description
ezcontourf	Easy filled contour plot of string expression.
vissuite	Help for visualization suite.
isosurface	Isosurface extractor.
isonormals	Isosurface normals.
isocaps	Isosurface end caps.
isocolors	Isosurface and patch colors.
contourslice	Contours in slice planes.
slice	Volumetric slice plot.
streamline	Streamlines from data.
stream3	3-D streamlines.
stream2	2-D streamlines.
quiver3	3-D quiver plot.
quiver	2-D quiver plot.
divergence	Divergence of a vector field.
curl	Curl and angular velocity of a vector field.
coneplot	Cone plot.
streamtube	Stream tube.
streamribbon	Stream ribbon.
streamslice	Streamlines in slice planes.
streamparticles	Display stream particles.
interpstreamspeed	Interpolate streamline vertices from speed.
subvolume	Extract subset of volume data set.
reducevolume	Reduce volume data set.
volumebounds	Return volume and color limits.
smooth3	Smooth 3-D data.
reducepatch	Reduce number of patch faces.
shrinkfaces	Reduce size of patch faces.

27

Using Color and Light

MATLAB provides a number of tools for displaying information visually in two and three dimensions. For example, the plot of a sine curve presents more information at a glance than a set of data points could. The technique of using plots and graphs to present data sets is known as ***data visualization.*** In addition to being a powerful computational engine, MATLAB excels in presenting data visually in interesting and informative ways.

Often, however, a simple 2-D or 3-D plot cannot display all the information one would like to present at one time. Color can provide an additional dimension. Many of the plotting functions discussed in previous chapters accept a *color* argument that can be used to add that additional dimension.

This discussion begins with an investigation of colormaps: how to use them, display them, alter them, and create them. Next, techniques for simulating more than one colormap in a *Figure* window or for using only a portion of a colormap are illustrated. Finally, lighting models are discussed, and examples are presented. As in the preceding chapters, the figures in this chapter do not exhibit color, although they do have color on a computer screen. As a result, if you are not following along in MATLAB, it may take some imagination to understand the concepts covered in this chapter.

27.1 UNDERSTANDING COLORMAPS

MATLAB uses a numerical array with three columns to represent color values. This array is called a ***colormap,*** and each row in the matrix represents an individual color using numbers in the range 0 to 1. The numbers in each row indicate the intensity of red, green, and blue making up a specific color. The table below illustrates the correspondence between the numerical values in a colormap and colors.

Red	Green	Blue	Color
1	0	0	Red
0	1	0	Green
0	0	1	Blue
1	1	0	Yellow
1	0	1	Magenta
0	1	1	Cyan
0	0	0	Black
1	1	1	White
0.5	0.5	0.5	Medium gray
0.67	0	1	Violet
1	0.4	0	Orange
0.5	0	0	Dark red
0	0.5	0	Dark green

The first column in a colormap is the intensity of red, the second column is the intensity of green, and the third column is the intensity of blue. Colormap values are restricted to the range from 0 to 1.

A colormap is a sequence of rows containing red-green-blue (RGB) values that vary in some prescribed way from the first row to the last. MATLAB provides a number of predefined colormaps as shown in the following table.

Colormap Function	Description
`hsv`	Hue-saturation-value colormap, begins and ends with red.
`jet`	Variant of `hsv` that starts with blue and ends with red.

Colormap Function	Description
`hot`	Black to red to yellow to white.
`cool`	Shades of cyan and magenta.
`summer`	Shades of green and yellow.
`autumn`	Shades of red and yellow.
`winter`	Shades of blue and green.
`spring`	Shades of magenta and yellow.
`white`	All white.
`gray`	Linear gray scale.
`bone`	Gray with a tinge of blue.
`pink`	Pastel shades of pink.
`copper`	Linear copper tone.
`prism`	Alternating red, orange, yellow, green, blue, and violet.
`flag`	Alternating red, white, blue, and black.
`lines`	Alternating plot line colors.
`colorcube`	Enhanced color cube.

By default, each of these colormaps generates a 64-by-3 array specifying the RGB descriptions of 64 colors. Each of these functions accepts an argument specifying the number of rows to be generated. For example, `hot(m)` generates an `m`-by-3 matrix containing the RGB values of colors ranging from black, through shades of red, orange, and yellow, to white.

Most computers can display at least 256 colors at one time in an 8-bit hardware color lookup table, although many now have display cards that can handle 24 bits or more, supporting more than 16 million colors. This means that conservatively up to three or four 64-by-3 colormaps can be in use at one time in different figures using a 256-color mode. Many more 64-by-3 colormaps can be supported with video cards set to greater color depths. If more colormap entries are used than can be supported in the hardware, the computer swaps out entries in its hardware lookup table. When this happens, the screen background colors change when MATLAB figures are plotted.

27.2 USING COLORMAPS

The statement `colormap(M)` installs the matrix `M` as the colormap to be used in the current *Figure* window. For example, `colormap(cool)` installs a 64-entry version of the `cool` colormap. `colormap default` installs the default colormap, usually `hsv` or `jet` depending on the default color scheme you have chosen with the `colordef` command.

Line-plotting functions such as `plot` and `plot3` do not use colormaps; they use the colors listed in the `plot` color and linestyle table. The sequence of colors used by these functions varies depending on the plotting style you have chosen. Most other plotting functions, such as `mesh`, `surf`, `contour`, `fill`, `pcolor`, and their variations, use the current colormap to determine color sequences.

Plotting functions that accept a *color* argument usually accept the argument in one of three forms:

1. A character string representing one of the colors in the `plot` color and linestyle table, for example, `'r'` or `'red'` for red.
2. A three-entry row vector representing a single RGB value, for example, `[.25 .50 .75]`.
3. An array. If the color argument is an array, the elements are scaled and used as indices into the current colormap.

27.3 DISPLAYING COLORMAPS

Colormaps can be viewed in a number of ways. One way is to view the elements in a colormap matrix directly, for example,

```
>> hot(8)
ans =
      0.33333            0            0
      0.66667            0            0
            1            0            0
            1      0.33333            0
            1      0.66667            0
            1            1            0
            1            1          0.5
            1            1            1
>> gray(5)
ans =
            0            0            0
         0.25         0.25         0.25
          0.5          0.5          0.5
         0.75         0.75         0.75
            1            1            1
```

The above example shows two standard colormaps. The first is an eight-element `hot` colormap, and the second is a five-element `gray` colormap. The gray colormap increments all three components equally, thereby producing various shades of gray.

A colormap is best visualized graphically. The `pcolor` and `rgbplot` functions are useful in this case, as in the following example.

```
>> n = 21;
>> map = copper(n);
>> colormap(map)
>> subplot(2,1,1)
>> [xx,yy] = meshgrid(0:n,[0 1]);
>> c = [1:n+1;1:n+1];
>> pcolor(xx,yy,c)
>> set(gca,'Yticklabel','')
>> title('Figure 27.1a: Pcolor of Copper')
>> subplot(2,1,2)
>> rgbplot(map)
>> xlim([0,n])
>> title('Figure 27.1b: RGBplot of Copper')
```

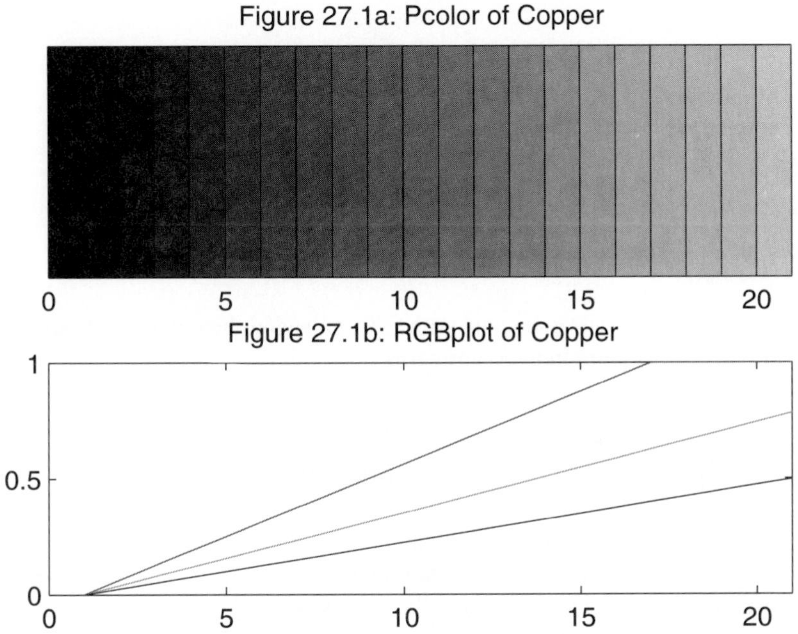

These figures show how a copper colormap varies from its first row shown on the left to its last row shown on the right. The function `rgbplot` simply plots the three columns of the colormap in red, green, and blue, respectively, thereby dissecting the three components visually.

When a 3-D plot is made, the color information in the plot can be displayed as auxiliary information in a colorbar using the `colorbar` function, for example,

```
>> mesh(peaks)
>> axis tight
>> colorbar
>> title('Figure 27.2: Colorbar Added')
```

Figure 27.2: Colorbar Added

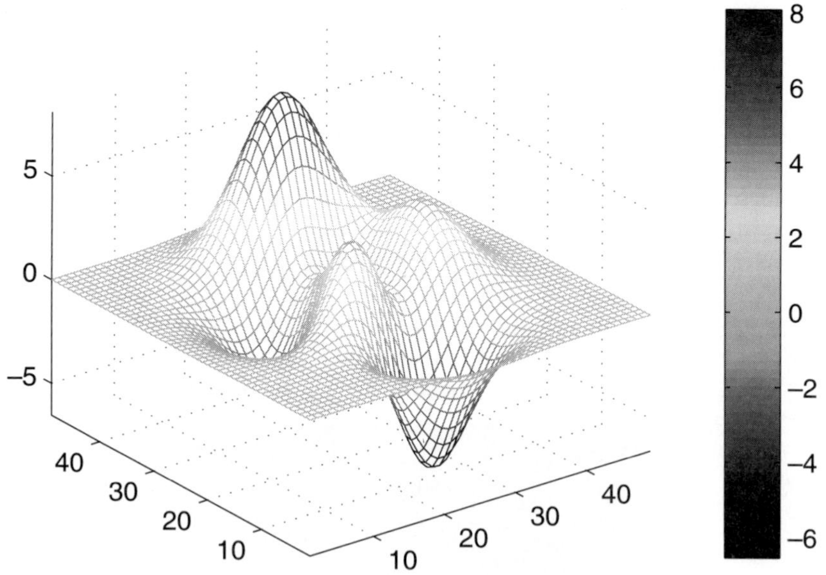

In this plot color is associated with the z-axis, and the colorbar associates z-coordinate values with the colors in the colormap.

27.4 CREATING AND ALTERING COLORMAPS

The fact that colormaps are arrays means that you can manipulate them exactly like other arrays. The function `brighten` takes advantage of this feature to adjust a given colormap to increase or decrease the intensity of the colors. `brighten(beta)` brightens (`0 < beta ≤ 1`) or darkens (`-1 ≤ beta < 0`) the current colormap. `brighten(beta)` followed by `brighten(-beta)` restores the original colormap. The command `newmap=brighten(beta)` creates a brighter or darker version of the current colormap without changing the current map. The command `mymap=brighten(cmap,beta)` creates an adjusted version of the specified colormap without affecting either the current colormap or the specified colormap `cmap`.

Colormaps can be created by generating an `m`-by-3 array `mymap` and installing it with `colormap(mymap)`. Each value in a colormap matrix must be between 0 and 1. If you try to use a matrix with more or less than three columns or containing any values less than 0 or greater than 1, `colormap` will report an error.

Colormaps can be converted between the red-green-blue (RGB) standard and the hue-saturation-value (HSV) standard using the `rgb2hsv` and `hsv2rgb` functions. MATLAB, however, always interprets colormaps as RGB values. Colormaps can be combined as well, as long as the result satisfies the size and value constraints. For example, the colormap called pink is simply

```
pinkmap = sqrt(2/3*gray + 1/3*hot);
```

Again, the result is a valid colormap only if all elements of the m-by-3 matrix are between 0 and 1 inclusive.

Normally, a colormap is scaled to extend from the minimum to the maximum values of your data, that is, the entire colormap is used to render your plot. You may occasionally wish to change the way these colors are used. The caxis function, which stands for ***color axis,*** allows you to use the entire colormap for a subset of your data range or to use only a portion of the current colormap for your entire data set.

[cmin,cmax] = caxis returns the minimum and maximum data values mapped to the first and last entries of the colormap, respectively. These are normally set to the minimum and maximum values of your data. For example, mesh(peaks) creates a mesh plot of the peaks function and sets caxis to [-6.5466, 8.0752], the minimum and maximum z values. Data points between these values use colors interpolated from the colormap.

caxis([cmin,cmax]) uses the entire colormap for data in the range between cmin and cmax. Data points greater than cmax are rendered with the color associated with cmax, and data points less than cmin are rendered with the color associated with cmin. If cmin is less than min(data) or cmax is greater than max(data), the colors associated with cmin or cmax will never be used. Only the portion of the colormap associated with data will be used. caxis('auto') or the command form caxis auto restores the default values of cmin and cmax. The following example illustrates color axis settings.

```
>> N = 17;
>> data = [1:N+1;1:N+1]';

>> subplot(1,3,1)
>> colormap(hsv(N))
>> pcolor(data)
>> set(gca,'XtickLabel','')
>> title('Figure 27.3: Auto Limits')
>> caxis auto      % automatic limits (default)

>> subplot(1,3,2)
>> pcolor(data)
>> axis off
>> title('Extended Limits')
>> caxis([-5,N+5]) % extend the color limits

>> subplot(1,3,3)
>> pcolor(data)
>> axis off
>> title('Restricted Limits')
>> caxis([5,N-5]) % restrict the color limits
```

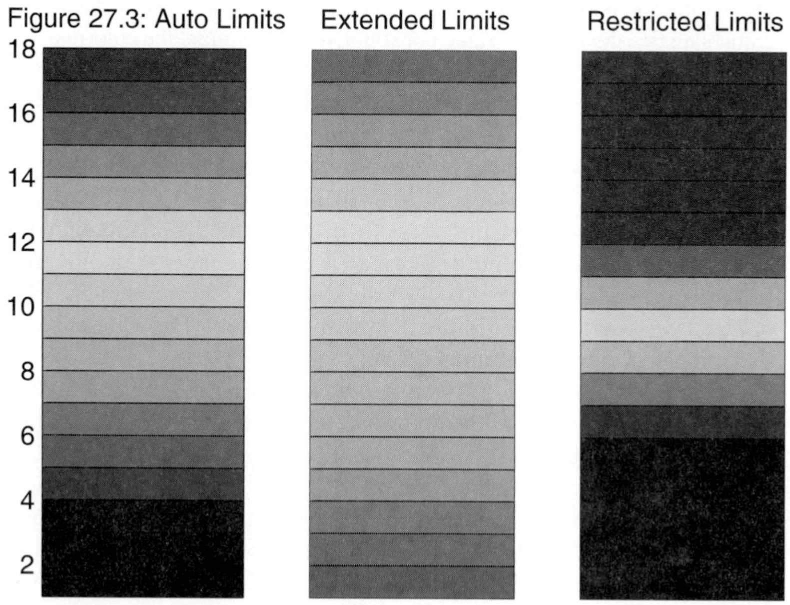

The first plot on the left is the default plot. This plot covers the complete colormap. In the center plot, the color axis is extended, forcing all plotted values to use a central subset of the colormap. In the plot on the right the color axis is restricted, forcing the colormap to cover a region in the center of the plot. The plot extremes simply use the colormap extremes.

27.5 USING COLOR TO DESCRIBE A FOURTH DIMENSION

Surface plots such as `mesh` and `surf` vary color along the z-axis unless a color argument is given, for example, `surf(X,Y,Z)` is equivalent to `surf(X,Y,Z,Z)`. Applying color to the z-axis produces a colorful plot but does not provide additional information since the z-axis already exists. To make better use of color, it is suggested that color be used to describe some property of the data not reflected by the three axes. To do so requires specifying different data for the color argument to 3-D plotting functions.

If the color argument to a plotting function is a vector or a matrix, it is scaled and used as an index into the colormap. This argument can be any real vector or matrix the same size as the other arguments. Consider the following example.

```
>> x = -7.5:.5:7.5;              % data
>> [X Y] = meshgrid(x);          % create plaid data
>> R = sqrt(X.^2 + Y.^2)+eps;    % create sombrero
>> Z = sin(R)./R;
```

```
>> subplot(2,2,1)
>> surf(X,Y,Z,Z)    % default color order
>> colormap(gray)
>> shading interp
>> axis tight off
>> title('Figure 27.4a: Default, Z')

>> subplot(2,2,2)
>> surf(X,Y,Z,Y)   % Y axis color order
>> shading interp
>> axis tight off
>> title('Figure 27.4b: Y axis')

>> subplot(2,2,3)
>> surf(X,Y,Z,X-Y) % diagonal color order
>> shading interp
>> axis tight off
>> title('Figure 27.4c: X - Y')

>> subplot(2,2,4)
>> surf(X,Y,Z,R)   % radius color order
>> shading interp
>> axis tight off
>> title('Radius')
```

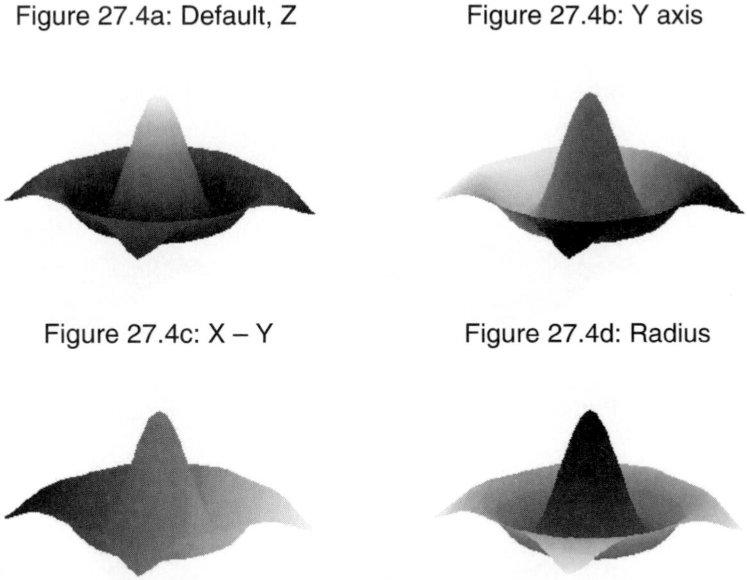

These subplots demonstrate four simple ways to use color as a fourth dimension. Whatever data is provided as the fourth argument to `surf` is used to interpolate the colormap. Any function of the first three arguments can be provided, or some completely independent variable works as well. Using the functions `del2` and `gradient` allows one to apply color with respect to curvature and slope, respectively, for example,

```
>> subplot(2,2,1)
>> surf(X,Y,Z,abs(del2(Z)))   % absolute Laplacian
>> colormap(gray)
>> shading interp
>> axis tight off
>> title('Figure 27.5a: |Curvature|')

>> subplot(2,2,2)
>> [dZdx,dZdy] = gradient(Z); % compute gradient of surface
>> Surf(X,Y,Z,abs(dZdx))      % absolute slope in x-direction
>> shading interp
>> axis tight off
>> title('Figure 27.5b: |dZ/dx|')

>> subplot(2,2,3)
>> surf(X,Y,Z,abs(dZdy))      % absolute slope in y-direction
>> shading interp
>> axis tight off
>> title('Figure 27.5c: |dZ/dy|')

>> subplot(2,2,4)
>> dR = sqrt(dZdx.^2 + dZdy.^2);
```

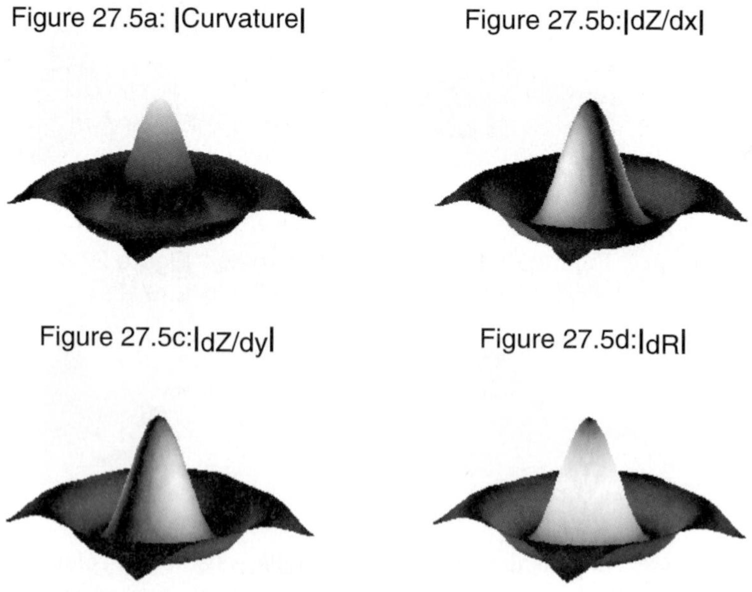

```
>> surf(X,Y,Z,abs(dR))          % absolute slope in radius
>> shading interp
>> axis tight off
>> title('Figure 27.5d: |dR|')
```

Note how color in these subplots provides an additional dimension to the plotted surface. The function del2 is the discrete Laplacian function that applies color based on the curvature of the surface. The function gradient approximates the gradient or slope of the surface with respect to the two coordinate directions.

27.6 LIGHTING MODELS

The graphics functions pcolor, fill, fill3, mesh, and surf, discussed in the previous chapters, render objects that appear to be well lit from all sides by very diffuse light. This technique emphasizes the characteristics of the objects in the *Figure* window and enhances the user's ability to visualize the data being analyzed. Although the data can be visualized quite clearly, the realism of the scene can be enhanced or diminished by creating different lighting effects.

The shading function selects faceted, flat, or interpolated shading. Examples of each of these were illustrated in the chapter on 3-D graphics. Although requiring more computational power and subsequently more time to render, interpolated shading of the objects in a scene can enhance the realism of the scene being rendered.

One or more light sources can be added to simulate the highlights and shadows associated with directional lighting. The function light creates a white light source infinitely far away along the vector [1 0 1]. Once the light source has been created, the lighting function allows you to select from four different lighting models: none (which ignores any light source), flat (the default when a light source is created), phong, and gouraud. Each of these models uses a different algorithm to change the appearance of the object. Flat lighting uses a uniform color for each face of the object. Gouraud lighting interpolates the face colors from the vertices. Phong lighting interpolates the normals at the vertices across each face and calculates the reflectance at each pixel. ***While colormaps are properties of Figure windows, light is a property or child of the axes.*** Therefore, each axes in a *Figure* window can be separately lit. Consider the following example.

```
>> subplot(2,2,1)
>> sphere
>> light
>> shading interp
>> axis square off
>> lighting none
>> title('Figure 27.6a: No Lighting')
```

```
>> subplot(2,2,2)
>> sphere
>> light
>> shading interp
>> axis square off
>> lighting flat
>> title('Figure 27.6b: Flat Lighting')

>> subplot(2,2,3)
>> sphere
>> light
>> shading interp
>> axis square off
>> lighting gouraud
>> title('Figure 27.6c: Gouraud Lighting')

>> subplot(2,2,4)
>> sphere
>> light
>> shading interp
>> axis square off
>> lighting phong
>> title('Figure 27.6d: Phong Lighting')
```

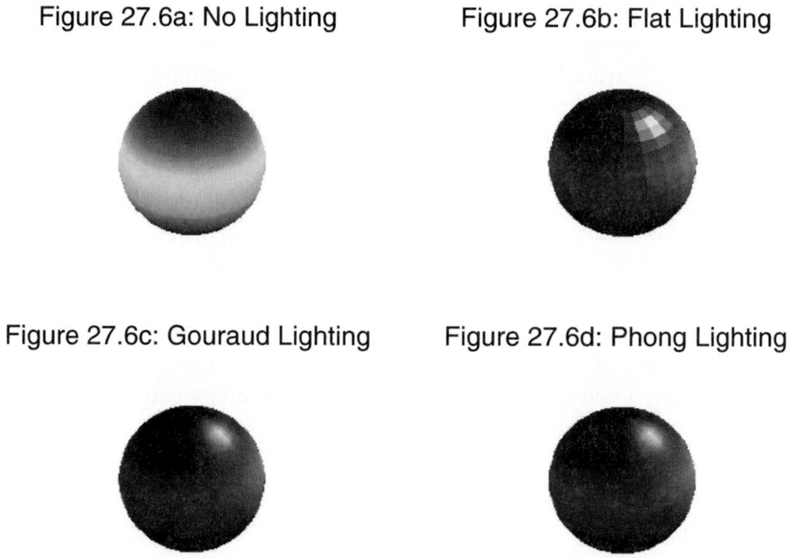

In addition to lighting, the appearance of objects in an axes can be changed by modifying the apparent reflective characteristics or ***reflectance*** of surfaces. Reflectance is made up of a number of components:

- **Ambient light**—strength of the uniform directionless light in the figure
- **Diffuse reflection**—intensity of the soft directionless reflected light
- **Specular reflection**—intensity of the hard directional reflected light
- **Specular exponent**—controls the size of the specular "hot spot" or spread
- **Specular color reflectance**—determines the contribution of the surface color to the reflectance.

Some predefined surface reflectance properties are available using the `material` function. Options include `shiny`, `dull`, `metal`, and `default` for restoring the default surface reflectance properties. The form `material([ka kd ks n sc])`, where `n` and `sc` are optional, sets the ambient strength, diffuse reflectance, specular reflectance, specular exponent, and specular color reflectance of objects in an axes, for example,

```
>> subplot(2,2,1)
>> sphere
>> colormap(gray)
>> light
>> shading interp
>> axis square off
>> material default
>> title('Figure 27.7a: Default Material')

>> subplot(2,2,2)
>> sphere
>> light
>> shading interp
>> axis square off
>> material shiny
>> title('Figure 27.7b: Shiny Material')

>> subplot(2,2,3)
>> sphere
>> light
>> shading interp
>> axis square off
>> material dull
>> title('Figure 27.7c: Dull Material')

>> subplot(2,2,4)
>> sphere
>> light
>> shading interp
>> axis square off
>> material metal
>> title('Figure 27.7d: Metal Material')
```

Figure 27.7a: Default Material

Figure 27.7b: Shiny Material

Figure 27.7c: Dull Material

Figure 27.7d: Metal Material

As shown above, the function `light` is fairly limited. It creates white light emanating from an infinite distance away along a given direction. In reality, `light` is a Handle Graphics object creation function. Handle Graphics functions are discussed in Chapter 30. The function `light` offers a variety of properties that can be set. For example, the light color, position, and style can be set, with style meaning that the light can be a point source at a given position or be infinitely far away along some vector:

```
>> Hl = light('Position',[x,y,z],'Color',[r,g,b],'Style','local');
```

This command creates a light source at position `(x,y,z)` using light color `[r,g,b]` and specifies that the position is a location `('local')` rather than a vector `('infinite')`. It also saves the handle of the *light* object (`Hl`), which can be used to change the properties of the light source at a later time. For example,

```
>> set(Hl,'Position',[1 0 1],'Color',[1 1 1],'Style','infinite');
```

sets the light source defined by the handle `Hl` back to its original default characteristics. For more information about Handle Graphics, see Chapter 30.

27.7 SUMMARY

The following table documents MATLAB functions for color and lighting.

Function	Description
`light`	Light object creation function.
`lighting`	Set lighting mode (`flat`, `gouraud`, `phong`, or `none`).
`lightangle`	Position light object in spherical coordinates.
`material`	Set material reflectance (`default`, `shiny`, `dull`, or `metal`).
`camlight`	Set light object with respect to camera.
`brighten`	Brighten or darken colormap.
`caxis`	Set or get color axis limits.
`diffuse`	Find surface diffuse reflectance.
`specular`	Find surface specular reflectance.
`surfnorm`	Compute surface normals.
`colorbar`	Create colorbar.
`colordef`	Define default color properties.
`colormap`	Set or get *Figure* window colormap.
`hsv2rgb`	Convert hue-saturation-value color values to red-green-blue model.
`rgb2hsv`	Convert red-green-blue color values to hue-saturation-value model.
`rgbplot`	Plot colormap.
`shading`	Surface shading (`flat`, `faceted`, or `interp`).
`spinmap`	Spin colormap.
`whitebg`	Change plot axes background color.
`graymon`	Set graphics defaults for grayscale monitors.
`autumn`	Colormap with shades of red and yellow.
`bone`	Gray scale colormap with a tinge of blue.
`cool`	Colormap with shades of cyan and magenta.
`copper`	Colormap with linear copper tone.

Function	Description
`flag`	Colormap with alternating red, white, blue, black.
`gray`	Colormap with linear gray scale.
`hot`	Colormap with black, red, yellow, and white.
`hsv`	Colormap based on hue, saturation, and value progression.
`jet`	Colormap variant of `hsv` that starts with blue and ends with red.
`lines`	Colormap based on line colors.
`prism`	Colormap with alternating red, orange, yellow, green, blue, and violet.
`spring`	Colormap with shades of magenta and yellow.
`summer`	Colormap with shades of green and yellow.
`winter`	Colormap with shades of blue and green.

28

Images, Movies, and Sound

MATLAB provides commands for displaying several types of images. Images can be created and stored as standard double-precision floating-point numbers (`double`) and optionally as 8-bit (`uint8`) or 16-bit (`uint16`) unsigned integers. MATLAB can read and write image files in a number of standard graphics file formats as well as use `load` and `save` to save image data in MAT-files. MATLAB provides commands for creating and playing animations as movies (sequences of frames). Sound functions are available as well for computers that support sound.

28.1 IMAGES

Images in MATLAB consist of a data matrix and usually an associated colormap matrix. There are three types of image data matrices, which are interpreted differently: indexed images, intensity images, and truecolor or RGB images.

An ***indexed image*** requires a colormap and interprets the image data as indices into the colormap matrix. The colormap matrix is a standard colormap: any `m`-by-3 array containing valid RGB data. Given an image data array `X(i,j)` and a colormap array `cmap`, the color of each image pixel P_{ij} is cmap(X(i,j),:). This implies that the data values in X are integers within the range [1 length(cmap)]. This image can be displayed using

```
>> image(X); colormap(cmap)
```

An ***intensity image*** scales the image data over a range of intensities. This form is normally used with images to be displayed in grayscale or one of the other monochromatic colormaps, but other colormaps can be used if desired. The image data is not required to be in the range [1 length(cmap)] as is the case with indexed images. The data is scaled over a given range, and the result is used to index into the colormap. For example,

```
>> imagesc(X,[0 1]); colormap(gray)
```

associates the value 0 with the first colormap entry, and 1 with the last colormap entry. Values in X between 0 and 1 are scaled and used as indices into the colormap. If the scale is omitted, it defaults to [min(min(X)) max(max(X))].

A ***truecolor*** or ***RGB image*** is created from an m-by-n-by-3 data array containing valid RGB triples. The row and column dimensions specify the pixel location, and the page or third dimension specifies each color component. For example, pixel P_{ij} is rendered in the color specified by X(i,j,:). A colormap is not required since the color data is stored within the image data array itself. If the host computer does not support truecolor images in hardware (e.g., it has an 8-bit display), MATLAB uses color approximation and dithering to display the image. For example,

```
>> image(X)
```

where X is an m-by-n-by-3 truecolor or RGB image, displays the image. X can contain uint8, unit16, or double data.

If images are displayed on default axes, the aspect ratio will often be incorrect and the image will be distorted. Issuing

```
>> axis image off
```

sets the axis properties so that the aspect ratio matches the image and the axis labels and ticks are hidden. To force each pixel in the image to occupy one pixel on the display requires setting *figure* and *axes* properties, as in the following example.

```
>> load clown        % sample image
>> [r,c] = size(X); % pixel dimensions
>> figure('Units','Pixels','Position',[100 100 c r])
>> image(X)
>> set(gca,'Position',[0 0 1 1])
>> colormap(map)
```

Here the *figure* is set to display exactly the same number of pixels as the image by setting its width and height equal to that of the image. Then the *axes* position is set to occupy the entire *figure* in normalized units.

MATLAB installations have a number of sample images in addition to `clown.mat` used in the above example. The `demos` subdirectory on the MATLAB path contains `cape.mat`, `clown.mat`, `detail.mat`, `durer.mat`, `flujet.mat`, `gatlin.mat`, `mandrill.mat`, and `spine.mat`. Each of these images can be displayed by issuing

```
>> load filename
>> image(X), colormap(map)
>> title(caption)
>> axis image off
```

28.2 IMAGE FORMATS

The default numerical data type in MATLAB is `double`. This refers to a double-precision, 64-bit, floating-point number. MATLAB has limited support for other formats such as the 16-bit character data type (`uint16`) and the 8-bit unsigned integer type (`uint8`) for images.

The `image` and `imagesc` commands can display 8- and 16-bit images without first converting them to the `double` format. However, the range of data values for `uint8` data is `[0 255]`, as supported in standard graphics file formats, and the range of data values for `uint16` is `[0 65535]`.

For indexed images, `image` maps the value 0 to the first entry in a 256-entry colormap and maps the value 255 to the last entry by automatically supplying the proper offset. Since the normal range of `double` data for indexed images is `[1 length(cmap)]`, converting between `uint8` and `double` or `uint16` and `double` requires shifting the values by 1. In addition, mathematical operations on `uint8` arrays are not defined. Therefore, to perform mathematical operations on unsigned integers, they must be converted to the `double` format. For example,

```
>> Xdouble = double(Xuint8) + 1;
>> Xuint8 = uint8(Xdouble - 1);
```

converts the `uint8` data in `Xuint8` to `double` and back. For 8-bit intensity and RGB images, the range of values is normally `[0 255]` rather than `[0 1]`. To display 8-bit intensity and RGB images, use the following commands.

```
>> imagesc(Xuint8,[0 255]); colormap(cmap)
>> image(Xuint8)
```

Conversions to `double` can also be normalized, for example,

```
>> Xdouble = double(Xuint8)/255;
>> Xuint8 = uint8(round(Xdouble*255));
```

The 8-bit color data contained in an RGB image is automatically scaled when it is displayed. For example, the color white is normally `[1 1 1]` when using doubles. If the same color is stored as 8-bit data, the color white is represented as `[255 255 255]`.

Although mathematical operations are not defined for `uint8` arrays, reading and writing files are defined, and so `imread`, `imwrite`, `save`, and `load` support `uint8` data. Standard MATLAB indexing and subscripting, and the `reshape`, `cat`, `permute`, `max`, `min`, and `find` functions are supported, as are the `[]` and `'` operators. To perform any other mathematical operation, first convert the data to double-precision format using the conversions suggested above. It is also possible to create your own methods for the `uint8` data type. The optional *Image Processing Toolbox* available for MATLAB contains many functions for manipulating images. This Toolbox is valuable if you regularly manipulate images.

28.3 IMAGE FILES

Image data can be saved to files and reloaded into MATLAB using many different file formats. The normal MATLAB `save` and `load` functions support image data in `double`, `uint8`, or `uint16` format in the same way that they support any other MATLAB variable and data type. When saving indexed images or intensity images with nonstandard colormaps, be sure to save the colormap as well as the image data as shown, for example,

```
>> save myimage.mat X map
```

MATLAB also supports several industry-standard image file formats using the `imread` and `imwrite` functions. Information about the contents of a graphics file can be obtained using the `imfinfo` function. The help text for `imread`, part of which is shown below, gives extensive information regarding image read formats and features.

```
>> help imread
 IMREAD Read image from graphics file.
    A = IMREAD(FILENAME,FMT) reads the image in FILENAME into
    A. If the file contains a grayscale intensity image, A is
    a two-dimensional array. If the file contains a truecolor
    (RGB) image, A is a three-dimensional (M-by-N-by-3) array.
    FILENAME is a string that specifies the name of the
    graphics file, and FMT is a string that specifies the
    format of the file. The file must be in the current
    directory or in a directory on the MATLAB path. If IMREAD
    cannot find a file named FILENAME, it looks for a file
    named FILENAME.FMT.

    The possible values for FMT include:
       'jpg' or 'jpeg' Joint Photographic Experts Group (JPEG)
       'tif' or 'tiff' Tagged Image File Format (TIFF)
       'gif'           Graphics Interchange Format (GIF)
```

```
      'bmp'          Windows Bitmap (BMP)
      'png'          Portable Network Graphics (PNG)
      'hdf'          Hierarchical Data Format (HDF)
      'pcx'          Windows Paintbrush (PCX)
      'xwd'          X Window Dump (XWD)
      'cur'          Windows Cursor resources (CUR)
      'ico'          Windows Icon resources (ICO)

   [X,MAP] = IMREAD(FILENAME,FMT) reads the indexed image in
   FILENAME into X and its associated colormap into MAP.
   Colormap values in the image file are automatically
   rescaled into the range [0,1].

   [...] = IMREAD(FILENAME) attempts to infer the format of the
   file from its content.

   Data types
   ----------
   In most of the image file formats supported by IMREAD,
   pixels are stored using 8 or fewer bits per color plane.
   When reading such a file, the class of the output (A or X)
   is uint8. IMREAD also supports reading 16-bit-per-pixel
   data from TIFF and PNG files; for such image files, the
   class of the output (A or X) is uint16.

   TIFF-specific syntaxes
   ----------------------
   [...] = IMREAD(...,IDX) reads in one image from a
   multi-image TIFF file. IDX is an integer value that
   specifies the order that the image appears in the file.
   For example, if IDX is 3, IMREAD reads the third image in
   the file. If you omit this argument, IMREAD reads the
   first image in the file.
```

The calling syntax for `imwrite` varies depending on the image type and file format as well. The help text for `imwrite`, part of which is shown below, gives extensive information regarding image save formats and features.

```
>> help imwrite
 IMWRITE Write image to graphics file.
   IMWRITE(A,FILENAME,FMT) writes the image A to FILENAME.
   FILENAME is a string that specifies the name of the output
   file, and FMT is a string the specifies the format of the
   file. A can be either a grayscale image (M-by-N) or a
   truecolor image (M-by-N-by-3).

   The possible values for FMT include:
```

```
   'tif' or 'tiff' Tagged Image File Format (TIFF)
   'jpg' or 'jpeg' Joint Photographic Experts Group (JPEG)
   'bmp'           Windows Bitmap (BMP)
   'png'           Portable Network Graphics (PNG)
   'hdf'           Hierarchical Data Format (HDF)
   'pcx'           Windows Paintbrush (PCX)
   'xwd'           X Window Dump (XWD)

IMWRITE(X,MAP,FILENAME,FMT) writes the indexed image in X,
and its associated colormap MAP, to FILENAME. If X is of
class uint8 or uint16, IMWRITE writes the actual values in
the array to the file. If X is of class double, IMWRITE
offsets the values in the array before writing, using
uint8(X-1). MAP must be a valid MATLAB colormap. Note
that most image file formats do not support colormaps with
more than 256 entries.

IMWRITE(...,FILENAME) writes the image to FILENAME,
inferring the format to use from the filename's extension.
The extension must be one of the legal values for FMT.

IMWRITE(...,PARAM1,VAL1,PARAM2,VAL2,...) specifies
parameters that control various characteristics of the
output file. Parameters are currently supported for HDF,
JPEG, TIFF, and PNG files.

Data types
----------
Most of the supported image file formats store uint8
data. PNG and TIFF additionally support uint16 data. For
grayscale and RGB images, if the data array is double, the
assumed dynamic range is [0,1]. The data array is
automatically scaled by 255 before being written out as
uint8. If the data array is uint8 or uint16, then it is
written out without scaling as uint8 or uint16,
respectively. NOTE: If a logical double or uint8 is
written to a PNG or TIFF file, it is assumed to be a
binary image and will be written with a bitdepth of 1.

For indexed images, if the index array is double, then the
indices are first converted to zero-based indices by
subtracting 1 from each element, and then they are written
out as uint8. If the index array is uint8 or uint16,
then it is written out without modification as uint8 or
uint16, respectively.

JPEG-specific parameters
------------------------
'Quality'      A number between 0 and 100; higher numbers
               mean quality is better (less image degradation
```

```
                 due to compression), but the resulting file
                 size is larger

TIFF-specific parameters
------------------------
'Compression'    One of these strings: 'none', 'packbits'
                 (default for nonbinary images), 'ccitt'
                 (default for binary images), 'fax3', 'fax4';
                 'ccitt', 'fax3', and 'fax4' are valid for
                 binary images only

'Description'    Any string; fills in the ImageDescription
                 field returned by IMFINFO

'Resolution'     A two-element vector containing the
                 XResolution and YResolution, or a scalar
                 indicating both resolutions; the default value
                 is 72

'WriteMode'      One of these strings: 'overwrite' (the
                 default) or 'append'
```

28.4 MOVIES

Animation in MATLAB takes one of two forms. First, if the computations needed to create a sequence of images can be computed quickly enough, *figure* and *axes* properties can be set so that screen rendering occurs sufficiently quickly so that animation is visually smooth. On the other hand, if computations require significant time or the resulting images are complex enough, one must create a movie.

In MATLAB, the functions `getframe` and `movie` provide the tools required to capture and play movies. `getframe` takes a snapshot of the current *figure,* and `movie` plays back the sequence of frames after they have been captured. The output of `getframe` is a structure containing all the information needed by `movie`. Capturing multiple frames is simply a matter of adding elements to the structure. Consider the following example.

```
% movie-making example: rotate a 3-D surface plot
[X,Y,Z]=peaks(50);           % create data
surfl(X,Y,Z)                 % plot surface with lighting
axis([-3 3 -3 3 -10 10])     % fix axes so that scaling does not change
axis vis3d off               % fix axes for 3D and turn off axes ticks etc.
shading interp               % make it pretty with interpolated shading
colormap(copper)             % choose a good colormap for lighting
```

```
for i=1:15                    % rotate and capture each frame
   view(-37.5+15*(i-1),30)   % change the viewpoint for this frame
   m(i)=getframe;            % add this figure to the frame structure
end
cla       % clear axis for movie
movie(m)  % play the movie
```

The above script file creates a movie by incrementally rotating the peaks surface and capturing a frame at every increment. Finally, the movie is played after clearing the *axes*. The variable m contains a structure array with each array element containing a single frame, for example,

```
>> m
m =
1x15 struct array with fields:
    cdata
    colormap

>> size(m(1).cdata)
ans =
   412   369     3
```

The color data holding the image cdata is a truecolor or RGB bitmap image. As a result, the complexity of contents of the *axes* does not influence the bytes required to store a movie. The size of the *axes* in pixels determines the size of the image and therefore the number of bytes required to store a movie.

28.5 IMAGE UTILITIES

Conversion between indexed images and movie frames is possible with the im2frame and frame2im functions. For example,

```
>> [X,cmap] = frame2im(M(n))
```

converts the nth frame of the movie matrix M into an indexed image X and associated colormap cmap. Similarly,

```
>> M(n) = im2frame(X,cmap)
```

converts the indexed image X and colormap cmap into the nth frame of the movie matrix M. Note that im2frame can be used to convert a series of images into a movie in the same way that getframe converts a series of *figures* or *axes* into a movie.

28.6 SOUND

MATLAB supports sound on PC platforms and on any UNIX platform with a /dev/audio device. sound(y,f,b) sends the signal in vector y to the computer's speaker at sample frequency f. Values in y outside the range [-1 1] are clipped. If f is omitted, the default sample frequency of 8192 Hz is used. MATLAB plays the sound using b bits/second if possible. Most platforms support b=8 or b=16. If b is omitted, b=16 is used.

The soundsc function is the same as sound except that the values in y are *scaled* to the range [-1 1] rather than clipped. This results in a sound that is as loud as possible without clipping. An additional argument is available that permits mapping a range of values in y to the full sound range. The format is soundsc(y,...,[smin smax]). If omitted, the default range is [min(y) max(y)].

Two industry-standard sound file formats are supported in MATLAB. NeXT/Sun audio format (*file*.au) files and Microsoft WAVE format (*file*.wav) files can be written and read.

The NeXT/Sun Audio sound storage format supports multichannel data for 8-bit mulaw, 8-bit linear, and 16-bit linear formats. The most general form of auwrite is auwrite(y,f,n,'*method*','*filename*'), where y is the sample data, f is the sample rate in hertz, b specifies the number of bits in the encoder, '*method*' is a string specifying the encoding method, and '*filename*' is a string specifying the name of the output file. Each column of y represents a single channel. Any value in y outside the range [-1 1] is clipped prior to writing the file. The f, n, and '*method*' arguments are optional. If omitted, f=8000, n=8, and '*method*'='mu'. The '*method*' argument must be either 'linear' or 'mu'. If the file name string contains no extension, '.au' is appended.

Conversion between mu-law and linear formats can be performed using the mu2lin and lin2mu functions. More information about the exact conversion processes involved with these two functions can be found using the on-line help.

Multichannel 8-bit or 16-bit WAVE sound storage format sound files can be created with the wavwrite function. The most general form is wavwrite(y,f,n,'*filename*'), where y is the sample data, f is the sample rate in hertz, b specifies the number of bits in the encoder, and '*filename*' is a string specifying the name of the output file. Each column of y represents a single channel. Any value in y outside the range [-1 1] is clipped prior to writing the file. The f and n arguments are optional. If omitted, f=8000 and n=16. If the file name string contains no extension, '.wav' is appended.

Both auread and wavread have the same syntax and options. The most general form is [y,f,b]=auread('*filename*',n) which loads a sound file specified by the string '*filename*' and returns the sampled data into y. The appropriate extension (.au or .wav) is appended to the file name if no extension is given. Values in y are in the range [-1 1]. If three outputs are requested as illustrated above, the sample rate in hertz and the number of bits per sample are returned in f and b, respectively. If n is given, only the first n samples are returned from each channel in the file. If n=[n1 n2], only samples from n1 through n2 are returned from each channel. The form [samples,channels]=wavread('*filename*','size') returns the size of the audio data in the file rather than the data itself. This form is useful for preallocating storage or estimating resource use.

28.7 SUMMARY

The table below summarizes the image, movie, and sound capabilities in MATLAB.

Function	Description
`image`	Create indexed or truecolor (RGB) *image* object.
`imagesc`	Create intensity *image* object.
`colormap`	Apply colormap to *image*.
`axis image`	Adjust axis scaling for *image*.
`uint8`	Conversion to unsigned 8-bit integer.
`uint16`	Conversion to unsigned 16-bit integer.
`double`	Conversion to double precision.
`imread`	Read image file.
`imwrite`	Write image file.
`imfinfo`	Image file information.
`getframe`	Place movie frame in structure.
`movie`	Play movie from movie structure.
`frame2im`	Convert movie frame to image.
`im2frame`	Convert image to movie frame.
`avifile`	Create `avi` movie file.
`addframe`	Add frame to `avi` movie file.
`close`	Close `avi` movie file.
`aviread`	Read `avi` movie file.
`aviinfo`	Information about an `avi` movie file.
`movie2avi`	Convert movie in MATLAB format to `avi` format.
`sound`	Play vector as sound.
`soundsc`	Autoscale and play vector as sound.
`wavplay`	Play WAVE format sound file.

Function	Description
`wavrecord`	Record sound using Windows audio input device.
`wavread`	Read WAVE format sound file.
`wavwrite`	Write WAVE format sound file.
`auread`	Read NeXT/SUN sound file.
`auwrite`	Write NeXT/SUN sound file.
`lin2mu`	Convert linear audio to mu-law.
`mu2lin`	Convert mu-law audio to linear.

29

Printing and Exporting Graphics

MATLAB graphics are very effective tools for data visualization and analysis. Therefore, it is often desirable to create hard-copy output or to use these graphics in other applications. MATLAB provides a very flexible system for printing graphics and creating output in many different graphics formats including EPS and TIFF. Most other applications can import one or more of the graphics file formats supported by MATLAB.

Perhaps the most important issue to recognize when printing or exporting graphics is that the *figure* is ***rerendered*** in the process. That is, what you see on the screen is *not* what you get on a printed page or in an exported file. By default, MATLAB can choose a different renderer (`painters`, `zbuffer`, or `OpenGL`), can change the *axes* tick mark distribution, and can change the size of the *figure* being printed and exported. Naturally, MATLAB provides the capability to enforce what-you-see-is-what-you-get (WYSIWYG), but this is not the default action taken.

In general, printing and exporting are not simple because there is an almost uncountable number of possible combinations involving printer drivers, printer protocols, graphics file types, renderers, bit-mapped versus vector graphics descriptions, dots-per-inch selection, color versus black and white, compression, platform limitations, and so on. Most of this complexity is hidden when default output is requested. However, when very specific printed characteristics are required, or when exporting a *figure* for insertion into a word processing or presentation document, the complexities of printing and exporting must be understood. In these cases, it is not uncommon to spend a significant amount of time tweaking output until it matches the characteristics desired.

This chapter introduces the printing and exporting capabilities in MATLAB. As in other areas, MATLAB provides menu items as well as *Command* window functions for printing and exporting. The menu approach offers convenience but limited flexibility, whereas the function approach offers complete flexibility but requires much more knowledge on the part of the user. The menu approach allows one to set characteristics for the current *figure* or perhaps the current session, but the function approach offers the added capability of setting default characteristics that carry over from one MATLAB session to the next.

> Accessing the on-line documentation for the function `print` by issuing `>> doc print` provides a great deal of information about printing and exporting.

29.1 PRINTING AND EXPORTING USING MENUS

When graphics are displayed in a *Figure* window, the top of the window contains a menu bar and possibly one or more toolbars. The menu bar has a number of menus including **File, Edit, View, Insert, Tools, Window,** and **Help.** Of these, the **File** menu lists menu items for printing and exporting the current *figure.* In addition, the **Edit** menu on PC systems contains menu items for exporting the current *figure* to the system clipboard. The **File** menu includes the menu items **Export, Page Setup, Print Setup, Print Preview,** and **Print.** Each of these items offers dialog boxes for setting various aspects of printing and exporting.

The **Export** menu item makes it possible to save the current *figure* in one of many graphics formats. The **Export** dialog box presents a **Save** dialog where the user chooses a directory, file name, and file type for the current *figure.* The size and features of the saved *figure* are determined by the settings selected in the **Page Setup** dialog box. The file type choices made available make default assumptions about the properties of the various file types. Exporting via the *Command* window provides more complete control over the exported *figure.*

Choosing the **Page Setup** menu item (or the `pagesetupdlg` command) opens a tabbed dialog box for setting a number of features used when a *figure* is rendered for printing or exporting. This dialog box is the primary place to specify the size, orientation, placement, and many of the features of the rendered *figure.*

Choosing the **Print Setup** menu item (or the `print -dsetup` command) on PC systems opens a standard dialog box for selecting a printer and options such as paper size, paper source, and orientation. On UNIX systems, the **Print Setup** menu item (or the `printdlg -setup` command) opens a dialog box identical to the **Print** dialog box except for the title of the box and the fact that the **OK** button closes the dialog box but does not send the *figure* to the printer or to a file. The UNIX **Print Setup** dialog box includes options for selecting a printer or a filename and a printer driver, *figure* size, axes and tick options, and an **Options** button providing access to a dialog box for setting many additional options including choosing a renderer and setting the output resolution. On both platforms, options chosen in this dialog box persist during a MATLAB session and override any like settings made in the **Page Setup** dialog box.

The **Print Preview** menu item (or the `printpreview` command) opens a window showing how the *figure* will be rendered on the printed page. Buttons are provided to call the **Page Setup** dialog box to make any necessary changes and the **Print** dialog box to print the *figure.*

The **Print** menu item (or the `printdlg` command) opens a standard **Print** dialog box on PC systems. From this dialog box, the printer and the number of copies can be chosen. The option to print to a file is available here as well. On UNIX systems, the printer or the filename, the printer driver, and options to freeze the axes and tick marks can be chosen. An **Options** button provides access to a dialog box for setting a variety of additional options, all of which also appear in the **Page Setup** dialog box.

> **Page Setup** options apply to the current *figure* and are saved with the current *figure.* **Print Setup** options persist through the current MATLAB session and override any like **Page Setup** options for the current *figure.* **Print** options apply only to the current *figure* and override any like options in **Page Setup** or **Print Setup** for the current *figure.*

These **File** menu items are sufficient for most printing and exporting jobs. *Command* window functions are required to gain more control over output or to set defaults that apply across MATLAB sessions.

On PC systems, the **Edit** menu provides export capabilities through the system clipboard. The **Copy Figure** menu item places the current *figure* on the clipboard based on the options set in the preferences dialog box opened by selecting the **Copy Options** menu item. The current *figure* can be copied in either bitmap (BMP) or enhanced meta file (EMF) format. A template can be used to change line widths and font sizes, as well as to set other default options for copy operations. These options apply only when a *figure* is copied to the clipboard using the **Copy Figure** menu item. They have no effect when printing or exporting a *figure* to a graphics file.

29.2 COMMAND LINE PRINTING AND EXPORTING

The function `print` handles all printing and exporting from the *Command* window. This single function offers numerous options specified as additional input arguments. The syntax for the command form of `print` is

```
>> print -device -option -option filename
```

where all parameters or arguments are optional. *-device* specifies the device driver to be used, *-option* specifies one or more options, and *filename* specifies the name of an output file if the output is not sent directly to a printer. Because of command-function duality, `print` can be called as a function as well. For example,

```
>> print('-device','-option','-option','filename')
```

is equivalent to the preceding `print` command statement.

In general, print options including *-device* can be specified in any order. Recognized print *-option* strings are described in the following table.

-option	Description
-adobecset	Select PostScript default character set encoding. (Early PostScript printer drivers and EPS file formats only.)
-append	Append *figure* to existing file. (PostScript printer drivers only.)
-cmyk	Print with CMYK colors instead of RGB colors. (PostScript printer drivers and EPS file format only.)
-device	Printer driver to be used.
-dsetup	Display the **Print Setup** dialog box. (Windows only.)
-f*handle*	Specify numerical *handle* of *figure* to print or export.
-loose	Use *loose* PostScript bounding box. (PostScript, EPS, and GhostScript only.)
-noui	Suppress printing of *uicontrol* objects.
-opengl	Render using OpenGL algorithm (bitmap format).
-painters	Render using Painter's algorithm (vector format).
-P*printer*	Specify name of printer to use. (UNIX only.)

-*option*	Description
-r*number*	Specify resolution in dots per inch (dpi). Settable for most devices for printing. Settable for built-in MATLAB file formats except EMF and ILL. Not settable for many GhostScript export formats. Default export resolution is 150 dpi for Z-buffer and OpenGL renderers, and 864 dpi for Painter's renderer.
-s*windowtitle*	Specify name of SIMULINK system window to print or export.
-v	Verbose. Display the **Print** dialog box. (Windows only.)
-zbuffer	Render using a Z-buffer algorithm (bitmap format).

29.3 PRINTERS AND EXPORT FILE FORMATS

The `print` function supports a number of output devices (printers and file types). Supported printers are shown in the first table below. Many of these printers are supported through the use of GhostScript printer drivers, which convert PostScript printer code to native printer code. This conversion process is transparent to the user but limits printable fonts to those supported in PostScript.

-*device*	Description
-dps	PostScript level 1, black and white, including grayscale.
-dpsc	PostScript level 1, color.
-dps2	PostScript level 2, black and white, including grayscale.
-dpsc2	PostScript level 2, color.
-dwin	Black and white, including grayscale. (Windows only.)
-dwinc	Color. (Windows only.)
-dbj10e	Canon Bubblejet BJ10e. (Uses GhostScript.)
-dbj200	Canon Bubblejet BJ200. (Uses GhostScript.)
-dbjc600	Canon Bubblejet 600/4000/70. (Uses GhostScript.)
-dln03	DEC LN03. (Uses GhostScript.)

-device	Description
`-depson`	Epson and compatible 9- or 24-pin dot-matrix printers. (Uses GhostScript.)
`-deps9high`	Epson and compatible 9-pin high-resolution printers. (Uses GhostScript.)
`-depsonc`	Epson LQ-2550 and compatible printers, including Fujitsu 3400/2400/1200. (Uses GhostScript.)
`-ddnj650c`	HP DesignJet 650C. (Uses GhostScript.)
`-ddjet500`	HP Deskjet 500. (Uses GhostScript.)
`-dcdjmono`	HP Deskjet 500C. (Uses GhostScript.)
`-dcdjcolor`	HP Deskjet 500C. (Uses GhostScript.)
`-dcdj500`	HP Deskjet 500C/540C. (Uses GhostScript.)
`-dcdj550`	HP Deskjet 550C. (Uses GhostScript.)
`-ddeskjet`	HP Deskjet and Deskjet Plus. (Uses GhostScript.)
`-dlaserjet`	HP Laserjet.
`-dljet3`	HP Laserjet III.
`-dljet2p`	HP Laserjet IIP.
`-dljetplus`	HP Laserjet+. (Uses GhostScript.)
`-dpaintjet`	HP Paintjet. (Uses GhostScript.)
`-dpjxl`	HP Paintjet XL. (Uses GhostScript.)
`-dpjxl300`	HP Paintjet XL300. (Uses GhostScript.)
`-dhpgl`	HP 7475A and compatible plotters.
`-dibmpro`	IBM 9-pin Proprinter. (Uses GhostScript.)

The function `print` also supports exporting to a file. Export file types are also specified by the *-device* option to `print`. Supported file formats are shown in the table below.

-device	Description
`-dbmp16m`	24-bit BMP. (Windows only.) (Uses GhostScript.)
`-dbmp256`	8-bit BMP with fixed colormap. (Windows only.) (Uses GhostScript.)

-device	Description
-dbmp	24-bit BMP. (Windows only.)
-dmeta	EMF. (Windows only.)
-deps	EPS level 1, black and white, including grayscale.
-depsc	EPS level 1, color.
-deps2	EPS level 2, black and white, including grayscale.
-depsc2	EPS level 2, color.
-hdf	HDF, 24 bit. (Windows only.)
-dill	Adobe Illustrator.
-djpeg -djpeg*NN*	JPEG, 24-bit, quality setting of 75. (Rendered using Z-buffer.) JPEG, 24-bit, quality setting of *NN*.
-dpbm	PBM plain format. (UNIX only.) (Uses GhostScript.)
-dpbmraw	PBM raw format. (UNIX only.) (Uses GhostScript.)
-dpcxmono	PCX, 1-bit. (Windows only.) (Uses GhostScript.)
-dpcx24b	PCX, 24-bit color. (Windows only.) (Uses GhostScript.)
-dpcx256	PCX, 8-bit color. (Windows only.) (Uses GhostScript.)
-dpcx16	PCX, 16-bit color. (Windows only.) (Uses GhostScript.)
-dpcx	PCX, 8-bit color. (Windows only.)
-dpgm	PGM portable graymap, plain. (UNIX only.) (Uses GhostScript.)
-dpgmraw	PGM portable graymap, raw. (UNIX only.) (Uses GhostScript.)
-dpng	PNG 24 bit.
-dppm	PPM portable pixmap, plain. (UNIX only.) (Uses GhostScript.)
-dppmraw	PPM portable pixmap, raw. (UNIX only.) (Uses GhostScript.)
-dtiff	TIFF. (Rendered using Z-buffer.)
-tiff	Add TIFF preview to EPS formats only. Must be used in addition to an EPS device specification.

MATLAB also provides methods for exporting images to graphics files. The functions `getframe`, `imwrite`, `avifile`, and `addframe` provide the capability to create and save image files from *figures*. See Chapter 28 for more information.

29.4 POSTSCRIPT SUPPORT

All PostScript devices and devices that use GhostScript offer limited font support. This includes devices that print as well as those that save images. The table below shows the supported fonts as well as common Windows fonts that map into standard PostScript fonts. Fonts not in the table below are mapped to `Courier`. The Windows devices `-dwin` and `-dwinc` use standard Windows printer drivers and therefore support all installed fonts.

PostScript Font	Windows Equivalent
`AvantGarde`	
`Bookman`	
`Courier`	`Courier New`
`Helvetica`	`Arial`
`Helvetica-Narrow`	
`NewCenturySchlBk`	`New Century Schoolbook`
`Palatino`	
`Symbol`	
`Times-Roman`	`Times New Roman`
`ZapfChancery`	
`ZapfDingbats`	

If your printer supports PostScript, a built-in PostScript driver should be used. Level 1 PostScript is an older specification and is required for some printers. Level 2 PostScript produces smaller and faster code than Level 1 and should be used if possible.

If you are using a color printer, a color driver should be used. Black-and-white or grayscale printers can use either driver. However, when a color driver is used for a black-and-white printer, the file is larger and colors are dithered, making lines and text less clear in some cases. When colored lines are printed using a black-and-white driver, they are converted to black. When colored lines are printed using a color driver on a black-and-white printer, the lines are printed in grayscale. In this case, unless the lines have sufficient width, they often do not have sufficient contrast with the printed page.

As implemented in MATLAB, PostScript supports *surfaces* and *patches* (only with triangular faces) that have interpolated shading. When printed, the corresponding PostScript files contain color information at the *surface* or *patch* vertices requiring the printer to perform the shading interpolation. Depending on the printer characteristics, this may take an excessive amount of time, possibly leading to a printer error. One way to solve this problem is to use flat shading along with a finer meshed surface. Another alternative that ensures that the printed output matches the screen image is to print using either the Z-buffer or an OpenGL renderer with a sufficiently high resolution. In this case the output is in bitmap format and may result in a large output file, but no interpolation is required by the printer.

29.5 CHOOSING A RENDERER

A renderer processes graphics data such as arrays of vertices and color data into a format suitable for display, printing, or export. There are two major categories of graphics formats: bitmap (or raster) graphics and vector graphics.

Bitmap graphics formats contain information such as color at each point in a grid. As the divisions between points decrease and the total number of points increases, the resolution of the resulting graphic increases and the size of the resulting file increases. Increasing the number of bits used to specify the color of each point in the grid increases the total number of possible colors in the resulting graphic and also increases the size of the resulting file. Increasing the complexity of the graphic has no effect on the size of the resulting output file.

Vector graphics formats contain instructions for recreating the graphic using points, lines, and other geometric objects. Vector graphics are easily resized and usually produce higher-resolution results than bitmap graphics. However, as the number of objects in the graphic increases, the number of instructions required to recreate the graphic increases, and the size of the resulting file increases. At some point, the complexity of the instructions can become too much for an output device to handle and the graphic simply cannot be output on the specific output device.

MATLAB supports three rendering methods: OpenGL, Z-buffer, and Painter's. Painter's uses vector format, while OpenGL and Z-buffer produce bitmaps. By default, MATLAB automatically selects a renderer based on the characteristics of the *figure* and the printer driver or file format used.

> The renderer MATLAB selects for printing or exporting is not necessarily the same renderer used to display a *figure* on the screen.

MATLAB's default selection can be overridden by the user, and this is often done to make the printed or exported *figure* look the same as it does on the screen or to avoid imbedding a bitmap in a vector format output file such as PostScript or EPS.

Some situations require specific renderers. For example,

- If the *figure* uses truecolor rather than a single color for surface or patch objects, the graphic must be rendered using a bitmap method to properly capture color.
- HPGL (`-dhpgl`) and Adobe Illustrator (`-dill`) output formats use the Painter's renderer.
- JPEG (`-djpeg`) and TIFF (`-dtiff`) output formats always use Z-buffer rendering.
- Lighting effects cannot be reproduced using the vector format Painter's renderer, and so a bitmap method must be used in this case as well.
- The OpenGL renderer is the only method that supports transparency.

The renderer used for printing and exporting can be chosen using dialog boxes or options to the `print` command, or by setting Handle Graphics properties. The dialog box opened by selecting the **Options** button in the **Print Setup** and **Print** dialog boxes on UNIX platforms and the **Axes and Figures** tab in the **Page Setup** dialog box on all platforms can be used to select a renderer. The `-zbuffer`, `-opengl`, and `-painters` options to the `print` command select a specific renderer when printing or exporting that overrides any other selections made.

29.6 HANDLE GRAPHICS PROPERTIES

A number of Handle Graphics properties influence the way graphics are printed or exported. Many of the options selected from printing and exporting dialog boxes make changes to these properties for the current *figure*. The following table lists the *figure* properties that influence printing and exporting.

'PropertyName'	'PropertyValue' choices, {default}	Description
Color	[RGB vector]	Sets *figure* background color.
InvertHardcopy	[{on} | off]	Determines whether *figure* background color is printed or exported. When set to on, forces a white *figure* background independent of the Color property.
PaperUnits	[{inches} | centimeters | normalized | points]	Units used to measure the size of a printed or exported *figure*.
PaperOrientation	[{portrait} | landscape | rotated]	Orientation of *figure* with respect to paper.

<table>
<tr><th>'PropertyName'</th><th>'PropertyValue'
choices, {default}</th><th>Description</th></tr>
<tr><td>PaperPosition</td><td>[left bottom ...
width height] vector</td><td>Position of figure on paper or in exported file. width and height determine the size of the figure printed or exported.</td></tr>
<tr><td>PaperPositionMode</td><td>[auto | {manual}]</td><td>Determines whether PaperPosition width and height are used. When set to auto, the figure is printed or exported using the Figure window displayed width and height; i.e., output is WYSIWYG.</td></tr>
<tr><td>PaperSize</td><td>[width height] vector</td><td>Paper size measured in PaperUnits.</td></tr>
<tr><td>PaperType</td><td>[{usletter} | uslegal |
A0 | A1 | A2 | A3 | A4 |
A5 | B0 | B1 | B2 | B3 |
B4 | B5 | arch-A |
arch-B | arch-C |
arch-D | arch-E | A |
B | C | D | E |
tabloid | <custom>]</td><td>Type of paper used. Selecting a PaperType sets the PaperSize accordingly.</td></tr>
<tr><td>Renderer</td><td>[{painters} |
zbuffer | OpenGL]</td><td>Display renderer.</td></tr>
<tr><td>RendererMode</td><td>[{auto} manual]</td><td>Determines how renderer is chosen. When set to auto, MATLAB chooses the renderer automatically and independently for display, printing, and export. When set to manual, the renderer set by the Renderer property is used for display, printing, and export.</td></tr>
</table>

Certain *axes* properties also influence printing and exporting. Particularly important are the *axes* tick mode properties:

```
XTickMode [ {auto} | manual ]
YTickMode [ {auto} | manual ]
ZtickMode [ {auto} | manual ]
```

When a *figure* is printed or exported, the resulting graphic is normally rendered at a different size than the *figure* on the screen. Since the width and height are different, MATLAB can rescale the number and placement of tick marks on each axis to reflect the new size. Setting the above properties to `'manual'` prevents MATLAB from changing the tick marks on the *axes* when the *figure* is printed or exported.

Some *line* properties can be used to advantage for output as well, for example,

```
Color: [ 3-element RGB vector ]
LineStyle: [ {-} | -- | : | -. | none ]
LineWidth: [ scalar ]
Marker: [ + | o | * | . | x | square | diamond | v | ^ | > | <
        | pentagram | hexagram | {none} ]
MarkerSize: [ scalar ]
MarkerEdgeColor: [ none | {auto} ] -or- a ColorSpec.
MarkerFaceColor: [ {none} | auto ] -or- a ColorSpec.
```

When colored lines are printed, the result depends on the capabilities of the output device and the printer driver. If a color printer and a color printer driver are used, the result is in color as expected. If a black-and-white printer driver is used, the result is black and white. If a color printer driver is used with a black-and-white printer, the result is grayscale. This can be a problem since grayscale is printed using dithering, which may lead to lines that are not distinct. A different but related problem can occur when printing in black and white. When multiple solid lines are printed in black, they lose the distinction color provides on the screen. In this case the *line* properties `'Color'`, `'LineStyle'`, `'LineWidth'`, and `'Marker'` can be used to add distinction to plotted lines.

Finally, it is often advantageous to modify *text* when printing or exporting *figures*. Useful *text* properties include the following.

```
Color: [ 3-element RGB vector ]
FontAngle: [ {normal} | italic | oblique ]
FontName: [ font name ]
FontSize: [ scalar ]
FontUnits: [ inches | centimeters | normalized | {points} | pixels ]
FontWeight: [ light | {normal} | demi | bold ]
```

Increasing the size of *text* strings such as titles and *axes* labels when printing or exporting to a smaller-sized graphic can often make the text easier to read. If the font used in the *figure* is not one of the 11 fonts supported by MATLAB for PostScript output listed above, changing the font to one of these 11 can prevent unwanted font substitution. Sometimes a bold font shows up better in printed output than a normal-weight font. Changes such as these can often improve the appearance of the printed or exported output. Font characteristics are particularly important when exporting graphics for inclusion in presentation software, where fonts must be large and distinct to be readable from across a large room.

29.7 SETTING DEFAULTS

MATLAB sets the following factory default options for printing and exporting.

- *Figure* size is 8-by-6 in.
- Orientation is portrait.
- *Figure* and *axes* background colors are inverted to white.
- US letter (8.5-by-11 in.) paper is used if available.
- *Figure* is centered on the paper.
- *Figure* is cropped.
- Output is RGB (not CYMK).
- Tick marks are recalculated.
- MATLAB chooses the renderer.
- Uicontrols print.
- Print device is `-dps2` on UNIX and `-dwin` on the PC platform.

The default print device is set in the `$TOOLBOX/local/printopt.m` file. Edit this file to change the default print device across MATLAB sessions. If you do not have write access to this file, edit the file using the command `edit printopt.m`, make your changes, save the `printopt.m` file into a local directory, and make sure the local directory is in the MATLABPATH before `$TOOLBOX/local`. For example, if you use a color PostScript printer for printed output on a UNIX platform, edit `printopt.m` and add the line `dev = '-dpsc2';` to the file at the location specified in the file.

Other option defaults can be changed by setting default properties in the `startup.m` file. For example, `set(0,'DefaultFigurePaperType','A4');` changes the default paper type to A4. The handle `0` addresses the *root* object. The property `'DefaultFigurePaperType'` sets the default figure `'PaperType'` property value. Adding the prefix `'Default'` to any Handle Graphics property name specifies that the accompanying property value should be used as the default. Default properties for a given object must be set at a higher level in the Handle Graphics hierarchy. For example, default *figure* properties must be set at the *root* object level, and default *axes* properties must be set at the *figure* object or *root* object level. Therefore, defaults are usually set at the *root* level. For example,

```
set(0,'DefaultFigurePaperOrientation','landscape');
set(0,'DefaultFigurePaperPosition',[0.25 0.25 10.5 8]);
set(0,'DefaultAxesXGrid','on','DefaultAxesYGrid','on');
set(0,'DefaultAxesLineWidth','1');
```

tells MATLAB to use the landscape mode, fill the page with the plot, print (and display) x- and y-axis grids, and display and print lines that are 1 point wide as defaults in all *figures* and *axes*.

Many other options can be set using Handle Graphics properties. Most printing and exporting properties are *figure* and *axes* properties. For more information on Handle Graphics properties and default values, see the next chapter.

29.8 SUMMARY

MATLAB provides a very flexible system for printing graphics and creating output in many different graphics formats. Most other applications can import one or more of the graphics file formats supported by MATLAB, but many have limited ability to edit the resulting graphic. The best results are achieved if the *figure* is edited and appropriate options are set before the *figure* is printed or exported. The most widely used, flexible output formats are PostScript, EPS, EMF, and TIFF. MATLAB contains native support for all these formats and uses Ghostscript to translate them into many others.

30

Handle Graphics

What is Handle Graphics? Handle Graphics is the name given to a collection of low-level graphics routines that do the work of generating graphics in MATLAB. Handle Graphics provides a high degree of control over graphics. These functions and options are commonly hidden inside higher-level graphics M-files. Handle Graphics lets you customize aspects of plots that cannot be addressed using the high-level commands and functions described in previous chapters. The *Figure* window toolbar and menus provide a GUI interface to many Handle Graphics features, making it less important for the casual MATLAB user to understand Handle Graphics.

This chapter is not an exhaustive discussion of Handle Graphics because simply too much detail is involved. The goal is to develop a basic understanding of Handle Graphics concepts and to present enough practical information so that this feature is accessible to even casual MATLAB users.

30.1 OBJECTS

Handle Graphics is based on the idea that every component of a visual aspect of MATLAB is an ***object,*** that each object has a unique identifier or ***handle*** associated with it, and that each object has ***properties*** that can be modified as desired. The word *object* appears in many areas of modern computing. Object-oriented programming languages, database objects, and operating system and application interfaces all use the concept of objects. An object is loosely defined as a closely related collection of data and functions that form a unique whole. In MATLAB, a graphics object is a distinct component that can be manipulated individually.

Everything created by a graphics command is a graphics object. These include *Figure* windows or simply *figures,* as well as *axes, lines, surfaces, text,* and others. These objects are arranged in a hierarchy of parent objects and associated child objects as diagrammed below.

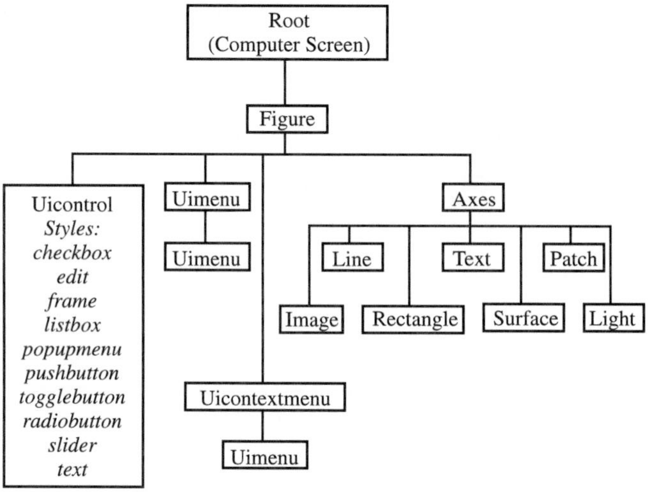

The computer screen itself is the *root* object and the parent of everything else. *Figures* are children of the *root; axes* and *user-interface* objects (to be discussed in the next chapter) are children of *figures.* And *line, rectangle, text, surface, light, patch,* and *image* objects are children of *axes.* The *root* can contain one or more *figures,* and each *figure* can contain one or more sets of *axes.* All other objects (except *uicontrol, uicontextmenu,* and *uimenu* objects discussed in the next chapter) are children of *axes* and display within an *axes.* All functions that create a graphics object create the parent object or objects if they do not exist. For example, if there are no *figures,* the `plot(rand(1,10))` function creates a new *figure* and a set of *axes* with predefined property values and then plots the *line* within these *axes.*

30.2 OBJECT HANDLES

Suppose you have three *figures* open with subplots in two of them and you want to change the color of a *line* on one of the subplot *axes.* How would you identify the *line* you wish to change? In MATLAB each object has an associated identifier, called a *handle,* which is a double-precision number. Each time an object is created, a unique handle is created for it. The handle of the *root* object, the computer screen, is always zero. The `Hf_fig=figure` command creates a new *figure* and returns its handle in the `Hf_fig` variable. *Figure* handles are normally integers and are usually displayed in the *Figure* window title bar. Other object handles are floating-point numbers in full MATLAB precision. All object creation functions return the handles of the objects they create. The following table lists the Handle Graphics objects in MATLAB.

Object	Description
root	Computer platform running MATLAB.
figure	Window on the computer screen.
uicontrol	User interface control in a *figure*.
uimenu	User interface menu in a *figure*.
uicontextmenu	User interface contextual menu in a *figure*.
axes	Rectangular coordinate system for plotting in a *figure*.
image	2-D picture in an *axes*.
light	Directional light source shining on an *axes*.
line	Line connecting data points on an *axes*.
patch	Polygonal area defined by vertices on an *axes*.
rectangle	Rectangular to elliptical shape on an *axes*.
surface	3-D representation of a surface on an *axes*.
text	Character string placed on an *axes*.

MATLAB commands are available to obtain the handles of *figures, axes,* and other objects. For example `Hf_fig=gcf` returns the handle of the current *figure,* and `Ha_ax=gca` returns the handle of the current *axes* in the current *figure.* These functions and other object manipulation tools are discussed later in this chapter.

To improve readability, in this text variables that contain object handles are given names beginning with a capital `H`, followed by a letter identifying the object type, then an underscore, and finally one or more descriptive characters. Thus, `Hf_fig` is a handle to a *figure,* `Ha_ax1` is a handle to an *axes* object, and `Ht_title` is a handle to a *text* object. When an object type is unknown, the letter `x` is used, as in `Hx_obj`. While handles can be given any name, following this convention makes it easy to spot handle variables in an M-file.

All MATLAB functions that create objects return a handle or a column vector of handles for each object created. Some plots are made up of more than one object. For example, a `mesh` plot consists of a single *surface* object with a single handle, while a `polar` plot consists of a number of *line* objects with individual handles associated with each *line*.

30.3 OBJECT PROPERTIES

All objects have a set of ***properties*** that define their characteristics. It is by setting these properties that one modifies how graphics are displayed. The properties associated with each object type (e.g., *axes, line, surface*) are unique, although a number of property names are common to all objects. Object properties can include such characteristics as an object's position, color, object type, parent object handle, child object handles, and many others. Each distinct object has properties associated with it that can be changed without affecting other objects of the same type.

Object properties consist of property ***names*** and their associated property ***values.*** Property names are character strings. They are typically displayed in mixed case with the initial letter of each word capitalized, for example, `'LineStyle'`. However, MATLAB recognizes a property regardless of case. In addition, you need use only enough characters to uniquely identify the property name. For example, the position property of an *axes* object can be called `'Position'`, `'position'`, or even `'pos'`.

When an object is created, it is initialized with a full set of default property values that can be changed in one of two ways. The object creation function can be issued with (`'PropertyName'`, `PropertyValue`) pairs, or property values can be changed after the object is created. For example,

```
>> Hf_1 = figure('Color','yellow')
```

creates a new *figure* with default properties, except that the background color is set to yellow rather than to the default color.

In addition to the *Figure* window menu and toolbar features in MATLAB, the function `inspect` provides a GUI for inspection and modification of object properties. To use this function simply issue `inspect(H)`, where `H` is the handle of the desired object.

30.4 `get` AND `set`

The two functions `get` and `set` are used to obtain or change Handle Graphics object properties. The function `get` returns the current value of one or more properties of an object. The most common syntax is `get(handle,'PropertyName')`. For example,

```
>> p = get(Hf_1,'Position')
```

returns the position vector of the *figure* having the handle `Hf_1`. Similarly,

```
>> c = get(Hl_a,'Color')
```

returns the color of an object identified by the handle Hl_a.

The function set changes the values of Handle Graphics object properties and uses the syntax set(*handle*,'*PropertyName*',*PropertyValue*). For example,

```
>> set(Hf_1,'Position',p_vect)
```

sets the position of the *figure* having the handle Hf_1 to that specified by the vector p_vect. Likewise,

```
>> set(Hl_a,'Color','r')
```

sets the color of the object having the handle Hl_a to red. In general, the set function can have any number of ('*PropertyName*',*PropertyValue*) pairs. For example,

```
>> set(Hl_a,'Color',[1 0 0],'LineWidth',2,'LineStyle','--')
```

changes the color of the *line* having the handle Hl_a to red, its line width to 2 points, and its linestyle to dashed.

In addition to these primary purposes, the get and set functions provide feedback about object properties. For example, set(*handle*,'*PropertyName*') returns a list of values that can be assigned to the object described by handle. For example,

```
>> set(Hf_1,'Units')
[ inches | centimeters | normalized | points | {pixels} | characters ]
```

shows that there are six allowable character string values for the 'Units' property of the *figure* referenced by Hf_1 and that 'pixels' is the default value.

If you specify a property that does not have a fixed set of values, MATLAB informs you of that fact, for example,

```
>> set(Hf_1,'Position')
A figure's 'Position' property does not have a fixed set of property values.
```

In addition to the set command, Handle Graphics object creation functions accept multiple pairs of property names and values. For example,

```
>> figure('Color','blue','NumberTitle','off','Name','My Figure')
```

creates a new *figure* with a blue background entitled 'My Figure' rather than the default window title 'Figure No. 1'.

As an illustration of the above concepts, consider the following example.

```
>> Hf_fig = figure  % create a figure
Hf_fig =
     1
>> Hl_light = light % add default light to an axes in the figure
Hl_light =
          107
>> set(Hl_light)    % find settable properties of light
        Position
        Color
        Style: [ {infinite} | local ]

        ButtonDownFcn: string -or- function handle -or- cell array
        Children
        Clipping: [ {on} | off ]
        CreateFcn: string -or- function handle -or- cell array
        DeleteFcn: string -or- function handle -or- cell array
        BusyAction: [ {queue} | cancel ]
        HandleVisibility: [ {on} | callback | off ]
        HitTest: [ {on} | off ]
        Interruptible: [ {on} | off ]
        Parent
        Selected: [ on | off ]
        SelectionHighlight: [ {on} | off ]
        Tag
        UIContextMenu
        UserData
        Visible: [ {on} | off ]

>> get(Hl_light)   % get all properties and names for light
        Position = [1 0 1]
        Color = [1 1 1]
        Style = infinite

        BeingDeleted = off
        ButtonDownFcn =
        Children = []
        Clipping = on
        CreateFcn =
        DeleteFcn =
        BusyAction = queue
        HandleVisibility = on
        HitTest = on
        Interruptible = on
        Parent = [108]
        Selected = off
        SelectionHighlight = on
        Tag =
        Type = light
```

```
UIContextMenu = []
UserData = []
Visible = on
```

The *light* object was used in the above example because it contains few properties. A *figure* was created and returned a handle. A *light* object was then created that returned a handle of its own. An *axes* object was also created since *light* objects are children of *axes*; the *axes* handle is available in the `'Parent'` property of the *light* object.

Note that the property lists for each object are divided into two groups. The first group lists properties that are unique to the particular object type, and the second group lists properties common to all object types. Note also that the `set` and `get` functions return slightly different property lists. The function `set` lists only properties that can be changed with the `set` command, while `get` lists all visible object properties. In the previous example, `get` listed the `'Type'` property while `set` did not. This property can be read but not changed; that is, it is a read-only property.

The number of properties associated with each object type is fixed in each release of MATLAB, but the number varies among object types. As shown above, a *light* object lists 3 unique and 18 common properties, or 21 properties in all. On the other hand, an *axes* object lists 93 properties. Clearly, it is beyond the scope of this text to thoroughly describe and illustrate all the properties of all 13 object types! However, they are listed in the Appendices.

As an example of the use of object handles, consider the problem of plotting a line in a nonstandard color. In this case, the line color is specified using an RGB value of `[1 .5 0]`, a medium-orange color.

```
>> x = -2*pi:pi/40:2*pi;              % create data
>> y = sin(x);                        % find sine of x
>> Hl_sin = plot(x,y)                 % plot sine and save handle
Hl_sin =
   59.0002
>> set(Hl_sin,'Color',[1 .5 0],'LineWidth',3) % Change color and width
```

Now add a cosine curve in light blue.

```
>> z = cos(x);                          % find cosine of x
>> hold on                              % keep sine curve
>> Hl_cos = plot(x,z);                  % plot cosine and save handle
>> set(Hl_cos,'Color',[.75 .75 1])      % color it light blue
>> hold off
```

It's also possible to do the same thing with fewer steps:

```
>> Hl_line = plot(x,y,x,z);        % plot both curves and save handles
>> set(Hl_line(1),'Color',[1 .5 0],'LineWidth', 3)
>> set(Hl_line(2),'Color',[.75 .75 1])
```

How about adding a title and making the font size larger than normal?

```
>> title('Handle Graphics Example') % add a title
>> Ht_text = get(gca,'Title')       % get handle to title
>> set(Ht_text,'FontSize',16)       % customize font size
```

The last example illustrates an interesting point about *axes* objects. Every object has a `'Parent'` property as well as a `'Children'` property, which contains handles to descendent objects. A *line* plotted on a set of axes has the handle of the *axes* object in its `'Parent'` property and the empty array in the `'Children'` property. At the same time, the *axes* object has the handle of its *figure* in its `'Parent'` property and the handles of *line* objects in the `'Children'` property. Even though *text* objects created with the `text` and `gtext` commands are children of *axes* and their handles are included in the `'Children'` property, the handles associated with the title string and axis labels are not. These handles are kept in the `'Title'`, `'XLabel'`, `'YLabel'`, and `'ZLabel'` properties of the *axes*. These *text* objects are always created when an *axes* object is created. The `title` command simply sets the `'String'` property of the title *text* object within the current *axes*. Finally, the standard MATLAB functions `title`, `xlabel`, `ylabel`, and `zlabel` return handles and accept property and value arguments. For example, the following command adds a 24-point green title to the current plot and returns the handle of the title *text* object.

```
>> Ht_title = title('This is a title.','FontSize',24,'Color','green')
```

In addition to `set` and `get`, MATLAB provides several other functions for manipulating objects and their properties. Objects can be ***copied*** from one parent to another using the `copyobj` function. For example,

```
>> Ha_new = copyobj(Ha_ax1,Hf_fig2)
```

makes copies of the *axes* object with handle `Ha_ax1` and all of its children, assigns new handles, and places the objects in the *figure* with handle `Hf_fig2`. A handle to the new *axes* object is returned in `Ha_new`. Any object can be copied into any valid parent object based on the hierarchy described earlier. Either one or both arguments to `copyobj` can be vectors of handles.

Note that any object can be ***moved*** from one parent to another simply by changing its `'Parent'` property value to the handle of another valid parent object. For example,

```
>> figure(1)
>> set(gca,'Parent',2)
```

moves the current *axes* and all its children from the *figure* having handle 1 to the *figure* having handle 2. Any existing objects in *figure* 2 are not affected except that they may become obscured by the relocated objects.

Any object and all of its children can be ***deleted*** using the `delete(handle)` function. Similarly, `reset(handle)` resets all object properties associated with `handle` except for the `'Position'` property to the defaults for that object type. If `handle` is a column vector of object handles, all referenced objects are affected by `set`, `reset`, `copyobj`, and `delete`.

The `get` and `set` functions return a structure when an output is assigned. Consider the following example.

```
>> lprop = get(Hl_light)
lprop =
           BeingDeleted: 'off'
             BusyAction: 'queue'
          ButtonDownFcn: ''
               Children: [0x1 double]
               Clipping: 'on'
                  Color: [1 1 1]
              CreateFcn: ''
              DeleteFcn: ''
       HandleVisibility: 'on'
                HitTest: 'on'
          Interruptible: 'on'
                 Parent: 108
               Position: [1 0 1]
               Selected: 'off'
     SelectionHighlight: 'on'
                  Style: 'infinite'
                    Tag: ''
                   Type: 'light'
          UIContextMenu: []
               UserData: []
                Visible: 'on'
>> class(lprop) % class of get(Hl_light)
ans =
struct
>> lopt = set(Hl_light)
lopt =
             BusyAction: {2x1 cell}
          ButtonDownFcn: {}
               Children: {}
               Clipping: {2x1 cell}
                  Color: {}
              CreateFcn: {}
              DeleteFcn: {}
       HandleVisibility: {3x1 cell}
                HitTest: {2x1 cell}
          Interruptible: {2x1 cell}
                 Parent: {}
               Position: {}
```

```
                Selected: {2x1 cell}
      SelectionHighlight: {2x1 cell}
                   Style: {2x1 cell}
                     Tag: {}
           UIContextMenu: {}
                UserData: {}
                 Visible: {2x1 cell}
>> class(lopt) % class of set(Hl_light)
ans =
struct
```

The field names of the resulting structures are the object property name strings and are assigned alphabetically. Note that even though property names are not case-sensitive, these field names are, for example,

```
>> lopt.BusyAction
ans =
    'queue'
    'cancel'
>> lopt.busyaction
??? Reference to non-existent field 'busyaction'.
```

Combinations of property values can be set using structures as well. For example,

```
>> newprop.Color = [1 0 0];
>> newprop.Position = [-10 0 10];
>> newprop.Style = 'local';
>> set(Hl_light,newprop)
```

changes the `'Color'`, `'Position'`, and `'Style'` properties but has no effect on any other properties of the *light* object. Note that you cannot simply obtain a structure of property values and use the same structure to reset the values, for example,

```
>> light_prop = get(Hl_light);
>> light_prop.Color = [1 0 0];   % change the light color to red
>> set(Hl_light,light_prop);    % reapply the property values
??? Error using ==> set
Attempt to modify read-only light property: 'BeingDeleted'.
```

Since `'BeingDeleted'` and `'Type'` are the only read-only properties of a *light* object, you can work around the problem by removing the `'BeingDeleted'` and `'Type'` fields from the structure, for example,

```
>> light_prop = rmfield(light_prop,'Type','BeingDeleted');
>> set(Hl_light,light_prop)
```

For objects with more read-only properties, all read-only properties must be removed from the structure to use it to set property values.

A cell array can also be used to query a selection of property values. To do so, create a cell array containing the desired property names in the desired order and pass the cell array to `get`. The result is returned as a cell array as well, for example,

```
>> plist = {'Color','Position','Style'}
plist =
    'Color'      'Position'    Style'
>> get(Hl_light,plist)
ans =
    [ double]    [1x3 double]    'local'
>> class(ans)
ans =
cell
```

One more point about the `get` function should be noted. If `H` is a vector of handles, `get(H,'`*`PropertyName`*`')` returns a cell array rather than a vector. Consider the following example, given a *Figure* window with four subplots.

```
>> Ha = get(gcf,'Children')       % get axes handles
Ha =
        15.0002
        13.0002
        11.0002
         9.0002
>> Ha_kids = get(Ha,'Children')  % get handles of axes children
Ha_kids =
    [    16.0002]
    [4x1 double]
    [    12.0002]
    [2x1 double]]
>> class(Ha_kids)
ans =
    cell
>> Hx = cat(1,Ha_kids{:})         % convert to column vector
Hx =
        16.0002
        26.0002
        24.0002
        18.0002
        22.0002
        12.0002
        14.0002
        10.0002
>> class(Hx)
ans =
    double
```

Now `Hx` can be used as an argument to Handle Graphics functions expecting a vector of object handles.

30.5 FINDING OBJECTS

As has been shown, Handle Graphics provides access to objects in a *figure* and allows the user to customize graphics using the get and set commands. The use of these functions requires that one know the handles of the objects to be manipulated. In cases where handles are unknown MATLAB provides a number of functions for finding object handles. Two of these functions, gcf and gca, were introduced earlier. For example,

```
>> Hf_fig = gcf
```

returns the handle of the current *figure,* and

```
>> Ha_ax = gca
```

returns the handle of the current *axes* in the current *figure.*

In addition to the above, MATLAB includes gco, a function to obtain the handle of the current object. For example,

```
>> Hx_obj = gco
```

returns the handle of the current object in the current *figure,* or alternatively,

```
>> Hx_obj = gco(Hf_fig)
```

returns the handle of the current object in the *figure* associated with the handle Hf_fig.

The current object is defined as the last object clicked on with the mouse within a *figure.* This object can be any graphics object except the *root.* When a *figure* is initially created, no current object exists and gco returns an empty array. The mouse button must be clicked while the pointer is within a *figure* before gco can return an object handle.

Once an object handle has been obtained, the object type can be found by querying an object's 'Type' property, which is a character string object name such as 'figure', 'axes', or 'text'. The 'Type' property is common to all objects. For example,

```
>> x_type = get(Hx_obj,'Type')
```

is guaranteed to return a valid object string for all objects.

When something other than the 'CurrentFigure', 'CurrentAxes', or 'CurrentObject' is desired, the function get can be used to obtain a vector of handles to the children of an object. For example,

```
>> Hx_kids = get(gcf,'Children');
```

returns a vector containing handles of the children of the current *figure.*

This technique of getting 'Children' handles can be used to search through the Handle Graphics hierarchy to find specific objects. For example, consider the problem of finding the handle of a green *line* object after plotting some data.

```
>> x = -pi:pi/20:pi;                    % create some data
>> y = sin(x); z = cos(x);
>> plot(x,y,'r',x,z,'g');               % plot lines in red and green

>> Hl_lines = get(gca,'Children');  % get the line handles
>> for k=1:size(Hl_lines)               % find the green line
>>   if get(Hl_lines(k),'Color') == [0 1 0]
>>     Hl_green = Hl_lines(k)
>>   end
>> end
Hl_green =
    58.0001
```

Although this method is effective, it becomes complicated when there are many objects. This technique also misses *text* objects in titles and axis labels unless these objects are tested individually.

To simplify the process of finding object handles, MATLAB contains the built-in function findobj, which returns the handles of objects with specified property values. Hx=findobj(*Handles*,'flat','*PropertyName*',*PropertyValue*) returns the handles of all objects in *Handles* whose '*PropertyName*' property contains the value *PropertyValue*. Multiple ('*PropertyName*',*PropertyValue*) pairs are allowed, and all must match. When *Handles* is omitted, the root object is assumed. When no ('*PropertyName*',*PropertyValue*) pairs are given, all objects match and all Handles are returned. When 'flat' is omitted, all objects in *Handles* ***and all decendants of these objects*** including axes titles and labels are searched. When no objects are found to match the specified criteria, findobj returns an empty matrix. Using the function findobj, the solution to the above example problem becomes one line:

```
>> Hl_green = findobj(0,'Type','line','Color',[0 1 0]);
```

It is possible to hide the visibility of specific handles by using the 'HandleVisibility' property common to all objects. This property is convenient because it keeps the user from inadvertently deleting or changing the properties of an object. When an object has its 'HandleVisibility' property set to 'off' or to 'callback', findobj does not return handles to these objects when called from the *Command* window. Hidden handles do not appear in lists of children or as the output of gcf, gca, or gco. However, when the property is set to 'callback', these handles can be found during the execution of a callback string. See Section 30.12 for information about callback strings.

30.6 SELECTING OBJECTS WITH THE MOUSE

The gco command returns the handle of the current object, which is the last object clicked on with the mouse. When a mouse click is made near the intersection of more than one object,

MATLAB uses rules to determine which object becomes the current object. Each object has a selection region associated with it. A mouse click within this region selects the object. For *line* objects the selection region includes the *line* and all if the area within a 5-pixel distance from the *line*. The selection region of a *surface, patch,* or *text* object is the smallest rectangle that contains the object. The selection region of an *axes* object is the *axes* box itself plus the areas where labels and titles appear. Objects within *axes,* such as *lines* and *surfaces,* are higher in the stacking order, and clicking on them selects the associated object rather than the *axes.* Selecting an area outside the *axes* selection region selects the *figure* itself.

When a mouse click is within the border of two or more objects, the ***stacking order*** determines which object becomes the current object. The stacking order determines which overlapping object is on *top* of the others. Initially, the stacking order is determined when the object is created, with the newest object at the top of the stack. For example, when you issue two `figure` commands, two *figures* are created. The second *figure* is drawn on top of the first. The resulting stacking order has *figure* 2 on top of *figure* 1, and the handle returned by `gcf` is 2. If the `figure(1)` command is issued or if *figure* 1 is clicked on, the stacking order changes. *Figure* 1 moves to the top of the stack and becomes the current *figure.*

In the preceding example, the stacking order was apparent from the window overlap on the computer screen. However, this is not always the case. When two *lines* are plotted, the second *line* drawn is on top of the first at the points where they intersect. If the first *line* is clicked on with the mouse at some other point, the first *line* becomes the current object but the stacking order does not change. A click on the intersecting point continues to select the second *line* until the stacking order is explicitly changed.

The stacking order is given by the order in which `'Children'` handles appear for a given object. That is, `Hx_kids=get(`*`handle`*`,'Children')` returns handles of child objects in stacking order. The first element in the vector `Hx_kids` is at the top of the stack, and the last element is at the bottom of the stack. The stacking order can be changed by changing the order of the `'Children'` property value of the parent object. For example,

```
>> Hf = get(0,'Children');
>> if length(Hf) > 1
     set(0,'Children',Hf([end 1:end-1]);
   end
```

moves the bottom *figure* to the top of the stack where it becomes the new current *figure.*

30.7 POSITION AND UNITS

The `'Position'` property of *figure* objects and most other Handle Graphics objects is a four-element row vector. As shown in the following figure, the values in this vector are `[left, bottom, width, height]`, where `[left, bottom]` is the position of the lower left corner of the object relative to its parent and `[width, height]` is the width and height of the object.

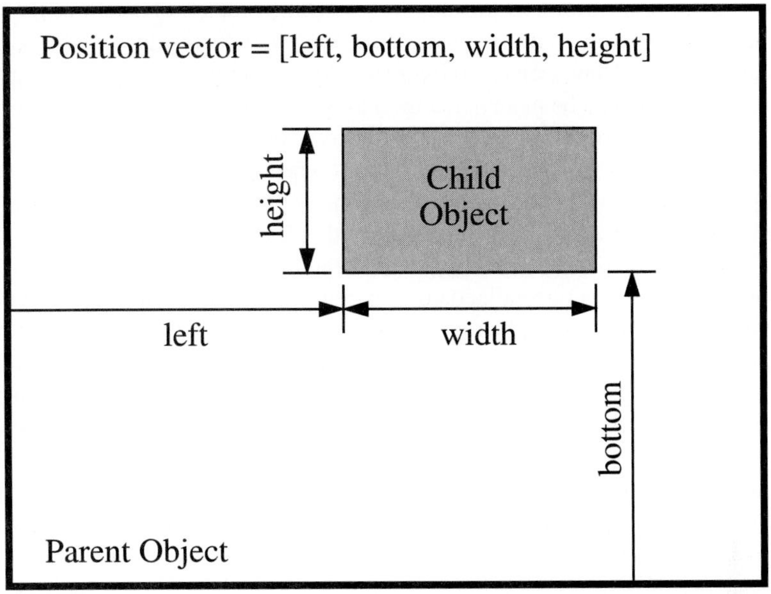

These position vector values are in units specified by the 'Units' property of the object. For example,

```
>> get(gcf,'Position')
ans =
   920   620   672   504
>> get(gcf,'units')
ans =
pixels
```

shows that the lower left corner of the current *figure* object is 920 pixels to the right and 620 pixels above the lower left corner of the screen and that the *figure* object is 672 pixels wide and 504 pixels high. ***Note that the* 'Position' *vector for a figure gives the drawable area within the figure object itself and does not include window borders, scroll bars, menus, or the title bar of the Figure window.***

Alternatively, *figures* have an undocumented 'OuterPosition' property that does include the window borders, for example,

```
>> get(gcf,'Position')       % drawable position
ans =
   920   620   672   504
>> get(gcf,'OuterPosition') % outside position
ans =
   916   616   680   531
```

Here, the outer position contains the left, bottom, width, and height of the outer boundary of the *Figure* window. When the *Figure* or *Camera* toolbar is displayed or hidden by making a choice from the **View** menu in a *Figure* window, either the drawable position or the outer position parameters can be maintained by setting the 'ActivePositionProperty' of the *figure.* Setting this property to 'Position' gives priority to the drawable position, thereby keeping the 'Position' values unchanged when toolbars are displayed or hidden. Setting this property to 'OuterPosition' gives similar priority to the 'OuterPosition' values, leaving them unchanged when toolbars are displayed or hidden.

The 'Units' property for *figures* defaults to pixels but can be inches, centimeters, points, characters, or normalized coordinates. Pixels represent screen pixels, the smallest rectangular object that can be represented on a computer screen. For example, a computer display set to a resolution of 800 by 600 is 800 pixels wide and 600 pixels high. Points are a typesetting standard, where 1 point is equal to 1/72 of an inch. Character units are units relative to the width of a character in the default system font. A value of 1 is equal to the width of the letter *x* in the default system font. Normalized coordinates are in the range 0 to 1. In normalized coordinates, the lower left corner of the parent is at [0, 0] and the upper right corner is at [1, 1]. Inches and centimeters are self-explanatory.

To illustrate various 'Units' property values, reconsider the above example:

```
>> set(gcf,'units','inches')     % INCHES
>> get(gcf,'position')
ans =
       7.9224        5.3362        5.7931        4.3448
>> set(gcf,'units','cent')       % CENTIMETERS
>> get(gcf,'position')
ans =
       20.108        13.544        14.703        11.027
>> set(gcf,'units','normalized')% NORMALIZED
>> get(gcf,'position')
ans =
      0.57438       0.51583          0.42          0.42
>> set(gcf,'units','points')     % POINTS
>> get(gcf,'position')
ans =
       570.41        384.21         417.1        312.83
>> set(gcf,'units','char')       % CHARACTERS
>> get(gcf,'position')
ans =
       153.17        38.688           112          31.5
```

All these values represent the same *figure* position relative to the computer screen for a particular monitor and screen resolution.

The position of *axes* objects are also four-element vectors having the same form, [left, bottom, width, height], but specify the object position relative to the lower left corner of the parent *figure*. ***In general, the*** 'Position' ***property of a child is relative to the position of its parent.***

To be more descriptive, the computer screen or *root* object position property is not called `'Position'` but rather `'ScreenSize'`. In this case, `[left, bottom]` is always `[0, 0]` and `[width, height]` are the dimensions of the computer screen in units specified by the `'Units'` property of the *root* object.

30.8 DEFAULT PROPERTIES

MATLAB assigns default properties to each object as it is created. The built-in defaults are referred to as ***factory*** defaults. To override these defaults, you must set or get the values using `set` and `get`. In cases where you want to change the same properties every time, MATLAB allows you to set your own default properties. It lets you change the default properties for individual objects and for object types at any point in the object hierarchy. When an object is created, MATLAB looks for a default value at the ***parent*** level. If no default is found, the search continues up the object hierarchy until a default value is found or until it reaches the built-in factory default.

You can set your own default values at any level of the object hierarchy by using a special property name string consisting of `'Default'` followed by the object type and the property name. The handle you use in the `set` command determines the point in the object parent-child hierarchy at which the default is applied. For example,

```
>> set(0,'DefaultFigureColor',[.5 .5 .5])
```

sets the default background color for all new *figure* objects to medium gray rather than the MATLAB default. This property applies to the *root* object (whose handle is always zero), and so all new *figures* will have a gray background. Other examples include the following.

```
>> set(0,'DefaultAxesFontSize',14)      % larger axes fonts - all figures
>> set(gcf,'DefaultAxesLineWidth',2)  % thick axis lines - this figure only
>> set(gcf,'DefaultAxesXColor','y')    % yellow X axis lines and labels
>> set(gcf,'DefaultAxesYGrid','on')    % Y axis grid lines - this figure
>> set(0,'DefaultAxesBox','on')        % enclose axes - all figures
>> set(gca,'DefaultLineLineStyle',':')% dotted linestyle - these axes only
```

When a default property is changed, only objects created *after* the change is made are affected. Existing objects already have property values assigned and do not change.

When working with existing objects, it is always a good idea to restore them to their original state after they are used. If you change the default properties of objects in an M-file, save the previous settings and restore them when exiting the routine, for example,

```
oldunits = get(0,'DefaultFigureUnits');
set(0,'DefaultFigureUnits','normalized');
    <MATLAB statements>
set(0,'DefaultFigureUnits',oldunits);
```

To customize MATLAB to use user-defined default values at all times, simply include the desired `set` commands in your `startup.m` file. For example,

```
set(0,'DefaultAxesXGrid','on')
set(0,'DefaultAxesYGrid','on')
set(0,'DefaultAxesZGrid','on')
set(0,'DefaultAxesBox','on')
set(0,'DefaultFigurePaperType','A4')
```

creates all *axes* with grids and an enclosing box turned on and sets the default paper size to `A4`. Defaults set at the *root* level affect every object in every *Figure* window.

There are three special property value strings that reverse, override, or query user-defined default properties. They are `'remove'`, `'factory'`, and `'default'`. If you've changed a default property, you can reverse the change, thereby resetting it to the original defaults using `'remove'`, for example,

```
>> set(0,'DefaultFigureColor',[.5 .5 .5])  % set a new default
>> set(0,'DefaultFigureColor','remove')    % return to MATLAB defaults
```

To temporarily override a default and use the original MATLAB default value for a particular object, use the special property value `'factory'`, for example,

```
>> set(0,'DefaultFigureColor',[.5 .5 .5])   % set a new user default
>> figure('Color','factory')   % figure using default color
```

The third special property value string is `'default'`. This value forces MATLAB to search up the object hierarchy until it encounters a default value for the desired property. If found, it uses this default value. If the *root* object is reached and no user-defined default is found, the MATLAB factory default value is used. This feature is useful when you want to set an object property to a default property value after it was created with a different property value, for example,

```
>> set(0,'DefaultLineColor','r')            % set default at the root level
>> set(gcf,'DefaultLineColor','g')          % current figure level default
>> Hl_rand = plot(rand(1,10)); % plot a line using 'ColorOrder' color
>> set(Hl_rand,'Color','default')           % the line becomes green
>> close(gcf)                               % close the window
>> Hl_rand = plot(rand(1,10)); % plot a line using 'ColorOrder' color again
>> set(Hl_rand,'Color','default')           % the line becomes red
```

Note that the `plot` command does not use *line* object defaults for the line color. If a color argument is not specified, the `plot` command uses the *axes* `'ColorOrder'` property to specify the color of each *line* it generates.

A list of all the factory defaults can be obtained by issuing

```
>> get(0,'factory')
```

Default properties that have been set at any level in the object hierarchy can be listed by issuing

```
>> get(handle,'default')
```

The *root* object contains default values for a number of color properties and the *figure* position at startup, for example,

```
>> get(0,'default')
ans =
                defaultTextColor: [0 0 0]
               defaultAxesXColor: [0 0 0]
               defaultAxesYColor: [0 0 0]
               defaultAxesZColor: [0 0 0]
           defaultPatchFaceColor: [0 0 0]
           defaultPatchEdgeColor: [0 0 0]
                defaultLineColor: [0 0 0]
     defaultFigureInvertHardcopy: 'on'
              defaultFigureColor: [0.8 0.8 0.8]
                defaultAxesColor: [1 1 1]
           defaultAxesColorOrder: [7x3 double]
           defaultFigureColormap: [64x3 double]
         defaultSurfaceEdgeColor: [0 0 0]
           defaultFigurePosition: [920 620 672 504]
```

Other defaults are not listed until they have been created by the user, for example,

```
>> get(gcf,'default')
ans =
0x0 struct array with fields:
>> set(gcf,'DefaultLineMarkerSize',10)
>> get(gcf,'default')
ans =
    defaultLineMarkerSize: 10
```

30.9 COMMON PROPERTIES

All Handle Graphics objects share the common set of object properties shown in the following table. See also Appendix A.

Property	Description
`BeingDeleted`	Set to `'on'` when object is about to be deleted. Undocumented in MATLAB 6.
`ButtonDownFcn`	Character string *callback* evaluated using `eval` in the *Command* window when the mouse button is pressed down with the cursor over the object. Callback is often a function call.
`Children`	Handles of visible children.

Property	Description
`Clipping`	Enable or disable clipping of *axes* children.
`CreateFcn`	Character string *callback* evaluated using `eval` in the *Command* window immediately *after* an object is created. Callback is often a function call.
`DeleteFcn`	Character string *callback* evaluated using `eval` in the *Command* window immediately *before* an object is deleted. Callback is often a function call.
`BusyAction`	Determines how callbacks to this object are interrupted by other callbacks.
`HandleVisibility`	Determines whether the object handle is visible in the *Command* window or while executing callbacks.
`HitTest`	Determines whether the object can be selected with the mouse and become the current object.
`Interruptible`	Determines whether callbacks to this object are interruptible.
`Parent`	Handle of parent object.
`Selected`	Determines whether when an object has been selected as the current object.
`SelectionHighlight`	Determines whether a selected object shows visible selection handles or not.
`Tag`	User-defined character string used to identify or *tag* the object. Often useful in association with `findobj`. For example, `findobj(0,'tag','mytagstring')`.
`Type`	Character string identifying object type.
`UIContextMenu`	Handle of contextual menu associated with an object.
`UserData`	Storage of any user-defined variable associated with an object.
`Visible`	Visibility of object.

Three of these properties contain *callback* character strings: `'ButtonDownFcn'`, `'CreateFcn'`, and `'DeleteFcn'`. Callback character strings, or simply *callbacks,* are passed to the `eval` function and executed in the *Command* window workspace. The `'Parent'` and `'Children'` properties contain handles of other objects in the hierarchy. Objects drawn on an *axes* are clipped at the *axes* limits if `'Clipping'` is `'on'` (the default for all except *text* objects). `'Interruptible'` and `'BusyAction'` control the behavior of callbacks if a later callback is triggered. `'Type'` is a string specifying the object type. `'Selected'` is `'on'` if this object is the `'CurrentObject'` of the *figure,* and `'SelectionHighlight'` determines if the object changes appearance when selected. `'HandleVisibility'` specifies whether the object handle is visible, invisible, or visible only to callbacks. The *root* `'ShowHiddenHandles'` property overrides the `'HandleVisibility'` property of all objects if needed. If `'Visible'` is set to `'off'`, the object disappears from view. It is still there and the object handle is still valid, but it is not rendered. Setting `'Visible'` to `'on'` restores the object to view. The `'Tag'` and `'UserData'` properties are reserved for the user. The `'Tag'` property is typically used to tag an object with a user-defined string. For example,

```
>> set(gca,'Tag','My Axes')
```

attaches the string `'My Axes'` to the current *axes* in the current *figure.* This string does not display in the *axes* or in the *figure,* but you can query the `'Tag'` property to identify the object. For example, when there are numerous *axes,* you can find the handle to the above *axes* object by issuing

```
>> Ha_myaxes = findobj(0,'Tag','My Axes');
```

The `'UserData'` property can contain any variable you wish to put into it. A character string, a number, a structure, or even a multidimensional cell array can be stored in any object's `'UserData'` property. No MATLAB function changes or makes assumptions about the values contained in these properties.

The properties listed for each object using the `get` and `set` commands are the documented properties. There are also undocumented or hidden properties used by MATLAB developers. Some of them can be modified, but others are read-only. Undocumented properties are simply hidden from view. These properties still exist and can be modified. The undocumented *root* property `'HideUndocumented'` controls whether `get` returns all properties or only documented properties. For example,

```
>> set(0,'HideUndocumented','off')
```

makes undocumented object properties visible within MATLAB. Since undocumented properties have been purposely left undocumented, one must be very cautious when using them. They are sometimes less robust than documented properties and are always subject to change. Undocumented properties may appear, disappear, change functionality, or even become documented in future versions of MATLAB.

30.10 NEW PLOTS

When a new graphics object is created using a low-level command such as `line` or `text`, the object appears on the current *axes* in the current *figure* by default. High-level graphics functions like `mesh` and `plot`, however, clear the current *axes* and reset most *axes* properties to their defaults before displaying a plot. As discussed earlier, the `hold` command can be used to change this default behavior. Both *figures* and *axes* have a `'NextPlot'` property used to control how MATLAB reuses existing *figures* and *axes*. The `hold`, `newplot`, `reset`, `clf`, and `cla` functions all affect the `'NextPlot'` property of *figures* and *axes*. `'NextPlot'` has three possible values:

```
>> set(gcf,'NextPlot')
    [ {add} | replace | replacechildren ]
>> set(gca,'NextPlot')
    [ add | {replace} | replacechildren ]
```

The default setting for *figures* is `'add'`; the default for *axes* is `'replace'`. When `'NextPlot'` is set to `'add'`, a new plot is added without clearing or resetting the current *figure* or *axes*. When the value is `'replace'`, a new object causes the *figure* or *axes* to remove all child objects and reset all properties except `'Position'` and `'Units'` to their defaults before drawing the new plot. The default settings clear and reset the current *axes* and reuse the current *figure*.

The third possible setting for `'NextPlot'` is `'replacechildren'`. This setting removes all child objects but does not change the current *figure* or *axes* properties. The command `hold on` sets both *figure* and *axes* `'NextPlot'` properties to `'add'`. The command `hold off` sets the *axes* `'NextPlot'` property to `'replace'`.

The `newplot` function creates a new *axes* following the above `'NextPlot'` guidelines. This function is meant to be called to create an *axes* that will contain children created by an object creation function such as `line`, `patch`, and so on, as opposed to a high-level graphics function such as `plot` or `surf`. The `newplot` function executes code similar to the following code segment.

```
function Ha = newplot
Hf = gcf;                          % get current figure or create one
next = lower(get(Hf,'NextPlot'));
switch next
  case 'replacechildren', clf;    % delete figure children
  case 'replace', clf('reset');   % delete children and reset properties
end
Ha = gca;                          % get current axes or create one
next = lower(get(Ha,'NextPlot'));
```

```
switch next
  case 'replacechildren', cla;    % delete axes children
  case 'replace', cla('reset');  % delete children and reset properties
end
```

30.11 RENDERING SPEED

There are many applications where one either wishes to show the evolution of a graphical solution as one or more properties of the solution change or to dynamically modify a graphical image in response to mouse feedback. In both these cases it is desirable to maximize the screen rendering speed and eliminate flicker. MATLAB *figure, axes, line, patch, rectangle,* and *surface* objects offer properties that influence rendering speed and flicker.

MATLAB *figures* have three properties that influence rendering speed: `'Renderer'`, `'DoubleBuffer'`, and `'BackingStore'`. `'Renderer'` refers to the underlying algorithm used to create or render a graphical image on the screen. This property has three possible values, `'painters'`, `'zbuffer'`, and `'openGL'`. Normally, MATLAB selects among the three renderers automatically based on the complexity of the graphics objects to be rendered and on the capabilities of the computer being used. For the most part MATLAB makes the optimum choice for each *figure.* However, in special cases the renderer can be specified by setting this property as desired.

`'BackingStore'` is normally set to `'on'` and controls the existence of a duplicate copy of the *Figure* window data. When multiple overlapping windows appear on a computer screen, having `'BackingStore'` set to `'on'` allows obscured or partially obscured *Figure* windows to be refreshed quickly from the off-screen copy when uncovered. When `'BackingStore'` is set to `'off'`, no off-screen copy is created, thereby increasing rendering speed but forcing a recomputation of graphical data when a *figure* is uncovered.

The *figure* `'DoubleBuffer'` property is normally set to `'off'`. Setting this property to `'on'` instructs MATLAB to draw graphics objects into an off-screen buffer and then dump the data to the screen when the buffer is fully updated. By drawing into an off-screen buffer rather than directly updating the screen, the rendering progress is hidden from the user. MATLAB sets this property to `'off'` because it is applicable only for graphics rendered using the Painter's algorithm. In addition, it produces flicker-free rendering only for simple graphics containing *lines,* such as those produced by the function `plot`. In addition, the *lines* rendered must have their `'EraseMode'` property set to the default `'normal'`. Graphics containing surfaces or many patches generally do not benefit from double-buffering.

When an *axes* is rendered using the Painter's algorithm, the amount of behind-the-scenes work done to render objects such as *lines* can be controlled by the `'DrawMode'` *axes* property. By default, this property is set to `'normal'`. However, setting it to `'fast'` sacrifices rendering accuracy for added speed. For Z-buffer and OpenGL rendering this property has no effect.

The graphics drawing objects *line, patch, rectangle,* and *surface* all have an `'EraseMode'` property that allows the user to specify how they are erased and rerendered. The default value for this property is `'normal'`, with `'none'`, `'background'`, and `'xor'` being alternatives. This property determines how these objects are rendered when they are redrawn because of a change in their own properties or the placement of other objects on top of them. For example, when `'EraseMode'` is set to `'none'`, the original object is not erased when its properties are changed; the modified object is simply rendered. In most cases this leaves the *axes* with undesirable ghosts. Setting `'EraseMode'` to `'background'` erases the original object by setting the pixels it occupies to the *axes* background color. This damages objects appearing beneath the original object. Setting `'EraseMode'` to `'xor'` erases and redraws the *line* by applying an exclusive OR operation on the color underneath the object. This does not damage objects beneath the changed object but can affect the color of the changed object. Given these property value descriptions, rendering speed is increased most dramatically with `'EraseMode'` set to `'none'`, but this results in ghosts that are undesirable in most cases. Setting `'EraseMode'` to `'xor'` or `'background'` offers a compromise between speed and rendering accuracy. In most cases, `'xor'` is the best choice for creating animations.

30.12 CALLBACKS

All Handle Graphics objects have the properties `'ButtonDownFcn'`, `'CreateFcn'`, and `'DeleteFcn'`. In addition *figures* have the properties `'CloseRequestFcn'`, `'KeyPressFcn'`, `'WindowButtonDownFcn'`, `'WindowButtonMotionFcn'`, and `'WindowButtonUpFcn'`, and the user interface functions have a property `'CallBack'`. The property values associated with each of these properties are character strings called ***callbacks.*** These callbacks are passed to `eval` in the *Command* window workspace for evaluation when specific user actions are taken. Since the strings are evaluated by `eval`, they can contain any sequence of valid MATLAB statements. In most cases they are function calls, often to the same function where the callbacks are defined. These callbacks form the basis for MATLAB's GUI features to be discussed in the next chapter. The setting of callback strings tells MATLAB to perform certain tasks in response to an action taken by the user.

The simplest callback is the close request callback, which is not empty by default, for example,

```
>> get(gcf,'CloseRequestFcn')
ans =
closereq
>> class(ans)
ans =
char
```

By default, when a *Figure* window is closed by clicking the close box in the *figure* title bar, the string `closereq` is passed to `eval`. This string is the name of a function in MATLAB that simply deletes the current *figure.* So by default, clicking the close box deletes the associated *Figure* window. This behavior can be changed simply by replacing the above string with another to be evaluated on a close request, for example,

```
>> set(gcf,'CloseRequestFcn','')
```

This replacement disables closure via the close box. The close request function is an empty string, and so no action is taken. This callback string can be any valid sequence of MATLAB statements. Therefore, the string could prompt the user for confirmation of the close request before actually doing it.

30.13 M-FILE EXAMPLES

There are many, many examples of Handle Graphics usage in MATLAB itself. Almost all the specialized plotting functions in the `specgraph` directory (`>> helpwin specgraph`) are composed of Handle Graphics functions. Even the M-file function `axis` is implemented using Handle Graphics function calls. This section provides further illustrations of Handle Graphics usage.

The function `mmis2d` shown returns logical True if an axis is a 2-D view of the *x-y* plane.

```
function [tf,xa,ya]=mmis2d(H)
%MMIS2D True for Axes that are 2D.
% MMIS2D(H) returns True if the axes having handle H displays
% a 2D viewpoint of the X-Y plane where the X- and Y-axes are
% parallel to the sides of the associated figure window.
%
% [TF,Xa,Ya]=MMIS2D(H) in addition returns the angles of x- and y-axes
%
% e.g., if the x-axis increases from right-to-left Xa=180
% e.g., if the y-axis increases from left-to-right Ya=0
% e.g., if the x-axis increases from bottom-to-top Xa=90

if ~ishandle(H)
     error('H Must be a Handle.')
end

if ~strcmp(get(H,'Type'),'axes')
```

```
    error('H Must be a Handle to an Axes Object.')
end
v=get(H,'view');
az=v(1); el=v(2);
tf=rem(az,90)==0 & abs(el)==90;

if nargout==3
    xdir=strcmp(get(H,'Xdir'),'reverse');
    ydir=strcmp(get(H,'Ydir'),'reverse');
    s=sign(el);

    xa=mod(-s*az - xdir*180,360);
    ya=mod(s*(90-az) - ydir*180,360);
end
```

This function makes use of the function `ishandle`, which returns logical True for arguments that are valid object handles. It checks to see if the supplied handle is that of an *axes* by getting the `'Type'` property. If successful, it then gets the `'View'` property to determine the requested output.

The function `mmgetpos` shown below finds the position of an object in a specific set of units. This function does the right thing in that it gets the current `'Units'` property, sets the units to the `'Units'` of the desired output, gets the `'Position'` property in the desired units, and then resets the `'Units'` property.

```
function p=mmgetpos(H,u,cp)
%MMGETPOS Get Object Position Vector in Specified Units.
% MMGETPOS(H,'Units') returns the position vector associated with the
% graphics object having handle H in the units specified by 'Units'.
% 'Units' is one of: 'pixels', 'normalized', 'points', 'inches', 'cent',
% or 'character'.
% 'Units' equal to 'data' is valid for text objects only.
%
% MMGETPOS does the "right thing", i.e., it: (1) saves the current units,
% (2) sets the units to those requested, (3) gets the position, then
% (4) restores the original units.
%
% MMGETPOS(H,'Units','CurrentPoint') returns the 'CurrentPoint' position
% of the figure having handle H in the units specified by 'Units'.
```

```
%
% MMGETPOS(H,'Units','Extent') returns the 'Extent' rectangle of the text
% object having handle H.
%
% 'Uimenu', 'Uicontextmenu', 'image', 'line', 'patch', 'surface',
% 'rectangle' and 'light' objects do NOT have position properties.

if ~ischar(u), error('Units Must be a Valid String.'), end
if ~ishandle(H), error('H is Not a Valid Handle.'), end
Htype=get(H,'Type');

if nargin==3 & ~isempty(cp) & ischar(cp)
     if strcmp(Htype,'figure') & lower(cp(1))=='c'
          pname='CurrentPoint';
     elseif strcmp(Htype,'text') & lower(cp(1))=='e'
          pname='Extent';
     else
          error('Unknown Input Syntax.')
     end
elseif H~=0
     pname='Position';
elseif H==0  % root object
     pname='ScreenSize';
else
     error('Unknown Input Syntax.')
end
hu=get(H,'units');
set(H,'units',u)
p=get(H,pname);
set(H,'units',hu)
```

The `mmzap` function shown below illustrates a technique that is very useful when writing Handle Graphics function M-files. It uses a combination of `waitforbuttonpress` and `gco` to get the handle to an object selected using the mouse. `waitforbuttonpress` is a built-in MATLAB function that waits for a mouse click or key press. Its help text is shown below.

```
>> help waitforbuttonpress

WAITFORBUTTONPRESS Wait for key/buttonpress over figure.
   T = WAITFORBUTTONPRESS stops program execution until a key or
   mouse button is pressed over a figure window. Returns 0
   when terminated by a mouse buttonpress, or 1 when terminated
```

```
by a keypress. Additional information about the terminating
event is available from the current figure.

See also GINPUT, GCF.
```

After a mouse button is pressed with the mouse pointer over a *figure,* gco returns the handle of the selected object. This handle is then used to manipulate the selected object.

```
function mmzap(arg)
%MMZAP Delete Graphics Object Using Mouse.
% MMZAP waits for a mouse click on an object in
% a figure window and deletes the object.
% MMZAP or MMZAP text erases text objects.
% MMZAP axes  erases axes objects.
% MMZAP line  erases line objects.
% MMZAP surf  erases surface objects.
% MMZAP patch  erases patch objects.
%
% Clicking on an object other than the selected type, or striking
% a key on the keyboard aborts the command.

if nargin<1, arg='text'; end

Hf=get(0,'CurrentFigure');
if isempty(Hf)
   error('No Figure Window Exists.')
end
if length(findobj(0,'Type','figure'))==1
     figure(Hf) % bring only figure forward
end
key=waitforbuttonpress;
if key  % key on keyboard pressed
     return
else    % object selected
     object=gco;
     type=get(object,'Type');
     if strncmp(type,arg,4)
          delete(object)
     end
end
```

The functions xlim, ylim, and zlim in MATLAB allow one to set and get axis limits for the three plot axes independently. There are no equivalent functions for grid lines. The function `grid` turns grid lines on and off along all three axes. To add this feature the function `mmxgrid` shown below allows one to turn grid lines on and off along the *x*-axis. With minor changes to `mmxgrid`, similar functions for the *y*-axis and *z*-axis are easily created as well.

```
function y=mmxgrid(arg)
%MMXGRID X-axes Grid Lines.
% MMXGRID ON adds grid lines along the X-axes of the
% current axes.
% MMXGRID OFF turns them off.
% MMXGRID by itself toggles the X-axes grid state.
%
% TF=MMXGRID returns logical True if the X-axes grid is ON.
% Otherwise it returns logical False.
%
% See also GRID, XLIM, XLABEL

if nargin~=0
   if ischar(arg)
      if length(arg)>1 & strncmpi(arg,'on',2)
         set(gca,'XGrid','on')
      elseif length(arg)>1 & strncmpi(arg,'off',3)
         set(gca,'XGrid','off')
      else
         error('Unknown Input Argument.')
      end
   else
      error('Character Input Argument Required.')
  end
elseif nargout~=0
   y=strcmp(get(gca,'XGrid'),'on');
else
   if strcmp(get(gca,'XGrid'),'on')
      set(gca,'XGrid','off')
   else
      set(gca,'XGrid','on')
   end
end
```

30.14 SUMMARY

Handle Graphics functions provide the ability to fine-tune the appearance of visual aspects of MATLAB. Each graphics object has a handle associated with it that can be used to manipulate the object. The following table documents Handle Graphics functions in MATLAB.

Function	Description
`get`	Get object properties.
`set`	Set object properties.
`gcf`	Get current *figure*.
`gca`	Get current *axes*.
`gco`	Get current object.
`findobj`	Find objects having specified properties.
`findall`	Find hidden and unhidden objects having specified properties.
`allchild`	Get hidden and unhidden children handles for an object.
`copyobj`	Copy object to new parent.
`root`	Root computer object, handle = 0.
`figure`	*Figure* object creation.
`axes`	*Axes* object creation.
`line`	*Line* object creation.
`text`	*Text* object creation.
`patch`	*Patch* object creation.
`rectangle`	*Rectangle* object creation.
`surface`	*Surface* object creation.
`image`	*Image* object creation.
`light`	*Light* object creation.
`uicontrol`	User interface *control* object creation.
`uimenu`	User interface *menu* object creation.
`uicontextmenu`	User interface *contextual menu* object creation.
`reset`	Reset object properties to default values.
`clf`	Clear current *figure*.
`cla`	Clear current *axes*.
`ishandle`	True for arguments that are object handles.

Function	Description
`delete`	Delete object.
`close`	Close *figure* using close request function.
`refresh`	Refresh *figure*.
`gcbo`	Get current callback object.
`gcbf`	Get current callback *figure*.
`closereq`	Default *figure* `'CloseRequestFcn'` callback.
`newplot`	Create *axes* with knowledge of `'NextPlot'` properties.

31

Graphical User Interfaces

This chapter introduces the graphical user interface features available in MATLAB. These features include menus, contextual menus, pushbuttons, scroll bars, radio buttons, toggle buttons, popup menus, and list boxes. In addition, it is possible to track mouse position and motion. These features are so extensive and detailed that an entire text could be devoted exclusively to them. Since that is not possible here, the best that can be hoped for is a useful introduction and several illustrative examples.

31.1 WHAT'S A GUI?

A user interface is the point of contact or method of interaction between a person and a computer or computer program. It is the method used by the computer and the user to exchange information. The computer displays text and graphics on the computer screen and may generate sounds with a speaker. The user communicates with the computer using an input device such as a keyboard, mouse, trackball, drawing pad, or microphone. The user interface defines the look and feel of the computer, operating system, or application. Often a computer or program is chosen on the basis of pleasing design and the functional efficiency of its user interface.

A graphical user interface, or GUI (pronounced *goo′ey*), is a user interface incorporating graphics objects such as windows, icons, buttons, menus, and text. Selecting or activating these objects in some way usually causes an action or change to occur. The most common activation method is to use a mouse or other pointing device to control the movement of a pointer on the screen and to press a mouse button to signal object selection or some other action.

In the same way that the Handle Graphics capabilities of MATLAB discussed in the previous chapter let you customize the way MATLAB displays information, the Handle Graphics user interface functions described in this chapter let you customize the way you interact with MATLAB.

This chapter illustrates the use of Handle Graphics *uicontrol, uimenu,* and *uicontextmenu* objects to add graphical user interfaces to MATLAB functions and M-files. *uimenu* objects create drop-down menus and submenus in *Figure* windows. *uicontrol* objects create objects such as buttons, sliders, popup menus, and text boxes. *uicontextmenu* objects create contextual menus that open over objects.

MATLAB includes an excellent example of its GUI capabilities in the `demo` command. To explore these demonstrations, simply issue the command

```
>> demo
```

31.2 WHO SHOULD CREATE GUIS AND WHY?

After running `demo` you are likely to ask yourself, "Why would I want to create a GUI in MATLAB?" Good question! The short answer is that you may not. Many people who use MATLAB primarily to analyze data, solve problems, and plot results may not consider GUI tools to be worth the effort. On the other hand, GUIs can be used to create very effective tools and utilities in MATLAB or to build interactive demonstrations of your work. The most common reasons to create a graphical user interface are the following.

1. You are writing a function that you will use over and over again and menus, buttons, or text boxes make sense as input methods.
2. You are writing a function or developing an application for others to use.
3. You want to create an interactive demonstration of a process, technique, or analysis method.
4. You think GUIs are neat and want to experiment with them.

Before we begin, remember that a basic understanding of Handle Graphics is a prerequisite for designing and implementing a GUI in MATLAB. If you skipped the previous chapter, you should go back and read it now. It is also helpful to read the MATLAB manual *Building GUIs with MATLAB.* This relatively small manual contains a wealth of information about the basics of good user interface design, along with a set of extensive examples that illustrate GUI programming in MATLAB.

31.3 GUI OBJECT HIERARCHY

As demonstrated in the previous chapter, everything created by a graphics command is a graphics object. These include *uimenu, uicontrol,* and *uicontextmenu* objects as well as *figures, axes,* and their children. The object hierarchy shown below shows that the computer screen itself is the *root* object and that *figures* are children of the *root; axes, uimenus, uicontrols,* and *uicontextmenus* are children of *figures.*

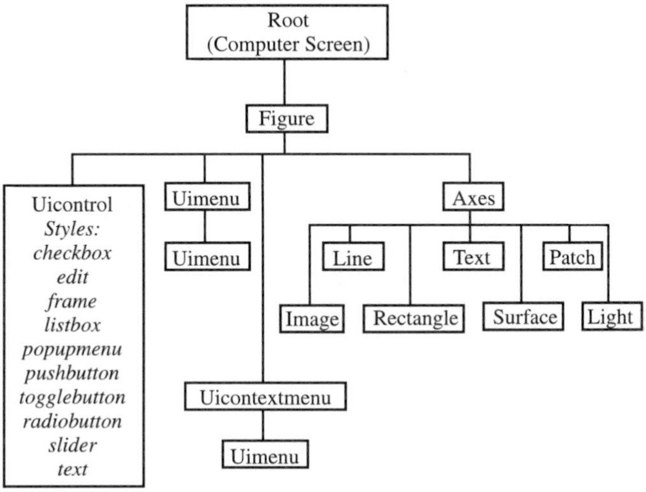

The *root* can contain one or more *figures,* and each *figure* can contain one or more sets of *axes* and their children. Each *figure* can also contain one or more *uimenus, uicontrols,* and *uicontextmenus* that are independent of the *axes.* While *uicontrol* objects have no children, they do have a variety of styles. However, both *uimenu* objects and *uicontextmenu* objects often have *uimenu* objects as children.

Graphical displays are generated differently on each computer platform that runs MATLAB. UNIX workstations use the X-Window System which has a number of window managers, such as Motif and CDE, to control the layout of the display. PCs rely on Microsoft Windows or Windows NT for window management. Although displays may be visually different on each platform, in most cases the Handle Graphics code is identical. MATLAB takes care of platform and window system differences internally. Functions incorporating Handle Graphics routines, including those using *uimenus, uicontrols,* and *uicontextmenus* objects, usually run on all platforms. Where known differences exist, they are pointed out later in this chapter.

31.4 MENUS

Menus are used in each windowing system to let users select commands and options. Commonly, there is a menu bar across the top of a window. When one of these top-level menus is selected by moving the pointer over the menu label and pressing the mouse button, a list of menu items drops down from the menu label. This type of menu is often called a pull-down menu. Menu items are selected by holding down the mouse button, moving the pointer over a menu item, and releasing the mouse button. MS Windows and some X-Window System platforms provide an additional method of selecting a menu item. Pressing and releasing the mouse button, or clicking, on a top-level menu opens the pull-down menu. Menu items can then be selected by moving the pointer over the menu item and clicking again. Selecting one of the menu items in the pull-down menu causes some action to occur.

A menu item can also act as a submenu with its own list of menu items. Submenu items display a small triangle or arrowhead to the right of the submenu label to indicate that there are more menu items available for this choice. When a submenu item is selected, another menu with more menu items is displayed in a pull-down menu to the right of the submenu item. This is sometimes called a ***walking menu.*** Selecting one of these items also causes some action to occur. Submenus may be nested, with the number of levels limited only by the windowing system used and available system resources.

The menu bar is located at the top of each *Figure* window and by default contains a number of default menu titles. Menu titles added by *uimenu* objects are positioned to the right of the last menu title. However, the standard menus and toolbars can be hidden by setting the `'Menubar'` property of *figures,* for example,

```
>> set(gcf,'menubar','none')   % hide standard menus
>> set(gcf,'menubar','figure') % display standard menus
```

31.5 MENU AND SUBMENU CREATION

Menu items and submenu items are created with the `uimenu` function in the same manner as other object creation functions. For example,

```
>> Hm_1 = uimenu(Hx_parent,'PropertyName',PropertyValue,...)
```

creates a *uimenu* item having the handle `Hm_1` and defined by `'PropertyName'`, `PropertyValue` pairs. `Hx_parent` is the handle of the parent object, which must be either a *figure* or another *uimenu.* When the parent object is a *figure,* the *uimenu* is a new menu in the *figure.* When the parent object is another *uimenu,* the *uimenu* is a submenu item of the parent menu. *Figure* windows that have their `'WindowStyle'` property set to `'modal'` are intended to be dialog boxes. Therefore, *uimenus* and standard menus exist in modal figures, but they are hidden and disabled.

31.6 MENU PROPERTIES

The table below shows the useful and unique Handle Graphics properties of *uimenus.*

uimenu Property	Description	Values, {default}
`Checked`	Visibility of check mark next to the *uimenu* item.	`'on'` or `{'off'}`

uimenu Property	Description	Values, {default}
`ForegroundColor`	Color of text label.	Colorspec {`[0 0 0]`}
`Label`	Menu label string.	Character string
`SelectionHighlight`	Object highlighted when selected.	{`'on'`} or `'off'`
`Separator`	Visibility of separator above the *uimenu* item.	`'on'` or {`'off'`}
`Visible`	Visibility of *uimenu* item. When invisible, the menu item is missing from the menu but still exists and has the same `'Position'` property.	{`'on'`} or `'off'`
`Accelerator`	Keyboard shortcut for *uimenu* item.	Single character
`Children`	Handles of submenus if present.	Vector
`Enable`	Enable or disable *uimenu.* When disabled, the menu item is visible but gray in appearance and not selectable.	{`'on'`} or `'off'`
`Parent`	Parent object. Either *figure, uimenu,* or *uicontextmenu*	Double
`Tag`	User-defined identifier.	Character string
`Type`	Object type. (Read-only.)	`'uimenu'`
`UserData`	User-defined variable storage.	Variable of any data type
`Position`	Relative menu position with respect to other *uimenus* in the same menu list. The number 1 is at the top of the menu.	Scalar
`Callback`	Character string evaluated when menu item is selected.	Character string

The most important properties of *uimenu* objects are the `'Label'` and `'CallBack'` properties. The `'Label'` property value is the visible string placed on the menu bar or in the pull-down menu to identify the menu item. The `'CallBack'` property contains the MATLAB string that is passed to `eval` for execution when the menu item is selected. Menu items that have child *uimenu* items do not execute callbacks. These menu items simply display their attached submenus.

The `'Accelerator'` and `'Label'` properties offer two approaches for selecting menu items without using the mouse. The `'Accelerator'` property defines a **Control** key equivalent for a *uimenu* item. That is, if `'x'` is the accelerator property value, holding down the **Control** key and pressing the **X** key forces the associated *uimenu* callback to execute without displaying the menu. Not all characters can be used for accelerators; each operating system has reserved accelerators for their standard menus.

Alternatively, a menu can be opened and items selected by pressing the **Alt** key followed by a shortcut character. The shortcut character is identified in a *uimenu* `'Label'` property by placing an ampersand (`&`) before the desired character. For example, `'&Grid'` creates the menu label string **Grid.** Similarly, `'G&rid'` creates the menu label **Grid.** When a menu is open, pressing the shortcut character on the keyboard executes the callback associated with that menu item.

31.7 MENU APPEARANCE

Many *uimenu* properties control aspects of the menu's appearance. `'Checked'` controls the visibility of a check mark next to a menu item. For features that are toggled on and off by a menu item, setting this property as part of a callback gives the user feedback about the current state of the feature. `'SelectionHighlight'` controls whether a menu item appears in contrasting colors as it is selected by the mouse. `'Separator'` determines whether a fine separator line appears above the menu item. This property is useful for logically grouping menu items. `'Visible'` controls *uimenu* visibility. When a menu or submenu is not visible, it does not appear but still exists. On the other hand, `'Enable'` controls the ability to select a menu item. When a menu item or submenu is disabled, it remains visible in a diminished state but cannot be selected. Finally `'Position'` controls placement of a *uimenu* relative to others in the same hierarchy. *uimenu* positions are numbered consecutively, with position 1 being at the top or leftmost position. All these appearance properties can be set on the fly, thereby allowing menus to change dynamically.

31.8 CONTEXTUAL MENUS

Contextual menus are similar to menubar menus except that they are attached to graphics objects within a *figure.* Contextual menus are usually opened by pressing the right mouse button over an object that has an attached contextual menu. In MATLAB the function `uicontextmenu` creates contextual menus, which are then attached to objects. ***uicontextmenus* are children of *figures* even though they are attached to other objects within a *figure.*** Once a *uicontextmenu* is created, it becomes the parent of one or more *uimenu* items. The appended *uimenu* objects have all the properties discussed in preceding sections of this chapter.

The table below shows the useful and unique Handle Graphics properties of *uicontextmenus.*

uicontextmenu Property	Description	Values, {default}
`Visible`	Visibility of *uicontextmenu* item. Set to `'on'` when the menu appears.	`'on'` or {`'off'`}
`Children`	Handles of *uimenu* objects.	Vector
`Parent`	Parent *figure* object.	Double
`Tag`	User-defined identifier.	Character string
`Type`	Object type. (Read-only.)	`'uicontextmenu'`
`UserData`	User-defined variable storage.	Variable of any data type

Contextual menus are created with the `uicontextmenu` function in the same manner as other object creation functions. For example,

```
>> Huix = uicontextmenu(Hf_parent,'PropertyName',PropertyValue,...)
```

creates a *uicontextmenu* object whose parent *figure* handle is *`Hf_parent`*, defined by *`'PropertyName'`*, *`PropertyValue`* pairs. The handle of the *uicontextmenu* is returned in `Huix`. This handle is used as the parent handle for *uimenu* objects that appear in the contextual menu. This handle is also placed in the `'UIContextMenu'` property of the graphics objects for which the contextual menu is to appear.

31.9 CONTROLS

Controls and menus are used by windowing systems on each computer platform to let users perform some action or to set an option or attribute. Controls are graphics objects such as icons, text boxes, and scroll bars used along with menus to create the graphical user interface implemented by the windowing system and window manager on your computer.

MATLAB controls are very similar to those used by the window manager. They are graphics objects that can be placed anywhere in a MATLAB *Figure* window and activated with the mouse. MATLAB controls include buttons, sliders, text boxes, and popup menus. Controls created by MATLAB have a slightly different appearance on MS Windows and X-Window System computer platforms, because of differences in the way the windowing systems render graphics objects. However, the functionality is essentially the same, and so the same MATLAB code creates the same objects that perform the same functions across platforms.

All controls in MATLAB are created with the function `uicontrol`. The general syntax is similar to that for `uimenu` and `uicontextmenu` discussed earlier. For example,

```
>> Hc_1 = uicontrol(Hf_fig,'PropertyName',PropertyValue,...)
```

creates a *uicontrol* object having handle `Hc_1`, defined by `'PropertyName'`, `PropertyValue` pairs. `Hf_fig` is the handle of the parent *figure* object.

31.10 CONTROL PROPERTIES

The table below shows the useful and unique Handle Graphics properties of *uicontrols.*

uicontrol Property	Description	Values, {default}
`BackgroundColor`	Background color of *uicontrol.*	Colorspec {system-dependent}
`Cdata`	Truecolor image displayed on *pushbutton* or *toggle button.*	3-D RGB array
`ForeGroundColor`	Color of text.	Colorspec `{[0 0 0]}`
`SelectionHighlight`	Object highlighted when selected.	`{'on'}` or `'off'`
`String`	Text for *uicontrol.*	Character string
`Visible`	Visibility of *uicontrol.*	`{'on'}` or `'off'`
`Enable`	Enable or disable *uicontrol.*	`{'on'}`, `'off'`, or `'inactive'`
`Parent`	Parent *figure* object.	Double
`Selected`	Identifies whether object is selected.	`'on'` or `{'off'}`
`SliderStep`	Slider or scroll bar step size.	Two-element vector
`Style`	Type of *uicontrol.*	`'pushbutton'`, `'togglebutton'`, `'radiobutton'`, `'checkbox'`, `'edit'`, `'text'`, `'slider'`, `'frame'`, `'listbox'`, `'popupmenu'`
`Tag`	User-defined identifier.	Character string
`ToolTipString`	String to display as a tool tip.	Character string.

uicontrol Property	Description	Values, {default}
`Type`	Object type. (Read-only.)	`'uicontrol'`
`UserData`	User-defined variable storage.	Variable of any data type
`Position`	Size and location of object.	`[left, bottom, width, height]` vector
`Units`	Units for `'Position'` property.	`{'pixels'}, 'normalized', 'inches', 'centimeters', 'points', 'characters'`
`FontAngle`	Character style.	`{'normal'},'italic','oblique'`
`FontName`	Font family.	Character string {system-dependent}
`FontSize`	Font size.	Size in `FontUnits` {system- dependent}
`FontUnits`	Font size units.	`{'points'}, 'normalized', 'inches', 'centimeters', 'pixels'`
`FontWeight`	Weight of text.	`{'normal'}, 'light', 'demi', 'bold'`
`HorizontalAlignment`	Text alignment.	`'left','center','right'`
`Callback`	Character string evaluated when *uicontrol* item is selected.	Character string
`UIContextmenu`	Handle of *uicontextmenu* associated with the object.	Double
`ListBoxTop`	Index of topmost string displayed in a list box.	Scalar
`Max`	Maximum value.	Scalar
`Min`	Minimum value.	Scalar
`Value`	Current value of *uicontrol.* Provides feedback about the current state.	Scalar or vector

The most important *uicontrol* property is `'Style'`. This property determines the type of *uicontrol* to be created. The style of a *uicontrol* determines the interpretation of many of the other properties.

31.11 CONTROL STYLES

MATLAB supports 10 *uicontrol* styles or types. Each of these creates a commonly known GUI object. This section introduces each of the *uicontrol* styles.

Pushbuttons. Pushbuttons, sometimes called *command buttons* or just *buttons,* are small, rectangular screen objects that usually contain a text label. Selecting a pushbutton with the mouse by moving the pointer over the object and clicking the mouse button causes MATLAB to perform the action defined by the object's callback string. Immediately after a pushbutton is pressed, it returns to its default up state. Pushbuttons are typically used to perform an action rather than change a state or set an attribute.

Toggle buttons. Toggle buttons are identical to pushbuttons except that they toggle between two states, up and down, when pushed. The `'Value'` property of a toggle button is set equal to the value specified by the `'Max'` property when the button is down or depressed. It is set equal to the value of the `'Min'` property when the button is up.

Radio buttons. Radio buttons consist of buttons containing a label and a small circle or diamond to the left of the label text. When selected, the circle or diamond is filled and the `'Value'` property is set to the value specified by the `'Max'` property, which is `1` by default; when unselected, the indicator is cleared and the `'Value'` property is set to the value specified by the `'Min'` property, which is `0` by default. Radio buttons are typically used to select one of a group of mutually exclusive options. To enforce this exclusivity, however, the callback string for each radio button must unselect all the other buttons in the group by setting the `'Value'` of each of them to `0` or to the value assigned to the `'Min'` property. This is only a convention, however. Radio buttons can be used interchangeably with check boxes, if desired.

Check boxes. Check boxes consist of buttons with a label and a small square box to the left of the label text. When activated, the control is toggled between checked and cleared. When checked, the box is filled or contains an `X` depending on the platform, and the `'Value'` property is set to the value specified by the `'Max'` property, which is `1` by default; when cleared, the box becomes empty and the `'Value'` property is set to the value specified by the `'Min'` property, which is `0` by default. Check boxes are typically used to indicate the state of an option or attribute. They are usually independent objects but can be used interchangeably with radio buttons, if desired.

Edit boxes. Editable text boxes display text in a box so that you can modify or replace the text string dynamically just as you would using a text editor or word processor. The new text string then becomes available in the `'String'` property of the *uicontrol.* Editable text boxes typically allow the user to enter text or a value. Editable text boxes can contain one or more lines of text. A single-line editable text box accepts one line of text from the user, while a multiline text box accepts more than one line of text. Single-line text entry is terminated by pressing the **Return** key. Multiline text entry is terminated with **Control-Return.** Multiline text boxes are created by setting the `'Max'` and `'Min'` property values to numbers such that `Max-Min>1`. The `'Max'` property does *not* specify the maximum number of lines. Multiline text boxes can have an unlimited number of lines. Multiline strings can be specified as a cell array of strings or a character array.

Text boxes. Static text boxes are controls that simply display a text string as determined by the `'String'` property. Static text boxes are typically used to display labels, user information, or current values. Static text boxes are static in the sense that the user cannot dynamically change the text displayed. The text can be changed only by changing the `'String'` property. Text strings are centered at the top of the text box. Text strings longer than the width of the text box ***word-wrap***; that is, multiple lines are displayed with the lines broken between words where possible. If the height of the text box is too small for the text string, some of text will not be visible. Multiline strings can be specified as a cell array of strings or a character array.

Sliders. Sliders, or ***scroll bars,*** consist of three distinct parts: the trough, or the rectangular area representing the range of valid object values; the indicator within the trough representing the current value of the slider; and arrows at each end of the trough. Sliders are typically used to select a value from a range of values. Slider values can be set in three ways. First, the indicator can be moved by positioning the mouse pointer over the indicator, holding down the mouse button while moving the mouse, and releasing the mouse button when the indicator is in the desired location. The second method is to click the mouse button while the pointer is in the trough, but to one side of the indicator. The indicator moves in that direction over a default distance equal to about 10% of the total range of the slider. Finally, clicking on one of the arrows at the ends of the slider by default moves the indicator about 1% of the slider range in the direction of the arrow. Sliders are often accompanied by separate text objects used to display labels, the current slider value, and range limits.

The `'Position'` property of *uicontrols* contains the familiar `[left bottom width height]` vector in units designated by the `'Units'` property. The orientation of a slider depends on the aspect ratio of `width` to `height`. A horizontal slider is drawn if `width > height`, and a vertical slider is drawn if `width < height`. On X-Window System platforms, the arrows appear only if one dimension is greater than four times the other. All sliders have arrows on other platforms.

The `'SliderStep'` property is a two-element vector `[arrow_step trough_step]` that controls the change in slider value when a slider arrow is clicked or the mouse is clicked in the slider trough. Default values are `[0.01 0.10]` for a change of 1% and 10% of the maximum slider value, respectively. Note that MATLAB enforces the requirement that `Max > Min` for sliders and that `Max` is at the top of a vertical slider and at the right end of a horizontal slider. If you require something different, for example, a vertical slider with values of `0` at the top and `10` at the bottom, use negative numbers for `'Min'`, `'Max'`, and `'Value'` and convert data as necessary using the `abs` function.

Frames. Frame *uicontrol* objects are simply opaque, shaded rectangular regions with a border. Frames are analogous to the `'Separator'` property of *uimenu* objects in the sense that they provide visual separation. Frames are typically used to logically group radio buttons or other *uicontrol* objects. Frames should be defined before other objects are placed within them. Otherwise, the frame may cover the other *uicontrols*.

List boxes. List box *uicontrol* objects look like multiline text boxes that allow users to select individual or multiple list entries with a mouse click. Individual list entries are specified by a cell arrays of strings, a padded string array, or a single string with a vertical bar `'|'` character used to separate list entries. When a list entry is selected with a mouse click, the `'Value'` property is updated with the index of the selected item.

If `Max-Min>1`, multiple list entries can be selected. Contiguous list entries are selected by dragging the mouse pointer over the desired entries or by selecting one item with a mouse click and selecting a second item while pressing the **Shift** key on the keyboard. Non-contiguous entries can be selected by pressing the **Control** key and selecting individual list entries. If multiple entries are selected, the `'Value'` property is updated with a vector of indices of the selections.

The size and placement of the list box is specified using the `'Position'` property. If the list box `'String'` values exceed the `width` or `height` of the list box *uicontrol,* horizontal and vertical scroll bars are added to the list box as necessary.

The list box callback string is evaluated whenever a mouse-button-up event changes the contents of the `'Value'` property. If you wish to allow multiple selections and take action only after all the selections have been made, do not use the list box `'Callback'` string. In this case, add a **Done** or **Apply** pushbutton and use its `'Callback'` string instead.

Alternatively, the use of a double-click can be sensed as part of the callback. List box *uicontrols* set the *figure* `'SelectionType'` property to `'normal'` for a single mouse click and to `'open'` for a double-click. The *uicontrol* callback can be designed to perform its function only after a double-click to indicate that the last selection has been made.

Popup menus. Popup menus are typically used to present a list of mutually exclusive choices to the user. These menus can be positioned anywhere in the *Figure* window. When closed, a popup menu appears as a rectangle or button containing the label of the current selection with a small raised rectangle or downward-pointing arrow beside the label to indicate that the object is a popup menu. When the pointer is positioned over a popup control and the mouse button is pressed, other choices appear. Moving the pointer to a different choice and releasing the mouse button closes the popup menu and displays the new selection. MS Windows and some X-Window System platforms allow the user to click on a popup menu to open it and then click on another choice to select it.

When a popup item is selected, the `'Value'` property is set to the index of the selected element of the vector of choices. Choice labels can be specified as a cell array of strings, a character array, or a single string separated by vertical bar `'|'` characters.

The `'Position'` property of a popup menu contains the familiar `[left bottom width height]` vector, where the `width` and `height` values determine the dimensions of the popup object. On X-Window Systems, these are the dimensions of the closed popup menu. When opened, the menu expands to display all the choices that can fit on the screen. On MS Windows systems, the `height` value is essentially ignored. These platforms create a popup menu tall enough to display one line of text regardless of the `height` value.

31.12 CONTROL SIZE AND FONT SELECTION

The `'Position'` and `'Units'` properties of *uicontrols* are used to locate objects in the *Figure* window. Given a *Figure* window of some size and the desired font for *uicontrols,* GUI layout is a problem in 2-D geometry. When designing a GUI, one must make *uicontrols* large enough to display all the desired text, and one must also decide if the GUI is to be resizable.

MATLAB's default *uicontrol* fonts were chosen to give the best appearance on each platform, and so use of the default *uicontrol* font is recommended unless you have special requirements. Portable or platform-independent code also works best using the default fonts.

Often sizing and placing *uicontrols* is a process of trial and error. Even when you are satisfied with the result, the appearance of the *figure* on another platform may be sufficiently different to require more adjustments. Often it is desirable to make *uicontrols* a bit larger than appears necessary, simply to ensure readability on all platforms.

Just because a *figure* has a default size, there is no guarantee that all *figures* on all platforms are that size. If you add *uicontrols* or *uimenus* to an existing *figure,* it may be smaller or larger than the default. In addition, the user can resize any *figure* at any time unless prevented from doing so by setting the *figure's* `'Resize'` property to `'off'`. Therefore, in general it is a good idea to specifically set the size of a *Figure* window to be used for a GUI.

Two things to consider when adding *uicontrols* to a *figure* that may be resized are the `'Units'` property and the restrictions imposed by fixed font size character strings. When the position of each *uicontrol* is specified in absolute units such as pixels, inches, centimeters, or points, resizing the window does not change the size or placement of them. The *uicontrols* maintain the same absolute position relative to the bottom and left sides of the *figure.* If the *figure* is made smaller, some of the *uicontrols* may move outside of the *figure* and will no longer be visible.

When the position of *uicontrols* is specified in normalized units, the *uicontrols* maintain their relative relationship to each other and to the *figure* itself when the *figure* is resized. However, there is a drawback in this case as well. If the *figure* is made smaller and the *uicontrols* are resized as a result, label strings may become unreadable since the font size is fixed. Any portion of a label outside the dimensions of the resized *uicontrol* is clipped.

There is no way to avoid this conflict between readable character strings of fixed size and GUI size. Good GUI layout practice usually leaves sufficient white space around *uicontrols* so that clipping does not occur in going from one platform to the next. If a GUI is meant to be resizable, the `'ResizeFcn'` callback property of the GUI *figure* can be used to move and reshape the *uicontrols* in response to a change in *figure* size.

31.13 CAPTURING MOUSE ACTIONS

GUI functions use the location of the mouse pointer and the status of mouse buttons to control MATLAB actions. This section discusses the interaction between pointer and object locations and mouse button actions and how MATLAB responds to changes or events, such as a button press, a button release, or pointer movement.

All Handle Graphics objects have a `'ButtonDownFcn'` property. *uimenus, uicontextmenus,* and *uicontrols* have a `'CallBack'` property that is central to their use. In addition, *figures* have `'WindowButtonDownFcn'`, `'WindowButtonUpFcn'`, and `'WindowButtonMotionFcn'` properties as well as `'KeyPressFcn'`, `'CloseRequestFcn'`, and `'ResizeFcn'` properties. All graphics objects also have `'CreateFcn'` and `'DeleteFcn'` properties. The value associated with each of these properties is a callback string that is passed to `eval` when the property is invoked. The pointer location determines which callbacks are involved and the order in which they are invoked when an event occurs.

The previous chapter contained a discussion of stacking order and object selection regions that is relevant to this discussion. MATLAB determines which callback is invoked based on three regions within a *figure.* When the pointer is within a Handle Graphics object as determined by its `'Position'` property, the pointer is considered to be `on` the object. If the pointer is not `on` an object but is within an object's selection region, the pointer is `near` the object. Finally, if the pointer is within the *figure* but not `on` or `near` another object, the pointer is `off` the other objects. When objects or their selection regions overlap, the stacking order determines which one is selected.

The selection region of Handle Graphics *line, surface, patch, text,* and *axes* objects was discussed in the previous chapter. *Uimenu* objects have no external selection region. The pointer is either `on` a *uimenu* object or it is not. *Uicontrols* have a selection region that extends about 5 pixels beyond the control's position in all directions. The pointer can be either `on` or `near` a control.

A ***button click*** is defined as the press and subsequent release of a mouse button while the mouse pointer is over an object. If the mouse pointer is over a *uimenu, uicontextmenu,* or *uicontrol* object, a button click triggers execution of the object's `'CallBack'` property string as long as the `'Enable'` property is set to `'on'`. The button press prepares the *uicontrol* and often changes the *uicontrol* or *uimenu* visually, and the button release triggers callback execution. If the mouse pointer is not `on` a *uicontrol* or *uimenu,* both button press and button release events are triggered as explained below.

When the mouse button is pressed, a ***button press*** event is created. When this happens with the pointer located within a *Figure* window, a number of different actions can occur, based on the location of the pointer and the proximity of Handle Graphics objects. If an object is selected, it becomes the current object. If no object is selected, the *figure* itself becomes the current object. The *figure's* `'CurrentPoint'` and `'SelectionType'` properties are also updated. The appropriate callbacks are then invoked.

The following table lists the pointer location options and the callbacks executed for a button press event.

Button Press Pointer Location	Action Taken
`on` a *uimenu* item if the `'Enable'` property is `'on'`.	Change *uimenu* appearance and prepare for a release event.

Button Press Pointer Location	Action Taken
`on` a *uicontrol* if the `'Enable'` property is `'on'`.	Change *uicontrol* appearance and prepare for a release event.
`on` a *uimenu* item if the `'Enable'` property is `'off'`.	Ignore button press.
`on` a *uicontrol* if the `'Enable'` property is `'off'` or `'inactive'`.	Evaluate *figure's* `'WindowButtonDownFcn'` callback and then *uicontrol's* `'ButtonDownFcn'` callback.
`on` or `near` any Handle Graphics object except for *uimenus* and *uicontrols*.	Evaluate *figure's* `'WindowButtonDownFcn'` callback and then the object's `'ButtonDownFcn'` callback.
Within a *figure* but not `on` or `near` any other object.	Evaluate *figure's* `'WindowButtonDownFcn'` callback and then *figure's* `'ButtonDownFcn'` callback.

Note that a button press event always invokes the *figure's* `'WindowButtonDownFcn'` callback before the selected object's `'ButtonDownFcn'` callback except when the pointer is `on` a *uicontrol* or *uimenu* object. When the pointer is `near` a *uicontrol* or `on` a *uicontrol* with the `'Enable'` property `'off'` or `'inactive'`, the *uicontrol's* `'ButtonDownFcn'` callback is invoked rather than the `'CallBack'` property after the *figure's* `'WindowButtonDownFcn'` callback has finished. The `'ButtonDownFcn'` callback of a *uimenu* is never invoked.

When the mouse button is released, a ***button release*** event is created. When this happens, the *figure's* `'CurrentPoint'` property is updated and the *figure's* `'WindowButtonUpFcn'` callback is invoked. If the `'WindowButtonUpFcn'` callback is not defined, the `'CurrentPoint'` property is not updated when the button is released.

When the pointer is moved within a figure, ***pointer movement*** events are created. When this happens, the *figure's* `'CurrentPoint'` property is updated and the *figure's* `'WindowButtonMotionFcn'` callback is invoked. If the `'WindowButtonMotionFcn'` callback is not defined, the `'CurrentPoint'` property is not updated when the pointer moves.

31.14 THE EVENT QUEUE

Because GUIs rely on human actions, GUI execution is based on the concept of an ***event queue.*** That is, a GUI is presented to the user. The user in turn interacts with the GUI in an essentially arbitrary way over time, with each interaction creating an event that is placed in the event queue. In addition, other commands that involve *Figure* window input or output generate events. Events include pointer movements and mouse button actions that generate callbacks, `waitfor` and `waitforbuttonpress` functions, and commands that redraw graphics such as `drawnow`, `figure`, `getframe`, or `pause`. Given all these events, MATLAB acts on them in the order in which they appear in the queue. MATLAB manages its event queue in a default manner that is appropriate in most cases. However, the common Handle Graphics object properties `'Interruptible'` and `'BusyAction'` can be used to specify particular actions.

In all cases a callback executes until it reaches a `waitfor`, `waitforbuttonpress`, `drawnow`, `getframe`, `pause`, or `figure` command. ***Callbacks that do not contain any of these commands cannot be interrupted.*** When one of these special commands is reached, MATLAB suspends execution of the callback and examines each of the pending events in the event queue. If the `'Interruptible'` property of the object with the suspended callback is set to `'on'`, which is its default value, all pending events are processed before the suspended callback is resumed. If the `'Interruptible'` property is set to `'off'`, then only pending screen update events are processed. At the same time, if the `'BusyAction'` property of the object with the suspended callback is set to `'cancel'`, the interrupting callback events are discarded. If the `'BusyAction'` property is set to `'queue'`, interrupting callback events are held in the event queue until the interrupted callback finishes. Even if an executing callback is not interruptible, pending screen update events are still processed when the callback reaches a `waitfor`, `waitforbuttonpress`, `drawnow`, `figure`, `getframe`, or `pause` command.

31.15 CALLBACK PROGRAMMING

Handle Graphics and GUI functions in particular make extensive use of callbacks to execute user selections. All these callback character strings are evaluated in the *Command* window workspace using the function `eval`. When the desired actions to be executed by a callback are simple, such as `close(gcbf)`, it is convenient to place the desired actions in the callback string itself. However, most of the time, the desired callback actions require many lines of MATLAB code, many of which produce intermediate variables. Writing all these lines as a single character string to be evaluated is generally not wise for a number of reasons.

First, quotes within the callback must be duplicated so that the quotes are interpreted correctly. Second, the *Command* window workspace becomes polluted by all the temporary variables created. Third, the long callback string is reinterpreted every time the callback is executed, which is relatively slow. And fourth, syntax errors in the callback string are not found until the callback is executed as opposed to when the GUI is created.

The preferred approach to callback programming is to call the function that creates the GUI itself with input arguments that uniquely determine the callback action requested. This approach is commonly called ***switchyard programming.*** For example, suppose a GUI function M-file `mygui.m` creates three pushbuttons, `Apply`, `Revert`, and `Done`, with the callbacks to these buttons being `mygui Apply`, `mygui Revert`, and `mygui Done`, respectively. Note that from command-function duality `mygui Apply` is the same as `mygui('Apply')`, and so on. Then the function `mygui` can implement the callback actions with a Switch-Case construction such as the following.

```
function mygui(arg)
%MYGUI Sample Switchyard Programming Example.

if nargin==0
   arg='Initialize';
end
switch arg
case 'Initialize'
   % code that creates the GUI and sets the callbacks

case 'Apply'
   % code that performs Apply button callback actions

case 'Revert'
   % code that performs Revert button callback actions

case 'Done'
   % code that performs Done button callback actions

otherwise
   % report error?
end
```

The above code segment is easy to read and does not suffer from any of the weaknesses identified earlier for the case where callback actions explicitly appear in the callback string. With the above approach, the GUI is created and managed all from one M-file. GUI creation causes the function to be compiled and loaded into memory. User interaction with the GUI issues callbacks that call the initializing function repeatedly.

The most difficult aspect of callback programming is retrieving data. It is not uncommon for callbacks to need specific handles or other data from the GUI or from another *figure*. Using the switchyard programming approach, each callback creates its own function workspace, which disappears after the callback completes its actions. Fortunately, MATLAB provides several approaches for retrieving or passing data to callbacks.

The functions `gcf`, `gca`, `gco`, `gcbo`, and `gcbf` provide easy access to current objects. In particular, `gcbo` and `gcbf` return handles to the current callback object and *figure*, respectively. Used within a callback, these functions provide access to the object and *figure* that generated the callback.

When other handles or data are required, they can be stored in the `'UserData'` property of an object whose handle is returned by one of the above functions. This is particularly useful when the data stored is a structure with different field names identifying the different data. For example, if variables `x`, `y`, and `z` are to be stored, they can be placed in a structure as `ud.x=x;`, `ud.y=y;`, and `ud.z=z;`. Then `set(H,'UserData',ud)` places the structure `ud` in the `'UserData'` storage location of the object having handle `H`. Later during a callback where `H` is known, the data can be retrieved by issuing `ud=get(H,'UserData')`.

This approach of using the `'UserData'` storage area works as long as you are guaranteed that your GUI has exclusive access to the `'UserData'` property. Setting `'HandleVisibility'` properties to `'Callback'` helps hide handles but does not absolutely ensure data security. When `'UserData'` storage cannot be reliably used, MATLAB provides application data storage. `'ApplicationData'` is a hidden property of all Handle Graphics objects that stores data similar to `'UserData'`. However, `'ApplicationData'` controls access to its data through the functions `getappdata`, `setappdata`, `rmappdata`, and `isappdata`. As a result, data can be reliably stored in graphics objects. These functions are described by their help text:

```
>> help getappdata

 GETAPPDATA Get value of application-defined data.
   VALUE = GETAPPDATA(H, NAME) gets the value of the
   application-defined data with name specified by NAME in the
   object with handle H. If the application-defined data does
   not exist, an empty matrix will be returned in VALUE.

   VALUES = GETAPPDATA(H) returns all application-defined data
   for the object with handle H.

>> help setappdata

 SETAPPDATA Set application-defined data.
   SETAPPDATA(H, NAME, VALUE) sets application-defined data for
   the object with handle H. The application-defined data,
   which is created if it does not already exist, is
   assigned a NAME and a VALUE. VALUE may be anything.

>> help rmappdata

 RMAPPDATA Remove application-defined data.
   RMAPPDATA(H, NAME) removes the application-defined data NAME,
   from the object specified by handle H.

>> help isappdata

 ISAPPDATA True if application-defined data exists.
   ISAPPDATA(H, NAME) returns 1 if application-defined data with
   the specified NAME exists on the object specified by handle H,
   and returns 0 otherwise.
```

Yet another alternative for data storage is provided through the use of ***persistent*** variables. Within a function M-file the function `persistent` can be used to declare one or more variables persistent, meaning that they do not disappear when a function terminates operation but rather remain in the function workspace for future calls to the function. Persistent variables are very much like global variables except that their scope is limited to the function where they are declared. The help text for `persistent` describes its usage as follows.

```
>> help persistent
 PERSISTENT Define persistent variable.
    PERSISTENT X Y Z defines X, Y, and Z as persistent in scope so that X,
    Y and Z maintain their values from one call to the next. PERSISTENT
    can only be used within a function.

    Persistent variables are cleared when the M-file is cleared from
    memory or when the M-file is changed. To keep an M-file in memory
    until MATLAB quits, use MLOCK.

    If the persistent variable does not exist the first time you issue
    the PERSISTENT statement, it will be initialized to the empty matrix.
    Also it is an error to declare a variable persistent if a variable
    with the same name exists in the current workspace.

    Stylistically, persistent variables often have long names with all
    capital letters, but this is not required.

    See also GLOBAL, CLEAR, MLOCK, MUNLOCK, MISLOCKED.
```

Finally, to gain access to `'UserData'` or application data storage, one must know the handle of the object holding the data. When this handle is not known, the `'Tag'` property and the function `findobj` are useful. By providing the desired object a unique `'Tag'` property string, `findobj` can be used to find the handle with the desired identifying tag. For example,

```
>> findobj(0,'Tag','MyUniqueTagString')
```

returns the handle to the object having the specified string.

31.16 M-FILE EXAMPLES

It is difficult to illustrate GUI programming with examples because GUI M-files are typically very long and their user-interactive nature makes it difficult to illustrate their results on a printed page. The best way to become familiar with GUI programming is to find a preexisting one in MATLAB or on a web site, open it in an editor to view the source code, and run it to see what the code produces. Comparing the visual operation of the GUI to the MATLAB code that produces it provides a wealth of information that cannot be gained in any other way.

Given that disclaimer, two GUI functions are illustrated in this section.

The function mmtext shown below demonstrates the use of multiple callbacks. This function allows graphical placement of text similar to the MATLAB function gtext. The added feature in mmtext is that the text can be dragged around the *axes* with the mouse after it has been placed.

```
function h=mmtext(arg)
%MMTEXT Place and Drag Text with Mouse.
% MMTEXT waits for a mouse click on a text object in the current figure
% then allows it to be dragged while the mouse button remains down.
%
% MMTEXT('whatever') places the string 'whatever' on the current axes
% and allows it to be dragged with the mouse
%
% Ht=MMTEXT('whatever') returns the handle to the text object.
%
% MMTEXT becomes inactive after the move is complete or no text
% object is selected.

if nargin==0, arg=0; end

if ischar(arg)  % user entered text to be placed
   Ht=text('Units','normalized',...
           'Position',[.5 .5],...
           'String',arg,...
           'HorizontalAlignment','center',...
           'VerticalAlignment','middle');
   if nargout>0, h=Ht; end
   mmtext(0)  % call mmtext again to drag it

elseif arg==0  % initial call, select text for dragging
   Hf=get(0,'CurrentFigure');
   if isempty(Hf)
      error('No Figure Window Exists.')
   end
   set(Hf,'BackingStore','off',...
          'DoubleBuffer','on',...
          'WindowButtonDownFcn','mmtext(1)')
   figure(Hf)  % bring figure forward

elseif arg==1 & strcmp(get(gco,'type'),'text') % text object selected
   set(gco,'Units','data',...
           'HorizontalAlignment','left',...
           'VerticalAlignment','baseline');
```

```
   set(gcf,'Pointer','topr',...
           'WindowButtonMotionFcn','mmtext(2)',...
           'WindowButtonUpFcn','mmtext(99)')

elseif arg==2  % dragging text object
       cp=get(gca,'CurrentPoint');
       set(gco,'Position',cp(1,1:3))

else           % mouse button up or incorrect object selected, rese
   set(gcf,'WindowButtonDownFcn','',...
           'WindowButtonMotionFcn','',...
           'WindowButtonUpFcn','',...
           'Pointer','arrow',...
           'DoubleBuffer','on',...
           'BackingStore','on')
end
```

The procedure used in `mmtext` is to set the `'WindowButtonDownFcn'` property of the *figure* to `'mmtext(1)'`, which is a callback to `mmtext`. Then `gco` is used to identify the handle of the selected text. Then the `'WindowButtonMotionFcn'` property of the *figure* is set to `'mmtext(2)'` and `'WindowButtonUpFcn'` is set to `'mmtext(99)'`. These three different numerical arguments to `mmtext` cause it to perform the desired operations. Finally, when the text move is completed, the callbacks are all reset to empty strings, thereby disabling text selection and dragging.

The next example, named `mmxy`, creates a *text* object that follows the mouse pointer around in an *axes*. The *text* object dynamically displays the *x-y* coordinates of the mouse pointer until the mouse button is pressed. When this occurs, the function returns the coordinates at the pointer location.

```
function out=mmxy(arg)
%MMXY Show and Get x-y Coordinates Using Mouse.
% MMXY shows the coordinates of the pointer location over the
% the current axes. Clicking the mouse button returns the
% coordinates at the pointer location.
```

```
persistent xy

if nargin==0 % initialize
   Hf=get(0,'CurrentFigure');
   if isempty(Hf) % do nothing if there is no figure
      return
   end
   Ha=get(Hf,'CurrentAxes');
   if isempty(Ha) % do nothing if there is no axes
      return
   end
   v=get(gca,'view');
   if any(v~=[0 90])
       error('MMXY works only for 2-D axes.')
   end
   xlim=get(gca,'XLim'); % get axes limits
   ylim=get(gca,'YLim');
   xy=[sum(xlim) sum(ylim)]/2;
   text('Parent',gca,... % create text to display coordinates
         'Position',xy,...
         'HorizontalAlignment','left',...
         'VerticalAlignment','bottom',...
         'Tag','MMXYtext')
   set(Hf,'Pointer','crossh',...        % change pointer
           'DoubleBuffer','on',...      % eliminate flickering
           'WindowButtonMotionFcn','mmxy move',... % motion callback
           'WindowButtonDownFcn','mmxy done')      % end callback
   figure(Hf) % bring current figure forward

   tf=waitforbuttonpress; % sit and wait for button press
   if ~tf % button press so return data
      out=xy;
   end

elseif strcmp(arg,'move') %'WindowButtonMotionFcn' callback
   cp=get(gca,'CurrentPoint'); % current mouse position
   xy=cp(1,1:2);
   Ht=findobj(gca,'Type','text','Tag','MMXYtext');
   set(Ht,'Position',xy,...
           'String',sprintf('x=  %.2g\ny= %.2g',xy))

elseif strcmp(arg,'done') % mouse click occurred, clean things up
   Ht=findobj(gca,'Type','text','Tag','MMXYtext');
   delete(Ht)
```

```
    set(gcf,'Pointer','arrow',...
            'DoubleBuffer','off',...
            'WindowButtonMotionFcn','',...
            'WindowButtonDownFcn','')
end
```

When called the first time, mmxy creates the *text* object and places it in the center of the current *axes,* changes the pointer shape, and sets up the 'WindowButtonMotionFcn' and 'WindowButtonDownFcn' callbacks. If a mouse button is clicked, the 'WindowButtonDownFcn' callback takes care of the cleanup. While waiting, pointer movement in the *figure* triggers the 'WindowButtonMotionFcn' callback, which updates the text string and its position. This function makes use of the function waitforbuttonpress, which halts operation until a button is pressed. Using this function keeps the first pass through the function from terminating until a button is pressed. In doing so, the persistent variable xy is continually updated in the motion callback. When a button is finally pressed, the first pass through the function copies the pointer location to the output variable and terminates execution.

31.17 GUIDE

GUIDE is a GUI tool supplied with MATLAB that has been designed to make building your own GUIs easier and faster. The function guide provides tools for creating, placing, aligning, and resizing *uicontrol* objects, a property editor and inspector that lists object properties and lets the user modify these properties interactively, and a menu editor for interactive editing and rearranging user-defined pull-down and contextual menus. GUIDE provides an interactive approach to GUI development and is good for laying out the geometry of a GUI. Past versions of this tool were not as productive as simply writing your own GUI M-file using the editor. GUIDE's greatest strength is in GUI object placement. When callbacks contain more than a single line of code, writing them in the M-file editor is still required. The authors found that writing GUI code using the M-file editor and following the layout guidelines in the MATLAB manual *Building GUIs with MATLAB* produced the most productive and most easily maintained GUIs. You may find that the new GUIDE in MATLAB 6 works well for you.

31.18 SUMMARY

Graphical user interface design is not for everyone. However, if you have a need for a GUI, it can be constructed in MATLAB. With the powerful numerical and graphical capabilities available in MATLAB, GUIs can become impressive tools for demonstrating and exploring a wide variety of technical data.

The following table summarizes the GUI functions available in MATLAB, including a number that have not been discussed elsewhere in this chapter. Further information regarding GUI construction can be found in the on-line documentation. A complete listing of GUI object properties can be found in the Appendices.

Function	Description
`uicontrol`	Create user interface control.
`uimenu`	Create user interface menu.
`uicontextmenu`	Create user interface contextual menu.
`drawnow`	Process all pending graphics events and update screen now.
`gcbf`	Get callback *figure* handle.
`gcbo`	Get callback object handle.
`dragrect`	Drag rectangles with the mouse.
`rbbox`	Capture position of a rubberband box.
`selectmoveresize`	Interactively select, move, and resize *axes* and *uicontrols*.
`waitforbuttonpress`	Wait for a key press or a button press over a *figure*.
`waitfor`	Block execution and wait for an event.
`uiwait`	Block execution and wait for resume.
`uiresume`	Resume execution of a blocked M-file.
`uistack`	Control the stacking order of objects.
`uisuspend`	Suspend the interactive state of a *figure*.
`uirestore`	Restore the interactive state of a *figure*.
`uiclearmode`	Clear the current interactive mode.
`guide`	Graphical user interface design environment.
`inspect`	Inspect object properties.
`align`	Align *uicontrols* and *axes*.
`propedit`	Property editor.

Function	Description
makemenu	Create *uimenu* structure.
umtoggle	Toggle checked status of a *uimenu* item.
getptr	Get *figure* pointer.
setptr	Set *figure* pointer.
hidegui	Hide or unhide GUI.
movegui	Move GUI window to a specified part of screen.
overobj	Get handle of object that pointer is over.
popupstr	Get popup menu selection string.
remapfig	Transform positions of objects in a *figure*.

32

Dialog Boxes

In the preceding chapter the tools available in MATLAB to create GUIs were discussed. These tools allow one to create user interfaces that perform almost any imaginable operation. As computers have evolved, a number of GUIs or dialog boxes have more or less become standard features. This chapter discusses the standard dialog boxes available within MATLAB. To be clear, these are not the dialog boxes one uses when interacting with MATLAB but rather dialog boxes that can be used in MATLAB programming and application development.

32.1 FILE SELECTION

Essentially every computer application offers the capability to open and save data files. To navigate the directory structure, operating systems or window managers provide dialog boxes to perform the tasks of identifying file names and directory paths. In MATLAB these tasks are performed by the functions `uigetfile` and `uiputfile`. Neither of these functions actually opens or saves a file. All they do is return a file name and a directory path that can be used along with the low-level file I/O functions in MATLAB to perform the open and save operations. (See Chapter 13 for information about the low-level file I/O functions in MATLAB.)

When possible, `uigetfile` and `uiputfile` use standard dialog boxes available on your computer platform. As a result, their layout varies from platform to platform, but their functionality does not. The help text for `uigetfile` describes its use.

```
>> help uigetfile

UIGETFILE Standard open file dialog box.
   [FILENAME, PATHNAME] = UIGETFILE('filterSpec', 'dialogTitle')
   displays a dialog box for the user to fill in, and returns the
   filename and path strings. A successful return occurs only if
   the file exists. If the user selects a file that does not exist,
   an error message is displayed, and control returns to the dialog box.
   The user may then enter another filename, or press the Cancel button.

   The filterSpec parameter determines the initial display of files in
   the dialog box. For example '*.m' lists all the MATLAB M-files.

   Parameter 'dialogTitle' is a string containing the title of the dialog
   box.

   The output variable FILENAME is a string containing the name of the
   file selected in the dialog box. If the user presses the Cancel button
   or if any error occurs, it is set to 0.

   The output parameter PATHNAME is a string containing the path of
   the file selected in the dialog box. If the user presses the Cancel
   button or if any error occurs, it is set to 0.

   [FILENAME, PATHNAME] = UIGETFILE('filterSpec', 'dialogTitle', X, Y)
   places the dialog box at screen position [X,Y] in pixel units.
   Not all systems support this option.

   See also UIPUTFILE.
```

Using `uigetfile` to find the `startup.m` file on the author's computer produces the following results.

```
>> [fname,dirpath] = uigetfile('*.m')
fname =
startup.m
dirpath =
C:\matlabR12\work\
```

Appending the file name to the directory path gives the unique file specification for `startup.m`, for example,

```
>> myfile = [dirpath fname]
myfile =
C:\matlabR12\work\startup.m
```

It is important to note that `uigetfile` is not limited to directories on the MATLAB search path. The directory path returned will be for whatever directory the dialog box points to when it is dismissed. In addition, dialog box positioning arguments do not work on Windows platforms. On platforms where they do work, position is specified in pixels relative to the upper left corner of the computer screen.

The function `uiputfile` is described by the following help text.

```
>> help uiputfile

 UIPUTFILE Standard save file dialog box.
    [FILENAME, PATHNAME] = UIPUTFILE('initFile', 'dialogTitle')
    displays a dialog box for the user to fill in and returns the
    filename and path strings.

    The 'initFile' parameter determines the initial display of files
    in the dialog box. Full file name specifications as well as wildcards
    are allowed. For example, 'newfile.m' initializes the display to
    that particular file and lists all other existing.m files. This may
    be used to provide a default file name. A wildcard specification such
    as '*.m' lists all the existing MATLAB M-files.

    Parameter 'dialogTitle' is a string containing the title of the dialog
    box.

    The output variable FILENAME is a string containing the name of the
    file selected in the dialog box. If the user presses the Cancel button
    or if any error occurs, it is set to 0.

    The output variable PATH is a string containing the name of the path
    selected in the dialog box. If the user presses the Cancel button
    or if any error occurs, it is set to 0.

    [FILENAME, PATHNAME] = UIPUTFILE('initFile', 'dialogTitle',X,Y)
    places the dialog box at screen position [X,Y] in pixel units.
    Not all systems support this option.

    Example:
            [newmatfile, newpath] = uiputfile('*.mat', 'Save As');

    See also UIGETFILE.
```

Using uiputfile to save a MAT-file in the work directory on the author's computer produces the following results.

```
>> [fname,dirpath] = uiputfile('*.mat')
fname =
mydata
dirpath =
C:\matlabR12\work\
```

Here, the string mydata was entered as the file name in the dialog box. Even though '*.mat' specified the file type, '.mat' was not automatically appended to the returned fname. It is up to the programmer to append the file extension.

32.2 COLOR SELECTION

Specifying colors in MATLAB based on RGB triples is straightforward but lacks visual feedback about the actual color specified by a given triple. In addition, most graphics objects have a 'Color' property that can be set. As described in its help text below, the function uisetcolor provides a GUI for choosing RGB triples or setting the color of a particular graphics object.

```
>> help uisetcolor

 UISETCOLOR Color selection dialog box.
    C = UISETCOLOR displays a color selection dialog appropriate to
    the windowing system, and returns the color selected by the
    user. The dialog is initialized to white.
    C = UISETCOLOR([R G B]) displays a dialog initialized to the
    specified color, and returns the color selected by the user.
    R, G, and B must be values between 0 and 1.
    C = UISETCOLOR(H) displays a dialog initialized to the color of
    the object specified by handle H, returns the color selected by
    the user, and applies it to the object. H must be the handle
    to an object containing a color property.
    C = UISETCOLOR(...,'dialogTitle') displays a dialog with the
    specified title.

    If the user presses Cancel from the dialog box, or if any error
    occurs, the output value is set to the input RGB triple, if provided;
    otherwise, it is set to 0.

    Example:
            hText = text(.5,.5,'Hello World');
            C = uisetcolor(hText, 'Set Text Color')
```

As with `uigetfile` and `uiputfile`, the function `uisetcolor` uses the standard color dialog box available on your computer platform when one is available. As a result, the layout and features of `uisetcolor` vary from platform to platform, but the functionality does not.

32.3 FONT SELECTION

Another built-in function named `uisetfont` provides a GUI for selecting fonts and font attributes as described in its help text below.

```
>> help uisetfont

 UISETFONT Font selection dialog box.
    S = UISETFONT(FIN, 'dialogTitle') displays a dialog box for the
    user to fill in, and applies the selected font to the input
    graphics object.
    All the parameters are optional.

    If parameter FIN is used, it must either specify a handle to a
    font-related text, uicontrol, axes object, or it must be a
    font structure.

    If FIN is a handle to an object, the font properties currently
    assigned to this object are used to initialize the font dialog box.

    If FIN is a structure, its fields must be some subset of
    FontName, FontUnits, FontSize, FontWeight, or FontAngle, and must
    have values appropriate for any object with font properties.

    If parameter 'dialogTitle' is used, it is a string containing the
    title of the dialog box.

    The output S is a structure. The structure S is returned with the
    font property names as fields. The fields are FontName,
    FontUnits, FontSize, FontWeight, and FontAngle.

    If the user presses Cancel from the dialog box, or if any error
    occurs, the output value is set to 0.

    Example:
          s = uisetfont(hText, 'Update Font');
          if isstruct(s)           % Check for cancel
             set(hText_2, s);
          end

    See also LISTFONTS
```

Using the function to choose Palatino 12-point italics produces the following results.

```
>> fc = uisetfont
fc =
      FontName: 'Palatino'
     FontUnits: 'points'
      FontSize: 12
    FontWeight: 'normal'
     FontAngle: 'italic'
```

Here `fc` is a structure containing the features chosen in the `uisetfont` GUI. The results are in the proper form to set the font properties of any *text* object.

32.4 M-FILE DIALOG BOXES

In addition to the built-in dialog functions discussed in earlier sections, MATLAB offers a number of dialog boxes implemented as M-file functions. Some of these functions prompt the user for input of some kind. The functions available include `axlimdlg`, `dialog`, `inputdlg`, `menu`, and `msgbox`.

The function `axlimdlg` provides a rudimentary dialog box for setting plot axes limits. The *Figure* window editing features in MATLAB 6 are much more comprehensive. The function `inputdlg` creates a set of text edit box *uicontrols* and prompts the user for input into each. This function is useful for prompting the user for a few values. `Menu` offers the user a selection of alternatives using *uicontrol* pushbuttons.

The functions `dialog` and `msgbox` are generic dialog box creation functions. Of these functions, `dialog` simply creates a *Figure* window with default properties set that are appropriate for *Figure* windows that do not contain any *axes* objects. *Figure* windows created using `dialog` use minimal system resources. For example, they do not allocate memory for a colormap. The function `msgbox` is used by all message dialog boxes and manages all the underlying activities required to put up a dialog box and accept input.

The standard message dialog boxes in MATLAB include `errordlg`, `helpdlg`, `questdlg`, and `warndlg`. These boxes display an appropriate icon along with at least one pushbutton to acknowledge and dismiss the dialog box. In addition to being helpful in application development, these functions are good examples of GUI construction to study. The help text for these dialog boxes shown below describes their usage.

```
>> help errordlg

 ERRORDLG Error dialog box.
   HANDLE = ERRORDLG(ErrorString,DlgName,CREATEMODE) creates an
   error dialog box which displays ErrorString in a window
   named DlgName. A pushbutton labeled OK must be pressed
   to make the error box disappear.
   ErrorString will accept any valid string input but a cell
   array is preferred.
```

```
>> help helpdlg

 HELPDLG Help dialog box.
   HANDLE = HELPDLG(HELPSTRING,DLGNAME) displays the
   message HelpString in a dialog box with title DLGNAME.
   If a Help dialog with that name is already on the screen,
   it is brought to the front. Otherwise a new one is created.
   HelpString will accept any valid string input but a cell
   array is preferred.

>> help warndlg

 WARNDLG Warning dialog box.
   HANDLE = WARNDLG(WARNSTRING,DLGNAME) creates an warning dialog box
   which displays WARNSTRING in a window named DLGNAME. A pushbutton
   labeled OK must be pressed to make the warning box disappear.

   HANDLE = WARNDLG(WARNSTRING,DLGNAME,CREATEMODE) allows CREATEMODE
   options that are the same as those offered by MSGBOX. The default
   value for CREATEMODE is 'non-modal'.
   WARNSTRING may be any valid string format. Cell arrays are
   preferred.

>> help questdlg

 QUESTDLG Question dialog box.
   ButtonName=QUESTDLG(Question) creates a modal dialog box that
   automatically wraps the cell array or string (vector or matrix)
   Question to fit an appropriately sized window. The name of the
   button that is pressed is returned in ButtonName. The Title of
   the figure may be specified by adding a second string argument.
   Question will be interpreted as a normal string.

   QUESTDLG uses WAITFOR to suspend execution until the user responds.

   The default set of buttons names for QUESTDLG are 'Yes','No' and
   'Cancel'. The default answer for the above calling syntax is 'Yes'.
   This can be changed by adding a third argument which specifies the
   default Button. i.e. ButtonName=questdlg(Question,Title,'No').

   Up to 3 custom button names may be specified by entering
   the button string name(s) as additional arguments to the function
   call. If custom ButtonName's are entered, the default ButtonName
   must be specified by adding an extra argument DEFAULT, i.e.

     ButtonName=questdlg(Question,Title,Btn1,Btn2,DEFAULT);

   where DEFAULT=Btn1. This makes Btn1 the default answer.
```

```
To use TeX interpretation for the Question string, a data
structure must be used for the last argument, i.e.

  ButtonName=questdlg(Question,Title,Btn1,Btn2,OPTIONS);

The OPTIONS structure must include the fields Default and Interpreter.
Interpreter may be 'none' or 'tex' and Default is the default button
name to be used.
```

32.5 SUMMARY

The dialog box functions available in MATLAB are summarized in the table below.

Function	Description
`axlimdlg`	Axes limits dialog box.
`dialog`	Create figure for dialog box or GUI.
`errordlg`	Error dialog box.
`helpdlg`	Help dialog box.
`inputdlg`	Input dialog box.
`listdlg`	List selection dialog box.
`menu`	Menu choice selection dialog box.
`msgbox`	Generic message dialog box.
`pagedlg`	Page position dialog box.
`pagesetupdlg`	Page setup dialog box.
`printdlg`	Print dialog box.
`printpreview`	Print preview dialog box.
`questdlg`	Question dialog box.
`uigetfile`	Standard open file dialog box.
`uiputfile`	Standard save file dialog box.
`uisetcolor`	Color selection dialog box.
`uisetfont`	Font and font attributes dialog box.
`waitbar`	Display wait bar.
`warndlg`	Warning dialog box.

33

MATLAB Classes and Object-Oriented Programming

MATLAB has a number of fundamental data types otherwise known as ***classes***. For example, arrays of numbers are commonly double-precision arrays. A variable containing such an array has a class called `double`. Similarly, character strings are another data type or class. Variables containing character strings have a class called `char`. Consider the following example.

```
>> pi          % a simple double
ans =
       3.1416
>> class(pi)
ans =
double
>> s = 'pi'    % a simple string
s =
pi
```

```
>> class(s)
ans =
char
```

Data types or classes in basic MATLAB include `double`, `char`, `logical`, `cell`, and `struct`. These data types are the most commonly used classes in MATLAB. In addition, MATLAB includes the lesser-used classes `sparse`, `function handle`, `inline`, `java`, `single`, and a variety of integer data types.

For each of these classes, MATLAB defines operations that can be performed. For example, addition is a defined operator for elements of the class `double` but is not defined for elements of the class `char` or for elements of the class `cell`.

```
>> x = pi+2
x =
        5.1416
>> y = 'hello' + 'there'
y =
   220   205   209   222   212
>> {'hello' 'there'}+{'sunny' 'day'}
??? Error using ==> +
Function '+' not defined for variables of class 'cell'.
```

Here adding two character strings created a numerical array rather than a character string. Rather than report an error, MATLAB chose to convert `'hello'` and `'there'` to their ASCII numerical equivalents and then perform element-by-element numerical addition. Even though MATLAB produced a result for this character string example, it did so only after converting the elements on the right-hand side to the class `double`. MATLAB does this implicit type or class conversion for convenience, not because addition is defined for character strings. On the other hand, trying to add two cell arrays produces an immediate error.

Starting with version 5, MATLAB added the ability to define new operations for the basic data types and more importantly added the ability to create user-defined data types or classes. Creating and using data types is called ***object-oriented programming*** (OOP), in which variables in each data type or class are called ***objects.*** Operations on objects are defined by methods that encapsulate data and overload operators and functions. The vocabulary of OOP includes terms such as *operator* and *function overloading, data encapsulation, methods, inheritance,* and *aggregation.* These terms and the fundamental principles of object-oriented programming in MATLAB are discussed in this chapter.

33.1 OVERLOADING

Before getting involved in the details of OOP and creating new variable classes, consider the process of overloading standard classes in MATLAB. The techniques used to overload standard classes is identical to that for user-created classes. So once overloading is understood for standard classes, it is straightforward for user-created classes.

When the MATLAB interpreter encounters an operator such as addition, or a function with one or more input arguments, it considers the data type or class of the arguments to the operator or function and acts according to the rules it has defined internally. For example, addition means to compute the numerical sum of the arguments if the arguments are numerical or can be converted to numerical values, such as character strings. When the internal rules for an operation or function are redefined, the operator or function is said to be ***overloaded.***

> ***Operator*** and ***function overloading*** allow a user to redefine what actions MATLAB performs when it encounters an operator or function. The collection of rules or M-files for redefining operators and functions is called ***methods.*** The files themselves are commonly referred to as method functions.

In MATLAB the redefined rules for interpreting operators and functions are simply function M-files stored in ***class directories*** just off the MATLAB search path. That is, class directories themselves are not and cannot be on the MATLAB search path, but they are and must be subdirectories of directories that are on the MATLAB search path. To find class subdirectories MATLAB requires that they be named as `@class`, where `class` is the variable class that the M-files in `@class` apply to. In addition, MATLAB supports multiple class directories. That is, there can be multiple `@class` directories just off the MATLAB path. When looking for functions in class directories, MATLAB follows the order given by the MATLAB search path and uses the first desired method function file found.

For example, if a directory `@char` appears just off the MATLAB search path, the M-files contained in this directory can redefine operations and functions on character strings. To illustrate this consider the function M-file `plus.m` shown below.

```
function s=plus(s1,s2)
% Horizontal Concatenation for char Objects.

if ischar(s1)&ischar(s2)
   s=cat(2,s1(:).',s2(:).');
elseif isnumeric(s2)
   s=double(s1)+s2;
else
   error('Operator + Not Defined.')
end
```

If this M-file is stored in any `@char` directory just off the MATLAB search path, addition of character strings is redefined as horizontal concatenation. For example, repeating the statement `y = 'hello' + 'there'` made earlier becomes

```
>> y = 'hello' + 'there'
y =
hellothere
```

MATLAB no longer converts the strings on the right-hand side to their ASCII equivalents and adds the numerical results! What MATLAB did was (1) interpret that character strings appear on both sides of the addition symbol +; (2) look down the MATLAB search path for an `@char` subdirectory; (3) find the one we created and look for a function M-file named `plus.m`; (4) find the above `plus.m` function, pass the two arguments to the addition operator to the function and let it determine what action to perform; and (5) finally return the function output as the result of the addition operation.

To speed operation MATLAB ***caches*** class subdirectories at startup. So for the above to work, one must create the subdirectory and M-file and then restart MATLAB or issue the `rehash` command to get MATLAB to cache the newly created class subdirectory and associated M-files.

When addition is performed between two different data types such as `char` and `double`, MATLAB considers the precedence and order of the arguments. For variables of equal precedence, MATLAB gives precedence to the leftmost argument to an operator or function, for example,

```
>> z = 2 + 'hello'
z =
   106   103   110   110   113
```

The classes `double` and `char` have equal precedence. As a result, MATLAB considers addition to be numerical and applies its internal rules converting `'hello'` to its ASCII equivalent and performing numerical addition. On the other hand, if the order of the operands above is reversed,

```
>> z = 'hello' + 2
z =
   106   103   110   110   113
```

MATLAB considers addition to be a `char` class operation. In this case the above `plus.m` function is called as `plus('hello',2)`. As written, `plus.m` identifies this mixed class call with `isnumeric(s2)` and returns the same result as `z = 2 + 'hello'`.

As illustrated above, a function named `plus.m` defines addition in a class subdirectory. To support overloading of other operators, MATLAB assigns the function names shown in the following table to operators.

<table>
<tr><th>Operator</th><th>Function Name</th><th>Description</th></tr>
<tr><td>a + b</td><td>plus(a,b)</td><td>Numerical addition.</td></tr>
<tr><td>a - b</td><td>minus(a,b)</td><td>Numerical subtraction.</td></tr>
<tr><td>-a</td><td>uminus(a)</td><td>Unary minus.</td></tr>
<tr><td>+a</td><td>uplus(a)</td><td>Unary plus.</td></tr>
<tr><td>a .* b</td><td>times(a,b)</td><td>Element-by-element multiplication.</td></tr>
<tr><td>a * b</td><td>mtimes(a,b)</td><td>Matrix multiplication.</td></tr>
<tr><td>a ./ b</td><td>rdivide(a,b)</td><td>Element-by-element right division.</td></tr>
<tr><td>a .\ b</td><td>ldivide(a,b)</td><td>Element-by-element left division.</td></tr>
<tr><td>a / b</td><td>mrdivide(a,b)</td><td>Matrix right division.</td></tr>
<tr><td>a \ b</td><td>mldivide(a,b)</td><td>Matrix left division.</td></tr>
<tr><td>a .^ b</td><td>power(a,b)</td><td>Element-by-element exponentiation.</td></tr>
<tr><td>a ^ b</td><td>mpower(a,b)</td><td>Matrix exponentiation.</td></tr>
<tr><td>a < b</td><td>lt(a,b)</td><td>Less than.</td></tr>
<tr><td>a > b</td><td>gt(a,b)</td><td>Greater than.</td></tr>
<tr><td>a <= b</td><td>le(a,b)</td><td>Less than or equal to.</td></tr>
<tr><td>a >= b</td><td>ge(a,b)</td><td>Greater than or equal to.</td></tr>
<tr><td>a ~= b</td><td>ne(a,b)</td><td>Not equal.</td></tr>
<tr><td>a == b</td><td>eq(a,b)</td><td>Equal.</td></tr>
<tr><td>a & b</td><td>and(a,b)</td><td>Logical AND.</td></tr>
<tr><td>a | b</td><td>or(a,b)</td><td>Logical OR.</td></tr>
<tr><td>~a</td><td>not(a,b)</td><td>Logical NOT.</td></tr>
<tr><td>a:d:b
a:b</td><td>colon(a,d,b)
colon(a,b)</td><td>Colon operator.</td></tr>
<tr><td>a'</td><td>ctranspose(a)</td><td>Conjugate transpose.</td></tr>
<tr><td>a.'</td><td>transpose(a)</td><td>Transpose.</td></tr>
</table>

Operator	Function Name	Description
`[a b]`	`horzcat(a,b)`	Horizontal concatenation.
`[a; b]`	`vertcat(a,b)`	Vertical concatenation.
`a(s1,s2,...)`	`subsref(a,s)`	Subscripted reference.
`a(s1,s2,...) = b`	`subsasgn(a,s)`	Subscripted assignment.
`b(a)`	`subsindex(a)`	Subscript index.
	`display(a)`	*Command* window output.
`end`	`end(a,k,n)`	Subscript interpretation of `end`.

Continuing with the above `char` class example, note that subtraction can be overloaded with the following function.

```
function s=minus(s1,s2)
% Subtraction for char Objects.
% Delete occurrences of s2 in s1.

if ischar(s1)&ischar(s2)
   s=strrep(s1,s2,'');
elseif isnumeric(s2)
   s=double(s1)-s2;
else
   error('Operator - Not Defined.')
end
```

As defined, subtraction is interpreted as the deletion of matching substrings, for example,

```
>> z = 'hello' - 'e'
z =
hllo
>> a = 'hello' - 2
a =
   102    99   106   106   109
```

Again the mixed-class case returns the MATLAB default action.

When multiple operators appear in a statement, MATLAB follows its usual order of precedence rules, working from left to right in an expression, for example,

```
>> a = 'hello' + ' ' + 'there'
a =
hello there
>> a - 'e'
ans =
hllo thr
>> a = 'hello' + ' ' + ('there' - 'e')
a =
hello thr
```

When a statement assigns a character string to an output without a terminating semicolon, MATLAB displays the string in the *Command* window. What is displayed in the *Command* window can be overloaded using the function `display.m`. While the default character display behavior of MATLAB is convenient, it can be overloaded with a function such as that shown below.

```
function display(s)
% Display for char objects.

isloose=strcmp(get(0,'FormatSpacing'),'loose');
ssiz=size(s);

if isloose, disp(' '), end
disp(['A Character Array of Size: ' mat2str(ssiz)])
if isloose, disp(' '), end
```

This function redefines how character strings are displayed in the *Command* window, for example,

```
>> 'hello'
A Character Array of Size: [1 5]
>> a = 'hello' + ' ' + 'there'
A Character Array of Size: [1 11]
>> format loose
>> a

A Character Array of Size: [1 11]
```

```
>> format compact
>> s=char('hello','there')
A Character Array of Size: [2 5]
```

The above discussion describes how MATLAB overloads operators. Overloading functions follows the same procedure. In this case, the function stored in the class subdirectory has the same name as that of the standard MATLAB function, for example,

```
function s=cat(varargin)
%CAT Concatenate Strings as a Row.

if length(varargin)>1 & ~ischar(varargin{2})
   error('CAT Not Defined for Mixed Classes.')
else
   s=cat(2,varargin{:});
end
```

This function overloads the function `cat` for character strings. It is called only if the first argument to the `cat` function is a character string; that is, it is of class `char`. If the first argument is numerical, the standard `cat` function is called, as in the example

```
>> cat('hello','there') % call overloaded cat
ans =
hellothere
>> cat('hello',2)       % call overloaded cat
??? Error using ==> char/cat
CAT Not Defined for Mixed Classes.

>> cat(2,'hello')       % call built-in cat
ans =
hello
```

In addition to the operator overloading functions listed in this section, MATLAB provides several OOP utility functions. They include `methods`, `isa`, `class`, `loadobj`, and `saveobj`. The functions `isa` and `class` help to identify the data type or class of a variable or object, for example,

```
>> a = 'hello';
>> class(a) % return class of argument
ans =
char
```

```
>> isa(a,'double') % logical class test
ans =
   0
>> isa(a,'char') % logical class test
ans =
   1
```

The function `methods` returns a listing of the methods or overloading operators and functions associated with a given class, for example,

```
>> methods cell

Methods for class cell:

deblank    ismember  setxor    strcat    union
intersect  setdiff   sort      strmatch  unique
```

This result shows that MATLAB itself has overloading functions that are called when input arguments are cell arrays. These functions extend the functionality of basic MATLAB functions to cell arrays without requiring the basic functions themselves to be rewritten to accept cell array arguments.

Finally, the functions `loadobj` and `saveobj` are called if they exist whenever the functions `load` and `save` are called with user-defined classes, respectively. Adding these functions to a class subdirectory allows one to modify a user-defined variable after a load operation or before a save operation.

33.2 CLASS CREATION

Operator and function overloading are key aspects of OOP. MATLAB's implementation relies on a simple scheme whereby the methods associated with a variable class are stored in class directories just off the MATLAB search path. The methods themselves are contained in standard M-files. (They can be P-file or MEX-file equivalents of M-files as well.) User-defined classes use the same scheme for method creation and storage. This section illustrates the creation of user-defined classes.

A new variable class is created when a class directory `@`*`classname`* is created and populated by at least two function M-files. The first M-file has the name *`classname`*`.m`, which is used to define the creation of variables in the new class. This M-file is called the ***constructor.*** The second M-file has the name `display.m` and is used to display the new variable in the *Command* window. No variable class is useful without additional method M-files, but the constructor and `display.m` are a minimum requirement.

In the vocabulary of OOP, the constructor creates an ***instance*** of the class. This instance is an object having methods that overload how operators and functions act in the presence of the object.

The constructor function *classname*.m is a standard function call with input arguments containing the data needed to create an output variable of the desired class. For greatest flexibility the constructor should handle three different sets of input arguments. Just as there are empty strings, arrays, cells, and so on, the constructor should produce an empty variable if no arguments are passed to it. On the other hand, if the constructor is passed a variable of the same class as that created by the constructor, the constructor should simply pass it as an output argument. Finally, if creation data is provided, a new variable of the desired class should be created. In this last case, the input data can be checked for appropriateness. Inside the constructor, the data used to create a variable of the desired class are stored in the fields of a structure. Once the structure fields are populated, the new variable is created by a call to the `class` function. For example, the constructor function for a rational polynomial object is shown below.

```
function r=mmrp(varargin)
%MMRP Mastering MATLAB Rational Polynomial Object Constructor.
% MMRP(p) creates a polynomial object from the polynomial vector p
% with 'x' as the variable.
% MMRP(p,'s') creates the polynomial object using the letter 's' as
% the variable in the display of p.
% MMRP(n,d) creates a rational polynomial object from the numerator
% polynomial vector n and denominator polynomial d.
% MMRP(n,d,'s') creates the rational polynomial using the letter 's' as
% the variable in the display of p.
%
% All coefficients must be real.

[n,d,v,msg]=local_parse(varargin); % parse input arguments
if isempty(v) % input was mmrp so return it
   r=n;
else
```

```
    error(msg) % return error if it exists
    tol=100*eps;
    if length(d)==1 & abs(d)>tol % enforce scalar d=1
         r.n=n/d;
         r.d=1;
    elseif abs(d(1))>tol % make d monic if possible
         r.n=n/d(1);
         r.d=d/d(1);
    else                  % can't be made monic
         r.n=n;
         r.d=d;
    end
    r.v=v(1);

    r=class(r,'mmrp');    % create object from parts
    r=minreal(r);         % pole-zero cancellation
end
```

To simplify the function, parsing of the input arguments is handled by a subfunction entitled `local_parse`. This function is not displayed, but it returns four outputs, `n`, `d`, `v`, and `msg`. The variables `n` and `d` are numerical row vectors containing the coefficients of the numerator and denominator of the rational polynomial, respectively. The variable `v` contains the string variable used to display the polynomial. Last, `msg` contains an error message if `local_parse` encounters invalid inputs.

Creation of the rational polynomial object is performed by the statement `r=class(r,'mmrp')`. This usage of the function `class` is valid only within the constructor itself. In other contexts `class` returns the character string name of the class of its single input argument. The above constructor considers all three sets of input arguments. If no input arguments exist, `n`, `d`, and `v` are returned to create an empty rational polynomial. If the input argument is a rational polynomial object, it is simply returned as the output argument. Finally, if data is supplied, a rational polynomial object is created. In the simplest case the denominator is simply equal to 1 and the display variable is `'x'`. The last assignment statement in `mmrp` passes the created rational polynomial to the overloaded function `minreal`, which returns a minimal realization of the object by canceling like poles and zeros.

Within the constructor it is important that the structure fields be created in the same order under all circumstances. Two structures containing the same fields cannot be equivalent unless the fields have been defined in the same order. Violation of this rule causes the created object to behave erratically.

Given the above constructor, the associated display.m file is shown below.

```
function display(r)
%DISPLAY Command Window Display of Rational Polynomial Objects.

loose=strcmp(get(0,'FormatSpacing'),'loose');
if loose, disp(' '), end
var=inputname(1);
if isempty(var)
     disp('ans =')
else
     disp([var ' ='])
end
nstr=mmp2str(r.n,r.v); % convert polynomial to string
nlen=length(nstr);
if length(r.d)>1 | r.d~=1
     dstr=mmp2str(r.d,r.v);
else
     dstr=[];
end
dlen=length(dstr);
dash='-';
if loose, disp(' '), end
if dlen % denominator exists
     m=max(nlen,dlen);
     disp('MMRP Rational Polynomial Object:')
     disp([blanks(ceil((m-nlen)/2)) nstr]);
     disp(dash(ones(1,m)));
     disp([blanks(fix((m-dlen)/2)) dstr]);
else
     disp('MMRP Rational Polynomial Object:')
     disp(nstr);
end
if loose, disp(' '), end
```

This function calls the function mmp2str to convert a numerical polynomial vector and a desired variable to a character string representation. This function exists elsewhere on the MATLAB search path, not in the @mmrp directory. If it existed in the class directory, MATLAB would not find it since the arguments to mmp2str are double and char, respectively, and not of class mmrp. As described in the last section, a method function is called only if the leftmost or highest-precedence input argument has a class that matches that of the method.

Within a method function, it is possible to act on objects as shown in the last assignment statement in the constructor `r=minreal(r)`, where the variable `r` on the right-hand side is an object having class `mmrp`. There are two exceptions to this property. ***The overloading functions*** `subsref` ***and*** `subsasgn` ***are not called when subscripted reference and subscripted assignment appear within a method function.*** This allows the user to more freely access and manipulate a class variable within a method function.

It is also possible to act on the data contained in an object by simply addressing the structure fields of the object as shown in numerous places within `display.m`. In this case, the class of the data determines how MATLAB acts.

> Outside method functions, for example, in the *Command* window, it is not possible to gain access to the fields of an object. Nor is it possible to determine the number of or names of the fields. This property is called data encapsulation.

The following examples demonstrate the creation and display of rational polynomial objects.

```
>> p = mmrp([1 2 3])
p =
MMRP Rational Polynomial Object:
x^2 + 2x^1 + 3

>> q = mmrp([1 2 3],[4 5 6],'z')
q =
MMRP Rational Polynomial Object:
0.25z^2 + 0.5z^1 + 0.75
------------------------
z^2 + 1.25z^1 + 1.5

>> r = mmrp(conv([1 2],[1 4]),conv([1 2],[1 3]))
r =
MMRP Rational Polynomial Object:
x^1 + 4
-------
x^1 + 3
```

Rational polynomial objects have little value unless operators and functions are overloaded. In particular, it is convenient to define arithmetic operations on `mmrp` objects. The following M-files define addition, subtraction, multiplication, and division for `mmrp` objects. Since multiplication and division offer multiple methods, they are all overloaded with the associated polynomial manipulation.

```
function r=plus(a,b)
%PLUS Addition for Rational Polynomial Objects.

if isnumeric(a)
      rn=mmpadd(a*b.d,b.n); % see chapter 19 for mmpadd
      rd=b.d;
      rv=b.v;
elseif isnumeric(b)
      rn=mmpadd(b*a.d,a.n);
      rd=a.d;
      rv=a.v;
else % both polynomial objects
      if ~isequal(a.d,b.d)
            rn=mmpadd(conv(a.n,b.d),conv(b.n,a.d));
            rd=conv(a.d,b.d);
      else
            rn=mmpadd(a.n,b.n);
            rd=b.d;
      end
      if ~strcmp(a.v,b.v)
            warning('Variables Not Identical')
      end
      rv=a.v;
end
r=mmrp(rn,rd,rv);
```

```
function r=minus(a,b)
%MINUS Subtraction for Rational Polynomial Objects.

r=a+(-b); % use plus and uminus to implement minus
```

```
function r=uminus(a)
%UPLUS Unary Minus for Rational Polynomial Objects.

r=mmrp(-a.n,a.d,a.v);
```

```
function r=times(a,b)
%TIMES Dot Times for Rational Polynomial Objects.

a=mmrp(a); % convert inputs to mmrp if necessary
b=mmrp(b);
rn=conv(a.n,b.n);
rd=conv(a.d,b.d);
if ~strcmp(a.v,b.v)
     warning('Variables Not Identical')
end
rv=a.v;
r=mmrp(rn,rd,rv);
```

```
function r=mtimes(a,b)
%MTIMES Times for Rational Polynomial Objects.

r=a.*b; % simply call times.m
```

```
function r=rdivide(a,b)
%RDIVIDE Right Dot Division for Rational Polynomial Objects.

a=mmrp(a); % convert inputs to mmrp if necessary
b=mmrp(b);
rn=conv(a.n,b.d);
rd=conv(a.d,b.n);
if ~strcmp(a.v,b.v)
     warning('Variables Not Identical')
end
rv=a.v;
r=mmrp(rn,rd,rv);
```

```
function r=mrdivide(a,b)
%MRDIVIDE Right Division for Rational Polynomial Objects.

r=a./b; % simply call rdivide.m
```

```
function r=ldivide(a,b)
%LDIVIDE Left Dot Division for Rational Polynomial Objects.

r=b./a; % simply call rdivide.m
```

```
function r=mldivide(a,b)
%MLDIVIDE Left Division for Rational Polynomial Objects.

r=b./a; % simply call rdivide.m
```

The above method functions are self-explanatory in that they implement simply polynomial arithmetic. Examples of their use include the following.

```
>> a = mmrp([1 2 3])
a =
MMRP Rational Polynomial Object:
x^2 + 2x^1 + 3
>> b = a + 2                    % addition
b =
MMRP Rational Polynomial Object:
x^2 + 2x^1 + 5
>> a - b                        % subtraction
ans =
MMRP Rational Polynomial Object:
-2
```

```
>> a + b                          % addition
ans =
MMRP Rational Polynomial Object:
2x^2 + 4x^1 + 8

>> 2*b                            % multiplication
ans =
MMRP Rational Polynomial Object:
2x^2 + 4x^1 + 10
>> a * b                          % multiplication
ans =
MMRP Rational Polynomial Object:
x^4 + 4x^3 + 12x^2 + 16x^1 + 15

>> b/2                            % division
ans =
MMRP Rational Polynomial Object:
0.5x^2 + x^1 + 2.5
>> 2/b                            % division
ans =
MMRP Rational Polynomial Object:
     2
---------------
x^2 + 2x^1 + 5
>> c = a/b                        % division
c =
MMRP Rational Polynomial Object:
x^2 + 2x^1 + 3
---------------
x^2 + 2x^1 + 5

>> d = c/(1+c)                    % mixed
d =
MMRP Rational Polynomial Object:
0.5x^2 + x^1 + 1.5
-------------------
x^2 + 2x^1 + 4

>> (a/b)*(b/a)                    % mixed
ans =
MMRP Rational Polynomial Object:
1
```

Given the polynomial functions available in MATLAB and the ease with which they can be manipulated, there are many functions that can be overloaded. For example, the basic MATLAB functions `roots` and `zeros` can be overloaded by the following method M-files.

```
function [z,p]=roots(r)
%ROOTS Find Roots of Rational Polynomial Objects.
% ROOTS(R) returns the roots of the numerator of R.
% [Z,P]=ROOTS(R) returns the zeros and poles of R in
% Z and P respectively.

z=roots(r.n);
if nargout==2
     p=roots(r.d);
end
```

```
function z=zeros(r)
%ZEROS Zeros of a Rational Polynomial Object.

z=roots(r.n);
```

The method function `roots` calls the basic MATLAB function `roots` because the arguments within the method are of class `double`. With the creation of the `zeros` method, the function `zeros` has two entirely different meanings depending on what its arguments are. The beauty of OOP is that functions can have multiple meanings or contexts without having to imbed them all in a single M-file. The class of the input arguments dictates which function is called into action.

Because of their utility in dealing with Handle Graphics objects, it is usually beneficial to overload the functions `set` and `get`. Mimicking their Handle Graphics usage, it is common to use them to set or get individual class structure fields, for example,

```
function set(r,varargin)
%SET Set Rational Polynomial Object Parameters.
% SET(R,Name,Value, . . .) sets MMRP object parameters of R
% described by the Name/Value pairs:
%
%  Name           Value
% 'Numerator'     Numeric row vector of numerator coefficients
% 'Denominator'   Numeric row vector of denominator coefficients
% 'Variable'      Character Variable used to display polynomial
```

```
if rem(nargin,2)~=1
   error('Parameter Name/Values Must Appear in Pairs.')
end
for i=2:2:nargin-1
   name=varargin{i-1};
   if ~ischar(name), error('Parameter Names Must be Strings.'), end
   name=lower(name(isletter(name)));
   value=varargin{i};
   switch name(1)
   case 'n'
      if ~isnumeric(value) | size(value,1)>1
         error('Numerator Must be a Numeric Row Vector.')
      end
      r.n=value;
   case 'd'
      if ~isnumeric(value) | size(value,1)>1
         error('Denominator Must be a Numeric Row Vector.')
      end
      r.d=value;
   case 'v'
      if ~ischar(value) | length(value)>1
         error('Variable Must be a Single Character.')
      end
      r.v=value;
   otherwise
      warning('Unknown Parameter Name')
   end
end
vname=inputname(1);
if isempty(vname)
   vname='ans';
end
r=mmrp(r.n,r.d,r.v);
assignin('caller',vname,r);
```

```
function varargout=get(r,varargin)
%GET Get Rational Polynomial Object Parameters.
% GET(R,Name) gets the MMRP object parameter of R described by
% one of the following names:
%
```

```
%  Name            Description
% 'Numerator'      Numeric row vector of numerator coefficients
% 'Denominator'    Numeric row vector of denominator coefficients
% 'Variable'       Character Variable used to display polynomial
%
% [A,B,. . .]=get(R,NameA,NameB,. . .) returns multiple parameters
% in the corresponding output arguments.

if (nargout+(nargout==0))~=nargin-1
   error('No. of Outputs Must Equal No. of Names.')
end
for i=1:nargin-1
   name=varargin{i};
   if ~ischar(name), error('Parameter Names Must be Strings.'), end
   name=lower(name(isletter(name)));
     switch name(1)
     case 'n'
       varargout{i}=r.n;
     case 'd'
       varargout{i}=r.d;
     case 'v'
       varargout{i}=r.v;
     otherwise
       warning('Unknown Parameter Name')
     end
end
```

These functions allow one to modify an `mmrp` object or to get data out of one. Consider the following example.

```
>> c  % recall data
c =
MMRP Rational Polynomial Object:
x^2 + 2x^1 + 3
---------------
x^2 + 2x^1 + 5

>> n = get(c,'n') % get numerator vector
n =
         1           2           3

>> set(c,'Numerator',[3 1]) % change numerator
```

```
>> c
c =
MMRP Rational Polynomial Object:
 3x^1 + 1
---------------
x^2 + 2x^1 + 5

>> class(c)  % class and isa know about mmrp objects
ans =
mmrp
>> isa(c,'mmrp')
ans =
   1
```

33.3 SUBSCRIPTS

Because of MATLAB's array orientation, user-defined classes can also make use of subscripts. In particular, `V(...)`, `V{...}`, and `V.field` are all supported. In addition, these constructions can appear on either side of an assignment statement. When they appear on the right-hand side of an assignment statement, one is referencing the variable `V`, and when they appear on the left-hand side, one is assigning data to some part of the variable `V`. These indexing processes are called subscripted reference and subscripted assignment, respectively. The method functions that control how they are interpreted when applied to an object are `subsref` and `subasgn`, respectively. These functions are not as straightforward to understand as other operator and function overloading methods. As a result, this section specifically addresses them. To facilitate this discussion, the `mmrp` object created in the preceding section is used in the examples.

When dealing with rational polynomials, there are two obvious interpretations for subscripted reference. For a rational polynomial object `R`, `R(x)`, where `x` is a data array, can return the results of evaluating `R` at the points in `x`. Alternatively, `R('v')`, where `'v'` is a single character, can change the variable used to display the object to the letter provided.

The part of the help text for `subsref` that describes how to write a `subsref` method is shown below.

```
B = SUBSREF(A,S) is called for the syntax A(I), A{I}, or A.I
when A is an object. S is a structure array with the fields:
    type -- string containing '()', '{}', or '.' specifying the
            subscript type.
    subs -- Cell array or string containing the actual subscripts.

For instance, the syntax A(1:2,:) invokes SUBSREF(A,S) where S is a
1-by-1 structure with S.type='()' and S.subs = {1:2,':'}. A colon
used as a subscript is passed as the string ':'.
```

```
Similarly, the syntax A{1:2} invokes SUBSREF(A,S) where S.type='{}'
and the syntax A.field invokes SUBSREF(A,S) where S.type='.' and
S.subs='field'.

These simple calls are combined in a straightforward way for
more complicated subscripting expressions. In such cases
length(S) is the number of subscripting levels. For instance,
A(1,2).name(3:5) invokes SUBSREF(A,S) where S is 3-by-1 structure
array with the following values:
    S(1).type='()'       S(2).type='.'        S(3).type='()'
    S(1).subs={1,2}      S(2).subs='name'     S(3).subs={3:5}
```

Based on the help text, if `R` is an `mmrp` object, `R(x)` creates `S.type='()'` and `S.subs=x`, where `x` contains the values where `R` is to be evaluated, not indices into an array. Similarly, `R('v')` creates `S.type='()'` and `S.subs='v'`. All other possibilities should produce an error.

Using this information leads to the `subsref` method function shown below.

```
function y=subsref(r,s)
%SUBSREF(R,S) Subscripted Reference for Rational Polynomial Objects.
% R('z') returns a new rational polynomial object having the same
% numerator and denominator, but using the variable 'z'.
%
% R(x) where x is a numerical array, evaluates the rational polynomial
% R at the points in x, returning an array the same size as x.

if length(s)>1
     error('MMRP Objects Support Single Arguments Only.')
end
if strcmp(s.type,'()') % R(x) or R('v')
   arg=s.subs{1};
   argc=class(arg);
   if strcmp(argc,'char')
      if strcmp(arg(1),':')
         error('MMRP Objects Do Not Support R(:).')
      else
         y=mmrp(r.n,r.d,arg(1)); % change variables
      end
   elseif strcmp(argc,'double')
```

```
      if length(r.d)>1
         y=polyval(r.n,arg)./polyval(r.d,arg);
      else
         y=polyval(r.n,arg);
      end
   else
      error('Unknown Subscripts.')
   end
else % R{ } or R.field
   error('Cell and Structure Addressing Not Supported.')
end
```

Examples using this method include the following.

```
>> c  % recall data
c =
MMRP Rational Polynomial Object:
 3x^1 + 1
---------------
x^2 + 2x^1 + 5

>> c = c('t') % change variable
c =
MMRP Rational Polynomial Object:
 3t^1 + 1
---------------
t^2 + 2t^1 + 5

>> x = -2:2
x =
  -2    -1     0     1     2
>> c(x)        % evaluate at points in x
ans =
         -1          -0.5           0.2          0.5      0.53846

>> c{3}        % try cell addressing
??? Error using ==> mmrp/subsref
Cell and Structure Addressing Not Supported.

>> c.n         % Try field addressing
??? Error using ==> mmrp/subsref
Cell and Structure Addressing Not Supported.
```

As stated earlier, outside method functions the field structure of objects is hidden from view. If it were not, issuing `c.n` above would have returned the numerator row vector from the object `c`. To enable this feature, it must be explicitly included in the `subsref` method as shown below.

```
function y=subsref(r,s)
%SUBSREF(R,S) Subscripted Reference for Rational Polynomial Objects.
% R('z') returns a new rational polynomial object having the same numerator
% and denominator, but using the variable 'z'.
%
% R(x) where x is a numerical array, evaluates the rational polynomial R
% at the points in x, returning an array the same size as x.
%
% R.n returns the numerator row vector of R.
% R.d returns the denominator row vector of R.
% R.v returns the variable associated with R.

if length(s)>1
   error('MMRP Objects Support Single Arguments Only.')
end
if strcmp(s.type,'()') % R( )
   arg=s.subs{1};
   argc=class(arg);
   if strcmp(argc,'char')
      if strcmp(arg(1),':')
         error('MMRP Objects Do Not Support R(:).')
      else
         y=mmrp(r.n,r.d,arg(1));
      end
   elseif strcmp(argc,'double')
      if length(r.d)>1
         y=polyval(r.n,arg)./polyval(r.d,arg);
      else
         y=polyval(r.n,arg);
      end
   else
      error('Unknown Subscripts.')
   end
elseif strcmp(s.type,'.') % R.field
   arg=lower(s.subs);
   switch arg(1)
   case 'n'
```

```
        y=r.n;
    case 'd'
        y=r.d;
    case 'v'
        y=r.v;
    otherwise
        error('Unknown Data Requested.')
    end
else % R{ }
    error('Cell Addressing Not Supported.')
end
```

Examples using this method include the following.

```
>> c.n  % return numerator
ans =
    3     1
>> c.v  % return variable
ans =
x
>> c.nadfdf % only first letter is checked
ans =
    3     1
>> c.t      % not n, d, or v
??? Error using ==> mmrp/subsref
Unknown Data Requested.
>> c.d(1:2) % we didn't include subaddressing in subsref
??? Error using ==> mmrp/subsref
MMRP Objects Support Single Arguments Only.
```

As stated earlier, the overloading functions `subsref` and `subsasgn` are *not* implicitly called when subscripted reference and subscripted assignment appear within a method function. Overloading the MATLAB polynomial evaluation function `polyval` demonstrates this fact as shown by the following method.

```
function y=polyval(r,x)
%POLYVAL Evaluate Rational Polynomial Object.
% POLYVAL(R,X) evaluates the rational polynomial R at the
% values in X.

if isnumeric(x)
   %y=r(x);        % what we'd like to do, but can't
   S.type='()';
   S.subs={x};
   y=subsref(r,S); % must call subsref explicitly
else
   error('Second Input Argument Must be Numeric.')
end
```

Because of how `subsref` is written for the `mmrp` object, polynomial evaluation is simply a matter of issuing `R(x)`, where `R` is an `mmrp` object and `x` contains the values where `R` is to be evaluated. Since this matches the expected operation of `polyval`, simply issuing `y=r(x)` within `polyval` should cause MATLAB to call the `subsref` method to evaluate the rational polynomial. This does not happen because MATLAB does not call `subsref` or `subsasgn` within methods. However, to force this to happen, one can explicitly call `subsref` with the desired arguments as shown above.

When dealing with rational polynomials, there is one obvious interpretation for subscripted assignment. For a rational polynomial object `R`, `R(1,p)= v`, where `p` is a numerical vector identifying variable powers and `v` is a numerical vector of the same length, the elements of `v` become the coefficients of the numerator polynomial associated with the powers in `p`. Likewise, `R(2,q) = w` changes the denominator coefficients for those powers identified in `q`.

The part of the help text for `subsasgn` that describes how to write a `subsasgn` method is shown below.

```
A = SUBSASGN(A,S,B) is called for the syntax A(I)=B, A{I}=B, or
A.I=B when A is an object. S is a structure array with the fields:
    type -- string containing '()', '{}', or '.' specifying the
            subscript type.
    subs -- Cell array or string containing the actual subscripts.

For instance, the syntax A(1:2,:)=B calls A=SUBSASGN(A,S,B) where
S is a 1-by-1 structure with S.type='()' and S.subs = {1:2,':'}. A
colon used as a subscript is passed as the string ':'.
```

```
Similarly, the syntax A{1:2}=B invokes A=SUBSASGN(A,S,B) where
S.type='{}' and the syntax A.field=B invokes SUBSASGN(A,S,B) where
S.type='.' and S.subs='field'.

These simple calls are combined in a straightforward way for
more complicated subscripting expressions. In such cases
length(S) is the number of subscripting levels. For instance,
A(1,2).name(3:5)=B invokes A=SUBSASGN(A,S,B) where S is 3-by-1
structure array with the following values:
    S(1).type='()'        S(2).type='.'        S(3).type='()'
    S(1).subs={1,2}       S(2).subs='name'     S(3).subs={3:5}
```

Based on this help text and the desired subscripted assignment, the following `subsasgn` method is created.

```
function a=subsasgn(a,s,b)
%SUBSASGN Subscripted assignment for Rational Polynomial Objects.
%
% R(1,p)=C sets the coefficients of the Numerator of R identified
% by the powers in p to the values in the vector C.
%
% R(2,p)=C sets the coefficients of the Denominator of R identified
% by the powers in p to the values in the vector C.
%
% R(1,:) or R(2,:) simply replaces the corresponding polynomial
% data vector.
%
% For example, for the rational polynomial object
%          2x^2 + 3x + 4
% R(x) = ---------------------
%         x^3 + 4x^2 + 5x + 6
%
% R(1,2)=5         changes the coefficient 2x^2 to 5x^2
% R(2,[3 2])=[7 8] changes x^3 + 4x^2 to 7x^3 + 8x^2
% R(1,:)=[1 2 3]   changes the numerator to x^2 + 2x + 3

if length(s)>1
    error('MMRP Objects Support Single Arguments Only.')
```

```
end
if strcmp(s.type,'()') % R(1,p) or R(2,p)
 if length(s.subs)~=2
    error('Two Subscripts Required.')
 end
 nd=s.subs{1}; % numerator or denominator
 p=s.subs{2};  % powers to modify
 if ndims(nd)~=2 | length(nd)~=1 | (nd~=1 & nd~=2)
    error('First Subscript Must be 1 or 2.')
 end
 if isnumeric(p) & ...
    (ndims(p)~=2 | any(p<0) | any(fix(p)~=p))
    error('Second Subscript Must Contain Nonnegative Integers.')
 end
 if ndims(b)~=2 | length(b)~=prod(size(b))
    error('Right Hand Side Must be a Vector.')
 end
 b=b(:).';     % make sure b is a row
 p=p(:)';      % make sure p is a row
 if ischar(p) & length(p)==1 & strcmp(p,':') % R(1,:) or R(2,:)
    if nd==1  % replace numerator
       r.n=b;
       r.d=a.d;
    else      % replace denominator
       r.n=a.n;
       r.d=b;
    end
 elseif isnumeric(p) % R(1,p) or R(2,p)
    plen=length(p);
    blen=length(b);
    nlen=length(a.n);
    dlen=length(a.d);
    if plen~=blen
       error('Sizes Do Not Match.')
    end
    if nd==1  % modify numerator
       r.d=a.d;
       rlen=max(max(p)+1,nlen);
       r.n=zeros(1,rlen);
       r.n=mmpadd(r.n,a.n);
       r.n(rlen-p)=b;
    else      % modify denominator
       r.n=a.n;
       rlen=max(max(p)+1,dlen);
```

```
        r.d=zeros(1,rlen);
        r.d=mmpadd(r.d,a.d);
        r.d(rlen-p)=b;
     end
  else
     error('Unknown Subscripts.')
  end
else % R{ } or R.field
   error('Cell and Structure Addressing Not Supported.')
end
a=mmrp(r.n,r.d,a.v);
```

Examples using this method include the following.

```
>> a = mmrp([3 1],[1 2 5 10]) % create test object
a =
MMRP Rational Polynomial Object:
     3x^1 + 1
-----------------------
x^3 + 2x^2 + 5x^1 + 10
>> a(1,:) = [1 2 4]     % replace entire numerator
a =
MMRP Rational Polynomial Object:
  x^2 + 2x^1 + 4
-----------------------
x^3 + 2x^2 + 5x^1 + 10
>> a(2,2) = 12          % replace x^2 coef in denominator
a =
MMRP Rational Polynomial Object:
   x^2 + 2x^1 + 4
------------------------
x^3 + 12x^2 + 5x^1 + 10
>> a(1,0) = 0           % replace 4x^0 with 0x^0
a =
MMRP Rational Polynomial Object:
    x^2 + 2x^1
------------------------
x^3 + 12x^2 + 5x^1 + 10
>> a(1,:)=a.d          % subsref and subsasn! (a.n and a.d cancel)
a =
MMRP Rational Polynomial Object:
1
```

33.4 CONVERTER FUNCTIONS

As demonstrated in earlier chapters, the functions `double`, `char`, and `logical` convert their inputs to the data type matching their name. For example, `double('hello')` converts the character string `'hello'` to its numerical ASCII equivalent. Whenever possible, methods for these converter functions should be included in a class directory. For `mmrp` objects `double` and `char` have obvious interpretations. The `double` method should extract the numerator and denominator polynomials, and the `char` method should create a string representation such as that displayed by `display.m`, for example,

```
function [n,d]=double(r)
%DOUBLE Convert Rational Polynomial Object to Double.
% DOUBLE(R) returns a matrix with the numerator of R in
% the first row and the denominator in the second row.
% [N,D]=DOUBLE(R) extracts the numerator N and denominator D
% from the rational polynomial object R.

if nargout<=1 & length(r.d)>1
   nlen=length(r.n);
   dlen=length(r.d);
   n=zeros(1,max(nlen,dlen));
   n=[mmpadd(n,r.n);mmpadd(n,r.d)];
elseif nargout<=1
     n=r.n;
else % nargout==2
     n=r.n;
     d=r.d;
end
```

```
function [n,d,v]=char(r)
%CHAR Convert Rational Polynomial Object to Char.
% CHAR(R) returns a 3-row string array containing R in the
% format used by DISPLAY.M
% [N,D]=CHAR(R) extracts the numerator N and denominator D
% as character strings from the rational polynomial object R.
% [N,D,V]=CHAR(R) in addition returns the variable V.

if nargout<=1
 nstr=mmp2str(r.n,r.v);
```

```
    nlen=length(nstr);
    if length(r.d)>1
       dash='-';
       dstr=mmp2str(r.d,r.v);
       dlen=length(dstr);
       m=max(nlen,dlen);
       n=char([blanks(ceil((m-nlen)/2)) nstr],...
          dash(ones(1,m)),...
          [blanks(fix((m-dlen)/2)) dstr]);
    else
       n=nstr;
    end
   elseif nargout>1
      n=mmp2str(r.n); % converts polynomial to string
      d=mmp2str(r.d);
   end
   if nargout>2
      v=r.v;
   end
```

33.5 PRECEDENCE, INHERITANCE, AND AGGREGATION

MATLAB automatically gives user-defined classes ***higher precedence*** than the built-in classes in MATLAB. Therefore, operators and functions containing a mixture of built-in classes and a user-defined class always call the methods of the user-defined class. While this default precedence is usually sufficient for simple classes, the presence of multiple user-defined classes requires that some mechanism exist to allow the user to control the precedence of classes with respect to one another, or perhaps to force a user-defined class to have lower precedence than a built-in class. The functions `inferiorto` and `superiorto` provide this capability within MATLAB. ***These functions must appear within the constructor function for a class.*** The arguments to both functions contain a list of character strings identifying the classes that have lower or higher precedence than the object created by the constructor. For example, `superiorto('double')` dictates that the object has higher precedence than double-precision variables, and `inferiorto('mmrp','char')` dictates that an object has lower precedence than `mmrp` and `char` objects.

For large programming projects it may be convenient to create a hierarchy of object types. In this case it may be beneficial to let one object type inherit methods from another type. In doing so, fewer methods need to be written and method modifications are more centralized. In the vocabulary of OOP, an object that inherits the properties of another is called a ***child*** class, and the class it inherits from is called the ***parent*** class. In the simplest case, a child class inherits methods from a single parent class. This is called ***simple inheritance.*** It is also possible for a child class to inherit methods from multiple classes, which is called ***multiple inheritance.***

In simple inheritance the child class is given all the fields of the parent class, plus one or more unique fields of its own. As a result, methods associated with the parent can be directly applied to objects of the child class. Quite naturally, methods of the parent class have no knowledge of the fields unique to the child and therefore cannot use them in any way. Similarly, fields of the parent class cannot be accessed by methods of the child. The child must use the methods it inherited from the parent to gain access to the parent fields. The `lti` object in the *Control Toolbox* is an example of a parent class having child classes `tf, zpk, ss, dss, frd.`

In multiple inheritance a child class is given all the fields of all parent classes, plus one or more unique fields of its own. As in simple inheritance, the parents and child do not have direct access to each other's fields. With multiple parents the complexity of determining which parent methods are called under what circumstances is more difficult to describe. Information and detailed examples regarding inheritance can be found in the MATLAB documentation.

In the `mmrp` class used as an example earlier, the object fields contained data that were elements of the MATLAB classes `double` and `char`. In reality there is no reason why object fields cannot contain other data types including user-defined classes. In the vocabulary of OOP this is called ***containment*** or ***aggregation.*** The rules for operator and function overloading do not change. Within method functions of one class, the methods of the classes of other classes are called as needed to operate on the fields of the original class.

34

MATLAB Programming Interfaces

MATLAB provides a number of ways to interface with external programs. C functions and FORTRAN subroutines can be called from MATLAB using MEX-files. Furthermore, MATLAB can perform computations and return the results to C or FORTRAN programs using the ***MATLAB Engine.*** MATLAB provides header files and libraries for creating and accessing standard MATLAB MAT-files. In addition, MATLAB can incorporate Java and can exchange data with PC applications using Dynamic Data Exchange (DDE) and act as an ActiveX server to communicate with Visual Basic (VB) applications or Visual Basic for Applications (VBA)-enabled PC applications such as Microsoft Excel, PowerPoint, and Word. The use of Java, DDE, and ActiveX are covered in the following chapters. This chapter focuses on interfacing with C and FORTRAN.

MATLAB supplies a rich set of external programming interfaces, much more than can be covered in this text. A comprehensive treatment of the MATLAB application programming interface (API) could easily fill a book by itself. This chapter and the next two chapters provide a constructive introduction, with examples, to the API features in MATLAB. The MATLAB documentation provides comprehensive treatment of this subject.

To avoid confusion, the discussions and examples in this chapter are based on using a C compiler on a UNIX platform. The examples in this chapter were developed and tested using the GCC compiler on a Linux i386 platform with the 2.2.14 kernel (glnx86 architecture). The LCC compiler supplied with MATLAB was used to test the examples on a Windows NT 4.0 Pentium PC (win32 architecture), and the G77 FORTRAN compiler was used to test FORTRAN code on a Linux platform.

34.1 ACCESSING MATLAB ARRAYS

Anyone writing programs to interface with MATLAB should have a basic understanding of the structure of MATLAB arrays. Any MEX, MAT, or Engine program must access MATLAB arrays to perform useful work. This section explains a little about how MATLAB stores arrays and lists the functions available for use in programs to access MATLAB arrays.

The MATLAB Array

MATLAB supports only one object—the MATLAB array. All MATLAB variables are MATLAB arrays. MATLAB array elements are composed of one of the six fundamental data types (double, uint8, char, cell, struct, or sparse) or another MATLAB array. All scalars and composite elements such as strings, vectors, matrices, cell arrays, structures, and objects are MATLAB arrays.

MATLAB stores array data in columnwise order. This fact is used later in the mmcellstr MEX-file (MEX Example 4) when data is extracted from a string buffer and reassembled into individual strings. The following example illustrates this data organization.

```
>> x = [1 2 3; 4 5 6; 7 8 9]
x =
       1    2    3
       4    5    6
       7    8    9

>> size(x)
ans =
       3    3

>> x(:)'
ans =
       1    4    7    2    5    8    3    6    9
```

Accessing MATLAB Arrays: The mxArray

A MATLAB array in C can be considered a new C data type—an object called an mxArray built from a C structure. The mxArray structure stores information about the type of array (double, sparse, cell, and so on), the array dimensions, and the data itself. The mxArray structure also stores type-specific information such as the complexity of a numerical array (real or complex), the number and names of fields of a structure or an object, and the indices and maximum number of nonzero elements of a sparse array. The MX functions are the methods used to access the characteristics and the elements of an `mxArray`.

Numerical matrices are stored as two vectors of doubles (or other numerical data types); one vector contains the real elements, and the second vector contains the imaginary elements. Two pointers are used to access the data; a pointer to the real vector (`pr`) and another pointer to the vector of imaginary numbers (`pi`). The `pi` pointer is `NULL` if the array is real. Strings are stored as 16-bit ASCII Unicode integers with no imaginary component. C strings are null-terminated, but MATLAB strings are not. The length of a MATLAB string is always available from the array dimensions.

Cell arrays are collections of arrays. The data vector contains pointers to other arrays. There is no imaginary component. Each pointer in the vector of pointers is considered to be a cell. Structures are stored as folded cell arrays in which each element of the data vector is a field. Each field is associated with a name stored in another structure element of the `mxArray`. Objects are stored as named structures (the class name) with registered collections of methods. There are no imaginary components of cell arrays, structures, or objects.

One of the elements of an `mxArray` is the size of the array implemented as a vector of integers. Each integer corresponds to the length of the associated dimension. If the number of elements in the vector is greater than 2, the `mxArray` is a multidimensional array. If any one of these dimensions is zero, the array is considered to be an empty array. Another `mxArray` structure element can be used to flag any noncomplex array as a logical array.

Sparse matrices consist of the elements described earlier; two numerical vectors along with pointers to the vectors. These vectors contain the nonzero elements of the matrix. Sparse arrays also contain the parameters `nzmax`, `ir`, and `jc`, where `ir` is a pointer to an array of the row indices of the corresponding nonzero elements and `jc` is a pointer to a vector of column indices. The maximum number of nonzero elements in the sparse matrix is stored in `nzmax`.

MX Functions

MATLAB provides more than 100 functions and subroutines to access and manipulate `mxArrays` from C or FORTRAN programs. Note that FORTRAN support for MATLAB data types is limited to double-precision data and strings, while C programs can access any MATLAB data type. The FORTRAN logical subroutines (`mxIs...`) return one (`1`) for True and zero (`0`) for False. The C `mxCreate...` functions normally come in two versions: an `mxCreate...Matrix` function for 2-D `mxArrays` and an `mxCreate...Array` version for *n*-D `mxArrays`. FORTRAN `mxCopyPtrTo...` functions are used to copy data from an `mxArray` into a FORTRAN array, and `mxCopy...ToPtr` subroutines are used to copy data from a FORTRAN array into an `mxArray`. These subroutines are often used to copy `mxArrays` into FORTRAN arrays, send the data to subroutines, and copy the resulting FORTRAN arrays back into `mxArrays`. Examples later in this chapter illustrate the use of many of these functions and subroutines. Complete lists of MX functions and subroutines including parameters and return values are included in the MATLAB documentation.

34.2 CALLING C OR FORTRAN FROM MATLAB

MEX-files are compiled C or FORTRAN functions that can be called from the MATLAB environment just as if they were M-file functions. Preexisting C functions or FORTRAN subroutines can be modified by adding a few lines of code to manage access to MATLAB data and functions. Compiling the modified code with the `mex` command produces a MEX-file that can be called from within MATLAB. Most computational functions perform faster and more efficiently using MATLAB M-files. However, certain operations such as For Loops are more efficiently implemented in C or FORTRAN. If you cannot eliminate iteration through vectorization, MEX-file creation may provide a viable solution.

Compiled MEX files have platform-specific file name extensions. For example, `dll` is the MEX-file extension on the Windows platform, and `mexsol` is the MEX-file extension for Sun Solaris platforms. On all platforms the `mexext` function returns the appropriate MEX-file extension.

Each MEX function you create should have an associated M-file (*myfunc*`.m`) to provide help text for the MEX function. The MATLAB documentation provides additional information about using other architectures and other compilers.

Preparing the MEX Environment

The MEX environment must be initialized to access an installed C or FORTRAN compiler. MATLAB supports a number of compilers, including those available for no charge. For example, the GCC compiler (including FORTRAN support) is available by download from many sources on the Internet including the GCC home page at `http://gcc.gnu.org/`. Another option is to use the LCC compiler supplied with MATLAB on the PC platform. Standard third-party ANSI C compilers and FORTRAN compilers are supported, such as the Microsoft and Borland compilers on the PC platform, the GCC compiler on the Linux and BSD platforms, and the vendor-supplied optional ANSI C compilers on Compaq, Sun, and HP workstations.

Certain compilers do not mask floating-point exceptions by default. MATLAB arrays allow nonfinite values such as `Inf` and `NaN`, which generate floating-point exceptions if they are not masked. The DEC FORTRAN compiler on the Alpha platform, Absoft FORTRAN under Linux, and Borland C++ on the Windows PC platform are all affected. The MATLAB documentation and the compiler documentation contain information describing ways to mask floating-point exceptions when compiling MEX, Engine, and MAT-file programs.

The command `>> mex -setup` selects the appropriate initialization or options file for the compiler and computer platform (operating system and architecture). The options file sets certain environment variables and specifies the locations of the appropriate header files and libraries for a platform and compiler. Once the MEX environment has been initialized, the command `>> mex myprog.c` compiles the MEX source file `myprog.c` into the compiled MEX-file `myprog.dll` (or `myprog.mexglx`, and so on). The `mex` command line option `-f` can be used to temporarily select a different initialization file if needed. The `-f` option is used later to compile MATLAB Engine and MAT programs. The `-v` option can be used to list the compiler settings and to observe the compile and link stages. The command `>> mex -help` provides a list of `mex` command line options. Other standard compiler options such as -c, -g, and -D are also supported by mex. Debuggers (such as dbx or gdb) can be used to debug MEX programs if the -g option is used. The mex command is implemented both as a function to be called from the MATLAB *Command* window and as a batch or script file for use outside the MATLAB environment. The MATLAB documentation contains more information about the mex command, command line options, supported compilers, and debugging procedures.

> MEX-files must be designed to operate as standard MATLAB functions using a variable number of input arguments and a variable number of output arguments. Normal MATLAB functions pass data by value rather than by reference. The inputs to a MEX function should never be modified. If the purpose of a function is to change the input, the changed value should be returned as an output. For example, if the function inc increments the value of an input variable b, the function should be called using the syntax b=inc(b).

MEX Source File Organization

MEX source code files can be divided into ***header, subroutine,*** and ***interface*** sections. The header section contains any necessary #include and #define directives. The interface section (also known as the ***gateway*** section in the MATLAB documentation) contains code to access MATLAB data and functions from your program. The subroutine section (also known as the ***computation*** section in the MATLAB documentation) actually performs operations on the data. This section can be written as a separate function or subroutine, or the code can be incorporated into the interface section.

In addition to any other necessary include files, the header section must contain an #include "mex.h" directive to provide support for MEX functions. The mex prefix designates functions that can be used only within MEX-files and operate in the MATLAB workspace. The "mex.h" header file also includes "matrix.h" to provide MX functions to support MATLAB data types along with the standard header files <stdio.h>, <stdlib.h>, and <stddef.h>. The mx prefix designates functions that operate on MATLAB data types.

The interface section is used to communicate with the MATLAB environment. The required function definition is the mexFunction statement. This is the entry point to the program and corresponds to the main function in a stand-alone C program. The mexFunction function definition is

```
void mexFunction( int nlhs,       mxArray *plhs[],
                  int nrhs, const mxArray *prhs[] )
```

The variable nlhs is an integer containing the number of left-hand-side (output) arguments corresponding to the number returned from the MATLAB nargout function. Similarly, nrhs contains the number of right-hand-side (input) arguments. prhs[] is an array of pointers to the input arguments. prhs[0] is a pointer to the first input argument, prhs[1] is a pointer to the second input argument, and so on. All MATLAB data types are MATLAB arrays, and so all input and output arguments to a MEX-file are the mxArray data type.

At the time the compiled MEX function is called, prhs contains pointers to the input arguments, while plhs contains null pointers. It is the responsibility of the programmer to create any output arrays and assign array pointers to the plhs pointer array. An output array can be created even if nlhs contains 0, indicating that no output arguments have been requested. If called from the *Command* window, any output is assigned to the ans variable in the MATLAB base workspace.

Workspace Issues

When a MATLAB M-file function is called, the function operates in a private workspace distinct from the MATLAB base workspace or the caller function workspace. Variables in the base or caller workspace are passed by value rather than by reference and are not affected by changes within the called function. The evalin and assignin functions are exceptions; these functions affect variables outside the current workspace.

MEX functions operate in their own environment in that the scope of local variables is limited to the MEX function itself. However, this environment is not a MATLAB workspace as such. MX functions (functions with the mx prefix) operate on MATLAB data types. MEX functions (functions with the mex prefix) operate within the MATLAB workspace itself. For example, the mexEvalString and mexCallMATLAB functions evaluate their string arguments in the caller workspace. The mexGetArray function copies a variable from a specified MATLAB workspace ('base', 'caller', or 'global') into an mxArray. mexGetArrayPtr gets a read-only pointer to a MATLAB variable. mexPutArray copies an mxArray into a specified MATLAB workspace. All other MEX functions operate in the caller workspace.

The final exception is the mexPrintf function for printing formatted strings. mexPrintf must be used rather than the standard C printf within MEX-files. This function calls the MATLAB printf function in the base workspace and prints in the *Command* window (and in the diary file if it is in use).

The following is a list of MEX functions available in C programs, FORTRAN programs, or both.

Function	C	F	Purpose
mexAtExit	C	F	Register a function to be called when the MEX-file is cleared.
mexCallMATLAB	C	F	Call a MATLAB function, M-file, or MEX-file.

Function	C	F	Purpose
mexErrMsgTxt	C	F	Issue an error message and return to MATLAB.
mexEvalString	C	F	Execute a MATLAB command in the caller workspace.
mexFunction	C	F	Entry point to the MEX-file.
mexFunctionName	C		Name of the current MEX function.
mexGet	C		Get the value of a Handle Graphics property.
mexGetArray	C		Get a copy of a variable from another workspace.
mexGetMatrix		F	Copy an mxArray from the caller workspace.
mexGetFull		F	Get the component parts of a double-precision mxArray.
mexGetArrayPtr	C		Get a read-only pointer to a variable from another workspace.
mexGetMatrixPtr		F	Get a pointer to an mxArray in the caller workspace.
mexGetGlobal		F	Get a pointer to a global mxArray.
mexGetInf		F	Get the value of infinity.
mexGetNaN		F	Get the value of NaN.
mexGetEps		F	Get the value of eps.
mexIsGlobal	C		True if the mxArray has global scope.
mexIsFinite		F	Determine whether or not the value is finite.
mexIsInf		F	Determine whether or not the value is infinite.
mexIsNaN		F	Determine whether or not the value is NaN.
mexIsLocked	C		True if the MEX-file is locked.

Function	C	F	Purpose
`mexLock`	C		Lock a MEX-file so it cannot be cleared from memory.
`mexUnlock`	C		Unlock a MEX-file so it can be cleared from memory.
`mexWarnMsgTxt`	C		Issue a warning message.
`mexPrintf`	C	F	ANSI C `printf`-style output routine.
`mexPutArray`	C		Copy an `mxArray` into a MATLAB workspace.
`mexPutMatrix`		F	Write an `mxArray` into the caller workspace.
`mexPutFull`		F	Create an `mxArray` in the caller workspace.
`mexSet`	C		Set the value of a Handle Graphics property.
`mexSetTrapFlag`	C	F	Control the response of `mexCallMATLAB` to errors.
`mexMakeArrayPersistent`	C		Make an `mxArray` persist after the MEX-file completes.
`mexMakeMemoryPersistent`	C		Make memory allocated by `mxMalloc` and `mxCalloc` persist.

MEX Example 1: `fact`

This basic example creates a MEX-file that computes the factorial function. Imbedded comments and error checking have been omitted.

```
/*
 * fact.c - returns the factorial of a nonnegative integer.
 *
 *   MATLAB usage:  p=fact(n)
 *
 * Mastering MATLAB 6 C MEX Example 1
```

```
 */

#include "mex.h"

void mexFunction( int nlhs,       mxArray *plhs[],
                  int nrhs, const mxArray *prhs[] )
{
    double n, j, *p;
    int i;

    n=mxGetScalar(prhs[0]);
    plhs[0]=mxCreateDoubleMatrix(1,1,mxREAL);
    p=mxGetPr(plhs[0]);

    j=1.0;
    for (i=n;i>1;i--)
      j=j*i;
    *p=j;
}
```

First, the `mex.h` header file is included. Then `mexFunction` is declared along with the required parameters. A few variables are declared, and the value of the input argument is obtained using the `mxGetScalar` function. An output matrix is created to be a 1-by-1 matrix of real doubles using the `mxCreateDoubleMatrix` function, and a C pointer is obtained using `mxGetPr`. The calculation is performed, and the result is assigned to the output matrix.

Issuing `>> mex fact.c` creates a MEX-file that can be called from MATLAB. The name of the resulting MEX-file depends on the computer platform: `fact.dll` on a Windows PC or `fact.mexglx` on a Linux platform. If the source C file contains an error, compiler error messages are displayed providing sufficient information to make the necessary corrections to the source code. No MEX output file is created if errors are found.

Running the compiled MEX-file produces output similar to the following.

```
>> x = 5
x =
     5
>> y = fact(x)
y =
   120
>> which fact
/home/work/matlab/fact.mexglx
```

Some of the more common MX and MEX functions are used in these examples, but many more are available. A complete list of MATLAB interface functions along with descriptions of their arguments and return values, called the MATLAB application programming interface, is available in both HTML and PDF formats. The HTML version can be viewed in the MATLAB Help Browser. The PDF versions of the API Guide and API Reference can be viewed using Adobe Acrobat Viewer or printed directly on a PostScript printer.

MEX Example 2: `mycalc`

This example introduces more elements. `mycalc` includes error checking and uses a subroutine to perform a calculation on the elements of an array. This style can be used to turn an existing C subroutine into a MEX-file by adding an interface section to a subroutine source code, including the `mex.h` directive, and compiling.

The `mycalc` MEX-file accepts a 2-D array of doubles and returns an array of the same size containing the results of the calculation on each of the input elements. The interface section is used to do some error checking, determine the dimensions of the input array, create C pointers to the input and output arrays, and call the subroutine to do the calculation.

```
/*
 * mycalc.c - calculates x^2-x+1/x for each element of an array.
 *
 *   MATLAB usage:  p=mycalc(n)
 *
 * Mastering MATLAB 6 C MEX Example 2
 */

#include "mex.h"

/* This is the original subroutine that performs the calculation. */
static void mycalc( double p[], double n[], int r, int c)
{
    int i;
    for (i=0;i<r*c;i++)
        p[i]=n[i]*n[i]-n[i]+1.0/n[i];
}

/* This is the interface to MATLAB data types and arguments. */
void mexFunction( int nlhs,       mxArray *plhs[],
                  int nrhs, const mxArray *prhs[] )
{
    double *p, *n;
```

```
    int r, c;

    /* Do some error checking. */
    if (nrhs != 1)
      mexErrMsgTxt("One input argument required.");
    else if (nlhs > 1)
      mexErrMsgTxt("Too many output arguments.");
    else if (!mxIsNumeric(prhs[0]))
      mexErrMsgTxt("Input must be numeric.");
    else if (mxIsComplex(prhs[0]))
      mexErrMsgTxt("Input must be real.");
    else if (mxGetNumberOfDimensions(prhs[0]) > 2)
      mexErrMsgTxt("N-Dimensional arrays are not supported.");

    /* Get the input array dimensions. */
    r=mxGetM(prhs[0]);
    c=mxGetN(prhs[0]);

    /* Create a matrix for the return argument */
    plhs[0]=mxCreateDoubleMatrix(r,c,mxREAL);

    /* Assign pointers to the parameters. */
    p=mxGetPr(plhs[0]);
    n=mxGetPr(prhs[0]);

    /* Do the actual calculation in a subroutine. */
    mycalc(p,n,r,c);
}
```

The subroutine is included first in the MEX C source file to avoid forward references and the necessity for a prototype statement. The `mexErrMsgTxt` function operates in the same way as the MATLAB `error` function. The error message text is printed in the MATLAB *Command* window, and the MEX function exits. Note that the standard C language double quotation marks (`"`) are used to delimit a string argument. The `mexWarnMsgTxt` function can be used to emulate the MATLAB `warning` function and prints the text string in the *Command* window without exiting the MEX-file.

The `mxGetM` and `mxGetN` functions return the number of rows and columns, respectively, of a 2-D `mxArray`. The statement

```
plhs[0]=mxCreateDoubleMatrix(r,c,mxREAL);
```

creates an `r`-by-`c` `mxArray` to contain real elements of MATLAB type `double`. The `mxCOMPLEX` flag rather than the `mxREAL` flag indicates the desire to create an array containing complex elements. C-style pointers to the mxArrays are returned by the mxGetPr function. mxGetPr returns a pointer to the real elements of an mxArray. (Use mxGetPi to get a pointer to the imaginary elements of a complex mxArray.) The final step is to call the subroutine mycalc with the appropriate arguments.

MEX Example 3: count

This example supports multidimensional arrays, uses #define statements to simplify the source code, and includes MATLAB help text for the count MEX-file.

```
/*
 * count.c - count occurrences of values in an array.
 *
 * MATLAB usage:  c=count(a,b,tol)
 *
 * Mastering MATLAB 6 C MEX Example 3
 */

#include <math.h>
#include "mex.h"

/* Define some variables to make life easier. */
#define A   prhs[0] /* Pointer to first right-hand-side argument  */
#define B   prhs[1] /* Pointer to second right-hand-side argument */
#define TOL prhs[2] /* Pointer to third right-hand-side argument  */
#define C   plhs[0] /* Pointer to first left-hand-side argument   */

void  mexFunction( int nlhs,       mxArray *plhs[],
                   int nrhs, const mxArray *prhs[] )

{
    int i, j, sizea, sizeb;
    double tol, vcount;
    double *a, *b, *c;

    /* Do some error checking */
    if (nrhs < 2)
      mexErrMsgTxt("Missing input arguments.");
    else if (nrhs > 3)
      mexErrMsgTxt("Too many input arguments.");
    else if (nlhs > 1)
      mexErrMsgTxt("Too many output arguments.");

    /* Get tolerance value if supplied, otherwise use EPS. */
```

```
if (nrhs == 3) {
  if (!mxIsNumeric(TOL) || mxIsComplex(TOL) ||
      mxGetNumberOfElements(TOL) != 1 )
    mexErrMsgTxt("TOL must be a real numeric scalar.");
  tol=mxGetScalar(TOL);
  if (tol < mxGetEps())
    mexErrMsgTxt("TOL must be a positive value.");
}
else
  tol=mxGetEps();

/* Make sure input arrays are non-complex numeric arrays. */
if (!mxIsNumeric(A) || !mxIsNumeric(B) ||
     mxIsComplex(A) || mxIsComplex(B))
  mexErrMsgTxt("Input arguments must be real of type double.");

/* Create the output mxArray the same size as A */
C=mxCreateNumericArray(mxGetNumberOfDimensions(A),
      mxGetDimensions(A),mxDOUBLE_CLASS,mxREAL);

/* Get the number of elements in A and B and create pointers */
/* to the input and output arrays. */
sizea=mxGetNumberOfElements(A);
sizeb=mxGetNumberOfElements(B);
a=(double *) mxGetPr(A);
b=(double *) mxGetPr(B);
c=(double *) mxGetPr(C);

/* Cycle through the elements of the arrays and count values */
for (i=0;i<sizea;i++) {
  vcount=0.0;
  for (j=0;j<sizeb;j++)
  if ((fabs(a[i]-b[j])) <= tol)
    vcount++;
  c[i]=vcount;
}
}
```

This example includes the standard `math.h` header file in addition to the `mex.h` file to support the `fabs` function used in the calculation section. Four `#define` statements are also used to reduce the amount of typing required and to improve the readability of the resulting code. The line

```
C=mxCreateNumericArray(mxGetNumberOfDimensions(A),
      mxGetDimensions(A),mxDOUBLE_CLASS,mxREAL);
```

is an example of an MX creation function for *n*-D mxArrays. Most mxArray creation functions have two distinct forms: a 2-D form and an *n*-D form. The 2-D version is

```
C=mxCreateNumericMatrix(mxGetM(A),mxGetN(A),mxDOUBLE_CLASS,mxREAL);
```

The 2-D form (mxCreate...Matrix) expects the number of rows and the number of columns as separate arguments. Any other arguments (the numerical class and the real/complex flag in this case) follow. The *n*-D form requires the number of dimensions and a vector of dimension sizes, followed by any other arguments. For example,

```
plhs[0]=mxCreateCellMatrix(3,4);
```

creates an empty 3-by-4 cell mxArray, while

```
plhs[0]=mxCreateCellArray(3,[2,3,4]);
```

creates a 3-D 2-by-3-by-4 cell mxArray.

The mxGetNumberOfElements function returns the total number of elements in an mxArray. This is the number passed to the subfunction rather than the dimensions of the arrays since the subroutine uses single-subscript addressing to process the array elements.

Finally, we create an M-file to provide appropriate MATLAB help text for the count function. The file is named count.m and is saved in the same directory as the count.mexglx MEX-file.

```
function c=count(a,b,tol)
%COUNT Count Occurrences of Values in an Array.
% COUNT(A,B) returns an array the same size as A whose i-th element
% contains the number of times A(i) appears in the array B.
% A and B must be Real arrays.
%
% COUNT implements the following:
%         c = zeros(size(A)));
%         for i=1:prod(size(A))
%             c(i)=sum(A(i)==B);
%         end
```

When MATLAB finds a MEX-file and an M-file in the same directory, the MEX-file is called to execute the function, while the M-file provides help text.

MEX Example 4: mmcellstr

The next example leaves the realm of numbers and enters the world of strings and cells. The mmcellstr function is a C MEX-file implementation of the MATLAB cellstr function. mmcellstr creates a cell array of strings from a character array. Each row of the character array is placed in an individual cell of a cell array.

This example demonstrates a number of new techniques including allocating memory in a MEX, file, handling empty arrays, and duplicating an array.

```
/*
 * mmcellstr.c - Create a cell array of strings from a 2-D character array.
 *
 * MATLAB usage: c=mmcellstr(s)
 *
 * Mastering MATLAB 6 C MEX Example 4
 */

#include "mex.h"

void mexFunction( int nlhs,       mxArray *plhs[],
                  int nrhs, const mxArray *prhs[] )
{
  int m, n, i, j;
  char *buf;
  char **line;

  /* Do some error checking */
  if (nrhs < 1)
    mexErrMsgTxt("Missing input argument.");
  else if (nrhs > 1)
    mexErrMsgTxt("Too many input arguments.");
  else if (mxGetNumberOfDimensions(prhs[0]) != 2)
    mexErrMsgTxt("Input must be 2-D.");
  else if (nlhs > 1)
    mexErrMsgTxt("Too many output arguments.");

/****** Start of Region 1 ******/
  /* If the input is already a cell array, duplicate it. */
  if (mxIsCell(prhs[0]))
    if (mxIsChar(mxGetCell(prhs[0],0))) {
      plhs[0]=mxCreateCellMatrix(mxGetM(prhs[0]),mxGetN(prhs[0]));
      plhs[0]=mxDuplicateArray(prhs[0]);
      return;
    }
/******  End of Region 1  ******/
```

```
  /* Make sure the input is a character array. */
  if (!mxIsChar(prhs[0]))
    mexErrMsgTxt("Input must be a character array.");

/****** Start of Region 2 ******/
  /* Handle the empty input case. */
  if (mxIsEmpty(prhs[0])) {
    plhs[0]=mxCreateCellMatrix(1, 1);
    mxSetCell(plhs[0],0,mxDuplicateArray(prhs[0]));
    return;
  }
/******  End of Region 2  ******/

  /* Determine the dimensions of the input structure array */
  m=mxGetM(prhs[0]);
  n=mxGetN(prhs[0]);

/****** Start of Region 3 ******/
  /* Stuff the input into a string buffer. */
  buf=mxCalloc(m*n,sizeof(char));
  buf=mxArrayToString(prhs[0]);

  /* Create line buffers for the individual strings. */
  for (i=0;i<m;i++)
    line[i]=mxCalloc(n+1,sizeof(char));
/******  End of Region 3  ******/

  /* Parse the buffer into individual lines. */
  for (j=0;j>n;j++)
    for (i=0;i<m;i++)
      line[i][j]=buf[i+m*j];

  /* Free the string buffer and create the output cell array. */
  mxFree(buf);
  plhs[0]=mxCreateCellMatrix(m, 1);

  for (i=0;i<m;i++) {
    /* For each line, remove trailing blanks... */
    j=n;
    while (--j >= 0)
      if (line[i][j] != ' ')
        break;
    line[i][j+1]='\0';
```

```
    /* insert the line into the output array... */
    mxSetCell(plhs[0],i,mxCreateString(line[i]));

    /* and free the line buffer memory. */
    mxFree(line[i]);
  }
}
```

After the header section and the function definition, some variables are defined. `buf` is a pointer to a character array (a string buffer), while `line` is a pointer to an array of character pointers. Memory is allocated for these buffers later in the function. Next comes some error checking. The next section deserves a closer look.

```
/****** Start of Region 1 ******/
  /* If the input is already a cell array, duplicate it. */
  if (mxIsCell(prhs[0]))
    if (mxIsChar(mxGetCell(prhs[0],0))) {
      plhs[0]=mxCreateCellMatrix(mxGetM(prhs[0]),mxGetN(prhs[0]));
      plhs[0]=mxDuplicateArray(prhs[0]);
      return;
    }
/******  End of Region 1  ******/
```

This section handles the case where the input is already a cell array of strings. In this case, the array is duplicated and passed to the output. First, we check that the input is a cell array (`mxIsCell`). If so, we check the class of the contents of a cell. `mxGetCell(prhs[0],0)` returns the contents of cell `0` of the input array. `mxIsChar` then determines if the element contains character data. The line

```
plhs[0]=mxCreateCellMatrix(mxGetM(prhs[0]),mxGetN(prhs[0]));
```

creates an output array with the same dimensions as the input array. Then `mxDuplicateArray` makes a ***deep*** copy of the input `mxArray` into the output `mxArray`. A deep copy duplicates all levels of an array; it is essentially a recursive copy. In this case, the line

```
plhs[0]=mxDuplicateArray(prhs[0]);
```

copies the entire contents of the input array into the output array. The function then returns to the calling workspace.

At this point, we have the correct number and type of arguments. In the third section, shown below, we obtain the dimensions of the input character array, allocate a character buffer of the correct size (`m*n`) using `mxCalloc`, and copy the character array into the new buffer as one long string using `mxArrayToString`. We then allocate a line buffer for each row in the input array. The size of each line buffer is the width of the character array plus one space for the C string terminator `'\0'`.

```
/****** Start of Region 3 ******/
  /* Stuff the input into a string buffer. */
  buf=mxCalloc(m*n,sizeof(char));
  buf=mxArrayToString(prhs[0]);

  /* Create line buffers for the individual strings. */
  for (i=0;i<m;i++)
    line[i]=mxCalloc(n+1,sizeof(char));
/******  End of Region 3  ******/
```

MEX-files should always use `mxCalloc` (or `mxMalloc`) to allocate memory and `mxFree` to return the allocated memory to the heap. These functions register the allocation and deallocation of memory with the MATLAB memory manager, which automatically frees all allocated memory when the function exits.

Since MATLAB arrays are stored columnwise, the buffer contains the input array elements in column order, similar to the result of using the MATLAB colon operator (`buf=chararray(:)`). The following section extracts the correct elements of `buff` into the line buffers, frees the string buffer memory, and creates the output cell array. Then each line is processed. A C string terminator (`'\0'`) is inserted into the buffer after the last nonblank character, and the line is copied and converted from a C string to a MATLAB string using `mxCreateString` and inserted into the output cell array using `mxSetCell`. Finally, the line buffer memory is freed using `mxFree`, and the next line is processed.

MEX Example 5: `mmv2struct`

The final MEX example illustrates a method of converting an M-file into an equivalent MEX-file. The function `mmv2struct.m` shown below packs and unpacks individual variables into a scalar structure.

```
function varargout=mmv2struct(varargin)
%MMV2STRUCT Pack/Unpack Variables to/from a Scalar Structure.
% MMV2STRUCT(X,Y,Z,...) returns a structure having fields X,Y,Z,...
% containing the corresponding data stored in X,Y,Z,...
% Inputs that are not variables are stored in fields named ansN
% where N is an integer identifying the Nth unnamed input.
%
% MMV2STRUCT(S)assigns the contents of the fields of the scalar structure
% S to variables in the calling workspace having names equal to the
% corresponding field names.
%
% [A,B,C,...]=MMV2STRUCT(S) assigns the contents of the fields of the
% scalar structure S to the variables A,B,C,... rather than overwriting
% variables in the caller. If there are fewer output variables than
% there are fields in S, the remaining fields are not extracted. Variables
% are assigned in the order given by fieldnames(S).

if nargin==0
    error('Input Arguments Required.')
elseif nargin==1                % Unpack Structure to Variables
    arg=varargin{1};
    if ~isstruct(arg)|length(arg)~=1
        error('Single Input Must be a Scalar Structure.')
    end
    names=fieldnames(arg);
    if nargout==0 % assign in caller
        for i=1:length(names)
            assignin('caller',names{i},getfield(arg,names{i}))
        end
    else % dump into variables in caller
        for i=1:nargout
            varargout{i}=getfield(arg,names{i});
        end
    end
else                            % Pack Variables into a Structure
   num=1;
   for i=1:nargin
      name=inputname(i);
      if isempty(name) % not a variable
         name=sprintf('ans%d',num);
         num=num+1;
      end
      eval(['y.' name '=varargin{i};'])
   end
   varargout{1}=y;
end
```

The same function written as a C MEX-file is shown below. Comparing the M-file to its MEX-file equivalent provides insight into the creation of MEX-files.

```
/*
 * v2struct.c - Pack/Unpack Variables to/from a Scalar Structure.
 *
 * MATLAB usage: s=mv2struct(x,y,z,...) s.x=x, s.y=y, etc.
 * MATLAB usage: mv2struct(s) a=s.a, b=s.b, etc.
 * MATLAB usage: [x,y,z,...]=mv2struct(s) x=s.a, y=s.b, etc.
 *
 * MEX file to implement the function mmv2struct.m.
 *
 * Mastering MATLAB 6 C MEX Example 5
 */

   #include "mex.h"
   #include <string.h>

   void mexFunction( int nlhs,       mxArray *plhs[],
                     int nrhs, const mxArray *prhs[] )
   {
     int i, j, nfields;
     char cmd[100], tmp[10];
     const char *ans = "ans";
     const char **fnames;
     char **name;

     /* Do some error checking */
     if (nrhs == 0)
       mexErrMsgTxt("Input Arguments Required.");

     else if (nrhs == 1) {   /* Unpack */
       if (!mxIsStruct(prhs[0]))
         mexErrMsgTxt("Single Input Must be a Scalar Structure.");
       else if (mxGetNumberOfElements(prhs[0]) != 1)
         mexErrMsgTxt("Single Input Must be a Scalar Structure.");

       nfields = mxGetNumberOfFields(prhs[0]);
       if (nlhs == 0)    /* Assign fields in the caller workspace */
         for (i=0;i<nfields;i++) {
           strcpy(cmd,mxGetFieldNameByNumber(prhs[0],i));
           strcat(cmd,"=");
           strcat(cmd,mxGetName(prhs[0]));
```

```
        strcat(cmd,".");
        strcat(cmd,mxGetFieldNameByNumber(prhs[0],i));
        mexEvalString(cmd);
      }
    else {              /* Assign fields to output variables */
      j=(nlhs<nfields)?nlhs:nfields;
      for (i=0;i<j;i++)
           plhs[i]=mxDuplicateArray(mxGetFieldByNumber(prhs[0],0,i));
    }
  }
  else {                /* Pack */
    /* Create a list of fieldnames. */
    fnames=mxCalloc(nrhs,sizeof(*fnames));
    for (i=0;i<nrhs;i++)  {
      name[i]=mxCalloc(BUFLEN,sizeof(char));
      if (*mxGetName(prhs[i]) != '\0')
        strcpy(name[i],mxGetName(prhs[i]));
      else {
        strcpy(name[i],ans);
        sprintf(tmp,"%d",i);
        strcat(name[i],tmp);
      }
      fnames[i]=name[i];
    }

    /* Create the output structure and free the allocated memory. */
    plhs[0]=mxCreateStructMatrix(1,1,nrhs,fnames);
    mxFree(fnames);
    for (i=0;i<nrhs;i++)
      mxFree(name[i]);

    /* Stuff the inputs into the structure fields. */
    for (i=0;i<nrhs;i++)
     mxSetFieldByNumber(plhs[0],0,i,mxDuplicateArray(prhs[i]));
  }
}
```

Windows PC Considerations

The previous examples were also compiled on a Windows PC using the LCC compiler supplied with MATLAB. While this compiler does not offer many features, it does produce functional MEX-files. The command

```
>> mex myprog.c
```

produces the MEX-file `myprog.dll` in the current directory. Adding the verbose (`-v`) option to the `mex` command line prints the compiler settings and shows the compile and link stages. The appropriate options file for this compiler was chosen previously using the `mex -setup` command. A different options file for an individual compilation can be specified by using the `-f` option. The `$MATLAB\bin\win32\mexopts` directory contains at least eight options files for different versions of the Borland, Microsoft, and Watcom compilers alone. The MATLAB documentation offers more details about configuring compilers and debugging MEX programs.

FORTRAN Considerations

FORTRAN MEX-files are limited to creating double-precision data and strings, while C-MEX-files can create any MATLAB data type. FORTRAN MEX-files support only `mxCreateFull`, `mxCreateSparse`, and `mxCreateString` `mxArray` creation functions. For this reason. FORTRAN MEX- and MX functions are listed separately in the MATLAB documentation. Note that FORTRAN source code is not case sensitive, and so `MXCREATEFULL`, `mxcreatefull`, and `mxCreateFull` are the same function. FORTRAN examples in this chapter continue to use mixed case to maintain consistency and make the FORTRAN code easier to read.

Since FORTRAN does not support new data types, MATLAB passes a special identifier of type `integer*4` called a ***pointer*** to the FORTRAN program for each input and output variable. These pointers can be used by MEX subroutines to obtain data in an appropriate FORTRAN native data type from the MATLAB arrays. Pointers must be declared as the default `integer*4` on all platforms except those using a 64-bit Alpha processor where pointers must be declared as `integer*8`.

Some FORTRAN compilers support the `%val` construct, which can be used to pass values from pointers obtained from functions such as `p=mxGetPr()` to subroutines. Otherwise, `mxCopy...` routines (such as `mxCopyPtrToReal8` and `mxCopyReal8ToPtr`) should be used to extract the data from the `mxArray`, pass it to the subroutine, and return the result to the `mxArray`.

In FORTRAN, the `mexFunction` subroutine definition is

```
subroutine mexFunction(nlhs, plhs, nrhs, prhs)
integer plhs(*), prhs(*)
integer nlhs, nrhs
```

where `nlhs` and `nrhs` contain the number of left- and right-hand-side arguments, respectively, and `plhs` and `prhs` are arrays of pointers to the arguments themselves.

The FORTRAN equivalent of the C MEX-file `fact.c` is

```
C-------------------------------------------------------------
C      fact.f - returns the factorial of a nonnegative integer.
C
C       MATLAB usage:  p=fact(n)
C
C      Mastering MATLAB 6 FORTRAN MEX Example 1

       subroutine mexFunction(nlhs, plhs, nrhs, prhs)
C-------------------------------------------------------------
C      These are pointers: integer*4 (integer*8 on Alphas)
C
       integer plhs(*), prhs(*)
       integer mxGetPr, mxCreateFull
       integer y_pr
C-------------------------------------------------------------
       integer nlhs, nrhs
       integer i
       real*8  x, y, mxGetScalar
C-------------------------------------------------------------
       x = mxGetScalar(prhs(1))
       plhs(1) = mxCreateFull(1, 1, 0)
       y_pr = mxGetPr(plhs(1))
C
       y = 1.0
       do 10 i=x,1,-1
          y = y * i
 10    continue
C
       call mxCopyReal8ToPtr(y, y_pr, 1)
       return
       end
```

Note that FORTRAN, like MATLAB, uses one-based array and loop indexing rather than the zero-based indexing used in C programs. Therefore, the pointer to the first right-hand-side (input) argument (`prhs[0]` in a C program) is `prhs(1)` in a FORTRAN program.

34.3 CALLING MATLAB FROM C OR FORTRAN

Just as you are able to call C or FORTRAN routines from MATLAB, you can also call MATLAB to perform operations in the background as part of some larger C or FORTRAN program. In MATLAB this is called the MATLAB Engine.

What Is It?

The MATLAB Engine consists of a communication library and a small collection of linkable routines that call MATLAB as a server process without linking in all of MATLAB. The MATLAB Engine allows you to start a MATLAB process, transfer data to MATLAB, execute MATLAB commands, capture the normal *Command* window output if desired, transfer data back to your program, and shut down the MATLAB process—all from within a C or FORTRAN program.

How It Works

The MATLAB Engine process runs in the background, separate from any interactive MATLAB session currently running. It does not interfere with any user running MATLAB. When an Engine process is started, a new MATLAB instance is created. This process is shared by all programs requesting access to a MATLAB Engine process on the specific host computer. An exclusive Engine process can be reserved in C programs, but the process is always shared in FORTRAN programs.

The `eng` prefix designates a MATLAB Engine function. MATLAB Engine functions available to C and FORTRAN programs are listed in the following table.

Function	C	F	Purpose
`engOpen`	C	F	Start up or share an instance of the MATLAB Engine.
`engOpenSingleUse`	C		Start an exclusive (nonshared) MATLAB Engine session.
`engPutArray`	C		Send a MATLAB array (`mxArray`) to the MATLAB Engine.
`engPutMatrix`		F	Send a MATLAB array (`mxArray`) to the MATLAB Engine.
`engOutputBuffer`	C	F	Create a buffer to store MATLAB text output.
`engEvalString`	C	F	Execute a MATLAB command within the MATLAB Engine.
`engGetArray`	C		Get a MATLAB array (`mxArray`) from the MATLAB Engine.
`engGetMatrix`		F	Get a MATLAB array (`mxArray`) from the MATLAB Engine.
`engClose`	C	F	Shut down the MATLAB Engine.

Engine Program Structure

The first step in using the MATLAB Engine is to open an Engine session using `engOpen` or `engOpenSingleUse`. Then create any `mxArrays` needed using the appropriate MX functions (such as `mxCreateDoubleMatrix`) and then use `mxSetName` to associate a MATLAB variable name with the `mxArray`. Populate the `mxArrays` and place them in the MATLAB environment using `engPutArray` (or `engPutMatrix` in FORTRAN programs). Create a buffer to capture *Command* window output if desired using `engOutputBuffer` and execute MATLAB commands using `engEvalString`. Recover any output `mxArrays` from the MATLAB environment using `engGetArray` (or `engGetMatrix`) and continue processing within the C or FORTRAN program. When done with the MATLAB environment, the process is terminated using `engClose`, and allocated memory for `mxArrays` is released using `mxDestroyArray`.

Engine Program Description

The `engOpen` function starts a MATLAB Engine session and returns a unique "Engine ID" which can be used to address this particular Engine. The function returns NULL if an error occurs. If the `engOpen` argument is NULL (`'\0'`), the Engine is started on the local computer using the command `matlab`. On a UNIX or Linux computer, the argument can be a host name. In this case, the Engine is started on the remote host using `rsh`. The `DISPLAY` environment variable is also set so that any graphics generated by the Engine (such as the result of a `plot` command) appear on the local computer display rather than on the computer running the Engine process. Appropriate permissions must be set to allow remote execution and to allow the remote computer to display on your computer screen. If the argument to `engOpen` is anything other than a host name (such as a string containing spaces, tabs, or nonalphanumerical characters), the string is executed literally to start an Engine process. You can take advantage of this facility to customize your Engine session, such as using `ssh` for encrypted communications with the remote host. The `engOpen` argument must be NULL on a Windows PC since remote execution is not supported on this platform. The MATLAB application installed on the local PC is started to service any Engine requests.

You must create any MATLAB variables to be used within the Engine environment. One way to create a MATLAB variable is to use the `engEvalString` function to evaluate a MATLAB command such as `y=-2*pi:pi/25:2*pi;` to create the variable `y` in the MATLAB workspace and assign values to `y`. Another method is to create a MATLAB array within your program and pass the resulting `mxArray` to the MATLAB Engine. For example, given a 1-by-10 array of double-precision data in the C variable `dataset`,

```
Engine *mat
mxArray *mydata = NULL;

mat = engOpen("\0");
mydata = mxCreateDoubleMatrix(1, 10, mxREAL);
mxSetName(mydata, "newdata");
```

```
memcpy((void *)mxGetPr(mydata), (void *)dataset, sizeof(dataset));
engPutArray(mat, mydata);
engEvalString("sqdata=newdata.^2;");
```

opens a connection to MATLAB on the local computer, creates an mxArray called mydata, associates the MATLAB variable name newdata with the mydata array, populates the array, sends the mydata array to the Engine, squares the elements of the array, and assigns the output to the MATLAB variable sqdata. The mxSetName function is required to assign a MATLAB variable name to the mxArray. This is the only way to identify the array in the MATLAB workspace. In this example, the C name and the MATLAB name are different to illustrate how each is used. Normally the same name is used to avoid confusion.

Once MATLAB performs the desired operations, the results must be passed back into your program. Once again, there are two ways to do this. The first method is to create a text buffer using the engCreateTextBuffer function to capture MATLAB text that is normally discarded, use the engEvalString function to generate the output text, and then parse the string buffer. For example,

```
char buf[256];
engOutputBuffer(mat, buf, 256);
engEvalString("disp(sum(sqdata))");
```

captures the output of the disp(sum(sqdata)) command as it would be displayed in the MATLAB *Command* window into the string buffer buf. The buffer can be parsed to extract the desired data.

```
double x;
x=atof(buf+2);
```

Each call to engEvalString replaces the data in the MATLAB output string buffer. Note that the first two characters of the output buffer always contain the MATLAB prompt characters ">>", and so the call to the atof function skips over these characters.

When the result is more substantial, you can retrieve one or more arrays from the MATLAB workspace. For example,

```
mxArray *sqdata = NULL;
double *sptr;

sqdata = engGetArray(mat,"sqdata");
sptr = mxGetPr(sqdata);
```

makes the mxArray sqdata available to your program. Use mxGetPr to get a C pointer to the real part of the mxArray. The other MX functions are also available to access the sqdata array.

Be sure to release the memory that was allocated to mxArrays when you are finished with them and close the MATLAB Engine when it is no longer needed.

```
mxDestroyArray(mydata);
mxDestroyArray(sqdata);
engClose(mat);
```

Compiling and Running Engine Programs

Programs that incorporate MATLAB Engine access functions must include the engine.h header file to support the MATLAB Engine functions in addition to any other necessary header files. The engine.h header file also includes matrix.h for MX function support. The compilation step uses the mex command with the engopts.sh options file in addition to any other compiler options. For example, if the MATLAB application is installed in /usr/local/matlab, the mex command to compile a C Engine program might be

```
mex -f /usr/local/matlab/bin/engopts.sh myprog.c
```

This command creates an executable program called myprog in the current directory and can be run from an operating system command prompt or by double-clicking on a Windows PC. If the standard options file does not meet your needs, make a local copy of engopts.sh and modify it as appropriate.

When the compiled Engine program is run, one or more MATLAB shared libraries are loaded as well. The operating system must be told where to look for these libraries. The LD_LIBRARY_PATH environment variable (or the equivalent on your platform) lists additional directories to be searched when the operating system cannot find all the required shared libraries in the standard system directories. You must add the appropriate system-specific MATLAB shared library directory to this list. If you have a Solaris operating system with MATLAB installed in the /opt/matlab directory and you are using a Bourne shell (sh, bash, ksh), the commands are

```
LD_LIBRARY_PATH=/opt/matlab/extern/lib/sol2:$LD_LIBRARY_PATH
export LD_LIBRARY_PATH
```

If you are using a C shell (csh, tcsh) on a Linux platform with libc2 C libraries and have MATLAB installed in the /usr/local/matlab directory, the command is

```
setenv LD_LIBRARY_PATH /usr/local/matlab/extern/lib/glnx86:$LD_LIBRARY_PATH
```

The platform-specific library directories (sol2, glnx86, lnx86, sgi, sgi64, win32, hp700, alpha, and ibm_rs) are located in the $MATLAB/extern/lib directory. Some platforms use a different environment variable to list additional shared library locations. The SGI64 platform uses LD_LIBRARY64_PATH rather than LD_LIBRARY_PATH. The HP700 platform uses SHLIB_PATH, and the IBM RS/6000 platform uses LIBPATH. The easiest way to set this variable is to add the appropriate command(s) to your shell startup script (.profile, .cshrc, .bashrc, .tcshrc, and so on).

Engine Example

So far, we have covered the individual elements of MATLAB Engine programs. Now it is time to put it all together. This example builds on the preceding sections to create a complete C program that uses the MATLAB Engine as a back-end computational engine. This program creates an array of data, sends the array to MATLAB, calculates the squares of the elements and the sum of the squares, and returns the results to the C program for printing. Comments have been added to explain how the pieces are combined.

```
/*
 * sos.c - Calculate the sum of the squares of the elements of a vector.
 *
 * Mastering MATLAB 6 C Engine Example 1
 *
 */

#include <stdio.h>
#include <string.h>
#include "engine.h"
#define  BUFSIZE 256

int main()
{
    Engine *mat;
    mxArray *mydata = NULL, *sqdata = NULL;
    int i, j;
    double x, *myptr, *sptr;
    char buf[BUFSIZE];
    double dataset[10] = { 0.0, 1.0, 2.0, 3.0, 4.0,
                           5.0, 6.0, 7.0, 8.0, 9.0 };

    /* Start the MATLAB Engine on the local computer. */
    if (!(mat = engOpen("\0"))) {
        fprintf(stderr, "\nCannot open connection to MATLAB!\n");
        return EXIT_FAILURE;
    }

    /* Create an mxArray and get a C pointer to the mxArray. */
    mydata = mxCreateDoubleMatrix(1, 10, mxREAL);
    myptr = mxGetPr(mydata);
```

```
    /* Associate a MATLAB variable name with the mxArray. */
    mxSetName(mydata, "newdata");

    /* Copy the dataset array to the new mxArray. */
    memcpy((void *)myptr, (void *)dataset, sizeof(dataset));

    /* Pass the mxArray to the Engine and square the elements. */
    engPutArray(mat, mydata);
    engEvalString(mat, "sqdata = newdata.^2");

    /* Create an output buffer to capture MATLAB text output. */
    engOutputBuffer(mat, buf, BUFSIZE);

    /* Calculate the sum of the squares and save the result in x. */
    engEvalString(mat,"disp(sum(sqdata))");
    x=atof(buf+2);

    /* Retrieve the array of squares from the Engine, */
    if ((sqdata = engGetArray(mat,"sqdata")) == NULL) {
        fprintf(stderr, "Cannot retrieve sqdata!\n\n");
        return EXIT_FAILURE;
    }

    /* and get a C pointer to the mxArray. */

    sptr = mxGetPr(sqdata);

    /* Print the results to stdout. */
    printf("\nThe inputs are:\n");
    for (i=0;i<10;i++)
      printf("%6.1f ",myptr[i]);
    printf("\n\nThe squares are:\n");
    for (i=0;i<10;i++)
      printf("%6.1f ",sptr[i]);
    printf("\n\nThe sum of the squares is %6.1f \n\n",x);

    /* Free the mxArray memory and quit MATLAB. */
    mxDestroyArray(mydata);
    mxDestroyArray(sqdata);
    engClose(mat);

    return EXIT_SUCCESS;
}
```

Windows PC Considerations

The previous example also compiles on a Windows PC using the LCC compiler. The command

```
>> mex -f c:\matlab6\bin\win32\mexopts\lccengmatopts.bat sos.c
```

produces the executable file `sos.exe` in the current directory. If you are not using the LCC compiler, specify the appropriate options file on the command line. The `$MATLAB\bin\win32\mexopts` directory contains at least eight options files for different versions of the Borland, Microsoft, and Watcom compilers alone. If you have trouble, use the verbose (`-v`) option to the `mex` command to view the compiler settings and the various steps in the compilation process.

MATLAB Engine programs link with DLL libraries in the `$MATLAB\bin\win32` directory. MATLAB adds this directory to your default path during installation so that Windows will be able to find the libraries. When executed from the command line or by double-clicking on the `sos.exe` file, a MATLAB session is run (minimized) to perform the calculations. It does not interfere with any interactive MATLAB session that may be open.

Consult the MATLAB documentation for more details about how to configure programming software to compile MEX and Engine programs and for debugging these programs within your software development environment.

FORTRAN Considerations

The same MATLAB Engine program written in FORTRAN requires only a few changes. Most Engine functions return a status value which is tested for errors. Also, the sum of the squares is printed as a character array to avoid extracting the numerical value from the text buffer and then printing it.

```
C
C   sos.c - Calculate the sum of the squares of the elements of a vector.
C
C   Mastering MATLAB 6 FORTRAN Engine Example 1
C
C==============================================================
      program main
C--------------------------------------------------------------
C     Pointers
C
      integer engOpen, engGetMatrix, mxCreateFull, mxGetPr
      integer mat, mydata, sqdata
```

```
C-----------------------------------------------------------------------
C     Other variable declarations
C
      double precision dataset(10), sqrs(10)
      integer engPutMatrix, engEvalString, engClose, engOutputBuffer
      integer temp, status
      character*256 buf
      data dataset / 0.0, 1.0, 2.0, 3.0, 4.0, 5.0, 6.0, 7.0, 8.0, 9.0 /
C-----------------------------------------------------------------------
C     Start the MATLAB Engine on the local computer.
C
      mat = engOpen('matlab ')
      if (mat .eq. 0) then
         write(6,*) 'Cannot open connection to MATLAB!'
         stop
      endif
C
C     Create an mxArray, associate a MATLAB variable name with the
C       mxArray, and copy the data into the array.
C
      mydata = mxCreateFull(1, 10, 0)
      call mxSetName(mydata, 'newdata')
      call mxCopyReal8ToPtr(dataset, mxGetPr(mydata), 10)
C
C     Pass the variable mydata into the MATLAB workspace.
C
      status = engPutMatrix(mat, mydata)
      if (status .ne. 0) then
         write(6,*) 'Cannot pass mydata to the Engine!'
         stop
      endif
C
C     Square the elements of the array.
C
      if (engEvalString(mat, 'sqdata = newdata.^2;') .ne. 0) then
         write(6,*) 'engEvalString failed'
         stop
      endif
C
C     Create an output buffer to capture MATLAB text output.
C
      if (engOutputBuffer(mat, buf) .ne. 0) then
         write(6,*) 'engEvalString failed'
         stop
      endif
```

```
C
C     Calculate the sum of the squares and capture the result.
C
      if (engEvalString(mat, 'disp(sum(sqdata))') .ne. 0) then
         write(6,*) 'engEvalString failed'
         stop
      endif
C
C     Retrieve the mxArray of squares from the Engine,
C     copy the data into an array of doubles, and print.
C
      sqdata = engGetMatrix(mat, 'sqdata')
      call mxCopyPtrToReal8(mxGetPr(sqdata), sqrs, 10)
C
 20   format(' ', G8.3, G8.3, G8.3, G8.3, G8.3, G8.3,
     & G8.3, G8.3, G8.3, G8.3)
      print *, 'The inputs are:'
      print 20, dataset
      print *, 'The squares are:'
      print 20, sqrs
      print *,  'The sum of the squares is ', buf(3:10)
C
C     Free the mxArray memory and quit MATLAB.
C
      call mxFreeMatrix(mydata)
      call mxFreeMatrix(sqdata)
      status = engClose(mat)
C
      if (status .ne. 0) then
         write(6,*) 'engClose failed'
         stop
      endif
C
      stop
      end
```

Note that if your FORTRAN compiler uses shared libraries, you must add the appropriate MATLAB shared library directory to your LD_LIBRARY_PATH (or equivalent) before executing any compiled Engine program. If you are using a Windows PC, the $MATLAB\bin\win32 directory was added to your default path during MATLAB installation so that Windows can find the MATLAB shared libraries (DLLs).

34.4 EXCHANGING DATA WITH MAT-FILES

There are several ways to exchange data with MATLAB and other programs. Most methods involve creating a data file to serve as an exchange medium. Selecting the appropriate method depends on the amount and format of the data to be imported or exported. In this section, reading and writing standard MATLAB MAT-files from C and FORTRAN are considered.

MAT-files

MAT-files are platform-independent in that platform differences (such as the native byte order) are identified in the MAT-file itself and MATLAB automatically translates the data format when loading data from the MAT-file. By supplying header files and libraries for use in your programs to read and write MAT-files, MATLAB provides these platform-independent features to C and FORTRAN programs as well as easy data exchange with MATLAB.

MAT Functions

The `mat` prefix designates a MATLAB function that operates on MAT-files. MATLAB MAT functions available to C or FORTRAN programs are listed in the following table.

MAT Function	C	F	Purpose
`matOpen`	C	F	Open a MAT-file.
`matClose`	C	F	Close a MAT-file.
`matGetDir`	C	F	Get a list of MATLAB arrays from a MAT-file.
`matGetFp`	C		Get an ANSI C file pointer to a MAT-file.
`matGetArray`	C		Read a MATLAB array from a MAT-file.
`matGetMatrix`		F	Read a MATLAB array from a MAT-file.
`matGetNextArray`	C		Read the next MATLAB array from a MAT-file.
`matGetNextMatrix`		F	Read the next MATLAB array from a MAT-file.
`matGetArrayHeader`	C		Load a MATLAB array header from a MAT-file.

MAT Function	C	F	Purpose
matGetNextArrayHeader	C		Load the next MATLAB array header from a MAT-file.
matGetString		F	Read a MATLAB string from a MAT-file.
matPutArray	C		Write a MATLAB array to a MAT-file.
matPutMatrix		F	Write a MATLAB array to a MAT-file.
matPutArrayAsGlobal	C		Write a global MATLAB array to a MAT-file.
matPutString		F	Write a MATLAB string to a MAT-file.
matDeleteArray	C		Delete a MATLAB array from a MAT-file.
matDeleteMatrix		F	Delete a MATLAB array from a MAT-file.

The `matGetArrayHeader` and `matGetNextArrayHeader` functions create `mxArrays` containing everything in the `mxArray` structure except the actual data itself. The `matGetDir` function creates a list of variable names and returns the number of MATLAB variables contained in the MAT-file. The `matGetArray` and `matGetMatrix` functions use the variable name to access the contents of the variables, while `matGetNext...` functions access the variables sequentially.

MAT Program Structure

C or FORTRAN programs that read or write MAT-files use MX functions to create MATLAB data arrays (`mxArrays`) in the same general way that MX functions are used in MEX-files or Engine programs. When creating a MAT-file, one first opens the MAT-file using `matOpen` and then creates, names, and populates `mxArrays` for each MATLAB variable, writes the `mxArrays` to the MAT-file using the appropriate `matPut...` functions, and finally closes the MAT-file using `matClose`. When reading data from a MAT-file, one first opens the MAT-file using `matOpen`, gets a list of the variables if desired using `matGetDir`, creates `mxArrays` using `matGetArray` or `matGetNextArray` (or `matGetMatrix`, `matGetNextMatrix`, or `matGetString` in FORTRAN), and finally closes the MAT-file using `matClose`.

Compiling and Running MAT Programs

Programs that incorporate MATLAB MAT-file access functions must include the `mat.h` header file to support the MATLAB MAT-file functions in addition to any other necessary header files. The `mat.h` header file also includes `matrix.h` for MX function support. The compilation step uses the `mex` command with the `matopts.sh` options file in addition to any other compiler options you may need. For example, if the MATLAB application is installed in `/usr/local/matlab`, the `mex` command to compile a C MAT program might be

```
>> mex -f /usr/local/matlab/bin/matopts.sh myprog.c
```

This command creates an executable program called `myprog` in the current directory and can be run from an operating system command prompt. The shared-library discussions in the Engine section relating to the UNIX and PC platforms apply here as well. An executable program created by the `mex` command uses shared libraries that must be found by your operating system when the program is run.

The Windows PC version uses the same options file that Engine programs do. Compiling the same `myprog.c` MAT program using the LCC compiler might use the command

```
>> mex -f c:\matlab6\bin\win32\mexopts\lccengmatopts.bat myprog.c
```

The compilation produces the executable file `myprog.exe` in the current directory, which can be run from a command prompt or by double-clicking on the file. If you are not using the LCC compiler, specify the appropriate options file on the command line.

MAT Program Example 1: `writemat`

The following C program creates a MAT-file containing a string and an array of doubles.

```
/*
 * writemat.c - Create a binary MAT file.
 *
 * Mastering MATLAB 6 C MAT-file Example 1
 *
 */

#include "mat.h"

int makemat(const char *filename,
            double *data, int m, int n,
            char *mmstr)
{
  MATFile *mfile;
  mxArray *mdata, *mstr;

  /* Open the MAT file for writing. */
  mfile = matOpen(filename, "w");
  if (mfile == NULL) {
    printf("Cannot open %s for writing.\n", filename);
```

```
    return(EXIT_FAILURE);
  }

  /* Create the mxArray to hold the numeric data.    */
  /* Note that the array dimensions are reversed.    */
  /* C uses row order while MATLAB uses column order. */
  /* The data array will be transposed in MATLAB.    */
  mdata = mxCreateDoubleMatrix(n,m,mxREAL);
  mxSetName(mdata, "mydata");

  /* Copy the data to the mxArray. Note that mxGetData is */
  /* similar to mxGetPr in that it returns a void pointer */
  /* while mxGetPr returns a pointer to a double.        */
  memcpy((void *)(mxGetData(mdata)), (void *)data,
                m*n*sizeof(double));

  /* Create the string array and set the variable name. */
  mstr = mxCreateString(mmstr);
  mxSetName(mstr, "mystr");

  /* Write the mxArrays to the MAT file. */
  matPutArray(mfile, mdata);
  matPutArray(mfile, mstr);

  /* Free the mxArray memory. */
  mxDestroyArray(mdata);
  mxDestroyArray(mstr);

  /* Close the MAT file. */
  if (matClose(mfile) != 0) {
    printf("Cannot close %s.\n",filename);
    return(EXIT_FAILURE);
  }

  return(EXIT_SUCCESS);
}

int main()
{
  int status;
  char *mmstr = "Mastering MATLAB Rocks!";
  double data[3][4] = {{  1.0,  2.0,  3.0,  4.0 },
                       {  5.5,  6.6,  7.7,  8.8 },
                       { -4.0, -3.0, -2.0, -1.0 }};
```

```
    status = makemat("mmtest.mat", *data, 3, 4, mmstr);
    return(status);
}
```

This program was compiled on both Linux and Windows PC platforms, and the results were identical. The resulting MAT-file was then loaded into a MATLAB session as follows.

```
>> clear all
>> load mmtest
>> whos
  Name          Size          Bytes  Class

  mydata        4x3              96  double array
  mystr         1x23             46  char array
Grand total is 35 elements using 142 bytes

>> mydata
mydata =
    1.0000    5.5000   -4.0000
    2.0000    6.6000   -3.0000
    3.0000    7.7000   -2.0000
    4.0000    8.8000   -1.0000

>> mystr
mystr =
Mastering MATLAB Rocks!
```

Note that the numerical array was transposed when loaded into MATLAB. This is because of the differences in the way that C and MATLAB store arrays: rowwise and columnwise, respectively. The FORTRAN version does not transpose the matrix since both MATLAB and FORTRAN store arrays in columnwise format. The following shows a FORTRAN version of the same program.

```
C
C   writemat.f - Create a binary MAT file.
C
```

```
C   Mastering MATLAB 6 FORTRAN MAT-file Example 1
C
C
      program writemat
C-----------------------------------------------------
C     Pointers.
C
      integer matOpen, mxCreateFull, mxCreateString
      integer matGetMatrix, mxGetPr
      integer mfile, mdata, mstr
C-----------------------------------------------------
C     Other variables
C
      integer status, matClose
      double precision dat(12)
      data dat / 1.0, 5.5, -4.0,
     &           2.0, 6.6, -3.0,
     &           3.0, 7.7, -2.0,
     &           4.0, 8.8, -1.0 /
C
C     Open MAT-file for writing.
C
      mfile = matOpen('mmtest.mat', 'w')
      if (mfile .eq. 0) then
         write(6,*) 'Can''t open ''mmtest.mat'' for writing.'
         stop
      end if
C
C     Create the mxArray to hold the numeric data.
C
      mdata = mxCreateFull(4,3,0)
      call mxSetName(mdata, 'mydata')
C
C     Copy the data to the mxArray.
C
      call mxCopyReal8ToPtr(dat, mxGetPr(mdata), 12)
C
C     Create the string array and set the variable name.
C
      mstr = mxCreateString('Mastering MATLAB Rocks!')
      call mxSetName(mstr, 'mystr')
C
C     Write the mxArrays to the MAT-file.
C
```

```
      call matPutMatrix(mfile, mdata)
      call matPutMatrix(mfile, mstr)
C
C     Free the mxArray memory.
C
      call mxFreeMatrix(mdata)
      call mxFreeMatrix(mstr)
C
C     Close the MAT file.
C
      status = matClose(mp)
      if (status .ne. 0) then
         write(6,*) 'Cannot close mmtest.mat'
         stop
      end if
C
      stop
      end
```

MAT Program Example 2: `whomat`

The next example reads a MAT-file and examines its contents. It then prints variable lists in formats similar to the MATLAB `who` and `whos` commands.

```
/*
 * whomat.c - Examine a binary MAT-file and print a list
 * of the contents (like "who" or "whos").
 *
 * Mastering MATLAB 6 C MAT-file Example 2
 *
 */

  #include "mat.h"
  #include <string.h>

  int whomat(const char *filename)
  {
```

```
MATFile *mfile;
mxArray *marray;
char **dir;
char siz[25], buf[10];
int i, j, k, num, nel, elsize, ndim, eltot, btot;
const int *dims;

/* Open the MAT-file for reading. */
mfile = matOpen(filename, "r");
if (mfile == NULL) {
  printf("Cannot open %s for reading.\n", filename);
  return(EXIT_FAILURE);
}

 /* Get the directory list and print in "who" format. */
dir = matGetDir(mfile, &num);
if (dir == NULL) {
  printf("Error reading the directory of %s.\n", filename);
  return(EXIT_FAILURE);
} else {
  printf("\n");
  printf("Variables in %s are:\n\n", filename);
  for (i=0; i<num; i++) {
    printf("%-10s",dir[i]);
    if (i>0 && i%4==0) printf("\n");
  }
}

/* Examine each variable and print a "whos" list. */
eltot=btot=0;
printf("\n\n  Name          Size          Bytes  Class\n\n");
for (i=0; i<num; i++) {
  marray=matGetArray(mfile, dir[i]);
  if (marray == NULL) {
    printf("Cannot read file %s.\n\n", filename);
    return(EXIT_FAILURE);
  }

  /* If marray is a cell array or structure array, then  */
  /* mxGetElementSize returns the size of a pointer; not */
  /* the size of all the elements in each cell or field. */
  /* To get the correct number of bytes would require    */
  /* traversing the array and summing leaf element sizes.*/
  /* Java arrays return 0x0 array dimensions and 0 size. */
```

```
      elsize=mxGetElementSize(marray);
      btot=btot+(nel*elsize);
      nel=mxGetNumberOfElements(marray);
      eltot=eltot+nel;
      ndim=mxGetNumberOfDimensions(marray);
      dims=mxGetDimensions(marray);
      siz[0]='\0';
      for (j=0; j<ndim; j++) {
        sprintf(buf,"%d",dims[j]);
        strcat(siz,buf);
        if (j<(ndim-1))
          strcat(siz,"x");
      }
      printf("  %-12s %-12s %5d  %s array\n", mxGetName(marray),
                siz,nel*elsize,mxGetClassName(marray));
      mxDestroyArray(marray);
    }
    printf("\nGrand total is %d elements using %d bytes\n\n",
              eltot,btot);

    /* Release the memory allocated for the directory. */
     mxFree(dir);

    /* Close the MAT file. */
    if (matClose(mfile) != 0) {
        printf("Cannot close %s.\n",filename);
        return(EXIT_FAILURE);
    }
    return(EXIT_SUCCESS);
}

int main(int argc, char **argv)
{
  int status;

  if (argc > 1)
    status = whomat(argv[1]);
  else{
    status = EXIT_FAILURE;
    printf("Usage: whomat <matfile>");
  }
  return(status);
}
```

The output of this program, while very similar to the output of the MATLAB `who` and `whos` commands for variables in the workspace, reports incorrect results for cell arrays, structures, and Java arrays. If `marray` is a cell array or structure array, then `mxGetElementSize(marray)` returns the size of a pointer, not the size of all the elements in each cell or field. To get the correct number of bytes would require traversing the array and summing leaf element sizes. If `marray` is a Java array, then `mxGetElementSize(marray)` returns zero and `mxGetDimensions(marray)` returns a pointer to a vector of zeros of length `mxGetNumberOfDimensions(marray)`. Adding support for these data types is left as an exercise for the reader.

34.5 SUMMARY

The MATLAB programming interfaces described in this chapter provide tools for maximizing MATLAB's productivity. MEX-files can be created to speed up loops that cannot be vectorized or to take advantage of previously written C functions or FORTRAN subroutines by adding a few lines of interface code. The resulting compiled MEX files can then be called from MATLAB just like M-file functions. MATLAB can be used as a back-end computational engine by your own programs to take advantage of MATLAB's computational speed, efficiency, and visualization functions. You can read and write MATLAB MAT-files from your own programs and transfer collections of variables and data into and out of MATLAB using simple `load` and `save` commands. All these ***hooks*** into the MATLAB environment add to the collection of tools you can use to solve problems or extend the capabilities of existing programs. Much more extensive documentation of the MATLAB API, including a complete list of MX functions and details of the internal structure of MAT-files, can be found in the MATLAB documentation.

35

Extending MATLAB with Java

35.1 JAVA OVERVIEW

MATLAB 6 features a redesigned graphical user interface called the MATLAB desktop, containing numerous windows and dialog boxes. These features were written in the Java programming language. Every installation of MATLAB now includes a Java virtual machine (JVM) integrated into MATLAB to support this new interface. This Java interpreter is used extensively within MATLAB as well as being the foundation of the redesigned user interface. Because Java is so thoroughly integrated into the MATLAB environment, the Java virtual machine is also available to the MATLAB user. Java classes, objects, and methods can be manipulated within MATLAB, both from the command line and from MATLAB functions. Java integration provides new opportunities to extend MATLAB in many different ways.

This chapter discusses the incorporation of Java into MATLAB. It is not an introduction to Java. The user is encouraged to consult a Java programming book to learn the details of the programming language. Only those features of Java that are useful in this chapter are covered here.

Java

Java is a programming language expressly designed for use in distributed environments on different kinds of computers under different operating systems. Java programs are compiled into Java platform-independent ***bytecode*** that can be run on any computer that has a Java virtual machine installed. The Java virtual machine is a program that interprets the bytecode into machine code that runs on the real computer hardware. This means that individual computer platform differences such as instruction lengths and data storage differences can be recognized and accommodated at the time the program is executed. Platform-specific versions of Java programs are no longer needed. A single Java program can produce the same results on any computer with a JVM.

Java is an object-oriented programming language. If you have experience with Java, C++, or one of a number of other programming languages, or if you are comfortable with MATLAB classes and objects, the concepts and terms used to describe Java may be quite familiar.

The language of Java includes the following terms.

- **Class**—A Java class consists of data specification (variables) and a collection of operations (methods) available to objects of this class. A Java class is a template definition of a particular kind of object.
- **Object**—A Java object is a specific instance of a particular Java class or subclass in the same way that a MATLAB structure object is an instance of a MATLAB `struct` class. An object contains real values instead of variables, and all the methods associated with the class can operate on any object instantiated from the class.
- **Method**—A method is a programmed procedure or operation that is defined as part of a class and is available for use by any object of that class. A Java method is analogous to a MATLAB class method; a function that operates only on objects of a specific class.
- **Variable** or **field**—A variable or field is the name associated with a value. Java variables are defined in Java classes. The terms field and variable are often used interchangeably.
- **Class library, toolkit,** or **package**—A package is a collection of related Java classes, such as the Abstract Windowing Toolkit (`java.awt.*`), providing windowing and GUI services, or the net class library (`java.net.*`), providing Internet and communications services.
- **Private/public**—Private fields are visible only within the class and can be changed only by public or private methods defined for the class. Private methods can be called only within the class and are not visible outside the class. Public fields and public methods are visible outside the class.
- **Static/Nonstatic**—Static fields and static methods are associated with classes rather than objects. Static fields are read-only; the contents cannot be changed. Static methods operate on classes. Nonstatic fields are associated with objects and often can be modified.
- **Final**—Final classes cannot have subclasses. Final variables or fields cannot be changed. Final methods cannot be overridden by subclasses. Private methods are ef-

fectively final. Variables labeled public static final are read-only class variables visible outside the class. By convention, public static final variable names use all capital letters.

The ability to access arbitrary Java classes in the MATLAB environment opens up almost unlimited possibilities beyond the traditional MATLAB environment. Some of these possibilities are explored in examples later in this chapter.

Why Use Java?

Why would anyone want to use Java? There are a number of reasons. Anyone familiar with object-oriented programming languages or with MEX-file programming in MATLAB should be comfortable using Java. You can access existing Java classes and methods to add functionality to MATLAB. You can use special-purpose prewritten Java classes to add unique functionality. You can also create your own Java classes and access them from within MATLAB. *The MathWorks Inc.* has also made it easy to pass data between MATLAB data types and Java objects by automatically casting between Java and MATLAB data types. MATLAB support for Java arrays makes interaction between MATLAB and Java even easier.

35.2 JAVA CLASSES

Java classes are the foundation of Java. MATLAB makes a number of standard and MATLAB-specific class packages available automatically. Making additional classes or class libraries available entails two steps. First you must tell MATLAB where to look for the `.class` or `.jar` files containing Java class definitions by adding entries to the `classpath.txt` file. Then you must refer to a class using the full class and package name or `import` the class or package into the MATLAB workspace.

Using Java Classes in MATLAB

The systemwide `classpath.txt` file located in the `$toolbox/local` directory specifies the locations of Java class definitions. This text file can be edited to make additional classes available to all MATLAB users. If this file is copied to the `$home/matlab` directory or to your current working directory, any changes made will affect only one user. To make individual `.class` files available, add the path to the directory containing the `.class` files to the `classpath.txt` file. Add the top directory of a class package directory tree to the `classpath.txt` file to add an entire package. Add the entire path to a `.jar` file (including the file name) to make an entire compressed Java archive available. The `classpath.txt` file is read only at startup, and so changes to the file are not recognized until MATLAB is restarted.

Once MATLAB knows where to look for Java classes, you can refer to any available class using the full class name. For example, `java.lang.String` refers to the `String` class contained in the `java.lang` class library.

35.3 JAVA OBJECTS

Java objects are created using either Java syntax or MATLAB syntax conventions. For example,

```
>> myFrameA = java.awt.Frame('A Cool Window');                % Java syntax

>> myFrameB = java_object('java.awt.Frame','Another Window'); % MATLAB syntax
```

creates two objects, both instances of the `java.awt.Frame` class. The `java_object` function is intended for unusual situations within functions and is rarely used. Java syntax is preferred.

The function `import` provides a shortcut method for referring to a given class within MATLAB. For example,

```
>> import java.awt.Frame

>> myFrameA = Frame; myFrameB = Frame;
```

creates two objects of the `java.awt.Frame` class. Future references to `Frame` refer to `java.awt.Frame`. Entire class libraries can be imported in the same manner. For example,

```
>> import java.awt.* java.net.* com.mathworks.ide.help.HelpBrowser
```

makes all `java.awt` classes, all `java.net` classes, and the `com.mathworks.ide.help.HelpBrowser` class available using shorthand notation. For example,

```
>> import java.awt.*

>> myButton = Button('Stop');
```

creates an instance of a `java.awt.Button` class. The `>> import` command with no arguments returns the current import list without adding to it. The `>> clear import` command clears the import list from the current workspace. Function import lists are cleared when the function returns.

Java Objects are References in MATLAB

It is important to understand that Java objects are ***references*** in MATLAB and are not copied on assignment or passed by value. A new reference is created whenever a Java object is assigned. When a Java object is passed to a function as an input argument, the variable name in the function is simply another reference to the original object. As an example, consider this short test function:

```
function javatest(obj)
% Test java object references

disp(obj.getLabel)                    % Display the object label
newRef=obj;                           % Create a new reference
set(newRef,'Label','Label One')       % Change the label using set()
disp(newRef.getLabel)                 % Display the new label
setLabel(newRef,'Label Two')          % Use the setLabel method
disp(newRef.getLabel)                 % Display the label again
newRef.setLabel('Label Three')        % Use Java object method syntax
disp(newRef.getLabel)                 % Display the label
```

To illustrate use of the above `javatest` function, first create an object of the `Button` class:

```
>> myBut = java.awt.Button('Label Zero')
 myBut =
 java.awt.Button[button1,0,0,0x0,invalid,label=Label Zero]
```

Then pass the `Button` to the `javatest` function:

```
>> javatest(myBut)
Label Zero
Label One
Label Two
Label Three
```

The `Button` object in the MATLAB base workspace has changed!

```
>> myBut
myBut =
 java.awt.Button[button1,0,0,0x0,invalid,label=Label Three]
```

But the `newRef` reference remains local to the function workspace and is unknown in the base workspace,

```
>> newRef
??? Undefined function or variable 'newRef'.
```

This occurs because Java objects are passed by reference rather than by value, and assignments simply create another reference. Changes made to the object referenced by `newRef` within the function affect the object referenced by `myBut` in the base workspace since they both refer to the same object. This is different from conventional MATLAB where data is passed and assigned by value, not by reference.

> Java objects are created by object constructor methods and destroyed by the `clear` function. Since every assignment creates a new object reference, Java objects cannot be duplicated. You cannot make a copy of any Java object.

Java arrays can be copied, but the elements of the new array are newly created references to the original objects.

35.4 JAVA METHODS

Java classes consist of data definitions and a collection of operations that can be performed on or by objects created from the class. The collection of operations, called methods, are the Java equivalent of operators and functions in MATLAB.

Invoking Methods on Java Objects

In the preceding example, the `Button's` Label property was changed within the `javatest` function in three different ways:

```
set(newRef,'Label','Label One')    % Change the label using set()
setLabel(newRef,'Label Two')       % Use the setLabel method
newRef.setLabel('Label Three')     % Use Java object method syntax
```

The first assignment uses the MATLAB `set` function overloaded for Java objects using the functional syntax: `set(object,property,value)`. The second assignment uses the `java.awt.Button` class `setLabel` method in a hybrid functional syntax: `method(object,value)`. The third assignment uses pure Java syntax: `object.method(value)`. All three variations are used in this example.

There is one more way to invoke a method on a Java object. The `java_method` command uses pure functional notation to invoke a method. For example,

```
java_method('setLabel',newRef,'Label Four')
```

also invokes the `setLabel` method on the `Button` object `newRef`. The `java_method` function is rarely used because Java or MATLAB syntax is preferred.

Getting Information About Classes and Objects

Classes are collections of variables and methods, and objects are instances of classes or subclasses. Each object inherits the methods and variables of the class. The `>> methods` command produces a list of the public methods available for a specific class, for example,

```
>> methods java.lang.Double

Methods for class java.lang.Double:

Double            floatValue        isNaN             shortValue
byteValue         getClass          longBitsToDouble toString
doubleToLongBits hashCode          longValue         valueOf
doubleValue       intValue          notify            wait
equals            isInfinite        notifyAll
```

Any object of the `java.lang.Double` class can use any of these methods. The argument to the `methods` command is the name of a Java class. A second argument `'-full'` produces a much more detailed list of methods, including information about their arguments and return values.

```
>> methods java.lang.Double -full

Methods for class java.lang.Double:

      Double(double)
      Double(java.lang.String) throws java.lang.NumberFormatException
      static java.lang.String toString(double)
      static java.lang.Double valueOf(java.lang.String) throws
      java.lang.NumberFormatException
      static boolean isNaN(double)
      static boolean isInfinite(double)
      static long doubleToLongBits(double)
      static double longBitsToDouble(long)
      java.lang.Class getClass()  % Inherited from java.lang.Object
      int hashCode()
      boolean equals(java.lang.Object)
      java.lang.String toString()
      void notify()  % Inherited from java.lang.Object
      void notifyAll()  % Inherited from java.lang.Object
      void wait(long) throws java.lang.InterruptedException
      void wait(long,int) throws java.lang.InterruptedException
      void wait() throws java.lang.InterruptedException
      int intValue()
      long longValue()
      float floatValue()
      double doubleValue()
```

```
byte byteValue()
short shortValue()
boolean isNaN()
boolean isInfinite()
```

The `fieldnames` command introduced in the discussion of structures in Chapter 7 has been overloaded to return information about the public fields or variables of a Java class or object, for example,

```
>> dObj = java.lang.Double(5.0);

>> fieldnames(dObj)
ans =
    'POSITIVE_INFINITY'
    'NEGATIVE_INFINITY'
    'NaN'
    'MAX_VALUE'
    'MIN_VALUE'
    'TYPE'

>> fieldnames(dObj,'-full')
ans =
    'static final double POSITIVE_INFINITY'
    'static final double NEGATIVE_INFINITY'
    'static final double NaN'
    'static final double MAX_VALUE'
    'static final double MIN_VALUE'
    'static final java.lang.Class TYPE'

>> fieldnames(java.awt.Dimension)
ans =
    'width'
    'height'

>> fieldnames(java.awt.Point,'-full')
ans =
    'int x'
    'int y'
```

35.5 OBJECT PROPERTIES

Java objects in MATLAB have properties just as Handle Graphics objects do. MATLAB has `get` and `set` methods to access some of the standard Java class methods and to add common properties to Java objects. For example, the `java.awt.Frame` object has a MATLAB property called `'Background'`. The MATLAB `get` and `set` methods implement the Java `getBackground` and `setBackground` methods to change this property.

For example, create a `java.lang.Double` object,

```
>> dObj = java.lang.Double(6.0)
dObj. =
6.0
```

and examine its properties:

```
>> get(dObj)

        Infinite = off
        Class = [ (1 by 1) java.lang.Class array]
        NaN = off

        BeingDeleted = off
        ButtonDownFcn =
        Children = []
        Clipping = on
        CreateFcn =
        DeleteFcn =
        BusyAction = queue
        HandleVisibility = on
        HitTest = on
        Interruptible = on
        Parent = []
        Selected = off
        SelectionHighlight = on
        Serializable = on
        Tag =
        Type = java.lang.Double
        UIContextMenu = []
        UserData = []
        ApplicationData = [ (1 by 1) struct array]
        Visible = on
```

The common MATLAB object properties are available including the `'Tag'` and `'UserData'` properties. The three object-specific properties, `'Infinite'`, `'Class'`, and `'NaN'`, are all read-only properties.

```
>> get(dObj,'Class')
ans =
class java.lang.Double
```

```
>> set(dObj,'Tag','MyDouble')
>> get(dObj,'Tag')
ans =
MyDouble
```

> Java objects do not have handles in the sense that Handle Graphics objects do. Java objects are not children of the *root* object and cannot be found by the `findobj` function or any other MATLAB search technique.

35.6 DATA EXCHANGE

Java classes and objects are distinct from MATLAB classes and variables. Moving data between different classes of objects or variables requires changing the form of the data.

Automatic Data Type Conversions

MATLAB and Java, as in any typed programming language or environment, use ***coercion*** or ***casting,*** a familiar concept to most programmers, to transfer data between data types or classes. Each class contains at least one class constructor method used to create an object from a different source data type. For example, arithmetic operations are undefined on the MATLAB `uint8` data type. Operations can be performed on `uint8` data by explicitly casting the values into the `double` data type, performing the operation, and casting the result back into the `uint8` data type, as in the following example.

```
>> x = uint8(3)
x =
     3
>> y = uint8(2)
y =
     2
>> z = x+y
??? Error using ==> +
Function '+' not defined for variables of class 'uint8'.

>> z = uint8(double(x)+double(y))
z =
     5
>> class(z)
ans =
uint8
```

MATLAB hides most of the complexity of Java data type conversion by automatically casting native MATLAB data types into standard Java classes as needed. In general, MATLAB numerical data types are converted to the most appropriate Java target data type. MATLAB strings and arrays of characters are converted to the java.lang.String class. Cell arrays of Java objects are converted to Java arrays of objects. Note that MATLAB arrays and Java arrays are not the same.

Java objects returned to MATLAB from Java methods are generally not automatically converted to MATLAB data types so that they can continue to be used by Java methods. There are two general exceptions. Numerical values returned from Java methods are converted to MATLAB data types: scalars are converted to MATLAB doubles, and numerical arrays are converted to arrays of the most appropriate MATLAB type to save storage space. Strings are the other exception. java.lang.String objects returned to MATLAB are converted to character arrays. Java String arrays are converted to cell arrays of strings. Java objects explicitly created in MATLAB retain their original Java object form, including java.lang.Double and java.lang.String objects.

Explicit Data Type Conversions

Explicit data type conversions are also possible using the functions double, char, struct, and cell. Java objects belonging to any Java Numeric class or subclass or any other Java class containing a toDouble method can be converted to a MATLAB double. Any Java object of the String class or any other Java class containing a toString method can be converted to a MATLAB char. Consider the following example.

```
>> wObj = java.lang.Double(3.12)
wObj =
3.12
>> wObj.intValue
ans =
     3
>> class(ans)
ans =
double
>> class(double(wObj))
ans =
double
>> sObj = java.lang.String('A Java String')
sObj =
A Java String
>> class(sObj)
ans =
java.lang.String
>> sObj.toUpperCase
ans =
A JAVA STRING
```

```
>> class(ans)
ans =
char
>> butObj = java.awt.Button('OK')
but =
java.awt.Button[button1,0,0,0x0,invalid,label=OK]
>> butObj.getSize
ans =
java.awt.Dimension[width=0,height=0]
>> class(ans)
ans =
java.awt.Dimension
```

Displaying Java Objects

Whenever a Java object is listed using the `disp` function or by omitting the semicolon on the command line, the `toString` method is used to display the object. The `toString` method for most Java objects returns a character string containing the class name and information about some of the variables associated with the object. Consider the example

```
>> butObj = java.awt.Button('OK')
butObj =
java.awt.Button[button0,0,0,0x0,invalid,label=OK]

>> f = java.awt.Frame('My Frame')
f =
java.awt.Frame[frame0,0,0,0x0,invalid,hidden,layout=java.awt.BorderLayout,
                resizable,title=My Frame] % (line wrapped for printing)
```

Objects of the `Numeric` and `String` classes and subclasses are again exceptions to the rule. `Numeric` Java types are displayed as strings containing the value of the number, and `String` types are displayed as a character array containing the text of the Java `String`.

Java objects are very similar to MATLAB structures in some respects. Java class fields (the same fields listed by the `fieldnames` command) can be converted to MATLAB structures and accessed using standard MATLAB syntax, as in the following example.

```
>> b = struct(butObj)
b =
             WIDTH: 1
            HEIGHT: 2
        PROPERTIES: 4
          SOMEBITS: 8
         FRAMEBITS: 16
           ALLBITS: 32
             ERROR: 64
             ABORT: 128
     TOP_ALIGNMENT: 0
```

```
      CENTER_ALIGNMENT: 0.5
      BOTTOM_ALIGNMENT: 1
        LEFT_ALIGNMENT: 0
       RIGHT_ALIGNMENT: 1

>> b.PROPERTIES
ans =
     4
>> class(ans)
ans =
double
```

This feature provides a way to capture the names and values of all the public fields or variables of a Java class, but the only way to change these values is by using appropriate Java methods on an object of the class if such methods are available. Note that these particular fields are likely to be public static final (the field names are capitalized) and as such cannot be changed at all.

35.7 JAVA ARRAYS

So far we have discussed passing singular Java objects between Java methods and the MATLAB environment. Some methods can handle or even expect arrays of objects, while others can return arrays of objects. Java arrays can be returned by Java methods or can be created by MATLAB commands.

Java arrays are based on the C language model and are significantly different from MATLAB arrays in their structure and in the way elements are accessed. Most of the time the differences do not matter, as MATLAB handles the conversion transparently.

Java Array Structure

Java arrays are always 1-D vectors. 2-D Java arrays are constructed as arrays of arrays. 3-D Java arrays are arrays of arrays of arrays. *n*-D Java arrays can be constructed in the same manner. This array structure is similar to that of nested cell arrays in MATLAB. Like cell arrays, nested Java arrays can be of different lengths. For example, 2-D MATLAB character arrays must have rectangular dimensions: each row must have the same number of columns. Cell arrays of strings, however, can contain strings of different lengths. Java arrays can contain arrays of different lengths as well. These types of arrays are sometimes termed ***ragged*** arrays. When methods return ragged, nonrectangular arrays, MATLAB stores them in cell arrays.

Accessing Elements of Java Arrays

Java array indexing, like C, is zero-based, while MATLAB uses one-based indexing. Java programs access elements of an array of length `N` using the indices `0` through `N-1`. MATLAB accesses the same elements using the indices `1` through `N`. For example, `myArray(4)` is used to access the fourth element of a Java array in MATLAB, while a Java program accesses the same element of the array using myArray[3]. Similarly, the element of a Java array that is accessed by myArray[2][4] in a Java program can be accessed by myArray(3,5) within MATLAB. However, MATLAB hides these differences. When a Java method is used or a Java array is accessed in the MATLAB environment, normal MATLAB syntax is used. MATLAB makes the necessary indexing conversions transparently. Consider the following example.

```
>> but1Obj = java.awt.Button('STOP')
but1Obj =
java.awt.Button[button0,0,0,0x0,invalid,label=STOP]

>> but2Obj = java.awt.Button('GO')
but2Obj =
java.awt.Button[button1,0,0,0x0,invalid,label=GO]

>> butArray = [but1Obj,but2Obj]
butArray =
java.awt.Button[]:
    [1x1 java.awt.Button]
    [1x1 java.awt.Button]

>> class(butArray)
ans =
java.awt.Button[]
>> size(butArray)
ans =
     2     1
>> getLabel(butArray(1))     % Functional syntax for the getLabel method
ans =
STOP
>> butArray(2).getLabel      % Java syntax for the getLabel method
ans =
GO
>> butArray(2).setLabel('YIELD')
>> but2Obj
but2Obj =
java.awt.Button[button1,0,0,0x0,invalid,label=YIELD]
```

Note that butArray is an array of ***references*** to the but1Obj and but2Obj objects. Changes made to these references change the original object.

Creating Java Arrays

Java arrays can be created as the output of the operation of a Java method, by concatenating objects or arrays, by extracting elements of existing Java arrays, by assignment to an array element, or by using the java_array function.

As shown in the preceding example, the standard array operators [] (and the cat function) can be used to concatenate Java objects into a Java array. If the objects are of the same class, the resulting array is of the same class as well. If the objects are arrays of the same class, the arrays are stacked. The length of the resulting array is the sum of the lengths of the individual arrays. If the objects are 2-D arrays that differ in the lengths of the second dimension, the result is a ragged array. If the objects are of different classes, the resulting array is of the java.lang.Object class and its length is the number of arrays being combined.

As with normal MATLAB arrays, you can also create a Java array by assigning an object to a specific element of a nonexistent array.

```
>> bigButArray(3,4) = java.awt.Button('YES')
bigButArray =
 java.awt.Button[][]:
     []      []      []                          []
     []      []      []                          []
     []      []      []    [1x1 java.awt.Button]
```

Extending an array can produce unexpected results. Because of the structure of Java arrays and the fact that they can be ragged, extending an existing Java array by assignment does not necessarily result in a rectangular array. Consider an example using the bigButArray from the previous example:

```
>> bigButArray(4,5) = java.awt.Button('NO')
bigButArray =
java.awt.Button[][]:
    {4x1 cell}
    {4x1 cell}
    {4x1 cell}
    {5x1 cell}
```

This adds a fourth element to the top-level Java array containing a 5-element Java array of Button objects. Each of the existing elements of the top-level array continue to contain 4-element Java arrays of Button objects. Because the resulting array is nonrectangular or ragged, MATLAB stores the result as a cell array of Java arrays.

Similarly, when the empty matrix is assigned to an entire row or column of a MATLAB matrix, MATLAB removes the row or column and collapses the resulting matrix dimensions. Since Java arrays can be ragged, they cannot be handled in the same way. When an entire row or column of a Java array is assigned the empty matrix, the dimensions do not change. The elements are simply assigned the Java NULL character, which MATLAB represents as the empty matrix.

The java_array function creates an unpopulated Java array (filled with NULL values) of a specific class using the syntax java_array('java class',m,n,p,...), where m, n, and p are array dimensions. For example, create a 3-by-4 empty Java array to contain Button objects,

```
>> buttonArray = java_array('java.awt.Button',3,4)
buttonArray =
java.awt.Button[][]:
     []     []     []     []
     []     []     []     []
     []     []     []     []
```

and use standard MATLAB assignment syntax and a `Button` constructor method to populate the array with new `Button` objects.

```
>> buttonArray(2,2) = java.awt.Button('MAYBE')
buttonArray =
java.awt.Button[][]:
     []                          []     []     []
     []     [1x1 java.awt.Button]     []     []
     []                          []     []     []
```

Accessing Java Array Elements

The elements of a Java object array can be accessed using the normal MATLAB array indexing syntax, as in the following example.

```
>> dArray = java_array('java.lang.Double',3,4)
dArray =
java.lang.Double[][]:
     []     []     []     []
     []     []     []     []
     []     []     []     []

>> for i = 1:3
     for j = 1:4
       dArray(i,j) = java.lang.Double(i*10+j);
     end
   end

>> dArray
dArray =
java.lang.Double[][]:
    [11]    [12]    [13]    [14]
    [21]    [22]    [23]    [24]
    [31]    [32]    [33]    [34]
```

Notice that the result is a Java array consisting of 3 elements displayed as rows; each of these elements contains another Java array consisting of 4 elements displayed as columns. The element referenced by `dArray[0][2]` in Java is the element referenced by `dArray(1,3)` in MATLAB:

```
>> dArray(1,3)
ans =
13.0
```

The second element of the top-level `dArray` is a 4-element Java array:

```
>> dArray(2)
ans =
java.lang.Double[]:
    [21]
    [22]
    [23]
    [24]
```

This is not the result you get when using the same syntax on a MATLAB array. Given a 3-by-4 MATLAB array `D` of doubles, `D(4)` and `D(1,2)` refer to the same individual array element.

Subarrays

Subsets of Java arrays can be accessed using familiar MATLAB array syntax. Consider the following example given the Java array `dArray` and the corresponding MATLAB array `D`.

```
>> dArray
dArray =
java.lang.Double[][]:
    [11]    [12]    [13]    [14]
    [21]    [22]    [23]    [24]
    [31]    [32]    [33]    [34]
>> D = double(dArray)
D =
    11     12     13     14
    21     22     23     24
    31     32     33     34
>> dArray(2,2:3)
ans =
java.lang.Double[]:
    [22]
    [23]
>> D(2,2:3)
ans =
    22     23
```

On the other hand, MATLAB uses column-oriented storage for array elements, whereas Java uses row-oriented storage for array elements. A 2-by-2 MATLAB array is stored as `[11 21 12 22]`, while a 2-by-2 Java array (a 2-element Java array containing 2-element Java arrays) is stored as `[11 12][21 22]`. When using the colon operator (`:`) to create a vector from an array, the result differs because of these storage differences.

```
>> dArray(:)
ans =
java.lang.Double[]:
    [11]
    [12]
    [13]
    [14]
    [21]
    [22]
    [23]
    [24]
    [31]
    [32]
    [33]
    [34]

>> D(:)
ans =
    11
    21
    31
    12
    22
    32
    13
    23
    33
    14
    24
    34
```

The colon operator allows assignment to every element of a Java array or subarray with a single statement by treating the array as a single vector, as in the example

```
>> dblArray = java_array('java.lang.Double',3,4)
dblArray =
java.lang.Double[][]:
     []      []      []      []
     []      []      []      []
     []      []      []      []
```

```
>> dblArray(:) = java.lang.Double(0)
dblArray =
java.lang.Double[][]:
    [0]    [0]    [0]    [0]
    [0]    [0]    [0]    [0]
    [0]    [0]    [0]    [0]

>> dblArray(2,:) = java.lang.Double(1)
dblArray =
java.lang.Double[][]:
    [0]    [0]    [0]    [0]
    [1]    [1]    [1]    [1]
    [0]    [0]    [0]    [0]

 >> dArray(:,3) = java.lang.Double(4)
dblArray =
java.lang.Double[][]:
    [0]    [0]    [4]    [0]
    [1]    [1]    [4]    [1]
    [0]    [0]    [4]    [0]
```

Remember that each of these elements is another reference to the same object. The original constructor assignment statement `dblArray(:)=java.lang.Double(0)` creates one `java.lang.Double` object containing the value `0` and a populated `dblArray` with 12 references to this object. Each subsequent assignment statement created one new object and multiple references to this object.

Duplicating Arrays

Assigning Java arrays creates new references as well. For example,

```
>> xArray = dArray
xArray =
java.lang.Double[][]:
    [11]    [12]    [13]    [14]
    [21]    [22]    [23]    [24]
    [31]    [32]    [33]    [34]
```

simply creates a new reference to `dArray` named `xArray`. You can also create a new object reference by assigning a name to a single element of an array:

```
>> xObj = dArray(2,3)
xObj =
23.0
```

In this example, `xObj` and `dArray(2,3)` reference the same object.

If you assign a top-level element of an array containing two or more levels, the result is another reference to the array. Contained in the top-level array. Consider the following example.

```
>> yArray = dArray(2)
yArray =
java.lang.Double[]:
    [21]
    [22]
    [23]
    [24]

>> yArray(2)=java.lang.Double(0)
yArray =
java.lang.Double[]:
    [21]
    [ 0]
    [23]
    [24]

>> dArray
dArray =
java.lang.Double[][]:
    [11]    [12]    [13]    [14]
    [21]    [ 0]    [23]    [24]
    [31]    [32]    [33]    [34]
```

This example creates `yArray` as a new reference to the second element of the top-level array in `dArray`.

You can create a new array from elements of a Java array (known as ***cloning*** in Java) by assigning a subset of the original Java array elements to a new variable.

```
>> zArray = dArray(1:2,2:3)
zArray =
java.lang.Double[][]:
    [12]    [13]
    [ 0]    [23]
```

In this example, `zArray` is a new array of `Doubles` containing new references to the original objects. For example, `zArray(1,1)` and `dArray(1,2)` point to the same object. However, if you *replace* an element of `zArray` with a new object, `dArray` is not affected.

```
>> zArray(2,2) = java.lang.Double(-1)
zArray =
java.lang.Double[][]:
    [12]    [13]
    [ 0]    [-1]

>> dArray
dArray =
java.lang.Double[][]:
    [11]    [12]    [13]    [14]
    [21]    [ 0]    [23]    [24]
    [31]    [32]    [33]    [34]
```

Replacing an element of zArray replaces the object reference with a new object and therefore does not affect dArray. However, the other elements in zArray are still references. Changes to ***attributes*** of these elements are changes to the original elements.

An entire Java array can be copied using the colon operator:

```
>> xArray = dArray(:,:)
xArray =
java.lang.Double[][]:
    [11]    [12]    [13]    [14]
    [21]    [ 0]    [23]    [24]
    [31]    [32]    [33]    [34]

>> xArray(2,3) = dArray(3,4)
xArray =
java.lang.Double[][]:
    [11]    [12]    [13]    [14]
    [21]    [ 0]    [34]    [24]
    [31]    [32]    [33]    [34]

>> dArray
dArray =
java.lang.Double[][]:
    [11]    [12]    [13]    [14]
    [21]    [ 0]    [23]    [24]
    [31]    [32]    [33]    [34]
```

The element at xArray(2,3) now contains a new reference to dArray(3,4), while dArray is unaffected.

A new array is also created when you concatenate Java arrays. Consider the example

```
>> a = dArray(1,3)
a =
13.0
```

```
>> b = dArray(3,2)
b =
32.0
>> c = [a b]
c =
java.lang.Double[]:
    [13]
    [32]
>> c(2) = dArray(3,3)
c =
java.lang.Double[]:
    [13]
    [33]
>> a
a =
13.0
>> b
b =
32.0
```

In general, a reference is created whenever you assign any Java object or array. A new array is created when you assign a subset of a Java array (or an entire array using the `(:,:)` notation) or concatenate Java arrays. The new array contains new references to the original array elements.

The statements

```
xArray = dArray;
yArray = dArray(2);
zObj = dArray(2,3);
```

create new references, while the statements

```
xArray = dArray(:.:);
yArray = dArray(2,:);
zArray = [dArray, dArray];
```

create new arrays containing additional references to the specified elements of the original array.

Java Array Size

Some MATLAB functions have been enhanced to support Java arrays, but full MATLAB functionality is not available because of the structure of Java arrays. For example, the `size` and `length` functions operating on a Java array return information about the top-level array only.

```
>> myArray = java_array('java.lang.Double',3,4)
myArray =
java.lang.Double[][]:
      []      []      []      []
      []      []      []      []
      []      []      []      []

>> size(myArray)
ans =
      3      1
>> length(myArray)
ans =
      3
```

To get information on other dimensions, you must specifically address an element of the top-level array.

```
>> size(myArray(1))
ans =
      4      1
>> length(myArray(2))
ans =
      4
```

The total number of elements in a Java array can be obtained using the `length` function.

```
>> length(myArray(:))
ans =
     12
```

Similarly, you can use the `end` keyword when addressing Java arrays, but only in the top-level reference (the first dimension).

```
>> myArray(2:end)
ans =
java.lang.Double[][]:
      []      []      []      []
      []      []      []      []
```

```
>> myArray(:,2:end)
ans =
java.lang.Double[][]:

>> myArray(2,2:end)
ans =
java.lang.Double[]:
```

35.8 JAVA FUNCTIONS

In addition to those mentioned previously, other MATLAB functions have been created or modified to support Java classes, objects, and methods. As noted earlier, `import` can be used to add to the Java class and package import list and allow shorthand references to Java classes. Java objects can be removed, and the import list can be cleared with the `clear` function. The `inmem` function has been enhanced to list the names of all the Java classes that have been loaded into the MATLAB workspace in an optional third output argument. The `exist` function now recognizes and identifies Java objects and arrays. The `class` function recognizes the class of Java objects and arrays, and the `isa` function can test the class of a Java object or array. The new `isjava` function can be used to determine whether or not a variable is a Java object.

The `fieldnames` function returns a list of the public fields of a Java class or object. The `methods` command lists the names of the methods available to operate on objects of specific Java classes. The `which` function has been enhanced to return a list of the loaded Java classes that contain a given method or combination of method and signature, for example,

```
>> which -all resize
java.awt.Button.resize                                     % Button method
java.awt.TextArea.resize                                   % TextArea method
java.awt.Frame.resize                                      % Frame method
/local/matlab6/toolbox/matlab/graph2d/@axisobj/resize.p  % axisobj method
/local/matlab6/toolbox/matlab/graph2d/@axisobj/resize.m  % Shadowed axisobj method
```

The `save` and `load` functions can store and recall Java objects and arrays in normal binary MAT-files. Java objects cannot be saved in ASCII-formatted files, however. Java exceptions are automatically caught and converted to normal MATLAB errors. The text of the exception is captured and can be displayed using `lasterr`.

The following table summarizes the MATLAB functions that support Java. Some are standard MATLAB functions that have been overloaded for Java, while others have been created specifically to support working with Java in MATLAB.

Function	Description
`methods`	List the public methods of a Java class.
`which`	Can return a list of matching methods in loaded Java classes.

Function	Description
fieldnames	List the public fields or variables of a Java class.
inmem	Can return a cell array of the names of all Java classes that have been loaded.
import	List or add to the Java class and package import list.
clear	Clear Java objects from the workspace or clear the Java class import list.
isjava	True if the argument is a Java object or Java array.
isa	Determine if a variable is a Java object of a specific class.
exist	Determine the nature of a variable; return 8 if the argument is a Java class.
class	Determine the class of a Java object.
double	Convert a Java object or array of class Numeric to MATLAB doubles.
char	Convert a Java object or array of class String to a MATLAB character array or to a cell array of strings.
struct	Create a structure from the public fields of a Java class or object.
save	Store variables including Java objects in a binary MAT-file.
load	Load variables including Java objects from a binary MAT-file.
[] and cat	Concatenate Java objects or arrays into a Java array.
java_array	Create a new Java array and populate it with NULL characters.
size	Return the size of the top-level array of a Java array.
length	Determine the length of the top-level array of a Java array.
java_method	Invoke a Java method on a Java object or Java array. (Not recommended.)
java_object	Create a Java object. (Not recommended.)

35.9 EXAMPLES

This section contains a number of examples that pull together many of the concepts and tools presented in this chapter to illustrate how Java can help to extend the capabilities of MATLAB. We start with few basic examples and proceed to more complete functions.

Example 1: whoami

This example uses elements of the `java.net` class library to return the host name and IP address of the computer running MATLAB.

```
function whoami
% Test function to illustrate the use of the java.net package.
%
% Mastering MATLAB 6 Java Example 1

% Use try and catch to avoid Java exception messages.
try
    me=java.net.InetAddress.getLocalHost;
catch
    error('Unable to get local host address.');
end

% Find my hostname and IP address
myname=me.getHostName;
myip=me.getHostAddress;

% and print the results.
disp(sprintf('My host name is %s',char(myname)));
disp(sprintf('My IP address is %s',char(myip)));
```

The `whoami` function produces results similar to the following.

```
>> whoami
My host name is www.phptr.com
My IP address is 204.179.152.74
```

Example 2: random

The next example uses the `java.util` package to generate a random number.

```
function num=random(varargin)
% Test function to illustrate the use of the java.util package.
%   Generate a random number between given limits (or 0:1).
```

```
%
% Mastering MATLAB 6 Java Example 2

% Check any input arguments.
if nargin == 0
  rmin=0; rmax=1;
elseif nargin < 3
  if nargin == 1
    lim = varargin{1};
  else
    lim = [varargin{1}, varargin{2}];
  end
  if isnumeric(lim) & length(lim) == 2
    rmin = min(lim); rmax = max(lim);
  else
    error('Invalid limits.');
  end
else
  error('Too many arguments.')
end

% Construct a Random object and generate a uniformly-
% distributed random number between the desired limits.
rNum = java.util.Random;
num = rNum.nextDouble * (rmax - rmin) + rmin;
```

The `random` function parses the input, creates a `Random` object, and uses the `nextDouble` method to obtain a uniformly distributed pseudorandom number. The `nextGaussian` method is available to generate a normally distributed random number. Other `Random` methods can be used to generate `integer`, `long`, or `float` values, or even a user-specified number of random bytes.

Example 3: `hithere`

This example creates a simple dialog box containing a line of text and a button. When the button is clicked, the dialog box exits.

```
% script hithere.m
% Example script to illustrate the use of the java.awt package.
```

```
%
% Mastering MATLAB 6 Java Example 3

% Create a Frame object and specify a 2x1 grid layout style.
dbox=java.awt.Frame('Hi There!');
dbox.setLayout(java.awt.GridLayout(2,1));

% Specify the window location, size and color. Use Java syntax
%    for the location, hybrid syntax for the size, and MATLAB
%    syntax to set the background color.
dbox.setLocation(50,50);
resize(dbox,200,100);
set(dbox,'Background',[.7,.8,.9]);

% Create a text label and a bright red button.
txt=java.awt.Label('Click the button to exit.',1);
but=java.awt.Button('Exit Button');
set(but,'Background',[1,0,0]);

% Define a callback for the button.
set(but,'MouseClickedCallback','dbox.dispose')

% Attach the label and button to the window.
dbox.add(txt);
dbox.add(but);

% The window is hidden by default. Make it visible.
dbox.show;
```

This example uses a script M-file rather than a function to avoid scoping issues with the `Button` callback. As with Handle Graphics objects, Java callbacks are strings that are passed to the `eval` function in the MATLAB base workspace. The following figure is an example of the dialog box generated by the `hithere.m` script.

Example 4: `netsearch`

This example uses the `java.net` package to manage Internet communication along with the `java.io` package to read a data stream. The `netsearch` function performs an Internet search and returns a cell array of the uniform resource locator (URL) strings found by the search engine. If no matches are found after contacting one search engine, another is tried.

```
function ulist=netsearch(varargin)
% MATLAB Java Demo function netsearch.m
%
%  Mastering MATLAB 6 Java Example 4
%    Open a connection to an Internet search engine using
%    Java networking toolkit objects and return the URLs
%    found by the search in a cell array.

% Import the java.net and java.io toolkits to save typing.
import java.net.* java.io.*

% Define the url for a search command and a target string
%     for each host to try in order.
s_host={'http://www.google.com/search?q=',    '<p><A HREF='
        'http://ink.yahoo.com/bin/query?p=', '<li><a href='};

nhosts=size(s_host,1);       % Number of search hosts defined
found=logical(0);            % Not yet found
ulist={};                    % Cell array to contain results

% Do some error checking.
if nargin < 1
  error('Nothing to search for.');
end
if nargout > 1
  error('Too many output arguments.');
end

% Create a search string from the input arguments.
for (idx=1:nargin)
  if ~ischar(varargin{idx})
    error('Search terms must be strings');
  else
    tmp_str=varargin{idx};

    % If this string argument contains spaces, quote the string
    % and replace the spaces with plus sign characters.
```

```
    if findstr(tmp_str,' ')
      tmp_str=['%22',strrep(tmp_str,' ','+'),'%22'];
    end

    % Build up the search string.
    if idx == 1
      s_str=tmp_str;
    else
      s_str=[s_str,'+',tmp_str];
    end
  end
end

% Start with the initial search host.
uidx=1;
hostidx=1;
while isempty(ulist) & (hostidx <= nhosts)

 % Construct a complete URL using the search string.
 s_url=[s_host{hostidx,1},s_str];

  % Create a URL connection to the search engine.
  searchHost=URL(s_url);

  % Open a buffered input stream reader to read one line at a time.
  shBuf = BufferedReader(InputStreamReader(searchHost.openStream));

  % Read the lines of the page returned by the search engine
  %   and extract any target URLs until the the page ends.
  linebuf=shBuf.readLine;
  while ~isempty(linebuf)
    linebuf=char(linebuf);
    found=strncmp(linebuf,s_host{hostidx,2},length(s_host{hostidx,2}));
    if found
      tmp=strtok(linebuf(length(s_host{hostidx,2})+1:end),'>');
      ulist{uidx}=strrep(tmp,'"','');
      uidx=uidx+1;
    end
    linebuf=shBuf.readLine;
    if isempty(linebuf)              % Check the next line as well.
      linebuf=shBuf.readLine;
    end
  end
  % We are done with the page so close the connection.
  shBuf.close;
```

```
  % If a target URL was not found, try the next host.
  if isempty(ulist)
    hostidx=hostidx+1;
  end
end

if isempty(ulist)
  ulist=[];
elseif length(ulist) == 1
  ulist=ulist{1};
end
```

The s_host array consists of two strings for each host. The first string contains the protocol, host, and search command portion of a search URL. The search terms are added to this string in an appropriate format to generate the complete URL string which is used to create a java.net.URL object. The openStream method is used on the searchHost object to open an Internet connection to the search host. An InputStreamReader object is created on this connection and passed to a BufferedReader to enable line-at-a-time processing of the input stream. The readLine method is then used to read one line at a time into a string buffer.

The second element of the s_host array is a target string. A web page is composed of text containing formatting and other codes called ***tags*** delimited by '<' and '>' characters. Each target URL (or ***hit***) that is found by a particular search engine is normally preceded by a specific character string in the page returned by the search URL. Each line of the web page is examined for the presence of this target string. If the string is found, the target URL is extracted and copied into the output cell array. When the page has been completely processed, the connection is closed. If no results are found, the next search host is contacted and the search continues. Note that web pages change over time and the strings in s_host may have to be modified appropriately.

Example 5: winfun

The next example is an expanded version of the hithere script in Example 3. This time, a window is created containing some buttons and menus with callbacks. The first time winfun is called, a window is constructed from java.awt toolkit objects, set to an initial state, and made visible. The function then exits. The Java objects still exist and are visible, but the object references (the variables) do not exist in the base workspace. If a button is pressed or a menu item selected, the associated object callback is executed. The callback calls the winfun function again (since the winfun function alone is known in the base workspace) with a unique argument. When `winfun` is called with an argument, the argument is passed to a local function to service the callback. Object references must be passed to the local function as well since the `local_callback` function executes in its own workspace. Finally, if the `winfun` function is called with no arguments but the Java objects still exist, the window is reset to the initial state and made visible again.

```
function winfun(varargin)
% MATLAB Java Demo function winfun.m
%
%  Mastering MATLAB 6 Java Example 5
%    Create a window with buttons, menus and text objects using
%    Java windowing toolkit objects within a function. Use a
%    local function to implement callbacks. Use persistent variables
%    to maintain visibility of the Java objects between calls.
%

% Import the entire Java Abstract Window Toolkit.
import java.awt.*

% Make sure we can find the Java objects when servicing callbacks.
persistent win ta mi abt mq ma txt

if isempty(win)  % Initial function call. Create the objects.

  % Start with some text for the About Box.
  txt=[' Cool Window version 1.3  ';...
       ' MM6 example function by  ';...
       'Mastering MATLAB authors  ';...
       'Hanselman and Littlefield '];

  % Reshape it for use in the textarea as well.
  tstr=reshape(txt',1,prod(size(txt)));

  % Create a window using the flow layout model (the simplest)
  %    and set the title. Set the layout using Java syntax.
  win=Frame('Cool Java Window');
  win.setLayout(FlowLayout);

  % Specify the window location, size and color. Use Java syntax
  %    for the location and size, and use MATLAB syntax to set
  %    the background color.
  win.setLocation(50,50);
  win.resize(340,160);
  set(win,'Background',[.7 .8 .9]);
```

```
% Create some menus: a 'File' menu and a 'Help' menu.
mf=Menu('File');
mh=Menu('Help');

% Create a 'Quit' menu item, define a callback to close the window,
%     and attach it to the File menu.
mq=MenuItem('Quit');
set(mq,'ActionPerformedCallback','winfun(''quit'')');
mf.add(mq);

% Create a 4x21 text area with no scroll bars (3).
ta=TextArea(tstr,4,21,3);
ta.setEditable(0);              % Don't let the user change the text.
set(ta,'Background',[1,1,.9]); % Set the text background color.

% Create a 'Show Info' menu item and attach it to the Help menu.
%    Show or hide the textarea when the menu item is selected.
mi=MenuItem('Show Info');
set(mi,'ActionPerformedCallback','winfun(''info'')');
mh.add(mi);

% Create an 'About' menu item and attach it to the Help menu.

ma=MenuItem('About');
set(ma,'ActionPerformedCallback','winfun(''about'')');
mh.add(ma);

% Create a menubar object, add the menus, and attach
%   the menubar to the window.
mb=MenuBar;
mb.add(mf); mb.add(mh);
mb.setHelpMenu(mh);       % Move the Help menu to the right side.
win.setMenuBar(mb);

% Create some buttons.
bs=Button('Shrink'); be=Button('Expand');
bl=Button('Left');   bu=Button(' Up ');
bd=Button('Down');   br=Button('Right');
bq=Button('Quit');

% Define callbacks for the buttons.
set(bs,'MouseClickedCallback','winfun(''shrink'')')
set(be,'MouseClickedCallback','winfun(''expand'')')
```

```
set(bl,'MouseClickedCallback','winfun(''left'')');
set(bu,'MouseClickedCallback','winfun(''up'')');
set(bd,'MouseClickedCallback','winfun(''down'')');
set(br,'MouseClickedCallback','winfun(''right'')');
set(bq,'MouseClickedCallback','winfun(''quit'')');

% Specify some colors for the buttons.
set(bs,'Background',[.5,1,1]);
set(be,'Background',[1,.5,1]);
set(bq,'Background',[1,.6,.6]);
set(bl,'Background',[.6,.5,.4],'Foreground',[1,1,1]);
set(bu,'Background',[.6,.5,.4],'Foreground',[1,1,1]);
set(bd,'Background',[.6,.5,.4],'Foreground',[1,1,1]);
set(br,'Background',[.6,.5,.4],'Foreground',[1,1,1]);

% Add the first row of buttons to the window. Objects will be
%    positioned in the order in which they are added.
win.add(bs); win.add(bl); win.add(bu);
win.add(bd); win.add(br); win.add(be);

% Attach the text area to the window, but don't display it yet.
win.add(ta); ta.hide;

% Now add the Quit button.
win.add(bq);

% Now that the main window has been created, it is time
%    to create a dialog box for the 'About' menu item.
abt = Dialog(win, 'About Winfun');
set(abt,'Background',[.95 .95 .95]);
abt.setLayout(GridLayout(5,1));

% Add some lines of text
abt.add(Label(txt(1,:))); abt.add(Label(txt(2,:)));
abt.add(Label(txt(3,:))); abt.add(Label(txt(4,:)));

% and a button bar to close the About box.
bok = Button('OK');
set(bok,'ActionPerformedCallback','winfun(''ok'')');
set(bok,'Background',[.6 .8 .8]);
abt.add(bok);

% Set the size of the dialog box but don't make it visible.
abt.resize(180,110);
% All done. Now show the main window and exit.
win.show;
```

```
elseif nargin == 0 % Subsequent user call.

  % Reset the hidden window to the initial state and show it.
  abt.hide; ta.hide; mi.setLabel('Show Info');
  win.resize(340,160); win.setLocation(50,50);
  win.show;

elseif nargin == 1 % Callback!

  % Pass object pointers and the input argument to a local
  %   subfunction to handle the callbacks.
  local_callback(win,ta,abt,mi,varargin{1});

else   % Should not get here. User call with an argument.
    error('Too many arguments.');
end
```

This example demonstrates many different ways to call methods on Java objects. It also shows how to use persistent variables to keep track of Java objects between function calls. The winfun.m file also contains the local function local_callback to handle object callbacks using the ***switchyard*** technique. Again, note that a number of Java objects (references) are passed to the callback function so that the references will be available in the callback function workspace.

```
function  local_callback(win,ta,abt,mi,arg);
% Local function for winfun.m to implement callbacks.

switch (arg)
  case 'shrink'   % Shrink width by 4 pixels, height by 2
    win.resize(win.getSize.width-4,win.getSize.height-2); win.show;
  case 'expand'   % Expand width by 4 pixels,height by 2
    win.resize(win.getSize.width+4,win.getSize.height+2); win.show;
  case 'left'     % Move 4 pixels to the left
    win.move(win.getLocation.x-4,win.getLocation.y); win.show;
  case 'up'       % Move 2 pixels higher
    win.move(win.getLocation.x,win.getLocation.y-2); win.show;
  case 'down'     % Move 2 pixels lower
    win.move(win.getLocation.x,win.getLocation.y+2); win.show;
```

```
  case 'right'    % Move 4 pixels to the right
    win.move(win.getLocation.x+4,win.getLocation.y); win.show;
  case 'info'     % Toggle visibility of the text area
    if (ta.isVisible)
      ta.hide; mi.setLabel('Show Info');
    else
      ta.show; mi.setLabel('Hide Info');
    end
    win.show;
  case 'about'    % Show the About Box to the right and lower
    abt.setLocation(...
       win.getLocation.x+win.getSize.width+20,win.getLocation.y+10);
    abt.show
  case 'ok'       % Hide the About Box
    abt.hide
  case 'quit'     % Hide both windows
    abt.hide; win.hide;
  otherwise       % Bad argument
    error('Invalid callback');
end
```

The callback argument determines which `case` statement is executed within the `switch` statement. When the argument is `shrink`, the size of the window object `win` is reduced by 4 pixels in the horizontal (`x`) direction and 2 pixels in the vertical (`y`) direction using the `resize` method. The `show` method is then used to redraw the window with the changed characteristics. Similarly, the `expand` argument increases the window size. The `up`, `down`, `left`, and `right` arguments change the window location using the `move` method.

When the `info` argument is invoked, the result depends on the state of the `ta` text area object. If `ta` is visible (as determined by the `isVisible` method), the text area is hidden and the menu item label is changed appropriately. If the text area is currently hidden, `ta` is made visible using the `show` method, and the menu item label is changed again. `win.show` is then called to refresh the window.

When the `about` argument is received, the dialog box `abt` is positioned to the right of the `win` window and made visible. When the `ok` argument is received, the `abt` dialog box is hidden. When `quit` is received, both the `win` window and the `abt` dialog box are hidden.

The following figure is an example of the windows generated by the `winfun` function.

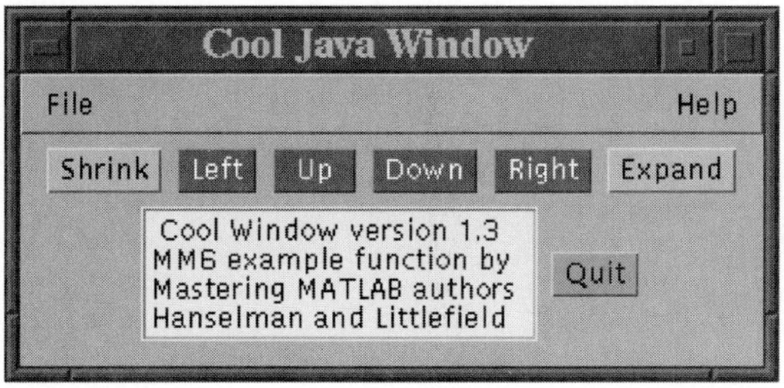

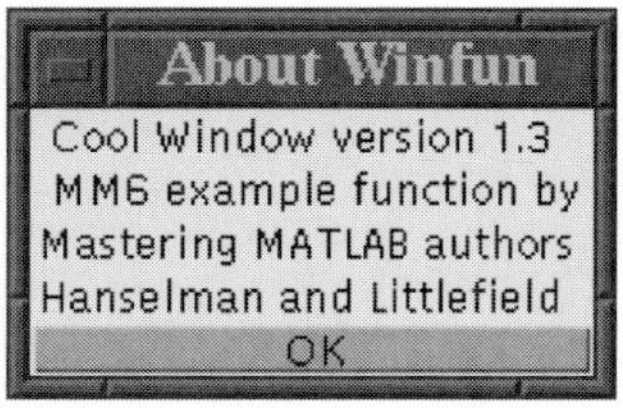

35.10 SUMMARY

Java is an object-oriented, platform-independent programming language that can be used to extend the scope of the MATLAB environment. Every installation of MATLAB 6 now includes a Java virtual machine integrated into MATLAB and available to the MATLAB user. Java classes, objects, and methods can be manipulated within MATLAB, both from the command line and from MATLAB functions. Java integration provides new opportunities to extend MATLAB in many different ways. While MATLAB currently incorporates Java, it is not possible to call MATLAB functions from Java. It is expected that this feature will appear in some future MATLAB release.

The examples in this chapter explore only a few of the possibilities opened up by the availability of Java objects and methods within MATLAB. The MATLAB documentation contains additional Java examples and more details on some of the topics discussed in this chapter. Perhaps the most important property of Java objects is that they are passed by reference, not by value.

> *Important:* Java objects are references in MATLAB. As a result, Java objects cannot be copied, only modified. In addition, Java objects never really disappear. The `clear` function removes references to these objects from the workspace, but the objects themselves may still exist. The Java `hide` method simply make objects invisible. The Java `dispose` method may remove some attributes of objects, but the objects may still exist. Finally, if one loses all references to a Java object by exiting a workspace or using the `clear` command, they cannot be retrieved. There is nothing similar to the `findobj` function for Java objects.

To end this chapter, we note that future versions of MATLAB are likely to greatly expand Java support. MATLAB appears to be moving toward an integrated development environment based on Java. Handle Graphics objects and Java graphics classes and objects are likely to converge. This all suggests that Java will play an increasing role in the future development of MATLAB.

36

Windows Application Integration

It is not always necessary to write your own applications in a programming language such as C or FORTRAN to get applications to communicate with each other. UNIX and Linux platforms use standard ***pipes*** to connect applications. Microsoft Windows applications use the DDE protocol or ActiveX, where ActiveX is a Microsoft implementation of the Component Object Model (COM) standard, to exchange data and communicate with other applications. Many commercial applications support ActiveX or DDE for interapplication communication on the Windows PC platform.

MATLAB supports both DDE and ActiveX in a limited capacity. It supports the creation of ActiveX objects within MATLAB to control other applications and can also act as an ActiveX server and respond to requests from other applications. ActiveX is available only on the `win32` platform under a Microsoft Windows operating system such as Windows 95, Windows 98, Windows NT, or Windows 2000.

36.1 ACTIVEX: CLIENT/SERVER COMMUNICATION

The ActiveX protocol specifies an object model and a collection of standard and custom interfaces that define each object's methods, properties, and events. Methods are actions that can be performed on or by an object (similar to MATLAB functions and object methods), properties are variables that determine the state of an object (similar to Handle Graphics properties), and events are notifications of changes in the state of an object that may trigger some action (similar to Handle Graphics or Java callbacks).

Applications that support ActiveX can support server functions (ActiveX Automation servers), client functions (ActiveX Automation clients or control containment), or both. ActiveX controls are objects that can be integrated into ***control containers*** (such as MATLAB *Figure* windows) by an ActiveX client application and are used to initiate an action by an ActiveX server application. ActiveX Automation servers are applications that can be controlled in some way by an ActiveX client or by an ActiveX control.

MATLAB ActiveX Support

MATLAB supports a limited set of ActiveX interfaces. It can act as an Automation server by exchanging data with other applications and executing commands in the MATLAB workspace, and it can act as an Automation client by exchanging data with other applications and controlling these Automation server applications (such as Microsoft Word, Excel, and PowerPoint) from the MATLAB command line or through M-files. MATLAB cannot be physically imbedded within other applications, but it can act as a control container by imbedding Automation server controls within MATLAB *Figure* windows similar to the way *uicontrols* are used.

MATLAB as Client

The `actxserver` function creates an `activex` object and opens a connection to an ActiveX Automation server. Similarly, the `actxcontrol` function creates an `activex` control that can be imbedded in a MATLAB container (such as a *Figure* window) to control an ActiveX Automation server. The functions (methods) that operate on `activex` objects are shown in the following table.

Method	Description
`actxserver`	Creates an `activex` server object to control an Automation server.
`actxcontrol`	Creates an `activex` control object to imbed within a MATLAB *Figure* window.
`invoke`	Invokes a method on an interface or displays a list of methods.
`set`	Sets a property on an interface.
`get`	Gets a property value from an interface or displays a list of properties.

Method	Description
`propedit`	Asks the control to display its built-in property page if it exists.
`release`	Releases an `activex` interface.
`send`	Displays a list of events.
`delete`	Deletes an `activex` object and all its interfaces.
`load`	Loads the property state of a control from a file.
`save`	Saves the property state of a control to a file.
`move`	Moves a control and returns the new position.

The `actxcontrol`, `actxserver`, `get`, and `invoke` functions can all return `activex` objects (or new ***interfaces*** to objects—essentially separate communication channels to objects), which can be controlled or queried using other `activex` functions or methods. The `release` function should be used to release the resources used by an `activex` object or interface when it is no longer needed. The `delete` function closes all connections and releases all resources when the server or control object is no longer needed.

Help text is available using the appropriate object method. For example,

```
>> help activex/delete
```

displays the help text for the `delete` method for `activex` objects.

A list of properties can be obtained using the form `get(axhandle)`, where `axhandle` is the `activex` object handle obtained from an `actxserver` or `actxcontrol` object creation method. The properties of a Word ActiveX server are as follows.

```
>> wordapp = actxserver('Word.Application')
wordapp =
    activex object: 1-by-1

>> get(wordapp)
    ActiveDocument = <Interface>
    ActivePrinter = HPPS on NE00:
    ActiveWindow = <Interface>
    AddIns = <Interface>
    Application = <Interface>
    Assistant = <Interface>
    AutoCaptions = <Interface>
    AutoCorrect = <Interface>
    BackgroundPrintingStatus = [0]
    BackgroundSavingStatus = [0]
    BrowseExtraFileTypes =
    Browser = <Interface>
```

```
Build = 8.0.5622
CapsLock = [0]
Caption = Microsoft Word
CaptionLabels = <Interface>
CommandBars = <Interface>
Creator = [1.29731e+009]
CustomDictionaries = <Interface>
CustomizationContext = <Interface>
DefaultSaveFormat =
DefaultTableSeparator = -
Dialogs = <Interface>
DisplayAlerts = [0]
DisplayAutoCompleteTips = <property unavailable>
DisplayRecentFiles = [-1]
DisplayScreenTips = [-1]
DisplayScrollBars = [-1]
DisplayStatusBar = <property unavailable>
Documents = <Interface>
EnableCancelKey = [1]
FileConverters = <Interface>
FileSearch = <Interface>
FindKey = <Interface>
FocusInMailHeader = [0]
FontNames = <Interface>
Height = [630]
International = <property unavailable>
IsObjectValid = <property unavailable>
KeyBindings = <Interface>
KeysBoundTo = <Interface>
LandscapeFontNames = <Interface>
Languages = <Interface>
Left = [401]
ListGalleries = <Interface>
MacroContainer = <Interface>
MailingLabel = <Interface>
MailMessage = <Interface>
MailSystem = [0]
MAPIAvailable = [0]
MathCoprocessorAvailable = [-1]
MouseAvailable = [-1]
Name = Microsoft Word
NormalTemplate = <Interface>
NumLock = [-1]
Options = <Interface>
Parent = <Interface>
Path = C:\PROGRA~1\MICROS~2\Office
PathSeparator = \
PortraitFontNames = <Interface>
PrintPreview = [0]
```

```
RecentFiles = <Interface>
ScreenUpdating = [-1]
Selection = <Interface>
ShowVisualBasicEditor = [0]
SpecialMode = [0]
StartupPath = c:\program files\microsoftoffice\office\startup
SynonymInfo = <Interface>
System = <Interface>
Tasks = <Interface>
Templates = <Interface>
Top = [38]
UsableHeight = [596]
UsableWidth = [530]
UserAddress =
UserControl = [0]
UserInitials = b
UserName = mm
VBE = <Interface>
Version = 8.0b
Visible = [0]
Width = [536]
Windows = <Interface>
WindowState = [0]
WordBasic = <Interface>
```

The command `>> invoke(axhandle)` returns a list of the methods available for the `axhandle` object. The methods available for the Word ActiveX server are as follows.

```
>> invoke(wordapp)
   Activate = Void Activate ()
   AddAddress = Void AddAddress (Variant(Pointer), Variant(Pointer))
   AutomaticChange = Void AutomaticChange ()
   BuildKeyCode = [ (1 by 102) char array]
   CentimetersToPoints = Float CentimetersToPoints (Float)
   ChangeFileOpenDirectory = Void ChangeFileOpenDirectory (String)
   CheckGrammar = Bool CheckGrammar (String)
   CheckSpelling = [ (1 by 303) char array]
   CleanString = String CleanString (String)
   DDEExecute = Void DDEExecute (Int, String)
   DDEInitiate = Int DDEInitiate (String, String)
   DDEPoke = Void DDEPoke (Int, String, String)
   DDERequest = String DDERequest (Int, String)
   DDETerminate = Void DDETerminate (Int)
   DDETerminateAll = Void DDETerminateAll ()
   GetAddress = [ (1 by 202) char array]
   GetSpellingSuggestions = [ (1 by 347) char array]
   GoBack = Void GoBack ()
   GoForward = Void GoForward ()
```

```
Help = Void Help (Variant(Pointer))
HelpTool = Void HelpTool ()
InchesToPoints = Float InchesToPoints (Float)
KeyString = String KeyString (Int, Variant(Pointer)[opt])
LinesToPoints = Float LinesToPoints (Float)
ListCommands = Void ListCommands (Bool)
LookupNameProperties = Void LookupNameProperties (String)
MillimetersToPoints = Float MillimetersToPoints (Float)
MountVolume = [ (1 by 111) char array]
Move = Void Move (Int, Int)
NewWindow = Variant(Pointer) NewWindow ()
NextLetter = Void NextLetter ()
OnTime = Void OnTime (Variant(Pointer), String, Variant(Pointer)[opt])
OrganizerCopy = Void OrganizerCopy (String, String, String, Vendor-Defined)
OrganizerDelete = Void OrganizerDelete (String, String, Vendor-Defined)
OrganizerRename = Void OrganizerRename (String, String, String, Vendor-Defined)
PicasToPoints = Float PicasToPoints (Float)
PointsToCentimeters = Float PointsToCentimeters (Float)
PointsToInches = Float PointsToInches (Float)
PointsToLines = Float PointsToLines (Float)
PointsToMillimeters = Float PointsToMillimeters (Float)
PointsToPicas = Float PointsToPicas (Float)
PrintOut = [ (1 by 359) char array]
Quit = Void Quit (Variant(Pointer)[opt], Variant(Pointer)[opt],
                  Variant(Pointer)[opt])
Repeat = Bool Repeat (Variant(Pointer)[opt])
ResetIgnoreAll = Void ResetIgnoreAll ()
Resize = Void Resize (Int, Int)
Run = Void Run (String)
ScreenRefresh = Void ScreenRefresh ()
SendFax = Void SendFax ()
ShowClipboard = Void ShowClipboard ()
ShowMe = Void ShowMe ()
SubstituteFont = Void SubstituteFont (String, String)
```

With this introduction, several examples are presented to illustrate the key features of ActiveX in MATLAB.

MATLAB Client Examples

This example uses MATLAB as an ActiveX client and Microsoft Word as an ActiveX server. The MATLAB M-file function `wordfig` copies the contents of the current (or specified) *Figure* window to the clipboard, starts a server instance of the Microsoft Word application, opens a selected document or creates a new document using the `uiputfile` dialog box to specify the filename, pastes the graphic at the ed of the document, closes the document, quits the Word application, and deletes the `activex` server object.

```
function wordfig(filespec,popt)
%WORDFIG Open a MSWord document and paste the current figure into it.
% WORDFIG Paste the current Figure window into a word document.
% WORDFIG(FILESPEC) Paste the current Figure window into the document
% named FILESPEC. Use the complete path to the document if necessary.
% WORDFIG(FILESPEC,POPT) Paste a Figure window into the document FILESPEC
% usingthe print options POPT (e.g. -f2 to select Figure window #2).
% If the FILESPEC argument is missing or empty, the uiputfile dialog box
% is used to select a file name.

% Create or verify a valid file name.
if nargin < 1 | isempty(filespec) | ~ischar(filespec)
  fname,dname]=uiputfile('*.doc','Modify or create the file:');
  if fname == 0, return, end
  filespec=fullfile(dname,fname);
end
[dname,fname,fext]=fileparts(filespec);
if isempty(dname), dname=pwd; end
if isempty(fext), fext='.doc'; end
filespec=fullfile(dname,[fname,fext]);

% Copy the current Figure window onto the clipboard.
if nargin < 2
  print('-dmeta');
else
  print('-dmeta',popt);
end

% Start an ActiveX session with MSWord.
wrd=actxserver('Word.Application');
wrd.Visible=1;  % Watch the action...

% Open or create a document.
if ~exist(filespec,'file')
  doc=invoke(wrd.Documents,'Add');
else
  doc=invoke(wrd.Documents,'Open',filespec);
end

% Insert some text at the end of the document.
myrange=doc.Content;
invoke(myrange,'InsertParagraphAfter');
invoke(myrange,'InsertAfter','--Figure Top Caption Goes Here--');
invoke(myrange,'InsertParagraphAfter');
```

```
% Paste AFTER the existing text.
invoke(myrange,'Collapse',0);
% Paste with "Picture Format" (1) and "Float Over Text" (3) options.
invoke(myrange,'PasteSpecial',0,0,1,0,3);
invoke(myrange,'InsertParagraphAfter');
invoke(myrange,'InsertAfter','--Figure Bottom Caption Goes Here--');
invoke(myrange,'InsertParagraphAfter');

% Save and close the document.
if ~exist(filespec,'file')
  invoke(doc,'SaveAs',filespec,1);
else
  invoke(doc,'Save');
end
invoke(doc,'Close');

% Quit Word and close the ActiveX server connection.
invoke(wrd,'Quit');
delete(wrd);
```

The next example uses MATLAB as an ActiveX client and Microsoft Excel as an ActiveX server. The MATLAB function `savexl` saves a 2-D MATLAB array in standard Excel spreadsheet format. `savexl` opens a connection to a server instance of the Microsoft Excel application, opens a new workbook, selects the appropriate range of cells, pastes a 2-D MATLAB array into the selected range of cells, saves the file as an Excel workbook, quits Excel, and deletes the `activex` server object.

```
function savexl(arr,filespec)
%SAVEXL Save a matrix to an Excel-format data file.
% SAVEXL(ARR) Save the matrix ARR to an Excel-format file ARR.XLS.
% SAVEXL(ARR,FILESPEC) Save ARR to the Excel-format file FILESPEC(.XLS).

% Get the name of the input variable and set a filename.
if nargin < 1
  error('Missing input argument.');
end
```

```
if ischar(arr) & size(arr,1) == 1  % Variable name supplied.
  vname=arr;
  try
    arr=evalin('caller',arr);
  catch
    error(['The variable ',arr,' does not exist.']);
  end
else                                 % Variable supplied.
  vname=inputname(1);
end
if isempty(vname) & nargin < 2
  error('No filename specified.');
end
if nargin > 1
  if isempty(filespec) | ~ischar(filespec)
    error('Invalid filename argument.');
  end
else
  filespec = [vname, '.xls'];
end
[dname,fname,fext]=fileparts(filespec);
if isempty(dname), dname=pwd; end
if isempty(fext), fext='.xls'; end
filespec=fullfile(dname,[fname,fext]);

% Determine the size of the input matrix.
if ndims(arr) > 2
  error('N-dimensional arrays are not supported.');
end
[m,n]=size(arr);

% Start an ActiveX session with MSExcel.
xl=actxserver('Excel.Application');
xl.Visible=1;  % Watch the action...

% Create a workbook and select a worksheet.
wb=invoke(xl.Workbooks,'Add');
sh=xl.Activesheet;

% Select a range of cells of the appropriate size.
r1='A1';
r2=get(sh,'Cells',m,n);
myrange=get(sh,'Range',r1,r2);
```

```
% Stuff the array into the range of cells.
set(myrange,'Value',arr);

% Save and close the Workbook.
invoke(wb,'SaveAs',filespec,1);
invoke(wb,'Close');

% Quit Excel and close the ActiveX server connection.
invoke(xl,'Quit');
delete(xl);
```

The resulting XLS-file can be reloaded into MATLAB using the `xlsread` command or the Import Wizard, which is available by selecting the **Import Data...** menu item in the **File** menu on the MATLAB desktop.

The final client example embeds an ActiveX control in a *Figure* window. MATLAB ships with a very simple ActiveX control (`mwsamp.ocx`) and associated type library (`mwsamp.tlb`) stored in the `$MATLAB\bin\win32` directory. The Mwsamp class contains one event (Click), two variables (Label and Radius), a few subroutines (Beep, Redraw, FireClickEvent, and so on), and a number of Get and Set functions. The `cdemo` function shown below creates a new *Figure* window with a `surf` plot, embeds an MWSAMP control in the corner of the *Figure* window, sets some control properties, and exits. When a mouse click event is detected within the control, the `cdemo` function is called again to service the callback. The control is deleted when the *Figure* window is closed.

```
function cdemo(varargin)
%CDEMO Sample function to manage an ActiveX object.
%  Function to create a sample ActiveX control. The function creates
%  a Figure window, adds a nice plot, creates an MWSAMP control,
%  embeds the control in the Figure window, sets the 'Label' and
%  'Radius' properties of the control, and invokes the 'Redraw'
%  method on the control.
%
%  CDEMO is also the event handler for this control. The only event
%  fired by the control is 'Click', which is fired when the user
```

```
%  clicks on the control with the mouse. The event handler changes
%  the text message in the control when the event is fired.
%  The control is deleted when the figure window is closed.

% Keep track of the click count and the control handle between calls.
persistent numclicks h

if nargin == 0      % Initial call-do the setup.
  numclicks=0;

  % Create a new Figure window and draw a nice plot.
  f = figure;
  surf(peaks);

  % Embed an MWSAMP ActiveX control in the lower left corner
  % of the Figure window and set the callback to recall this
  % function (cdemo).
  h = actxcontrol('MWSAMP.MwsampCtrl.1',[0 0 90 90],f,'cdemo');

  % Set the initial label and circle radius in the control
  % showing two methods of setting the property values.
  set(h,'Label','Click Here');
  h.Radius=28;

  % Redraw the control with the new properties.
  invoke(h,'Redraw');

else    % This section handles the callback. If a mouse click event
        % is detected, the first argument will be a string that
        % resolves to the value -600. No other events are supported.

  if ~ischar(varargin{1})
    error('Invalid input.');
  end

  % Increment the click total, change the label, and redraw.
  if str2num(varargin{1}) == -600
     numclicks = numclicks + 1;
     h.Label=['Click #',num2str(numclicks)];
     invoke(h,'Redraw');
  else
    error('Invalid input.');
  end
end
```

MATLAB as Server

MATLAB can act as an ActiveX Automation server when called by an ActiveX client such as Visual Basic, Visual Basic for Applications, or Visual C++. Microsoft Excel, Microsoft PowerPoint, or another ActiveX client application can be an Automation controller as well. The client application can start and stop an instance of MATLAB, pass arrays back and forth from the MATLAB workspace, and execute MATLAB commands in the MATLAB workspace. The MATLAB Engine on the Windows PC platform and the MATLAB Notebook are both implemented using MATLAB as an ActiveX Automation server.

The registered MATLAB ActiveX object name is **Matlab.Application.** MATLAB provides the following Automation methods to ActiveX client applications.

String Result = **Execute**(*String* Command)

String CharArray = **GetCharArray**(*String* Name, *String* Workspace)

Void **PutCharArray**(*String* Name, *String* Workspace, *String* CharArray)

Void **GetFullMatrix**(*String* Name, *String* Workspace, *(Double)** Pr, *(Double)** Pi)

Void **PutFullMatrix**(*String* Name, *String* Workspace, *(Double)** Pr, *(Double)** Pi)

Void **MaximizeCommandWindow()**

Void **MinimizeCommandWindow()**

Void **Quit()**

Result is the text returned in the *Command* window when the **Command** argument is executed in the MATLAB workspace. **CharArray** is a character array containing a string value. **Name** is the variable name in the MATLAB workspace. **Workspace** is one of "base" or "global". **Pr** is a pointer to an array of doubles representing the real component of a MATLAB numerical array. **Pi** is a pointer to an array of doubles representing the imaginary component of a MATLAB numerical array. If there is no imaginary component, **Pi** should point to an empty array.

The easiest way to create an Excel VBA macro is to record a new macro and edit the resulting VBA code. For example, open Excel and select the menu item **Tools/Macro/Record New Macro....** Give your macro a name in the dialog box (the following example uses the name "Square") and click on the **OK** button. Then click on the **Stop Recording** button in the next dialog box. This creates an empty macro. Now select the **Tools/Macro/Macros...** menu item and click on the **Edit** button. Now you can edit the macro, save the result, and run the macro whenever you wish.

Example

This is an example of an Excel macro that starts MATLAB as an Automation server, passes the contents of cells B3:E8 to a MATLAB array, squares the contents of the array, passes back the result, and inserts the result in cells B12:E17 in the Excel spreadsheet. It also passes a string value obtained from cell B1 to MATLAB, appends " squared (in MATLAB)" to the string, passes back the result, and inserts this result in cell B10. The MATLAB server is then closed.

```
Sub Square()
'
' Square Macro
' Square the contents of cells B3:E8 and place the result in B12:E17.
' Also append the phrase " squared (in MATLAB)" to a string from B1
' and place the result in B10.

' First define the variables.
Dim MatLab As Object
Dim Result, NewString As String
Dim MReal(6, 4) As Double
Dim MImag() As Double
Dim RealValue As Double
Dim i, j As Integer

' Invoke MATLAB.
Set MatLab = CreateObject("Matlab.Application")

' Fill the Mreal array with data from the sheet.
For i = 0 To 5
   For j = 0 To 3
   MReal(i,j)=ActiveSheet.Range(Cells(i+3,j+2),Cells(i+3,j+2)).Value
   Next j
   Next i

' Send the string and data from the spreadsheet to MATLAB.
Call MatLab.PutCharArray("instr", "base", ActiveSheet.Range("B1:B1").Value)
Call MatLab.PutFullMatrix("a", "base", MReal, Mimag)

' Send MATLAB some commands to execute.
Result = MatLab.Execute("b=a.^2;")
Result = MatLab.Execute("outstr=[instr, ' squared (in MATLAB)']")

' Retrieve the results and stuff them into spreadsheet cells.
Call MatLab.GetFullMatrix("b", "base", MReal, MImag)
ActiveSheet.Range("B12:E17").Value = MReal
ActiveSheet.Range("B10:B10").Value = MatLab.GetCharArray("outstr", "base")
'
End Sub
```

Given the following illustrative spreadsheet contents, the results of applying the `Sub Square()` macro appear in the succeeding spreadsheet illustration.

	Input array of numeric values			
	1	2	3	4
	2	3	4	5
	3	4	5	6
	4	5	6	7
	5	6	7	8
	6	7	8	9

The result after the macro is run is

	Input array of numeric values			
	1	2	3	4
	2	3	4	5
	3	4	5	6
	4	5	6	7
	5	6	7	8
	6	7	8	9
	Input array of numeric values squared (in MATLAB)			
	1	4	9	16
	4	9	16	25
	9	16	25	36
	16	25	36	49
	25	36	49	64
	36	49	64	81

Of course this example is of very limited practical value. However, it provides a solid foundation for further development.

The Visual Basic environment provides some tools that help determine the appropriate objects and methods for communicating with other ActiveX applications in addition to the MATLAB `get` and `invoke` methods illustrated above. The Object Browser can be used to determine the objects available in each of the object libraries (such as the Excel library or the MSForms library). The objects and members (properties, events, and functions) are searchable, and context-sensitive help is available.

36.2 DYNAMIC DATA EXCHANGE

Prior to the client/server capabilities of ActiveX, Microsoft created a mostly peer-to-peer interapplication communication protocol called Dynamic Data Exchange. DDE enables two cooperating applications to exchange data and execution strings (commands) using the Windows clipboard. One application can also register a request for notification of updates when certain data changes in the other application. This DDE functionality has been incorporated into the more flexible ActiveX protocol. DDE is still supported for existing code, but ActiveX is normally used for new implementations.

DDE connections between applications are called ***conversations.*** Each application has a unique ***service name*** to identify the application. Each conversation is identified by a service name and a ***topic*** known to both applications. Each application supports a System topic, and most support one or more additional topics. The application that initiates a DDE request is designated the ***client,*** and the application that answers the request is designated the ***server*** for the duration of the conversation.

A typical DDE conversation starts with application A requesting a conversation with an instance of application B. The conversation consists of a service name/topic pair. If application B (identified by service name) recognizes the topic, then it establishes a conversation with application A. The elements of the conversation are items that are passed between the applications using the Windows clipboard. All applications support the Text format for data exchange. Some applications support additional data formats such as Bitmap and MetaFilePict for graphics and XLTable format for Excel spreadsheet data. MATLAB supports only the Text format when operating as a DDE client, but supports Text, XLTable, and MetaFilePict formats when operating as a DDE server.

An ActiveX connection request can invoke an instance of an application (launch the application) to service a client request, but a DDE conversation can be initiated only between applications that are already running.

MATLAB as a DDE Client

The DDE functions supported by MATLAB are listed in the following table.

Function	Description
`ddeadv`	Set up an advisory link between MATLAB and a DDE server application.
`ddeexec`	Send an execution string to a DDE server application.
`ddeinit`	Initiate a DDE conversation between MATLAB and another application.
`ddepoke`	Send data from MATLAB to a DDE server application.
`ddereq`	Request data from a DDE server application.

Function	Description
`ddeterm`	Terminate a DDE conversation between MATLAB and a server application.
`ddeunadv`	Release an advisory link between MATLAB and a DDE server application.

These functions are used by MATLAB to manage DDE connections to other applications acting as DDE servers. Examples of DDE servers include Microsoft Excel, Word, Access, and PowerPoint.

As a server, Microsoft Excel supports two kinds of topics. The System topic and a topic consisting of the name of a workbook that is open in Excel or the name of a spreadsheet in the open workbook. A Microsoft Excel item is any cell reference: an individual cell or a range of cells. Microsoft Word supports the System topic and the name of an open document in Word. A Microsoft Word item is any bookmark in the open document. Consult the on-line help or the printed documentation for these and other DDE applications for details about the topics and the items they support.

The following is an example of a DDE conversation between MATLAB (the client) and an open copy of Excel (the server). First, we request a connection to the System topic (every DDE application supports the System topic).

```
>> xls = ddeinit('excel','system')
>> xls =
    4.7836e-299
```

The return value is the handle assigned to the conversation. A failed request returns a handle value of `0`. Next, we request a list of the items available under the System topic using the standard SysItems item. The optional third argument is a format vector. The first element indicates the clipboard format (`1` for Text—the only format supported by MATLAB as a client). The second element determines how the result is stored: `0` to interpret the data as numerical values (the default) and `1` to interpret the data as a character string. These requests are for items that return tab-delimited character strings.

```
>> s = ddereq(xls,'SysItems',[1 1])
s =
SysItems    Topics  Status  Formats Selection   Protocols   EditEnvItems
```

Query each of them for more detail,

```
>> t = ddereq(xls,'Topics',[1 1])
t =
[:]:    [Book1]Sheet1   [Book1]Sheet2   [Book1]Sheet3   System

>> t = ddereq(xls,'Status',[1 1])
t =
Ready
```

```
>> t = ddereq(xls,'Formats',[1 1])
t =
XlTable Microsoft Excel 8.0 Format  Biff4   Biff3   SYLK
Wk1 Csv Unicode Text    Text    Rich Text Format    DIF Bitmap
Picture (Enhanced Metafile) Printer_Picture Screen Picture EMF

>> t = ddereq(xls,'Selection',[1 1])
t =
[Book1]Sheet1!R1C1

>> t = ddereq(xls,'Protocols',[1 1])
t =
StdFileEditing  Embedding

>> t = ddereq(xls,'EditenvItems',[1 1])
t =
StdHostNames    StdTargetDevice StdDocDimensions
```

and close the connection

```
>> status = ddeterm(xls)
status =
     1
```

This shows that the open workbook named `Book1` contains three worksheets named `Sheet1`, `Sheet2`, and `Sheet3`, that Excel is ready to converse, that Excel supports many clipboard formats, that the currently selected cell is row 1 column 1, and other details. Excel supports the System topic and one topic for each of the available worksheets. The worksheet topics support only one item type: a range of cells.

The next example opens a conversation with one of the worksheets. First, create a magic square and plot the resulting surface.

```
>> m = magic(10);
>> h = surf(m);
```

Open a connection to a worksheet and insert the data into a range of cells.

```
>> xl = ddeinit('excel','Sheet1');
>> range = 'r1c1:r10c10';
>> status = ddepoke(xl,range,m);
```

Now set up a link between the spreadsheet data and MATLAB to trigger a callback if any data in the range of cells changes.

```
>> status = ddeadv(xl,range,'disp(''Spreadsheet data change alert!'')');
```

The third argument is the callback passed to eval. Now any time a change is made to the contents of one or more of these cells in the spreadsheet, a message is displayed in the *Command* window.

Now close this link and open another. This time, when a change is made to the spreadsheet, the link passes the range of data back to MATLAB in the variable z and the callback updates the plot with the new data. The presence of the fourth argument notifies the server to send back data in addition to sending a signal to MATLAB to execute the callback.

```
>> status = ddeunadv(xl,range1);
>> status = ddeadv(xl,range,'set(h,''ZData'',z); set(h,''CData'',z);','z');
```

Make some extensive changes to the data to see the effect on the plot.

```
>> status = ddepoke(xl,'r1c1:r9c9',magic(9));
```

Change some data yourself to see how it affects the plot. When you are finished, close the link and terminate the conversation.

```
status=ddeunadv(xl,range1);
status=ddeterm(xl);
```

The ddeexec function passes a command to the DDE server to be evaluated. For example,

```
status=ddeexec(xl,'[formula.goto("r3c5")]');
```

makes the cell in row 3 column 5, the current cell. Consult the documentation for your DDE server application for a list of supported commands.

MATLAB as a DDE Server

The DDE service name for MATLAB is, naturally enough, **MATLAB.** MATLAB supports two topics when operating as a DDE server: System and Engine. The valid items for each of these topics are listed in the following table.

Topic	Item	Description
System	SysItems	A tab-delimited list of items supported under the System topic (SysItems, Format, and Topics).
	Format	A tab-delimited list of supported formats (Text, MetaFilePict, and XLTable).

Topic	Item	Description
	`Topics`	A tab-delimited list of supported topics (`System` and `Engine`).
`Engine`	`EngEvalString`	Item name (if required by the client calling syntax) when a command is sent for evaluation.
	`EngStringResult`	String result of a DDE `execute` command.
	`EngFigureResult`	Graphical result of a DDE `execute` command.
	<matrixname>	The name of the matrix to be created, updated, or returned.

DDE client applications open a conversation with MATLAB using the service name **MATLAB** and either the System or Engine topic. The MATLAB Engine topic supports three client request operations: sending data to MATLAB, receiving data from MATLAB, and sending a command to MATLAB to be executed.

The client can send data using the DDE `poke` operation where the item is the name of the matrix to create or update and the format of the poke data is Text or XLTable. The client can request data from MATLAB using the DDE `request` operation in three forms. To request the contents of an array, the item is the name of the matrix to send and the data format is Text or XLTable. To request the text output from a previous MATLAB command, the item is `EngStringResult` using the Text format. To request graphical output from a previous MATLAB command, the item is `EngFigureResult` and the format is MetaFilePict. Some clients are able to receive only Text from a `request` operation. For these clients, MATLAB provides the ability to specify item `EngFigureResult` with the Text format. In this case, the result is a status string. If the string is "Yes", the figure is available on the clipboard for the client to retrieve. If the operation fails, the text returned is "No".

The client can send a command to MATLAB using the DDE `execute` operation. The item is `EngEvalString` and the format of the command is Text. Some clients omit the item and just send the command. MATLAB accepts either form.

Consult the documentation for your DDE client application or programming language for the appropriate syntax for writing DDE programs or functions to connect to an instance of MATLAB.

36.3 MATLAB NOTEBOOK

The MATLAB Notebook lets you access MATLAB as an ActiveX server from within a Microsoft Word document without actually writing your own programs. Microsoft Word for

Windows 95 (Word 7), Word 97, and Word 2000 are the only word processors supported by the MATLAB Notebook and must be purchased and installed separately on your Windows 95, Windows 98, Windows NT 4.0, or Windows 2000 computer. Using the Notebook, you can create a report with MATLAB commands and the resulting MATLAB output imbedded within the document itself. The Notebook is implemented using a predefined collection of Microsoft Word macros and ActiveX controls that allow you to connect to a MATLAB session from a Word document called an M-book. This functionality is automatically available when you install MATLAB on a `win32` PC platform along with Microsoft Word or Office.

The Notebook uses a Microsoft Word template to embed controls within your document. The command `>> notebook -setup` initializes the Notebook. You are asked to select the version of Word you are using (95, 97, or 2000), the location of the Microsoft Word program (using a dialog box), and the location of a template file (such as `normal.dot`) using another dialog box. A new template file called `m-book.dot` is then copied into each of these directories. The next time you use the `notebook` command, the Microsoft Word application is opened using the `m-book.dot` template. If a filename argument is supplied, Word attempts to open the requested file. If no argument is supplied, a new M-book document is opened.

Word macros are disabled in a default Microsoft Word installation. If you have Word macros disabled, you will see a dialog box asking for permission to enable macros in this document. If you accept, the document will be opened. You must enable macros to use the Notebook functionality. You can enable macros only in the document by selecting the **Enable Macros** button. You can enable macros in all documents by deselecting the "**Always ask...**" checkbox in the dialog box. However, enabling macros globally can be a potential security risk since macro viruses have been detected in certain Word documents distributed by e-mail and by other means.

When an M-book is opened using the `notebook` command from MATLAB or by opening an M-book from Microsoft Word, a new **Notebook** menu appears next to the **Table** menu in the Word application menus. The **Notebook** menu items enable operations such as defining or undefining MATLAB input statements or ***cells,*** grouping and ungrouping these cells, defining calculation zones within the document, and evaluating cells, calculation zones, or the entire M-book. When an input cell is evaluated, the statement is sent to MATLAB for evaluation and the results (either the command-line results, a plot, or both) are inserted in the M-book document following the input statement.

For example, consider the following illustrative M-book.

MATLAB Notebook Example 1

Assignment #2

Create a 3-by-3 magic square

m=magic(3)

square the elements of the magic square

m2=m.^2

and plot the result

plot(1:9,m2(:))

When the three MATLAB statements are selected and the **Notebook/Define Input Cell** menu item is selected for each of the statements, the resulting M-book appears as follows.

MATLAB Notebook Example 1

Assignment #2

Create a 3-by-3 magic square

```
[m=magic(3) ]
```

square the elements of the magic square

```
[m2=m.^2 ]
```

and plot the result

```
[plot(1:9,m2(:)) ]
```

The command text in the input cells changes to a fixed-point font, and the cells are delimited by square brackets (the brackets do not appear when the document is printed). If the **Notebook/Evaluate M-book** menu item is then selected, the application connects to an open MATLAB session or starts a new MATLAB session, evaluates the MATLAB statements, and inserts the results in the M-book as shown below.

MATLAB Notebook Example 1

Assignment #2

Create a 3-by-3 magic square

```
[m=magic(3) ]

[m =

     8     1     6
     3     5     7
     4     9     2 ]
```

square the elements of the magic square

```
[m2=m.^2 ]

[m2 =

    64     1    36
     9    25    49
    16    81     4 ]
```

and plot the result

```
[plot(1:9,m2(:)) ]
```

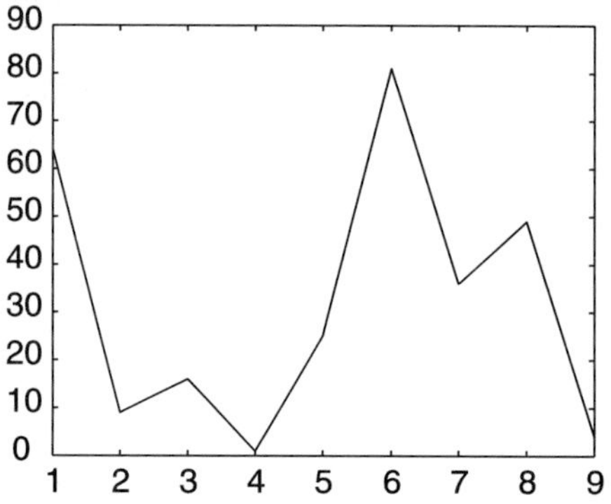

The Notebook can be used to create an annotated record of a MATLAB session (think of it as a very fancy `diary` command) or to insert MATLAB examples into a report. Any changes made to an input cell are reflected in the output cell whenever the input cell is evaluated. In that respect an M-book is a dynamic document.

Unlike MATLAB Engine sessions, M-books share the base workspace with any currently open interactive MATLAB session. In addition, all M-books in a Word session share a single instance of MATLAB and all share the same MATLAB workspace. Thus, if you have multiple documents open, all variables are shared among all M-books and any interactive session; a change to a variable in one M-book is a change to variables of the same name in other M-books and in the interactive session as well. Also, since you can define and undefine input cells and calculation zones, data dependencies can be easily broken by these changes. The **Purge Output Cells** and **Evaluate M-book** menu items should be selected periodically to ensure data consistency. When you evaluate any input cell or an entire M-book, text output is replaced, but graphical output is replicated. For example, if the M-book is evaluated a second time without first purging the output cells, the previous document will contain two graphs at the end of the document.

The *MathWorks Inc.* sells a product called *Excel Link* as an extra-cost toolbox that provides similar functionality for the Microsoft Excel spreadsheet application. Data exchange and MATLAB commands can be easily controlled from within Excel. If your work requires moving large amounts of data between Excel and MATLAB or using Excel to analyze MATLAB results, the time saved by purchasing *Excel Link* may be well worth the cost of the toolbox.

36.4 SUMMARY

The simplicity of using pipes to connect the standard input and standard output of applications on UNIX and Linux platforms has enabled widespread interapplication communication for many years. Standardized protocols for communication between applications on the Windows PC platform is now available as well. MATLAB supports the Microsoft Dynamic Data Exchange and ActiveX protocols to enable MATLAB to operate as a client or as a server for other DDE or ActiveX-enabled applications such as Microsoft Word, Excel, and PowerPoint.

37

Getting Help

With each major release the help capabilities of MATLAB have improved significantly. MATLAB 6 is no exception. In MATLAB 5 help could be viewed in a GUI-based *Figure* window using the function `helpwin`. More substantial HTML-based documentation could be viewed in a standard web browser using the `helpdesk` function. These functions supplemented the historical *Command* window functions `help` and `lookfor`. As versions have changed, old help functions have changed too. Some have become obsolete, and others have been grandfathered but now do different things. This chapter introduces the primary help capabilities available in MATLAB, including resources available via the Internet.

37.1 *COMMAND* WINDOW HELP

Before MATLAB included GUI features, help was available in the *Command* window using the functions `help` and `lookfor`. These basic functions remain available today. For example,

```
>> help sqrt

 SQRT   Square root.
    SQRT(X) is the square root of the elements of X. Complex
    results are produced if X is not positive.

    See also SQRTM.
```

shows the help text for the function `sqrt`. In general the function `help` is useful if you know the name of a particular function but are unsure of its input or output arguments. In the above, function names are capitalized only to give them visual distinction. All functions in MATLAB are called using lowercase arguments. For example,

```
>> SQRT(2)
??? Capitalized internal function SQRT; Caps Lock may be on.
```

shows that MATLAB guesses that you mean `sqrt(2)` because `SQRT(2)` is not the square root function.

If you are unsure which function performs a given task but you know a keyword that is related to the function, the function `lookfor` is helpful. Consider the following example.

```
>> lookfor inverse
INVHILB Inverse Hilbert matrix.
ACOS    Inverse cosine.
ACOSH   Inverse hyperbolic cosine.
ACOT    Inverse cotangent.
ACOTH   Inverse hyperbolic cotangent.
ACSC    Inverse cosecant.
ACSCH   Inverse hyperbolic cosecant.
ASEC    Inverse secant.
ASECH   Inverse hyperbolic secant.
ASIN    Inverse sine.
ASINH   Inverse hyperbolic sine.
ATAN    Inverse tangent.
ATAN2   Four quadrant inverse tangent.
ATANH   Inverse hyperbolic tangent.
ERFINV  Inverse error function.
INV     Matrix inverse.
PINV    Pseudoinverse.
IFFT Inverse discrete Fourier transform.
IFFT2 Two-dimensional inverse discrete Fourier transform.
IFFTN N-dimensional inverse discrete Fourier transform.
IFFTSHIFT Inverse FFT shift.
IPERMUTE Inverse permute array dimensions.
UPDHESS Performs the Inverse Hessian Update.
INVHESS Inverse of an upper Hessenberg matrix.
```

The function `lookfor` opens all the function M-files on the MATLAB search path, looks for the given keyword on the first comment line (i.e., the H1 help line), and returns the lines where a match is found.

37.2 THE HELP BROWSER

In MATLAB 6, help functions beyond `help` and `lookfor` have been consolidated in the Help Browser or simply the *Help* window. This window can be opened by choosing **Help** from the **View** menu on the MATLAB desktop or by typing `helpwin` at the MATLAB prompt. In addition to a text area for displaying help text, the *Help* window offers a help navigator that contains user-selectable tabs for *Contents, Index, Search,* and *Favorites.* The *Contents* tab provides a table of contents to all on-line documentation for MATLAB and all toolboxes. The *Index* tab provides an index to all on-line help entries. The *Search* tab allows one to search on-line documentation. And finally, the *Favorites* tab provides a user listing of favorite help entries. These features are easier to explore first-hand than they are to illustrate in a text, and so the user is encouraged to explore the Help Browser for themselves.

The *Help* window equivalent to the function `help` is `helpwin`. For example,

```
>> helpwin sqrt
```

displays the same help text as `>> help sqrt`, but it does so in the *Help* window. Behind the scenes MATLAB opens the file `sqrt.m`, reads the help text found there, converts the file to HTML format, and displays the HTML text in the *Help* window. In the process, capitalized function names are converted to lowercase, and functions listed on the `See also` line are converted to HTML links to the named functions. In addition, if the function has more extensive on-line documentation, a link to that documentation appears at the top of the displayed help text. If you create your own toolbox or collection of function M-files, `helpwin` will display help text as described here for these functions as well. If the argument to `helpwin` is the name of a toolbox directory, the `Contents.m` file in that directory is opened and displayed in the *Help* window.

The function `doc` bypasses M-file help text and goes directly to on-line documentation. For example,

```
>> doc print
```

displays the on-line documentation for the function `print`, which contains much more information than is available from `>> helpwin print`.

The functions `whatsnew` and `whatsnew` *`toolbox`* display release notes and last minute changes for MATLAB or a selected toolbox in the *Help* window. Behind the scenes `whatsnew` *`toolbox`* opens and displays the `Readme.m` file for the toolbox in the *Help* window.

37.3 INTERNET RESOURCES

The Mathworks Inc., the makers of MATLAB, was one of the first 100 commercial sites on the Internet. Their web site, `http://www.mathworks.com`, provides a wealth of information covering all aspects of MATLAB. There is simply too much on their web site to discuss here. In addition, as with most sites, features and links come and go, making it difficult to accurately describe what is available at any given time. Two of the most useful features of *The Mathworks Inc.* web site are the solution search engine, which provides answers to common technical support questions, and the repository of user-contributed and Mathworks-contributed function M-files. You should be able to find *Mastering MATLAB 6* listed on their web site as well.

If you are in the middle of a MATLAB session, you need not leave MATLAB to go to their web site. The MATLAB Help Browser accepts URLs and serves as a simple web browser. Alternatively, any other web browser will do.

In addition to the wealth of information on *The Mathworks Inc.* web site, the Internet newsgroup `comp.soft-sys.matlab` is an unmoderated forum for discussion of MATLAB topics. Many very knowledgeable people monitor this newsgroup regularly and contribute answers to posted questions. The MATLAB newsgroup is a good place to ask questions that are not easily answered through on-line help. In fact, *The Mathworks Inc.* staff often respond to posted questions. The authors of *Mastering MATLAB 6* monitor the newsgroup daily to answer questions and to identify topics pertinent for inclusion in this text. Even if you do not post questions to the newsgroup, simply monitoring the threads provides a wealth of MATLAB knowledge.

37.4 *MASTERING MATLAB 6* HELP

In addition to the help capabilities available in MATLAB, the authors of this text provide two services. First, we maintain the Mastering MATLAB web site at `http://www.eece.maine.edu/mm`. At this web site you will find a downloadable collection of script M-files to generate all the figures in the text. These M-files spare you from having to type all the code found in the text into the *Command* window. In addition, the Java, MEX, and function M-file code that appears in the text is available for download. You can also find a listing of errata for the text, as well as links to other MATLAB-related areas on the Internet. Second, the authors provide an email address, `mm@eece.maine.edu`, for your comments and feedback. We encourage you to submit errata, to give us feedback that will help us make the next edition of the text better, and to ask questions about the examples and content of *Mastering MATLAB 6*. You may submit general questions about MATLAB as well, but we might not provide an answer if that answer can be found easily using the documentation that comes with MATLAB.

37.5 SUMMARY

The table below summarizes the important aspects of this chapter.

Item	Description
`help` *`functionname`*	Display help for function *`functionname`* in the *Command* window.
`lookfor` *`keyword`*	Keyword search of M-files using the string *`keyword`*.
`helpwin` *`functionname`*	Display help for the function *`functionname`* in the *Help* window.
`doc` *`functionname`*	Display on-line help for the function *`functionname`* in the *Help* window.
`helpbrowser`	Open the *Help* window to documentation home page.
`whatsnew`	Display Release Notes or `Readme.m` toolbox file.
`http://www.mathworks.com`	*The Mathworks Inc.* web site.
`comp.soft-sys.matlab`	The MATLAB newsgroup.
`http://www.eece.maine.edu/mm`	*Mastering MATLAB 6* web site.
`mm@eece.maine.edu`	E-mail to *Mastering MATLAB 6* authors.

38

Examples, Examples, Examples

38.1 VECTORIZATION

It's been said that a picture is worth a thousand words. Likewise, when it comes to software, an example is worth a thousand words. This chapter is devoted to extensive examples. Most examples are chosen to show the process of ***vectorizing code.*** Vectorizing in this context means to write or rewrite code so that scalar operations on array elements are replaced by array operations. For example,

```
>> for i=1:n
      y(i) = sin(2*pi*i/m);
   end
```

is replaced by the vectorized code

```
>> i = 1:n;
>> y = sin(2*pi*i/m);
```

The For Loop above represents poor programming practice. Not only is the For Loop unnecessary as seen by its vectorized equivalent, it's very slow since memory is reallocated for the variable `y` each time through the loop (see Section 5.13).

Contrary to what some may believe, vectorizing does not mean eliminating *all* For Loops. For Loops do serve a purpose; after all, MATLAB wouldn't include them as a control flow structure if they didn't. For Loops are often a good choice when (1) the amount of code to be interpreted within the loop is small, even if this code requires substantial floating-point operations, (2) the code within the loop makes minimum calls to M-file functions, (3) no memory is allocated or reallocated after the first pass through the loop, or (4) when using a For Loop eliminates the need to create arrays larger than the computer can access with minimum delay. Obviously, the last case is not only platform-dependent but also dependent on the attributes of an individual platform.

While vectorization leads to efficient MATLAB programming, it does have a down side. That is, vectorized code is often more difficult to read or follow. The above example is clearly an exception to this fact—the vectorized code is much easier to read than the nonvectorized code. The above example represents a simple, easy-to-learn vectorization. Most often it is the more difficult or less obvious vectorization challenges that lead to code that is more difficult to follow.

Vectorizing code makes use of a small number of MATLAB operators and functions. These operators and functions generally involve the manipulation of indices or the replication of arrays and can be divided into three categories as shown in the tables below. The first two categories are basic internal MATLAB capabilities and are therefore fast. The last category consists of optimized M-file code for implementing common array manipulation functions.

Operator	Description
`:`	Colon notation. `n:m` creates a row array that starts with `n` and ends with `m`. `n:inc:m` creates a row array that starts with `n`, counts by `inc`, and ends at or before `m`. As an array index, `:` means take all elements. Also, `A(:)` on the right-hand side of an equal sign means reshape `A` as a column vector. On the left-hand side of an equal sign `A(:)` means fill contents of `A` with results of the right-hand side without reallocating memory for `A`.
`.'`	Nonconjugate transpose. Exchange rows for columns.
`[]`	Brackets. Array concatenation.

Built-in Function	Description
`all(x)`	True if all elements of `x` are nonzero.
`any(x)`	True if any elements of `x` are nonzero.
`cat(Dim,A,B,...)`	Concatenate `A, B, ...` along dimension `Dim`. (Faster than `[]`.)

Built-in Function	Description
cumsum(x)	Cumulative sum of elements of vector x.
diff(x)	Difference between elements in x.
end	Last index. Inside array index identifies the last element along given dimension.
find(x)	Find indices where x is nonzero.
logical(x)	Convert x to logical data type to enable logical array addressing.
permute(A,Order)	Generalized transpose. Rearranges the dimensions of A so that they are in the order specified by the vector Order.
prod(x)	Product of elements in x.
reshape(A,r,c)	Reshape array A to be r-by-c.
sort(x)	Sort array x in ascending order.
sum(x)	Sum of elements in x.

M-file Function	Description
ind2sub(Size,idx)	Convert single indices in idx to array subscripts of an array having dimensions Size.
ipermute(A,Order)	Generalized transpose. Inverse of permute(A,Order).
kron(A,B)	Kronecker tensor product of A and B.
meshgrid(x,y)	Mesh domain generation from vectors x and y.
repmat(A,r,c)	Replicate array A creating an r-by-c block array.
shiftdim(A,n)	Shift dimensions of A by integer n.
squeeze(x)	Remove singleton dimensions from array A.
sub2ind(Size,r,c)	Convert array subscripts r and c of an array having dimensions Size to single indices.

38.2 UP-DOWN SEQUENCE

As a first example, consider the following simple algorithm. Let *N* be some positive integer. If *N* is even, divide it by 2. On the other hand, if it is odd, multiply it by 3 and add 1. Repeat until N becomes 1. This algorithm has some interesting properties. It appears to converge to 1 for all numbers N. Some numbers require many iterations to converge. Others such as $N = 2^m$ converge very quickly. While it is interesting to study the sequence of values generated by different values of N, let's just compute the number of iterations required to achieve convergence.

First, let N be a scalar. That is, let's write the algorithm for a single number. The following script M-file implements the above algorithm.

```
% updown1.m
% up-down algorithm

N = 25;       % number to test
count = 0;    % iteration count
while N>1
   if rem(N,2)==0 % even
      N=N/2;
      count=count+1;
   else           % odd
      N=(3*N+1)/2;
      count=count+2;
   end
end
count  % display iteration count
```

The above code directly implements the algorithm with one exception. When an odd number is multiplied by 3 and has 1 added, the resulting number is automatically even. As a result, the next pass through the algorithm always divides by 2. Since this always occurs, the divide-by-2 step is included and the count is incremented by 2 to reflect the fact that two steps are taken.

Next, consider letting N be an array of numbers each of which we wish to find the iteration count. The most direct approach is to use a For Loop as shown in the following script M-file.

```
% updown2.m
% up-down algorithm

Nums = 25:50;  % numbers to test
for i=1:length(Nums)
   N=Nums(i);  % number to test
   count = 0;  % iteration count
```

```
    while N>1
      if rem(N,2)==0 % even
         N=N/2;
         count=count+1;
      else           % odd
         N=(3*N+1)/2;
         count=count+2;
      end
    end
    Counts(i)=count;
end
results=[Nums' Counts']
```

Here the earlier scalar algorithm appears within a For Loop. At the beginning of the loop the *i*th element of the vector `Nums` is copied into `N`. The algorithm then runs to completion, and the iteration count is copied into the *i*th element of `Counts`. Finally all results are displayed. This code segment violates a key memory allocation guideline, namely, the variable `Counts` is reallocated to a larger size at every pass through the For Loop. Therefore, the first vectorization step is to preallocate all elements of `Counts` as shown below.

```
% updown3.m
% up-down algorithm

Nums = 25:50;               % numbers to test
Counts=zeros(size(Nums)); % preallocate array
for i=1:length(Nums)
    N=Nums(i);  % number to test
    count = 0;  % iteration count
    while N>1
      if rem(N,2)==0 % even
         N=N/2;
         count=count+1;
      else           % odd
         N=(3*N+1)/2;
         count=count+2;
      end
    end
    Counts(i)=count;
end
results=[Nums' Counts']
```

Now every time through the For Loop simply inserts the current `count` into a preexisting location in `Counts`. Preallocation is always a first and most important step in vectorization.

There must be a way to vectorize this algorithm so that the For Loop is unneeded. The function `rem` returns an array the same size as its input, and so all numbers can be tested simultaneously at every iteration of the While Loop. Using this fact leads to the following script M-file.

```
% updown4.m
% up-down algorithm

Nums = 25:50;            % numbers to test
N=Nums;                  % duplicate numbers
Counts=zeros(size(N));   % preallocate array
idx=find(N>1);           % indices of not done values
while ~isempty(idx)
   odd=logical(rem(N(idx),2)); % True where odd
   oidx=idx(odd);        % indices where odd
   eidx=idx(~odd);       % indices where even

   N(eidx)=N(eidx)/2;              % operate on all evens
   Counts(eidx)=Counts(eidx)+1;    % increment even counts

   N(oidx)=(3*N(oidx)+1)/2;        % operate on all odds
   Counts(oidx)=Counts(oidx)+2;    % increment odd counts

   idx=find(N>1);        % eliminate converged values from
                         % further consideration
end
results=[Nums' Counts']
```

When considering all elements simultaneously, we must find some way of not operating on array elements that have already converged to 1. The statement `idx=find(N>1);` returns the indices in `N` that haven't converged. Inside the While Loop odd and even values are separated by the logical statement `odd=logical(rem(N(idx),2));`. Then logical addressing is used to identify indices in `idx` that contain nonconverged odd and even values. These indices are stored in the arrays `oidx` and `eidx`, respectively. Once these indices are known, it's simply a matter of doing what the algorithm says and incrementing the counts accordingly. Finally, the last statement inside the While Loop, `idx=find(N>1);`, eliminates converged values from further consideration. The While Loop terminates when all the elements have converged.

A comparison of the two preceding implementations shows that the latter vectorized version uses much more memory than the prior scalar version. This latter version creates a number of arrays of length up to `length(Nums)`, whereas the scalar version allocates only one array of length equal to `length(Nums)`. Vectorization is fine as long as MATLAB has access to the required memory. When the number or size of arrays gets too large, vectorization can fail to speed up the execution of an algorithm.

The above M-file represents good use of vectorization. The code is straightforward and readable. However, it can be vectorized further. Using the MATLAB profiler, the line `idx=find(N>1);`, consumes significant time when `N` is large. In addition this function acts on the entire length of `N` at every iteration even when there are only a few values remaining that satisfy the requirement. Therefore, to speed the algorithm up further it is necessary to remove elements from `N` as they converge. Since we want the values and iteration counts at the end, the elements removed from `N` and their counts must be placed in separate arrays. Following these guidelines leads to the following script M-file.

```
% updown5.m
% up-down algorithm

Nums = 25:50;            % numbers to test
N1=length(Nums);         % number of values
N=Nums;                  % duplicate numbers
Counts=zeros(size(N));   % preallocate array
Ndone=Counts;            % preallocate array
Cdone=Counts;            % preallocate array
n=0;                     % pointer

while n<N1
   odd=logical(rem(N,2)); % True where odd
   even=~odd;             % True where even

   N(even)=N(even)/2;              % operate on all evens
   Counts(even)=Counts(even)+1;    % increment even counts

   N(odd)=(3*N(odd)+1)/2;          % operate on all odds
   Counts(odd)=Counts(odd)+2;      % increment odd counts

   done=(N==1);    % True for converged values
   Nd=sum(done);   % Number of converged values

   if Nd>0  % Purge N and Counts of converged values
      idx=n+(1:Nd);               % where to store converged data
      Ndone(idx)=Nums(done);      % store converged values
      Cdone(idx)=Counts(done);    % store converged counts
      Nums(done)=[];              % throw out converged values
      N(done)=[];                 % and converged iterations
```

```
      Counts(done)=[];          % and converged counts
      n=idx(end);               % last element in Ndone and Cdone
   end
end
[Nums,idx]=sort(Ndone); % sort results
Counts=Cdone(idx);      % shuffle Counts to match Nums
results=[Nums' Counts']
```

In this script M-file `Ndone` and `Cdone` are used to store values and iteration counts of the elements that have converged. Using the moving pointer `n`, data are placed in these variables as they converge and are deleted from `Nums`, `N`, and `Counts`. After `N` and `Counts` are updated according to the algorithm, the logical indices and number of converged values are found. The If-End construction copies converged data and then deletes it from further consideration. To be fair, the final results accumulated in `Ndone` and `Cdone` are sorted so that they appear in the same order as in the preceding implementations.

Given the script M-files `updown3.m`, `updown4.m`, and `updown5.m`, we can test them for speed by using the profiler or by simply using the functions `tic` and `toc`. If the statement `Nums = 25:50;` is removed from each file along with the last statement `results=[Nums' Counts']`, then the following script M-file tests the execution speed of the three implementations.

```
% testupdown.m
% script file to test updown implementations

times=zeros(1,3);
Nums=1e3:1e4;          % numbers to test

tic
updown3                % For Loop implementation
times(1)=toc;

tic
updown4                % First vectorization
times(2)=toc;

tic
updown5                % Second vectorization
times(3)=toc;

relspeed=times/min(times) % relative speed results
```

With `Nums=1e3:1e4` as shown above, the relative speed results of the algorithms on the author's computer are 9.1, 1.3, and 1.0, respectively. That is, the For Loop implementation is 9.1 times slower than the second vectorization, and the first vectorization is 30% slower than the second. If `Nums` is changed to `Nums=1e5:2e5`, the relative speed results are 7.1, 1.3, and 1.0, respectively. With the larger number of elements, the vectorized approaches are now not as fast because of their large intermediate arrays. Overall, the final implementation is the fastest, uses the most memory, and is the most difficult to read. Though not uniformly true, these properties are commonly true for well optimized code.

38.3 VANDERMONDE MATRIX

There are a number of numerical linear algebra problems that require the generation of a Vandermonde matrix. For a vector $\boldsymbol{x}$, a Vandermonde matrix has the form

$$V = \begin{bmatrix} x_1^m & x_1^{m-1} & \cdots & x_1 & 1 \\ x_2^m & x_2^{m-1} & \cdots & x_2 & 1 \\ \vdots & \vdots & \ddots & \vdots & \vdots \\ x_n^m & x_n^{m-1} & \cdots & x_n & 1 \end{bmatrix}$$

As shown, the columns of V are element-by-element powers of the components of $\boldsymbol{x}$. Let's consider a variety of approaches to constructing this matrix.

The first approach that comes to mind is the straightforward application of a For Loop as in the following script M-file.

```
% vander1.m
% construct a Vandermonde matrix.

x=(1:6)';     % column vector for input data
m=5;          % highest power to compute
V=[];

for i=1:m+1   % build V column by column
   V=[V x.^(m+1-i)];
end
```

The above approach builds `V` column by column, starting from an empty matrix. There are a number of weaknesses in this implementation, the most obvious being that memory is reallocated for `V` each time through the loop. So the first vectorization step is to preallocate `V` as shown in the M-file below.

```
% vander2.m
% construct a Vandermonde matrix.

x=(1:6)';         % column vector for input data
m=5;              % highest power to compute
n=length(x);      % number of elements in x
V=ones(n,m+1);    % preallocate memory for result

for i=1:m         % build V column by column
   V(:,i)=x.^(m+1-i);
end
```

Here V is initialized as a matrix containing all ones. Then the individual columns of V are assigned within the For Loop. The last column is not assigned in the For Loop since it already contains ones and there is no use in computing x.^0. The above code is the implementation found in the vander function in MATLAB. There are still two problems with the above code. First, the columns of V are explicitly computed without making use of prior columns, and second, the For Loop should be able to be eliminated. The script M-file below solves the first problem.

```
% vander3.m
% construct a Vandermonde matrix.

x=(1:6)';         % column vector for input data
m=5;              % highest power to compute
n=length(x);      % number of elements in x
V=ones(n,m+1);    % preallocate memory for result

for i=m:-1:1      % build V column by column
   V(:,i)=x.*V(:,i+1);
end
```

Now the columns of V are assigned starting with the second last column and proceeding backward to the first. This is done because the ith column of V is equal to the $(i + 1)$th column multiplied elementwise by x. This is the implementation found in the MATLAB function polyfit.

At this point the above implementation cannot be optimized further without eliminating the For Loop. Eliminating the For Loop requires some ingenuity and a lot of familiarity with the functions in MATLAB. Using the array manipulation tables found earlier in this chapter, the functions `repmat` and `cumprod` offer some promise. The script M-file below demonstrates an approach that uses `repmat`.

```
% vander4.m
% construct a Vandermonde matrix.

x=(1:6)';          % column vector for input data
m=5;               % highest power to compute
n=length(x);       % number of elements in x

p=m:-1:0;          % column powers
V=repmat(x,1,m+1).^repmat(p,n,1);
```

This implementation uses `repmat` twice, once to replicate `x` creating a matrix of `m+1` columns each containing `x`, and the second time to create a matrix containing the powers to be applied to each element of the matrix containing `x`. Given these two matrices, element-by-element exponentiation is used to create the desired result. As with `vander2.m`, this implementation explicitly computes each column without using information from other columns. The function `cumprod` solves this problem as shown in the script M-file below.

```
% vander5.m
% construct a Vandermonde matrix.

x=(1:6)';          % column vector for input data
m=5;               % highest power to compute
n=length(x);       % number of elements in x

V=ones(n,m+1);
V(:,2:end)=cumprod(repmat(x,1,m),2);
V=V(:,m+1:-1:1);
```

Here the function `cumprod` is used to compute the columns of `V` after using `repmat` to duplicate `x`. Since `cumprod` proceeds from left to right, the final result is found by reversing the columns of `V`. This implementation uses only one M-file function, `repmat`. Eliminating this function by array addressing should lead to the fastest possible implementation. Doing so leads to the script M-file below.

```
% vander6.m
% construct a Vandermonde matrix.

x=(1:6)';         % column vector for input data
m=5;              % highest power to compute
n=length(x);      % number of elements in x

V=ones(n,m+1);
V(:,2:end)=cumprod(x(:,ones(1,m)),2);
V=V(:,m+1:-1:1);
```

Given the six implementations above, let's test them using `tic` and `toc`. By removing the first two lines, `x=(1:6)';` and `m=5;`, the following script M-file tests the execution speed of the implementations.

```
% testvander.m
% script file to test vandermonde implementations

x=randn(10000,1);   % column vector for input data
m=100;              % highest power to compute
times=zeros(1,5);

tic
vander1
times(1)=toc;

tic
vander2
times(2)=toc;

tic
vander3
times(3)=toc;
```

```
tic
vander4
times(4)=toc;

tic
vander5
times(5)=toc;

relspeed=times/min(times) % relative speed results
```

Running this script file produces the following results on the author's computer.

```
relspeed =
     24.194        1.632            1     7.2114      2.057     2.0563
```

What's going on here? The last implementation should be the fastest since it utilizes the most vectorized solution. Surprisingly, `vander3.m` is the fastest despite the fact that it uses a For Loop! These results are important because they point out the fact that eliminating all For Loops does not necessarily produce the fastest code. Sometimes preallocation and careful use of For Loops to minimize memory use produce optimum code.

In the process of eliminating the For Loop, the last three implementations use more memory. The two fastest implementations, `vander2.m` and `vander3.m`, use preallocation and a For Loop. Given that the only difference between `vander5.m` and `vander6.m` is `repmat(x,1,m)` versus `x(:,ones(1,m))`, calling `repmat` does not appear to produce a significant degradation in performance.

The values for `x` and `m` in `testvander.m` were chosen so that the implementations run slow enough to give reliable elapsed time values. As a result, `testvander.m` compares the implementations for very large arrays. As an alternative, the implementations can be tested using smaller arrays by running each implementation many times before computing elapsed times. The script file below uses For Loops to iterate each implementation.

```
% testvander2.m
% script file to test vandermonde implementations

x=randn(100,1);       % column vector for input data
m=10;                 % highest power to compute
N=1:500;
times=zeros(1,6);
```

```
tic
for i=N, vander1, end
times(1)=toc;

tic
for i=N, vander2, end
times(2)=toc;

tic
for i=N, vander3, end
times(3)=toc;

tic
for i=N, vander4, end
times(4)=toc;

tic
for i=N, vander5, end
times(5)=toc;

tic
for i=N, vander6, end
times(6)=toc;

relspeed=times/min(times) % relative speed results
```

The Vandermonde matrix now has only 100 rows and 11 columns, which is much smaller than the 10,000-by-101 matrix in `testvander.m`. Running this script file produces the following results on the author's computer.

```
relspeed =
       2.5134      1.209      1.1444      3.8931      1.5075     1
```

Things have changed! With smaller arrays, the vectorized solution `vander6.m` becomes the fastest. In addition, the use of the M-file `repmat` in `vander5.m` creates a significant speed penalty of approximately 50%. The optimum For Loop implementation `vander3.m` remains competitive, incurring only a 14% speed penalty. Even the worst-case implementation, `vander1.m`, is only 2.5 times worse than `vander6.m`, as opposed to being 24 times worse in the large array case in `testvander.m`.

So which of the above implementations is the best? For very large arrays `vander3.m` is the fastest, and for array sizes most likely to occur in applications `vander6.m` is the fastest. The MATLAB function `polyfit` uses the `vander3.m` implementation. Strict vectorization is optimum if memory requirements do not stress memory management capabilities of a computer platform. On the other hand, variable memory preallocation and judicious use of For Loops to minimize memory demands are best if problem size becomes very large. Given the deteriorating numerical properties of Vandermonde matrices as their dimension rises, they are much more likely to be useful in applications where matrix sizes are relatively small. As a result, `vander6.m` is generally the best algorithm.

38.4 REPEATED VALUE CREATION AND COUNTING

This section considers the following problem. Given a vector $\boldsymbol{x}$ containing data and a vector $\boldsymbol{n}$ of equal length containing nonnegative integers, construct a vector where $x(i)$ is repeated $n(i)$ times for every ith element in the two vectors. For example, $\boldsymbol{x} = [3 \quad 2 \quad 0 \quad 5 \quad 6]$ and $n = [2 \quad 0 \quad 3 \quad 1 \quad 2]$ would produce the result $\boldsymbol{y} = [3 \quad 3 \quad 0 \quad 0 \quad 0 \quad 5 \quad 6 \quad 6]$. Note that since $n(2)$ is zero, $x(2)$ does not appear in the result $\boldsymbol{y}$.

In addition to repeated value creation, the inverse problem of identifying and counting repeated values is also of interest. Thus, given the example $\boldsymbol{y}$ above, find the vectors $\boldsymbol{x}$ and $\boldsymbol{n}$ that describe it.

Consider repeated value creation first. As always, the nonvectorized or scalar approach is straightforward as shown in the script M-file below.

```
% repeat1.m
% repeated value creation and counting

x = [3 2 0 5 6];   % data to repeat
n = [2 0 3 1 2];   % repeat counts

y=[];
for i=1:length(x)
   y=[y repmat(x(i),1,n(i))];
end
```

In this implementation the result is built using brackets to concatenate the repeated values next to each other. Preallocating space for the result `y` is the first step toward vectorization. In addition, zero values in `n` can be eliminated from consideration. Performing these steps leads to the script M-file below.

```
% repeat2.m
% repeated value creation and counting

x = [3 2 0 5 6];  % data to repeat
n = [2 0 3 1 2];  % repeat counts
nz=(n~=0);
n=n(nz);             % eliminate zero counts
x=x(nz);             % eliminate corresponding data
y=zeros(1,sum(n));   % preallocate array

idx=1;               % pointer into y
for i=1:length(x)
   y(idx:idx+n(i)-1)=repmat(x(i),1,n(i));
   idx=idx+n(i);     % next pointer location
end
```

Here, `sum(n)` is the total number of elements in the result, and the variable `idx` is used to identify where the next data is to be placed in `y`. The only remaining way this For Loop approach can be improved is to eliminate the function call to `repmat`. As we saw earlier, the overhead of calling an M-file function each time through the loop slows the implementation down. Rather than consider this incremental improvement, let's find a way to eliminate the For Loop.

To determine how to proceed, it is beneficial to look at how `x` is related to `y`. After eliminating zero counts in the example being considered, `x`, `n`, and `y` are

```
>> x
x =
     3     0     5     6
>> n
n =
     2     3     1     2
>> y
y =
     3     3     0     0     0     5     6     6
```

If we can create an index vector `idx = [1 1 2 2 2 3 4 4]`, then `x` is related to `y` as

```
>> idx =[1 1 2 2 2 3 4 4];
>> y = x(idx)
y =
     3     3     0     0     0     5     6     6
```

So rather than concentrate on getting the values of x into the correct places in y, if we can generate an index vector for x with the desired values, finding y simplifies to just one statement, y = x(idx). This is a common situation when vectorizing. The indices are often more important than the data itself.

The relationship between n and idx above is straightforward. In addition, since idx looks like a cumulative sum, there's a chance that the cumsum function will be useful. When we can generate an array of ones and zeros at the indices where idx changes value, then idx is indeed a cumulative sum, for example,

```
>> tmp = [1 0 1 0 0 1 1 0]
tmp =
     1     0     1     0     0     1     1     0
>> idx = cumsum(tmp)
idx =
     1     1     2     2     2     3     4     4
```

The nonzero values in tmp are related to n. To discover this relationship, look at its cumulative sum:

```
>> csn = cumsum(n)
csn =
     2     5     6     8
```

If the last value in csn is discarded and 1 is added to the remaining values, the indices of all 1s in tmp are known, except for the first which is always 1. Therefore, the indices of all 1s can be computed. Consider the example

```
>> tmp2 = [1 csn(1:end-1)+1]
tmp2 =
     1     3     6     7
```

That's it. The values in tmp2 identify the 1s to be placed in tmp. All other values in tmp are 0. Now all that remains is creating tmp. This is easily done, as in the following example.

```
>> tmp = zeros(1,csn(end)) % preallocate with all zeros
tmp =
     0     0     0     0     0     0     0     0
>> tmp(tmp2) = 1           % poke in ones with scalar expansion
tmp =
     1     0     1     0     0     1     1     0
>> idx = cumsum(tmp)       % form the desired cumsum
idx =
     1     1     2     2     2     3     4     4
>> y = x(idx)              % idx does the rest!
y =
     3     3     0     0     0     5     6     6
```

Using the above approach, a vectorized implementation of creating repeated values is shown in the script M-file below.

```
% repeat3.m
% repeated value creation and counting

x = [3 2 0 5 6];  % data to repeat
n = [2 0 3 1 2];  % repeat counts

nz=(n~=0);
n=n(nz);              % eliminate zero counts
x=x(nz);              % eliminate corresponding data

csn=cumsum(n);                   % cumulative sum of counts
tmp=zeros(1,csn(end));           % preallocate memory
tmp([1 csn(1:end-1)+1]) = 1;  % poke in ones
idx=cumsum(tmp);                 % index vector
y=x(idx);                        % let array indexing do the work
```

About the only improvement that can be made in the above implementation is variable reuse that eliminates memory reallocation. The variables `tmp` and `idx` and `y` have the same size and are not needed simultaneously. Therefore, two fewer memory allocations for an array the size of the output are required if the data contained in these variables share the same MATLAB variable. Doing so leads to the M-file shown below.

```
% repeat4.m
% repeated value creation and counting

x = [3 2 0 5 6];  % data to repeat
n = [2 0 3 1 2];  % repeat counts

nz=(n~=0);
n=n(nz);              % eliminate zero counts
x=x(nz);              % eliminate corresponding data

csn=cumsum(n);              % cumulative sum of counts
y=zeros(1,csn(end));        % preallocate memory once!
```

```
y([1 csn(1:end-1)+1]) = 1; % poke in ones
y(:)=cumsum(y);            % index vector
y(:)=x(y);                 % let array indexing do the work
```

Now, after eliminating zero elements in n and creating csn, memory is allocated for only one variable the size of the result. The last three statements in the M-file simply store the right-hand-side results in the memory previously allocated to y. Note that if the left-hand side of the last two statements did not include the (:), memory allocations for new arrays named y would occur on each line. For further information on arrays and memory allocation, see Section 5.13.

As was done in preceding sections, the data creation statements in these script files are removed (actually commented out by placing a % before them) and a script file is written to perform timing analysis. The first script M-file is shown below.

```
% testrepeat
% script file to test repeat implementations

xdata=rand(1,100);                  % data to test
ndata=repmat([3 8 2 1 0 6 9 5 7 4],1,100/10); % counts

N=1:500;
times=zeros(1,4);

x=xdata;  % refresh data
n=ndata;
tic
for i=N, repeat1, end
times(1)=toc

x=xdata;  % refresh data
n=ndata;
tic
for i=N, repeat2, end
times(2)=toc;

x=xdata;  % refresh data
n=ndata;
tic
for i=N, repeat3, end
```

```
times(3)=toc;

x=xdata;  % refresh data
n=ndata;
tic
for i=N, repeat4, end
times(4)=toc

relspeed=times/min(times)
```

Since x and n are modified within the implementations, the data is refreshed as shown. The data in the above script file is relatively small; x and n contain only 100 elements, and the algorithm result contains 450 elements. Running the script file several times and averaging the results give a relative speed vector of

```
relspeed =
        45.975         39.985         1.0347              1
```

Obviously, the two For Loop implementations are very slow compared to the vectorized cases. In addition, the last implementation, repeat4.m, just edges out repeat3.m as the fastest algorithm. On several runs of the script file, repeat3.m was faster than repeat4.m, but on average the above results hold. Therefore, for a relatively small data set, repeat4.m with its minimum array creation is arguably the best.

The above script file was rerun with a larger data set to see what influence array size has on the result. Letting xdata grow to 10,000 elements produces an average relative speed vector:

```
relspeed =
        610.52         66.909              1              1
```

Clearly, repeat1.m has essentially failed. The fact that it reallocates memory each time through its For Loop makes it a factor of 600 times slower than the vectorized approaches and about 10 times slower than repeat2.m, which uses a For Loop but preallocates memory. What's most interesting here is that repeat3.m and repeat4.m still show no measurable difference on average on the author's computer. Perhaps your computer offers more definitive results.

Let's move on to the inverse of the above algorithm, namely, repeated value identification and counting. That is, starting with $\boldsymbol{y}$, find $\boldsymbol{x}$ and $\boldsymbol{n}$ (except for any zero count values of course). Again the most obvious solution is nonvectorized and uses a For Loop as shown in the script M-file below.

```
% repeat5.m
% repeated value creation and counting
% inverse operation

y = [3 3 0 0 0 5 6 6]; % data to examine

x=y(1);                   % beginning data
n=1;                      % beginning count
idx=1;                    % index value
for i=2:length(y)
   if y(i)==x(idx)        % value matches current x
      n(idx)=n(idx)+1;    % increment current count
   else                   % new value found
      idx=idx+1;          % increment index
      x(idx)=y(i);        % poke in new x
      n(idx)=1;           % start new count
   end
end
```

Here a simple If-Else-End construction is used to decide if a particular element of `y` is a member of the current repeated value. If it is, the count is incremented. If it is not, a new repeat value is created. Though it is not obvious, each time the Else section is executed, memory is reallocated for `x` and `n`.

The next step is to use preallocation as shown in the script M-file below.

```
% repeat6.m
% repeated value creation and counting
% inverse operation

y = [3 3 0 0 0 5 6 6]; % data to examine

x=zeros(size(y));         % preallocate results
n=x;

x(1)=y(1);                % beginning data
n(1)=1;                   % beginning count
idx=1;                    % index value
for i=2:length(y)
```

```
    if y(i)==x(idx)      % value matches current x
       n(idx)=n(idx)+1; % increment current count
    else                 % new value found
       idx=idx+1;        % increment index
       x(idx)=y(i);      % poke in new x
       n(idx)=1;         % start new count
    end
end
nz=(n==0);  % find elements not used
x(nz)=[];   % delete excess allocations
n(nz)=[];
```

Since the length of x and n are unknown, but they cannot be any longer than y, x and n are preallocated to have the same size as y. At the end, the excess memory allocations are discarded.

Vectorizing this algorithm requires study of an example. Consider the y vector that was the result of applying the creation algorithm to the original x and n data:

```
>> y
y =
     3     3     0     0     0     5     6     6
```

Because of the structure of this vector, the MATLAB function diff must be useful, for example,

```
>> diff(y)
ans =
     0    -3     0     0     5     1     0
```

If this vector is shifted one element to the right, the nonzero elements line up with places in y that represent new repeated values. In addition, the first element is always a new repeated value. So, using logical operations, the repeated values can be identified, for example,

```
>> y
y =
     3     3     0     0     0     5     6     6
>> tmp = [1 diff(y)]~=0
tmp =
     1     0     1     0     0     1     1     0
```

Given the logical variable tmp, the vector x is found by logical addressing,

```
>> x = y(tmp)
x =
     3     0     5     6
```

Finding the repeat counts `n` associated with each value in `x` takes further study. The repeat counts are equal to the distance between the ones in `tmp`. Therefore, finding the indices associated with `tmp` is useful, for example,

```
>> find(tmp)
ans =
     1     3     6     7
>> diff(ans)
ans =
     2     3     1
```

The difference in indices gives the repeat count for all but the last repeated element. The function `diff` misses this count because there is no marker identifying the end of the array, which marks the end of the last repeated value. Appending one nonzero to `tmp` solves this problem, for example,

```
>> find([tmp 1])
ans =
     1     3     6     7     9
>> n = diff(ans)
n =
     2     3     1     2
```

The inverse algorithm is now known. Implementing it leads to the script file below.

```
% repeat7.m
% repeated value creation and counting
% inverse operation

y = [3 3 0 0 0 5 6 6]; % data to examine

tmp=([1 diff(y)]~=0);
x=y(tmp);
n=diff(find([tmp 1]));
```

The above implementation demonstrates the compactness of vectorization. This solution requires 3 lines of code, compared to the 17 used in `repeat6.m`. This implementation also demonstrates the difficulty often encountered in reading vectorized code. These 3 lines are essentially meaningless unless one executes and views the results of each line with a simple example.

Before concluding, it is important to note that the above implementation fails if `y` contains any `Inf` or `NaN` elements. The function `diff` returns `NaN` for differences between `Inf` elements, as well as for differences containing `NaN` elements. Because of the utility of creating and counting repeated values, it is encapsulated in the function `mmrepeat` shown below.

```
function [y,m]=mmrepeat(x,n)
%MMREPEAT Repeat or Count Repeated Values in a Vector.
% MMREPEAT(X,N) returns a vector formed from X where X(i) is repeated
% N(i) times. If N is a scalar it is applied to all elements of X.
% N must contain nonnegative integers. N must be a scalar or have the same
% length as X.
%
% For example, MMREPEAT([1 2 3 4],[2 3 1 0]) returns the vector
% [1 1  2 2 2  3]    (extra spaces added for clarity)
%
% [X,N]=MMREPEAT(Y) counts the consecutive repeated values in Y returning
% the values in X and the counts in N. Y=MMREPEAT(X,N) and [X,N]=MMREPEAT(Y)
% are inverses of each other if N contains no zeros and X contains unique
% elements.

if nargin==2 % MMREPEAT(X,N)
    xlen=length(x);
    nlen=length(n);
    if ndims(x)~=2 | prod(size(x))~=xlen
       error('X Must be a Vector.')
    else
       [r,c]=size(x);
    end
    if any(n<0) | any(fix(n)~=n)
       error('N Must Contain NonNegative Integers.')
    end
    if ndims(n)~=2 | prod(size(n))~=nlen | (nlen>1 & nlen~=xlen)
       error('N Must be a Scalar or Vector the Same Size as X.')
    end
    x=reshape(x,1,xlen); % make x a row vector

    if nlen==1 % scalar n case, repeat all elements the same amount
       if n==0 % quick exit for special case
          y=[];
          return
       end
```

```
      y=x(ones(1,n),:); % duplicate x to make n rows each containing x
      y=y(:);           % stack each column into a single column
      if r==1           % input was a row so return a row
         y=y.';
      end
   else % vector n case
      iz=find(n~=0);         % take out elements to be repeated zero times
      x=x(iz);
      n=n(iz);
      csn=cumsum(n);
      y=zeros(1,csn(end));  % preallocate temp/output variable
      y(csn(1:end-1)+1)=1; % mark indices where values increment
      y(1)=1;               % poke in first index
      y=x(cumsum(y));       % use cumsum to set indices
      if c==1               % input was a column so return a column
         y=y.';
      end
   end
elseif nargin==1 % MMREPEAT(Y)
   xlen=length(x);
   if ndims(x)~=2 | prod(size(x))~=xlen
      error('Y Must be a Vector.')
   else
      [r,c]=size(x);
   end
   x=reshape(x,1,xlen); % make x a row vector
   xnan=isnan(x);
   xinf=isinf(x);
   if any(xnan|xinf) % handle case with exceptions
       ntmp=sum(rand(1,4))*sqrt(realmax); % replacement for nan's
       itmp=1/ntmp;                        % replacement for inf's
       x(xnan)=ntmp;
       x(xinf)=itmp.*sign(x(xinf));
       y=[1 diff(x)]~=0;          % places where distinct values begin
       m=diff([find(y) xlen+1]); % counts
       x(xnan)=nan;               % poke nan's and inf's back in
       x(xinf)=inf*x(xinf);
   else % x contains only algebraic numbers
       y=[1 diff(x)]~=0;          % places where distinct values begin
       m=diff([find(y) xlen+1]); % counts
   end
   y=x(y); % the unique values
   if c==1
       y=y.';
   end
```

```
else
    error('Incorrect Number of Input Arguments.')
end
```

38.5 CIRCULAR ADDRESSING

This section considers rotating the elements of a vector to different positions and creating matrices from vectors, with different rows or columns containing rotated copies of the vector. Consider the following example.

```
>> x = 1:8    % test vector
x =
     1     2     3     4     5     6     7     8
>> n = 3      % shift amount
n =
     3

>> y = x([n+1:end 1:n])      % shift left
y =
     4     5     6     7     8     1     2     3
>> y = [x(n+1:end) x(1:n)] % shift left
y =
     4     5     6     7     8     1     2     3

>> y = x([end-n+1:end 1:end-n])      % shift right
y =
     6     7     8     1     2     3     4     5
>> y = [x(end-n+1:end) x(1:end-n)] % shift right
y =
     6     7     8     1     2     3     4     5
```

Note that the shift amount can be interpreted as a shift left or a shift right. In addition, a shift can be implemented in two ways. One can concatenate the required indices then address x or concatenate the individually indexed pieces of x.

If the sign of n is used to determine the shift direction, with positive n signifying shift right, one could use an If-Else-End construction to implement the shifting or one could use the function mod, for example,

```
>> t = -4:4       % sample data
t =
    -4    -3    -2    -1     0     1     2     3     4
```

```
>> n = 3
n =
     3
>> mod(t,n)      % count 0 thru 2
ans =
     2     0     1     2     0     1     2     0     1
>> mod(t-1,n)+1 % count 1 thru 3
ans =
     2     3     1     2     3     1     2     3     1
```

The mod function returns the modulus or signed remainder after division. By subtracting 1, finding the modulus, and then adding 1, the mod function counts 1 through n repeatedly. Applying this method to the above indexing problem gives

```
>> x = 1:8
x =
     1     2     3     4     5     6     7     8
>> n = 3
n =
     3
>> y = x(mod((1:end)-n-1,end)+1) % shift right
y =
     6     7     8     1     2     3     4     5

>> n = -3
n =
    -3
>> y = x(mod((1:end)-n-1,end)+1) % shift left same as above
y =
     4     5     6     7     8     1     2     3
```

In this case, the remainder of all indices (1:end) with n+1 subtracted is found with respect to the length of x. The above scheme works when one dimension of a higher-dimension array is shifted as well, for example,

```
>> x = magic(5)
x =
    17    24     1     8    15
    23     5     7    14    16
     4     6    13    20    22
    10    12    19    21     3
    11    18    25     2     9
>> y = x(mod((1:end)-n-1,end)+1,:) % shift rows up 3
y =
    10    12    19    21     3
    11    18    25     2     9
```

```
    17    24     1     8    15
    23     5     7    14    16
     4     6    13    20    22
>> y = x(:,mod((1:end)-n-1,end)+1) % shift columns left 3
y =
     8    15    17    24     1
    14    16    23     5     7
    20    22     4     6    13
    21     3    10    12    19
     2     9    11    18    25
```

There are occasions when a matrix is composed by placing shifted versions of a vector in its rows or columns. Using a For Loop is the most straightforward way of performing this step, for example,

```
% cirle1.m
% circular addressing
x=-3:3;          % data to work on
n=1;             % shift per row
r=5;             % total number of rows

lx=length(x);
y=zeros(r,lx);    % preallocate result
y(1,:)=x;         % first row is x

for i=2:r
   tmp=y(i-1,:); % row to shift
   y(i,:)=tmp(mod((1:lx)-n-1,lx)+1);
end
```

Here an `r`-by-`lx` array is formed by repeatedly shifting the vector `x` and placing the elements sequentially in the rows of the result. As demonstrated in earlier sections of this chapter, the result `y` was preallocated before the For Loop. The above script M-file produces the result

```
>> y
y =
    -3    -2    -1     0     1     2     3
     3    -3    -2    -1     0     1     2
     2     3    -3    -2    -1     0     1
     1     2     3    -3    -2    -1     0
     0     1     2     3    -3    -2    -1
```

The shift amount need not be fixed but can vary row by row, as in the following example.

```
% cirle2.m
% circular addressing

x=-3:3;          % data to work on
n=[1 2 -3 0];    % relative shift
r=5;              % total number of rows
lx=length(x);
y=zeros(r,lx);    % preallocate
y(1,:)=x;         % first row is x

for i=2:r
   tmp=y(i-1,:); % row to shift
   y(i,:)=tmp(mod((1:lx)-n(i-1)-1,lx)+1);
end
```

This script M-file produces the result

```
>> y
y =
     -3    -2    -1     0     1     2     3
      3    -3    -2    -1     0     1     2
      1     2     3    -3    -2    -1     0
     -3    -2    -1     0     1     2     3
     -3    -2    -1     0     1     2     3
```

The above process can be vectorized further by studying how the indices of x appear in the final result. To simplify this discussion let the shift amount be constant from row to row as in the example

```
% cirle3.m
% circular addressing

x=-3:3;          % data to work on
n=1;             % relative shift
r=5;             % total number of rows
```

```
lx=length(x);
y=zeros(r,lx);    % preallocate
y(1,:)=x;         % first row is x
idx=zeros(r,lx); % capture indices
idx(1,:)=1:lx;

for i=2:r
   tmp=y(i-1,:); % row to shift
   idx(i,:)=mod((1:lx)-(n+i-2)-1,lx)+1;
   y(i,:)=tmp(idx(i,:));
end
idx
```

The above script M-file produces the index array

```
>> idx
idx =
     1     2     3     4     5     6     7
     7     1     2     3     4     5     6
     6     7     1     2     3     4     5
     5     6     7     1     2     3     4
     4     5     6     7     1     2     3
```

This array can be decomposed into the sum of two arrays, for example,

```
>> idxa = repmat(1:7,5,1)          % repeat x indices
idxa =
     1     2     3     4     5     6     7
     1     2     3     4     5     6     7
     1     2     3     4     5     6     7
     1     2     3     4     5     6     7
     1     2     3     4     5     6     7
>> idxb = repmat(-n*(0:4)',1,7)  % row shifts
idxb =
     0     0     0     0     0     0     0
    -1    -1    -1    -1    -1    -1    -1
    -2    -2    -2    -2    -2    -2    -2
    -3    -3    -3    -3    -3    -3    -3
    -4    -4    -4    -4    -4    -4    -4
>> idxa+idxb  % sum
ans =
     8     9    10    11    12    13    14
     7     8     9    10    11    12    13
```

```
     6     7     8     9    10    11    12
     5     6     7     8     9    10    11
     4     5     6     7     8     9    10
>> mod(idxa+idxb-1,7)+1  % wrap to array bounds
ans =
     1     2     3     4     5     6     7
     7     1     2     3     4     5     6
     6     7     1     2     3     4     5
     5     6     7     1     2     3     4
     4     5     6     7     1     2     3
```

The result immediately above is the desired index array. The decomposition of the indices produces two arrays that match the output of the `meshgrid` function. As a result, the above implementation can be written as shown in the script M-file below.

```
% cirle4.m
% circular addressing

x=-3:3;          % data to work on
n=1;             % relative shift
r=5;             % total number of rows
lx=length(x);

[idxa,idxb]=meshgrid(1:lx,-n*(0:r-1));
idx=mod(idxa+idxb-1,lx)+1; % wrap indices
y=x(idx);        % final result by indexing
```

The above result contains no For Loops. However, it does create three temporary indexing arrays the size of the result. Therefore, for very large arrays the For Loop approach may likely be faster, but for smaller arrays the above approach is significantly faster. Once again, the vectorized implementation above is more difficult to read than the For Loop implementation.

Because of the utility of the above implementation, it is encapsulated in the M-file function `mmwrap` as shown below.

```
function y=mmwrap(x,s,n)
%MMWRAP Form Matrix From Circular Shifted Vector.
```

```
% MMWRAP(X,S,N) returns a matrix created by repeated circular
% shifting of the vector X. If X is a row vector, the result has
% circularly shifted rows. If X is a column vector, the result
% has circularly shifted columns. X is always the first row
% or column of the result.
% If S is a scalar each row or column is shifted S elements from
% the previous row or column. If S is positive the shift is to the
% right or down. Negative S shifts to the left or up.
% N is the total number of rows or columns to create.
%
% If S is a vector, the i-th element of S determines the shift for
% the (i+1)-th row or column relative to the preceding one.
% If S is a vector, N is ignored and length(S)+1 rows or columns
% are created.

xsiz=size(x);
xlen=length(x);
if ndims(x)>2 | prod(xsiz)~=xlen
   error('X Must be a Row or Column Vector.')
end
if nargin<2
   error('Two or Three Input Arguments are Required.')
end
s=s(:);
slen=length(s);
if any(fix(s)~=s)
   error('S Must Contain Integers.')
end
if slen==1 & nargin==2
   error('Missing Third Input Argument.')
elseif slen==1
   if length(n)>1 | fix(n)~=n
      error('N Must be an Integer.')
   end
   s=-s*(0:n-1);
else
   s=[0; -cumsum(s)];
end
x=x(:).';  % consider row case for now
[idxa,idxb]=meshgrid(1:xlen,s);
idxa=mod(idxa+idxb-1,xlen)+1; % wrap indices
y=x(idxa);
```

```
if diff(xsiz)<0 % input was a column so return column orientation
   y=y.';
end
```

38.6 INDEXING ARRAY SEGMENTS

Logical expressions and the `find` function allow one to easily identify indices in an array that satisfy some criteria. There are applications where one wishes to address segments of an array based on starting indices and a segment width, ending indices and a segment width, or starting and ending indices. For example, given a vector of starting indices $\boldsymbol{i}$ = [1 5 13 22] and a segment width $w = 3$, one may wish to create an index vector ***idx*** = [(1:3), (5:7), (13:15), (22:24)]. Or given a vector of starting indices $\boldsymbol{i}$ = [1 5 13 22] and a vector of ending indices $\boldsymbol{j}$ = [2 9 15 30], one may wish to create an index vector ***idx*** = [(1:2), (5:9), (13:15), (22:30)]. This section addresses this problem.

Solving this problem using a For Loop is straightforward, for example,

```
% segment1.m
% indexing array segments

i = [1 5 13 22]; % test data
j = [2 9 15 30];

idx=[];
for k=1:length(i)
   idx=cat(2,idx,i(k):j(k));
end
```

Here the `cat` function is used instead of brackets just to show that there is an alternative to brackets for concatenation. This implementation suffers from repeated memory allocation since the size of `idx` increases each time through the For Loop. It is possible to preallocate memory for the result. To do so, we need to figure out the size of the result and how to organize placing segments in it. Since the indices cumulate, the function `cumsum` may be helpful. Consider the following example.

```
>> run = j-i+1       % length of each run
run =
     2     5     3     9
>> ij = cumsum(run) % end of each run in result
ij =
     2     7    10    19
>> ii = ij-run+1     % start of each run in result
ii =
     1     3     8    11
```

The variable `run` is the run length of each segment. Therefore, the sum of the elements of `run` is equal to the number of elements in the result. This value is given by the last element in the cumulative sum `ij`. The elements in `ij` mark the last index of each run in the result. The first element of each run in the result is found by subtracting the run length from the last element and adding 1. Using the above guidelines leads to the following script M-file that preallocates the result.

```
% segment2.m
% indexing array segments

i = [1 5 13 22]; % test data
j = [2 9 15 30];

run=j-i+1;               % length of each run
ij=cumsum(run);          % last index of each run
ii=ij-run+1;             % first index of each run
idx=zeros(1,ij(end));    % preallocate result

for k=1:length(i)
   idx(ii(k):ij(k))=i(k):j(k);
end
```

This implementation still suffers from having a For Loop. Given the straightforward nature of this problem, there must be a completely vectorized solution. When we study the symbolic result ***idx*** = [(1:2), (5:9), (13:15), (22:30)], shown earlier, the result can be computed if the right-hand side can be written as a string. Once the string is found, the function eval can be used to generate the result. Of course, this method is not viable if constructing the string requires a For Loop. Fortunately, the function sprintf is vectorized, for example,

```
>> sprintf('%d:%d,',[i;j])
ans =
1:2,5:9,13:15,22:30,
>> class(ans)
ans =
char
```

Except for the final comma above, the output of sprintf characterizes the indices to be created. The MATLAB interpreter considers commas to be white space, and so the last comma does not produce an error. Adding opening and closing brackets completes the string. Consider the example

```
% segment3.m
% indexing array segments

i = [1 5 13 22]; % test data
j = [2 9 15 30];

idx=eval(cat(2,'[',sprintf('%d:%d,',[i;j]),']'));
```

While this implementation is compactly written and vectorized, the function eval calls the entire MATLAB command interpreter to evaluate the string on the right-hand side. As a result, it incurs significant overhead. However, it is likely to be faster than the For Loop implementations.

Vectorizing this problem without using eval requires study of the solution and working backward. The solution of the above example is

```
>> i    % lower end of segments
i =
     1     5    13    22
>> j    % upper end of segments
j =
     2     9    15    30
>> idx % result
idx =
  Columns 1 through 12
     1     2     5     6     7     8     9    13    14    15    22    23
  Columns 13 through 19
    24    25    26    27    28    29    30
```

The result looks like a cumulative sum with jumps. In fact `idx` can be decomposed into two pieces whose sum gives the desired result when passed to `cumsum`. They are

```
>> idxa = ones(1,19) % unit counts for cumsum
idxa =
  Columns 1 through 12
     1     1     1     1     1     1     1     1     1     1     1     1
  Columns 13 through 19
     1     1     1     1     1     1     1
>> idxb = [0 0 2 0 0 0 0 3 0 0 6 0 0 0 0 0 0 0 0] % jump amounts
idxb =
  Columns 1 through 12
     0     0     2     0     0     0     0     3     0     0     6     0
  Columns 13 through 19
     0     0     0     0     0     0     0
>> cumsum(idxa+idxb) % final result
ans =
  Columns 1 through 12
     1     2     5     6     7     8     9    13    14    15    22    23
  Columns 13 through 19
    24    25    26    27    28    29    30
```

Here `idxa` is a vector that `cumsum` uses to count by 1 and `idxb` is a vector that forces `cumsum` to take the jumps seen in the result. The indices where nonzeros appear in `idxb` are at the beginning of segment runs (except for the first), and their values are equal to 1 less than the difference between the end of one run and the start of the next. Given this description, the above scheme is implemented in the script M-file below.

```
% segment4.m
% indexing array segments

i = [1 5 13 22]; % test data
j = [2 9 15 30];
n=length(i);
run=j-i+1;              % length of each run
ij=cumsum(run);          % last index of each run

idx=ones(1,ij(end));    % preallocate result

idx(1)=i(1);             % poke in first value
idx(1+ij(1:end-1))=i(2:n)-j(1:n-1); % poke in jumps
idx=cumsum(idx);1
```

At this point it is worthwhile to compare the performance of these implementations. As was done in preceding sections, the data creation statements in these script files are commented out by placing a % before them, and a script M-file is written to perform timing analysis. This script M-file is shown below.

```
% testsegment
% script file to test segment implementations

i=10*(1:1000);
j=i+5;

N=1:100;
times=zeros(1,4);

tic
for t=N, segment1, end % no preallocation
times(1)=toc;

tic
for t=N, segment2, end % For Loop
times(2)=toc;

tic
for t=N, segment3, end % EVAL
times(3)=toc;

tic
for t=N, segment4, end %cumsum
times(4)=toc

relspeed=times/min(times)
```

Running this M-file and creating a result having length 6000 give the following relative speed results.

```
relspeed =
      122.09      24.455      139.82           1
```

Decreasing the result length by a factor of 10 gives the following relative speed results.

```
relspeed =
      14.833      9.3333      47.967           1
```

Perhaps the most amazing aspect of the above results is how slow the single-statement implementation using `eval` and `sprintf` is. It is even slower than the implementation that reallocates memory every step. (People have noted the slow speed of `sprintf` on the MATLAB Newsgroup, and so it may be the function dominating the poor performance of this implementation.) The fully vectorized approach is clearly superior for both large and small arrays, with the For Loop approach using memory preallocation much better than either of the remaining approaches. Relative to the fully vectorized implementation, the other implementations decrease in performance as the array size grows.

Because of the utility of the above array segment implementation, it is encapsulated in the function `mmakeidx` as shown below.

```
function idx=mmakeidx(lo,hi)
%MMAKEIDX Make Index Vector From Limits.
% MMAKEIDX(Lo,Hi) creates an index vector from the vectors Lo and Hi.
%
% Lo and Hi are vectors containing low and high indices of segments
% to be addressed.
% MMAKEIDX returns [Lo(1):Hi(1) Lo(2):Hi(2) ... Lo(end):Hi(end)].

if nargin~=2
   error('Two Input Arguments Required.')
end
if any(fix(lo)~=lo)|any(fix(hi)~=hi)
   error('Lo and Hi Must Contain Integers.')
end
if length(lo)~=length(hi)
   error('Lo and Hi Must Have the Same Length.')
end
if any((hi-lo)<0)
   error('Lo(i) Must be Less Than Hi(i).')
end

n=length(lo);

run=hi-lo+1;           % length of each run
last=cumsum(run);      % last index of each run

idx=ones(1,last(end)); % preallocate result
idx(1)=lo(1);          % poke in first value
idx(1+last(1:end-1))=lo(2:n)-hi(1:n-1); % poke in jumps
idx=cumsum(idx);
```

38.7 VECTOR SUBDIVISION

This section considers the problem of subdividing a vector. For example, if $\boldsymbol{x} = [4 \quad 5 \quad 7 \quad 6]$, subdividing this vector by 2 gives $\boldsymbol{y} = [4 \quad 4.5 \quad 5 \quad 6 \quad 7 \quad 6.5 \quad 6]$. Similarly, subdivision by 4 produces $\boldsymbol{y} = [4 \quad 4.25 \quad 4.5 \quad 4.75 \quad 5 \quad 5.5 \quad 6 \quad 6.5 \quad 7 \quad 6.75 \quad 6.5 \quad 6.25 \quad 6]$. Subdivision by n inserts $n - 1$ equally spaced elements between each element in the original vector. If N is the length of $\boldsymbol{x}$, the length of the result is $N + (n - 1)(N - 1)$.

Implementing vector subdivision using a For Loop is straightforward, as shown in the script M-file below.

```
% subdiv1.m
% subdivide a vector

x = [4 5 7 6]; % test data
n = 4;         % number of subdivisions

N=length(x);   % length of data

y=zeros(1,N+(n-1)*(N-1)); % preallocate result
f=(0:n-1)/n;   % fractional spacing between elements
idx=1;         % index for result

for i=1:n-1
   dx=x(i+1)-x(i);                 % difference
   y(idx:idx+(n-1))=x(i)+f*dx; % place values
   idx=idx+n;                      % update index
end
y(end)=x(end); % place last value
```

This implementation preallocates memory for the result, and the variable `f` contains the fractional or normalized spacing between subdivided elements, for example,

```
>> n
n =
     4
>> f
f =
              0           0.25            0.5           0.75
```

The product of `f` and `dx` denormalizes the spacing. In each pass through the For Loop the difference between the elements of `x` is found. Then `n` elements of the result `y` are computed by adding the denormalized spacing to the current value of x. After the For Loop finishes its work, the final value of y is inserted.

The above implementation can be improved in several ways while retaining the For Loop. For example, all element differences can be computed outside the loop by using the function diff. Rather than address incremental improvements, let's find an implementation that eliminates the For Loop.

The process used in the For Loop implementation can be extended to eliminate the For Loop by letting the problem extend into two dimensions and then collapsing it back into one. Consider the example

```
>> xx = repmat(x(1:end-1),n,1)   % replicate x to n rows
xx =
     4     5     7
     4     5     7
     4     5     7
     4     5     7
>> ff = repmat((0:n-1)'/n,1,N-1) % replicate f to N-1 columns
ff =
             0             0             0
          0.25          0.25          0.25
           0.5           0.5           0.5
          0.75          0.75          0.75
>> dx = diff(x)                  % all differences
dx =
     1     2    -1
>> ddx = repmat(dx,n,1)          % replicate differences to n rows
ddx =
     1     2    -1
     1     2    -1
     1     2    -1
     1     2    -1
```

The last element in x is ignored because it simply becomes the last element in the result. The variables xx, ff, and ddx are all the same size and contain the information needed to implement the subdivision on all elements of x simultaneously using element-by-element array arithmetic. The product ff.*ddx contains all denormalized spacings, which need to be added to the values in xx, for example,

```
>>y = xx+ff.*ddx
y =
             4             5             7
          4.25           5.5          6.75
           4.5             6           6.5
          4.75           6.5          6.25
```

The columns here contain the desired results. Reshaping and adding the final element of x completes the implementation, for example,

```
>> y = [y(:)' x(end)]
y =
  Columns 1 through 6
         4       4.25        4.5       4.75          5        5.5
  Columns 7 through 12
         6        6.5          7       6.75        6.5       6.25
  Column 13
         6
```

Putting these pieces together leads to the following script M-file.

```
% subdiv2.m
% subdivide a vector

x=[4 5 7 6]; % test data
n=4;         % number of subdivisions

N=length(x); % length of data

xx=repmat(x(1:end-1),n,1);   % replicate x
ff=repmat((0:n-1)'/n,1,N-1); % replicate normalized spacing
ddx=repmat(diff(x),n,1);     % replicate differences in x
y=xx+ff.*ddx;                % compute results
y=[y(:)' x(end)];            % back to 1-D
```

The above implementation illustrates the common vectorization technique of extending a problem to higher dimensions, using array operations on the higher-dimension data and then collapsing the result back to the desired dimensions. In the process of doing so, significant temporary memory is used to speed the algorithm.

Because of the utility of the above implementation for vector subdivision, it is encapsulated in the function M-file `mmsubdiv` shown below.

```
function xx=mmsubdiv(x,n)
%MMSUBDIV Subdivide Vector Values.
% MMSUBDIV(X,N) returns a vector formed from X where successive values
```

```
% are subdivided into N intervals marked by N-1 linearly spaced points.
%
% For example, MMSUBDIV(X,2) returns the vector:
%
% [X(1) 0.5*(X(1)+X(2)) X(2) 0.5*(X(2)+X(3)) X(3) ...]
%
% The output vector contains N*(length(X)-1)+1 points.

if ndims(x)~=2 | prod(size(x))~=length(x)
     error('X Must be a Vector.')
else
     [r,c]=size(x);
end
x=x(:)'; % make x a row vector
xlen=length(x);
n=abs(round(n(1)));
if n<2
      xx=reshape(x,r,c);
else
      xx=repmat(x(1:end-1),n,1);
      d=repmat((0:n-1)'/n,1,xlen-1);
      dx=repmat(diff(x),n,1);
      xx=xx+d.*dx;

      xx=[xx(:); x(xlen)];
      if c>1, xx=xx'; end
end
```

38.8 FINDING INDICES

This section considers the MATLAB function `find` and extending its capabilities. The function `find` returns indices where its argument is True (nonzero), for example,

```
>> x = rand(4)
x =
      0.20277      0.19881      0.93181      0.52515
      0.19872     0.015274      0.46599      0.20265
      0.60379      0.74679      0.41865      0.67214
      0.27219       0.4451      0.84622      0.83812
```

```
>> idx = find(x>=0.5)
idx =
     3
     7
     9
    12
    13
    15
    16
```

In this form the indices returned are single indices. That is, they are what would be returned if the `find` function were called as `idx = find(x(:)>=0.5)`. Alternatively, `find` returns row and column indices. Consider the example

```
>> [i,j] = find(x>=0.5);
>> i' % display as a row
ans =
     3     3     1     4     1     3     4
>> j' % display as a row
ans =
     1     2     3     3     4     4     4
```

Here the pairs `i(k)` and `j(k)` identify the row and column indices, respectively, of values where `x>=0.5` is True.

When the input argument to `find` is *n*-D and two output arguments are provided, `find` returns row and column indices of the 2-D equivalent of its argument. That is, an input variable `arg` is reshaped as `reshape(arg,size(arg,1),prod(size(arg))/size(arg,1))`, for example,

```
>> c = cat(3,magic(4),eye(4)) % 3-D array
c(:,:,1) =
    16     2     3    13
     5    11    10     8
     9     7     6    12
     4    14    15     1
c(:,:,2) =
     1     0     0     0
     0     1     0     0
     0     0     1     0
     0     0     0     1
>> [i,j] = find(c==1)    % find unity values
i =
     4
     1
     2
     3
     4
```

```
j =
     4
     5
     6
     7
     8
>> cc = reshape(c,4,8)   % make 2-D
cc =
    16     2     3    13     1     0     0     0
     5    11    10     8     0     1     0     0
     9     7     6    12     0     0     1     0
     4    14    15     1     0     0     0     1
>> [i,j] = find(cc==1)   % find returns same values
i =
     4
     1
     2
     3
     4
j =
     4
     5
     6
     7
     8
```

There are occasions when the above uses for the `find` function are not specific enough. For example, sometimes the first or last element in each row (or column) of an array satisfying some criteria is desired. The `find` function can be used to return these indices. The most straightforward approach uses a For Loop as shown in the script M-file below.

```
% find1.m
% extending find

x=[4 9 1 0 3 4 0
   8 2 7 1 0 0 0
   3 7 1 9 0 2 5
   9 5 2 8 2 1 0
   8 5 2 7 5 8 3]; % test data

xr=size(x,1);  % row dimension of x
j=zeros(xr,1); % preallocate result

% find last element equal to 1 in each row
```

```
for i=1:xr
   tmp=find(x(i,:)==1);
   if ~isempty(tmp) % beware of empties
      j(i)=tmp;
   end
end
```

This implementation simply treats each row as a separate vector. If no element equal to 1 is found in a row, `find` returns an empty matrix. In this case, the result keeps its default value of zero for that row. The result produced by the above script file is

```
>> j
j =
     3
     4
     3
     6
     0
```

Using the two output argument form of the `find` function on the above test data produces

```
>> [r,c] = find(x==1)
r =
     1
     3
     2
     4
c =
     3
     3
     4
     6
```

Here `c` contains the nonzero elements of `j`. As a result, the two-output argument form of `find` can be used to solve the problem at hand. It's just a matter of indexing, for example,

```
>> j = zeros(size(x,1),1) % preallocate zeros
j =
     0
     0
     0
     0
     0
```

```
>> j(r) = c % poke data into j based on r and c
j =
     3
     4
     3
     6
     0
```

Since there is only one element equal to 1 in each row of x, this indexing scheme is fairly straightforward. It also works when there are multiple True elements per row, for example,

```
>> x  % show test data again
x =
     4     9     1     0     3     4     0
     8     2     7     1     0     0     0
     3     7     1     9     0     2     5
     9     5     2     8     2     1     0
     8     5     2     7     5     8     3
>> [r,c] = find(x~=0); % find last non zero element
>> length(r)           % too many Trues to show
ans =
    28
>> j = zeros(size(x,1),1); % preallocate zeros
>> j(r) = c
j =
     6
     4
     7
     6
     7
```

The statement j(r) = c assigns the elements of j numerous times based on the indices in r and c. However, because find searches down the rows starting with the first column and ending with the last, the final assignments to j are the last on each row. The following script M-file illustrates this fact more clearly with a simpler example.

```
% find2.m
% extending find

x=[0 9 7 0 0 0
   5 0 0 6 0 3
   0 0 0 0 0 0
   8 0 4 2 1 0] % test data
```

```
[r,c]=find(x~=0);
rt=r' % display as r and c as rows
ct=c' % to save space
j=zeros(size(x,1),1);
j(r)=c
```

Running the above script M-file produces the following output in the *Command* window.

```
x =
     0     9     7     0     0     0
     5     0     0     6     0     3
     0     0     0     0     0     0
     8     0     4     2     1     0
rt =
     2     4     1     1     4     2     4     4     2
ct =
     1     1     2     3     3     4     4     5     6
j =
     3
     6
     0
     5
```

Based on the above data, `j(1)` is assigned twice, once with `c(3)` and then with `c(4)`. Similarly, `j(2)` is assigned three times, once with `c(1)`, then `c(6)`, and then `c(9)`. The element `j(3)` is not assigned because the number 3 does not appear in `r`. Finally, `j(4)` is assigned four times, once with `c(2)`, then `c(5)`, then `c(7)`, and finally with `c(8)`.

The above process also allows one to find the last row where each column is True, for example,

```
>> i = zeros(size(x,2),1); % preallocate result
>> i(c) = r
i =
     4
     1
     4
     4
     4
     2
```

This also works because for each column the last True row appears last and becomes the last index assigned to the variable `i`.

There are two approaches to finding the first True elements in a row or column. One can either reverse or flip the row or column order of the input data, or one can flip the order of the output of arguments from `find`. After doing so, the last elements assigned to `i` and `j` are the first elements found. Consider the following example.

```
>> x  % recall test data
x =
     0     9     7     0     0     0
     5     0     0     6     0     3
     0     0     0     0     0     0
     8     0     4     2     1     0
>> rf = r(end:-1:1);        % flip r
>> cf = c(end:-1:1);        % flip c
>> j = zeros(size(x,1),1); % preallocate results
>> i = zeros(size(x,2),1);
>> j(rf) = cf  % first nonzero element per row
j =
     2
     1
     0
     1
>> i(cf) = rf % first nonzero element per column
i =
     2
     1
     1
     2
     4
     2
```

Because of the utility of the above implementation, it is encapsulated in the function M-file `mmfindrc` shown below.

```
function idx=mmfindrc(x,dim,flag)
%MMFINDRC Find First or Last Nonzero Indices per Row or Column.
% MMFINDRC(X,Dim,Flag) returns a vector whose i-th element contains
% the index of the First/Last nonzero column/row of X for the i-th
% row/column of X.
% X is the 2-D array to be searched.
% Dim is the dimension to accumulate indices along.
% Dim=1 returns a vector of length equal to the row dimension of X.
% Dim=2 returns a vector of length equal to the column dimension of X.
% Flag indicates whether the first of last element is returned.
```

```
% Flag='first' returns the First nonzero.
% Flag='last' returns the Last nonzero.
% If Flag is not given, 'last' is assumed.

if nargin~=2 & nargin~=3
   error('Two or Three Input Arguments Required.')
end
xsiz=size(x);
if ndims(x)~=2 | min(xsiz)<=1
   error('Vectors and N-D Arrays are Not Allowed.')
end
if length(dim)>1 | fix(dim)~=dim | dim<1 | dim>2
   error('Dimension Argument Must be 1 or 2.')
end
if nargin==2
   flag='last';
end
if ~ischar(flag)
   error('Flag Input Argument Must be a String.')
end
first=lower(flag(1))=='f'; % default is 'last'
[r,c]=find(x);
if dim==1 & ~first
   idx=zeros(xsiz(1),1);
   idx(r)=c;
elseif dim==2 & ~first
   idx=zeros(xsiz(2),1);
   idx(c)=r;
elseif dim==1 & first
   idx=zeros(xsiz(1),1);
   idx(r(end:-1:1))=c(end:-1:1);
elseif dim==2 & first
   idx=zeros(xsiz(2),1);
   idx(c(end:-1:1))=r(end:-1:1);
end
```

To illustrate use of the function `mmfindrc` consider the following example.

```
>> s = char('January','February','March','April')
s =
January
February
March
April
```

```
>> ~isspace(s)
ans =
     1     1     1     1     1     1     1     0
     1     1     1     1     1     1     1     1
     1     1     1     1     1     0     0     0
     1     1     1     1     1     0     0     0
>> mmfindrc(~isspace(s),1) % find last nonspace per row
ans =
     7
     8
     5
     5
>> mmfindrc(s=='r',2)       % find last 'r' per column
ans =
     0
     0
     4
     2
     0
     1
     2
     0
```

38.9 DIFFERENTIAL SUMS

This section considers computing the differential sum between elements in an array. That is, if $\boldsymbol{x} = [3 \quad 1 \quad 2 \quad 6 \quad 3 \quad 1 \quad -1]$, then the differential sum of $\boldsymbol{x}$ is $\boldsymbol{y} = [4 \quad 3 \quad 8 \quad 9 \quad 4 \quad 0]$. This is the dual or complement of the MATLAB function `diff`. Just as with `diff`, we wish to create a function that works along any dimension of its input, no matter how many dimensions the input has. Before generalizing to the n-D case, let's consider the vector and matrix cases. The vector case is straightforward, for example,

```
>> x = [3 1 2 6 3 1 -1]
x =
     3     1     2     6     3     1    -1
>> x(1:end-1)
ans =
     3     1     2     6     3     1
>> x(2:end)
ans =
     1     2     6     3     1    -1
>> y = x(1:end-1)+x(2:end)
y =
     4     3     8     9     4     0
```

Simple array addressing is all that is required, and the above approach works if `x` is either a row or a column vector. When the input is a matrix, the default action is to perform a differential sum down the columns, which is along the row dimension, as in the example

```
>> x = magic(4) % 2-D data
x =
    16     2     3    13
     5    11    10     8
     9     7     6    12
     4    14    15     1
>> y = x(1:end-1,:)+x(2:end,:)
y =
    21    13    13    21
    14    18    16    20
    13    21    21    13
```

It is also desirable to be able to specify an operation across the columns, which is along the column dimension, for example,

```
>> y = x(:,1:end-1)+x(:,2:end)
y =
    18     5    16
    16    21    18
    16    13    18
    18    29    16
```

Here the row and column indices are reversed from the preceding row operation. This operation along the column dimension can be performed by the preceding row operation if `x` is transposed first and then transposed again after the operation. Consider the following example.

```
>> tmp = x'; % transpose data
>> y = tmp(1:end-1,:)+tmp(2:end,:);
>> y = y'    % transpose result
y =
    18     5    16
    16    21    18
    16    13    18
    18    29    16
```

This can also be accomplished with the n-D functions `permute` and `ipermute`, which are generalizations of the transpose operator, as in the example

```
>> tmp = permute(x,[2 1])
tmp =
    16     5     9     4
     2    11     7    14
     3    10     6    15
    13     8    12     1
```

```
>> y = tmp(1:end-1,:)+tmp(2:end,:);
>> y = ipermute(y,[2 1])
y =
    18     5    16
    16    21    18
    16    13    18
    18    29    16
```

Before extending this to the *n*-D case, consider the 3-D case since it relatively easy to visualize, for example,

```
>> x = cat(3,hankel([3 1 6 -1]),pascal(4))
x(:,:,1) =
     3     1     6    -1
     1     6    -1     0
     6    -1     0     0
    -1     0     0     0
x(:,:,2) =
     1     1     1     1
     1     2     3     4
     1     3     6    10
     1     4    10    20
>> y = x(1:end-1,:,:)+x(2:end,:,:) % diff sum along row dimension
y(:,:,1) =
     4     7     5    -1
     7     5    -1     0
     5    -1     0     0
y(:,:,2) =
     2     3     4     5
     2     5     9    14
     2     7    16    30
```

Note that the same process occurs here but that added colons are required to reach both pages of `x`. If the `1:end-1` and `2:end` indices are moved to other dimensions, the differential sum moves to that dimension, for example,

```
>> y = x(:,:,1:end-1)+x(:,:,2:end)
y =
     4     2     7     0
     2     8     2     4
     7     2     6    10
     0     4    10    20
```

This is the differential sum between the two pages of `x`.

The above example points to one way to generalize this algorithm to *n* dimensions. The indices into `x` on the right-hand side are comma-separated lists. Therefore, if we create cell arrays containing the desired indices, the differential sum can be computed using comma-separated list syntax, for example,

```
>> y = x(1:end-1,:,:)+x(2:end,:,:) % duplicate this case
y(:,:,1) =
     4     7     5    -1
     7     5    -1     0
     5    -1     0     0
y(:,:,2) =
     2     3     4     5
     2     5     9    14
     2     7    16    30

>> c1 = {(1:3) ':' ':'}   % first set of indices
c1 =
    [1x3 double]    ':'    ':'
>> c2 = {(2:4) ':' ':'}   % second set of indices
c2 =
    [1x3 double]    ':'    ':'

>> y = x(c1{:})+x(c2{:})  % use comma separated list syntax
y(:,:,1) =
     4     7     5    -1
     7     5    -1     0
     5    -1     0     0
y(:,:,2) =
     2     3     4     5
     2     5     9    14
     2     7    16    30
```

The above example demonstrates the power of comma-separated list syntax. In the above the keyword `end` could not be used because it has meaning only when used directly as an index to a variable. As a result, `c1` and `c2` contain the actual numerical indices.

The following script file generalizes the above implementation for computing differential sums.

```
% diffsum1.m
% compute differential sum along a given dimension

x = cat(3,hankel([3 1 6 -1]),pascal(4)) % data to test
dim=1  % dimension to work along

xsiz=size(x)
xdim=ndims(x)

tmp=repmat({':'},1,xdim) % cells of ':'
c1=tmp;
```

```
c1{dim}=1:xsiz(dim)-1     % poke in 1:end-1
c2=tmp;
c2(dim)={2:xsiz(dim)}     % poke in 2:end

y=x(c1{:})+x(c2{:})       % comma separated list syntax
```

With no semicolons at the end of the statements, diffsum1 above produces the following output.

```
x(:,:,1) =
     3     1          -1
     1     6    -1     0
     6    -1     0     0
    -1     0     0     0
x(:,:,2) =
     1     1     1     1
     1     2     3     4
     1     3     6    10
     1     4    10    20
dim =
     1
xsiz =
     4     4     2
xdim =
     3
tmp =
    ':'    ':'    ':'
c1 =
    [1x3 double]    ':'    ':'
c2 =
    [1x3 double]    ':'    ':'
y(:,:,1) =
     4     7     5    -1
     7     5    -1     0
     5    -1     0     0
y(:,:,2) =
     2     3     4     5
     2     5     9    14
     2     7    16    30
```

Here x is the input data and dim is the dimension chosen for computing the differential sum. Using information about the size and dimensions of x, repmat can produce a cell array for addressing all elements in all dimensions of x. Then indices are inserted into the proper cells to create c1 and c2 as shown earlier. Finally, comma-separated list syntax is used to generate the final result.

The above procedure can be encapsulated in a function M-file as shown below.

```
function y=mmdiffsum1(x,dim)
%MMDIFFSUM Differential Sum of Elements.
% MMDIFFSUM(X) for vector X is [X(1)+X(2) X(2)+X(3) ... X(n-1)+X(n)]
% For matrix X, MMDIFFSUM is the differential sum down each column,
% X(1:n-1,:)+X(2:n,:). For N-D arrays, MMDIFFSUM(X) is the differential
% sum along the first nonsingleton dimension of X.
%
% MMDIFFSUM(X,DIM) returns the differential sum along the dimension DIM.
%
% Example: If X = [0 1 2
%                  3 4 5]
%
%          then MMDIFFSUM(X) and MMDIFFSUM(X,1) is [3 5 7]
%          and MMDIFFSUM(X,2) is [1 3
%                                 7 9]
%
% If SIZE(X,DIM)==1, the result is empty.
%
% See also DIFF, CUMSUM.

if nargin==1   % dim not given
  dim=min(find(size(x)>1)); % find first nonsingleton dimension >1
end
if isempty(x)  % empty x
   y=x;        % no work, just return empty
   return
end
xdim=ndims(x);
if prod(size(dim))~=1 | ... % check for weird dim
   round(dim)~=dim | ...
   dim<1 | ...
   dim>xdim
   error('Can''t Decipher DIM Variable.')
end
xsiz=size(x);
tmp=repmat({':'},1,xdim); % cells of ':'
c1=tmp;
c1{dim}=1:xsiz(dim)-1;    % poke in 1:end-1
c2=tmp;
c2(dim)={2:xsiz(dim)};    % poke in 2:end

y=x(c1{:})+x(c2{:});      % comma-separated list syntax
```

The above function M-file is not the only way to compute differential sums for an arbitrary *n*-D array. Earlier the functions `permute` and `ipermute` were used to transpose `x` so that the desired dimension for computing the sum was the row dimension. Applying this procedure to the 3-D example above gives the following script M-file.

```
% diffsum2.m
% compute differential sum along a given dimension

x = cat(3,hankel([3 1 6 -1]),pascal(4)) % data to test
dim=3  % dimension to work along

xsiz=size(x);
n=xsiz(dim);                 % size along desired dim
xdim=ndims(x);               % # of dimensions

perm=[dim:xdim 1:dim-1]      % put dim first
x=permute(x,perm)            % permute so dim is row dimension
x=reshape(x,n,prod(xsiz)/n)  % reshape into a 2D array

y=x(1:n-1,:)+x(2:n,:)       % Differential sum along row dimension

xsiz(dim)=n-1                % new size of dim dimension
y=reshape(y,xsiz(perm))      % put result back in original form
y=ipermute(y,perm)           % inverse permute dimensions
```

Here the variable `perm` forms a permutation vector for transposing `x` so that the differential sum is computed along the row dimension. After permuting, `x` is reshaped into a 2-D array. For 3-D `x` this means block-stacking the pages of `x` as additional columns. Then the differential sum is computed, and the array result is reshaped and inverse-permuted to its original shape using the fact that its size along the chosen dimension has decreased by 1. With no semicolons at the end of the statements, `diffsum2` above produces the following output.

```
x(:,:,1) =
     3     1     6    -1
     1     6    -1     0
     6    -1     0     0
    -1     0     0     0
x(:,:,2) =
     1     1     1     1
     1     2     3     4
     1     3     6    10
     1     4    10    20
```

```
dim =
     3
perm =
     3     1     2
x(:,:,1) =
     3     1     6    -1
     1     1     1     1
x(:,:,2) =
     1     6    -1     0
     1     2     3     4
x(:,:,3) =
     6    -1     0     0
     1     3     6    10
x(:,:,4) =
    -1     0     0     0
     1     4    10    20
x =
  Columns 1 through 12
     3     1     6    -1     1     6    -1     0     6    -1     0     0
     1     1     1     1     1     2     3     4     1     3     6    10
  Columns 13 through 16
    -1     0     0     0
     1     4    10    20
y =
  Columns 1 through 12
     4     2     7     0     2     8     2     4     7     2     6    10
  Columns 13 through 16
     0     4    10    20
xsiz =
     4     4     1
y(:,:,1) =
     4     2     7     0
y(:,:,2) =
     2     8     2     4
y(:,:,3) =
     7     2     6    10
y(:,:,4) =
     0     4    10    20
y =
     4     2     7     0
     2     8     2     4
     7     2     6    10
     0     4    10    20
```

The above procedure can be encapsulated in a function M-file as shown below.

```
function y=mmdiffsum2(x,dim)
%MMDIFFSUM Differential Sum of Elements.
% MMDIFFSUM(X) for vector X is [X(1)+X(2) X(2)+X(3) ... X(n-1)+X(n)]
% For matrix X, MMDIFFSUM is the differential sum down each column,
% X(1:n-1,:)+X(2:n,:). For N-D arrays, MMDIFFSUM(X) is the differential
% sum along the first non-singleton dimension of X.
%
% MMDIFFSUM(X,DIM) returns the differential sum along the dimension DIM.
%
% Example: If X = [0 1 2
%                  3 4 5]
%
%          then MMDIFFSUM(X) and MMDIFFSUM(X,1) is [3 5 7]
%          and MMDIFFSUM(X,2) is [1 3
%                                 7 9]
%
% If SIZE(X,DIM)==1, the result is empty.
%
% See also DIFF, CUMSUM.

if nargin==1
  dim=min(find(size(x)>1));       % find first nonsingleton dimension >1
end
if isempty(x)  % empty x
   y=x;        % no work, just return empty
   return
end
xdim=ndims(x);
if prod(size(dim))~=1 | ... % check for weird dim
   round(dim)~=dim | ...
   dim<1 | ...
   dim>xdim
   error('Can''t Decipher DIM Variable.')
end
xsiz=size(x);
n=xsiz(dim);

perm=[dim:xdim 1:dim-1];       % put dim first
x=permute(x,perm);             % permute so dim is row dimension
x=reshape(x,n,prod(xsiz)/n);   % reshape into a 2D array

y=x(1:n-1,:)+x(2:n,:);         % Differential sum along row dimension
```

```
xsiz(dim)=n-1;                  % new size of dim dimension
y=reshape(y,xsiz(perm));        % put result back in original form
y=ipermute(y,perm);             % inverse permute dimensions
```

If you've been following along with the prior sections of this chapter, you are probably wondering which of the two function M-files is the fastest. The function `mmdiffsum1` clearly uses less memory since the output `y` is computed directly from the input `x`, whereas `mmdiffsum2` reassigns `x` and `y` several times and calls the M-file functions `reshape` and `ipermute`. As a result, `mmdiffsum1` should be faster. Once comma-separated list syntax is understood, it also becomes easier to read. On the author's computer neither implementation outperformed the other consistently.

38.10 ARRAY EXPANSION

MATLAB performs scalar expansion. That is, given an array $\boldsymbol{A}$ and a scalar x, $\boldsymbol{A} + x$ is automatically interpreted as adding x to each element of $\boldsymbol{A}$, for example,

```
>> A = magic(5)
A =
    17    24     1     8    15
    23     5     7    14    16
     4     6    13    20    22
    10    12    19    21     3
    11    18    25     2     9
>> x = 2
x =
     2
>> A+x
ans =
    19    26     3    10    17
    25     7     9    16    18
     6     8    15    22    24
    12    14    21    23     5
    13    20    27     4    11
```

In a sense MATLAB expanded the scalar `x` to become a 5-by-5 array containing `x` in every element location and then performed element-by-element addition. Scalar expansion also applies in assignment statements, for example,

```
>> A(2:4,3:4) = 0
A =
    17    24     1     8    15
    23     5     0     0    16
     4     6     0     0    22
    10    12     0     0     3
    11    18    25     2     9
```

This sets rows 2, 3, and 4 in the third and fourth columns to zero. Here MATLAB expanded the scalar zero to a 3-by-2 array of zeros and assigned them to a submatrix within `A`.

This section considers the extension of scalar expansion to higher dimensions. In the simplest case it means replicating a vector so that operations with matrices are defined. In general, it means replicating any lower-dimensional array so that operations with higher-dimension arrays are defined.

Expanding a vector to a matrix has been demonstrated in a number of places in this text. For example,

```
>> x = 1:5
x =
     1     2     3     4     5
>> A+x(ones(5,1),:) % same as A+repmat(x,5,1)
ans =
    18    26     4    12    20
    24     7     3     4    21
     5     8     3     4    27
    11    14     3     4     8
    12    20    28     6    14
```

Here the row vector `x` is replicated to 5 rows and then added to `A`. As a result, *i* is added to the *i*th column of `A`. This process is easily extended to higher dimensions as well, with the inherent increase in indexing complexity. Consider the example

```
>> A = cat(3,magic(4),eye(4)) % 3-D data
A(:,:,1) =
    16     2     3    13
     5    11    10     8
     9     7     6    12
     4    14    15     1
A(:,:,2) =
     1     0     0     0
     0     1     0     0
     0     0     1     0
     0     0     0     1
>> x = (-1:2)' % column vector
x =
    -1
     0
     1
     2
```

```
>> A+repmat(x,[1 4 2]) % replicate and add
ans(:,:,1) =
    15     1     2    12
     5    11    10     8
    10     8     7    13
     6    16    17     3
ans(:,:,2) =
     0    -1    -1    -1
     0     1     0     0
     1     1     2     1
     2     2     2     3
```

Here the column vector x was replicated to 4 columns and 2 pages and then added to A. While this example replicated a vector, any lower-dimension array can work, for example,

```
>> y = cat(3,ones(1,4),2*ones(1,4)) % 1 row, 4 columns, 2 pages
y(:,:,1) =
     1     1     1     1
y(:,:,2) =
     2     2     2     2
>> A+repmat(y,[4 1 1]) % replicate and add
ans(:,:,1) =
    17     3     4    14
     6    12    11     9
    10     8     7    13
     5    15    16     2
ans(:,:,2) =
     3     2     2     2
     2     3     2     2
     2     2     3     2
     2     2     2     3
```

In this trivial example, 1 is added to the first page, and 2 is added to the second page of A.

Given this background we wish to construct a function that automates the above process. Technically speaking, we wish to expand all singleton dimensions of an array to match those of another array. Nonsingleton arrays sizes must match between the two arrays. In the preceding example, y has a singleton row dimension and nonsingleton column and page dimensions that match those of A.

To implement this function it is necessary to recognize that every array has an unlimited number of trailing singleton dimensions, that is, higher dimensions of size equal to 1. Consider the example

```
>> x = 1:5
x =
     1     2     3     4     5
```

```
>> size(x)
ans =
     1     5
```

The function size returns a vector of length 2 for x above. However, x also has one page. That is, size(x) could have returned [1 5 1]. In fact size(x) could have returned an array of any length greater than or equal to 2, with all elements beyond the second equal to 1. Clearly, there is no practical reason to do so, and MATLAB stops at the last nonsingleton dimension.

In the 3-D example above, y has dimensions of 1-by-4-by-2 and A has dimensions of 4-by-4-by-2. In addition, the repmat function specified [4 1 1] for the replication of y to match A. The correspondence between the dimensions of y and A and the repmat replication vector is as follows.

```
>> ysiz = size(y)
ysiz =
     1     4     2
>> Asiz = size(A)
Asiz =
     4     4     2
>> rep = ones(1,length(Asiz)) % singleton replication vector
rep =
     1     1     1
>> rep(ysiz==1)=Asiz(ysiz==1) % poke in required nonsingletons
rep =
     4     1     1
>> all(ysiz(ysiz~=1)==Asiz(ysiz~=1)) % must be True
ans =
     1
```

As shown, all singleton dimensions of y, that is, those for which ysiz==1, must be replicated to match the corresponding dimension of A. In addition, all nonsingleton dimensions of y, that is, those for which ysiz~=1, must match corresponding dimensions of A.

Using the above information as a guide, the function mmx shown below implements generalized expansion.

```
function y=mmx(a,b)
%MMX Expand Singleton Dimensions.
% MMX(A,B) expands A by replication to match the size of B so that
% arithmetic and logical operations between A and B are defined.
%
% All nonsingleton dimensions of A must match those of B.
```

```
% All singleton dimensions of A are replicated to match those of B.

asiz=[size(a) ones(1,ndims(b)-ndims(a))]; % add singletons to A to match B
bsiz=size(b);

if length(asiz)>length(bsiz) % can't make a larger array smaller!
    error('A Cannot Have More Dimensions than B.')
end

ns=(asiz>1);               % nonsingleton dims of A
sd=(~ns);                  % singleton dims of A
if all(asiz==bsiz)         % no work to do, A is already as big as B
    y=a;

elseif all(ns==0)          % A is a scalar (protect next test from empties)
    y=repmat(a,bsiz);      % expand scalar A to the size of B

elseif any(asiz(ns)~=bsiz(ns))
    error('All NonSingleton Dimensions of A Must Match Those of B.')

else                       % finally, do it
    rep=ones(size(bsiz)); % start with single replication of all dimensions
    rep(sd)=bsiz(sd);      % poke in replications of A required to match B
    y=repmat(a,rep);       % let repmat do the nitty-gritty work
end
```

To demonstrate the above function, reconsider several examples in this section.

```
>> A = cat(3,magic(4),eye(4)) % 3-D data
A(:,:,1) =
    16     2     3    13
     5    11    10     8
     9     7     6    12
     4    14    15     1
A(:,:,2) =
     1     0     0     0
     0     1     0     0
     0     0     1     0
     0     0     0     1
```

```
>> x = (-1:2)' % column vector
x =
    -1
     0
     1
     2
>> A+mmx(x,A) % expand x to match A and add
ans(:,:,1) =
    15     1     2    12
     5    11    10     8
    10     8     7    13
     6    16    17     3
ans(:,:,2) =
     0    -1    -1    -1
     0     1     0     0
     1     1     2     1
     2     2     2     3

>> y = cat(3,ones(1,4),2*ones(1,4))
y(:,:,1) =
     1     1     1     1
y(:,:,2) =
     2     2     2     2
>> A+mmx(y,A) % expand y to match A and add
ans(:,:,1) =
    17     3     4    14
     6    12    11     9
    10     8     7    13
     5    15    16     2
ans(:,:,2) =
     3     2     2     2
     2     3     2     2
     2     2     3     2
     2     2     2     3
```

This utility function hides the details of array expansion from the user and generally makes code easier to read. Some have suggested that MATLAB implement this feature as a native part of the MATLAB language, just as scalar expansion was added previously. Until that time, if it ever occurs, the function `mmx` will perform this valuable task.

38.11 STRUCTURE MANIPULATION

Structures are a convenient data structure in MATLAB. They allow one to group associated data into a single variable and use descriptive field names to identify different data contained within the structure. Once created, structures are a convenient way to pass data to a function, to store data in the `'UserData'` property of a graphics object, as application data associated with a graphics object, or for holding all Handle Graphics properties of an object.

Given the utility and convenience of structures, this section discusses several techniques for their manipulation, including structure concatenation, renaming fields, reordering fields, and removing fields. There are no built-in functions for performing these tasks, and of these only removing fields is implemented as an M-file function.

Structure manipulation functions operate just like other functions in that structure inputs are manipulated to create a new structure that is returned by the function. So when fields are removed from a structure, a new structure is simply created that does not contain the fields chosen for removal. Likewise, when structures are concatenated, a new structure is created whose fields contain the union of the fields of the two input structures.

First, consider the process of gathering variables and storing them as fields within a single structure, with field names matching variable names. Performing this task in the *Command* window is straightforward; one just assigns fields to like-named variables, for example,

```
>> a = eye(2) % test data
a =
     1     0
     0     1
>> b = 'String'
b =
String
>> c = cell(2)
c =
     []     []
     []     []
>> y.a = a; % store variables in a structure
>> y.b = b;
>> y.c = c
y =
    a: [2x2 double]
    b: 'String'
    c: {2x2 cell}
```

The inverse of this process is also useful. For example, if a structure such as y above is stored in the 'UserData' property of a graphics object and then recalled during a callback, it may be convenient to recreate the original variables in the workspace. Consider the example

```
>> a = y.a
a =
     1     0
     0     1
>> b = y.b
b =
String
>> c = y.c
c =
     []     []
     []     []
```

This process of packing and unpacking variables is encapsulated in the M-file function mmv2struct as shown below.

```
function varargout=mmv2struct(varargin)
%MMV2STRUCT Pack/Unpack Variables to/from a Scalar Structure.
% MMV2STRUCT(X,Y,Z,...) returns a structure having fields X,Y,Z,...
% containing the corresponding data stored in X,Y,Z,...
% Inputs that are not variables are stored in fields named ansN
% where N is an integer identifying the Nth unnamed input.
%
% MMV2STRUCT(S)assigns the contents of the fields of the scalar structure
% S to variables in the calling workspace having names equal to the
% corresponding field names.
%
% [A,B,C,...]=MMV2STRUCT(S) assigns the contents of the fields of the
% scalar structure S to the variables A,B,C,... rather than overwriting
% variables in the caller. If there are fewer output variables than
% there are fields in S, the remaining fields are not extracted. Variables
% are assigned in the order given by fieldnames(S).

if nargin==0
    error('Input Arguments Required.')
elseif nargin==1                  % Unpack Structure to Variables
    arg=varargin{1};
    if ~isstruct(arg)|length(arg)~=1
        error('Single Input Must be a Scalar Structure.')
    end
    names=fieldnames(arg);
    if nargout==0 % assign in caller
        for i=1:length(names)
            assignin('caller',names{i},getfield(arg,names{i}))
        end
    else % dump into variables in caller
        for i=1:nargout
            varargout{i}=getfield(arg,names{i});
        end
    end
else                              % Pack Variables into a Structure
   num=1;
   for i=1:nargin
      name=inputname(i);
      if isempty(name) % not a variable
         name=sprintf('ans%d',num);
```

```
        num=num+1;
      end
      eval(['y.' name '=varargin{i};'])
    end
    varargout{1}=y;
end
```

This function makes straightforward use of For Loops, `varargin`, `varargout`, `inputname`, `assignin`, `getfield`, and `eval`. The presence of For Loops is unavoidable here. However, their presence does not make this function slow since the number of iterations is typically limited. That is, one seldom packs or unpacks hundreds or thousands of variables. Usage of this function is demonstrated as follows.

```
>> avar = rand(10,1);
>> bvar = 'A Character String';
>> cvar = {eye(2) 'Hello' []};
>> y = mmv2struct(avar,bvar,pi,cvar) % pack variables
y =
    avar: [10x1 double]
    bvar: 'A Character String'
    ans1: 3.1416
    cvar: {[2x2 double]  'Hello'  []}

>> clear avar bvar cvar  % clear variables
>> who
Your variables are:

y

>> mmv2struct(y) % unpack variables
>> who
Your variables are:

ans1      avar      bvar      cvar      y

>> [a,b,c,d] = mmv2struct(y) % unpack into new variables
a =
      0.61543
      0.79194
      0.92181
      0.73821
      0.17627
      0.40571
```

```
        0.93547
         0.9169
        0.41027
        0.89365
b =
A Character String
c =
         3.1416
d =
    [2x2 double]    'Hello'     []
```

The MATLAB function `rmfield` removes fields from a structure by copying all fields except those to be removed into a new structure. To implement this process `rmfield` uses the functions `getfield` and `setfield` iteratively over all fields and over all structure array elements. That is, `rmfield` contains two nested For Loops, one a loop over all retained fields and the other a loop over all array elements. This is necessary because the functions `getfield` and `setfield` get or set the contents of a single field of a single array element at a time. Therefore, if the structure being manipulated contains many array elements or many field names, `rmfield` can be relatively slow. Fortunately, this process can be vectorized by using the functions `struct2cell` and `cell2struct`. These built-in functions convert a structure into a cell array, and vice versa. Once a structure has been converted to an equivalent cell array, it is simply a matter of deleting the desired fields and reconstructing the remaining structure. A side benefit is that the fields to be deleted can be returned as a separate structure. In doing so, a structure can be split in two as well.

Without the complications of *n* dimensions, `struct2cell` and `cell2struct` are simple to use, for example,

```
>> y  % recall prior structure
y =
    avar: [10x1 double]
    bvar: 'A Character String'
    ans1: 3.1416
    cvar: {[2x2 double]  'Hello'  []}
>> c = struct2cell(y) % convert to a cell array
c =
           [10x1 double]
    'A Character String'
    [             3.1416]
           { 1x3 cell  }
>> f = fieldnames(y)  % capture field names
f =
    'avar'
    'bvar'
    'ans1'
    'cvar'
>> z = cell2struct(c,f) % convert back to a structure
z =
    avar: [10x1 double]
```

```
     bvar: 'A Character String'
     ans1: 3.1416
     cvar: {[2x2 double]  'Hello'  []}
>> isequal(y,z)
ans =
     1
```

If the field `ans1` is to be removed from the structure `y`, the preceding example becomes

```
>> c = struct2cell(y) % convert to a cell array
c =
            [10x1 double]
     'A Character String'
     [            3.1416]
            { 1x3 cell  }
>> f = fieldnames(y)  % capture field names
f =
     'avar'
     'bvar'
     'ans1'
     'cvar'
>> f(3) = [] % throw out 'ans1'
f =
     'avar'
     'bvar'
     'cvar'
>> c(3) = [] % throw out data in 'ans1'
c =
            [10x1 double]
     'A Character String'
            { 1x3 cell  }
>> z = cell2struct(c,f) % convert back to a structure
z =
     avar: [10x1 double]
     bvar: 'A Character String'
     cvar: {[2x2 double]  'Hello'  []}
```

The function `mmrmfield` shown below encapsulates the use of `struct2cell` and `cell2struct` for the removal of fields from a structure. In addition, it handles the general *n*-D structure array case and gives the option of returning the removed portion as well.

```
function [ss,r]=mmrmfield(s,fdel)
%MMRMFIELD Remove Structure Fields.
% MMRMFIELD(S,FName) removes the field identified by the string
```

```
% FName from the structure S.
% If FName is a string array or cell array of strings, all
% specified fields are removed.
%
% [S,R]=MMRMFIELD(S,FName) returns S with fields removed in the
% structure S and the removed fields in the structure R.

if nargin~=2
   error('Two Input Arguments Required.')
end
if ~isstruct(s)
   error('First Argument Must be a Structure.')
end
if ~ischar(fdel)&~iscellstr(fdel)
   error('Second Argument Must be a String Array or Cell Array.')
end
if ischar(fdel)          % convert to cells if char array
   fdel=cellstr(fdel);
end
fnames=fieldnames(s);    % get field names of structure
nf=prod(size(fdel));     % number of fields
idx=zeros(nf,1);         % preallocate
for i=1:nf
   tmp=find(strcmp(fnames,fdel(i)));
   if isempty(tmp)
      error(sprintf('A Field Named  %s  Does Not Exist in S.',fdel{i}))
   end
   idx(i)=tmp(1);        % get index of fieldname to delete
end
c=struct2cell(s);              % convert structure to cells
args=repmat({':'},1,ndims(s)); % generate :,:,... for indexing

if nargout==2  % return removed fields
   r=cell2struct(c(idx,args{:}),fnames(idx),1);
end
c(idx,args{:})=[];          % throw out field data to delete
fnames(idx)=[];             % throw out field names to delete
ss=cell2struct(c,fnames,1); % build new structure from remains
```

The function `mmrmfield` again points to the tradeoff between speed and memory requirements. The function `mmrmfield` is much faster than `rmfield` in MATLAB, but it requires duplication of all the data in the structure when it is converted to a cell array. As long as there is sufficient memory available, `mmrmfield` is superior to `rmfield`.

Concatenating structures is the opposite of removing fields. If two structures have the same size or dimensions and different field names, they can be combined into a single structure having field names that are the union of those of the two original structures. Once again the functions struct2cell and cell2struct allow this process to be vectorized. After both structures are converted to cell arrays, the cell arrays and field names are concatenated, and then the resulting cell array is converted back to a structure. This process is encapsulated in the function mmstructcat shown below.

```
function s=mmstructcat(s1,s2)
%MMSTRUCTCAT Concatenate Structures.
% MMSTRUCTCAT(S1,S2) forms a new structure by combining the fields
% of structures S2 and S1. S1 and S2 must have the same dimensions.
% Duplicate field names in S1 and S2 are not allowed.

if ~isstruct(s1) | ~isstruct(s2)
    error('Arguments Must be Structures.')
end
s1siz=size(s1);
s2siz=size(s2);
if any(s1siz~=s2siz) % potential dimension mismatch
   if min(s1siz)==1 & min(s2siz)==1 % both vectors, so
      s1=reshape(s1,1,prod(s1siz)); % change to rows and
      s2=reshape(s2,1,prod(s2siz)); % allow concatenation
   else
      error('Arguments Must Have the Same Size.')
   end
end
c1=struct2cell(s1);  % vectorized approach
f1=fieldnames(s1);
c2=struct2cell(s2);
f2=fieldnames(s2);
try % this fails if field names are not unique
   s=cell2struct([c1;c2],[f1;f2],1);
catch
   error('S1 and S2 Must Contain Unique Field Names.')
end
```

The above function illustrates practical use of a Try-Catch block. Rather than explicitly checking to see if f1 and f2 contain unique field names, the above lets cell2struct flag the error and the catch block returns a tailored error message.

The utility of the functions cell2struct and struct2cell make it easy to rename and reorder the fields of a structure. While renaming and reordering fields do not change the data stored, they are helpful for organizing the visual display of structure content. In addition, since two structures containing the same fields and data are equal only if the fields are created in the same order, reordering fields is a valuable utility. The processes of renaming and reordering fields are encapsulated in the functions `mmrnfield` and `mmrofield` as shown below.

```
function ss=mmrnfield(s,oldname,newname)
%MMRNFIELD Rename Structure Fields.
% MMRNFIELD(S,OldName,NewName) returns the structure S with the
% field name denoted by the string OldName changed to NewName.
% Oldname must exist in S.
%
% If OldName and NewName are cell arrays of equal length, each
% field name in OldName is changed to the corresponding element
% in NewName.

if nargin~=3
   error('Three Input Arguments Required.')
end
if ~isstruct(s)
   error('First Argument Must be a Structure.')
end
if ~(ischar(oldname)|iscellstr(oldname))&...
   ~(ischar(newname)|iscellstr(newname))
   error('Last Two Arguments Must be Strings or Cell Strings.')
end
if ischar(oldname)   % convert to cell
   oldname=cellstr(oldname);
end
if ischar(newname)   % convert to cell
   newname=cellstr(newname);
end
nold=length(oldname);
if nold~=length(newname)
   error('OldName and NewName Must Have the Same Length.')
end
fnames=fieldnames(s);      % get field names of structure
idx=zeros(nold,1);         % indices of oldname in fnames
for i=1:nold
   tmp=find(strcmp(fnames,oldname{i}));
   if isempty(tmp)
      error(sprintf('Structure Does Not Contain Field Name %s',oldname{i}))
   end
```

```
   idx(i)=tmp;
end
fnames(idx)=newname;        % change names of desired fields
c=struct2cell(s);           % convert structure to cell
ss=cell2struct(c,fnames,1);% rebuild structure with changed names
```

```
function ss=mmrofield(s,ord)
%MMROFIELD Reorder Structure Fields.
% MMROFIELD(S,Order) returns the structure S with the
% field names reordered according to the variable Order.
%
% MMROFIELD(S,'alpha') reorders the structure so the field
% names appear in alphabetic order.
% MMROFIELD(S,'reverse') reorders the structure so the
% field names appear in reverse alphabetic order.
%
% MMROFIELD(S,Idx) where Idx is a permutation of the indices
% of the field names of S, reorders the structure to match
% the order given by Idx.

if nargin~=2
   error('Two Input Arguments Required.')
end
if ~isstruct(s)
   error('First Argument Must be a Structure.')
end
dims=size(s);
c=struct2cell(s(:)); % reshape to 1-D for now

if ischar(ord) % 'alpha' or 'reverse'
   [fnames,idx]=sort(fieldnames(s));
   if strncmpi(ord,'r',1)
      idx=idx(end:-1:1);
      ss=cell2struct(c(idx,:),fnames(end:-1:1),1);
   elseif strncmpi(ord,'a',1)
      ss=cell2struct(c(idx,:),fnames,1);
   else
      error('Unknown String Second Argument.')
   end
```

```
elseif isnumeric(ord)   % Idx input
   fnames=fieldnames(s);
   nfn=length(fnames);
   if nfn~=length(ord)
      error('Incorrect Number of Field Names Provided.')
   end
   if ~isequal(1:nfn,sort(ord(:)'))
      error('Idx Does Not Contain Field Name Indices.')
   end
   ss=cell2struct(c(ord,:),fnames(ord),1);
else
   error('Unknown Second Argument.')
end
ss=reshape(ss,dims); % reshape back to original dims
```

38.12 SUMMARY

This chapter has demonstrated numerous examples of MATLAB programming. Vectorization was defined as writing code so that scalar operations on array elements are replaced by native array operations. Vectorization is not simply the avoidance of For Loops. This chapter brings together many of the ideas and functions discussed elsewhere in the text. From that point of view, it finally put all the pieces together in a way that promotes synergy. Of the countless examples that could have been considered, this chapter concentrated on those that involve indexing, *n*-D arrays, vectorization, and structure manipulation. This chapter could easily have gone for another 100 pages or more. It is hoped that these examples promote more efficient MATLAB programming.

A

Common Handle Graphics Properties

This appendix lists properties and associated values that are common to all Handle Graphics objects. Default values are shown in braces, for example, {default}. Some properties have no meaning to some objects.

`'BusyAction'  'cancel' | {'queue'}`

Determines how to deal with interruptions by other object callbacks, that is, what action to take if a callback to the object is busy. If the 'Interruptible' property of an object is 'off', 'cancel' discards callbacks that interrupt the object, and 'queue' places the interrupting callback in the event queue to be executed after the current callback terminates. If the 'Interruptible' property of the object is 'on', 'BusyAction' has no effect.

`'ButtonDownFcn'` *string*

Specifies the character string to be evaluated when you press a mouse button with the pointer over the object but not over any child or parent object.

`'Children'` *vector*

Contains a vector of handles to all child objects. The order in which the handles appear is the stacking order with the topmost object appearing first. Rearranging the vector rearranges the stacking order.

`'Clipping'` `{'on'} | 'off'`

Specifies whether children of *axes* objects only are clipped to the *axes* plot box.

`'CreateFcn'` *string*

Specifies the callback string evaluated just after the object is created. Must be set as a default property, for example, `set(0,'DefaultAxesCreateFcn','grid off')`.

`'DeleteFcn'` *string*

Specifies the callback string evaluated just prior to deleting the object.

`'HandleVisibility'` `{'on'} | 'callback' | 'off'`

Specifies whether the object's handle can be seen from the *Command* window or callbacks. When set to `'callback'`, the object's handle is visible from callbacks but not from the *Command* window. When a handle is invisible, it does not show up on a list of children nor can it be found by the `findobj` function. However, if the handle is known, it can still be accessed by `get` and `set`. The *root* property `'ShowHiddenHandles'` overrides this property.

`'HitTest'` `{'on'} | 'off'`

Determines whether the object is selectable by a mouse click and can become the current object.

`'Interruptible'` `{'on'} | 'off'`

Specifies whether the object's callbacks are interruptible by other callbacks.

`'Parent'` *handle*

Parent object handle as shown on page 497.

`'Selected'  'on' | 'off'`

Specifies whether the object is selected. Selection handles are shown if the `'SelectionHighlight'` property is `'on'`.

`'SelectionHighlight'  {'on'} | 'off'`

Specifies whether selection handles are shown when `'Selected'` is `'on'`.

`'Tag'` *`string`*

Character string specified by the user to tag the object so that it is easily found using `findobj`.

`'Type'` *`string`*

Read-only property that returns a lowercase string identifying the object type.

`'UIContextMenu'` *`handle`*

Handle of a *uicontextmenu* object to be associated with the object.

`'UserData'` *`variable`*

Storage location for the contents of a variable of any class. Accessible by using `get` and `set`.

`'Visible'  {'on'} | 'off'`

Determines whether the object is visible on the screen. The functions `get` and `set` work on invisible objects.

B

Axes *Object Properties*

This appendix lists the unique properties and associated values or their description for the *axes* object. Default values are shown in braces, for example, {default}. Unless stated otherwise, all properties can be set. Properties common to all objects are shown in Appendix A.

'ALim' [*amin amax*]

Specifies a two-element vector that determines how MATLAB maps the 'AlphaData' property values of *image, patch,* and *surface* objects to the *figure*'s 'Alphamap' property values.

'AlimMode' {'auto'} | 'manual'

Specifies whether the 'ALim' property is automatically adjusted by MATLAB. Setting the 'ALim' property sets this property to 'manual'.

`'AmbientLightColor'` *`ColorSpec`*

Specifies the color of the ambient light that shines uniformly on all objects in the *axes*. One or more visible *light* objects must be present. `Colorspec` is a three-element RGB vector or the string name of a standard color.

`'Box'` `'on'` | `'off'`

Specifies whether the *axes* are enclosed in a box for 2-D views or in a cube for 3-D views.

`'CameraPosition'` `[x, y, z]`

Specifies the position from which the camera views the *axes* scene in *axes* coordinates.

`'CameraPositionMode'` `{'auto'}` | `'manual'`

Specifies whether MATLAB automatically adjusts the camera position such that the camera lies a fixed distance from the camera target along the azimuth and elevation specified by the `'View'` property. Set to `'manual'` if `'CameraPosition'` is set.

`'CameraTarget'` `[x, y, z]`

Specifies where in *axes* coordinates the camera points to.

`'CameraTargetMode'` `{'auto'}` | `'manual'`

Specifies whether MATLAB automatically positions the camera target at the centroid of the *axes*. Set to `'manual'` if `'CameraTarget'` is set.

`'CameraUpVector'` `[x, y, z]`

Specifies the rotation of the camera around the viewing axis defined by the `'CameraTarget'` and the `'CameraPosition'` properties. `'CameraUpVector'` is a three-element vector; for example, `[0 1 0]` specifies the positive *y*-axis as the up direction. The default for 3-D views is `[0 0 1]`, which defines the positive *z*-axis as the up direction.

`'CameraUpVectorMode'` `{'auto'}` | `'manual'`

Specifies whether the `'CameraUpVector'` is the default or is user-specified. If `'CameraUpVector'` is set, this property is set to `'manual'`.

`'CameraViewAngle'` $0 \leq angle \leq 180$ degrees

Specifies the camera field of view. Larger angles make the object appear smaller.

`'CameraViewAngleMode'  {'auto'} | 'manual'`

Specifies whether `'CameraViewAngle'` is set automatically by MATLAB to the minimum angle that captures the entire *axes* scene. If `'CameraviewAngle'` is set, this property is set to `'manual'`.

`'CLim'  [`*`cmin cmax`*`]`

Specifies a two-element vector that determines color axis limits.

`'CLimMode'  {'auto'} | 'manual'`

Specifies whether `'CLim'` is automatically adjusted by MATLAB. Setting the `'CLim'` property sets this property to `'manual'`.

`'Color'  {'none'} |` *`ColorSpec`*

Specifies the color of the *axes* background. `'none'` specifies a transparent axis. *`ColorSpec`* is a three-element RGB vector or the string name of a standard color.

`'ColorOrder'` *`m-by-3 array`*

Specifies a sequence of `m` RGB values to use for line plots.

```
'CurrentPoint'  [xback,yback,zback;...
                  xfront,yfront,zfront]
```

Contains the pointer location of the last mouse button click in the *axes* in data coordinates. The 2-by-3 array contains the coordinates of two data points that lie on a line perpendicular to the plane of the screen passing through the pointer.

`'DataAspectRatio'  [`*`dx dy dz`*`]`

Specifies the relative scaling of *axes* data units. For example, [1 2 3] causes the length of one unit of data in the x-direction to be the same length as two units in the y-direction and three units in the z-direction.

`'DataAspectRatioMode'  {'auto'} | 'manual'`

Specifies whether MATLAB automatically adjusts the `'DataAspectRatio'`. If `'DataAspectRatio'` is set, this property is set to `'manual'`.

`'DrawMode'   {'normal'} | 'fast'`

Specifies the tradeoff between drawing speed and accuracy for the Painter's rendering method.

`'FontAngle'   {'normal'} | 'italic' | 'oblique'`

Specifies the character slant to be used for *axes* text.

`'FontName'   string`

Specifies the font family to be used for *axes* text. Using `'FixedWidth'` sets the font to that stored in the *root* object property `'FixedWidthFontName'`.

`'FontSize'   number`

Specifies the font size in units specified by the `'FontUnits'` property.

```
'FontUnits'   {'points'} | 'normalized' | 'inches' |...
              'centimeters' | 'pixels'
```

Specifies the units for font size. `'normalized'` is with respect to *axes* height.

`'FontWeight'   'light' | {'normal'} | 'demi' | 'bold'`

Specifies the font weight.

`'GridLineStyle'   '-' |'--'| {':'} | '-.' | 'none'`

Specifies the line style used to draw grid lines.

`'Layer'   {'bottom'} | 'top'`

Specifies the placement of tick marks and grid lines with respect to *axes* children.

`'LineStyleOrder'   LineSpec`

A character string with line styles and markers separated by vertical bars | which are used when creating multiple line plots. MATLAB cycles through these styles and markers *after* using all the colors in the `'ColorOrder'` property. The default is `'-'`.

`'LineWidth'   scalar`

Specifies the line width of *axes* lines in points (1 point = 1/72 inch). The default is 0.5 point.

`'NextPlot'  'add' | {'replace'} | 'replacechildren'`

Specifies where to draw the next plot using high-level plotting functions such as `plot`:

> `'add'`—add plot to existing *axes,* that is, `hold on`.
> `'replace'`—issue `cla reset` and then plot.
> `'replacechildren'`—issue `cla` and then plot.

`'PlotBoxAspectRatio' [`*`px py pz`*`]`

Specifies the relative *x*-, *y*-, and *z*-direction scaling of the *axes* plot box (the total rectangular area within the *figure* used by the *axes*).

`'PlotBoxAspectRatioMode'  {'auto'} | 'manual'`

Specifies whether MATLAB automatically adjusts axis scaling. Setting `'PlotBoxAspectRatio'` sets this property to `'manual'`.

`'Position'  [`*`left bottom width height`*`]`

Specifies the *axes* position in standard position rectangle format with respect to the lower left-hand corner of the *figure* window as shown on page 477. Units are defined by the `'Units'` property.

`'Projection'  {'orthographic'} | perspective`

Specifies the type of graphics projection used.

`'TickDir'  'in' | 'out'`

Specifies the direction of axis tick marks. `'in'` is the default for 2-D views. `'out'` is the default for 3-D views.

`'TickDirMode'  {'auto'} | 'manual'`

Specifies whether MATLAB automatically adjusts the tick mark direction as the view changes.

`'TickLength'  [`*`2DLength 3DLength`*`]`

A two-element vector that specifies the tick mark length for 2-D and 3-D views, respectively. The lengths are normalized lengths with respect to the longest visible *x*-, *y*-, or *z*-axis lines.

`'Title'` *`handle`*

Contains the handle to the *text* object that is used for the *axes* title.

```
'Units'  'pixels' | {'normalized'} | 'inches' |...
         'centimeters' | 'points' | 'characters'
```

Specifies the units of measurement for the *axes* object `'Position'` property.

`'View'  [Azimuth Elevation]`

Two-element vector that specifies the *axes* viewpoint. This property is superseded by *axes* camera properties but remains a convenient way to set simple viewpoints. *Azimuth Elevation* are defined in degrees as shown on page 398.

`'XAxisLocation'  'top' | {'bottom'}`

Specifies the location of *x*-axis tick marks and labels.

`'YAxisLocation'  'right' | {'left'}`

Specifies the location of *y*-axis tick marks and labels.

`'XColor', 'YColor', 'ZColor'  ColorSpec`

Specifies the color of axis lines, tick marks, tick mark labels, and axis grid lines on the associated axis. *Colorspec* is a three-element RGB vector or the string name of a standard color.

`'XDir', 'YDir', 'ZDir'  {'normal'} | 'reverse'`

Specifies the direction of increasing values with respect to a right-hand coordinate system on the associated axis.

`'XGrid', 'YGrid', 'ZGrid'  'on' | {'off'}`

Determines the presence of axis grid lines on the associated axis.

`'XLabel', 'YLabel', 'ZLabel'  handle`

Contains the handle of respective axis *text* object labels.

`'XLim', 'YLim', 'Zlim'  [min max]`

Specifies a two-element vector containing the minimum and maximum values of the associated axis.

`'XLimMode', 'YLimMode', 'ZLimMode'  {'auto'} | 'manual'`

Specifies whether the respective axis limits are chosen automatically by MATLAB. If `'Xlim'`, `'Ylim'`, and `'Zlim'` are set, the respective `'XLimMode'`, `'YLimMode'`, and `'ZLimMode'` properties are set to `'manual'`.

`'XScale', 'YScale', 'ZScale'  {'linear'} | 'log'`

Specifies the axis scaling for the associated coordinate axis.

`'XTick', 'YTick', 'Ztick'` *vector*

Specifies a vector of monotonically increasing data values that identify the tick mark locations on the associated coordinate axis. For no tick marks, set equal to an empty array `[]`.

`'XTickMode', 'YTickMode', 'TickMode'  {'auto'} | 'manual'`

Specifies whether the respective axis tick vectors are generated automatically by MATLAB. If `'XTick'`, `'YTick'`, and `'ZTick'` are set, the respective axis tick mode is set to `'manual'`.

`'XTickLabel', 'YTickLabel', ' ZTickLabel'` *string*

Specifies the character string labels to be placed at the tick mark locations on the associated axis. `string` can be specified as a cell array of strings, a string matrix, a character string with tick labels separated by vertical slash characters, or a numerical vector that is internally converted to a string matrix.

`'XTickLabelMode', 'YTickLabelMode', 'ZTickLabelMode'  {'auto'} | 'manual'`

Specifies whether the respective axis tick labels are generated automatically by MATLAB. If `'XTickLabel'`, `'YTickLabel'`, and `'ZTickLabel'` are set, the respective axis tick label mode is set to `'manual'`.

C

Figure *Object Properties*

This appendix lists the unique properties and associated values or their description for the *figure* object. Default values are shown in braces, for example, {default}. Unless stated otherwise, all properties can be set. Properties common to all objects are shown in Appendix A.

'Alphamap' *m-by-1 numerical array*

Specifies the transparency map of *image, patch,* and *surface* objects.

'BackingStore' {'on'} | 'off'

Specifies whether a copy of the *figure* is stored in an off-screen pixel buffer. An 'off' setting speeds animations, but bringing the *figure* to the front requires more time since the *figure* must be rerendered rather than being copied from the off-screen buffer.

`'CloseRequestFcn'` *`string`*

Specifies a callback routine that is evaluated whenever you initiate the process of closing the *figure* in a way other than by using the `delete` command. The default callback is `closereq`, which uses `delete(get(0,'CurrentFigure'))`.

`'Color'` *`Colorspec`*

Specifies the color of the *figure* background. *`Colorspec`* is a three-element RGB vector or the string name of a standard color.

`'Colormap'` *`m-by-3 numerical array`*

Specifies an `m`-by-3 array of RGB values that define `m` colormap colors for the rendering of *surface, image,* and *patch* objects.

`'CurrentAxes'` *`handle`*

Specifies the handle of the current *axes.* The current *axes* need not be the topmost *axes.* If there are no *axes* objects in the *figure,* `get(gcf,'CurrentAxes')` returns an empty array. The function `gca` returns this property.

`'CurrentCharacter'` *`character`*

Read-only property containing the last key pressed with the mouse pointer over the *figure* window.

`'CurrentObject'` *`handle`*

Contains the handle of the object that is under the current point as defined by the `'CurrentPoint'` property. The handle returned is the topmost object in the stacking order. The function `gco` returns this handle.

`'CurrentPoint'` `[`*`x y`*`]`

A two-element vector that specifies the *x*- and *y*-coordinates of the last mouse button click in the *figure* in units defined by the `'Units'` property. Measurements are with respect to the lower left-hand corner of the *figure.*

`'Dithermap'` *`m-by-3 array`*

Specifies the colormap used for true-color data on pseudocolor displays.

`'DithermapMode' 'auto' | {'manual'}`

Specifies how dithered displays are generated:

> `'manual'`—use the `'Dithermap'` array.
> `'auto'`—generate a dither map based on the colors currently displayed.

`'DoubleBuffer' on | {'off'}`

Produces flicker-free rendering for simple animations by rendering into an off-screen buffer and then dumping the updated image to the *figure*. Useful for simple animations that contain *line* and *text* objects whose `'EraseMode'` property is set to `'normal'`. The *figure* `'Renderer'` property must be set to `'painters'`.

`'FileName'` *`string`*

File name used by GUIDE to store a GUI created in the *figure*.

`'FixedColors'` *`m-by-3 array`*

Read-only RGB array of fixed colors appearing in a *figure* that are not obtained from the *figure* colormap.

`'IntegerHandle' {'on'} | 'off'`

Specifies whether the *figure* handle is an integer or a floating-point number.

`'InvertHardcopy' {'on'} | 'off'`

Specifies whether printed *figures* appear as colored objects on a white background (`'on'`) or print as shown in the *figure* (`'off'`).

`'KeyPressFcn'` *`string`*

Specifies a callback that is evaluated when a key is pressed while the mouse pointer is within the *figure* window.

`'Menubar' 'none' | {'figure'}`

Specifies the presence of a menu bar in the *figure*.

`'MinColormap'` *`scalar`*

Specifies the minimum number of system color table entries used by MATLAB to store the *figure* colormap. The default is 64.

`'Name'` *`string`*

Specifies the title displayed in the *figure* window title bar. For example, `set(gcf,'Name','Hi Jack')` generates a *figure* window title bar `'Figure No. 1: Hi Jack'`. Set the *figure* `'NumberTitle'` property to `'off'` to hide the `'Figure No. 1'` prefix in the title bar.

`'NextPlot'  {'add'} | 'replace' | 'replacechildren'`

Specifies the *figure* to be used for the next graphics function:

> `'add'`—use the current *figure*.
> `'replace'`—issue `clf reset` and then use the current *figure*.
> `'replacechildren'`—issue `clf` and then use the current *figure*.

See the `newplot` function for additional information.

`'NumberTitle'  {'on'} | 'off'`

Specifies whether the *figure* window title bar contains the string `'Figure No. N'`, where `N` is the *figure* handle.

`'PaperOrientation' {'portrait'} | 'landscape'`

Specifies horizontal (landscape) or vertical (portrait) paper orientation for printed *figures.*

`'PaperPosition'` `[`*`left bottom width height`*`]`

Specifies the location of the *figure* on the printed page in standard position rectangle format when `'PaperPositionMode'` is set to `'manual'`. Units are defined by the `'PaperUnits'` property.

`'PaperPositionMode'  'auto' | {'manual'}`

Specifies whether figures are printed using the `'PaperPosition'` property information or are `'auto'` printed WYSIWYG, centered on the page.

`'PaperSize'` `[`*`width height`*`]`

Specifies the size of the current paper type in units defined by the `'PaperUnits'` property. If set to nonstandard values, `'PaperType'` is set to `'<custom>'`.

```
'PaperType'  {'usletter'} | 'uslegal' | 'tabloid' | 'A0' |...
             'A1' | 'A2' | 'A3' | 'A4' | 'A5' |...
             'B0' | 'B1' | 'B3' | 'B4' | 'B5' |...
             'arch-A' | 'arch-B' | 'arch-C' | 'arch-D' |...
             'arch-E' | 'A' | 'B' | 'C' | 'D' | 'E' |...
             'tabloid' | '<custom>'
```

Specifies the current paper type.

```
'PaperUnits'  'normalized' | {'inches'} |...
              'centimeters' | 'points'
```

Specifies the units used for paper properties.

```
'Pointer'  'crosshair' | {'arrow'} | 'watch' |...
           'topl' | 'topr' | 'botl' | 'botr' |...
           'circle' | 'cross' | 'fleur' |...
           'left' | 'right' | 'top' | 'bottom' |...
           'fullcrosshair' | 'ibeam' | 'custom'
```

Specifies the mouse pointer used in the *figure*.

'PointerShapeCData'   *16-by-16 array*

Defines the mouse pointer used when the 'Pointer' property is set to 'custom'. Each element specifies a pixel, with element (1,1) being the upper left corner, using the values

1—color pixel black.

2—color pixel white.

NaN—make pixel transparent.

'PointerShapeHotSpot'   [*i j*]

Two-element vector that specifies the row and column indices in 'PointerShapeCData' indicating the pointer's selection spot. The default location is (1,1).

'Position'   [*left bottom width height*]

Specifies the *figure* position in standard position rectangle format with respect to the lower left-hand corner of the screen as shown on page 477. Units are defined by the 'Units' property.

'Renderer'   'painter' | 'zbuffer' | 'OpenGL'

Specifies the rendering method used for both the screen and printing. The default value depends on what is rendered and on the computer platform.

`'RendererMode'  {'auto'} | 'manual'`

Specifies whether MATLAB selects the best rendering mode automatically and individually for the screen and printer.

`'Resize'  {'on'} | 'off'`

Specifies whether the *figure* is resizable by the user.

`'ResizeFcn'  string`

Specifies a string that is evaluated immediately after the *figure* window has been resized by the user.

`'SelectionType'  'normal' | 'extended' | 'alt' | 'open'`

Read-only property that specifies the type of mouse selection made:

> `'normal'`—single-click leftmost mouse button.
> `'extended'`—**Shift**-click leftmost mouse button.
> `'alt'`—**Ctrl**-click left mouse button.
> `'open'`—double-click any mouse button.

`'ListBox'` style *uicontrol* objects set `'SelectionType'` to `'normal'` to indicate a single mouse click and set it to `'open'` to indicate a double mouse click.

`'ShareColors'  {'on'} | 'off'`

Specifies whether the *figure* shares slots in the system color table. An `'on'` setting is more efficient, while an `'off'` setting may speed *figure* rerendering.

```
'Units'  {'pixels'} | 'normalized' | 'inches' |...
         'centimeters' | 'points'
```

Specifies the units of measurement for *figure* object properties.

`'WindowButtonDownFcn'  string`

Specifies a callback string that is evaluated when you press a mouse button down while the mouse pointer is in the *figure* window.

`'WindowButtonMotionFcn'  string`

Specifies a callback string that is evaluated when you move the mouse within the *figure* window.

`'WindowButtonUpFcn'` *string*

Specifies a callback string that is evaluated when you release a mouse button after a `'WindowButtonDownFcn'` event has occurred in the *figure* window.

`'WindowStyle'  {'normal'} | 'modal'`

Specifies the *figure* window style. A `'modal'` window is primarily for dialog boxes and GUIs where the user must respond before being able to bring another window forward.

`'XDisplay'` *display (X-Windows only)*

Specifies the display name of the X server.

`'XVisual'` *string (X-Windows only)*

Specifies the characteristics of the display.

`'XVisualMode' [ {'auto'} | 'manual' ]` *(X-Windows only)*

Specifies whether MATLAB determines the display characteristics.

D

Image *Object Properties*

This appendix lists the unique properties and associated values or their description for the *image* object. Default values are shown in braces, for example, `{default}`. Unless stated otherwise, all properties can be set. Properties common to all objects are shown in Appendix A.

`'AlphaData'` *m-by-n array*

Specifies the transparency of each element in the *image* data.

`'AlphaDataMapping'  {'none'} | 'direct' | 'scaled'`

Specifies the transparency mapping method.

`'Cdata'` *m-by-n or m-by-n-by-3 array*

The *image* data as specified by any one of the three image interpretation methods.

`'CdataMapping'  {'direct'} | 'scaled'`

Specifies whether colors are direct or scaled indexed. This property has no effect when true-color or RGB color is used.

`'EraseMode'  {'normal'} | 'none' | 'xor' | 'background'`

Specifies the procedure MATLAB uses to draw the object:

- `'normal'`—redraw the display, performing all tasks required to ensure that all *axes* objects are rendered correctly.
- `'none'`—do not redraw anything.
- `'xor'`—draw and erase the object by eXclusive-ORing (XOR) it with the color underneath it. Other covered objects are not destroyed.
- `'background'`—erase the object by redrawing it in the *axes* background color. Other covered objects are destroyed.

`'XData'  {[1 size(Cdata,2)]}`

A two-element vector specifying the *x*-coordinate centers of the *image* elements.

`'YData'  {[1 size(Cdata,1)]}`

A two-element vector specifying the *y*-coordinate centers of the *image* elements.

E

Light *Object Properties*

This appendix lists the unique properties and associated values or their description for the *light* object. Default values are shown in braces, for example, `{default}`. Unless stated otherwise, all properties can be set. Properties common to all objects are shown in Appendix A.

`'Color'` *`ColorSpec`*

Specifies the color of the *light* object. *`ColorSpec`* is a three-element RGB vector or the string name of a standard color.

`'Style'  {'infinite'} | 'local'`

Specifies the light source style as being parallel (infinitely far away) or divergent (local).

`'Position'  [`*`x y z`*`]`

Vector containing the *x*-, *y*-, and *z*- coordinates of the *light* object in *axes* data units.

F

Line *Object Properties*

This appendix lists the unique properties and associated values or their description for the *line* object. Default values are shown in braces, for example, `{default}`. Unless stated otherwise, all properties can be set. Properties common to all objects are shown in Appendix A.

`'Color'` *`ColorSpec`*

Specifies the color of the *line* object. *`ColorSpec`* is a three-element RGB vector or the string name of a standard color.

`'EraseMode'  {'normal'} | 'background' | 'xor' | 'none'`

Specifies the procedure MATLAB uses to draw the object:

`'normal'`—redraw the display, performing all tasks required to ensure that all *axes* objects are rendered correctly.

`'none'`—do not redraw anything.

'xor'—draw and erase the object by eXclusive-ORing (XOR) it with the color underneath it. Other covered objects are not destroyed.

'background'—erase the object by redrawing it in the *axes* background color. Other covered objects are destroyed.

```
'LineStyle'  {'-'} | '--' | ':' | '-.' | 'none'
```

Specifies the line style to be used for the *line*.

```
'LineWidth'  scalar
```

Specifies the line width of the *line* in points (1 point = 1/72 inch). The default is 0.5 point.

```
'Marker'   '+' | 'o' | '*' | '.' | 'x' | 'square' |...
           'diamond' | 'v' | '^' | '>' | '<' |...
           'pentagram' | 'hexagram' | {'none'}
```

Specifies the marker character symbol placed at the *line* data points.

```
'MarkerEdgeColor' ColorSpec | 'none' | {'auto'}
```

Specifies the color of the marker or the edge color for filled markers:

ColorSpec—defines the color to use.

'none'—specifies no color, which makes nonfilled markers invisible.

'auto'—sets 'MarkerEdgeColor' to the same color as the 'Color' property.

```
'MarkerFaceColor' ColorSpec | {'none'} | 'auto'
```

Specifies the fill color for markers that are closed shapes:

ColorSpec—defines the color to use.

'none'—makes the marker interior transparent.

'auto'—sets the fill color to the *axes* color.

```
'MarkerSize'  scalar
```

Specifies the size of the marker in points. The default size is 6 points, except for '.' which is drawn at one-third the specified size.

```
'XData'  array
```

Array containing *x*-coordinates defining the *line*.

`'YData'` *array*

Array containing *y*-coordinates defining the *line*.

`'ZData'` *array*

Array containing *z*-coordinates defining the *line*.

G

Patch *Object Properties*

This appendix lists the unique properties and associated values or their description for the *patch* object. Default values are shown in braces, for example, `{default}`. Unless stated otherwise, all properties can be set. Properties common to all objects are shown in Appendix A.

`'AlphaDataMapping'  'none' | 'direct' | {'scaled'}`

Specifies the transparency mapping method.

`'AmbientStrength'` $0 \leq scalar \leq 1$

Specifies the ambient light strength of one or more visible *light* objects illuminating the *axes*.

`'BackFaceLighting'  'unlit' | 'lit' | {'reverselit'}`

Specifies how faces are lit when their vertex normals point away from the camera.

`'CData'` *m-by-n or m-by-n-by-3 array*

Specifies the color of the *patch* object. You can specify a color for each vertex, a color for each face, or a single color for the entire *patch.* The data can be numerical values that are scaled to map linearly into the current colormap, integer values that are used directly as indices into the current colormap, or arrays of RGB values.

`'CDataMapping'  {'scaled'} | 'direct'`

Specifies whether colors are direct or scaled indexed. This property has no effect when truecolor or RGB color is used.

`'EdgeAlpha'` {*scalar*} | `'flat'` | `'interp'`

Specifies the transparency of the edges of *patch* faces. Scalar values must be between 0 (invisible) and 1 (opaque), inclusive, with 1 being the default value.

`'EdgeColor'` {*ColorSpec*} | `'none'` | `'flat'` | `'interp'`

Specifies how color is applied to *patch* edges:

- *ColorSpec*—a three-element RGB vector or the string name of a standard color.
- `'none'`—the edges are not drawn.
- `'flat'`—the color of each vertex controls the color of the edge that follows it.
- `'interp'`—interpolated coloring is used.

`'EdgeLighting'  {'none'} | 'flat' | 'gouraud' | 'phong'`

Specifies the algorithm used to calculate the effect of *light* objects on *patch* edges.

`'EraseMode'  {'normal'} | 'none' | 'xor' | 'background'`

Specifies the procedure MATLAB uses to draw the object:

- `'normal'`—redraw the display, performing all tasks required to ensure that all *axes* objects are rendered correctly.
- `'none'`—do not redraw anything.
- `'xor'`—draw and erase the object by eXclusive-ORing (XOR) it with the color underneath it. Other covered objects are not destroyed.
- `'background'`—erase the object by redrawing it in the *axes* background color. Other covered objects are destroyed.

`'FaceAlpha'  {scalar} | 'flat' | 'interp'`

Specifies the transparency of *patch* faces. Scalar values must be between 0 (invisible) and 1 (opaque), inclusive, with 1 being the default value.

`'FaceColor'  {ColorSpec} | 'none' | 'flat' | 'interp'`

Specifies how color is applied to the *patch* face:

> `ColorSpec`—a three-element RGB vector or the string name of a standard color.
> `'none'`—the faces are not drawn.
> `'flat'`—the color of the first vertex controls the color of the face.
> `'interp'`—interpolated coloring is used.

`'FaceLighting'  {'none'} | 'flat' | 'gouraud' | 'phong'`

Specifies the algorithm used to calculate the effect of *light* objects on *patch* faces.

`'Faces'  m-by-n array`

Specifies the connection array that identifies which vertices in the `'Vertices'` property are connected. The faces array defines `m` faces with up to `n` vertices each. Each row designates the connections for a single face, and the number of elements in the row that are not `NaN` defines the number of vertices for the face. The `'Faces'` and `'Vertices'` properties provide an alternative and often more efficient way to specify a *patch.*

`'FaceVertexAlphaData'  m-by-1 vector`

Face and vertex transparency data when patches are defined by `'Faces'` and `'Vertices'` properties.

`'FaceVertexCData'  scalar, vector, or matrix`

Specifies the color of *patches* defined by the `'Faces'` and `'Vertices'` properties when `'FaceColor'`, `'EdgeColor'`, `'MarkerFaceColor'`, or `'MarkerEdgeColor'` is set properly. The data can be numerical values that are scaled to map linearly into the current colormap, integer values that are used directly as indices into the current colormap, or arrays of RGB values.

`'LineStyle'  {'-'} | '--' | ':' | '-.' | 'none'`

Specifies the line style used for *patch* edges.

`'LineWidth'` *scalar*

Specifies the line width of *patch* edges in points (1 point = 1/72 inch). The default is 0.5 point.

```
'Marker'   '+' | 'o' | '*' | '.' | 'x' | 'square' |...
           'diamond' | 'v' | '^' | '>' | '<' |...
           'pentagram' | 'hexagram' | {'none'}
```

Specifies the marker character symbol placed at *patch* vertices.

`'MarkerEdgeColor'` *ColorSpec* `| 'none' | {'auto'} | 'flat'`

Specifies the color of the marker or edge color for filled markers:

> *ColorSpec*—defines the color to be used.
> `'none'`—specifies no color, which makes nonfilled markers invisible.
> `'auto'`—sets `'MarkerEdgeColor'` to the same color as the `'EdgeColor'` property.

`'MarkerFaceColor'` *ColorSpec* `| {'none'} | 'auto' | 'flat'`

Specifies the fill color for markers that are closed shapes:

> *ColorSpec*—defines the color to be used.
> `'none'`—makes the marker interior transparent.
> `'auto'`—sets the fill color to the *axes* color.

`'MarkerSize'` *scalar*

Specifies the size of the marker in points. The default size is 6 points, except for `'.'` which is drawn at one-third the specified size.

`'NormalMode'` `{'auto'} | 'manual'`

Specifies whether MATLAB or user-provided vertex normal vectors are used.

`'SpecularColorReflectance'` $0 \le scalar \le 1$

Specifies the color of light reflected from the object. If set to 0, the reflected light is the color of the object and the light source. If set to 1, the reflected light is that of the light source only.

`'SpecularExponent'` *scalar* ≥ 1

Specifies the size of the specular spot where light reflects. Most materials have exponents in the range of 5 to 20.

`'SpecularStrength'` $0 \leq$ *scalar* ≤ 1

Specifies the intensity of the specular component of the light falling on the *patch.*

`'VertexNormals'` *matrix*

If the `'NormalMode'` property is set to `'auto'`, `'VertexNormals'` contains the MATLAB-generated normals used to perform lighting calculations. If `'NormalMode'` is set to `'manual'`, the user must supply this matrix.

`'Vertices'` *matrix*

Contains the *x*-, *y*-, *z*-coordinates for each vertex. See the `'Faces'` property for more information.

`'XData'` *vector* or *matrix*

Contains the *x*-coordinates of the points at the vertices of the *patch.* If `'XData'` is a matrix, each column represents the *x*-coordinates of a single face of the *patch.*

`'YData'` *vector* or *matrix*

Contains the *y*-coordinates of the points at the vertices of the *patch.* If `'YData'` is a matrix, each column represents the *y*-coordinates of a single face of the *patch.*

`'ZData'` *vector* or *matrix*

Contains the *z*-coordinates of the points at the vertices of the *patch.* If `'ZData'` is a matrix, each column represents the *z*-coordinates of a single face of the *patch.*

H

Rectangle *Object Properties*

This appendix lists the unique properties and associated values or their description for the *rectangle* object. Default values are shown in braces, for examples, `{default}`. Unless stated otherwise, all properties can be set. Properties common to all objects are shown in Appendix A.

`'Curvature'` `[w h]`

Specifies the horizontal or vertical *rectangle* curvature. Elements are between 0 and 1, inclusive. The first element is the fraction of the *rectangle* width that is curved. The second element is the fraction of the *rectangle* height that is curved. For example, if `[w h] = [0 0]`, a rectangle is drawn. If `[w h] = [1 1]`, an ellipse is drawn. If a scalar is given, it applies to both the width and height.

`'EdgeColor'` {*ColorSpec*} | `'none'`

Specifies how color is applied to *rectangle* edges:

ColorSpec—a three-element RGB vector or the string name of a standard color.

`'none'`—the edges are not drawn.

`'EraseMode'` {`'normal'`} | `'none'` | `'xor'` | `'background'`

Specifies the procedure MATLAB uses to draw the object:

`'normal'`—redraw the display, performing all tasks required to ensure that all *axes* objects are rendered correctly.

`'none'`—do not redraw anything.

`'xor'`—draw and erase the object by eXclusive-ORing (XOR) it with the color underneath it. Other covered objects are not destroyed.

`'background'`—erase the object by redrawing it in the *axes* background color. Other covered objects are destroyed.

`'FaceColor'` {*ColorSpec*} | `'none'`

Specifies how color is applied to *rectangle* faces:

ColorSpec—a three-element RGB vector or the string name of a standard color.

`'none'`—the edges are not drawn.

`'LineStyle'` {`'-'`| `'--'` | `':'` | `'-.'` | `'none'`

Specifies the line style used for the *rectangle.*

`'LineWidth'` *scalar*

Specifies the line width of the *rectangle* in points (1 point = 1/72 inch). The default is 0.5 point.

`'Position'` [*x y width height*]

Specifies the location and size of the *rectangle* in data units of its parent *axes.* *x* and *y* are the left and bottom coordinates of the rectangle.

I

Root *Object Properties*

This appendix lists the unique properties and associated values or their description for the *root* object. Default values are shown in braces, for example, {default}. Unless stated otherwise, all properties can be set. Properties common to all objects are shown in Appendix A.

'CallbackObject' *handle*

Read-only property that returns the handle of the object whose callback routine is currently executing. This property is returned by the function gcbo.

'CurrentFigure' *handle*

Returns the handle of the current *figure* if it exists; otherwise returns an empty matrix. set(0,'CurrentFigure',Hf) makes the *figure* having handle Hf the current figure. This property is returned by the function gcf.

`'Diary'  'on' | {'off'}`

Used by `diary` command to enable creation of a diary file.

`'DiaryFile'  string`

File name of a diary file.

`'Echo'  'on' | {'off'}`

Used by the `echo` command to enable echoing of script files into the *Command* window.

`'ErrorMessage'  string`

Returns the text of the last error message generated. Can be set to any string.

`'FixedWidthFontName'  string`

String specifying a platform-dependent, fixed-width font that promotes platform-independent GUIs. Setting any `'FontName'` property to `'FixedWidth'` uses this font. Normally this property is set by MATLAB, but it can be set by the user as well.

```
'Format'   'short' | 'shortE' | 'shortG' | 'long' |...
           'longE' | 'longG' | 'bank' | 'hex' | '+' | 'rat'
```

Used by the `format` command to set the *Command* window output format.

`'FormatSpacing'  'compact' | 'loose'`

Used by the `format` command to set the *Command* window output spacing.

`'Language'  string`

String specifying the language used.

`'PointerLocation'  [x y]`

Returns the instantaneous x- and y-coordinates of the mouse pointer measured from the lower left-hand corner of the screen, in units specified by the `'Units'` property. Can be used to place the mouse pointer at a specific location.

`'PointerWindow'  handle`

Read-only property that returns the handle of the *Figure* window containing the mouse pointer at any instant. If the mouse is not over a MATLAB window, 0 is returned.

`'RecursionLimit'  integer`

Specifies an upper limit for recursive function calls.

`'ScreenDepth'` *`integer`*

Specifies the numerical bit depth of the computer screen.

`'ScreenSize'` `[`*`left bottom width height`*`]`

Read-only property that returns the screen size in standard position rectangle format. Units are defined by the `'Units'` property.

`'ShowHiddenHandles'` `'on' | {'off'}`

Globally enables or disables the visibility of hidden object handles, that is, objects whose `'HandleVisibility'` property has been set `'off'`.

```
'Units'  {'pixels'} | 'normalized' | 'inches' |...
         'centimeters' | 'points' | characters
```

Specifies the unit of measurement for other *root* object properties.

J

Surface *Object Properties*

This appendix lists the unique properties and associated values or their description for the *surface* object. Default values are shown in braces, for example, {default}. Unless stated otherwise, all properties can be set. Properties common to all objects are shown in Appendix A.

'AlphaData' *m-by-n array*

Specifies the transparency of each face or vertex of the *surface*.

'AlphaDataMapping' 'none' | 'direct' | {'scaled'}

Specifies the transparency mapping method.

'AmbientStrength' $0 \leq scalar \leq 1$

Specifies the ambient light strength of one or more visible *light* objects illuminating the *axes*.

`'BackFaceLighting'` `'unlit' | 'lit' | {'reverselit'}`

Specifies how faces are lit when their vertex normals point away from the camera.

`'CData'` *m-by-n* or *m-by-n-by-3 array*

Specifies the color of each vertex in the *surface* object. The data can be numerical values that are scaled to map linearly into the current colormap, integer values that are used directly as indices into the current colormap, or arrays of RGB values.

`'CDataMapping'` `{'scaled'} | 'direct'`

Specifies whether colors are direct or scaled indexed. This property has no effect when truecolor or RGB color is used.

`'DiffuseStrength'` $0 \le$ *scalar* ≤ 1

Specifies the diffuse light strength of one or more visible *light* objects illuminating the *axes.*

`'EdgeAlpha'` `{`*scalar*`} | 'flat' | 'interp'`

Specifies the transparency of the edges of the *surface.* Scalar values must be between 0 (invisible) and 1 (opaque), inclusive, with 1 being the default value.

`'EdgeColor'` `{`*ColorSpec*`} | 'none' | 'flat' | 'interp'`

Specifies how color is applied to *surface* edges:

ColorSpec—a three-element RGB vector or the string name of a standard color.
`'none'`—the edges are not drawn.
`'flat'`—the color of each vertex controls the color of the edge that follows it.
`'interp'`—interpolated coloring is used.

`'EdgeLighting'` `{'none'} | 'flat' | 'gouraud' | 'phong'`

Specifies the algorithm used to calculate the effect of *light* objects on *surface* edges.

`'EraseMode'` `{'normal'} | 'none' | 'xor' | 'background'`

Specifies the procedure MATLAB uses to draw the object:

`'normal'`—redraw the display, performing all tasks required to ensure that all *axes* objects are rendered correctly.
`'none'`—do not redraw anything.

`'xor'`—draw and erase the object by eXclusive-ORing (XOR) it with the color underneath it. Other covered objects are not destroyed.

`'background'`—erase the object by redrawing it in the *axes* background color. Other covered objects are destroyed.

```
'FaceAlpha'  {scalar} | 'flat' | 'interp' | 'texturemap'
```

Specifies the transparency of *surface* faces. Scalar values must be between 0 (invisible) and 1 (opaque), inclusive, with 1 being the default value.

```
'FaceColor'  {ColorSpec} | 'none' | 'flat' |...
             'interp' | 'texturemap'
```

Specifies how color is applied to *surface* faces:

ColorSpec— three-element RGB vector or the string name of a standard color.

`'none'`—the faces are not drawn.

`'flat'`—the color of the first vertex controls the color of the face.

`'interp'`—interpolated coloring is used.

`'texturemap'`—texture-maps the `'CData'` array to the surface.

```
'FaceLighting'  {'none'} | 'flat' | 'gouraud' | 'phong'
```

Specifies the algorithm used to calculate the effect of *light* objects on *surface* faces.

```
'LineStyle'  {'-'} | '--' | ':' | '-.' | 'none'
```

Specifies the line style used for *surface* edges.

```
'LineWidth'  scalar
```

Specifies the line width of *surface* edges in points (1 point = 1/72 inch). The default is 0.5 point.

```
'Marker'  '+' | 'o' | '*' | '.' | 'x' | 'square' |...
          'diamond' | 'v' | '^' | '>' | '<' |...
          'pentagram' | 'hexagram' | {'none'}
```

Specifies the marker character symbol placed at *surface* vertices.

`'MarkerEdgeColor'` *`ColorSpec`* `| 'none' | {'auto'}`

Specifies the color of the marker or the edge color for filled markers:

> *`ColorSpec`*—defines the color to be used.
> `'none'`—specifies no color, which makes nonfilled markers invisible.
> `'auto'`—sets `'MarkerEdgeColor'` to the same color as the `'EdgeColor'` property.

`'MarkerFaceColor'` *`ColorSpec`* `| {'none'} | 'auto'`

Specifies the fill color for markers that are closed shapes:

> *`ColorSpec`*—defines the color to be used.
> `'none'`—makes the marker interior transparent.
> `'auto'`—sets the fill color to the *axes* color.

`'MarkerSize'` *`scalar`*

Specifies the size of the marker in points. The default size is 6 points, except for `'.'` which is drawn at one-third the specified size.

`'MeshStyle'` `{'both'} | 'row' | 'column'`

Specifies whether to draw row, column, or both row and column edge lines.

`'NormalMode'` `{'auto'} | 'manual'`

Specifies whether MATLAB or user-provided vertex normal vectors are to be used.

`'SpecularColorReflectance'` $0 \leq scalar \leq 1$

Specifies the color of light reflected from the object. If set to 0, the reflected light is the color of the object and the light source. If set to 1, the reflected light is that of the light source only.

`'SpecularExponent'` $scalar \geq 1$

Specifies the size of the specular spot where light reflects. Most materials have exponents in the range of 5 to 20.

`'SpecularStrength'` $0 \leq scalar \leq 1$

Specifies the intensity of the specular component of light falling on the *surface*.

`'VertexNormals'` *matrix*

If the `'NormalMode'` property is set to `'auto'`, `'VertexNormals'` contains the MATLAB-generated normals used to perform lighting calculations. If `'NormalMode'` is set to `'manual'`, the user must supply this matrix.

`'XData'` *vector* or *matrix*

Specifies the x-coordinates of *surface* points. If `'XData'` is a vector, it is converted to a column and is replicated until it has the same number of columns as the data in the `'ZData'` property.

`'YData'` *vector* or *matrix*

Specifies the y-coordinates of *surface* points. If `'YData'` is a vector, it is converted to a row and replicated until it has the same number of rows as the data in the `'ZData'` property.

`'ZData'` *matrix*

Specifies the z-coordinates of *surface* points.

K

Text *Object Properties*

This appendix lists the unique properties and associated values or their description for the *text* object. Default values are shown in braces, for example, {default}. Unless stated otherwise, all properties can be set. Properties common to all objects are shown in Appendix A.

'Color' *ColorSpec*

Specifies the color of the *text* object. *ColorSpec* is a three-element RGB vector or the string name of a standard color.

'Editing' 'on' | {'off'}

Enables or disables in-place editing of the *text* object. Can be applied to a single *text* object at a time. When set to 'on', the object appears in an editable box with an I-beam cursor. Clicking in the *figure* window outside the object terminates editing and sets 'Editing' to 'off'. Alternatively, editing can be set 'off'.

`'EraseMode'   {'normal'} | 'none' | 'xor' | 'background'`

Specifies the procedure MATLAB uses to draw the object:

- `'normal'`—redraw the display, performings all tasks required to ensure that all *axes* objects are rendered correctly.
- `'none'`—do not redraw anything.
- `'xor'`—draw and erase the object by eXclusive-ORing (XOR) it with the color underneath it. Other covered objects are not destroyed.
- `'background'`—erase the object by redrawing it in the *axes* background color. Other covered objects are destroyed.

`'Extent' [`*`left bottom width height`*`]`

Read-only property that returns the size and position of the text string in standard position rectangle form using units specified by the `'Units'` property.

`'FontAngle'   {'normal'} | 'italic' | 'oblique'`

Specifies the character slant to be used.

`'FontName'`   *`string`*

Specifies the font family to be used. Using `'FixedWidth'` sets the font to that stored in the *root* object property `'FixedWidthFontName'`.

`'FontSize'`   *`number`*

Specifies the font size in units specified by the `'FontUnits'` property.

```
'FontUnits'   {'points'} | 'normalized' | 'inches' |...
              'centimeters' | 'pixels'
```

Specifies the units for font size. `'normalized'` is with respect to the *axes* height.

`'FontWeight'   'light' | {'normal'} | 'demi' | 'bold'`

Specifies the font weight.

`'HorizontalAlignment'   {'left'} | 'center' | 'right'`

Specifies the horizontal justification of the *text* with respect to its `'Position'` property.

`'Interpreter'   {'tex'} | 'none'`

Specifies whether the *text* string should be parsed for TeX instructions.

`'Position'  [x y z]`

Vector containing the *x*-, y-, and optional *z*- coordinates of the *text* object in units specified by the `'Units'` property. The default *z*-coordinate is zero.

`'Rotation'  scalar`

Specifies *text* angular orientation in degrees. Compass East is 0 degrees. Compass North is 90 degrees.

`'String'  string`

Specifies the text string to be displayed. `string` can be a single string, a string array, or a cell array of strings. String arrays and cell arrays of strings create multiple text lines.

```
'Units'  'pixels' | 'normalized' | 'inches' |...
         'centimeters' | 'points' | {'data'}
```

Specifies the units of measurement for *text* `'Extent'` and `'Position'` properties. All units except `'data'` are with respect to the lower left-hand corner of the *axes* plot box. `'data'` implies use of the data coordinates of the underlying *axes*.

```
'VerticalAlignment'  'top' | 'cap' | {'middle'} |...
                     'baseline' | 'bottom'
```

Specifies the vertical justification of the *text* with respect to its `'Position'` property.

L

Uicontextmenu *and* Uimenu *Object Properties*

UICONTEXTMENU PROPERTIES

The list below contains the unique properties and associated values or their description for the *uicontextmenu* object. Default values are shown in braces, for example, `{default}`. Unless stated otherwise, all properties can be set. Properties common to all objects are shown in Appendix A.

`'Callback'` *`string`*

Specifies a string to be evaluated when the right mouse button is clicked with the mouse pointer over an object for which the *uicontextmenu* object is defined. A *uicontextmenu* with children executes its callback routine before displaying submenus. A *uicontextmenu* without children executes this string when you release the mouse button.

`'Position'` *[left bottom]*

Specifies the position of a visible *uicontextmenu* in pixels from the lower left-hand corner of its parent *figure* object.

UIMENU PROPERTIES

The list below contains the unique properties and associated values or their description for the *uimenu* object. Default values are shown in braces, for example, `{default}`. Unless stated otherwise, all properties can be set. Properties common to all objects are shown in Appendix A.

`'Accelerator'` *character*

Specifies the keyboard equivalent for the menu item. The keyboard equivalent is **Control-***character.* Accelerators work only for menu items that directly execute a callback routine, not for items that bring up other menus.

`'Callback'` *string*

Specifies the string to be evaluated when you select the *uimenu* object. A *uimenu* object with children (submenus) executes its callback routine before displaying the submenus. A *uimenu* without children executes its callback routine when the mouse button is released.

`'Checked'  'on' | {'off'}`

Specifies whether a check mark appears next to the menu item. This property is not set automatically by selecting a menu item.

`'Enable'  {'on'} | 'off'`

Specifies whether the *uimenu* object is enabled. When `'off'`, the *uimenu* label is dimmed and it cannot be selected.

`'ForegroundColor'` *ColorSpec* (X-Windows only)

Specifies the color of the *uimenu* label string. *ColorSpec* is a three-element RGB vector or the string name of a standard color.

`'Label'` *string*

Specifies the character string to place on the menu item. An `&` character forces the next character to appear underlined on the menu and allows it to be selected by pressing the underlined character.

`'Position'` *`scalar`*

Specifies the relative menu position on the menu bar or within a menu. Top-level menus are placed from left to right on the menu bar according to the value of their `'Position'` property, with 1 representing the leftmost position. Individual items within a given menu are placed from top to bottom according to the value of their `'Position'` property, with 1 representing the topmost position.

`'Separator'` `'on' | {'off'}`

Specifies the presence of a menu separator above the menu item.

M

Uicontrol *Object Properties*

This appendix lists the unique properties and associated values or their description for the *uicontrol* object. Default values are shown in braces, for example, `{default}`. Unless stated otherwise, all properties can be set. Properties common to all objects are shown in Appendix A.

`'BackgroundColor'` *`ColorSpec`*

Specifies the background color used to fill the *uicontrol* object. *`ColorSpec`* is a three-element RGB vector or the string name of a standard color. The default color is system-dependent and can be retrieved by issuing `get(0,'DefaultUicontrolBackgroundColor')`.

`'Callback'` *`string`*

Specifies the character string to be evaluated when you activate the *uicontrol* object, for example, push a `'pushbutton'` or drag a `'slider'`. `'frame'` and static `'text'` *uicontrol* styles do not invoke callbacks.

`'CData'` *m-by-n-by-3 array*

Truecolor image to be displayed on `'pushbutton'` or `'togglebutton'` *uicontrol* styles.

`'Enable'  {'on'} | 'inactive' | 'off'`

Specifies whether the *uicontrol* object is enabled. When `'on'`, the callback string is evaluated when the *uicontrol* is selected. When `'off'`, the *uicontrol* label string is dimmed. When `'inactive'`, the *uicontrol* is not dimmed. When `'off'` or `'inactive'`, the callback string is not evaluated, but the `'ButtonDownFcn'` property is functional.

`'Extent'  [0 0` *width height*`]`

A read-only property that returns the size of the text string used to label the *uicontrol* in standard position rectangle form using units specified by the `'Units'` property. Useful to determine the *uicontrol* size required to hold the desired label string.

`'FontAngle'  {'normal'} | 'italic' | 'oblique'`

Specifies the character slant to be used.

`'FontName'` *string*

Specifies the font family to be used. Using `'FixedWidth'` sets the font to that stored in the *root* object property `'FixedWidthFontName'`.

`'FontSize'` *number*

Specifies the font size in units specified by the `'FontUnits'` property.

```
'FontUnits'  {'points'} | 'normalized' | 'inches' |...
             'centimeters' | 'pixels'
```

Specifies the units for font size. `'normalized'` is relative to the height of the *uicontrol.*

`'FontWeight'  'light' | {'normal'} | 'demi' | 'bold'`

Specifies the font weight.

`'ForegroundColor'` *ColorSpec*

Specifies the color of the text labeling the *uicontrol.* `ColorSpec` is a three-element RGB vector or the string name of a standard color. The default color is black.

`'HorizontalAlignment'` `{'left'} | 'center' | 'right'`

Specifies the horizontal justification of the *uicontrol* label string with respect to its `'Position'` property. On Windows PCs, this property affects only `'edit'` and `'text'` style *uicontrols.*

`'ListboxTop'` *`scalar`*

For `'listbox'` style *uicontrols,* specifies the index of the topmost string displayed in the list box.

`'Max'` *`scalar`*

For `'radiobutton'` and `'checkbox'` style *uicontrols,* `'Max'` is the contents of the `'Value'` property when the *uicontrol* is `'on'`. For `'slider'` style *uicontrols,* `'Max'` is the largest value you can select, and it must be greater than the value specified by the `'Min'` property. The default value is 1. For `'edit'` style *uicontrols,* if `'Max' - 'Min'` > 1, the `'edit'` box accepts multiline input strings. For `'listbox'` style *uicontrols,* if `'Max'-'Min' > 1`, multiline selection is allowed. If `'Max' - 'Min'` ≤ 1, only a single line selection is allowed.

`'Min'` *`scalar`*

For `'radiobutton'` and `'checkbox'` style *uicontrols,* `'Min'` is the contents of the `'Value'` property when the *uicontrol* is `'off'`. For `'slider'` style *uicontrols,* `'Min'` is the smallest value you can select, and it must be less than the value specified by the `'Max'` property. The default value is 0. For `'edit'` style *uicontrols,* if `'Max'-'Min'` > 1, the `'edit'` box accepts multiline input strings. If `'Max'-'Min' ≤ 1`, only a single line is accepted. For `'listbox'` style *uicontrols,* if `'Max'-'Min' > 1`, multiline selection is allowed. If `'Max' - 'Min' > 1`, only a single line selection is allowed.

`'Position'` `[`*`left bottom width height`*`]`

Specifies the *uicontrol* position in standard position rectangle format with respect to the lower left-hand corner of the *figure* window. Units are defined by the `'Units'` property. The height of `'popupmenu'` style *uicontrols* on Windows PCs is set by the font, and *`height`* is ignored.

`'SliderStep'` `[`*`arrow_step trough_step`*`]`

Specifies the normalized amount, 0 to 1, of the `'Max'` − `'Min'` distance used as a slider step size. *`arrow_step`* is the slider movement made for clicks on the arrows. *`trough_step`* is the slider movement made for clicks in the trough.

```
'String'   string
```

Specifies the *uicontrol* label string displayed on push buttons, toggle buttons, radio buttons, check boxes, static text, editable text, list boxes, and popup menus. Multiple items in a popup menu or list box can be specified as a cell array of strings, a string matrix, or within a single string separated by vertical slash characters. Line breaks in multiple-line editable text or static text controls occur between each row of a string matrix or each cell of a cell array of strings. Vertical slash characters are not interpreted as line breaks. The text modified in an `'edit'` style *uicontrol* is returned in this property.

```
'Style'   'pushbutton' | 'togglebutton' |'radiobutton' |...
          'checkbox' | 'edit' | 'text' | 'slider' |...
          'frame' | 'listbox' | 'popupmenu'
```

Specifies the *uicontrol* object style to be created.

```
TooltipString   string
```

Specifies the tool tip to be displayed when the user moves the mouse pointer over the *uicontrol* and leaves it there momentarily.

```
'Units'   {'pixels'} | 'normalized' | 'inches' |...
          'centimeters' | 'points'
```

Specifies the units of measurement for *uicontrol* object properties.

```
'Value'   scalar or vector
```

Contains the current value of the *uicontrol:*

> `'Radiobutton'` and `'Checkbox'`—`'Max'` when `'on'`, `'Min'` when `'off'`.
> `'Slider'`—a number representing the slider position.
> `'PopUpMenu'`—an index of the item selected.
> `'ListBox'`—a vector of indices of items selected.
> `'Togglebutton'`—`'Max'` when the button is down, `'Min'` when the button is up.

Other *uicontrol* styles do not set this property.

Index